The Reverent
Discipline

The Reverent Discipline

ESSAYS IN
LITERARY CRITICISM
AND CULTURE

George A. Panichas

WITH A FOREWORD BY G. WILSON KNIGHT

THE UNIVERSITY OF TENNESSEE PRESS
KNOXVILLE

Library of Congress Cataloging in Publication Data

Panichas, George Andrew.
   The reverent discipline.
     CONTENTS: The writer and society: some reflections.—Promise
of greatness: the war of 1914–1918.—The end of the lamplight.
[etc.]
    1. Literature—History and criticism. I. Title.
PN511.P16   809   73–15749
         ISBN 0–87049–149–0

Foreword

BY G. WILSON KNIGHT

The discussion of literature has in our time taken on an importance and intensity unlike anything in the past. It is as though the investigation has become a prime necessity without which literature itself can no longer fulfill its purpose.

Ours is an era of uncentered thinking and ungeared emotions. The prophecy of disintegration with which Pope concluded *The Dunciad* has been fulfilled. The process was delayed for a while by the spiritual and revolutionary movements of the Romantic period, which simultaneously let off steam and tapped energies that served, paradoxically, as a stabilizing power for another century, until the explosion of the First World War. Previous to that, much of our traditional culture was, though increasingly threatened, intact. In Britain the national imagination, including aristocratic valuations, was still alive in the Edwardian era. Culture was less talked of than in the blood. All that has gone. War or no war, the time was perhaps ripe for it, and that is why T. S. Eliot's *The Waste Land* had so immediate and pervasive an appeal.

In the days of classical education it seemed unnecessary for universities to have departments of English. Our own literature was expected to be naturally assimilated as part of an educated man's culture, and there was accordingly the less reason for intensive discussion. But, after the spread of scientific education accompanied by a scant reliance on Greek and Latin, new needs have arisen, and the more so since our prevailing world-view has become so imaginatively febrile. The Victorian and Edwardian eras took for granted much in literature that we have to have explained to us, or have to explain, laboriously, to ourselves. They may not have known so much, intellectually, but they may not have needed to. Though we today have a far greater knowledge of the intricacies of a Shakespearean play, it is likely that many an educated Victorian was more emotionally at home with its central powers. Whatever may have been its failings, a Beerbohm-

Tree production of Shakespeare had qualities of amplitude and reverence outside our ken. For us much has become alien which to our forefathers was instinctively apprehended, and yet we half recognize our need to reincorporate what has been lost.

Professor Panichas' book is one great plea for such an incorporation. His survey is wide. Mainly, one is aware of his deep sympathy with Edwardian culture, at its most infectious in his excellent handling of Vivian de Sola Pinto's fascinating reminiscences in *The City That Shone*; and also of his acute diagnoses of what has followed since. His own position is defined as "Christian Humanist" or "Christian Hellenist." His Greek ancestry may be felt empowering his Hellenism; his Christianity is liberal and undogmatic. From such acceptances he discusses his various writers and their concern with the dominant issues of our century. To this investigation he brings what so many of his contemporaries lack: balance, urbanity, and courtesy.

He also brings a yet greater quality: a refusal to be dominated by negations. He is always ready to recognize what is positive, as preeminently in his essay on the First World War and the human qualities generated and involved (originally composed as an introduction to his collection of war records, *Promise of Greatness*). Even when handling the ultimate negation of death, his approach is inspiring, as when he tells us how the experiences of those who fought awoke in them mysterious perceptions:

> At the front death is the overwhelming fact. The magnitude of death creates speechless horror; the thought of death fills immensity. There is hardly a boundary line between the dead, the dying, and the living. (42)

That war had its heroisms; but, despite all that was truly great, this newly terrible, mechanized, and crushing holocaust left our culture parched of vigor, enduring "tragedy without vision" (52). Probably no finer assessment of the issues involved on both sides of the argument, the heroism and its result, has been composed.

Professor Panichas' survey is throughout dispassionate, seeing not merely the bad, but what is today so much harder, the good. Though dispassionate, it is a survey that takes account of and understands the passions of others. It is at once interpretative and critical. Repeatedly he emphasizes the need for standards; but also, with an equal—or greater—emphasis, the need for humility. These two emphases are covered by his title: *The Reverent Discipline*.

The two are, however, not easily combined. I have always had my own difficulties with "criticism," as such, and especially where "morals" are in question. This might be called a distinguishing feature of my own literary commentaries from those of Dr. F. R. Leavis which, though on an admittedly subtle level, have a strongly "moral" tone. One difficulty is that the word "moral" itself is dangerous; by derivation "morality" signifies social custom, accepted ways, and so on. Neither are we helped by "ethics," which has a similar connotation. Nor is the danger only verbal; we too readily attribute a final authenticity to judgments that are themselves merely dictated by local and ephemeral custom. In a recent article on "John Ford: Dramatist of the Heart" (contributed to the 1971 *Transactions of the Devonshire Association*, England), I have been at pains to show how Ford's *dramatic artistry* is used to honor actions which are socially unacceptable. That is the way of drama. Again and again its heroes are morally subversive; and even when the play's framework is "morally" sound, that frame would be nothing without the heroes, whose dark powers are what we pay to witness and enjoy. We can only suppose that they house energies which we, in actual life, may hope to develop, control, and transmute, so that, following Nietzsche (*Thus Spake Zarathustra*, "Of Delights and Passions," I.5), our "devils" become "angels."

For me, the issue is raised by Professor Panichas' handling of Dostoevsky's Stavrogin. He comes down rather heavily on Stavrogin's satanic attributes. They are there, of course, and a rational defense is difficult, if not impossible; all I can do is to urge that we should at least counter our sense of damnation by reading the relevant pages in Middleton Murry's *Dostoevsky*.

The prevailing moral, or sociological, emphasis of contemporary criticism derives from the will to relate literature, or imagination, to actual life. As I have said, we are today suffering a divorce of a new kind, and that is why we strive so urgently to—in Forster's famous phrase—"connect." On every page Professor Panichas and the writers he is discussing are urgently engaged in this task, this quest. And yet morality by itself is not enough. In life nothing may be as important as right action. But what *is* right action? Conceptually it can only be defined by vague and general phrases such as the "love" of the New Testament, and even that breaks down if we apply it too widely. It certainly helps little in wartime. Then there is the animal creation to be considered. And where do we stop, and why? I doubt if we can go much further than John Masefield, writing in *King Cole*, on the bright powers stirring humanity: "To thoughts like planets and to acts like flowers." To that we can all, surely, subscribe. True righteousness can only be defined by poetry.

Our best "moral" or "sociological" critics do, of course, admit the subtleties. They know that this is a very complex matter. But there is one element they do *not* normally observe: the supernatural or, as some prefer, the paranormal. Again and again it is supposed that if literature is to have relevance to affairs, that relevance must be moral. But what of the metaphysical, or spiritual? The New Testament places the love of God before the love of man; and Masefield's line has its "planets" first and the "flowers" after.

What is so important in Professor Panichas' book is that he, who can write so convincingly and authoritatively on the need for "values" and "standards"—and is, as I am not, to this extent at home with many of the viewpoints of modern criticism—yet counters this with an insistence that no valid literary standards can be based on the ephemeral. They are "resistant to the transient and the merely experimental":

> Standards are the discriminating formulation of truths that measure man against the greater truths of eternity. They are a bulwark against formlessness and falseness; inevitably they are rooted in hierarchy—a hierarchy of merit. (171)

That is nobly stated; but where are we to look for direction? To the New Testament? To *Thus Spake Zarathustra*? To both, surely; but also *to all great works that have stood the test of centuries.* Our own, human, ratification is our ultimate authority: the truth, and the standards, are within us. All we need is to shatter the iron curtain debarring "common sense" from "imagination": we must learn to believe what we imagine.

That such a curtain exists is clear enough. Great literature, from early times until today, has been saturated in extrasensory acceptance—and so, outside our universities, has human nature. Year by year the opposition between the experience of centuries and our modern seats of learning has become more patent. The prospect is, however, brightening. I would point to the spiritualistic advances of our time, to the growing interest in magic, and, among the many relevant recent books, to my brother W. F. Jackson Knight's posthumous *Elysion* and the challenge of Colin Wilson's *The Occult.* Modern literature and modern criticism are insistent on the need to relate literature to life, the imagination to actuality. In both the actuality of human existence and its expression in great literature, a spiritual dimension is evident in every age, including our own. But literary exegesis has remained blind to it; academic and ecclesiastical barriers constrict our understanding of those very psychic facts which are the indispensable link for a newly invigorated culture.

For these powers Professor Panichas' approach has room; whatever his reaction to my present statements may be, it will, I know, be characterized by the same urbanity, the same insight, and the same generosity that he applies throughout. But an apology is scarcely needed. In treating of the two peak figures in his survey, Dostoevsky and Lawrence, he himself powerfully emphasizes their prophetic function.

An exquisite and detailed care is devoted to his account of Father Zossima in *The Brothers Karamazov*. Dostoevsky's saint is characterized by a "refined" and "pristine" Christianity so purged of accretions that it exists as a universal (252). It is a saintliness simultaneously of earth and of the beyond, "rooted in the sacred mystery of the created world" (253):

> Makar and Father Zossima are images of a divine *sophia*, earthly and yet metaphysical. Dramatically they reflect Dostoevsky's own contemplation of the theme of mystical naturalism that is intrinsic in a spiritual vision which never loses sight of a supernal power, but that concurrently bathes in the majesty of the immediate physical world in which God's immanence remains as an irrevocable, interpenetrating hint of a higher dimension.... (254)

Father Zossima, we are told, denotes "experience beyond art, vision beyond reality, spirit beyond flesh, life beyond death" (260). The study is completed by Alyosha, the boy-disciple who is to take the old man's teaching into the world and who has contact with him after his death through an experience of extrasensory perception, followed by a sense of the sacred majesty of earth and sky: "For Alyosha this mystical experience has as its media vision and voice, supersensual auditory and visual intuitions which bring man's finite being, his 'seeing self,' into contact with the Infinite Being, the Absolute" (273). So Father Zossima visited the soul of Alyosha. There was a direct communion, and communication, between the dead saint and the living boy.

For Dostoevsky, saintliness is one with earth-magic; in Lawrence the powers of earth-creation expand to the mystical. One of Professor Panichas' finest essays is concerned with Lawrence's insight into ancient Greece. This is not the Greece of surface harmony and rational control. He shows that Lawrence was drawn rather to the more unruly powers, seeing Cassandra as "a great woman saint," "one of the world's great figures," a medium "of the deepest truth," through whom "the truth came as through a fissure from the depths and the burning darkness that lies out of the depth of time" (337–38). Lawrence continues:

> It is necessary for this great type to re-assert itself on the face of the earth. It is not the salon lady and the blue stocking—it is not the critic and judge, but the priestess, the medium, the prophetess. . . . She is one of the world's great figures, and what the Greeks and Agamemnon did to her is symbolic of what mankind has done to her since—raped and despoiled and mocked her, to their own ruin. (338)

Naturally enough Lawrence preferred the pre-Socratic philosophers, especially Heracleitus, to Socrates and Plato, turning to them as he turned to "the Etruscans, the Aztecs and the Red Indians," in whom he found a vital abundance untainted by attenuating doctrines.

This living abundance is one with an insight into experience beyond death. Nothing in Professor Panichas' book is more happily told than the story of Lawrence's attainment, in *Last Poems*, to the new, beyond-earthly insight of "The Ship of Death," having worked through the torments of physical existence to become "an apocalyptic poet transcending empirical realities" (346).

If literary criticism is to have standards involving hierarchies of value, they must accord primacy to such central statements as these from Dostoevsky and Lawrence; otherwise our supposed "standards" are little better than an insidious technique of literary castration. Only those, like Professor Panichas, who deeply respond to the centralities are likely to have standards which we can respect. Though normally disclaiming criticism in favor of interpretation, I myself have "standards," as when I rate John Cowper Powys and Francis Berry in the forefront of modern letters, using standards derived from a recognition of powers to which modern criticism has remained cold.

In an article entitled "Imagining Science" (*The Listener*, London, November 18, 1971), Dr. George Steiner has recently urged, as have others before him, that our literary intelligence should be far more at home than it is with the world of scientific advance; but what he has to say must be linked to what John Cowper Powys (in *In Spite Of*) and Colin Wilson (in *The Occult*) have to say when they tell us that in the development of psychic activity lies our next step in human evolution. It is, really, all one question, since any "science" worthy of its name will, or should, include psychic experience and phenomena. To do this it will have to respect the evidence while simultaneously honoring and exercising the imagination, which Shelley in his *Defence of Poetry* calls "that imperial faculty whose throne is curtained within the invisible nature of man." It may well be that, as Dr. Steiner tells us, scientists themselves suffer from a certain loneliness in their hazardous and often terrifying specializations, cut off as they are from communal understanding. They too most surely need "standards," for without them science may only too rapidly become nightmare. If literature needs science, science needs literature; for literature at its best, in the past and today, represents just that total, imaginative and psychic, awareness, or the striving for it, which we so sorely need.

Here, in the following pages, are our witnesses; and in our search for such guidance we can do no better than start with the rich storehouse of vital thinking incorporated into Professor Panichas' survey.

Preface

∽

The special but always living and relevant ways in which literary and cultural values touch and connect; the ways in which visionary art and moral significance have a common frontier; the ways in which criticism, in both its function and its pursuit, is applicable to and useful for elucidating larger cultural themes, questions, and stresses in their literary, social, and religious contexts—these matters provide the unifying principle as well as the organizing pattern of the essays written during the last sixteen years included in this volume.

As a generalist critic and as a Christian Humanist, I have presented my interests and opinions concerning some central problems of "Culture and Society," especially as these problems have been confronted by men of genius and men of letters in the modern world. It is inevitable that, as the greater and darker problems of the modern world lie behind the particular problems of literature, an essential task of criticism is that of searching for and apprehending ultimates in the relations between "Art and Morality." That these problems are by no means ephemeral, and that not only the creative artist but also the professional critic and, indeed, any man of vision must return again and again to the past, as a source of inspiration, or meditation, or wisdom, or for standards, attests to the significance of what, in the end, becomes the crossing point of "Ancients and Moderns."

Since life, society, and civilization may be seen through all literature, the essays in this book cut through cultural and national boundaries. My choice of subjects—or better, my exploration of the human imagination—has always been a synthesizing one, and one spiritually akin to literature that in its universal aspects expresses humanity. Erich Auerbach's statements that "our philological home is the earth: it can no longer be the nation," and that "we must return, in admittedly altered circumstances, to the knowledge that prenational medieval culture already possessed: the knowledge that the spirit is not national," express my own beliefs. And when I assert that the nature of my sympathy is Christian Humanist, I want to emphasize a transcending temper rather than a rigorism informing my literary and cultural investigations. My feeling is that the social significance of art is best characterized by what, to quote Carl Jung, "is constantly at work educating the spirit of the age, conjuring up the forms in which the age is most lacking."

The title of this volume, *The Reverent Discipline*, should suggest my aims and evoke the guiding spirit of my efforts. It is a title, I might add, that I decided upon after having for long at the back of my mind, and after much study and thought, Lawrence's words (found in his *Phoenix: The Posthumous Papers of D. H. Lawrence* [1936]), "To my thinking, the critic, like a good beadle, should rap the public on the knuckles and make it attend during divine service. And any good book is divine service." These words, together with the title of this work, epitomize my view of literary criticism, in all its elements and touches, as being indispensable to the educative process. The exercise of criticism—the critical act—must be at once firm and controlled in its achievement of balance and coherence, clarity and order, those elements which civilized thought and sensibility require for their very survival. Criticism without standards must remain incomplete and inclusive. Standards, after all, are what define the strengths and the possibilities of the critical discipline as a force, as a moral force, in life. The case for standards of criticism, at any rate, has been variously stated by a number of great twentieth-century critics, beginning with T. S. Eliot and continuing (dauntlessly) with F. R. Leavis, who warns in one of his most admirable essays, "Towards Standards of Criticism" (1933):

> Literary criticism provides the test for life and concreteness; where it degenerates, the instruments of thought degenerate too, and thinking, released from the testing and energizing contact with the full living consciousness, is debilitated, and betrayed to the academic, the abstract, and the verbal. It is of little use to discuss values if the sense of value in the concrete—the experience and perception of value—is absent.

But, if balance is one of the aims of criticism (as I seek to indicate in the essay "The Writer and Society: Some Reflections"), then the discipline of criticism implies a further humane refinement, a refined enthusiasm as opposed to an indulgence in emotion; it implies *reverence*, "the highest of human feelings," to use Carlyle's description of Boswell's feelings for Dr. Johnson. Undoubtedly, the problems of the modern age have been so difficult and so absorbing that the need for and the defense of standards have become urgent. And in this necessarily contentious process—for there are, as Eliot maintained, definite positions to be taken and principles to be applied when one must reject something and select something else—the element of reverence as a resource of criticism has been too often and too easily neglected or forgotten or condemned, even by a figure no less than E. M. Forster, who, no doubt echoing his Bloomsbury connection, declared that "Reverence is fatal to literature." It is time to reinstate reverence in the critical discipline, to give it its rightful share of significance among the other critical standards and criteria ("balance and coherence, clarity and order"), to benefit by its humanizing power. No doubt reverence is the most fragile of critical faculties, perhaps because it is the least empirical. It rarely makes for fuss or for controversy. There is something wondrous about it that makes Lawrence's metaphor, "any good book is divine service," more meaningful. Reverence, thus, implies a certain immanence as well as fear and awe, with a notion of wonder (as connoted by the Greek word for reverence, σέβας). And, as anyone attending divine service will disclose, it also connotes deep respect, humility, honor, and meditation—meditation above all—in the presence of otherness.

Reverence in its critical context serves to educe a larger, more resilient vision and a deeper understanding of a world in which man continuously searches for a basic orientation in his situation. And in this search, in this charting of ways, standards and discipline are required sources of strength and direction. They represent scrupulosity of thought and are essential to human improvement. They epitomize the critical process in its discovery of truth, of that truth which José Ortega y Gasset defines as "what quiets an anxiety in our intelligence." A consonant experience of reverence, which in the critical process constitutes a difference of quality of perception, of level and power, is also needed if judgment is to be heightened. For it can exert a balance by offsetting the extreme, corruptive push of the empirical on the one side and the anarchic on the other, perhaps the two most predominant forces of disorientation in modern life. It needs to be appealed to and grasped as a critical desideratum. Reverence has hidden depths which conceptual thought cannot reach, but of which it has immense need. Reverence is a paradigm that sanctifies and saves. Reverence connotes other possibilities of response and attention, of knowledge and presence. It is discovery, discovery of another dimension. It is the finest offshoot of the revelation of order.

I am not asking for any softening of the standards of criticism. I am asking that the critical discipline be given, in a positive and humane sense, the higher task of continuing standards while at the same time going beyond them. The transfiguration of the critical discipline into the reverent discipline represents, as I see it, the attainment of a standard of standards. It takes into account "the highest of human feelings" without compromising them. And it helps to incorporate this reconciling element into the social fabric where, in a time of irreverence, it is needed most—and needed desperately. If discipline equips us with the sense of precise discrimination, if it enables us to scrutinize and to appraise, then reverence ennobles the critical function with magnanimity of response in the experience and affirmation of the greatness of the creative imagination. It brings into proximity the humane and the sacred. Without discipline, reverence—reverence for the work of art—is empty of value and false of feeling. Without reverence, discipline is too mechanical, even arid, an exercise of fact and virtue. (The import of what I am merely suggesting here is detailed in my essay "Toward a Metaphysics of Art.") For discipline and reverence are, or should be, interdependent in their critical intentions. Discipline strives to give order to vision; reverence gives a certain rhythm of sensibility and sanctity to vision. Each complements the other. Joined, they help to order and to mediate a fullness of vision.

My concept of literary criticism as a discipline owes a great deal to the thought and the influence of the work of Dr. Leavis, especially as it is vigorously set forth in his essay quoted above, as well as in his other writings such as *The Common Pursuit* (1952) and *D. H. Lawrence: Novelist* (1955). The consistency of his critical theory is marked by a sustained devotion and courage of purpose which few other critics can ever hope to equal. His work, particularly as it is expressed in ceaseless concern for critical standards *and* for relevant attention to the problems of contemporary civilization, has helped to stimulate the movement of my own critical thinking. But though my concern with critical standards and with civilization, in their constant interaction, has remained steadfast, the movement of my critical thought has gone in another direction. To put it in another way, my critical thought has searched for another form for the enlargement of comprehension. I have, as this collection of essays should confirm, sought for what lies beyond discipline, though I could never have grasped the significance of this critical direction without the prior, intrinsic recognition of criticism *as* discipline. The form of this enlarged view—and I am not speaking here of modification, inasmuch as I believe that discipline and reverence are interdependent and coextensive—represents for me a kind of double rhythm which the title of this volume should convey.

Eliot's essay "Religion and Literature" (1935) marks an important point of connection in my developing critical theory and practice.

The opening paragraph of this essay, especially the last sentence of it—

> Literary criticism should be completed by criticism from a definite ethical and theological standpoint. In so far as in any age there is common agreement on ethical and theological matters, so far can literary criticism be substantive. In ages like our own, in which there is no such common agreement, it is the more necessary for Christian readers to scrutinize their reading, especially of works of imagination, with explicit ethical and theological standards. The "greatness" of literature cannot be determined solely by literary standards; though we must remember that whether it is literature or not can be determined only by literary standards.

—underlines the critical enlargement which I think is necessary. That, as Eliot maintains, "the application of our religion to the criticism of any literature" is inescapable, and that literary judgments cannot, or should not, be separated from religious judgments, and that what one reads directly affects the whole of what one is, not only one's literary taste, but also one's moral and religious being, are conclusions which have had for me an increasing force of truth. But in a highly secular age, when the liberal-minded take pride in their liberalizing advances (doubts about which I raise in the essay "Ideologues of Mediocrity"), the need to make the religious connections that Eliot alludes to is often frowned upon. We should be reminded of everything, it seems, but not of metaphysical and theological assumptions: of the supernatural, of conscience, of the inner life, of evil, sin, guilt, suffering, wisdom, redemption, discipline—and reverence. It is my hope that the essays in this book will remind the reader that criticism has a strong role to play in connecting literature and life in immediate and existential ways, while at the same time criticism remains ever aware of the fundamental limitations of the temporal and the external and of the ultimate binding of the temporal and the eternal. My concept of humanism should be understood in the context of this statement; hence, by way of distinguishing, I would uphold a sacramental rather than a secular humanism.

A coalescing critical and religious humanism has relevance to the meaning of civilization, as some of my essays particularly in the section "Ancients and Moderns" and as my recurrent accent on Hellenism seek to demonstrate. Together they can work to construct mutually corrective values and also a center of judgment. It is this belief that is implicit in my choice of Christian Humanist to describe my own sympathy (though I could just as easily, and for the same purpose, have said Christian Hellenist) in exploring the relations between literature and religion in the ways Eliot suggests. Again, the stress should fall on sympathy rather than on doctrine and dogma, which lead to preconceptions, preconditions, sanctions, and programs. Problems and not prescriptions—the interacting problems of literature and culture—shape the essential and the commanding concern of these essays. As Leavis expresses it: "The problem is to go beyond the words on the page without losing touch with them; to develop a technique for keeping the sensibility always in control in one's inevitable dealings with abstractions and 'precipitates from the memory.' " Insofar as these problems take us back to abiding moral bases, then the temper of my approach and scope is Christian and Humanist. I much prefer, to use a common expression, the wisdom of ages to the wisdom of the age. The epigraphs to this book should further clarify the specifics of what I am suggesting.

We are now in the midst of a battle to maintain and promulgate civilized standards in opposition to the drift toward barbarism, a drift that has accelerated in the modern world. If provincialism and demoralization are to be contained, moreover, then literary criticism must be viewed in its wholeness rather than its parts. The value and influence of the generalist, as opposed to the *spécialiste*, can scarcely be overestimated in this connection. Literary criticism in the light of what I call a reverent discipline implies a recovery of values and of directions. This recovery means a consequent (re)awareness of the Judaeo-Christian tradition as the background of our civilization. Critics who refuse to acknowledge this fact, or who reject its pertinence, are precisely those *spécialistes* who would limit the full play of the critical spirit. That the critical spirit cannot be divorced from a clear-cut scale of moral values and from religious roots is what is at the origin of the critical thrust of this book, what, in short, informs that sense of enlargement relating to a beginning and an end.

One must not expect criticism to be an invincible force. The critic, even if he is militant, even if he is a warrior in his own right, can hardly issue victory proclamations. His *raison d'être* is ever so tenuous, and his work has no measurable destiny. When he refuses to believe this fact and dares to fight against it, society, which knows where the existent power lies, has a way of telling him exactly where he stands. What is the value of criticism if, in its most pragmatic aspects, it seems so peripheral to the battle of life? Answers are far from simple, and perhaps there is no final answer. But this much at least is certain: the critical function in its innermost essences has prophetic power. Not that criticism predicts the future; rather it helps achieve the future. It helps save the future by its search for and vigilant defense of excellence. Like the work of the best teacher, criticism can never

be weighed, although one knows when it has done its work by enlarging one's perception of the quality of life. Criticism is a moral
form of reflection arising out of the recognition of limitations and
the affirmation of the possibilities of vision and individual talent.
Criticism that is critical expresses real spiritual energy and satisfies
a real spiritual need.

My emphasis thus far has been on points of connection and of reconciliation as they have helped to mold my approach to literature
and culture. Yet I can hardly conclude this prefatory statement without mentioning something that, for the critic, is both immediate and
personal. For though one must necessarily discuss critical concepts,
principles, laws, methods, aims, phases, techniques, systems, and
requirements, one should not fail to speak about the emotional self
that complements the intellectual self. A special and a clarifying need
exists to say something about "our own person," about knowing oneself and what prompts one, in a critical sense, to be and to reflect in
the world. Any explanation of this side of the critic is not easy. Critics
"are different fauna from people," says Lawrence, he himself being
among the greatest critics. The attempts to label and hence identify
critics are many. I am thinking here of Eliot's categories of modern
literary critics, beginning as he does about the year 1826 with the
work of Sainte-Beuve—"the Professional Critic," "the Critic with
Gusto," "the Academic and Theoretical Critic," the critic who is also
a poet, and so on. Eliot's classifications no doubt are part of an
attempt to know the critic's qualities and "temperament." (The historian of criticism, René Wellek, has devoted an entire lifetime and
many books—"books about books about books," as one writer has
said—to this subject. Some of my own essays in the last section of this
book share in the task.)

What we need to know, finally, is the modern critic himself as he
pursues his constantly expanding task of orientation and construction, as he speculates and scrutinizes and seeks bearings—analyzes,
interprets, connects, judges. But no amount of scholarship or indisputable critical precept can ever make for complete criticism. The critic's
own "sincere and vital emotion," with all his complexity of feelings,
as Lawrence maintains, must never be depreciated. For instance, what
makes Macaulay unsatisfactory, Lawrence believes, is that "he prefers
a fine effect to the sincere statement of the aesthetic and emotional
reaction." By no means am I using Lawrence's words here to dignify
what, in the contemporary jargon of students and teachers who ought
to know better, goes by the term "visceral reaction," as irresponsible a
reaction as there ever was, against which Lawrence posits this neces-

sary corrective: "A critic must be emotionally alive in every fibre, intellectually capable and skilful in essential logic, and then morally very honest." We need, in other words, to know about the critic's evolving sense of completeness in precisely the responsible ways Lawrence sees it: to know, too, that the critic does reveal something of himself in his critical function. That it is possible, if not tempting, to romanticize this aspect of the critic's work goes without saying. But, in the attempt to preclude such a critical deflection, we can commit an oversight that diminishes the very understanding of the consummate nature of critical achievement. We forget the critic himself.

Here I can merely suggest that just as there is a psychology of art, so too is there a psychology of criticism. And if there is a creative impulse, there is also a critical impulse. It hardly needs stressing that this comparison is not to equate creative genius with critical practitioner, or the critic's function with the artist's purpose. ("You cannot," avers Eliot, "fuse creation with criticism as you can fuse criticism with creation. The critical activity finds its highest, its true fulfilment in a kind of union with creation in the labour of the artist.") The word *genius* should accentuate the fineness of imaginative vision that Henry James, in his Preface to *The Spoils of Poynton*, talks about with specific reference to the "germs" of the creative process: "Such is the interesting truth about the stray suggestion, the wandering word, the vague echo, at touch of which the novelist's imagination winces as at the prick of some sharp point: its virtue is all in its needle-like quality, the power to penetrate as finely as possible." (The first paragraph of James's Preface should be studied carefully for its insights into the mystery and the miracle of imaginative creation and its concept of the worth of art.) What James writes is sufficient to remind us that the critic's work, in its cognitive aspects and its permeating bias, must speak also in terms of the personal and the conscious. The critic—to apply James's word—is "ruminant." Where the artist finds, the critic seeks.

But I should not want to press the subject too far. I am content to end with a quotation from an essay in John Middleton Murry's book *Discoveries* (1924). The passage crystallizes some of the points I have been struggling to hint at in these last few paragraphs. For the measure of criticism that Murry takes is contributive to a deeper appreciation of the point of view and the meaning, the metaphysics, of what for me is *the reverent discipline*:

> After all, I believe that criticism is a personal affair, and that the less we critics try to disguise this from ourselves, the better. On what ex-

cites and attracts and fascinates us in pursuit of our own completion, in obedience, if you like, to our own secret rhythm which we also must have if our work is to be vital at all—on that alone we shall have something to say worth hearing.

G.A.P.

Contents

༄

The Reverent
Discipline

✍ Then it seems to me a good critic should give his reader a few standards to go by. He can change the standards for every new critical attempt, so long as he keeps good faith. But it is just as well to say: This and this is the standard we judge by.

—D. H. LAWRENCE: "John Galsworthy," in *Phoenix*

✍ I have suggested that the liberal attitude towards literature will not work. Even if the writers who make their attempt to impose their "view of life" upon us were really distinct individuals, even if we as readers were distinct individuals, what would be the result? It would be, surely, that each reader would be impressed, in his reading, merely by what he was previously prepared to be impressed by; he would follow the "line of least resistance," and there would be no assurance that he would be made a better man. For literary judgment we need to be acutely aware of two things at once: of "what we like," and of "what we ought to like." Few people are honest enough to know either. The first means knowing what we really feel: very few know that. The second involves understanding our shortcomings; for we do not really know what we ought to like unless we also know why we ought to like it, which involves knowing why we don't yet like it. It is not enough to understand what we ought to be, unless we know what we are; and we do not understand what we are, unless we know what we ought to be. The two forms of self-consciousness, knowing what we are and what we ought to be, must go together.

—T. S. ELIOT: "Religion and Literature," in *Selected Essays*

✍ The true literary critic must have a humanistic philosophy.

—J. MIDDLETON MURRY: "The Function of Criticism," in *Aspects of Literature*

✍ Situations differ, opportunities vary, I know, but it will always be necessary to insist (and in a more than theoretical way) that criticism is a collaborative and creative interplay. It creates a community and is inseparable from the process that creates and keeps alive a living culture; that creates a civilization, in so far as a civilization is something more than a matter of material conditions and externalities of social behaviour. If you believe that literature matters, you are committed to believing that.

—F. R. LEAVIS

I

Culture and Society

And every civilization, when it loses its inward vision and its cleaner energy, falls into a new sort of sordidness, more vast and more stupendous than the old savage sort.

—D. H. LAWRENCE

ᔓ

1

The Writer and Society: Some Reflections

∾

Any discussion of the relationship between literature and society leads to inevitable and thorny problems. The nature of some of these problems can perhaps best be captured by way of warning, as found in René Wellek and Austin Warren's *The Theory of Literature*: "But literature is no substitute for sociology or politics. It has its own justification and aim."[1] Such a warning is not without precedent, nor without celebrated proponents and antagonists. From an early time in the history of aesthetics, works of literary art have prompted varying, often opposing, aesthetic responses. Plato, it will be remembered, equated the study of art with the study of moral values; and Aristotle equated art with poetic values and with the study of aesthetics.

Proponents of what can be called the purist, or formalist, point of view judge a work of art according to criteria of craftsmanship. What matters is the purity of the imagination as it is communicated by its "structure of words," by form, by technique—"technique as discovery," as the phrase goes—set forth in transcendent detachment. A work of art is an expression and ordering of vision, its style achieved through the "organization of originality," to use Paul Valéry's phrase. The creator must be judged not as a "thinker," or as an ideologue, or as a dialectician, or a didactician, but rather as an artist. His is "the struggle—which alone constitutes life for a poet" as T. S. Eliot predicates (he is talking about Shakespeare), "to transmute his personal and private agonies into something rich and strange, something universal and impersonal."[2] And the artist must be judged according to how far he has managed to separate himself from the subjective world and thus, through the "continual extinction of personality," to purify himself in relation to his art. James Joyce, in a well-known passage in *A Portrait of the Artist as a Young Man*, suggests some of the formulary principles of this aesthetic approach: "The artist, like the

5

God of the creation, remains within or behind or beyond or above his handiwork, invisible, refined out of existence, indifferent, paring his fingernails."

Those who dissent from this view see the artist and his work in less exclusive and autonomous dimensions. For the social critic the functions and the frontiers of art are much deeper and much wider. For him literature is a never-ending process and not some autotelic end in itself. He finds the values of art interacting with and even blending with other values—economic, religious, moral, philosophical, historical, political. He agrees with Charles Augustin Sainte-Beuve that "no aspect of human life is alien to literature." Literature is not merely the narrative of an age, but "an invitation to action." Ultimately what and how the artist writes interweaves with the world in which he lives, with the people whom he observes, with the civilization and the conduct which he comprehends in his vision. In this respect the artist is a poet in the ancient Hellenic sense of a creator, one who conveys wisdom and who helps to form what is sometimes described as "the normative consciousness" of the human race. Leo Tolstoy crystallized these views when he wrote: "Art, like speech, is a means of communication, and therefore of progress, i.e., of the movement of humanity forward toward perfection."[3]

Twentieth-century critics have often echoed the Tolstoyan view of art by emphasizing "a sociological criticism of literature" and a "historical interpretation of literature," "literature as equipment for living," in Kenneth Burke's phraseology. Since man is in the highest degree a historical being, then all his creative efforts must be seen in their historical and cultural facets, for, as Matthew Arnold would have it, these creative efforts are "a criticism of life." The creative imagination must, under the circumstances, address itself to the overarching question of how man lives. The great artist is he who speaks about life and the possibilities of life. If his vision is achieved by intrinsic values, his view of life has extrinsic cognitive values. In turn, literary criticism ought to be, as Edmund Wilson, echoing the ideas of Hippolyte Taine and Sainte-Beuve, writes in *Axel's Castle*, "a history of man's ideas and imaginings in the setting of the conditions which have shaped them."[4]

The metaphysic of the artist and how it is incorporated in his vision are controlling factors in the creative imagination and in its "powerful and profound applications of ideas to life," to quote Arnold again. The artist, if he speaks to life and for life, can rarely avoid responding to the world around him. This does not mean that he must be subservient to a metaphysic. Rather, he reveals the power of his creative imagination in direct relationship to his ability to transcend a metaphysic without consciously ignoring or dispensing with its integral substances as these affect human experience. His art is, perhaps in the final sense, a mediation between his metaphysic—his cognitive view of life: the life of man and the meaning of the world—and his vision, his revelation, which, through the organic processes of craftsmanship, helps us to understand the infinite variety of existence. Henry James, who for too long has been identified with the exponents of what goes under the (misleading) rubric of "pure art," addresses himself to the relation between art and metaphysic, between literature and society, when he writes:

> The great question as to a poet or a novelist is, How does he feel about life? what, in the last analysis, is his philosophy? When vigorous writers have reached maturity, we are at liberty to gather from their works some expression of a total view of the world they have been so actively observing. This is the most interesting thing their works offer us. Details are interesting in proportion as they contribute to make it clear.[5]

Clearly, the distempers of the twentieth century have sharpened some of the attitudes toward what exactly the relationship is between literature and society, or, as James would have it, what some of the ways are in which an artist expresses in his writings "a total view of the world." Modern history has strengthened the position of the social critic, while that of the critic as purist has steadily weakened. Today we need only think of the immensely diminished status of the New Critics to gauge the truth of this fact. Even the currently widespread usage of the words "relevance" and "meaning" should underline, with respect to both the study and the criticism of literature, the direction of things. More than at any other time in history, literature today is seen against, and appraised in the light of, major historical events, forces, and ideas. The historical situation, in effect, is always there, even central to the literary imagination. The vision of the artist is not able to distance the reality of history, even, it seems, the "dialectical vision of history" which constitutes the major concern of Marxist critics like Georg Lukács and Ernst Fischer. This is by no means to claim that literature has become dialectic and ideology (except, of course, for Soviet literature). It does mean that twentieth-century literature reflects historical developments and that it is impelled and colored by social and political developments. And it means, necessarily, that we must be able, as Lionel Trilling writes, "to see literary situations as cultural situations."[6]

To a large degree, history, not literary aesthetic, dictates sensibility and belief in twentieth-century literature. Any consideration

of the major works of the imagination during this century corroborates this generalization. When Joseph Conrad, in his novel *Victory,*
saw this age as one "in which we are camped like bewildered travellers
in a garish, unrestful hotel," he was prophetically evoking the condition of twentieth-century life. Immediately behind Conrad's insight
were the radical transformations of culture being occasioned by
Marxism, Darwinism, and Freudianism. Before him lay the succes-
sions to a pervasive disequilibrium: "the growing murderousness of
the world"; the erosion of the "ancient edifices"; the heightened tensions between man's "inner life" and his "outer life"; the ascendancy
of science and technology; the spread of anxiety, alienation, uprootedness, as well as a growing uniformity and standardization, particularly
as disclosed in political movements like Stalinism, Fascism, Nazism,
and in other forms of modern tyranny enforcing "the collectivist
discipline."

This rather bare summary of the human condition in the twentieth
century is given here not only to emphasize the broken world which a
modern writer cannot escape and which helps to mold his vision, but
also to instance the despiritualizing scope of twentieth-century life.
In *Man in the Modern World,* Karl Jaspers suggests some of the
deeper ideological significances of "epochal" changes gradually destroying the life of man and his acceptance of transcendent values:

> There were periods in which man felt his world to be durable, an un-
> changing intermediate between the vanished Golden Age and the End
> that would come in due course when the Almighty's purposes were ful-
> filled. Man accommodated himself to life as he found it, without wish-
> ing to change it. His activities were limited to an endeavour to better
> his own position amid environing circumstances deemed to be substan-
> tially unalterable. Within these circumstances he had safe harbourage,
> linked as he was both with heaven and with earth. The world was his
> own world, even though it was of no account, because for him true
> being existed only in a transcendental realm.[7]

Jaspers published his book in 1931; in his Foreword to the 1951 edition he writes: "The facts remain unaltered," as indeed they remain
now, two decades later. Man remains passive before the mechanized
nature of mass-order and technical life-order.

The social and religious implications of Jaspers' *Man in the Mod-
ern World* are given their literary and critical relevance in Edwin
Muir's *Essays on Literature and Society,* chiefly in such chapters as
"The Political View of Literature," "The Decline of the Novel," and
"The Natural Man and the Political Man." As these titles indicate,
Muir concerns himself with some of the ideological problems one en-

counters in modern literature, especially in prose fiction. The world in cultural transformation that Jaspers examines is the world that Muir identifies as the novelist's. It is a world in upheaval. And the upheaval is explained by, is the result of, ideological change—that change in attitude toward life which Jaspers traces and which, in the historical limit-situation, is reflected in actual historical movements and conflicts. Above all, Muir shows how the writer responds to ideology, how his vision, as it is ordered by his craft and by his use of language, re-creates the impact of this response. In this connection the aesthetic question itself is not a matter of literature versus ideology, but of literature *and* ideology, or, as Muir points out, a question of defining "the difference between the position of the novelist fifty or a hundred years ago and his position today."

Inevitably this difference of position is a difference of ideology resulting from the writer's changed and changing "total view of the world." Muir admits his concern with a novelist's "story," with his "grammatical construction," with his "skill in insinuating explanatory and qualifying clauses and all sorts of parentheses." But he is also preoccupied with some of the ideological changes peculiar to the modern age and the modern novelist, who all along has been listening to and recording the "voices of a new world." However, Muir recognizes in modern works of art a difference of tone and account and meaning: a difference of orientation and approach, of sensibility. This difference is ideological, Muir insists, and he associates it with a story that has no ending because the modern novelist's "sentence remains hanging in the air." And the reasons for this suspension are dependent on the force and on the thrust of ideology. As Muir explains it:

> This is another way of saying that the contemporary novelist has an imaginative grasp of origins but not of ends. There was a time when the novelist . . . had a grasp of both. To have this is a mark of that order of thought and imagination which is generally called classical. Our own order is not a classical order; we have a grasp of origins but not of ends; our existence, like our works, is an unfinished sentence.[8]

Basically, then, what literature in the twentieth century has reflected is an unimpeded secularization of history. This secularization has been accompanied by great changes in the view of man and his universe and by the proliferation of new and revolutionary ideas affecting one's conception of life. The traditional novel, Muir notes, was a story of time against a pattern of permanence, whereas the modern novel has become a story of time against a background of time. Even in the works of Henry Fielding and Jane Austen a concern with eternal truths still prevailed. New and unsettling ideas, whether about evil or God or moral values, had not yet overwhelmed, secularized, the concept of life. A certain sense of permanence, human and super-human, still prevailed, even as the ideas of the Enlightenment gathered momentum. Muir goes on:

> But they [Fielding and Jane Austen] lived in an order in which everybody possessed without thinking about it much the feeling for a permanence above the permanence of one human existence, and believed that the ceaseless flux of life passed against an unchangeable background. Men still felt this whether they were Christians or not. They felt also that there was a relation between the brief story of man and that unchangeable order; and this sentiment, in whatever terms it was held, was the final earnest of the completeness of their conception of life.[9]

The history of the modern novel is in essence the history of the mutation of this concept; it is the history of ideological change, of a fervent interplay of ideas. And the interplay of ideas has revolved around the total rearrangement of society. The portrayal of man in the modern novel gives an index to the process of this rearrangement and evinces the spirit and the direction of changing ideological forces. There has emerged, Muir believes, "a new species of the natural man dovetailed into a biological sequence and a social structure." Natural man "is simply a human model capable of indefinite improvement on the natural plane; the improvement depending ultimately on the progress of society, and of things in general."[10]

Muir's observations point to the great power wielded by ideas, which are inevitable to the creative process. The writer, particularly the novelist, cannot avoid contact with these ideas as they touch and shape his attitudes toward life. Increasingly the writer has been compelled to speak out on major issues. "Today everything is changed," Camus writes, "and even silence has dangerous implications." Increasingly the writer has viewed himself as an "architect of history," to borrow John Dos Passos' apt description. Unable to escape history, the writer becomes its conscience as well as its consciousness. Henry Miller has gone so far as to claim that the man who is to be called a poet must be "capable of profoundly altering the world." At no other time in the history of literature have writers responded so intensely to the problems of man in society as in the twentieth century. How is man ruled and what is his place in society? how will life and culture survive? how will man's freedom be saved? how will the economic questions be solved?—these are some of the disturbing questions that modern writers have had to deal with precisely because they have been among the most stubborn, painful questions confronting man in this century. The traditional role of the writer as storyteller has merged with what can be termed the prophetic role, whereby the writer combines craft with moral and ultimately apocalyptic meaning, becoming a "spokesman of tragic times" of whom much is expected. "It may well be that at this point in history," according to one critic, "we all need the aid of the novelist's imagination simply to help us imagine what seems to be more and more unimaginable...."[11]

During the twentieth century we have come to rely a great deal on the writer to help us understand a world in the midst of ideological turmoil and cultural fragmentation. We have come to identify him with concern, candor, and courage. To him we have turned for the help we seem unable to get from the traditional sources of state, school, and church. Often, too, we have heeded the voice of the writer when other voices have been silenced or corrupted. It is the writer in his "meditation on history" who can achieve "metapolitical objectivity" and can even be (in the extreme Marxist view) an "engineer of human souls" who can be of use in bringing about "a decent ordering of human affairs." When Simone Weil, that most passionate Platonist of modern philosophers, asserts, "I believe in the responsibility of the writers of recent years for the disaster of our times," she helps to define, despite the perverseness of her contention, the magnified power of the writer in the modern world. As standards and values have collapsed, the need for them has become more manifestly urgent. To turn to literature in order to understand better social and political matters can equip one with those advantages of discrimination and discipline that are all too often missing or neglected in other areas of culture. "Art-speech is the only truth," we hear D. H. Lawrence saying to us.

II

Increasingly unable to separate himself from the moral and political events of his time, the modern writer, like Jean-Paul Sartre in his celebrated manifesto, has had to address himself to the question "What is literature?" This question, especially in the years following World War I, became more pronounced as writers became more aware of their place in the historical process and its concomitant "tragic sense of life." In the years since World War II, this question has become for the writer a central question—as central, in fact, as "What is 'the future of mankind'?" Indeed, the shaping, the demanding, spirit of literature in the twentieth century can be said to be precisely this question. ("The past," as Irving Howe notes, "was devoted to answers; the modern period confines itself to questions."[12]) The writer, Sartre believes, "establishes a historical contact among men who are steeped in the same history and who likewise contribute to its making." His literary work is an appeal, and its value is commensurate with this appeal. One of the main results of this concept of art, its function and responsibility in the twentieth century, has been the writer's sense of commitment—an awareness of one's literary contribution as an involvement in the problems and disasters of the age, as well as an awareness that, in Sartre's words, "the written work can be an essential condition of action, that is, the moment of reflective consciousness."

The historic and essentially aristocratic case against a "committed literature" has been argued by Eliot, who insisted that "the meddling of men of letters in practical affairs ... is only one phenomenon of a general confusion." Yet even Eliot did not rule out the presence, or the passion, of ideological elements in matters of art. "If there is a right relation of emotion to thought in practical affairs," he stipulates, "so there is in speculation and art too." What Eliot and others sharing his view have feared is that writers, misled by their own social-political illusions, may become theorists who impose a form of political ideology on their writings. The condemnation of a "committed literature" is best stated in Julien Benda's famous work *La Trahison des Clercs*. Published in 1927, this book in many ways sparked the antipodal position taken by Sartre in his *Qu'est-ce que la littérature?* (1947). No other two books better define some of the problems which have beset both the theory and the criticism of literature in the modern age. Benda looks back to the past; Sartre is the voice of the present, if not the future. The sharpness of the debate between the two is illustrated in Sartre's pointed attack on Benda:

> If the writer has chosen, as Benda has it, to talk drivel, he can speak in fine, rolling periods of that eternal freedom which National Socialism, Stalinist communism, and the capitalist democracies all lay claim to. He won't disturb anybody; he won't address anybody. Everything he asks for is granted him in advance.[13]

Sartre's voice, not Benda's, rings louder. Modern literature reflects not only the writer's awareness of his social responsibility, but his involvement in what Benda derided as "the realism of the multitude." What Benda feared—the man of letters exercising "political passions with all the characteristics of passion"[14]—characterizes, some believe, the state of literature today. Is not Sartre's concept of the writer's social responsibility precisely that ideology, so suspect to men like Eliot and Benda, which has led to a mutation of literature? And is not the steady collapse of standards, of delicacy and restraint, evident in the whole of literature as it all too easily becomes, say, physiology on the one hand and politics on the other? When ideology invades literature, it is claimed, it produces an extreme individualism of views and no clear rules regarding the limitations of a literary work. Ideology personalizes art; and the artist, as Eliot once wrote about Lawrence, becomes a propagandist, a "promoter of personality," a "seeker for myths." As such, the ideological element as a standard of *engagement* is an intrusion into literature which introduces problems alien to "the pursuit of criticism" and the judgment of an artist's achievement, which, Eliot declared, is not required to serve or be aware of certain ends or beliefs, "and indeed performs its function, whatever that may be, according to various theories of value, much better by indifference to them." "The poet makes poetry," Eliot states, "the metaphysician makes metaphysics, the bee makes honey, the spider secretes a filament; you can hardly say that any of these agents believes: he merely does."[15]

Whatever the problems of criticism or the pronouncements of critics may be, it is certain that creative artists in the modern age are increasingly preoccupied with social problems as a whole and with political problems in particular. For the modern writer politics in all its forms—as theory, as commitment, as action—has become a matter of consciousness and of conscience. Aesthetic considerations are invariably colored by social-political demands. In effect, the writer as seen in his art and in his actions has, sometimes reluctantly, at other times fearlessly and confidently, ventured into the public realm. He has, to use Robert Lowell's image, gone into "the bullring." If he has rendered the experience of this "bullring," it can also be said that the political situation, especially since 1918, that comprises this experience has affected the theory and execution of his art. The essentially patrician attitude that "a creator is one who makes others create" has been steadily transformed into the populist belief that a creator is one who makes others act. It is the recognition of this fact—that man's destiny is primarily one of action—that the modern writer has disclosed with his creative powers.

To preserve, as Joseph Conrad advised, "an attitude of perfect indifference ... because directly the 'Fiat!' has issued from his lips, there are the creatures made in his image that'll try to drag him down from his eminence,—and belittle him by their worship":[16]—to preserve this aesthetic attitude has become an increasingly difficult goal for the creative artist in the twentieth century. For, as political situations have changed and polarized, as national interests have given way to international problems, as the emphasis on theological and ontological issues has been transferred to ethical and political formulations, in short, as social-political dialectic has replaced metaphysical concepts, with the unpolitical and even the antipolitical attitude toward culture definitely waning and, in some ways, extinct, modern literature has witnessed the invasion of its aesthetic sanctuary. Writers have become protesters and partisans. Their writings have as themes "resistance, rebellion, and death." As Lionel Trilling reminds us in *Beyond Culture*: "Modern literature . . . is directed toward moral and spiritual renovation: its subject is damnation and salvation. It is a literature of doctrine which, although often concealed, is very aggressive."[17] Ever present is the secular world and secular man; and ever present, too, is an intensifying concern with the salvation of man in an existential cultural situation. "A man's— and how much more an artist's—[political] opinions are today bound up with the salvation of his soul," writes Thomas Mann, who fled from Nazi Germany in 1936.

Just how aggressive, even belligerent, the writer has become was illustrated at the Chicago Conspiracy Trial when the poet Allen Ginsberg took the stand and recited from his poem "Howl." Wheeling in his chair and pointing an accusing finger at the seventy-four-year-old judge, Ginsberg intoned: "Moloch the vast stone of war! Moloch the stunned governments! / Moloch whose ear is a smoking tomb! Moloch whose blood is running money!" Such passionate, frightening words remind us that not infrequently the poet combines the rage of his inspiration with action, whether in the "guerrilla theater" at Chicago or in ancient Judah to which the "weeping poet," that first great pacifist, the prophet Jeremiah, addressed his words of terror and doom, from the day he was first divinely "set . . . over the nations and over the kingdoms, to root out, and to pull down, and to destroy, and to throw down, to build, and to plant."[18] Artists in the twentieth century, it could be said, have been lavish in the renderings of their vision that they have addressed to modern man. Undoubtedly, their visions have not always been rendered with striking artistic success. Not all writers have become acceptable members of a "priesthood of craftsmanship." Perhaps there have been too many words and too much anger to permit unqualified achievement. But modern history has been a history of men who live in "dark times," so that the artist, so much more sensitive to the darkness of his world, has not been immune to making propaganda an impelling determinant of his art. George Orwell asserts "that every artist is a propagandist . . . in the sense that he is trying, directly or indirectly, to impose a vision of life that seems to him desirable."[19]

The interrelations of radical politics and radical literature were most apparent in the 1930's, a period that, as William Phillips points out, despite contradictions, illusions, and duplicities, was a time "when responsibility meant responsibility to ideas and convictions, justice seemed more important than expediency, the greater good meant more than the lesser evil, dreams seemed more cogent than reality."[20] In the United States, where the Great Depression had as profound an impact on American cultural life and thought as the Great War had had on the European consciousness, radical fiction, or "proletarian literature" as it is referred to, was induced by a Marxist view of society. In the forefront of "American literary communism" were writers like James T. Farrell and Waldo Frank. Preceding them, in the early part of the 1900's, were writers like Jack London and Upton Sinclair, who were responsive to the principles of socialism. The phenomenon of this literary responsiveness to, this quarrel with, society was peculiarly American. It was, Daniel Aaron has told us, as empirical as it was evangelical, as intense as it was uneasy and ambivalent, as didactic as it was angry and impatient.[21]

Moods of social protest in the thirties were not limited to the American scene or to writing. In the "English thirties poetry" the relationships of literature and society were evident in the belief that public poetry, as opposed to private poetry in the form of "heightened conversation," was what was demanded if the experience of literature was to be made accessible to all people. Poets like Stephen Spender, W. H. Auden, Louis MacNeice, and C. Day Lewis saw their proper functions as being not merely the mouthpiece of a community, but also its critical faculty and its conscience. More than contemplation and sensitive perception were demanded of the poet. "I would have a poet," MacNeice writes in *Modern Poetry: A Personal Essay*, "able-bodied, fond of talking, a reader of the newspapers, capable of pity and laughter, informed in economics, appreciative of women, involved in personal relationships, actively interested in politics, susceptible to physical impressions." And poetry itself, either as entertainment or as criticism, MacNeice declares, "is only valuable if it can add something to the experience of its public, this addition often consisting merely in the illumination of that public's own experience."[22]

On the Continent, throughout the 1930's and the 1940's, the political plays of the German Marxist Bertolt Brecht illustrated brilliantly the connections between the "didactic play" and social purposes. Brecht sought to represent human conditions in a world of economic rapaciousness, war, prejudice, brutality, political evil. For Brecht the theater was necessarily an "epic theater": externalizing, argumentative, didactic, one in which the spectator becomes an active observer and arouses his will to action, calling for decisions and a world outlook. This theater, by "making gestures quotable," demands a struggle of social convictions. For Brecht the social-political situation served to catalyze both his view and his practice of dramatic art. He showed how political consciousness inspires art, how social background and dialectic can inhere in the artist's imagination and give rise to art. In the long run what writers like Brecht do in their works (whatever the genre) is to remind us that the social-political element plays its appropriate role in the artist's vision and technique, activates this vision, and in times of intense ideological turmoil assumes a prominence in and even a technical and at times innovative direction of works of art. Certainly, when considering the literature of the 1930's, one cannot ignore some of the implicit and explicit political elements at work in the writer's imagination. One cannot disregard the truth of the contention that "the essential life of a period is best understood through its literature; not because of what the literature describes, but because of what it embodies."[23]

Here we can well be reminded of the difficulties which, in the twentieth century, arise concerning the purpose of the artist and the task of the critic. A classic illustration of these difficulties was the awarding of the first Bollingen Prize for Poetry to Ezra Pound for *The Pisan Cantos* as "the highest achievement of American poetry in 1948." Judges were the Fellows in American Letters of the Library of Congress, consisting of Léonie Adams, Conrad Aiken, W. H. Auden, Louise Bogan, Katherine Garrison Chapin, T. S. Eliot, Paul Green, Robert Lowell, Katherine Ann Porter, Karl Shapiro, Theodore Spencer, Allen Tate, Willard Thorp, and Robert Penn Warren. Aware of the controversy that would surround their choice, in the light of Pound's career as a fascist and an anti-Semite, the judges were careful to issue this statement: "To permit other considerations than that of poetic achievement to sway the decision would destroy the significance of the award and would in principle deny the validity of that objective perception of value on which civilized society must rest." (Goethe's belief that more is permitted to poets than to ordinary mortals—"*Dichter sündgen nicht schwer*"—can be adduced at this point.) Both the choice of Pound and the judges' statement were unsettling. No other literary event could better focus on the debate between those who see literature in its social and cultural implications and those who see it in its purist callings: between the judgment of imagination as dialectic and of imagination as art.

William Barrett, an editor of the *Partisan Review*, reflected the acerbity of this debate when, writing in the April 1949 issue, he questioned the merits of the choice of *The Pisan Cantos* and specifically "the validity of aesthetic principles" employed by the judges. Barrett emphasized that we could not easily "forget all about the humanly ugly attitudes" of which Pound was a spokesman and which recur in some of the poems comprising *The Pisan Cantos*. With evident dissatisfaction, he also used the Pound case to confront the aestheticians who formulated the criteria for the award—"the validity of that objective perception of value," to recall the most important of their critical standards—with the question: "How far is it possible, in a lyric poem, for technical embellishment to transform vicious and ugly matter into beautiful poetry?"

Reaction to Barrett was heated. Of the Bollingen jurors who replied in the May 1949 issue of the *Partisan Review*, Tate was the most outraged. Barrett, he felt, had in essence charged the Bollingen jurors with anti-Semitism. "I hope that persons who wish to accuse me of cowardice and dishonor will do so henceforth personally, in my presence, so that I may dispose of the charge at some other level than the public discussion. Courage and honor are not subjects of literary controversy, but occasions for action." Barrett was not to be intimidated. Tate's "challenge to a personel duel," he noted, "is strictly extra-curricular sport—having nothing to do with the public issue." Thus Karl Shapiro, who had voted against Pound, said in his "statement of principle" that "the poet's political and moral philosophy ultimately vitiates his poetry and lowers its standards as a literary work." Artists everywhere "should stand against this poet for his greater crime against civilization." In Pound's *The Cantos*, Shapiro concluded, fascism is undeniably "one of the 'myths.'" The question that remains to be answered is, "Through his experience with vicious and ugly ideas, what poetic insights into our world has this poet given us?" These (ungracious) facts in the "Case of Ezra Pound" are given here not to rekindle old feuds, but rather to show the acrimony that surrounds a discussion of literature and society generally and of literature and politics specifically. Barrett and Shapiro, in the questions they raised, underline a position taken by critics concerned with the mythopoeic and moral functions of art, with what Sartre speaks of as the writer's social responsibility in an age of acute historical awareness.

A more recent example of the trend this questioning has led to is John R. Harrison's *The Reactionaries: A Study of the Anti-Democratic Intelligentisa,* in which W. B. Yeats, Wyndham Lewis, Ezra Pound, T. S. Eliot, and D. H. Lawrence are selected as the literary-ideological exemplars of the "anti-democratic intelligentsia" in the twentieth century. Harrison summarizes the purpose of his work and the overall direction of his arguments and conclusions in these words: "What Yeats, Pound, Lewis and Eliot wanted in literature was bareness, a hard intellectual approach ruled by the authority of strict literary principles. They rejected the humanist tradition in literature, and in society, the democratic humanitarian tradition. The same principles governed their social criticism as their literary criticism, and led them to support the fascist cause, either directly, as Pound and Lewis did, or indirectly, as Yeats and Eliot did."[24] This book was much discussed by the literary establishment. It was often applauded. In England, Anthony Burgess, writing in the *Spectator,* observed: "Mr. Harrison is really very good and very fair.... He states where the reactionaries went wrong, and—if we regard the politics of men of letters as of any interest at all—we shall not be unhappy to find him right."[25] In the United States, Philip Rahv, writing in *The New York Review of Books,* largely endorsed Harrison's findings, though he quibbled with the "gummy use of the label 'fascist.' " What the five writers discussed by Harrison, Rahv said, "can be truly accused of is presumption in undertaking to speak portentously about matters they knew little about. This presumption by quite a few men of letters is a cultural phenomenon—a symptom of certain antinomian qualities intrinsic to the literature of the modern age. ..."[26]

The weakness inherent in these critical views becomes as apparent and disputable as, in its peculiar ways, the Marxist view of literature as an "ideological superstructure," the values of which stem from determinations of its "objective reality." The problem with Harrison's study is perhaps also a problem of the social and cultural approach to literature as a whole: excessive reliance on empirical presuppositions, which become in the end an oversimplified aesthetic, no less harmful and limited than the Marxist conclusion. Harrison fails in his work because, unlike Irving Howe in *Politics and the Novel,* he is not concerned, as he should be, with "perspectives of observation" but rather with "categories of classification." Implicit in this latter concern is the danger of the disparity that one writer detects in *The*

Reactionaries when he states: "The book's chief limitation is that Mr. Harrison never faces the central question raised by the awkward social attitudes of his subjects. If it is accepted that some or all of them were among the finest artists of their time, how was it that their art found so much nourishment in authoritarian ideas?"[27]

That "perspective of observation" which Harrison lacks is afforded by Stephen Spender in an essay, "Writers and Politics," in which he discusses *The Reactionaries,* Conor Cruise O'Brien's *Writers and Politics,* and Peter Stansky and William Abraham's *Journey to the Frontier,* a study dealing with the participation of two promising young writers, John Cornford and Julian Bell, in the Spanish Civil War, 1936–1938.[28] Spender discusses precisely those problematic aspects of the relationship between a writer and society which are too often ignored or oversimplified. A writer's politics, he shows, cannot be discarded from an imaginative work of art. The "appeal of politics in the guise of metaphor," as seen in Pound's case, was tempting to writers united in "their condemnation of a society which they saw as the disintegration of civilization." "The temptation for the poet," Spender observes, "is to take over the rhetoric of political will and action and translate it into the rhetoric of poetry without confronting the public rhetoric of politics with the private values of poetry." In a country like France, he emphasizes, where "there is a tradition of intellectually respect-worthy opinion about politics to which the writer can relate his own views," it is not difficult to judge seriously and even accurately a writer's expressed opinions. But because no such tradition exists in England and America, the ways in which the writer intervenes in politics "tend to be sporadic and occasional and perhaps not consistent with his truest, that is his most imaginative insights."

Spender's observations comprise a basic corrective attitude that can hardly be stressed enough in "the pursuit of criticism" relating to the writer and society. Writers between 1910 and 1930 were sensitive to a society which they saw as representing the decay of civilization and as constituting a real and a potential destroyer of the imagination. Indeed, Spender feels, the politics, even the excrescences of the political beliefs, of writers like Yeats, Eliot, Pound, Lewis, and Lawrence showed only "that they cared less for politics than for literature." The upshot of all this is, he insists, that a writer's political gestures and attitudes are often largely rhetorical; that, in the case of the five writers in question, the political elements "are secondary effects of their thoughts about the tragedy of culture in modern industrial societies." Spender's insistence on the necessity to keep in mind the infinitely subtle facets of the artistic imagination in relation to social-political ideas and movements becomes all the more necessary if "categories of classification" are to be avoided.

What, then, can make the writer different (and at the same time insist on that difference in any judgment of his vision as it is consummated in his art) from a political activist? What can distinguish the subtlety of art, even in its politics, from the politics of ideology? Certainly, as Spender asserts, with Yeats, Eliot, Pound, Lewis, and Lawrence, the difference in all its nuances remains inescapable precisely because it is wrought in paradox, which no critical efforts can explain away. The explanation lies in the vision that the imagination finally renders. What Spender achieves in the following passage is precisely that "perspective of observation" that makes criticism legitimate and shows how the subject of literature and society can be of value if the criteria of interpretation do not in themselves become politicized:

> There was, then, the paradox that the reactionaries who were on the side of the past, the dead, had to live for the sake of literature, whereas circumstances drove the most sincere anti-Fascists—men like Cornford, Bell, [Ralph] Fox and [Christopher] Caudwell—to death as absolution in a cause which they had made absolute. The reactionaries wrote out their tragic sense of modern life. The Cornfords and Bells lived and died the tragedy.

Spender's observations trenchantly demonstrate that the subject of the writer and society demands responsible inquiry. Harrison's *The Reactionaries* (even the choice of title conveys dangerous implications) is an example of what can go wrong, particularly of what can go wrong when one's view of his role as a critic discloses both general confusion and, worse, a failure, or an inability, to define or apply the standards of criticism which are necessary in examining a writer's social and political beliefs and expressions. Only when Spender's essay is read as a corrective to Harrison's work are we able to grasp the complexities which determine a writer's relationship to society. The assessment of such a relationship involves at once larger and more intricate considerations: the need to be aware of the full power of the ideological forces which comprise the social-political structure and of the way in which dialectical elements affect a writer's vision. The dangers, the disparities, of such critical assessment can polarize into positions impervious to the complexity of a social-literary integration and also to the miracle of imaginative vision, the creative process, as it transcends social doctrine and programs to become art. One can never disregard the mysterious hidden patterns of the creative process and the creative paradoxes that defy rigid aesthetic classification. Ernst Cassirer in his magisterial *An Essay On Man* reminds us of the nonempirical, aesthetic "forms" of the imagination when he writes:

> ... it is not the same thing to live in the realm of forms as to live in that of things of the empirical objects of our surroundings. The forms of art, on the other hand, are not empty forms. They perform a definite task in the construction and organization of human experience. To live in the realm of forms does not signify an evasion of the issues of life; it represents, on the contrary, the realization of one of the highest energies of life itself. We cannot speak of art as "extrahuman" or "superhuman" without overlooking one of its fundamental features, its constructive power in the framing of our human universe.[29]

Intrinsic literary and cultural values to be realized in the examination of the relationships between literature and society are possible only if certain cautions are kept in mind: if, that is, any critical attempt in this direction is not to be muted in its effectiveness because of the need to correct it, as Spender's essay on *The Reactionaries* demonstrates. This is not to say that such an examination of the problem can ever be final. It is to insist that the examination of literary and cultural interrelationships can be (aesthetically) both elucidation, or illumination, and (culturally) "correction of taste." By relevant, one means, as a start, the critic's "sense of the past," a recognition that, to quote from Lionel Trilling's *The Liberal Imagination*, "the literary work is ineluctably a historical fact, and, what is more important ... its historicity is a fact in our aesthetic experience."[30] Trilling shows that this historical sense, central to the aesthetic faculty, reconciles the experience of literature with a sense of the age, with the question of cultural continuity, with the meaning of life and the destiny of man. Ultimately what this historical sense does is to complement the discipline of literary studies and criticism, and thus enable one to see literature in its living relationships with the whole of society, as L. C. Knights sees these relationships in his *Explorations* (and earlier in his pioneering *Drama and Society in the Age of Jonson*) in which he writes:

> ... in an attempt to understand the quality of living in a past period— to understand, that is, all those intangible modes of being which are only hinted at in the documents on which economic and political history is based—the study of that period's literature is central, and some degree of *critical* ability is indispensable to the historian of culture.[31]

A "disciplined exploration" of literature, Knights contends, remains indispensable to an understanding of society, that is, to an understanding of the organization of life, the ordered human community—that "system or mode of life adopted by a body of individuals for the purpose of harmonious co-existence or for mutual benefit, defence, etc.," to cite one working definition. Criticism and history, as Knights discloses, have their interacting roles to play in their cultural contexts insofar as both relate to the larger questions of life, thought, and literature: "What, in the given age, were the main lines of force as expressed in human thought and action? What were the underlying, conscious or unconscious motives and energies which shaped its art and philosophy, its social, moral and legal codes, no less than its scientific, industrial and political achievements?"[32] Answers to these questions, Knights asserts, can be realized through a proper correlation between criticism and history, "with a view to that wider and deeper understanding of the sources of cultural health."

The critical study of the literature of a period in relation to its sense of the social realities, its cultural artifacts, its civilization, is conducive to "the first-hand apprehension of realized values," which in themselves arise from the fact that literature provides important evidence of the prevailing culture precisely because "it is itself a large part *of* that culture in its intellectual aspects, and it can only be used as 'evidence' when it has been assessed critically as literature." To work back through literature to the life of the time can provide, according to Knights, three essential advantages: first, that of giving evidence of style and language, which in their viable differences are "conditioned by social factors which they can be made, in part, to reveal"; second, that of revealing the tastes and intellectual ability of the audience for which the literature was intended and, more specifically, "how the interests reflected in literature of different degrees of popularity were formed"; and third, that of determining what comprises the highly subtle (and problematical) relationship between the standards a writer adopts and "current social codes," the determination of which "demands a cultivated literary sense as well as historical knowledge."[33]

Knights's observations remind us of the constant need for critics to exert special cautions in investigating the relationships between literature and society. There is a need to avoid the practice of those critics who view an imaginative artist as one whose mind is too fine to be violated by ideas, to borrow here words that Eliot applied to Henry James. This attitude reduces literature either to the dead ends of formalism, which rejects viewing literature in terms of cultural concerns, or to obscurantism. Likewise, there is a need to avoid another form of literary theory, the Marxizing, which examines art in canonical terms of the dialectical method and historical structural-ism, in terms of the canon laid down by Marx himself when he wrote in his Preface to the *Critique of Political Economy*: "The methods of production in material life determine the general character of the social, political, and spiritual process of life. It is not the conscious-ness of men that determines their being, but, on the contrary, their social being determines their consciousness." (In various ways it is this Marxist principle that Knights tests, and then corrects, in his work, as English social critics of the New Left like Richard Hoggart, in *The Uses of Literacy*, and Raymond Williams, in *Culture and Society, 1780–1950*, have also done in recent years.)

Of the two extremes, the Marxist sensibility has played a more important role in sharpening, as George Steiner calls to our attention, the critic's sense of time and place and in contributing "a sociological awareness to the best of modern criticism." "A vital tradition [like the Marxist], vital even in its polemics, is not a luxury but a rigorous need," Steiner observes.[34] But criticism, if it is not to be made im-perfect by what is restrictive and doctrinaire, and if it is to transcend a tolerant eclecticism, which in time is reduced to what has been labeled a "pluralistic ambiguity," needs to adhere to the caution of balance. And this balance can be achieved only by recognizing the primacy of the creative process, which, as one social scientist notes, "transcends the horizon of society, only when integrating the hell and paradise of human life into the symbols of the whole, a task which the sociologist [for example] is incapable of realizing."[35] Dr. F. R. Leavis, whose writings are paradigms of how literary and cultural elements can be vigorously balanced and sustained in works of criti-cism, alludes to some of the cautions emphasized above in the follow-ing remarks;

> Without the sensitizing familiarity with the subtleties of language, and the insight into the relations between abstract or generalizing thought and the concrete of human experience, that the trained frequentation of literature alone can bring, the thinking that attends social and politi-cal studies will not have the edge and force it should.[36]

Some of the critical writings of George Orwell can serve as addi-tional examples of how disciplined criticism and keen historical and social awareness can work together—in fact, how each is indispens-able to the other—illustrating, in the end, how responsible criticism is established on the principle that "the judgments the literary critic is concerned with are judgments about life," to use Leavis' phraseology. A glance at any part of the four-volume edition of *The Collected Essays, Journalism and Letters of George Orwell* should remind one of the clarity and the honesty of Orwell's work as a critic and thinker. That he was no more than an "apologist for cynicism," "a reactionary rebel," "a peculiarly complex and ambiguous man," "a writer of brilliant perception, but also of ridiculous quirks and oddities," or that the effect of his entire thought "is an effect of paradox," or that he was a "nagger . . . who extended discomfort into agony"—these are the recurrent and at present fashionable charges which diminish in their substance as one examines Orwell's writings on the relationships between the writer and society. In the early forties Orwell defined his approach to this subject in a concluding statement to his essay on William Butler Yeats: ". . . a writer's political and religious beliefs are not excrescences to be laughed away, but something that will leave their mark even on the smallest detail of his work."[37] Modern critics have in fact come to be concerned precisely with the problems which Orwell underlines here.

Perhaps the best example of Orwell's social criticism is his essay on Rudyard Kipling[38] (though his essays on Charles Dickens, Jonathan Swift, or P. G. Wodehouse, as well as his "Politics and the English Language," could as easily serve the purpose). The occasion for this essay was the publication of *A Choice of Kipling's Verse* (1941), containing a long introduction by T. S. Eliot. In Kipling, Orwell saw a writer who could stand toward H. G. Wells as a corrective: a writer, in other words, "who was not deaf to the evil forces of power and military 'glory.' " Unlike Wells who "is too sane to understand the modern world," Orwell contends, "Kipling would have understood the appeal of Hitler, or for that matter of Stalin, whatever his attitude towards them might be."[39] Orwell made these observations in an earlier essay, "Wells, Hitler and the World State." The essay on Kipling, as a kind of follow-up, contains Orwell's evaluation of Kipling's work and of his reputation as a poet. In contrast to Eliot's "defensive" position on Kipling ("answering the shallow and familiar charge that Kipling is a 'Fascist' "), Orwell begins by admitting that Kipling "*is* a jingo imperialist, he *is* morally insensitive and aesthetically disgusting." He nevertheless believes that one must go on to try to find out why Kipling "survives while the refined people who have sniggered at him seem to wear badly." The first clue to any understanding of Kipling, he shows, is that morally or politically Kipling "was *not* a Fascist." Rather, his outlook was pre-Fascist, the nineteenth-century imperialist outlook as opposed to that of the modern gangster. Kipling, Orwell goes on to state, belonged to the period 1885–1902; and though the Great War and its aftermath embittered him, "he shows little sign of having learned anything from any event later than the

Boer War." As a result, "all his confidence, his bouncing vulgar vitality, sprang out of limitations which no Fascist or near-Fascist shares."

By identifying himself with the official class, Kipling possessed "a sense of responsibility," or as Eliot writes: ". . . he was aiming to communicate the awareness of something in existence of which he felt that most people were very imperfectly aware. It was an awareness of grandeur, certainly, but it was much more an awareness of responsibility."[40] Orwell particularly singles out "the middle-class Left" for their aversion to Kipling:

> All left-wing parties in the highly industrialised countries are at bottom a sham, because they make it their business to fight against something which they do not really wish to destroy. They have internationalist aims, and at the same time they struggle to keep up a standard of life with which those aims are incompatible. We all live by robbing Asiatic coolies, and those of us who are "enlightened" all maintain that those coolies ought to be set free; but our standard of living, and hence our "enlightenment," demands that the robbery shall continue. A humanitarian is always a hypocrite, and Kipling's understanding of this is perhaps the central secret of his power to create telling phrases. It would be difficult to hit off the one-eyed pacifism of the English in fewer words than in the phrase, "making mock of uniforms that guard you while you sleep."

The indictment is both tough and jarring. No wonder E. M. Forster says that "no one can embrace Orwell's works who hopes for ease. Just as one is nestling against them, they prickle." Yet, feelings and political implications notwithstanding, Orwell's words point to the essential nature of the task in judging Kipling's work and reputation from the viewpoint of a poet's special "grasp of function" to convey, as Eliot felt, "a simple forceful statement rather than a musical pattern of emotional overtones." The middle-class Left, Orwell insists, sniggered at Kipling because they hated him for his sense of responsibility, quite as much as for his cruelty and vulgarity. And an aesthetic judgment on Kipling's work must always return to "his sense of responsibility, which made it possible for him to have a worldview, even though it happened to be a false one."

Although one may disagree with, even snigger at, some of the social-political attitudes in Kipling's work, one cannot, Orwell argues, say that they are frivolous attitudes: "The fact is that Kipling, apart from his snack-bar wisdom and his gift for packing much cheap picturesqueness into a few words . . . is generally talking about things that are of urgent interest." His thought, if vulgar, is permanent, so that much of his poetry gives "pleasure to people who know what poetry means." Kipling can best be described "simply as a good bad poet": "He is as a poet what Harriet Beecher Stowe was as a novelist. And the mere existence of this kind, which is perceived by generation after generation to be vulgar and yet goes on being read, tells something about the age we live in." A good bad poem Orwell defines as "a graceful monument to the obvious," recording in memorable form "some emotion which very nearly every human being can share." As a good bad poet who was a Conservative identifying himself with the ruling power and not the opposition, Kipling, Orwell maintains, enjoyed the advantage of having "a certain grip of reality."

Of course, "Kipling sold out to the British governing class, not financially but emotionally," a fact that helped to warp his political judgment, "for the British ruling class were not what he imagined, and it led him into abysses of folly and snobbery." On the other hand, and most important, Kipling "gained a corresponding advantage from having at least tried to imagine what action and responsibility are like." The business of the critic is to save the writer from misunderstanding and, in the case of Kipling, from the misrepresentation that can arise from the conscious or unconscious surrender to political theory or notion. The critic must rise above such a weakness if he is to be capable of judging the value of a writer, in the way that Orwell judges Kipling throughout his essay and, exemplarily, in this final judgment:

> It is a great thing in his favour that he is not witty, not "daring," has no wish to *épater les bourgeois*. He dealt largely in platitudes, and since we live in a world of platitudes, much of what he said sticks. Even his worst follies seem less shallow and less irritating than the "enlightened" utterances of the same period, such as Wilde's epigrams or the collection of cracker-mottoes at the end of *Man and Superman*.

IV

As the modern world has increasingly come to mean alienation, situation, history, to cite Sartre's triad, the aesthetic function of art has reflected change. Literature has become much more than mere "aesthetic experience," an "intransitive apprehension" of aesthetic object. To stay inside a self-contained work of art is deemed neither feasible nor desirable. The modern artist has come to see his role as one not of entertainment, but rather of the expression of meaning, the communication of insight into some aspect of reality and human experience, the questioning and the redefining of life-values. Sartre has gone so far as to claim that the empire of meaning is prose. And

Leavis has gone on to claim that "it is the great novelists above all who give us our social history; compared with what is done in *their* work—their creative work—the histories of the professional social historian seem empty and unenlightening."[41] Such claims, coming from two writers profoundly dissimilar in critical temperament and approach, point to the extension of aesthetic boundaries in the twentieth century and to the recognition of art as a force for life.

Modern artists have more and more affirmed their place in the world in all its predicament and paradox. What has become less acceptable is precisely the kind of remoteness from the human spectacle that Ezra Pound admired in Joyce's *A Portrait of the Artist as a Young Man*: ". . . I think the book hard, perfect stuff. I doubt if you could have done it in the 'lap of luxury' or in the whirl of a metropolis with the attrition of endless small amusements and endless calls on one's time, and endless trivialities of enjoyment (or the reverse)."[42] Rather it is the artist's sense of responsibility and his commitment that inform his role in the world and in the creative process: "For me," asserts the Italian novelist and politician Ignazio Silone, "writing has not been, and never could be, except in a few favored moments of grace, a serene aesthetic enjoyment, but rather the painful and lonely continuation of a struggle."[43] That art must reveal this struggle and, in the end, help change the world instead of just reflecting it, illustrates the kind of aesthetic transformation that has ripened in the twentieth century. (In some ways this transformation has accompanied the socialist view of life as an instrument of social influence in dynamic relation to the "meaning of life" and in terms of what Ernst Fischer speaks of as "a large vision of the future, a hopeful historical perspective."[44])

Not unexpectedly, academic literary study has also been undergoing sharp changes, with old, established, essentially conservative attitudes being rejected or at least challenged. (Tate's contention that "Pound's language remains our particular concern," despite the fact that his verbal sensibility is at the mercy of "Icarian self-indulgences," is an example of a literary attitude now being challenged.[45]) Particularly in the United States the rise of "the dissenting academy," to borrow the title of a volume of essays edited by Theodore Roszak, is in fact everywhere apparent among scholars in the various humanistic disciplines; and everywhere in the "multiversity" protests are being heard against "mindless specialization and irrelevant pedantry," against the "tradition of official conformity," against the "condition of entrenched social irrelevance" that has characterized American academics to the extent that this condition, as Roszak suggests, can be "condemned as an act of criminal delinquency."[46] More than ever the feelings of protesting scholars, teachers, and students are angry, their tempers radical. Genuine "humanist" social responsibility, "critical social relevance," it is claimed, has been sacrificed or betrayed. Louis Kampf in his essay "The Scandal of Literary Scholarship," which significantly (symptomatically?) is the first essay in *The Dissenting Academy*, bitterly attacks the proliferation of "criticism without real social relevance." The academic bureaucracy, commercial values (or the lack of any values), careerism ("making it"?), the pervasive absence of any sense of commitment in literary criticism are what have led to "this sellout," Kampf charges. "The study of literature must begin with an exploration of our social needs," he insists.[47]

Dissenting literary scholars, even if they constitute a small but militant minority, "a phalanx from the left," as it has been described, are asking questions which demand answers. ("Dangerous as it is," Kampf notes, "we may have to accept some student's honest feeling that, for example, Milton's use of pastoral in 'Lycidas' is a foolish irrelevance."[48]) Behind this dissatisfaction is a growing belief that the critical discipline itself must be "liberated," to apply here the widely used terminology of Herbert Marcuse; that the critical faculty, as a form of moral discrimination, must not be surrendered to "the forces of domination" in an advanced industrial society "organized as things and instrumentalities." Criticism, like the art it mediates, must contain "the rationality of negation" and be part of "the Great Refusal," to borrow Marcuse's terms once more.[49] What activist critics are often decrying is the habit of both scholar and teacher to dissociate literature from life and thought, or as Diana Trilling has well expressed the crux of the problem: "The teaching of modern subjects in our universities, especially literature, proceeds of course on some unadmitted (because inadmissible) assumption of a drastic discontinuity between art and life."[50]

Not to be overlooked is the anti-Arnoldian thesis advanced by one critic. "The mainstream of modern critical interpretation of literature," this radical energumen states, "though it would claim for itself an objective, scientific basis, can be reasonably seen as the development of what is only implied in Arnold, the administration of literature." Arnold's politics and his culture, in effect, are not unrelated, but are connected by ideas of centralization, control, and administration, precisely the elements that have made "literature seem unusable in fighting those tendencies in society."[51] Another critic asserts that not only must there be a complete repudiation of "reactionary formalism," but also a fearless radicalization of the teaching and criticism of literature by teachers and scholars who "are bringing some politics into the classrooms . . . [and] have even removed their ties."[52] And, if one is to judge by the continuing protests, there appears to be little let-up in the offing. Literary orthodoxy is under pressure, even as literary philistinism is in retreat. Compartmentalization, and departmentalization, of Literature is surely coming to an end. Thus, if some of the outcries and gestures of the radical critics often seem intemperate, or if some of their solutions (e.g., the "radicalized curriculum") are shockingly simplistic, their pleas for a revaluation of both the teaching and the criticism of literature, freed at last from "administrative" control by academy and by academic coterie alike, is not without that desired quality of integrity that both dignifies the creative act and validates the critical function.

For some, no doubt, it is tempting to discredit the views of the radical critics; and no doubt there are good reasons for opposing them. After all, removing one's tie does not exactly give a critic any credentials or any critical insights into literature. Neither the radicalization nor the politicalization of literature and of literary studies is the answer. We need merely consider the happenings of the thirties to see some of the consequences of a radicalized literature: to see, that is, some of the aberrations that emerged in those years in the course of "literary class war." There were, to be sure, some valuable contributions to the study of literature in terms of its relevance to man and society, especially in a time of economic deprivation. Not a few men of letters dared to make what Arthur Koestler calls "the journey into communism." Granville Hicks illustrated what he called "the clarifying effect of revolutionary allegiance," and his book *The Great Tradition* was an outgrowth of the American experience. Although Hicks's interpretation of American literature was characterized, it was charged, by a "mechanical Marxism," its thesis that revolutionary writing since the Civil War was at the heart of the American tradition could not be discounted.

But for Hicks and for other "comrades of the Pink decade"— Koestler, André Gide, and Richard Wright come immediately to mind—the journey into communism was followed by a return from it. Communism became the "god that failed." In 1940, in a retrospective mood, as he looked back to the form and results of his "allegiance," Hicks concluded: "Politics is no game for a person whose attention is mostly directed elsewhere."[53] These are more than words of repudiation; they bring to the forefront the problem of the radicalization of literature as well as the subject of the relationship of the writer, both artist and critic, to the human condition in its social-political ramifications. And again questions of legitimacy and of function arise, as do words of caution. For, above all, what literature must be saved from is the narrow critical and mechanical strictures that limit the value of Hicks's *The Great Tradition*. The "closed myth of concern" that Northrop Frye sees as shackling Marxist writing is one way of describing something that writers must avoid. The insistence on making literature relevant in terms of social needs or action can easily lead to a form of this closed myth. "Not only is there always a pressure within society to close its mythology," Frye reflects, "but the efforts to keep it open have to be strenuous, constant, delicate, unpopular, and above all largely negative."[54] (Frye here makes more meaningful Edwin Muir's fear that "when the natural man becomes political, there seem to be only two directions in which he can advance: towards Communism or towards Fascism."[55])

Thus we are returned inevitably to the cautionary note struck earlier, and to the critical ambivalence that any discussion of literature and society arouses. And we are returned particularly to the fact that though the so-called administration of literature often leads to what is pedantic, the element of discipline in the form of resistance to the expedient and imperfect, to the quantitative as opposed to the qualitative (the closed myth of concern as opposed to the open myth), cannot be ignored in the study of literature. The disciplinary element is a mainstay of civilization itself, as Yeats reminds us:

> A civilization is a struggle to keep self-control, and in this it is like some great tragic person, some Niobe who must display an almost superhuman will or the cry will not touch our sympathy. The loss of control over thought comes towards the end; first a sinking in upon the moral being, then the last surrender, the irrational cry, revelation—the scream of Juno's peacock.[56]

In this struggle for the survival of civilization, the critical process remains fundamental. To be vigorous in the best cultural sense, this process must at the same time transcend categorizations of conservative versus modern, reactionary versus liberal. Indeed, perhaps what most harmed the proletarian critics of the thirties and, earlier, the critics of "the conservative mind" (Irving Babbitt and Paul Elmer More, for instance) was an inability to transcend the limitations of their social or classical presuppositions.

As modern writers have steadily disclosed their concern with social and political issues, the result of this concern has been the emergence of what is called a radical literature. Yet critics must remember that radical literature is not to be evaluated in terms of radical politics. "Maybe the lesson of the 30's," William Phillips points out, "is that radical politics has not been able to escape the dilemma of being distorted by power or left hanging without power, while literature to be radical need not—perhaps cannot—be tied to radical politics."[57] These words bring attention to problems that today require careful thought. The differences between radicalization and politicalization are always in need of being identified. One important service a critic can do is to assess some of the radical— radical in the sense of the socially aware, relevant, exigent, and radical in terms of the modern temper—techniques and tendencies, as language and meaning in literature. But this critical task has to be free from any imposition of a blatantly political attitude. The critic best fulfills his function by discerning the radical and the political without surrendering to either one or both elements. Criticism, at its best and most helpful, is an exercise in freedom; and though it can be radical, it cannot be political, cannot subscribe to a theory of politics.

By no means should these remarks imply that the responsible critic must be "scientific," "objective," or "scholarly." With respect to the function and the pursuit of criticism, these adjectives of criteria have long been misapplied, to the point of the irrelevance that activist writers are now castigating. "Criticism can never be a science: it is, in the first place, much too personal," D. H. Lawrence avers, "and in the second, it is concerned with values that science ignores."[58] Lawrence helps to define the limits of criticism, even as he suggests its responsibilities and challenges. Modern literary studies, or, in a more technical sense, "English studies," have not always been alert to Lawrence's words. In fact, though it is getting rather late in the century, English studies are just beginning to explore what literature has to say about man in his social and political lives. It has taken a long time to unload some of the old, stifling attitudes toward the relations between literature and society, attitudes that, in the grip of parochial specialisms, have been hostile to probing the dynamic relations between a writer and society.

The impatience shown in recent years by activist critics is not unwarranted, despite some of their shock tactics and rhetoric (the title of an essay by one such critic, "The Teaching of Literature in the Highest Academies of the Empire," shows just how self-deceiving the rhetoric becomes). It *is* unwarranted when it begins to tie criticism exclusively to the "desperate need of social change," at which point the critical task becomes as distorted as it has all along been constricted by administrators of literature. It is probably with such facts in mind that one scholar and teacher, Richard Poirier, warns: "English studies cannot be the body of English literature but it can be at one with its spirit: of struggling, of wrestling with words and meaning. Otherwise English studies may go one of two ways: it can shrink, hopefully in a manner as distinguished and health-giving as that which accompanied the retrenchment of Classics departments; or it can become distended by claims to a relevance merely topical."[59]

The spirit of "literary revolutionism" is powerful, and for the critic it poses special problems. More and more demands are being made that literary scholarship should be allied with political activism; that the critic play his appropriate political role in opposing some of the wrongs in society, such as "social mechanisms," "industrial capitalism," the "system of acculturation"; that the critic who judges literature should judge it in accordance with the ways in which literature is, or is not, attuned to pressing social issues and promulgates political action and social change; that the act of criticism, given the revolutionism of the age, must be seen within "social contexts" if it is in any way to be deemed useful. The critic is being asked to be more than what he is: to be, at the same time, political scientist, economist, religious thinker, philosopher, social historian, and theorist. Yet it is too easily forgotten that "the basic experience of everyone is the experience of human limitation."[60] Criticism, then, finds itself in something of a condition of crisis requiring redefinition of tasks, concepts, and approaches. Obviously, the activist critics do not have a solution, their preoccupation with immediate and often local and temporary social needs (in literary contexts) being in itself symptomatic of party-spirit and provincialism. In one major respect, nevertheless, this crisis has had the fortunate consequence of forcing critics and teachers of literature to review the nature of their work, their function, and to reappraise their ends and values. "Criticism," as William Hazlitt writes in his famous essay, "is an art that undergoes a great variety of changes, and aims at different objects at different times."

Today, when one thinks of the way in which the world is "turning and turning in the widening gyre," the need for critical perspective and for an understanding of man and of his society is itself critical. Imaginative literature as the book of life contains countless clues to this understanding. It can provide us not only with an understanding of what life is, but also with a vision of the world in which human experience achieves its quintessence, its concreteness and meaning as a whole. Toward the achievement of this understanding the critic can be of considerable service, service that reaches beyond mere literary code and that is both relevant and responsible. "The central problem of literary criticism," Theodore Spencer wrote back in the early and uncertain years of World War II, "is not only a problem of form, not only a problem of literary value—it is the problem of what it means to be a conscious being in a world that may darken to annihilation."[61] It is in the process of his criticism that the critic registers this greater consciousness, and he can—he must—do so above party feelings and ideologies. "His job, as the trustee of tradition," to quote Spencer again, "is to know as fully, as quantitatively, as possible, what is included in human experience, and on the basis of that knowledge to be as dispassionate as he is aware."[62]

Admittedly a critic cannot always be a "trustee of tradition." But, if he is in any way to begin to fulfill his function as a critic, he should be aware, supremely aware. For the modern critic this desideratum connotes, more than anything else and more than at any other time in history, an awareness of relationships that connect (and *connect*, not *exist between*) literature and other areas of human effort. It is true enough, as Richard Hoggart has warily said, that "if we forget the 'celebratory' or 'playful' element in literature we will sooner or later stop talking about literature and find ourselves talking about history or sociology or philosophy—and probably about bad history and bad sociology and bad philosophy." But just as importantly, and more relevantly, Hoggart does not fail to add that literature "has to do with language exploring human experience, in all its flux and complexity. It is therefore always in an active relation with its age; and some students of literature—many more students of literature than at present—ought to try to understand these relationships better."[63] This statement, it becomes indisputably evident in our world, affirms the positive, the legitimate, as well as the living and central, connection inherent in the very words: the Writer and Society.

2

Promise of Greatness:
The War of 1914–1918

∽

No one who was born and has lived in the twentieth century has been spared from war, from either the reality or the constant thought and threat of war. This century has seen wars fought with ever-increasing ferocity. Perhaps no other war stirs the emotions more or exerts more lasting interest than does World War I, the Great War of 1914–18, the Great War for Civilization. Although more than a half century has passed since the Armistice of November 11, 1918, in the memories of the survivors, those who fought and those who did not, in the imaginations of those unborn at the time, the Great War holds a place of importance which grows stronger as the events come gradually to belong to a past which gives rise to legend, song, and poetry— to the tale of war: the mingling of romance and history into which war has merged from the earliest of times.

War as we have experienced it in this century can hardly arouse exaltation. We now see the utter devastation and meaninglessness of war, those cruel realities that the bloodstained face of history has taken on. We have had to learn to confront war not as abstraction, but as actuality, "the great unequal battle . . . between the forces of terror and the forces of dialogue," as Albert Camus expressed it. War has made us and our age harder and more cynical. Certainly men today refuse to connect the waging of war with the mystique of adventure: the fulfillment of some inborn promise, the matchless opportunity to display a chivalrous temper. It seems that we have learned war's lessons of illusion and disillusion. The rhetoric of war, which we find as deplorable as it is irresponsible, has no place in a world where nuclear annihilation poses the final menace— and the final madness.

Our attitude toward war, expressed nowadays in such militant and clamorous ways, underlines the fact that the twentieth century is no longer young or naïve. When we consider some of the immediate responses to the declaration of war in August 1914, we recognize the innocence of youth on the threshold of a new age in an old world with which the century began. C. E. Montague later wrote in *Disenchantment*, "All the air was ringing with rousing assurances."[1] "The air is better to breathe than it has been for years," declared Walter Raleigh.[2] In Vienna, Sigmund Freud exclaimed, "All my libido is given to Austro-Hungary."[3] In France one writer expected that the war would be "amusing," another that it would provide the opportunity to "picnic on the grass."[4] And in Germany one thinker asserted that because his nation had discovered the factor of a higher organization, the war would provide the occasion for reorganizing Europe—and, concurrently, for realizing the German dream of the *Kolossal.*[5] Time and history had not yet run out of promises for the generation of 1914–18. The experience of the war harmonized with the language of heroism, as the early years of the war amply demonstrated. These years held golden moments, "the eve of our crowning hour," according to a soldier-poet. Many men who enlisted in that war felt they were fighting not only for age-old concepts, but also for the sake of changing the world and shaping a new destiny.

Fifty years later we come to realize that the Great War in its early stages was fought not so much to destroy an enemy as to defend and extend the possibilities of civilization, and precisely that civilization which Henry James envisioned as the way "to find and to make the earth a friendlier, an easier, and especially a more various sojourn."[6] It is on transcendent levels of the abstract, the ideal, and the romantic that we first view the waging of this war. Comradeship, splendor, glory, honor, love, and sympathy were still to retain those values vital to a humane civilization. The war was seen in 1914 as a conflict "between sisters, between Martha and Mary, the efficient and intolerant against the casual and sympathetic,"[7] between the real and the unreal, the effete and the vital, the conscious and the unconscious, the *homo contrahumanus* and the *homo humanus.* For many of its participants and nonparticipants as well, this war acted as "a great remedy" and "a great experience," a breakthrough at long last from the dream world of the nineteenth century. "You won't catch me complaining of any war—much less of a great war like this that we wage on both sides like mystics for a reason beyond reason," Robert Frost wrote in a letter dated September 17, 1914.[8]

Combatants were characterized again and again by an enthusiasm bordering on religious frenzy. For not a few, the war at the front was transposed into a religious experience which provided a heightening, a lucidity, and a freedom, emerging from shared suffering and death, that no human action could approximate. In battle one experienced

35

a "compelling fascination ... that lies ... [in] War's power": "Once
you have lain in her arms you can admit no other mistress. You may
loathe, you may execrate, but you cannot deny her."[9] The war served
as a baptism into reality, a tragic, even ecstatic dimension of life that
a soldier-priest, Pierre Teilhard de Chardin, envisioned as "an urgent
invitation to prayer" while one lived "in a forward-looking tension."
Only at the front, with "its noble struggles" and "its impassioned
quests," in the ever present shadow of danger, Teilhard de Chardin
believed, could one attain a fully conscious state, a new form of soul,
"to be healed and made perfect," and experience there, in "the thick
of human endeavour, and with no stopping for breath," what he could
not experience anywhere else: that sense of exaltation which comes
with "fulfilling a function far higher than that of the individual."[10]
Charles Hamilton Sorley, despite a "mute and burning rage and an-
noyance and sulkiness," felt something of the same when he confessed
that in battle "one learns to be a servant. The soul is disciplined."[11]

This was far from assuming some merely sentimental attitude or
some lingering heroic dream evoked by schoolboy memories of the
"plains of windy Troy," which elated Rupert Brooke upon his departure for the Dardanelles in late February 1915. "Will Hero's Tower
crumble," he asked, "under the 15″ guns? Will the sea be polyphlois-
bic and wine-dark and unvintageable? Shall I loot mosaics from St.
Sophia, and Turkish Delight, and carpets? Should we be a Turning
Point in History? Oh God!"[12] For many of the fighting men, the war
was much more than the excitation of the "confident and glorious
hopes" that stirred in Brooke. And it was much more, surely, than
what H. G. Wells described with commanding import when he asserted; "This, the greatest of all wars, is not just another war—it is
the last war!"[13] For some men the war meant the renovation of mankind by the creation of a "great society" and a "new map of Europe."
As one young French novelist wrote to Romain Rolland, "History
will tell of us, for we are opening a new era in the world."[14] For others
it signified the ultimate confrontation of the realities which lie far
beyond and far deeper than just "a necessity of honour," for which
one statesman pleaded, or an opportunity to "travel along the road
of human destiny and progress, at the end of which we shall see
the patient figure of the Prince of Peace, pointing to the Star of
Bethlehem that leads us on to God," as one English journalist
averred.[15]

Hence for some of the fighting men the war—"the whole sad man-
made complication," as Rainer Maria Rilke termed it—transcending
the romantic and idealistic, transcending, too, what some fighting

men designated as "a state of primal innocence," the war enabled one to grasp a better concept of the nature of man and of life as a whole. It disclosed that evil in the world is not rooted merely in oppression, but is an intrinsic part of the nature of things. The realities of the condition of man and of life at the front; the nightmare of slaughter and wooden crosses that the Great War became—these were facts that unmasked the demonic character of man who had sinned and fallen. Life at the front was thus the furthest extension of man's essential condition: his weakness and imperfectibility strained to their most extreme limits. "In this war, then, we are fighting for no great *liberation of mankind*," T. E. Hulme wrote from the trenches, "for no great jump upward, but are merely accomplishing a work, which, if the nature of things was ultimately 'good,' would be useless, but which in this actual 'vale of tears' becomes from time to time necessary, merely in order that bad may not get worse."[16]

The war suddenly awakened the 1914 generation from the comparative ease and comfort and orderliness of an older, more stable way of life. Left behind was the leisurely world of European society before 1914—when education was centered in the classics, when cricket and the hunt were often more important than international affairs, when private life was valued, when writing poetry and exploring the countryside were sources of quiet joy—a world still close to Thomas Hardy's "indispensable conditions of existence [which] are attachment to the soil of one particular spot by generation after generation."[17] Even as it caused incredulity, disarray, and anguish, the declaration of war awakened dreams of glorious exploits echoing once more to the roll of drums. Stefan Zweig, reflecting on the reasons why Europe went to war, suggests that it was not because of ideologies or even provocative acts, but rather because of a "surplus of force, a tragic consequence of the internal dynamism that had accumulated in those forty years of peace and now sought violent release."[18] Those who had come to manhood under the discipline of the old tradition had suddenly to face the demands of a new age. The war was as much an awakening to these demands as it was a military event. And one of the clearest demands after that "monstrous August" was that the war must correspond with the essential character of a civilization which was becoming increasingly industrialized.

The military conduct of the war mirrored a great transition. Dreams of cavalry charges, of open warfare with dashing officers leading professional soldiers into the fray, into a struggle of strength and skill and courage, had to give way, at a tremendous expense of lives and material, to the grim exigencies of a fighting front thick with barbed wire and gashed by trenches. This was the new war in a new age. It was a total, an absolute war; it involved many nations and war fronts and was fought with revolutionary tactics and with new weapons of annihilation: airplanes, submarines, tanks, trench bombs, poison gas. In short, modern warfare was to prescribe the methods of wholesale violence. At the same time, disclosing the denial of personality, it was a struggle directed against men as objects. As such, this war was to be a portent of an age progressively sacrificing the personal to the needs of machine-made mass civilization. "As a man as of a knife: does it cut well? Nothing else mattered," D. H. Lawrence wrote in *Women in Love*, which "took its final shape in the midst of the period of war."[19] His words illustrate the objectivization that war in the modern industrial world has since procured on demand time and time again.

That the Great War was to be the source of many achievements in prose, poetry, drama, and in autobiography and memoirs is not surprising. Literature, after all, reflects both the values and the impulses of an age. For the generation of 1914 these impulses were eminently generous. The drabness of mechanical civilization had not yet conditioned men who, even in the cockpit of slaughter and in the darkness of battle, still apprehended the call of beauty, the passage of the seasons, the spirit of place. Just as war had a deeply religious dimension for some of its combatants, so too did it have a deeply poetic dimension when the creative and destructive instincts, imagination and power, strove for expression. Undoubtedly the immediate scenes of fighting, the desolate, defiled, charred, scarred landscape, now beyond description, strange and dead, inhuman, empty, were not without their communicable, and incommunicable, impressiveness. Men who had lived in Arcadia were now trapped in Armageddon, but the past lingered precariously in their memory. In the tension between terror and memory was born art, which, as André Gide has told us, "is born of constraint, lives by struggle, dies of freedom."

The literature of the war, as written by participants and by survivors both during and after the conflict, invariably reflects a yearning for truth, a struggling search for some deep understanding of war that, never ignoring the passion of the experience, yet attains the detachment necessary to measure it. What we detect so often in the generation and in the literature of 1914–18 is an intensity of awakening to reality and to truth. Many of the combatants recognized as never before the problematic human situation and discovered truth of self. Bodily and mentally, men rose through the experience of war to the experience of self-meaning. Many of the recollections of the war verbalize the process of discovering some truth of self, of life. Thus, for many soldiers, regardless of nation, the Great War as the home of their youth dramatized in extremity what the world included.

Reading the reminiscences of life at the front, we are struck by how long the soldiers had to wait for things to happen. Determination itself was tested by a war in which time had come to a desperate standstill. "There really seems no reason why the Germans and ourselves," said French President Raymond Poincaré at the end of the first year, "should not stand facing one another for all eternity."[20] Indeed, it was a war in which there was as much a despair of time as there was of death. The oppressiveness of time served to signify an agonizing sense of unreality and an awareness of an isolated world reduced to devastation and putrefaction. This world, where life and death at last became one, represented for some of the soldiers a nightmarish eternity. At the front, the alternating periods of violence and of stillness, of savage bombardments followed by sudden silence, blended to render time dimensionless, indistinct. Time, it seems, had also become the victim of destruction and death. Endurance, if anything, had to take the place of time and the place of faith.

If the war meant anguish, it also meant "the infinite pain of self-realization," to use a phrase of William Butler Yeats, who dismissed the war as a "bloody frivolity." In one sense, perhaps, true heroism was to be experienced in such an awakening. Now there was a growing awareness of the value of simply doggedly hanging on in an interminable conflict of great military "offensives" and "deadlocks." But the war also meant a more passionate awakening than just learning how to endure. This was an experiential awareness on the part of men sharing dangers, undergoing the drudgery of war in the trenches, having the same fears, disappointments, complaints, resentments, irritations, disgusts, the same hopes and dreams and enthusiasms, fighting and surviving, or dying, in a world which they alone knew. Endurance, which must inevitably consist in physical and spiritual weariness that defies death and nothingness, was made more achievable by a confraternity of men in arms and by a sense of identity that could be grasped only in the most extraordinary of human situations. This shared identity was not established just on the fact of youth in sight of chaos or on intense comradeship emerging in a world from which there was no easy escape. After all, no lines of discrimination based on class or favor could exist among men thrown together in a war that imposed on them an equivalent danger and

equivalent conditions of fighting and dying. When time had no meaning and when civilized living had been necessarily reduced in space
to the rubble of no-man's-land, men sought their remaining human
identity through communion with one another. Beyond this identity
there could be nothing else that counted.

In one another the soldiers fighting at the front grew to greatness.
In a world where everything seemed to be in a state of collapse, ranging from the failures of leadership at home and at the front to the
failures of the announced promise of "victory" battles, they looked
for something surer than mere promises or the vagaries of faith. And
they found this assurance in fellowship with their comrades. Exposed
to maximum dangers, the men in the front lines learned to speak
a language based on a unity of experience. They had found promise
and truth in one another, even as they learned to accept and inspire
one another. Not seldom, in fact, soldiers who had been returned to
civilian areas for rest and recuperation yearned to be sent back to the
battlefield. (Recovering from war wounds in England, Siegfried Sassoon felt the "awful attraction" that the war held over his mind, and
he was "disquieted by a craving to be back on the Western Front as
an independent contemplator."[21]) Their feelings for one another
were a mixture of respect and pity, based on an experience of life
born, tested, and renewed in the heat of conflict. As their accounts
demonstrate, these men did not hate utterly. For them the war, much
deeper than the fastness of hate, was the passion of its suffering, when
in the course of cruel history "I hear, through dead men's drums, the
riddled lads / Strewing their bowels from a hill of bones, / Cry Eloi
to the guns"[22]—the suffering, that is to say, mitigated by a common
human identity and fulfilled in a common judgment: when all are
to blame, all are accused.

The many brave acts of the men who fought in this war must not
be judged by the traditional criterion of prowess or the old concept
of the heroic man of action. This was an altogether new, mechanized
war, ungraced by those inexpressibly strange felicities and nobilities
engendered by older wars, even at their most savage heights. The
Nietzschean view of men who wage war for the "pleasures of victory
and cruelty" so as to be "purified" by their triumphs over the elements and other men, and thus become "the archetypes of moral
beauty," could hardly be defended or exemplified in a war that
wrought indiscriminate annihilation. There was nothing beautiful
or glorious about this war. Bravery was no longer some spectacular
process; when it appeared, it was usually against a dehumanized background of ugliness and disbelief. Essentially a brave act had to be

achieved not in some encounter with other men, but against the mechanical might of the weapons of destruction produced by a new science and engineering. Bravery, like heroism, was radically transformed in act and meaning in a conflict in which, as it transpired, there could be neither complete victory nor complete defeat.

These observations do not imply that soldiers in this war were not as brave as soldiers in past wars. On the contrary, the men at the front disclosed a bravery all the more astonishing when one considers their inexperience and the awesome surprise they must have often felt in contending not with other human beings, but with the depersonalized ways of modern warfare based on tactics and maneuvers and executed by great armored forces. Bravery became more a matter of holding on tenaciously, even miraculously, against innumerable forms of mechanized power that could bring death swiftly, unexpectedly, at any time, in any place. For many soldiers bravery became a realized inner experience of surmounting fear of the senseless and the pitiless, while at the same time appreciating such things as chance, luck, and fate. It became passive, rather than exhibitive. In other words, bravery was something that a soldier had first to search for, discover, and exert in himself, and as such it was to be attained anonymously: in the common soldier—the "nobody" as he was sometimes known—struggling to survive a mass killing process which ultimately flouted any distinction between bravery or cowardice.

As the war went on, especially after the Battle of the Somme and the failure of the "Great Advance" in 1916, and as the casualties, the disappointments, and the horrors accumulated, the realization grew that this was a "murder war" now further and further removed from any struggle for civilization, certainly from that phantom civilization which Matthew Arnold once saw as the humanization of man in society. At the front, in the midst of endless barbed-wire entanglements, of advances counted by the inches, of murderous artillery bombardments that led to the disappearance of entire villages and to the creation of cemeteries of mud for men and animals alike, the presage of death became the most immediate fact of life. Military leadership, professionally—and professedly—concerned with what T. E. Lawrence has described as "the whole house of war in its structural aspect, which was strategy, in its arrangements, which were tactics, and the sentiment of its inhabitants, which was psychology,"[23] frequently failed to sustain the soldiers' enthusiasm and trust and, worse, to understand the hell of this war. Errors in judgment, inexcusably inadequate communication, recklessness, bungling, stubbornness, caprice, irresponsibility, amateurishness, and stupidity, especially on the part of the military mandarins, led to unnecessary death and maiming, as well as to the cynicism that the fighting men increasingly felt and that in some French Army units even erupted into mutiny—in "the house of war" the meed of valor must yet inevitably vie with the spirit's ruin.

Of all the experiences of war, what remains unwavering in the survivors' recollections is the omnipresence of death. And it is the immensity, the ugliness and horror of death that haunt their memories. The scenes in which the soldiers depict death are touched not so much by mystery or fear as by incomprehensibility. At the front, death was to come suddenly and with a wide range of devastation. Often it was the unnaturalness of the scenes of death that seemed grotesque. Death came with mechanical force, with an objective relentlessness and an instantaneousness beyond belief. Though some of the survivors recall separate examples of death wounds and death experiences, it is more usual for them to depict scenes of collective death. We are thus reminded of a war in which entire armies disappeared; death was as massive in its results as it was incontrovertible in its power. Awesomeness and powerlessness, consequently, characterize the responses of the fighting men to the constant danger of death cheaply but efficiently accomplished by the engines of war.

Oftentimes the survivors recall scenes in which the living and the dead come together. A soldier seeking refuge and protection in some pithole finds his only other companion to be a dead soldier. Or, as he threads his way in the dark, he stumbles against a dying man. Or, as he is digging, he unearths a khaki-clad corpse covered by debris in the wake of an earlier artillery bombardment. And too, there are the memories of mass graves, of burying parties, of smelling corpses being eaten by packs of roaming dogs, of young and strong bodies deformed beyond recognition. And we are ever aware of the appalling number of casualties, in a war in which one day alone could bring death and wounds to many thousands of men and one year to well over a million. At the front death is the overwhelming fact. The magnitude of death creates speechless horror; the thought of death fills immensity. There is hardly a boundary line between the dead, the dying, and the living. It has been said that although death destroys a man, the idea of death saves him. But for the men at the front, death was the major fact of life: the incessant vision of the wounded and the dying exceeded pity and prayer alike.

Yet self-pity and sentimentality, offshoots of great spiritual and physical crises, are singularly lacking in these responses. Even where the scenes of death become dread images of mass slaughter, they reflect immense pain and a stark recognition of some tremendous force let loose, bringing infinite ruin. Often, therefore, death is seen in the metaphorical guise of madness; it is what could not possibly be real because of its sheer inhumanness, but which in its enormity and momentum moves at last beyond the consciousness of the real and the moral. That life has been violated and blasphemed in man's least sacrosanct moments is what often informs some of the immediate responses to the scenes of death. The victory of a profane spirit becomes an overarching fact. That the word "monstrous" appears repeatedly in the survivors' recollections is not without significance. This power that brings death is mechanical and conscienceless; it inflicts death with a kind of measured, passionless intensity. The battle scenes of death reveal the marks of a power that crushes once it strikes, reaping men in swaths.

In the concluding pages of *The Magic Mountain*, Thomas Mann describes the Great War as "The historic thunder-peal, of which we speak with bated breath, [and which] made the foundations of the earth to shake. . . ."[24] By the time of the Armistice, the war had become an experience of the abyss, not only for the fighting men on both sides, but also for entire civilian populations, especially in the immediate areas of the hostilities. This shaking of the foundations of European civilization was brutally evident in every phase of life. After 1918 the values of a settled civilization were gone. The years of the war remained as the chief remembrance of things past, and the future was uncertain. The war had destroyed a sense of security and stability, and 1918 was to become a date signaling the crises of civilization that have marked the rest of the twentieth century. Those who lost their lives lost all their bitterness. But those who survived felt sorrow without end. Recalling the upheavals of the war, Leonard Woolf remarks in *Downhill All the Way*: "In 1914 in the background of one's life and one's mind there was light and hope; by 1918 one had unconsciously accepted a perpetual public menace and darkness and had admitted into the privacy of one's mind or soul an iron fatalistic acquiescence in insecurity and barbarism."[25]

Here Woolf underlines what can be described as the "deaths in belief" that the generation of 1914–18 suffered. The war was especially disastrous for idealistic thought, for the innocence of an optimist faith, for the liberal doctrine, for the humanist creed, and for the old ideals of classicism and education. More than anything else, the war had unmasked the most diabolic tendencies and weaknesses of man and his society. Neither the values of a civilization founded on what the English philosopher G. E. Moore termed the "divine voice of a plain common-sense" nor G. Lowes Dickinson's melioristic vision of a world in which man can stretch "feelers into the Dark, laying hold there of stuff, and building mythologies and poems, the palaces of splendid hopes and desires," could possibly withstand the ravages of this war. Modern civilization, in the wake of war, was to become the hostage of a world in which a glorified "authentic present" and a "massive incertitude" (to use here a phrase of Ezra Pound's) agitated to replace the traditions and values that the war had destroyed. Civilization in the period following 1918 was witness both to a dying order and to a world striving to be reborn. But the possibility of resurrection in a world defiled beyond recognition was not without its frightening limitations. "The post-war generation had to live," one writer lamented, "and the war-generation had nothing to give them to live by."[26]

There are always those, of course, who, like Conrad Aiken, suggest that "The history of war / is the history of mankind,"[27] who suggest that war in the historical process is ultimately a dynamic, cleansing, and creative experience which helps to teach nations and humanity self-knowledge and to release new energy. But the Great War was to destroy such a myth! After the Armistice nothing could be more painfully obvious than the absurdity of the promises of war. For what remained—had to remain—was the physical and spiritual shattering that this war had brought to European civilization, not the least of which were the staggering statistics of nearly nine million men in uniform killed and more than twenty-one million wounded. Figures by themselves cannot relate a tragedy. Nor can mere descriptions of a holocaust convey its full meaning. The outer crisis of this war— the death of man by man, the destruction, the absurdity, the defilement—was inevitably transcribed into an inner crisis of mind and soul: the alienation, meaninglessness, cynicism, hate, despair, confusion, suspicion, fear, and doubt that possess modern man even in the midst of his triumphs in science and technology. The legacy of the Great War, as its survivors' reminiscences reveal and as history attests, was the death of man in flesh and in spirit. Perhaps this is the one truth that can be discovered in the midst of struggle and destiny in those years of conflict.

When the war ended, a feeling of futility set in, a realization that, in the end, little had been gained and much had been lost. This sense of futility is communicated by the survivors over and over again. It haunts their memories and stamps their apprehension of the emptiness of life. A broken promise and a broken world were the most direct results of the war. The war dramatized disorder, division, and catastrophes. Beyond these tangible manifestations of an annihilative spirit, it also led to a deadening process in the hearts of men. Civilized living, it can be asserted, is nourished by a sense of discrimination, which war blunts and gradually displaces. "Pathos, piety, courage—they exist, but are identical, and so is filth. Everything exists, nothing has value."[28] Thus E. M. Forster sums up the senselessness of existence, and no words could better capture what the Great War finally legislated. More than anything else, in the collapse of the discriminating, civilizing faculty, the war revealed that barbarism is a force which constantly threatens civilization, that civilization itself must occupy a tenuous position in a world in which supreme acts of might indicate not only the relative worth of life, but its worthlessness as well. For the survivors the war was to produce a clearer, more terrifying recognition of the finite conditions of man's existence.

Barbarism was not confined to the fronts. Nor was it merely resorted to and executed in the service of force and slaughter. Barbarism is as much a dehumanizing process as it is a brutal action or reaction; its eruptions and effects are to measured in terms not of one area of antagonisms, but of a total human situation. If barbarism quickens in the midst of the cannonade and the battle cries of the killing instinct—if, that is, it is a special condition, even requirement, of what happens in warfare—it is also something that embraces what can be called the public life, or the everyday life distant from the war front. During the Great War civilian populations could hardly escape the impact of the war either physically or spiritually. The barbarism of the war was extended to include those men and women not immediately involved. Perhaps one of the most far-reaching, brutalizing effects of the war was the surfacing of a crisis of trust between participant and nonparticipant, a breakdown of communication between them. One of the soldiers in Henri Barbusse's *Under Fire*, returning to the front after two months' sick leave, brings out this lack of communication when he cries: "I'm fed up—*that's* what I am! The people back there, I'm sick of them—they make me spew, and you can tell 'em so!"[29] It was the very nature and irrationality of the war that made more difficult the possibility of authentic dialogue between those who were fighting and those not fighting. (G. E. Moore, for example, admitted that he never felt anything about the war at all. To him it made no difference: "None. Why should it?" he snapped to Lytton Strachey.[30])

The barbarism of the war at the front was not without its counterpart in the public life that managed to go on in apparent safety behind the lines. And among civilian populations, the Great War brought out some of the least desirable qualities and responses. Writing from London in October 1917, D. H. Lawrence bitterly complained that "People are not people any more: they are factors, really ghastly, like lemures, evil spirits of the dead."[31] For Lawrence the war signified "destruction and dying and corruption," "so much hate . . . and disintegration," when "massive creeping hell is let loose." Lawrence did not serve in the war, but his insights into the condition of the men and women who lived during the war years have a special significance insofar as they help convey the spirit of the barbarism that possessed whole populations. Its manifestations were numerous. "Talkers," "word makers of war," statesmen, and profiteers (war's "vested interests bawling patriotically and making money"[32]) united to oil the propaganda machines and to inflame public opinion with atrocity stories and spy scares. Religious leaders, preaching "the Gospel of the Spiked Helmet" and exhorting "Christ-loving soldiers," claimed that the choice had to be made between "the nailed hand" and "the mailed fist." Young women presented white feathers to men who for one reason or another were not serving in the armed forces. And some parents publicly displayed their sons' military medals—and their sons—with a sense of pride tantamount to the most glossy barbarism.

Nothing ever remains sacred in war, which embodies disorder and affliction *ne plus ultra*. No one was to be immune from the barbarism that war provokes or blameless in the savageries committed against civilized life and thought. War generates habits of violence. It muddles human consciousness. It accentuates the ceaseless struggle between barbarism and its proper opposite, civilization. The Great War proved that the barbaric element, far from having been refined out of existence, remains a perpetual threat in a world of immense technological progress. Europe in the course of the war saw the deterioration of rational, civilizing values, particularly the value of life, not only in the destruction and death on the war fronts, but also in the widespread demoralization of life distant from the front. The Great War increasingly absorbed the energies of soldier and civilian alike. Tested and pressured by a war augmented by the inexorable powers of the newly evolved and evolving technique and apparatus of an industrial society, the very structure and consciousness of Europe crumbled. For European civilization, therefore, the Great War meant both death and world-weariness: death for the soldier, world-weariness for the civilian. It compelled the depersonalization of life, as well as its sacrifice to a mechanized materialism abrogating all human value. "The terrible, terrible war," to cite Lawrence once more, "made so fearful because in every country practically every man lost his head, and lost his own centrality, his own manly isolation in his own integrity, which alone keeps life real."[33]

The war, transforming men, transformed Europe. More than anything else, it shattered man's inner life by destroying faith in himself and in his own worth. By 1918 the soul had been humiliated. With the end of the war European man was to be acutely aware of the deceptiveness of his prewar belief, fashioned in more spacious, less thought-tormented days, that his refinement and essential civilization had at last, in this century and in this world, defeated barbarism. Immunity from the barbarism of the subhuman and the antihuman was to be one of modern man's serious deaths in belief. For the "European spirit" and the "European mind" the Great War showed civilization in that "rhythm of disintegration," as Arnold Toynbee calls it,[34] which was equated with "breakdown," "collapse," "paralysis." The war constituted a multiple barbarism of might, the fundamental, most exhaustive consequence of modern man's capacities and progress, his technical resources, his industries—his audacity. Europe submitted to this might, to this technique, and the disaster was incalculable: it had to be appraised on a scale of consequence and change greater than in any previous conflict, involving not localized objectives and limited fighting numbers and fronts, but a total society, in which the whole was at war with its parts. Superseding the "old geometry of history" and "the old mechanics of power," the war showed that "melodic history" was no longer possible.[35] The meaning of history, like the spirit and mind of Europe, could hardly remain the same after the events of 1914–18.

"We later civilizations . . . we too now know that we are mortal," Paul Valéry wrote in 1919, his famous words arising from the depths of the ruins and the anguish of the Great War.[36] The passage from war to peace, he believed, was darker and more dangerous than the passage from peace to war. "Peace," he continued, "is perhaps that state of things in which the natural hostility between men is manifested in creation, rather than destruction as in war."[37] Valéry's remarks stress the mortality of European civilization and of the European psyche that the war had evinced. The problems of the "great peace" after the military crisis was over were to agonize the conscience of Europe throughout the years before the next war. The war itself was an omen of the peace that ensued: the exhaustion of a civilization in spirit and in mind, as much as in body.

47

Sir Herbert Read notes that the Great War has not yet been, nor in all probability will be, the subject of a tragedy or of a great epic work by any of its survivors. Rather, the war's tragic meaning will have to be discovered, and its human drama rendered, in the various reminiscences and reflections that have been appearing since 1914. Yet if the Great War, with the passage of over half a century, has not lent itself to tragic or epic expression, it has, in the divers literary forms that have been written, disclosed what is just as imperishable and just as sacred a manifestation of the creative spirit: prophetic vision. This vision arises from a special knowledge, in itself a result of experiencing some historical happening in civilization at its midnight hour, and communicates with a sense of urgency a special revelation, that burden of vision which a Hebrew prophet depicted as his responsibility to "Write the vision and make it plain, upon tables, that he may run that readeth it."[38] No less than other celebrated writers in the great prophetic tradition which extends back to the ancient Hebrews, the survivors of the Great War often "see" and "speak" in their writings with a prophetic power that reveals hidden truths. And like great prophets who see more than they ought to see, they speak directly from the inner fact of things, with an immediacy of experience and concern that endows their vision with a truth no less significant or imperative than that with which the ancient prophet demanded of his people: "Hear this word."

Prophetic literature is a "literature of crisis." It emerges in the midst of breakdown. It is addressed to men who do not know, who do not understand. It decries the violation of the dignity of life. It protests against human debasement. It speaks not only of what is happening or has happened, but also of what can happen. The prophetic voice has no finality in the historical setting in which suffering is uncircumscribed. With the pain of experience and with a compassion and a pathos that endure, the prophet's words register a special awareness, beyond experience itself—even beyond man himself. Prophets, Paul Tillich suggests, "are like the refined instruments which register the shaking of the earth on far-removed sections of its surface."[39] These words crystallize some of the essential qualities and functions of the writings of those who fought in the Great War. These writings summon us to take part in the crisis of a guilt-ridden epoch, to recognize a historical situation, and to fathom its disaster as it is re-created in words—in the vision—that echo the Hebrew prophet's own lament: "The harvest is past, the summer is ended, and we are not saved."[40] The prophetic spirit, Martin Buber maintains, "instils the vision in the people for all time to come. It lives

within the people from then on as a longing to realize a truth."[41]
Approached from this view, the literature of war becomes prophecy.
Such literature, we can well agree with Sir Herbert, contains "the
raw material for tragedy," "the substance of a world tragedy"; but it
remains for prophecy to give it universal significance.

Far from simplifying or sentimentalizing the problem of war, as
Douglas Jerrold feared,[42] these writings are prophetic in their warnings. They are quintessentially part of the historical process and
witness to "the rebelliousness of the hour" rather than to "the
struggle for revelation." Once the war had ended, Rilke remarked,
"the world passed out of the hands of God into the hands of men."
In an age that has been increasingly concerned with the problematic
relation between man and man, not between man and God, it is to
this truth that the war writers turn our attention. The war writer
as prophet unveils the spirit of an age in which man, cut off from
God and the old value system, is also cut off from other men. The
war itself epitomized this schism. The soldier-prophet registers its
pain and terror. Indeed, the experience and the forces of terror in
this century are announced, are prophesied, in the writings that
came out of 1914–18. An event like Virginia Woolf's suicide in
1941 can be connected with the terror, the fanaticism, the violence,
which the Great War unleashed. Her suicide note summarizes the
terror that appeared with such "unparalleled" savagery in 1914 and
was to continue into World War II. Besides, it shows how defenseless
a private life, and civilization with it, is in the presence of fear and
force, "the last arguments" which, Clive Bell says,[43] the Great War
confirmed. "I feel certain [Virginia Woolf wrote] that I am going mad
again. I feel we can't go through another of those horrible times.
And I shan't recover this time. I begin to hear voices, and I can't
concentrate.... I can't fight any longer."[44]

Military despotism, the herd instinct, barbarism—the Great War
signaled the entry of these forces of terror into modern life, as the
wheels of the universe seemed to roll backward. When the Belgian
city of Louvain, with its great library, its art treasures, its famous
public buildings, was burned and devastated and its civilian population mercilessly slaughtered in the early days of the war, it was made
clear that in a modern "murder war" nothing is preservable, least
of all the amenities and sanctities of civilization. From the very
beginning of the conflict, the pleas of Hermann Hesse, in Berne, to
artists and thinkers not to be engulfed by the war spirit—"*O Freunde,
nicht diese Töne!*"[45]—or the counsel of Romain Rolland, in Geneva,
to remain "*au-dessus de la mêlée*," were destined by and large to be

ignored or received as the foolish ideas of "pacifists" and "defeatists." Any expectation of discovering after 1914 "the moral equivalent of war" became redundant. As the war dragged on year in and year out, so did all hope and faith vanish. In the resultant conditions of life, the boredom and the dreariness at the front and away from the front, 1914–18 may be seen as years that lie, in Barbara Tuchman's words, "like a band of scorched earth dividing that time from ours."[46] There died in those lost years—years wrenched from the body of life—the hopes for civilization that life enjoins. This war served as a prologue to an age, particularly to that modern spirit of discontent and endless groping for meaning, for values that the conflict had all along proved valueless.

As some of the survivors stress, perhaps the greatest casualty of the war was the collapse of the established values of a social order, of European civilization, extending back to the French Revolution. Although it had survived the conflagrations of 1830, 1848, 1870, this civilization was unequal to the struggle posed by the Great War. It was unequal to this struggle not because the struggle was no longer considered necessary or right, but because civilization was unready for the radical nature of a time when history was being emptied of its past. The Great War degraded the civilizing reticences, whether in the methods and weapons of modern warfare or in the cause and manner of death. What the survivors often decry in their writings is the obscenity of the war and, in turn, the obscenity of the "modern mind." On the front lines, as well as at home, among statesmen, priests, and generals, among soldiers, parents, and wives—allies and enemies alike—everyone had submitted to the obscene process of the war, to that "modern mind" which, outdistancing itself in its inventions and capacity for invention, had depraved itself. A war that for many started somehow with a vague dream of a better world gradually brought the realization that civilization was reverting to the obscenities of life at its most primitive level. That this shock was overpowering and even impossible to fathom becomes the burden of the message of the literature of the Great War and the source of its prophecy.

Many writers depict the Great War as a tragedy in the history of European civilization. Certainly when the period of this "war-disease" is examined; when the war's barbarism, both "scientific" and "systematic," is seen in all its pain and horror; when European society was reduced to a collective state of destruction or one awaiting destruction; when the spirit of the time was no more than a "hymn to hate," with the voices of reason and compassion giving way to those of violence—"Have no fear, our force will slay theirs," the French philosopher Henri Bergson asserted,[47] and his words summed up the sentiments on both sides, as even intellectuals and academicians affirmed that force contains the only solutions—it is not difficult to detect the tragic ramifications of this war: the calamity, anguish, despair, oppressiveness, pathos, and the fatefulness which are the constants of all tragedy, classical and modern. Characterized by ugliness, cynicism, insensitivity, scorn, and criminality, it was tragedy that was mean-spirited, without the beauty, wisdom, or the nobility and humanism that redeem tragedy and man. In the tragedy of this war, man's puniness was laid bare with devastating contempt: man was nothing, degraded to instrumentality by an obscene mechanical process. The tragedy of the Great War was a modern tragedy of obscenity, when neither man's understanding nor his virtues could resemble or equal those endemic to the ascendant rhythm of ancient tragedy. Such a tragedy could hardly conclude except on the humiliating note of insult and sneer, as the spectacle of the postwar period, right up to 1939, iterated with multiplying examples.

By no means should these remarks imply that the generation of 1914–18 was unequal to or incapable of tragedy. Their writings on the war show only too clearly a grasp of the tragic elements that no survivor of World War II has yet to disclose. The generation that fought in the Great War was a generation made for suffering and heroism in a "war against war." That they were an unsuspicious generation with a passion for idealism, justice, and freedom; that they were responsive to "cause" and "principle" and "duty"; that they were as proud and self-confident as they were romantic and naïve; that they were a generation that believed in creative reason, in progress and civilization, and hence in man's destiny—these are the qualities that the men of 1914 reveal without conscious effort. But if this generation was worthy of heroic attitudes and gestures that still looked back to early times, they were not ready for the changes that affected tragic experience in the modern world. For millions of men the experience of the war was tragic in its physical and mental suffering; in its exposure of the inchoate evil and the chaos existent in the visible world; in its desperation and dilemma, as well as in its hopelessness. But although the phenomenal experience of the war was for many men tragic, the vision implicit in tragedy was not. The mechanical nature of modern warfare had neutralized both men and values. Life had been terribly cheapened; suffering itself had been devalued.

The ultimate meaning of the war had been translated into something soulless, into a state that gravitated not to a higher recognition of human value, but to meaninglessness.

Finally, the war constituted an unelevated tragedy, lifted to no noble scale or design, and thus holding no visionary, no revivifying meaning for man and his world. In place of magnanimity, which is intrinsic to the experience of tragedy with its "divine worth of tones and tears," the war ordained a squalid human destiny, one of bondage to distortions and perverseness. If the historical situation was conducive to tragic experience, with the warning to man not to boast in his strength as applicable to European man in 1914–18 as it was to the ancient Greek heroes, the unnatural and immoral conditions of the war failed, necessarily, to produce vision. A war that violated and scorned the dignity of and reverence for life precluded tragic vision—precluded, that is, the possibility of a deep, redeeming awareness of man's place in the modern world. A sense of nothingness, of futility, of cynicism and alienation from the past ("No more Hope, no more Glory, no more parades for you and me any more," wrote Ford Madox Ford[48]), which the conflict resulted in, signified not the attainment of vision, and thus of truth and value, but the impasse of despair and the death of hope in the midst of the obscene. The Great War became tragedy without vision, the experience of evil and suffering without value, without the culminating affirmation and decisiveness that bring with them even a fleeting comprehension of victory over the seal of man's betrayal and condemnation.

"The war," wrote Benedetto Croce, "which had been announced to the peoples with the promise of a general catharsis, in its course and its end was completely untrue to this promise."[49] Not a transfiguring nobility but a sense of disgust beyond despair marked the temper of Europe by November 11, 1918. The very sordidness of the war, the whole demeaning process of its rapacity, had cheated man of any positiveness of a tragic vision, of something valuable and lasting in life and in the universe, some conception of wisdom and regeneration. War, once again, but on a more monstrous scale, had not enlarged the meaning of life, had not, in an integrally tragic sense, revealed either humility or enlightenment, or shown man, trapped by conflict, a different shape of his destiny. No longer was it even a matter of optimism or pessimism. At the end of the war, man's apathy, his smallness, and, indeed, his loathsomeness informed the prevailing view of events and consequences. More than life itself had died in the conflict. Max Ernst, the German painter who had fought at the front and been wounded, said that the question the war finally posed for him was: "How to overcome the disgust and fatal boredom that military life and the horrors of war create. Howl? Blaspheme? Vomit?"[50] His words epitomize the feelings of men who, recognizing the fact that with *this* war senselessness had made its appearance in society, wanted to spit in the eye of the world, as well as the mood that swept over postwar Europe, when, as Aldous Huxley was to write, "To-morrow . . . will be as awful as to-day."[51]

That the Great War could go beyond a tragedy of phenomena to become a tragedy of vision, that tragedy which Karl Jaspers defines as "the measure of man's greatness in breakdown and failure,"[52] transcending man's "limit-situation," remained an unfulfilled promise. The promise of greatness with which the war was at first identified, when, as a poet rhapsodized, the time was ripe "To win Eternity / And claim God's kiss,"[53] was dead by 1918. Dramatizing the precariousness of human meaning and truth, the war had in the end hardly affirmed "the measure of man's greatness." What happened in 1914–18 disclosed once again that "Every truth we may think complete will prove itself untruth at the moment of shipwreck."[54] The Great War, marking the triumph of such a "moment," annulled not alone the human possibility, but also man's expedition toward the goal which Jaspers sees as holding the only promise of greatness capable of overcoming the expiration of hope itself. "This is the vision of a great and noble life: to endure ambiguity in the movement of truth and to make light shine through it; to stand fast in uncertainty; to prove capable of unlimited love and hope."[55]

3

The End of the Lamplight

ဢ

"Though the world might conceivably be pushed back to the pattern of 1938, there can be no more question of restoring the Edwardian age than of reviving Albigensianism."[1] So George Orwell wrote in 1948. Today the finality of this statement is undeniable. The England of the era of the 1890's through August 1914 is difficult to recognize in the England of today. It was a gilded age associated with the aristocracy and the upper and governing classes, with empire, wealth, peace, leisure, and superfluity, with the cultivation and enjoyment of a refined cultural ethos. It was also an age too often impervious to the less privileged social classes and their conditions. "We are not concerned with the very poor. They are unthinkable, and only to be approached by the statistician or the poet," wrote E. M. Forster in *Howards End* (1910). Even this enlightened "liberal humanist" could not reconcile himself to the increasingly problematic aspects of the changing landscape of an urban, industrialized England.

To create high civilization based on humanism and individualism, and on capitalism and liberalism, was a major goal in the Edwardian Age. Yet this civilization, some would claim, was narrow in its valuations, rooted as these were in the spirit of coterie, in traditionalism, in defined but outdated standards of attitude and hierarchy. "The Edwardian was a dreadful age," one critic asserts unequivocally, "an age of repulsive insensitivity in the reactionary and secure, and of imperceptive, doctrinaire arrogance on the part of the reformers."[2] This not uncommon journalistic oversimplification fails to tell the whole truth, even as it keeps current some misconceptions about the Edwardian Age. Clearly it will take time to appraise Edwardian life in an objective light and to see it in its many-sided perspectives. Some advances, however, are occasionally evident. Samuel Hynes's *The Edwardian Turn of Mind* (1968) is one of these. It focuses on the irregularities of this age, its troubled, dramatic, and odd place in history, coming as it did between the nineteenth and twentieth centuries: "... it was not quite Victorian, though conservatives tried to make it so, nor was it altogether modern, though it contained the beginnings of many ideas that we recognize as our own." Pointing to the encounter between the old and the new in Edwardian England, Hynes observes that this meeting "cannot be described simply in terms of generations, or of classes, or of political parties." He then goes on to this conclusion, which in a corrective sense should serve as the best way to *begin* to approach the Edwardian Age:

> The sides were not clearly drawn, loyalties were shifting and uncertain, and even within single groups or movements there were curious anomalies.... The extraordinary crudity and violence with which many Edwardians faced the issues of their time [in politics, in science, in morals, in the arts] may in part be explained by the circumstance that they were often uncertain of where they stood and of who stood with them.[3]

To see the Edwardians as Hynes wants us to see them is no easy matter. For if the Edwardians are to be saved from the sociology of politics *per se*, they are also to be saved from dogmatism in any modern form or idea. Present-day activists, impatient of tradition, would dismiss the Edwardians as effete and dilettante, and would not turn to them for heroic revolutionary prototypes. An elegant philosopher-statesman like Arthur James Balfour could hardly rival a militant confrontationist like Che Guevara. Nor could the philosophy of friendship expounded by G. E. Moore in *Principia Ethica* compete with the philosophy of violence in Herbert Marcuse's *Negations*. The Edwardians' idea of a cultured tradition, based on civilization, on art, and on personal relationships, will not find much favor in times of radical thought and change. The reasons for this are not difficult to see when considering the Edwardians. There was their gentility, their charm and urbanity, their chivalry, this latter quality nowhere better demonstrated than in the immediate response to the coming of war in 1914. There was their view of good manners and rules of personal conduct and mien, even when public propriety and private indulgence contradicted each other. There was their sense of humor and of dignity, an awareness of the decorum so much renounced today by teacher and student alike. There was their notion of family loyalty and of friendship as the foundations of society. These were some of the distinguishing marks of the Edwardian Age that prompted many who lived in that era to believe that a more civilized period in human life was beginning. Plato, that great teacher of hierarchy, would no doubt have enjoyed an Edwardian "symposium."

The qualities of a cultured tradition are nowhere better displayed than in Lady Cynthia Asquith's three books of "memories of peoples, places and moods," *Haply I May Remember, Remember And Be*

Glad, and her posthumous *Diaries 1915–1918.** Students of the period
1900–18, that is, before and after the beginning of the war—the before
and the after, according to one writer, marking the same kind of division as B.C. and A.D.[4]—will find these volumes invaluable in evoking
a spirit of place and time and in revealing a pattern of life and an
attitude of mind that abruptly, permanently, vanished "after the
bombardment." "Looked back upon through the dust of a world
disrupted," Lady Cynthia recalls, "our way of life does indeed appear
to belong to an almost mythological existence" (*R,* 64). And certainly the contrasts between life today and life then are so acute
that looking back invites an incredibility which one finds in a myth.
It is as if we were in another century, so much has the world
changed since 1914, become "technologized" in an age bringing
with it, as Joseph Conrad believed, "the creeping paralysis of a
hopeless outlook."

In the two books dealing essentially with the period before the
Great War, Lady Cynthia discloses a pervasive optimism and a verve
characteristic of an upbringing that was confident and comfortable
and that did not know, or rarely visualized, the emotional disabilities
and lifelong insecurity which molded, threatened, and demoralized
the lives of the less privileged. Even in her diaries, written in the
midst of war and the personal tragedies that it brought to her and
to her family, a stoic self-possession and a civilized determination remained. Lady Cynthia epitomizes the often-made contention that
those belonging to the privileged economic and intellectual classes
(or *élite,* though this word has its distasteful connotations) are less
apt to give in to pathos and dreariness. But whatever the psycho-
sociological merits of these observations, Lady Cynthia evinces a
moral courage and an honesty that bespeak her background and that
endeared her to a maverick like D. H. Lawrence. Orwell's praise
of Sir Osbert Sitwell's autobiography comes readily to mind here;
his words can just as convincingly be applied to Lady Cynthia's
collection of memories of an era that she remembers "happily" and
"gladly":

> In many ways it is a grave handicap to remember that lost paradise
> "before the war"—that is, before the other war. In other ways it is an
> advantage. Each generation has its own experience and its own wisdom,
> and though there is such a thing as intellectual progress, so that the

* All quotations from Lady Cynthia Asquith's books are included in the text
and are referred to by abbreviations and page number: *H* for *Haply I May Remember* (London, 1950); *R* for *Remember And Be Glad* (London, 1952); and *D* for
Diaries 1915–1918 (New York, 1969), ed. E. M. Horsley.

ideas of one age are demonstrably less silly than those of the last—still, one is likelier to make a good book by sticking to one's early-acquired vision than by a futile effort to "keep up." The great thing is to be your age, which includes being honest about your social origins.[5]

Of "social origins" Lady Cynthia's could not have been more fortunate. Born in 1887, Cynthia Charteris was the eldest daughter of Lord and Lady Elcho, after 1914, Lord and Lady Wemyss. Her mother was descended from George Wyndham, the first Baron Leconfield, the natural son of the third Earl of Egremont, who was probably the father of the Whig premier Lord Melbourne. "Mary Wemyss will always be remembered by those who knew her," an appreciator states, "as one of the last enchantments of the old world. . . . in all that she did or said there was a perfect rightness combined with perfect naturalness."[6] In 1910, Cynthia herself married Herbert (nicknamed "Beb") Asquith (1881–1947), son of H. H. Asquith, Liberal prime minister in the years 1908–16. Three years after the death of his first wife, Helen Melland, in 1891, H. H. Asquith had married Margot, daughter of Sir Charles Tennant. Obviously, Lady Cynthia's range of friends and acquaintances, in the upper classes, in her own family circle as well as in those immediately outside of it, was extensive. A constant interaction of life, literature, and politics perhaps best describes her life until she died in 1960.

Lady Cynthia's memoirs, portraying the immense scope and meaningfulness of this interaction, which in the end must earn it the broader term of civilization, will bring to mind what George Santayana celebrated as a way of life combining those excellences of "order without constraint, leisure without apathy, seclusion without solitude, good manners without punctilio, emulation without intrigue, splendour without hollowness."[7] If this modern Latin philosopher and poet acclaimed British civilization, it was another writer and supreme craftsman, Henry James, who embraced it with a resolve scarcely less than love, culminating in his becoming a naturalized British subject on July 26, 1915, with no less the prime minister himself, Mr. Asquith, along with Edmund Gosse, J. B. Pinker, and G. W. Prothero acting as his sponsors. European civilization in general and British civilization in particular represented to James a golden age, only to be violated forever in that "monstrous August" of 1914. This conflict brought with it, James lamented in his letters, "a huge horror of blackness," "the plunge of civilization into this abyss of blood and darkness," "this colossal convulsion" and "huge immorality, the deep conspiracy for violence, for violence and wrong." "You and I," he cried to one of his correspondents, "the ornaments of our generation, should have been spared this wreck of our belief that through the long years we had seen civilization grow and the worst become impossible."[8]

James's words, uttered with the deepest emotion, expressing his sad farewell to a civilization now menaced by "these horrors," can be better understood as one follows Lady Cynthia's "sifting" of her memories of an age when men and women were "speeding into the sunset." The stability of this era can often be directly identified with one's house and attachment to place. With a vividness born of love, Lady Cynthia recalls in *Haply I May Remember* the houses in which she lived—Stanway, her family's home in the Cotswolds, "where naturally my roots are deeper and more widely spread than anywhere"; Gosford, the Scottish home of her father's father; and Clouds, the Wiltshire home of her mother's family. What impresses one in reading her descriptions of these houses is that she endows each one with a life and character of its own, each house becoming a personification, a living heart. To contemporary man, who lives in flux and who is too often an anonymous transient in an ugly apartment building or in a dull house lost in the vast sameness of suburbia, Lady Cynthia's devoted account of her houses, each with its "layers upon layers of memories," may sound strange and anachronistic. Yet her memories of these old houses elicit a tranquil condition of life, a sense of beauty and permanence, as well as a sense of the past prescribing a continuity of existence, tradition, and civilization. The chaos of our modern urban areas reminds us how greatly cultural continuity has diminished in the irreversible tide of technological progress. Indeed, we are reminded more than anything else how much the automobile has replaced the house as an operative center of living. We often hear people voicing their love of their motor car, giving it life and blood in a name, speaking of it as a person, celebrating its power; but rarely do we hear such terms of intimacy and respect given to one's house. Such, in the (mechanized) swiftness of time, has been a change of roles! Not again, or infrequently, it is sad to think, will one express a sentiment like the following in which Lady Cynthia voices her special love for Stanway:

> As a child I loved my home precisely as one loves a human being—loved it as I have loved very few human beings. I could never go away without a formal leave-taking. "How are you?" I would ask on return, gazing up at the gabled front to absorb its beauty like a long, lovely draught, and I fancied that it smiled back a welcome (*H*, 6).

Lady Cynthia's memories become more of a caress than merely a recollection. "Even had I, immediately I grew up," she writes, "left

Stanway for ever, it would still be the haunt of a myriad unfading remembrances, as to all of us must surely be the place where, living through the timeless dawn of life, we first opened our eyes on grass, trees and sky; first 'felt through all our fleshly dress bright shoots of everlastingness'; first perceived the eternal sight and the eternal laugh" (*H*, 1). Her description of the house, inevitably and intensely touched by nostalgia, but also, and much more importantly, by an innermost appreciation of beauty (after 1914, it seems, things became more dark and somber, more ugly), is not so much an aesthetic response as a warm glow of love. Even when a local decorator would be called in, Lady Cynthia notes, it was to renovate but never to innovate. Lady Cynthia's pastoral picture of Stanway confirms the truth of what Leonard Woolf, himself an equally dynamic contemporary of Lady Cynthia, speaks of as the fact that "the deepest and most permanent effect upon oneself and one's way of living is the house in which one lives. The house determines the day-to-day, hour-to-hour, minute-to-minute quality, colour, atmosphere, pace of one's life; it is the framework of what one does, of what one can do, and of one's relations with people."[9] Lady Cynthia writes:

> The house is built of time-tinted golden Cotswold stone. Approached through the arch of the beautiful Inigo Jones Gatehouse, the west front of the house with its four wide sixteenth-century gables, numerous mullioned windows, and one huge oriel, closely overlooks the village church and the huddled graves of the rude forefathers. The southern wing faces a lawn skirted by a wood of yew trees that makes a dark background in the spring for the brief, shimmering, waxen glory of a large magnolia tree. Queened over by the great tulip tree, the eastern lawns stretch out until the ground rises in a sudden steep bank up to the long wide grass terrace that was once a pond and is still called the canal. . . . The most striking thing about the house is the beauty of the golden hue of its mellowed stone softened by centuries' growth of silver and yellow lichen and thickly clustered over with great masses of magnolia and clematis leaves. More than any other building I know, the house seems to have a face—an actual countenance with an expression that changes like that of a living creature. At times, it looks withdrawn into itself, utterly aloof, benign; at others sheltering and steeped in memories, as though its golden walls had participated in the joys and sorrows of all the generations who have lived within them and were still ready to throb in sympathy with their descendants (*H*, 4–6).

Both in the memoirs and in the diaries what is in vigorous evidence is the depth and magnitude of life going on in the old house, the center of a remarkable family and also of some remarkable men and women who gathered there to take advantage of Lady Wemyss' ceaseless hospitality. Her guests were many and brilliant, holding the most divergent views; and their conversations glittered. The art of conversation, which has today all but died out, was then still an implicit aspect of society. Lady Cynthia recalls the "glowing, winged hours" when she heard many gifted talkers—Arthur Balfour as the *arbiter elegentiarum*, Walter Raleigh, J. M. Barrie (Lady Cynthia was his secretary from 1918 until his death in 1937), George Wyndham, Harry Cust, Charles Whibley, H. G. Wells, Beatrice Webb, Evan Charteris, Hugh Cecil, Maurice Baring, Lady Desborough—"now at their serious, now at their nonsense best—debate with a zest, a gaiety, a courtesy and mutual appreciation" in "tournaments of wit and wisdom" (*H*, 13–14). Expressing his gratitude to Lady Wemyss, Sir Osbert Sitwell states that it was in a house like Stanway "that I first learned that the ordinary, quiet life of a family—something which we had never experienced in our own homes—could be absorbing and delightful. . . ."[10]

And always these gatherings, as Lady Cynthia shows, were characterized by ease, as well as éclat. The house itself, "a Liberty Hall both to children and dogs," was never lavish in its luxuries but had an uncluttered spaciousness and a "restful shabbiness," with plenty of deep chairs and well-worn sofas giving "the sense that there was not much to be afraid of spoiling or breaking." The light-heartedness, the informality of the house parties, not without their occasional fun and games, physical as well as intellectual—such constituted the setting of Lady Cynthia's early life, providing an interplay of rank and privilege and intelligence, contributing abundantly to that irrepressible self-confidence with which her generation, it was believed, was being conducted into Paradise.

Perhaps the most singular feeling that the memoirs (and the era) communicate is that of happiness: the happiness of being with one's family and with friends of all ages, living in secure and comfortable surroundings, enjoying life without the nagging and irascibility and sense of exclusion, even alienation, which accompany straitened circumstances; the happiness that comes with maturing intellectual discovery and creative aspiration and that must belong to the refining influences of a way of life free from "the fret, the hurry, the stir." It was a happiness seen here in calm but rich human development, cultivated for its own glory and values in their own moments, "each moment deemed an eternity," as Epicurus would have it. It was a happiness of acceptance of the serious and the pleasurable, not far out of line, in fact, with Epicurus' doctrine of attaining "stabilized pleasure." It was, in a word, the happiness born of balance and redeemed by love, and in the end it accounts for the attitude of mind that Lady Cynthia discloses with gentle resplendence.

How and why this happiness worked is precisely the story told in these memoirs. Lord and Lady Wemyss, their daughter recalls, did not always share the same views or like, or expect to like, the same people. Lord Wemyss displayed occasional sulkiness, which, Lady Cynthia declares, "affected me like a thunder-clap; and when he wouldn't, or couldn't, talk, I could never help listening to his silence." "His sudden moods," she continues, "were as communicable as they were unpredictable; but however glum he might be, there was always the chance, and a very good chance too, of his suddenly brightening up to become more amused and amusing than all the rest of the company put together" (*R*, 17). Lady Cynthia's recollection of her father underlines the power of a sense of humor—most civilized and liberating of human qualities—to sustain happiness.

The chapter entitled "Edwardian Girlhood" in *Remember And Be Glad* is illuminating in its depiction of the customs, conventions, and taboos of Lady Cynthia's world, "before the shattering years." She points out that girls of her class lacked independence. A girl could not attend a dance without a chaperon. Traveling alone was prohibited. When it came to mending or washing or sewing or cooking, an upper-class Edwardian girl knew nothing: "Everything was done for us," Lady Cynthia cries, with a touch of regret. She recalls that modern standards of hygiene and comfort did not exist then, and things like hot water, easy chairs, and electric lights were not quickly accepted. When one wealthy Victorian lady was asked whether she intended to install a bathroom in her house, her reply was: "No, thank Heaven, I'm none so dirty as that!" Young men and women continued to call each other by their surnames until they were friends of long standing. Lady Cynthia instances this formality of address as a symptom of the strong lines of demarcation between the sexes. In country houses, she notes, the frontier between the drawing room and the smoking room was sharply drawn. As for the kind of things young people discussed, she says that certain subjects, like homosexuality, were never mentioned, though, as she emphasizes, taboos were slowly beginning to crumble and a new freedom of speech was to emerge, until one bewildered father complained: "My daughter talks about anything. In fact she hardly talks about anything else." Though admitting to moods of depression, shyness, and self-dissatisfaction, Lady Cynthia insists that at least one of the blessings of her generation "lay in our not being modern psychology-ridden .... we had not yet been taught how to be unhappy in any of the myriad new ways this branch of science has discovered for us." Even when they were given to intro-spection and to analyzing one another, she tells us, "our interest was personal, not pathological." And, in the center of this, she points out that the most salient characteristic of life before 1914 was the great interest taken in individuals, the family going "into Committee for days at a time when some decision affecting one of its members had to be made, say, the choice of a school or a profession . . . . Nothing ever seemed to happen casually."

In spite of the fact that girls of her class had neither jobs nor house-work to do, Lady Cynthia "can't remember ever wanting to kill a single hour of time." Reading aloud was still very popular, especially when several friends read a Shakespeare play in parts. Learning poetry by heart was another pastime. Many young people kept "Commonplace books," large albums bound in white vellum or Florentine paper, in which they copied their best-loved poems. "Al-most every single poem in *The Shropshire Lad* found its way into my Commonplace book, and most of Meredith's *Modern Love*." Lady Cynthia notes that the poets she loved in her teens were William Morris, Yeats, Francis Thompson, Flecker, Villon, Ronsard, and Verlaine. Among her favorite prose writers she includes Dickens, Meredith, and Hardy. Anthony Trollope's work, she recalls, was never mentioned in her girlhood. "He was a delight saved up to be a solace through the First World War and returned to in the Second." Maeterlinck, Rostand, Anatole France, Tolstoy, and Turgeniev were also loved. Some contemporary writers she singles out for praise are Bennett, Wells, Chesterton, A. E. W. Mason, W. H. Hudson, Arthur Machen. Her favorite literary critic was Walter Raleigh, who in 1904 became the first holder of the new chair of English literature at Oxford. Lady Cynthia's education, it should be noted, was mostly private, never formal "in the sense of any systematic training of my mind." (Her vignettes of her various teachers, in the chapter entitled "Education?" in *Haply I May Remember*, are unforgettable.)

That hers was an epoch of violent contrasts between luxury and poverty, Lady Cynthia does not deny. Yet she also cites the presence of hope in life for

> I think most of us, sharing as we did the more or less general belief in a benevolent civilisation, felt a confident certainty in the inevitability of Progress. It might be, indeed was, deplorably slow, but it was assumed to be sure. Thus our world appeared to be at the same time improving

and yet stable. Above all, peace had come to seem the natural state between the great nations. Yes, military music spoke to me only of the
past—of "old, unhappy far-off things, and battles long ago." Surely,
surely never again would social progress be retarded by a great war?
(*R*, 113)

But the Great War did come, suddenly, "like a chasm in a smooth
road," as Virginia Woolf wrote. Just how shattering the war was for
Lady Cynthia, in what ways it fractured and ultimately destroyed
the equilibrium of life memorialized in *Haply I May Remember*
and *Remember And Be Glad*, the pain and the anguish that it brought
with it, her diaries, begun on April 15, 1915 (when Duff Cooper, later
Lord Norwich, presented her with the first blank, handsomely bound
volume) and continuing until the early part of October 1918, chronicle with a power and a trenchancy no less than Sir John Evelyn's or
Sir Harold Nicolson's. The world before 1914, as portrayed by Lady
Cynthia, brings to mind the innocent "state of the human soul" found
in Blake's *Songs of Innocence*; the world of the diaries is that of his
Songs of Experience, with "youth to slaughterhouses led" and "The
Human Form a fiery Forge,/ The Human Face a Furnace seal'd."

What especially strikes the reader coming to the diaries after the
memoirs is the frenzied pace and the atmosphere of chaos that Lady
Cynthia re-creates. There is something almost maddening about it,
as if she and her class now recognize the end of an era, but feel the
need to cling to it with a fury of desperation. In these diaries we view
a world in collapse. Again and again she records her difficulty in
believing what is happening as she views her husband and brothers
and friends going off to war—men volunteering to step "Into the
grandeur of our fate," as Laurence Binyon wrote, and with "faith and
fire within us / Men who march away," as Thomas Hardy believed.[11]
All the leisure and happiness of the past are seen suddenly, steadily
slipping away, surrendering to the urgencies that overtake life in
time of war:

It is difficult to recognise one's own identity these days; the whole of
life has become such a melodrama that one always feels in a dream
(*D*, 9):

to the new demands being shouted amid sensational scenes in the
streets:

London, I think, looks distinctly more abnormal now—more soldiers,
more bandages and limps, and more nurses—quite a sensational sense of
strain. Raw recruits led by band still make one cry and everywhere the
rather undignified, bullying posters—very, very dark night (*D*, 17):

to the eventual recognition of the nightmare of hopelessness affecting the very center of one's being:

> Such ghastly depression—life seems a sheer nightmare, every prospect a horror, every retrospect a pain. Pangs of the past and fears of the future, with terrible lassitude (*D*, 272).

And, as 1918 draws to a close, there is a final human breaking point—the exhaustion of all energy, patience, and courage—and a final reckoning of all that has happened and been lost—the chaos, disillusion, and death—with the sight of peace in the midst of degradation. On the verge of a brief nervous breakdown (in itself, surely, an epiphany of the human condition at its most dismal point), Lady Cynthia writes with prophetic insight in her diary of October 7, with which the book concludes:

> I am beginning to rub my eyes at the prospect of peace. I think it will require more courage than anything that has gone before. It isn't until one leaves off spinning round that one realises how giddy one is. One will have to look at long vistas again, instead of short ones, and one will at last fully recognise that the dead are not only dead for the duration of the war (*D*, 480).

Often the mood is one of sadness in the presence of death. There are the usual dinner parties at the Ritz Hotel, the Café Royal, and elsewhere, as well as entertainments and short holidays, but all these pale before the news of the war as it comes closer to home with the posting of the casualty lists, with more frequent memorial services held at Saint Paul's Cathedral or at St. Martin-in-the-Fields for close friends and relatives killed in battle, with the Zeppelin attacks on London. We see Lady Cynthia and her patrician circle, particularly those belonging to the informal "society" called "The Corrupt Coterie" (the Asquiths, Charterises, Grenfells, Herberts, Horners, Listers, Mannerses, Tennants, and Trees), weave in and out of 10 Downing Street, attend picture exhibitions, have their portraits painted by Augustus John, Ambrose McEvoy, or John Singer Sargent, visit palmists, participate in fiery debates about conscription, play tennis or cards, make gossip ("There has been an article in the *Vigilante* accusing the wives of Cabinet ministers of lesbianism"), attend Harry Lauder's musical play or see Mary Anderson in Gilbert's *Comedy and Tragedy*, go to " 'Poets' Reading' in aid of the Star and Garter Fund" (e.g., Belloc, Binyon, Cammaerts, Davies, Hewlett, Walter de la Mare, Newbolt, Owen Seaman, Margaret Woods, Yeats), contribute to the war effort in various voluntary capacities, make love (Sir Claud Russell, Charles Whibley, and Bernard Cyril Freyberg were forever pursuing Lady Cynthia, just to kiss her hand), or exchange the latest stories of men in search of love and fun, especially the Prince of Wales ("So far, he dances most with Rosemary and also motors with her in the daytime. No girl is allowed to leave London during the three weeks of his leave and every mother's heart beats high"), go off for a "dentist" ("a pre-arranged tête-à-tête"), and traffick in "dewdrops" ("a compliment retailed to you by some third person"), its opposite being a "spike."

But it is death that stalks the diaries. From beginning to end, nothing that Lady Cynthia and her family and friends do or say mitigates its presence. The announcement of the death of Rupert Brooke, a protégé of Sir Edward Marsh, the latter a close friend of the Asquiths, inspires this entry for April 27, 1915: ". . . it does stab one to think of his beautiful young poet's face with the cornfield head. He had the most lovely *regard* I have ever seen I think" (*D*, 12). In the same year the news of the deaths in battle of William and Julian Grenfell, called Castor and Pollux by Maurice Baring, dealt a heavy blow to Lady Cynthia. In *Remember And Be Glad* she notes that these early friends ("little curly-headed boys in white the first time they came to Stanway") would for her always be "eternally young, their bright images guard[ing] the memory of the youth and hope which once we shared." Now their deaths fill Lady Cynthia with anguish and remind her that "We have all been caught up into a Greek tragedy and are but gradually beginning to realise it . . . . Soon one will hardly remember who is alive and who is dead. In a sense Death is really becoming annihilated—the division grows narrower and narrower" (*D*, 31, 62). Death came even closer to Lady Cynthia in the same year, when her youngest brother, Yvo Charteris (b. 1896), was killed while leading an attack only a few weeks after having gone out to the Western Front as a captain. Lady Cynthia's entry for the day on which she received this news by telephone catches all the anguish of her loss. No more soul-shaking entry in the diaries is to be found than that in which she laments the loss of Yvo:

> Then I knew and rushed upstairs, and gradually the horrible pain penetrated. Oh how it hurts and how little one ever faced the possibility for an instant! Darling, darling little Yvo—the perfect child and youth. How can one not be going to see him again? None of the others could have quite emptied the future for each of us quite like him. He was the greatest luxury in one's life with his overwhelming charm—his brilliancy, sweetness, and that supernatural sympathy and understanding. One looked forward to him always as an ever-increasing joy. There was something so expectant about him, with his interest and amusement in life, it was like someone just sitting down to a wonderful banquet. How can

one believe it, that it should be the object to kill Yvo? That such a joy-dispenser should have been put out of the world on purpose. For the first time I felt the full mad horror of the war . . . (*D*, 90).

By the end of 1915 Lady Cynthia comprehended the tragedy of the war as one bringing with it the end of an old world and prescribing a condition of death that must be endured:

> Oh why was I born for this time? Before one is thirty to know more dead than living people? Stanway, Clouds, Gosford—all the settings of one's life—given up to ghosts. Really, one hardly knows who is alive and who is dead. One thing is that now at least people will no longer bury their dead as they used. Now they are so many one *must* talk of them naturally and humanly, not banish them by only alluding to them as if it were almost indelicate (*D*, 97).

Another blow was to strike the Charteris family in the following year, when the eldest son, Hugo (b. 1884), holder of the courtesy title Lord Elcho, died in the disastrous battle of Katia, a year after embarking for Egypt with his Yeomanry. Since his name was not listed among the casualties in the original report, his family hoped for his survival. A telegram from the Red Cross, with the words *"Un Lord Elcho fait prisonier à Katia est interné à Damascus,"* at first provided relief and hope, but it was later canceled by the official certification of his death. One will not easily forget the picture of Lord Elcho's wife receiving confirmation of the death of her husband. The poignancy of this scene, Lady Cynthia writes, "was so inconceivably beyond anything in my experience that I don't feel as if I could ever be unhaunted by it for a minute" (*D*, 183).

Lord Elcho represented "something special to his own generation," Lady Cynthia declares. "Sense of humor, sense of justice, sense of obligation—all three seemed equally but quite unclashingly developed" (*H*, 161–162). His death in battle—when he was "twice wounded, once in the arm and once in the leg—but continuing wholly regardless of pain and fire to encourage his men," as some of the survivors of his troop afterward said, was in keeping with his qualities. R. C. Sherriff's essay "The English Public Schools in the War" (1914–18), in which he praises the young company officers who, like Lord Elcho, an old Etonian, were usually public school products, for their heroic leadership (in contrast with the generals, who had lost personal touch with the common soldier), repeatedly stresses that the common soldier turned instinctively to these junior officers, by no means soldiers in the professional sense, "who lived with him and talked to him as a human being like themselves and helped him hold onto a shred of pride and self-respect." "The common soldier," Sherriff concludes, "liked them because they were 'young swells,' and with few exceptions the young swells delivered the goods."[12] If we are to understand the humanity and the vision of the war generation which Lord Elcho personified (even when this vision, especially after the battles of 1916, led to disillusionment and, as C. E. Montague said, the bottom fell out of the fighting men's paradise[13]), Lord Elcho's letter to his mother upon Yvo's death conveys the humanizing instincts of a generation whose destiny, to quote Sir Herbert Read, was "as tragic as the destiny of the heroes of a Greek drama":[14]

Darling Mum,
   I have absolutely nothing to say. When your own mother and brother are concerned, it is futile to talk of sympathy, and the one consolation for me is that—if any comfort is to be extracted, or if the best thought is of any use, which of course it is—your soul is big enough, large enough, for that purpose. The mere thought of your tackling it strengthens me. That sounds selfish and detached, but I have such faith in you—I suppose the misery of people like Ettie [Lady Desborough] breaks the shock. A woman with sympathy loses many sons before her own. If anything could dwarf one's own tragedy, it is the agony of millions of others, but it doesn't—it's the other way about. One's sluggish imagination is stimulated and one merely realises for the first time other people's miseries as well as one's own. The only sound thing is to hope the best thing for one's country, and to expect absolutely nothing for oneself in the future. To write down everyone one loves as dead, and then—if any of us are left—we shall be surprised. To think of one's country's future and one's own happy past. The first is capable of vast improvement—as for the second, when all is said and done, we were a damned good family. Qua *family* as good as Clouds. I couldn't have had more joy out of anything than I have from my family. I'm glad we had that bit with Yvo at Hunstanton. I wish I had seen him as a Guardsman. What letters! The first one (thousand singing legs) perfect description and atmosphere—the second one full of jolly thought and not the least self-conscious. Bless him. I am so awfully sorry for Papa who loved him. Tell him how much I feel for him. He must write his sons off and concentrate upon his grandchildren who, thank God, exist. . . . I should rather have stayed here on the chance of Balkans as Cavalry. Gallipoli is terribly dull but *unberufen* very safe now, except for sickness. We have had very few men and no officers hit since August 22nd. But the gloom, and boredom, and discomfort of life there seems the limit.
   Goodbye darling—I love you till all is blue.
                                        Ego* (*D*, 186)

*Lord Elcho's family nickname, because of his babyish attempts to pronounce the name Hugo.

A glance at the index to Lady Cynthia's diaries will reveal the range of her friendships among the most famous and powerful figures of her time. The index could be easily be labeled a catalogue of celebrities. Lady Cynthia's description of her dining with Lord and Lady Curzon ("Such a snob party—nearly all Viceroys—the last they give before they are really in the grip of rations" [*D*, 412]), along with Lord Crewe, Lord Hardinge, the Lansdownes, the Salisburys, Lord Farquhar, and General Sir John Cowans, is just one example of what recurs throughout these pages. No name of importance connected with the war, the government, the nobility, or with art, literature, and music seems to be omitted as Lady Cynthia records her day-by-day activities. Her reflections on the figures whom she met in the course of her endless, energetic movement in society are incisive. One cannot afford to miss her uninhibited responses. Balfour has a charm that is as radiant as ever: "He really is in a class quite, quite alone. Oddly enough, in spite of his divine amiability and sweetness and easiness, I should still feel shy alone in a room with him." Winston Churchill "has genius and imagination. . . . More than most people I suppose he has the defects of his qualities, and would always be a source of danger, pining for despotism, seeing himself as a Napoleon and inclined to be unconstitutional. A brilliant, audacious layman is bound to exasperate the experts under him . . ." (*D*, 23). Prime Minister Asquith "presents the most extraordinary mellow serenity to the world, and is an imperturbable buffer between himself and all crises private and public. I have never before seen him look tired, worried, busy, or preoccupied, and I have seen him weathering a good many storms now, but this time he looked really rather shattered with a sort of bruised look in his eyes . . ." (*D*, 25). General Kitchener looks "*so* different from the poster—and my own conception of him—*very* mossy and gentle old gentleman" (*D*, 134). Horatio Bottomley, the editor of the rabidly patriotic weekly *John Bull* and a great speaker for army recruitment, brings this reaction: "Heard the renowned Bottomley speak a few straight words from the 'shoulder,' as it is called. What a scoundrel he looks, but he does speak well! He is staying in this hotel and looks too revolting at close quarters" (*D*, 255). F. E. Smith (later Earl of Birkenhead) "is a magnificent bounder, and I can't help liking him. His appearance is like something in a novelette—the Zeppelin-like cigar always in his mouth and the reliefs of good living on his face" (*D*, 303). The war poet Siegfried Sassoon, she notes after meeting him at a dinner given by the celebrated hostess Lady Sibyl Colefax, "was in khaki: at first I only noticed his sticking-out ears and obvious embarrassment, but a closer scrutiny revealed great charm and a certain sweetness and grave strength in his countenance" (*D*, 366).

Of great interest are the sections of the diaries concerning Bernard Cyril Freyberg, a New Zealander who became the youngest brigadier-general in the British Army, winning the Victoria Cross in 1916. (After distinguished service in World War II, he was governor-general of New Zealand.) Lady Cynthia met Freyberg in 1916, when he was a colonel, and they became close friends. "He interests me enormously. I love his lack of humour, his frank passion for fighting and his unconcealed dread of peace. Life appears to hold no other interest for him. He wonders what he will do when it is all over" (*D*, 261). For Lady Cynthia, Freyberg represented a fascinating military type—ambitious, ruthless, self-reliant, blunt, grim—in violent contrast to most of the other men she knew, especially, as she wrote, "a wonderful contrast to [D. H.] Lawrence," who apparently met Freyberg and must have heard much about him from Lady Cynthia. It is altogether possible that Lawrence had Freyberg in mind when he created the figure of Captain Herbertson, an officer of the Guards, in the chapter "The War Again" in *Aaron's Rod* (1922), a postwar novel of disillusionment. Lawrence depicted Captain Herbertson as a man who "had the war at the back of his mind, like an obsession," who

> was not conceited—he was not showing off—far from it. It was the same thing here in this officer as it was with the privates, and the same with this Englishman . . . and every time it was the same hot, blind, anguished voice of a man who had seen too much, experienced too much, and doesn't know where to turn. None of the glamour of returned heroes, none of the romance of war: only a hot, blind, mesmerised voice, going on and on, mesmerised by a vision that the soul cannot bear.

This passage returns us to the man who in Lady Cynthia's diaries was indeed preoccupied with war and, as Lawrence wrote, bore "the hot, seared burn of unbearable experience, which did not heal nor cool":

> We had [writes Lady Cynthia] an orgy of military shop from Freyberg—hours and hours of it. I must say he never bores me. It interests me to see him sitting there with his, in a way, boyish snub face with its extraordinary, almost grim, determination and feel his ambition and energy and practical ability is working away like machinery all the time inside him (*D*, 381).

But of all the figures who appear in the diaries, none exerts the power of mystery and paradox, or exemplifies the visionary elements associated with a prophetic poet, that D. H. Lawrence does. He conveys a dramatic, exciting quality, and his words and movements are not unlike the strophe and antistrophe of an ancient Greek chorus. Even when he is not present or when his voice is not heard, his shadow and the echo of his words loom large. Lawrence first met the Herbert Asquiths toward the end of July 1913, when he was brought by Edward Marsh to Kingsgate, near Broadstairs, Kent, where the Asquiths had taken a small house. (A patron of poets, Marsh was during this time editor of the *Georgian Poetry* anthologies, to which Lawrence contributed poems in 1912; he also served as Winston Churchill's private secretary, 1905–15 and 1917–22.) In her chapter on Lawrence in *Remember And Be Glad*, Lady Cynthia recalls this first meeting with much feeling. Noting that she and her husband knew only that Lawrence wrote poetry, that he was a coal miner's son, and that he was tubercular, she goes on to measure the effect of his presence: ". . . a slender, lithe figure stepped lightly into the room, [and] we both realised almost with a shock of collision that something new and startling had come into our lives. . . . Some electric, elemental quality gave him a flickering radiance. Apart from this strange otherness, one could see at once that he was preternaturally alive" (*R*, 133). Herbert Asquith in his chapter on Lawrence in *Moments of Memory* also recalls this meeting with Lawrence: "a poet living on a plane far removed from the dust of politics, but more deeply in revolt against the values of the age than any political leader."[15]

Lawrence, we know from his poetry and prose, was often critical of the upper classes, whom he attacked as "just a bloody sham," "just fantasies of self-importance," "sphinxes of self-consciousness." "So up I started climbing," he writes in a satirical poem, "The Saddest Day,"

> to join the folks on high,
> but when at last I got there
> I had to sit down and cry.

And in another poem, "Up He Goes!—," he refuses to be impressed by "a damn fraud":

> They're not any better than we are,
> the upper classes—they're worse.
> Such bloomin' fat-arsed dool-owls
> they aren't even fit to curse![16]

Yet, these sharp satirical thrusts, found in his *Pansies* (1929), along with some of his devastating portrayals of the upper classes in his novels *Women in Love, Aaron's Rod, St. Mawr,* and *Lady Chatterley's Lover,* should be kept in perspective. To an extent they can be explained as resentments and prejudices rooted in a working-class background. But for the most part they were the angry and bitter reactions of a man who believed that the whole of British society, beginning, obviously, with the ruling classes, had submitted to the mechanical spirit of nullity and debasement that he connected with World War I, both in the years of the struggle and in its aftermath. What distinguishes Lawrence's views of the entire class structure (and what became evident to those who, like Lady Cynthia, admired and respected him) was his transcendent grasp of a "classless truth" (to use F. R. Leavis' words), nowhere better expressed than in these words from *Women in Love*:

> "In the spirit, I am separate as one star is from another, as different in quality and quantity. Establish a state on *that*. One man isn't any better than another, not because they are equal, but because they are intrinsically *other*, that there is no term of comparison. The minute you begin to compare, one man is seen to be far better than another, all the inequality you can imagine, is there by nature."[17]

Lawrence liked the Asquiths as much as they liked him. "Jolly nice folk," he wrote;[18] and his relations with them remained amicable to the end. They were civilized, intelligent, stimulating, and, not least, sympathetic people with whom he could discuss books and ideas and with whom he shared a belief that the Great War would lead to the breakdown of life. It is a tribute to Lady Cynthia and to the measure of her influence on Lawrence and of his faith in her that some of his finest letters are those he wrote to her about World War I. "The War," he moaned to her, "finished me: it was the spear through the side of all sorrows and hopes."[19] Certain aspects of Lawrence's relations with the Asquiths can also be established in a story like "The Ladybird" (1923), the outgrowth of an earlier story, "The Thimble" (1916), in which some of the war experiences of the Asquiths are rendered, albeit in a germinal sense. Lady Cynthia questioned the "word-picture" of herself in "The Thimble" ("He has quite gratuitously put in large feet"), but generally approved of the characterization: "I think some of his character hints are damnably good. He has kept fairly close to the model in the circumstances." The opening paragraph of "The Ladybird," with the substitution of a proper name, is an incisive comment on Lady Cynthia:

> How many swords had Lady Beveridge in her pierced heart! Yet there always seemed room for another. Since she had determined that her heart and kindness should never die. If it had not been for this determination she herself might have died of sheer agony, in the years 1916 and 1917, when her boys were killed, and her brother, and death seemed to be mowing with wide swaths through her family.

(Lawrence's volume of poetry *Bay* [1919], containing mostly war poems, was dedicated to Lady Cynthia. And when he chose Constance Chatterley as the name of the heroine in his most controversial and last novel, it is suggested, he had in mind the name of Cynthia Charteris.[20])

The sense of isolation and repression that Lawrence experienced during 1914–18 was undoubtedly assuaged by his friendship with people in high places, who were equally troubled about the state of civilization and the prospects of humanity. When in November 1915 his novel *The Rainbow* was officially suppressed by the authorities, it was Philip Morrell who asked questions in the House of Commons. Lawrence's physical and financial deprivations during these years, especially after his and his wife's expulsion from Cornwall in October 1917 on silly spy charges, were lessened as a result of assistance from or through Lady Cynthia. And it was people like Lady Cynthia who, he believed, would help him to found a new community somewhere, "our new community in the midst of this old one." ("He repeatedly urged us to join this community, not a very practical suggestion as Beb was in the Army" [*R*, 137].) Lawrence may have found the upper and middle classes "broad and shallow and passionless," as compared with the working class, that was "narrow, but still fairly deep and passionate." But it was in the upper class that the poet of the religion of the blood found intellectual peers who *understood* the pain and despair of his vision of a war-weary world in dissolution to which he gave utterance in a passage like the following from a letter to Lady Cynthia:

> When I drive across this country, with autumn falling and rustling to pieces, I am so sad, for my country, for this great wave of civilisation, 2000 years, which is now collapsing, that it is hard to live. So much beauty and pathos of old things passing away and no new things coming: this house of the Ottoline's [Lady Ottoline Morrell's house, Garsington Manor, Oxford]—it is England—my God, it breaks my soul—their England, these shafted windows, the elm-trees, the blue distance—the past, the great past, crumbling down, breaking down, not under the force of the coming birds, but under the weight of many exhausted lovely yellow leaves, that drift over the lawn, and over the pond, like the soldiers, passing away, into winter and the darkness of winter—no, I can't bear it. For the winter stretches ahead, where all vision is lost and all memory dies out.[21]

Both in the memoirs and in the diaries Lady Cynthia's depiction of Lawrence gives us a picture of a poet much gentler and more humane than that generally given either by some of Lawrence's other contemporaries or by Lawrence himself. His lightness, his intuition, his gentleness are emphasized. Interestingly, Lady Cynthia comments on Lawrence's sense of humor, a quality, it is agreed, lacking in his writings: "There is so much delicious laughter in him which he entirely extinguishes on paper." Nor does she fail to mention Lawrence's wife, Frieda:

> I find them the most intoxicating company in the world. I never hoped to have such mental pleasure with anyone. It is so wonderful to be such a perfect *à trois*. I am so fond of her. She has spontaneousness and warm cleverness, and such adoration and understanding of him. He interests and attracts me. His talk is so extraordinarily real and living— such humour and yet so much of the fierceness and resentment which my acquiescent nature loves and covets. He is a Pentecost to one, and has the gift of intimacy and such perspectiveness that he introduces one to oneself (*D*, 18–19).

Lawrence's ability to heighten life is appreciatively remarked upon: "In his talk there is none of the crudeness and occasional ugliness (the result of over-emphasis) one finds in his book[s], but he has passionate resentment against the existing frame and values of life" (*D*, 19). Like others who knew Lawrence, she recalls his voice, "with its layers of harshness and softness," blending earnestness and "delicious whimsicality," humor, anger, resentment. (Certainly, of twentieth-century authors, Lawrence, Joyce, and Ezra Pound have had the most fascinating speaking voices.)

Interesting, even charming, pictures of Lawrence are given. There is one showing him, Lady Cynthia, and her son Michael going for a walk: "He pushed the pram. Michael's hair and his beard were a perfect match. We looked a funny sight. We went to the Zoo and enjoyed it very much. . . . He liked Lawrence very much" (*D*, 295). There is another showing Lawrence turning up in Augustus John's studio where the famous painter was doing a new version of a portrait of Lady Cynthia. "John asked Lawrence to sit for him, and Lawrence admired the large designs of the studios, but maintained an ominous silence as regards my pictures." "Let the dead paint the dead," Lawrence then intoned to John. Looking at other paintings in the studio, he commented on Margot Howard de Walden's portrait, "Who is that bird?" The painting of Bernard Shaw with closed eyes he thought "very true symbolism" (*D*, 361). (Duncan Grant and Mark Gertler were other artists who received equally caustic treatment from Lawrence.) Nevertheless it is Lawrence's steady denunciation of the war that predominates in most references to him. Lady Cynthia's entries echo the peculiar intensity and bitterness of Lawrence's views and idiom. "The war," she writes just after visiting the Lawrences in Hampstead, "is driving him quite mad with rage—he just sits and gibbers with fury. He sees no hope in the country, nothing but war, and the war he sees as the pure *suicide* of humanity—a war without *any* constructive ideal in it, just pure senseless destruction" (*D*, 89).

Lawrence's fiercest recollection of the war years is found in the chapter entitled "The Nightmare" in *Kangaroo* (1923). Some of the passages reveal that for Lawrence it was the later years of the war that were the worst: "Awful years—'16, '17, '18, '19—the years when the damage was done. The years when the world lost its real manhood." "From 1916 to 1919 a wave of criminal lust rose and possessed England, there was a reign of terror, under a set of indecent bullies like Bottomley of *John Bull* and other bottom-dog members of the House of Commons." What is particularly revealing in his outbursts is that he excludes Prime Minister Asquith from reprehension. "I respect the Prime Minister," he wrote in a letter, "because I believe in his real *decency* and I think Lloyd Georges are toads."[22] In the "Nightmare" chapter he differentiates between the periods before and after Asquith's fall from office in 1916, that is, between the quiet human decency and orderly life that Asquith personified and the exacerbated opportunism and bulliness which followed; between the spirit of patriotism and belief in democracy that impelled many men to enter the war and, after 1916, the collapse of all integrity in England, the capitulation to a debased spirit, "the unspeakable baseness of the press and the public voice, the reign of that bloated ignominy, *John Bull*." "The torture was steadily applied," Lawrence wrote in his novel, "during those years after Asquith fell, to break the independent soul in any man who would not hunt with the criminal mob." Just how distressing Asquith's fall from power was, with all its implications, is registered in this passage concerning Richard Lovat Somers' (that is, Lawrence's) gathering crises and his belief that the free England had now died, that "the old spirit died for ever in England," that "this England of the peace was like a corpse":

> Spring came—and one morning the news that Asquith was out of the government, that Lloyd George was in. And this was another of Somers' crises. He felt he must go away from the house, away from everywhere. And as he walked, clear as a voice out of the moors, came a voice saying: "It is the end of England. It is the end of old England. It is finished. England will never be England any more."

In matters of politics Lawrence spoke as a prophet, not as a politi-

cal realist. His views were more intuitive than anything else: "Politics
—what are they? Just another extra-large, commercial wrangle over
buying and selling—nothing else."[23] The Great War reinforced these
feelings, and as the years passed, his distrust of politicians and political schemes increased. It is interesting, therefore, to study Lawrence's
reactions to H. H. Asquith. As seen above, he connected Asquith with
"the old England," the England that Lawrence related to a particular
life-ethos: belief in society, in love, in friends. It is evident that he
respected Asquith for his dignity, his reticence, his sense of honor, his
detestation of demagoguery and of all affectation, in short, for his
personification of the highest traditions of public life. He could hardly
ignore, moreover, his sharing with Asquith, who was born in the
small Yorkshire town of Morley where his father was a wool spinner
and weaver, a nonconformist puritan background. It would be safe
to assume, then, that Lawrence identified Asquith with a way of life
and an attitude of mind more than with a particular class.

But Asquith and those like him, Lawrence thought, "softly found-
ered" and then "went right under," unable to deter the coming of
"that *John Bull* government," as "agonies gave way to tortures."
These words in *Kangaroo* regarding Asquith and his followers are
also pertinent here: "The well-bred, really cultured classes were on
the whole passive resisters. They shirked their duty. It is the business
of people who really know better to fight tooth and nail to keep up a
standard, to hold control of authority. *Laisser-aller* is as guilty as the
actual, stinking mongrelism it gives place to." For Lawrence this
"stinking mongrelism" was epitomized by Lloyd George, who, he
wrote, "stands for nothing, and is nothing," representing "the Horatio
Bottomley Lloyd George world," "mean and paltry in spirit."[24] Indeed, in his bleakest moments of despair, Lawrence thought it best
that Asquith depart from office so that Lloyd George could at last
take over and more quickly bring on the ultimate breakdown in a
hopeless world, as this passage from a letter, dated December 5, 1916,
illustrates:

> The war is beyond weariness; it has reached the stage of stony oppres-
> sion. And though I think Asquith is by far a more decent man than
> Lloyd George or any of the others, yet I wish he would clear out, and
> leave them to it. The debacle would come the quicker. It is bound to
> come, the great smash-up in this country—and oh, oh God, if it would
> only come quickly. But it will never take place while Asquith holds the
> Premiership. He is too much the old, stable, measured, *decent* England.
> Alas and alack, that such an England must collapse and be trodden
> under the feet of swine and dogs. But so it is, by the decree of unalter-

able faith. And therefore, the longer the old decency remains standing, the longer the tops of our heads will tickle, expecting it to come crashing down on us. It is this sword of Damocles business which one cannot bear. But sleep—sleep in your soul—everything will come, and will go, in the end.[25]

The passage of time was to corroborate Lawrence's historical judgments and prophetic insights, for with the fall of Asquith, the "last of the Romans," much more was to disappear from English life. "Of all the British statesmen and politicians whom I have known . . . Mr. Asquith . . . has always seemed to me the most satisfactory representative," Sir Thomas Beecham (1879–1961), conductor, impresario, and astute political observer, wrote in his autobiography. "More human and less abstract than those two brilliant bachelors, Lord Balfour and Lord Haldane, and of a solidity, reliability, and poise less conspicuous in the younger stars of the political firmament, his resignation of the Premiership in 1916 was not the unqualified advantage to the country as has been so often alleged."[26] "With him," Roy Jenkins declares in his biography, "there died the best part of the classical tradition in English politics."[27]

It should not go unnoticed that Lawrence, like Lady Cynthia, distrusted *demos*. His criticisms of the industrial masses, however, like his criticisms of the upper classes, were formed by a discriminating and impersonalizing intelligence and by a directing protest against and despair of the material and technological spirit which he felt led to dehumanizing emptiness. The Asquiths, on the other hand, disliked the populace for other, less moral, and certainly less defensible reasons, born of those ingrained class prejudices that, at the turn of the century, prompted one typical "True-Blue" Tory spokesman to assert: "I like a society properly ordered in ranks and classes. I like my butcher or my gardener to take off his hat to me, and I like, myself, to stand bareheaded in the presence of the Queen. . . . I prefer a society where people have places and know them."[28] The entries in Lady Cynthia's diaries are more subtle than this Tory's open scorn of "the whole democratic movement." ("Do what you may," he insists, "it will always be a few people that will govern."[29]) In one entry she speaks of the "ghastly population in the hotel," also noting to her husband that these people "represented England and were what he was really fighting for." Such was his agreement, it seems, that "he nearly resigned his commission" (*D*, 50). On another occasion, after dining at a hotel, she concludes: "Population worse than ever" (*D*, 53). On still another occasion she writes: "Dined in table d'hôte—loathsome population" (*D*, 174). And then there is her description of a journey by train which she blandly admits she and Charles Whibley spent "discussing the ugliness of the travellers" (*D*, 209).

Attitudes like these were endemic to the coterie world and to "the Edwardian turn of mind." Sir Osbert Sitwell, in describing some of the sumptuous entertainments given during the summers of 1913 and 1914, went so far as to point out that "As guests, only the poor of every race were barred. Even foreigners could enter, if they were rich."[30] Such examples of indulgent living, according to one writer on social questions, C. F. G. Masterman (1874–1927), were not only vulgar but "a loss that falls on all."[31] As late as 1940, Margot Asquith complained in a letter to the *Daily Telegraph*: "Since most London houses are deserted there is little entertaining . . . in any case, most people have to part with their cooks and live in hotels." Commenting on this letter in his wartime diary, Orwell rejoined, "Apparently nothing will ever teach these people that the other 99% of the population exists."[32] Another representative of this "turn of mind," Sir Harold Nicolson, who insisted that one's friends should be "well-read and well-bred," becomes, in Martin Green's opinion, "a discarded cultural image," a type that with its "governessy refinement and upliftingness," "has outlived its usefulness." In its place has come a new British type, "the decent man—as opposed to the gentleman—or the Anglo-Saxon moralist, or the Anglo-Saxon rebel."[33] Its most obvious representatives, we are told, are D. H. Lawrence, Orwell, and Dr. Leavis. Not that Lady Cynthia was ever unprepared for such reactions to people like herself and to her age: "One can hardly believe," she writes in one of her earliest entries with specific references to her reading Richardson's *Pamela*, "our habits and values will ever seem as incredibly quaint to our descendants as those of our ancestors, thus portrayed, do to us" (*D*, 5).

One of the major strengths of the memoirs and diaries is Lady Cynthia's gift for evoking the spirit of an age without romanticizing it. To view her writings only insofar as they explain a *Zeitgeist* or are pregnant with political or sociological implications and influences is to violate the deeply personal values her work conveys. The story Lady Cynthia records is one that underscores a way of life lost and a generation departed. Her story unfolds as happiness gives way to cruel destiny, with disorder and death threatening, as Vera Brittain wrote in her poem "The War Generation: Ave,"

> . . . to dethrone
> Those dreams of happiness we thought secure;
> While, imminent and fierce outside the door,
> Watching a generation grow to flower,
> The fate that held our youth within its power
> Waited its hour.[34]

In the end Lady Cynthia's life and work will be connected with a memory of beauty transcending the uncertainty of life. Those seeking answers to what went wrong or why her generation was unprepared for slaughter must come away instead with a sense of beauty in personal life. Her writings, singularly free of attitudinizing, render a history of personal experience in dramatic contexts. The human and the emotional dimensions of life prevail here, not its abstract critical intellectualization and dialecticism. Appropriately, the frontispiece to her *Diaries 1915–1918* is a reproduction of her portrait by Augustus John, done in 1917 and called "Portrait of a Lady in Black," now in the Art Gallery of Ontario. This portrait accentuates the personal tone of all her work. It gives clues to Lady Cynthia's strength of beauty and attests to the accuracy of L. P. Hartley's descriptions in his Foreword to the *Diaries*: "Dazzling [and] enchanting . . . she seemed all fire and air"; "her face often showed that she had more than her share of sorrows, but she made light of them"; she had "the physical and mental graces that were the vesture of her spirit and that are, for each of her friends, a treasured possession"; "a stable bedrock of character and a strong practical sense"; "a mysterious, a moonlit, leprechaun quality that was not quite of this world" (*D*, ix–x).

The strongly personal elements that this portrait suggests and that in their own history and time comprise a memory of beauty, cannot be separated from the fate which history in upheaval makes inevitable. For this memory of beauty was to be transformed into the fact of conflict. The antithesis of the human values revealed in the portrait of Lady Cynthia is caught in a painting, "Conflict," by C. R. W. Nevinson (1889–1946), one of the first official war artists for England during World War I.[35] "Conflict," in its semi-Cubist style, shows three pairs of powerful, naked men entwined in mortal struggle, seen against a dark, bare, rocky background. Clenched fists are pounding the sides and backs of men gradually succumbing to greater, brutal force. The faces of the men locked in physical combat are indistinct; there are only some hard lines suggesting conscienceless cruelty. Desperation, ugliness, terror: these are the themes of Nevinson's painting, which in effect announces the transition to the "modern world" and the "modern consciousness."

Civilization without beauty remains inconsummate. Without friendship it must die. Lady Cynthia Asquith possessed both the attribute of beauty and the capacity for friendship, qualities which brought out the best in the people who were fortunate enough to know her and which helped to sustain the process of civilization in a difficult and perilous time. Frieda Lawrence wrote in her memoir: "Cynthia seemed to me lovely as Botticelli's Venus. . . . [She] was always a loyal friend, even through the war, when friends were rare."[36] No other tribute could have been better expressed—or more deserved.

4

King of Bloomsbury

In her diary entry for July 15, 1918, Lady Cynthia Asquith tells of lunching with her "literary mentor," Charles Whibley, at the Café Royal in London.[1] He "iconoclasted a good many tin gods," she says of this well-known literary critic, who "had the reputation of writing the best English of the day," and who, according to T. S. Eliot, could be counted with Léon Daudet and Charles Maurras as being "the three best writers of invective of their time."[2] Lady Cynthia goes on to note: "He fulminated against Lytton Strachey, condemning *Eminent Victorians* as mere journalese, and complaining of his total lack of grammar." If Lady Cynthia's "literary mentor" attacked a book that was causing considerable stir because of its blasphemous view of the Victorian Age, her friend the "Professor," Walter Raleigh, found *Eminent Victorians* "a delight," "pure joy," "very swell." "More power to your elbow! And don't worry, the noise is produced by the din you have made," he wrote to Strachey, who had studied under Raleigh while attending Liverpool University College from 1897 to 1899.[3]

When *Eminent Victorians* appeared in 1918, it put Strachey in the front rank of contemporary authors and brought him the fame for which he hankered. But among the members of the Bloomsbury Group, Strachey had been a famous name since its inception in 1907, the original group consisting of Strachey, John Maynard Keynes, Virginia and Leonard Woolf, Vanessa and Clive Bell, Desmond and Molly MacCarthy, Duncan Grant, E. M. Forster, Roger Fry, Adrian Stephen, and Saxon Sydney-Turner. If Virginia Woolf, as is alleged, reigned as Queen of Bloomsbury, Strachey reigned as king. The truth of this fact is fully confirmed by Michael Holroyd's two-volume biography, which in scope, content, and execution is a superb literary monument, as fitting a memorial as any monarch would wish.*

***Lytton Strachey: A Critical Biography*, 2 vols. (New York, 1968).

Surely Holroyd has saved the author of *Eminent Victorians* from those who, to quote a feverish reviewer in *The Cambridge Quarterly*, would have avoided what they consider Holroyd's greatest error: "to defend Strachey's posturings, and to praise his work . . . [for] the task is impossible. Lytton Strachey was not a 'mind'; as such he deserves to die."[4] The tone of this stricture is precisely the tone that Holroyd shuns, and the absence makes his two volumes excellent reading. We can imagine the results if the reviewer in *The Cambridge Quarterly* had been assigned the task of writing the biography of Strachey. (In a review of Holroyd's first volume, Malcolm Muggeridge generously admits, "I shudder to think what might have been made of this material [Strachey's correspondence] in less meticulous hands; mine for instance."[5])

In Holroyd, Strachey has been singularly favored with a biographer who presents all the facts of Strachey's life and circle without the biases that could easily mar any biography, let alone *the* biography of the King of Bloomsbury, whom F. R. Leavis has dismissed as follows: "Articulateness and unreality cultivated together, callowness disguised from itself in articulateness; conceit casing itself safely in a confirmed sense of high sophistication; the uncertainty as to whether one is serious or not taking itself for ironic poise: who has not at some time observed the process?"[6]

Inevitably, any assessment of Strachey's place in the history of English literature, and of the significance of the Bloomsbury Group, must confront the criticism of Leavis and his adherents. Both Strachey and Bloomsbury are repugnant to the Leavisites and are equated with devitalization, snobbism, shallowness, dilettantism, sham. Even E. M. Forster, despite a tenuous connection with Bloomsbury, is reprimanded for lacking the "personal vigour" and the "intellectual strength which impresses as the best source of vitality,"[7] to quote the words of Mrs. (Q. D.) Leavis—words peculiar to the Leavis view of Bloomsbury and of any creative writer failing to live up to the "refreshing sardonic" qualities of Leavis' bellwether, D. H. Lawrence, who detested Bloomsbury and satirized it in his short novel *St. Mawr* (1925):

> Believe in nothing, care about nothing: but keep the surface easy, and have a good time. *Let us undermine one another. There is nothing to believe in, so let us undermine everything. But look out! No scenes, no spoiling the game. Stick to the rules of the game. Be sporting, and don't do anything that would make a commotion. Keep the game going smooth and jolly, and bear your bit like a sport. Never, by any chance, injure your fellow man openly. But always injure him secretly. Make a*

*fool of him, and undermine his nature. Break him up by undermining
him, if you can. It's good sport.*

It is interesting to recall here that in November 1915, Strachey and
the Lawrences attended a party given by Dorothy Brett in her London studio. Strachey didn't venture to have himself introduced, he
wrote to David Garnett, though he "examined [the Lawrences] closely
and carefully for several hours." He found Lawrence "so pathetic,
miserable, ill, and obviously devoured by internal distresses." Of
Frieda he wrote: "I was surprised to find that I liked her looks very
much—she actually seemed (there's no other word for it) a lady."[8] It
should be added that Strachey, who never thought highly of Lawrence's writings, was outraged by the prosecution and the suppression
of *The Rainbow* (1915). Years later he also protested against the police seizure of Lawrence's paintings exhibited in June and July 1929
at the Warren Gallery in London, even though he dismissed the pictures as "poor." Strachey could not "abide" the prophetic strain in
Lawrence's writings. Lawrence, on the other hand, could not approve
of Strachey's Bloomsbury ethos: "Curse the Strachey who asks for a
new religion—the greedy dog," he wrote Lady Ottoline Morrell. "He
wants another juicy bone for his soul, does he? Let him start to fulfill
what religion we have." And, regarding Strachey's first book, *Land-
marks in French Literature* (1912), he wrote: "I still don't like Strachey—his French literature neither—words—literature—bore."[9]

Lawrence's criticisms of Bloomsbury and of Strachey reecho in
Leavis' views and in the pages of *Scrutiny*, the quarterly Leavis
edited between 1932 and 1953. To read Lawrence on Bloomsbury is
to read Leavis and, then, to read Leavis' followers, like T. R. Barnes,
who, reviewing Strachey's *Characters and Commentaries* (1933) in
Scrutiny, made this comment on Strachey: "Incapable of creation in
life or in literature, his writings were his substitute for both."[10]
Leavis' response to Strachey, and to Bloomsbury, uncovers some curious facets of the history of English literature and criticism in the
twentieth century. That the two men represent antithetical literary
forces is evident. For the difference between the Leavis outlook and
the Strachey outlook is as sharp, in terms of literary taste and criticism, as is the difference between D. H. Lawrence and James Joyce
in terms of the novel and the novelist's technique. Leavis upholds a
strongly moral, social, and vital strain in literature, in the teaching of
literature, and in criticism. His views are hard and rational: "We believe . . . that literary criticism is not a mystic rapture but a process of
the intelligence."[11] For Leavis, to quote Henry James, the critic must

be absolutely "damned critical—for it's the only thing to be, and all else is damned humbug."[12]

The critical act predicates for Leavis "moral discrimination, and judgment of relative human value." In time the critic will be forced to become "explicitly a moralist." As a critic who emphasizes "life" in its concreteness and immediacy, Leavis is preoccupied with the English provincial tradition, as opposed to that of London, with its clubs, its brassy journalism, its spirit of coterie, and its literary poses— with all of which Bloomsbury has been identified. His interest in non-English literature is only token and there is even disparagement of classical studies, facts prompting Professor René Wellek to single out Leavis' "provinciality and insularity."[13] Any art or criticism which is playful, impressionistic, rhetorical, ornamental, or formalistic he finds meaningless. According to a recent critic, Leavis' own style of writing "expresses a personality—it is always recognizable": "It is not a style that readily allows profitable argument or discussion. It is expressive of personal evaluations, and presents these with an impressive authority, an authority dependent on the style: everyone has noticed how disciples of Leavis echo his verbal manner."[14] The "verbal manner" is there, unmistakenly, in some of the critical reactions to Holroyd's *Lytton Strachey*, and brings our attention to the appropriateness of Wellek's contention that "There is a Leavis position, even an orthodoxy which can be described and criticized."

It would not be farfetched to point out that the irreconcilability of the Leavis and the Strachey literary positions can be likened to that of the Stoics and the Epicureans in the philosophical framework of Hellenistic times. In his unbending characteristic of judging, punishing, and chastising, knowing neither pity nor indulgence; in his stress on "life" in terms of moral growth; in his struggles for literary "standards" and "discrimination"; in his rationalistic and dogmatic critical approaches, his famous "revaluations" of literature, e.g., the elevation of D. H. Lawrence or the "dislodgment" of Milton—in these and in other aspects of his teaching and criticism, Leavis, like the Stoic sage who declared that philosophy is the "exercise" of an art to achieve "Wisdom," stresses the disciplined study of literature in "the great tradition" (Jane Austen, George Eliot, Henry James, Joseph Conrad, D. H. Lawrence) that can lead to a better life and to an "organic community." There is something of the Roman in Leavis and his followers: that tendency toward severity. Leavis himself is something of a modern Cato (234–149 B.C.): the literary "censor" of the English cultural scene who resembles the famous Roman moralist seeking to defend Rome's "primitive integrity" against "the hydra-like luxury and effeminacy of the time."[15]

On the other hand, Strachey—and Bloomsbury—in style and taste, are the modern English equivalent of ancient Epicureanism. A relaxed nonconformity; a marked gentility, a love of quietude and safety, equitably shared by selected and, above all, civilized "old friends"; a profound skepticism and a reverence for the private, "inner" life; a respect for intelligent conversation, carried on in the felicitous London confines of Bloomsbury as a modern Epicurean garden; an enlightened view of God and of death; a severe indictment of Christianity (though Dostoevsky's *The Brothers Karamazov* nearly converted Strachey), especially a Victorian mold of it as crystallized in *Eminent Victorians* in the chapter on Cardinal Manning; an appreciation of "stabilized pleasure" as an intrinsic part of human happiness—these were some of the traits that the King of Bloomsbury and his retinue perpetuated. What Bertrand Russell has to say concerning "the world of Lytton Strachey" has astringent relevance here:

> The tone of the generation some ten years junior to my own was set mainly by Lytton Strachey and Keynes. It is surprising how great a change in mental climate those ten years had brought. We were still Victorian; they were Edwardian. We believed in ordered progress by means of politics and free discussion. The more self-confident among us may have hoped to be leaders of the multitude but none of us wished to be divorced from it. The generation of Keynes and Lytton did not seek to preserve any kinship with the Philistine. They aimed rather at a life of retirement among fine shades and nice feelings, and conceived of the good as consisting in the passionate mutual admirations of a clique of the élite.[16]

In Strachey's life we are in the presence of "an amused Epicurean Zeus," to use the phrase of F. L. Lucas. It was a life that dramatized precisely the traits enumerated above, with one chief difference being Strachey's obsessive homosexuality. Certainly the style of Strachey's life with its parties, gossip, and travels, with its involved homosexual love affairs, aberrational in character (Strachey wanted to play the feminine role in his affairs with a continuing series of male lovers), with its appetite for jokes and clever remarks at the expense of innocent bystanders and acquaintances, as well as good friends, including one's host or hostess, is a style that can hardly lend itself to the fancy of the Leavisite view of life and literature. (Cicero's feeling that Epicureanism corrupted Roman lives "with bowered seclusion, luxury, ease, indolence, and sloth" can be seen as an equivalent feeling that Leavis and his followers have all along held with respect to Bloomsbury.[17])

Despite his personal idiosyncrasies and what some critics have thought to be the absurdity of his style, in life as in literature, Strachey gained popularity and was to have a marked influence on English life. It is in opposition to this influence, in its very nature and form, that we can discern what we have termed the Leavisite outlook. In matters of life, Strachey represents to the Leavisites a sickening and, to use a favored Lawrentian word, a "disintegrating" human personality peculiar to members of the Cambridge and Bloomsbury "gang," of whom Lawrence wrote: "Their attitude is so irreverent and blatant. They are cased each in a hard little shell of his own, and out of this they talk words."[18] And in matters of literature, as already indicated, Strachey obviously represents the blatancies of what Leavis terms "the literary racket" with its "prepossession, conceit, and insensibility so potently banded" in a spirit "inimical to criticism, that is, to intelligence."[19]

The significance of the Leavisite objections can be better understood when one considers the evident homosexual tone and climate of the English world during and after Strachey's time—in business, government, teaching, and journalism: in short, in the essential makings and functions of English cultural life and taste in the years between the two world wars. Leavisites contend that the Strachey outlook, by its unwholesomeness, damaged irreparably the cultural vitality of English life, especially in the years following the Great War when English society sorely needed vigorous, healthy-minded leadership and guidance, emotionally and intellectually, to withstand the inevitable disillusionments that the war caused.

Goronwy Rees points out that between 1918 and 1939 the English universities (Oxford and Cambridge) were deeply affected by homosexuality; that this fact also significantly influenced those who studied in the universities during this period—an influence that most probably continued when some of the graduates came into positions of importance—and that the positions occupied by such persons in English life had "given them a distinctive and identifiable influence on English life as a whole."[20] Rees's uneasy feelings about "a significant stratum of English life [the extent of homosexuality] ... still to be uncovered" can be correlated with the Leavisite objections to the effects of the Strachey attitude, in particular, and of the Bloomsbury ethos, in general. The homosexual element, which Strachey espoused with intense dedication, could not but contribute to the kind of softness that in the end led to the appeasement of Hitler, nowhere better dramatized than in Neville Chamberlain's mission to Munich. Homosexuality, in this connection, reflected a facet of decadence, and in the years from 1933 to 1939 this decadence was duly recorded in the decline of English political thought. In the final analysis, what Leavis deplores in Bloomsbury is this decadent tone, this lack of toughness and vitality.

As a writer and a personality, Strachey had much impact on his times. But his times, and his contemporaries, were in need of examples of emotional and intellectual toughness. Strachey and his circle, however, were disinclined to sacrifice (even in the midst of the Great War) what was funny and gay. Holroyd's biography, to quote *Punch*, takes us "back to an infinitely remote, deliciously leisured world of long vac, reading parties and shy, homosexual *schwärmerei*, where you can imagine Goldie Lowes Dickinson dancing elegant little fairy dances on the King's lawn in front of Gibbs Building."[21] At the same time it takes us back to a crucial period of English civilization which demanded of both its legislators and its littérateurs something more than gay reading parties and fairy dances on lawns that would eventually be the targets of deadly Messerschmitts.

Interestingly, some reviewers of Holroyd's volumes have complained that the portrayal of Strachey's life fails to appreciate its pervasive comic elements. Leonard Woolf, a confidant of Strachey's, protests that the biography lacks humor and misleadingly depicts Strachey's life as a never ending "state of passion, passionate love, passions of ecstasy or despair." Hence, Strachey is invariably revealed as "dying of love." Yet, Woolf avers, Strachey did not have any strong passions or emotions. "He loved to dramatize himself, his friends, and his loves. And he was hardly ever completely serious when he had his pen in his hand, writing the tragedy or comedy of his perpetual love affairs to Maynard Keynes, James [Strachey], or me."[22] Woolf's comments give all the more reason why Strachey's life is, in the end, the tragedy it is found to be in the pages of Holroyd's biography. It is exactly the tragic dimension of Strachey's life that a moral critic who writes in almost athletic terms of disapproval, like Leavis, and a Bloomsbury compatriot, like Woolf, cannot see. In the case of the former, a severe literary puritanism and a deep self-righteousness rule out any compassionate response to the fatuity of it all. In the case of Woolf, the requisites of loyalty and friendship preclude an objective view. And in these reasons, too, we can understand why Holroyd, given his dispassionate point of view—for he is neither a Leavisite nor a bedazzled spectator of glittering biography—has proved to be a brilliant biographer.

Holroyd's biography gives us an amazingly impressive understanding of a writer who, as Anthony West observes, transcending his writing, lived for something greater: "personal relationships and their analysis in conversation," the belief that "the personal life is the essence and the public performance no more than its shadow."[23] More importantly, it also enables us to fathom the tragedy of a man who was sick throughout his life and died of cancer at the age of fifty-two; who was unhappy in his family life and in his school years until he entered Cambridge University; who failed to get firsts in his university studies, as well as a much-desired fellowship at Cambridge; who, for a major part of his career, was faced with financial plight; who suffered from a kind of nomadism (though not on D. H. Lawrence's global scale); who, above all, demonstrated in his sexual habits and anomalies an unrequited passion no less consuming than what André Gide in *The Immoralist*, Thomas Mann in *Death in Venice*, Yukio Mishima in *Confessions of a Mask*, and E. M. Forster in *Maurice* depict as the intolerable condition of their protagonists, who happen to be homosexuals, searching for the love that, as Lord Alfred Douglas writes, "dare not speak its name."

No doubt Strachey's life had its comedy and its cleverness, but this part of his life was built on words, of which Bloomsbury had a plenitude. (Strachey, for example, described Aldous Huxley as "a piece of seaweed," and his friend Virginia Woolf, who also had a gift for epistolary invective, wrote of poor Middleton Murry as "a moon calf looking youth.") But even as he was debunking a Victorian past with furious irreverence, there wove through his life an underlying sense of disappointment, an element of dissatisfaction, of futility, emptiness, and desperation that no glibness could hide. The sadness of Strachey's life—the sadness of all life which Virginia Woolf in *Jacob's Room* speaks of as "brewed by the earth itself.... We start transparent, and then the cloud thickens. All history backs our pane of glass. To escape is vain"—cannot easily be disregarded on the basis of Strachey's literary accomplishment or comic posturings. Ultimately Holroyd's biography communicates an overarching sadness and pathos. It is the kind of sadness that has its literary counterparts in André Gide's impassioned confessions in his letters to Paul Claudel, in the poetic erotica of C. P. Cavafy, and in Oscar Wilde's *De Profundis*. The tone of this sadness evinces an inner paralysis, a sterility, an incompletion.

Even as he joked and laughed and scorned, Strachey, who detected the subtlest psychic tones in the lives of Florence Nightingale, General Gordon, Queen Elizabeth I, and the Earl of Essex—deep, troubling tones which other commentators could never hear, even as close as a heartbeat—Strachey could not have eluded tones that reverberated in his own being and that exposed his own malaise and provoked an awareness of those terrible mortal limitations which he sought in vain to overcome or escape. Strachey testifies to the pathos of his own condition in a letter to Dora Carrington, a gifted painter he met in 1915 and with whom he lived until his death in 1932. (In 1922 Carrington, as she was called, married Ralph Partridge, one of Strachey's lovers. His relationship to Carrington continued, though it now became a convenient *ménage à trois*.) Sexual love, however, was impossible for them: Strachey was homosexual and Carrington disliked, as David Garnett asserts, being a woman, a dislike that "gave her a feeling of inferiority so that normal and joyful relationship was next to impossible." In his reply to a letter from Carrington, in which she bemoaned the crippling limitation and the emotional impermanence of their relationship, Strachey replied:

> Your letter made me cry, I feel a poor old miserable creature, and I may have brought more unhappiness to you than anything else. I only pray that it is not so, and that my love for you, even though it is not what you desire, may make our relationship a blessing to you—as it has been to me.
>
> Remember that I too have never had my moon! We are all helpless in these things—dreadfully helpless. I am lonely and I am all too truly growing old, and if there was a chance that your decision meant that I should somehow or other lose you, I don't think I could bear it.[24]

In his life as in his art, with Voltaire as his bible and the eighteenth century as his example, Strachey chose the way of the Enlightenment, of which he was a fervent modern champion and in which he saw his own and the world's salvation. But it was an enlightenment founded on the illusion of man's sinlessness. Although he did not look deep within himself to meditate and to discover himself completely, the King of Bloomsbury could hardly have overlooked either the sadness of his own life or the tragedy of the human condition. Man must, John Milton reminds us, "Some time let Gorgeous Tragedy / In Scepter'd Pall come sweeping by."

5

Three English Lives

ARNOLD TOYNBEE, VIVIAN DE SOLA PINTO,
LEONARD WOOLF

へりく

The publication of an ever-increasing number of biographies, letters, memoirs, reminiscences, and critical studies shows that British (and European) civilization in the years before and after the Great War is being scrutinized from different angles. It is an age that is often associated with crisis, internal and external, and with some tremendous, but for the most part vaguely defined, breakthrough. It is an age which exerts its fascinations. Some writers look back to the three or four decades before 1914 to determine the reasons for the disintegration of particular values, especially in the years *l'entre deux guerres*. Other writers look back to this period in an attempt to contrast some of the brave new directions taken since 1914 by modern society. Some reflect nostalgically on this period. Others welcome a release from what are considered its archaic ways and its provincialism. Such interest is possibly symptomatic of our own generation's state of soul and of mind, as well as its quest for identity, or self-understanding, or a better comprehension of its roots or (inescapably) its uprootedness.

Journey Through Despair, 1880–1914, by John A. Lester, Jr.,* is a thoughtful, if not exhaustive, result of an interest in a phase of modern British civilization going back before the outbreak of World War I and yet belonging, intrinsically, to contemporary England. Focusing on the "transformations in British literary culture" from the death of Thomas Carlyle to World War I, this book contemplates not merely defilement in the broadest cultural framework, but, particularly, the despair that ravaged "man's imaginative orientation to the world" at a time when "the old bases of significant imaginative life were indefensible." Lester states his purpose in these words:

*Princeton, N. J., 1968.

89

"This book is an attempt to describe the bewilderment and to define the critical challenge which confronted the imagination in this period, and to trace the most characteristic responses which that crisis provoked."

The three main divisions of *Journey Through Despair* can be conveniently summarized as follows: Part I, "The Challenge," delineates the drift toward disillusionment in man's material life, thought, and imagination. The whole of this period is called "transitional," with "the transit not yet completed," inasmuch as moods and doubts still remain. In outlining the nature of the challenge posed by "the new cosmology," Lester emphasizes the problems caused by Darwinism, with the resultant need for man to learn how "to survive in a wilderness of choice and change."

Part II, "Responses in Three Modes," attempts to show some responses to the challenge as revealed in the emotions, the mind, and the imagination. There developed a pessimism caused by "the death of God" and the banishment of certitudes and of hope. Such tendencies as the glorification of the "eternal Nowness" and of a return to nature were offshoots of this emotional crisis. Attempts to discover other faculties of cognition emerged, at times in paradoxical ways—on the one hand, the empirical investigation of facts and a rational study of their consequences; on the other, the quest for nonlogical faculties of cognition, such as a recognition of the powers of the unconscious and of the instinctive forces (even extending to a fascination with psychical research and occultism). The "rage for art" became apparent chiefly as a means of escape from despair and as the only note of promise in a disordered world. "Art became the antithesis and the antagonist of nature and science, of both abstraction and intellection." This quotation from William Butler Yeats supports Lester's judgment: "The arts are . . . about to take upon their shoulders the burdens that have fallen from the shoulders of priests, and to lead us back upon our journey by filling our thoughts with the essences of things, and not with things."

Part III, "Applications," considers three themes in the literature of the period: the mask, ecstasy, and the will to believe. Some writers, like Oscar Wilde and Yeats, employed the mask to depersonalize the work of art. This mask served "as protective shell to a wounded sensibility," "as a projective conception of the varieties and heights of being which man might achieve," "as an aesthetic means of striking an aesthetic attitude, calm, serene, and outside the flux of time." The longing for ecstatic experience was revealed in D. H. Lawrence's eros, in Richard Jefferies' nature, in James Joyce's epiphany. Ecstasy became "an end in itself, a justifying reward in a world in which rewards were few." Ultimately, what we discover in this period, Lester concludes, is that in the midst of the collapse of absolutes it still remained man's task to "find and fabricate illusions and *believe* in them," to affirm that "man must *be* and must *find significance in being.*" Here Joseph Conrad is cited as exemplifying how the imagination can respond to the challenge of the "crisis of despair." "The human heart," Conrad writes in *Lord Jim*, "is vast enough to contain all the world. It is valiant enough to bear the burden."

These conclusions are bound to elicit general agreement. Some cultural historians see the war of 1914–18 as the consummate result of exactly that cultural debilitation which the author traces in literary and ideational areas. Nevertheless, Lester's book leaves the impression that he was somehow bending a great segment of cultural history to accommodate his thesis. His findings are too one-sided, too overworked in the portrayal of despair. For if this was a period when despair seemed overwhelming, it was also a period of quiet contentment. In England, as Virginia Woolf asserts in her essay "The Leaning Tower," many writers still enjoyed "the advantages of the tower class," when reading, listening, discussing aesthetic emotions and traveling, as well as leisure and tranquillity, were luxuries of life not yet destroyed by a war that, in 1914, came crashing "like a chasm in the smooth road."

Journey Through Despair is curiously deficient in its awareness of a settled civilization and even of a pastoral *ethos* that still distinguished English life from 1880 to 1914. But its deficiency, one might say, recommends this book, insofar as it prompts disagreements and, more importantly, calls for the correction of a thesis that the author charts with an often grim academic passion. It is true that during this period English civilization was insulated and detached from that of the Continent. Writers like H. G. Wells, Arnold Bennett, John Galsworthy, and even Thomas Hardy typified the English mind in isolation before 1914. With Lawrence, Joyce, Eliot, Aldous Huxley, and Wyndham Lewis, especially as their works revealed the modern spirit at the end of World War I, the provincialism and the narrowness of late Victorian and of Edwardian England were outgrown. Their works communicated, even as they were informed by, changing history: "they have got the whole of human history inside their heads," to use one description emphasizing changes in the literary climate. Thus the writers of the postwar period, as George Orwell wrote in *The Listener* (March 19, 1942), "broke the cultural circle in which England had existed for something like a century. They re-established contact with Europe, and they brought back the sense of history and the possibility of tragedy."

Yet the acquisition of this historical sense was not without its pains. The "drift toward disillusionment" that Lester finds in the years 1880–1914 was a condition of the postwar period. The differences between the periods before and after the war are indisputably clear in Lawrence's *Women in Love,* a novel that focuses on the death of civilization. In it one reads a statement like this: "There is a phase in every race ... when the desire for destruction overcomes every other desire." Such words capture a frightening sense of loss: the loss of the "old agricultural past," the loss of that warm feeling of communion of life in the English Midlands that Lawrence's poem "Piano" evokes:

> In spite of myself, the insidious mastery of song
> Betrays me back, till the heart of me weeps to belong
> To the old Sunday evenings at home, with the winter outside
> And hymns in the cosy parlor, the tinkling piano our guide.

The Great War separated two worlds, two consciousnesses, two tempers, even as it introduced modern literature. One can think here of no more startling contrasts than those between the prewar poems of Rupert Brooke, such as these lines from his "Flight":

> Voices out of the shade that cried,
>   And long noon in the hot calm places,
> And children's play by the wayside,
>   And country eyes, and quiet faces—
> All these were round my steady paces.

and these lines from Siegfried Sassoon's "To Any Dead Officer," written just before the United States entered the war:

> Good-bye, old lad! Remember me to God,
>   And tell Him that our Politicians swear
> They won't give in till Prussian Rule's been trod
>   Under the Heel of England.... Are you there? ...
> Yes ... and the War won't end for at least two years;
> But we've got stacks of men.... I'm blind with tears,
>   Staring into the dark. Cheero!
> I wish they'd killed you in a decent show.

Brooke's dream world came to an end with a war that led straight to Sassoon's despair. Orwell comes closest to the mark when he reminds us that with the new writers, immediately after the war, "something has been punctured. To begin with, the notion of progress has gone by the board. They don't any longer believe that men are getting better and better by having lower mortality rates, more effective birth control, better plumbing, more aeroplanes and faster motor cars. Nearly all of them are homesick for the remote past. . . ."

A more balanced outlook than Lester's is needed if the period is to be rightly understood. One should reexamine, for instance, the early works of two novelists whom Lester enlists for support—E. M. Forster and D. H. Lawrence. Could we not declare that in *The Longest Journey* (1907) Forster in effect sanctions a way of life that *Journey Through Despair* equates with *angst*? And is it not significant that Forster himself admitted that he stopped writing novels because the world after the Great War had drastically changed from the Edwardian world he knew? Significantly, Forster's posthumous novel, *Maurice*, contains a revealing "Terminal Note," dated September 1960. In it Forster declares that this novel is set about 1912, in the England before World War I, the England "where it was possible to get lost" in "the greenwood," i.e., the England to which *The Longest Journey* also belongs. What Forster says in the following quotation from the "Terminal Note" gives a vivid picture of English life before 1914 and summarizes, too, the dehumanizing losses suffered in the years after 1914:

> Our greenwood ended catastrophically and inevitably. Two great wars demanded and bequeathed regimentation which the public services adopted and extended, science lent her aid, and the wildness of our island, never extensive, was stamped upon and built over and patrolled in no time. There is no forest or fell to escape to today, no cave in which to curl up, no deserted valley for those who wish neither to reform nor corrupt society but to be left alone. People do still escape, one can see them any night at it in the films. But they are gangsters, not outlaws, they can dodge civilization because they are part of it.

If we want evidence from one who did not belong to "the tower class," if we want a novel from the working class, then we can turn to Lawrence's *The Rainbow* (1915). No other novel better illustrates the point raised here. Despair was not the all-consuming force that Lester's book makes it out to have been. The first part of this novel is like a hymn to an older, happier generation living on Marsh Farm, with its seasonal rhythm of life, its beauties, its peace and orderliness. Nor is it insignificant that in *Lady Chatterley's Lover* (1928), for all its immaturities and misjudgments in taste, Lawrence still yearns for the Eden of the English Midlands, not yet transformed into the amorphous and ugly industrial world that Nottingham and London came to symbolize. Lawrence, no less than Forster, was profoundly appreciative of "the last moment of the greenwood." In the short novel *The Captain's Doll* (1923), he writes such nostalgic words as these:

"It seemed lovely: almost like before the war: almost the same feeling of eternal holiday, as if the world was made for man's everlasting holiday."

And if an American spectator of the English scene is also needed, for the sake of further confirmation, there is George Santayana, whose *Soliloquies in England and Later Soliloquies* (1922), written during his stay in England between 1914 and 1918, begins by memorializing not a world of despair, but a world of "contentment in solitude, fair outward ways, manly perfection and simplicity," a world in which "cataclysms are rare"—or were until that "monstrous August" of 1914. In his Prologue, Santayana also transcribes "some desperate verses" he wrote in those years. Admitting that he is "hardly a poet in the magic sense of the word," he does not ask the reader "to admire his three sonnets, but to believe them." The first, "A Premonition," with the subtitle, "Cambridge, October 1913," returns one to Forster's England of the soon-to-be-lost "greenwood" and to Lawrence's England of "man's everlasting holiday":

> Grey walls, broad fields, fresh voices, rippling weir,
> I know you well: ten faces, for each face
> That passes smiling, haunt this hallowed place,
> And nothing not thrice noted greets me here.
> Soft watery winds, wide twilight skies and clear,
> Refresh my spirit at its founts of grace,
> And a strange sorrow masters me, to pace
> These willowed paths, in this autumnal year.
> Soon, lovely England, soon thy secular dreams,
> Thy lisping comrades, shall be thine no more.
> A world's loosed troubles flood thy gated streams
> And drown, methinks, thy towers; and the tears start
> As if an iron hand had clutched my heart,
> And knowledge is a pang, like love of yore.

To modify even more assiduously the thesis of *Journey Through Despair*, one may turn to the autobiography of a continental writer, Stephan Zweig's *The World of Yesterday*. Perhaps its most vivid pages are those in which Zweig evokes the idyll of the European way of life before 1914. He speaks of this period as "the Golden Age of Security," when life had its fixed values, when wars and revolutions were given little thought, when radicalism and violence were kept in check, when the private life was still protected from oppressive bureaucratic and collectivist practices. "It was an ordered world . . . , a world without haste," writes Zweig.

Zweig's words receive endorsement in the life story of three representatives of an age to which feelings of despair have been so readily and mistakenly ascribed. These three English representatives are the historian Arnold Toynbee (b. 1889), the teacher and scholar Vivian de Sola Pinto (1895–1969), and the political thinker, writer, and editor Leonard Woolf (1880–1969). The ethos molding their lives and their achievements bespeaks an age in which humanistic civilization was ascendant. Not grim despair, but a steady sentience and a steady faith in man and in man's ability to diminish his limitations characterizes their outlooks. Invariably each reveals a reverence for the intellect, friendship, and the arts. Each disdains cruelty and intolerance, ugliness and barbarism. Each was a product of a classical education that disciplined the intellect without either emptying it of enthusiasm or making it the slave of specialism. What one finds in each man is the avoidance of extremes and the informing presence of a balance in his view of life. Even the Great War, in all its horrors, did not break this humanistic attitude. In fact, the conflict itself emphasized the need to hang on to this attitude, at all costs, if barbarism were to be resisted.

If modern literature was to stress the depth of what had been lost, these three modern men of letters were to be spokesmen for a way of life that, though crippled and scarred, survived because it contained what is best in the Judaeo-Christian and Graeco-Roman civilizations. Toynbee, Pinto, and Woolf can be seen as cultural synthesists helping to maintain those standards that make for the continuity of wisdom. It can happen that humanism becomes the victim of despair; but its essential value, its gospel of faith, is its transcendent and creative love of the mystery and wonder of the world. In Toynbee, Pinto, and Woolf this transcendence and creativeness give to their humanism an enduring significance. These three English lives—indeed, these three priests of humanism—should disarm even the most intransigent skeptic.

ARNOLD TOYNBEE

Arnold Toynbee's life and work have been marked not only by his immense accomplishments as a moral and prophetic historian—"our more slender but no less weighty Gibbon," as Sir Harold Nicolson once described him[1]—but also by the many gifted men and women whom he has met and known. These people are the subjects of his book *Acquaintances*.[2] All now dead, most of them were brilliant, some could be counted as geniuses, and all were vital and active, very much committed in their particular fields. They all had "style."

Toynbee has chosen his subjects on the basis of their being of "general interest." He notes that his relations with them "were of different degrees of intimacy, ranging from mere acquaintance to close friendship." The sketches are mainly of people who made their reputations either in the world of arts and letters or in the world of politics. In this respect they could be said to comprise the intelligentsia, but without the pejorative connotations this word often arouses. Consistently, he writes of them with *pietas,* a feeling that is abundantly vindicated both by their character and their contributions to civilized living. The interest that these people hold for us is heightened by the fact that they lived and worked during the greater part of the twentieth century. In reading about them—what they were like as human beings, how they played important roles in history, why and when they acted as they did—we are able to gain new insights into the intellectual life of this century.

For the most part, Toynbee's "acquaintances" were intellectuals; that is, they were preoccupied with ideas and books and often at the same time active in public life. In the United States it has been only in recent years that intellectuals have started to participate in politics, but in England and in Europe as a whole, as Toynbee shows, it has long been traditional for a man of letters to have a political life as well. (The use of the title "Dr." to describe the credentials of a European scholar-statesman still confuses some Americans, who associate this title exclusively with their physicians!). The range and depth of the intellectual interests of Toynbee's English friends could well be described as astonishing. Sir Alfred Zimmern, author of the monumental work *The Greek Commonwealth* and a popular teacher of ancient history at Oxford in the early 1900's, became an expert in international relations. During the interwar years he held an annual summer school at Geneva when the Assembly of the League of Nations was in session, with Zimmern himself giving a running commentary on the Assembly's proceedings. Lord Bryce, the famous historian and author of *The Holy Roman Empire* and *The American Commonwealth,* served as a member of Gladstone's cabinet and later as British ambassador to the United States. Colonel T. E. Lawrence, whose career in World War I and espousal of the Arab cause were remarkable, achieved success also as a linguist, a scholar, and an author.

But there was nothing insular about Toynbee's circle. There are a number of recollections of non-English notables. Field Marshall Jan Smuts is one of these. Toynbee points out that General Smuts's book *Holism,* which he read in the early summer of 1927, was an important influence as he was just beginning work for *A Study of History.* Indeed, "this book of General Smuts's has continued to be one of my guides on my own mental voyage of exploration." W. L. Westermann, the German-American scholar and papyrologist, is another acquaintance whom Toynbee met during the 1919 peace conference in Paris and from whom he learned much about the American way of life. (Westermann was then head of the Turkish section of the American delegation.) Sri Jawaharlal Nehru is yet another acquaintance, whom Toynbee met in the 1930's and then on two later occasions, in 1957 and in 1960, and about whom he writes warmly and objectively: "Since his death Jawaharlal Nehru has been suffering the same treatment as T. E. Lawrence. The debunkers have been busy with him. Yet, after the vultures have finished their scavenging work, Nehru, too, will still be the great man that he was—great, though human; human, so lovable."

Throughout, the recollections are written in a magnanimous spirit. Grace of style and simplicity of approach are ever present. Toynbee knows exactly on what aspects of his subjects' lives to fasten, and, unlike many other modern biographers, he has a disdain for trivia. Invariably he records the specific impressions people made on him and their influences on his life and work. The complexity and richness of the relationships are delineated. There is no doubt of Toynbee's gift and reverence for friendship. The portrait of Montague John Rendall, first a Second Master (*Ostiarius*) and later Head Master (*Informator*) at Winchester College, which Toynbee attended from 1902 to 1907, is especially generous in showing the large and permanent place in one's life a gifted teacher of the humanities can have. (The impersonality so apparent, and endemic, in American education today, with its emphasis on bigness, inevitably points a contrast.) With rare vividness, Toynbee pays tribute to Rendall's "noble" gifts as a teacher—after a lapse of more than fifty years! "Mr. Rendall's passion for beauty," Toynbee recalls, "was matched by his missionary zeal for communicating this to everyone within his range; and this was his *forte*. His passion was infectious; for he had a remarkable power of making the beauty, latent in things, come alive."

Toynbee's penetrating insights into the personalities of his friends and acquaintances help one to understand the paradoxes in people. These personal elements, however, are not exploited in order to startle or scandalize, but rather they are appraised forthrightly but charitably. The tone of Toynbee's sketches is never rash or cruel; it has a civilized quality that could be profitably emulated by other modern biographers. Sir Lewis Namier "was invincibly lovable, from first to last; and ... [he] needed to be invincibly lovable if a friendship with him was to last, for his character had another vein in it which, unsubdued, put his lovableness to a searching test. If you crossed Lewis on some issue which, for him, was of importance, he was capable of declaring war on you, however old and close a friend of his you might be; and, in making war, he was always vehement, sometimes vindictive, and occasionally even venomous—*impiger, iracundus et acer*, in fact." Sidney and Beatrice Webb were unjustly labeled inhuman ("a pair of inhuman dissectors of sensitive human tissue"), says Toynbee, who met the famous couple before the end of World War I. "In their private life," he insists, "the Webbs were not in the least inhuman. Not only did they love each other deeply; they were rather more demonstrative than most English people are in displaying their feelings for each other in the presence of their friends. They were not shy; I have seen them even playful; and their friends received their share of this engaging warmth of feeling."

Equally illuminating is Toynbee's essay on T. E. Lawrence, who, he emphasizes, had in him an element of greatness which will never disappear no matter what his detractors say. Though egotism played some part in Lawrence's character, he was essentially "a particular type of British idealist." His inability to settle down to civilian life after the war—and he had his pick of attractive positions in each of his fields of activity—was the result of his difficulty to readjust to peacetime, a failing common to other combatants. Toynbee's description of Lawrence is astute, as he is seen in Paris in 1919 trying to promote the Arab cause. The following exchange between Clemenceau and Lawrence, as reported by Toynbee, is arresting:

> "You know, Colonel Lawrence," said Clemenceau, as his opening gambit, "you know that France has been interested in Syria ever since the Crusades." "Yes," Lawrence answered, "but the Syrians won the Crusades, and they have never forgotten that." Apparently this had not occurred to Clemenceau before. He had no reply, so the conversation ended there. . . . Lawrence's power revealed itself visually. Lawrence was, in fact, like a chameleon. When he was not in action, he had a deceptive appearance of being insignificant.... In action, Lawrence's spirit, like Achitophel's, "o'er informed the tenement of clay."

Toynbee never fails to laud men of integrity. C. P. Scott, editor of the *Manchester Guardian*, is praised by Toynbee for allowing him to report firsthand the Greek massacres of the Turks in the second battle of Inönu during the Graeco-Turkish war in 1921. Though pro-Greek, the paper published these reports and thus defied external pressures exerted by British liberal circles. "The *Manchester Guard-ian* stood," Toynbee states, ". . . for publishing the truth, as it saw it, without fear or favour. In my brief term of temporary service on the *Guardian*'s staff, I had the paper's high standard of probity borne in on me by finding myself one of its beneficiaries."

Lord Samuel, the first High Commissioner for Palestine under the mandate, is the subject of the last sketch in the book. In 1909 or 1910, while studying at Balliol, Toynbee had his first glimpse of Lord Samuel, then Postmaster-General. Some time after the First World War, he had his first meeting with him as a cabinet minister in the course of an informal conference on the Middle East. Some of Toynbee's comments on Lord Samuel are most revealing, for they crystal-lize precisely those vanishing human values that Toynbee honors and that make for statesmanship. "Lord Samuel was open-minded, dis-cerning, free from self-conceit. . . . The salient feature in his character was his integrity; the next most striking feature was his common sense. The two factions of the fractured Liberal Party found in him a conciliator on whose rectitude and reasonableness both sides could rely." In old age, in spite of bereavement and physical infirmities, Lord Samuel's "spirit never closed in on itself. Till his death, he re-tained his lifelong interest in human affairs, and his lifelong concern for their betterment. If one ends like that, one has indeed done well." These words sum up Toynbee's concept of worthy human character and the life of value. It is possibly an old-fashioned, didactic concept. But it is one that, by its edge and force, tells the difference between civilization and barbarism.

Toynbee's "acquaintances" demonstrate time and again a respect for the habits and standards of serious moral evaluation, as well as a necessity for discrimination and integrity. They were men and women who stood for the humane and humanizing elements of life. They belonged to a world which now contrasts starkly with a world in which functional specialisms and scholar-pedants have replaced the humanities and humanists, a world in which the managerial experts, the technicians, statisticians, and public relations men, obsessed with the superficialities of image and the intricacies of power, have come gradually to constitute and to mold a new society. (We need hardly be reminded that today we have a plethora of politicians, but no great statesmen!) If Toynbee communicates a certain nostalgia, it is for the values and disciplines which make for dignity and integrity.

By and large *Acquaintances* revolves around World War I, includ-ing the years immediately before and after. Of essays on other sub-jects, there is "Bonn in Nazi-Time," which re-creates the frightening

atmosphere of a nation in which anti-intellectualism was rampant
and "meanness" and brutality ascendant. There is also "A Lecture
by Hitler," which recounts Toynbee's meeting with Hitler in 1936.
"Most of the time, my eyes were following Hitler's hands. He had
beautiful hands. He used them to accompany his words; and his gestures were eloquent, as well as graceful. His voice, too, was, unexpectedly to me, agreeably human in its pitch and cadence—human,
that is, so long as he was not talking about Russia." The ethos that
this book conveys, and in a deep sense sanctifies, is one that belongs
to British character and civilization formed "before the war." Toynbee's "exclusive and intense" education, chiefly his training in Greek
and Latin at Winchester and later in ancient history at Oxford (1907–
11), testifies to a background in the *Literae Humaniores*, which before 1914 occupied a central position in the education peculiar to the
British middle class, to the members, that is, of "the tower class" who,
according to Virginia Woolf, "have sat upon the same kind of chair—
a raised chair."[3] This education helped to stamp Toynbee's attitude
of mind as well as his ethos with a pervasive humanism. The four
leading characteristics which E. M. Forster attributes to the humanist—curiosity, a free mind, belief in good taste, and belief in the human race—are those of Toynbee himself.[4]

Throughout, Toynbee discloses great respect for a generation in
which intellectuals possessed the virtue of public spirit—e.g., Sir
James Headlam-Morley, Lord Bryce, Lionel Curtis, Gilbert Murray,
and J. W. Mackail. Interestingly, too, he indicates the profound concern that he and others belonging to the 1914–18 generation had for
promoting peace in the wake of a cataclysmic war. (In conversations
with his son Philip, Toynbee has stressed that, between past and
present, "1914 was the watershed date ... much more than the outbreak of the second war. Because the second was implicit in the
first."[5]) Having known peace, prosperity, and certitude before 1914,
Toynbee confesses to a longing for prewar humanist culture and for
what he has called a "unity of outlook." His middle-class upbringing, his work in the British Foreign Office, his scholarly pursuits—all
these are reflected in his belief that since 1914 civilization has been
in a state of progressive disintegration. Not that Toynbee longs to
return to the past. "I feel a relief that it's gone," he said to his son.
"The sight, when I was small, of children in rags and beggars in the
street was very painful. I am very glad that has gone."[6] What these
biographical sketches indicate is Toynbee's affirmation of what Simone Weil terms "the idea of value" in human life.

The changes in human affairs within his lifetime are surveyed and commented on by Toynbee in *Experiences*, his sequel to *Acquaintances*.[7] In this autobiographical volume he is an observer and appraiser, as well as the subject and the narrator. Personal reminiscence and historical reflection comprise the dual substance of *Experiences*. The England before 1914 is evoked. Born into the British middle class in 1889, he offers many insights into the late Victorian and the Edwardian way of life. In particular he recalls his own schooling, first at a boarding school in Kent, Wootton Court, then at a great public school, Winchester College, and finally at the University of Oxford, where he studied at Balliol College (1907–11). His education, in keeping with the pedagogical theories of that time, was classical, and as such it was characterized precisely by those elements of stability and security which are in themselves integral to the classical outlook. As a result, Toynbee's formative mental and spiritual world was rooted in the Graeco-Roman evaluation. Perhaps the most positive effect of this education, he points out, was that it gave him a certain disinterested view of the world, so that he was saved from overestimating the importance of modern Western civilization. As a humanist student of the classics taught to see Graeco-Roman life as a unity, he also acquired the lifelong conviction that human affairs are not intelligible until they are seen as a whole, that is, until they are seen synoptically. Although his classical education prevented him from making himself at home in the physical sciences and in higher mathematics, its values have been inestimable in other, more important ways:

> My spiritual home [he writes] in the Graeco-Roman World has, as things have turned out, been of great practical help to me. It has been a haven of stability in the midst of a welter of change. In the living world into which I have been born, a placid phase of history has been swept away by a turbulent phase within my lifetime, but my footing in my Classical World has moderated for me the shock of this transition. In the barbarians' postscript to history, one paragraph has been followed by another. But history itself—that is, Greek and Roman history—still remains what it has always been.

This grounding in the classical world and outlook can be seen in Toynbee's intellectual history and in his rejection of narrow, compartmentalized education, especially the forms of specialization which now seem to have proliferated. It accounts for Toynbee's predilection for great men, either as leaders or thinkers, or as both, in whom "all-roundness," their special "un-modern" sense of "comprehensive-mindedness," was a key to their greatness: e.g., General Smuts, Albert Einstein, Winston Churchill, and such Western historians as Clarendon, Gibbon, Freeman, Bury, Theodor Mommsen, and Eduard Meyer. In this respect, Terence's words, *Homo sum, nihil humanum a me alienum puto*—"I am a human being, so there is nothing human that I do not feel to be my concern"—have served as Toynbee's inspiration.

Toynbee maintains that his own classical education has saved him from the "cult of specialization": "I have never made the choice between being an historian of politics, economics, religion, the arts, science, or technology; my conscious and deliberate aim has been to be a student of human affairs studied as a whole. I have rebelled against their being partitioned into the so-called 'disciplines.'" Humanist by training and humanist in practice, Toynbee has attempted to expand his intellectual horizon systematically and to bring, historically, religiously, philosophically, "within my range of vision, and my range of action, all the other societies, of the same species as the Graeco-Roman society, that have come and gone up to date." Despite his own "slight distaste for the modern Western civilization which has now pervaded the whole surface and air-envelope of our planet," Toynbee's classical and humanist ethos leads him to this conclusion:

> I feel confident that the tradition of the past is also "the wave of the future." We are now moving into a chapter of human history in which our choice is going to be, not between a whole world and a shredded-up world, but between one world and no world. I believe that the human race is going to choose life and good, not death and evil.

Toynbee shows a particular awareness of the great changes of fortune that England has experienced over the last eighty years. These changes constitute a "historic drama," to which he returns repeatedly in *Experiences*. The chapter entitled "The Shattering of the Victorian Illusion of Stability" contains a fine account of the state of the world in which Toynbee was growing up, when "security and stability were in the ascendant, and it looked as if people of my age would live to see these two amenities become prevalent all over the world." No chapter in the book catches better what it was like to be living in England during the years before World War I—the Great War as it was called until the fall of France in 1940, before which the British sought "to avoid admitting to themselves that they were now engaged in a war of the same magnitude." Here Toynbee describes the well-being of middle-class society, constituting a minority, he asserts, but one large enough to be a self-contained society of "gentlefolk" in which "one's prospects in life were fantastically promising compared with those of any child in 1969." Side by side with shocking inequality in the distribution of power, wealth, and opportunity were, on the other hand, such things as financial rewards for hard work, freedom of travel, and prevailing law and order in most Western countries. "The ensuing Edwardian Age," Toynbee writes, "was really the Victorian Age's twilight hour; but most of us who lived through it were not conscious of the fading of light." It was not until August 1914, he goes on to show, that the illusion "of a stable world had been shattered by a thunderbolt." "Since that moment I have seen the World with different eyes and have found that it is not the kind of world, until then, that I had naïvely imagined it to be."

With Toynbee, as with so many of his contemporaries lucky enough to survive the events of 1914–18, the war was a violent shock, an awakening to reality and to the sharp limits of human feeling vaguely intuited by Toynbee himself while traveling on the island of Crete in March 1912. On that occasion he happened to have as a companion an old man driving two mules. To Toynbee's question about why some villages along the edge of the fertile plain were deserted, the old man replied: " 'Those villages? Why, the Muslims lived there. But in ninety-seven [1897, the year of the Cretan massacres] ... we cut them all [up]—men, women, and children—cut them [up]'; and he drew his hand expressively across his throat, while his voice rose to a shrill scream and his eyes gleamed as he gloated over this delicious memory." Toynbee's distress over "a vein of diabolical evil in all human nature," of which he had had a glimpse in Crete, was to achieve its quintessence in August 1914. His Cretan experience, Toynbee reflects, was to convey to him that, despite all of man's "civilizing habits," "no one can go bail for the moral integrity of any individual human being or any human community. No one can guarantee that anyone will be proof against all temptations. Under temptation, the volcano may suddenly erupt, even when its fires have been dormant for so long that they have been deemed to be extinct."

For Toynbee, as for "European Man," the Cretan peasant's words not only crystallized a sad human truth, but also contained a prophecy. August 1914: this date, "graven on our hearts," was indeed a portentous rupture in England's history—"the break" that was all the more clear and sharp for Toynbee and his generation, because, as he points out, "By August 1914 Britain had been exempt from engagement in any great war for almost a century. For us the last great war had ended on 18 June 1815, at Waterloo." For Toynbee and many others of his class, Victorian and Edwardian England had provided the semblance of security and confidence, but not for the kind of human reactions that the Cretan peasant adumbrated. The third chapter in the book, "August 1914," suggests the reasons why war and the subject of war preoccupy Toynbee both in his reminiscences and in his historical studies. To his generation, the war of 1914–18 marked the end of an interlude of innocence and the beginning of the experience of war that in the twentieth century has become almost incessant. It signaled the cruel, rapacious element in human nature which the old Cretan revealed but which Toynbee first thought impossible in civilized life. The opening paragraph of "August 1914" measures the shock that this war caused and tells why for Toynbee and his contemporaries the shock was greater and deeper than that produced by World War II:

> August 1914: "the very word is like a bell"; and the dead to whom it tolls us back are the men of many nations, on both sides of the front, whose lives were taken in the course for the four following sacrificial years. August 1914: Why is it that, at least for English people of my generation, the naming of this date still moves us so deeply? August 1914 has receded, by now, more than half a century into the past, and in the meanwhile there has been a second world war. Why does not the mention of the date September 1939 have the same effect on us? One reason is, I think, that one cannot feel the same shock for the second time with the same intensity. In 1939 the outbreak of a world war was no longer a new experience for us. In some ways the second experience was the more excruciating of the two; for, this time, we had seen the coming war bearing down on us far ahead of its outbreak; it did not burst upon us out of the blue, like a thunder-clap. Moreover, our experience of the the First World War had told us, in advance, what tribulations we had now to expect to undergo once again. Yet, just because of this excruciating foreknowledge, the shock, on the second occasion, was not so violent.

Because of dysentery, which he had contracted in Greece in 1912, Toynbee himself was disqualified for combat service. Nevertheless, he was involved in government work in the Foreign Office and he participated in the Paris Peace Conference in 1919, as he also did in 1946. "Uncanny and disquieting" is how he describes these two experiences. "The experience of two recurring Paris peace conferences," he says, "makes it difficult not to become convinced that the recurrence is the way in which the Universe really works." The many hours he spent at both conferences in minor jobs gave him rare opportunities for observation and made up "a pricelessly valuable part of my education." The 1919 peace conference was "stormy"; that in 1946 was "glacial." "In 1919 the principal representatives of the powers had been in human enough relation with each other to be able to quarrel; and they had commanded the necessary means of linguistic communication for quarreling vocally, thanks to Clemenceau's being able to speak English." But in 1946 interchanges between the delegates were channeled through interpreters, and the long process of translation led to boredom. The use of interpreters, he adds, can lead, as it did on occasion, to a distortion of the meaning of the delegates' words—not a conscious distortion, but rather one created by intonation. Readers who remember the 1946 conference will appreciate Toynbee's description of the chief Soviet delegate, V. M. Molotov:

> ... Molotov always remained formidably bland. I noticed that there was not a wrinkle on his lofty forehead, though one knew that he had gone through personal ordeals that would have broken any ordinary human being's nerve. Molotov's self-control would have been the envy and admiration of a Stoic, Epicurean, or Buddhist. Molotov's invulnerability ... and imperturbability ... —the austere ideals of Greek and Indian philosophies of detachment—were practical, and apparently effortless, accomplishments; and this serenity of Molotov's was, of course, a winning card.

Interspersed throughout *Experiences* are Toynbee's reflections, which embody a quiet and often inspiring wisdom, the outgrowth of a great historian's meditations on life, and which at the same time return us to Toynbee's grounding in ancient civilization. They bring to the forefront just how permanent the wisdom of the Graeco-Roman world is in the life and thought of a man who has drunk at the ancient springs. In these reflections Toynbee wears, naturally, the mantle of the old sages and seers. And we are ever aware of a man who has absorbed the ideas of the great teachers, e.g., Plato, Aristotle, Zeno, Epicurus, Lucretius, Cicero. Of death Toynbee says: "Death does eventually release each of us, in turn, from the burdens and injustices of this life. Death is, in fact, our eventual saviour from the tyranny of human society in this world—a tyranny that is tolerable, if at all, only because it has an inexorable time-limit." And he has this thought on bereavement: "The greatest happiness in life is mutual love, and therefore the greatest sorrow, next to sorrow for one's sins, is not for anything—not even for the worst thing—that can happen to oneself; it is sorrow for the suffering of the people whom we love, and it is sorrow over our parting from them if we outlive them." But the wisdom that he has derived from the past is as applicable to man's external as to his internal world. Speaking of war, of "the change in its character and in people's attitude," he observes: "The general lesson is that any country which has so far been invariably victorious in a series of past wars is likely to become a menace both to itself and to the rest of the World." His disturbing (and perhaps prophetic) criticism of what he speaks of as the "Germanization" of the American people's attitudes is worthy of consideration:

> The American people have succumbed to militarism; and, even if this lapse proves to be only temporary in the United States, as it seems already to have proved to be in Japan and Germany, it has revealed to the rest of the World an aspect of America that is as disconcerting as it has been unexpected. Even if the American people retrieve McCarthy's tyranny, the World's "image" of America will never again be the same as it was before.

Only to religion does Toynbee give attention comparable to that he gives to war. His creed consists of a single article: *Deus est mortali iuvare mortalem* ("For a human being, God is the act of helping another human being"). The humanist temper is obviously at the center of this view. By religion Toynbee means "a human being's relation to an ultimate reality behind and beyond the phenomena of the Universe." He categorically rejects certain fundamental tenets of his own ancestral religion. The Virgin birth, the Resurrection, and the Ascension he finds irreconcilable with his understanding of the universe. Miracle is "intrinsically illogical." God and love, he claims, are identical, but he does not share the Christian certainty that the God who is love is omnipotent. Here he stands not with Irenaeus, but with Marcion, who believed in a god who is both unlovingness and unlovableness, and for whom "the god who is love is a stranger in the creator-god's universe, and mankind, in virtue of its capacity for loving, is also a stranger there." Love, Toynbee concludes, is not omnipotent, even as there is no omnipotent force governing the universe. Theologically, Toynbee's belief approaches Epicurus' doctrine that the gods, who are innumerable and who live in the *metakosmia*, in the spaces between worlds, are "the paragons of the good life" and create "no trouble for themselves and seek to cause none to others."[8]

Among the historical higher religions, Zoroastrianism presents the fewest problems to Toynbee: "Zoroastrians see life as the arena of warfare between good and evil; and this picture seems to me to correspond to what we know of the spiritual structure of human nature." Each man, endowed with consciousness, is compelled to make choices between life and good, on the one side, and death and evil, on the other. Original sin "is born afresh in every child that is brought into the world." Hence, the conflict in each man's soul will continue as long as mankind survives. Expressing his disdain for the "unverified and unverifiable dogmas" that are offered as shortcuts for elucidating the mystery of existence, Toynbee also warns that "man's constant yearning to see rest and security is an infirmity against which he should be on his guard." Religiously, then, he asserts that his is the "way of exploration": "My aim is to have the maximum of religion with the minimum of religion." And except for one, perhaps, he is thus ineligible for membership in any of the historical religious communities. The exception is Hinduism, "to which I might conceivably gain admittance . . . for Hinduism is catholic in the sense of being comprehensive, not catholic in the Catholic Christian Church's original sense of being a particular religion's universally recognized standard form. Hinduism might admit me. In the hierarchy of castes, I should rank below the sweepers."

Toynbee voices regret for being cut off from membership in any of the historical religious communities, insofar as religion is not just a personal affair between a human being and the ultimate spiritual reality but also a social affair whereby human beings enter communion with each other. He notes that he is in fact "a representative of a large and increasing fraction of the human race that has lost its attachment to its ancestral religious community." Yet he expects that Christianity and other religious communities will eventually liberalize their tenets and practices so as to readmit ex-members like himself. Besides, there are limits to his agnosticism. For though he has rejected particular religious beliefs, he has come to think that religion itself "is an intrinsic faculty of human nature." Being human involves having religion; and "human beings who declare that they have no religion are deceiving themselves through failing to search their own hearts." Undoubtedly Christianity has "paid the extreme penalty for its persistent fanaticism and factiousness." But "Modern Western Man's" efforts to replace his ancestral religions by some other religion have not been either happy or successful. The emergence in the modern age of three post-Christian ideologies, Nationalism, Individualism, and Communism, has led to results "still more wicked than the worst that have ever been perpetrated in the name of Christianity. Modern Man's state in the age of agony and atrocity that dawned in 1914 has been even worse than Western Man's state was in the age of the Catholic-Protestant war of religion." This worst state, he nonetheless feels, has now turned out not to be the last. Thus he applauds the *aggiornamento* of the Roman Catholic Church, as well as the Ecumenical Movement.

> We are now moving into an age [he continues] in which the range of choice will be wider and the exercise of the freedom to choose will become more frequent. We can look forward to a coming stage in mankind's religious history at which a person's religion will be, not the one

that he has inherited, but the religion that he has chosen for himself when he has come of age—a religion which may or may not be the one in which he has been born and brought up. This is a spiritual gain for future generations of mankind that has already been brought within sight by the change of heart which has overtaken the adherents of the diverse historic religions in our time.

Interestingly, Toynbee is not as optimistic when he discusses other cultural conditions and directions. He is strongly distrustful, for example, of the adverse consequences of increasing specialization which he sees directly or indirectly reflected in the misuse and abuse of the most advanced devices of science and technology and in the collectivist and bureaucratic tendencies found in every department of life. Technological and scientific advances, far from solving human problems, have led to "unintended consequences." Noting that he is very much a dissenter from the nineteenth-century middle-class creed, he is still inclined to look at some things with middle-class eyes. And neither the British welfare state nor the British industrial worker meets with his full approval. In both he cites elements of immaturity and irresponsibility. British workers, in spite of immense economic and social gains, "are still fighting the nineteenth-century battle on the home front that began to become out of date when, a century ago by now, Britain lost her brief monopoly of being the 'unchallengeable workshop of the World.'" The development of trade union organization has given industrial workers "the power to maintain and extend the restrictive practices that were their nineteenth-century defence against overwork and unemployment." In the wake of these developments, British currency has depreciated and foreign markets have been lost. "I fear," he writes, "it may be that the provision of social services, not accompanied by an education in the middle-class standard of foresight and responsibility, has fostered the childish-minded short-sightedness that was the British industrial workers' inevitable attitude in the pre-welfare-state age."

Other unfortunate manifestations, he feels, are to be seen in education, where egalitarianism all too often leads to a general leveling-down. What Toynbee underlines here is the major problem besetting modern Western society: the quantitative versus the qualitative values that must, in the end, be chosen as the basis for the "new society." The debate between those who choose the former and those who choose the latter still rages, and Toynbee shows an awareness of some of the paradoxes. It is evident that quantitative schemes, which are ascendant, will really lead to greater problems in the guise of conformism in public and private life and in the deterioration of aesthetic taste, with the proliferation of what is ugly and gray in living patterns. Toynbee points to housing developments as an example of quantitative solutions. "High-rise" buildings, he contends, are often damaging to the landscape as ugly architectural schemes that inevitably work against "spirit of place." Even more importantly, such buildings contribute to further depersonalization and communal immobilization in a technocratic way of life. "These pitfalls," he reflects, "are genuine and unavoidable consequences of slum-clearance and large-scale standardized municipal housing. They are unfortunate consequences; yet who would be prepared, on that account, to pronounce that municipal re-housing is a social evil? We are left with a puzzle on our hands. A good move has had some unintended bad results that are disconcerting."

On the title page of *Experiences* appear these words from Psalm 104: "Man goeth forth to his work and to his labour until the evening." This epigraph is not without an informing significance in Toynbee's life and work, in which intellectual honesty combines with hard work, impelled by his conscience as duty and by the need to see and understand. As a historian, he emphasizes that his love for facts is neither functional nor specialistic. "I love them as clues to something beyond them—as clues to the nature and meaning of the mysterious Universe in which every human being awakes to consciousness." That he has chosen to work in history has its essential reason: "Because, for me, this is the pursuit that leads, however haltingly, towards the *Visio Beatifica*." His words return us to his humanist faith and to his deep spirit of optimism and tolerance that, despite the increasing brutalization of life since 1914, inhere in his ultimate view of life. Despite the heightening demands of "the Computer Age" and the pressures of living in the "Brave New World," Toynbee believes that the outer life need not be the oppressor of the private life, that the private life can still be sustained in time of turmoil. In a humanist way he counsels modern man to seek for "the inward spiritual grace of serenity." The achievement of this serenity, he confesses, entails suffering in the midst of a world which man cannot escape. "The serenity that can give a human being," he asserts, "the spiritual strength to live in 'Brave New World' as an uneffaced person is the serenity that does not seek to barricade itself against the assaults of suffering but embraces suffering for the sake of following the lead of love."

Toynbee affirms here precisely that liberal and humanist faith that shone so brightly, and with such promise and inspiration, before 1914. It is a faith that E. M. Forster calls up in these words: "I belong to the fag-end of Victorian liberalism and can look back to an age whose challenges were moderate in their tone, and the cloud on whose horizon was no bigger than a man's hand. In many ways it was an admirable age. It practised benevolence and philanthropy, was humane and intellectually curious, upheld free speech, had little colour prejudice, believed that individuals are and should be different, and entertained a sincere faith in the progress of society."[9] Forster's words crystallize in many ways the classical liberal humanist tradition that Toynbee exemplifies by background, training, temper, concern, and personal relationships. It is a tradition founded on the three interdependent qualities of friendship, balance, and serenity without which life remains a burden of despair. It is a tradition characterized by a ceaseless pursuit of truth, as Toynbee's own "acquaintances" and "experiences" disclose.

VIVIAN DE SOLA PINTO

The late Vivian de Sola Pinto's autobiography,* confined to the years 1895–1922, takes its title from these words in John Bunyan's *The Pilgrim's Progress*:

> Now just as the Gates were opened to let in the men, I looked in after them, and, behold, the City shone like the sun; the streets also were paved with gold, and in them walked many men, with crowns on their heads, palms in their hands, and golden harps to sing praises withal.
> There were also of them that had wings, and they answered one another without intermission, saying, "Holy, holy, holy is the Lord." And after that they shut up the gates, which when I had seen I wished myself among them.

Bunyan's words, placed as an epigraph on the title page, are magical and visionary in the picture they give and the feelings they evoke. If they are in themselves numinous words, compelling almost a mystical sense of wonder and even of ecstasy, they are also appropriately chosen words which help to convey a writer's recollection of an age in English life that has now vanished. For the world into which Pinto was born, middle class, comfortable, secure, was not unlike Bunyan's "shining city." If one happened to be well placed in English society in those years, enjoying the benefits of houses in the city and the country, the advantages of an expensive education, the joys of long holidays in England and on the Continent, in short, the experience

The City That Shone (New York, 1969).

of a pleasant idyll, then no doubt Bunyan's "streets paved with gold" and "men with crowns on their heads, [and] palms in their hands" were familiar sights. This autobiography reminds us of a way of life that, before 1914, marked an epoch of peace and, better, of civilization—the civilization of an England, and of a Europe, which Henry James so perceptively evoked in some of his novels and which even a rebellious D. H. Lawrence could celebrate for its "spirit of place."

For Pinto and his generation the Edwardian years were not merely an era of peace and hope, but also a pastoral era when England had not yet been overcome by those conditions of life that the Great War later announced in such brutal tones and gestures: mechanization, depersonalization, hardness, uprootedness. A stable rhythm and harmony of life still existed in a world that, as Pinto writes on the first page of his memoir, was

> without motor-cars, aeroplanes, radio, television, electric light or telephones, a world in which gentlemen wore high stiff white collars, top hats and frock coats and ladies bonnets, shawls, chignons and bustles, a world where the pockets of rich men were full of golden sovereigns, and middle-class houses were full of servants, where soldiers wore tight scarlet tunics and pillbox caps, and where the streets of London were full of jingling hansoms, smart carriages and lumbering four-wheelers.

Perhaps another way to distinguish this age is to say that it was poetic. In *The City That Shone* the most poetic sections are those that recall the attributes of this age, its mood, temper, atmosphere, color, and music—the music of Edward Elgar, for instance, which some readers will surely hear accompanying the rich stream of life which Pinto recreates for us in this scene of London "before the internal-combustion engine put an end to it":

> Early in the morning came the milkman with his cry of "Milko!" and his cart full of great brassbound cans, drawn by a slowly ambling piebald horse. Later in the morning came the butcher's boy in his blue apron, bowling along in his little cart at a smart trot. Then there were the coalheavers with their sou'wester hats who hurled the contents of their sacks down chutes into the cellars with which most houses were equipped at that date. There were the great drays of the breweries, Barclay and Perkins and Ind Coope, drawn by huge horses with tufted fetlocks and a peculiar dancing walk. Hopkins's dray-horses with "bright and battering sandal." There were men with shaggy brown bears on chains, "German bands," Italian organ-grinders with monkeys on their barrel-organs and dark-eyed female assistants with big ear-rings and bright handkerchiefs tied round their heads, who came to the doors with tambourines to make collections, ballad-singers, male and female chanting doleful ditties in strange whining voices, collectors of rags, bottles and old iron, "needy knifegrinders" with their whirring wheels, women

selling herrings and vegetables on barrows, an endless stream of colourful and vocal humanity. In the afternoon came the muffin man with a tray covered with green baize on his head, ringing his handbell. . . . Twilight brought the lamplighters, silent, mournful-looking men dressed in black, carrying long poles which magically kindled the yellow flame of the gas lights in street-lamps.

This is a memorable picture of London at the turn of the century. And it reminds us just how far distant the Edwardian world is in the past and, too, how much drabber and grayer life has become in the age of the computer and the technocrat. We need not, of course, approve of the economics of this period, or the class barriers and the inequities that existed. But neither can we ignore the tragedy of ugliness that awaited British civilization in the wake of the war of 1914–18. In the sections relating to his Edwardian childhood, Pinto manages to give us something of the aesthetics of an age, an awareness of life not yet fully regulated by a time clock and packaged in efficient capsules. There is in these pages a consciousness of life not yet collectivized and organized to the extent that it loses its meaning, its radiance and buoyancy, as it is progressively subordinated to a machine consciousness. A certain sense of orderliness, together with an atmosphere of security, confidence, and love, informs the pages which recapture Pinto's formative years.

What is both intriguing and revealing about this book is that though the Edwardian Age is often condemned for its "suburban niceness," its stuffiness, its middle-class conformities and philistinism, its "vulgar bourgeois pretentiousness"—an age when, Pinto declares, "life was too easy, too comfortable, too soft and, as it were, padded . . . [and] everything seemed hollow, trivial and uninspiring"—the condemnation is never entirely vindicated or convincing. There is not, in other words, a conclusive, irreversible rejection. The voice of one's developed social consciousness is, to be sure, present in these reminiscences. But also present is an innermost appreciation of a magical and often exquisite civilized world, "with its homes and its family life and its comparative peace" as E. M. Forster has memorialized it. Pinto attacks some aspects of his pre-war environment as being "hollow, trivial and uninspiring," but like others he "doth protest too much." Here, he brings to mind the commensurate truth and the paradox of Forster's words, "I am actually what my age and my upbringing have made me—a bourgeois who adheres to the British constitution, adheres to it rather than supports it. . . ."[10]

The point that I am driving at is that some autobiographers are occasionally enigmatically reticent about their true "loyalties" to their early environment. In an almost unconscious pattern of recall, Pinto's memory of his late Victorian and Edwardian days, of his life until 1914, is precisely the one in the book that excites in him, and in his style, an informing joy of detailed recollection. Emotionally and intellectually, this is the period, with its aura of civilized values and amenities, that gives him the greatest delight and inspiration. His criticisms of his age stem from a mental, self-conscious attitude, when, as in the following passage, not the "emotional mind" or "demon," but rather "the voice of the commonplace me" (to use D. H. Lawrence's phraseology) is heard:

> But was it really the best of all possible worlds? Very early I began to feel doubtful about this. My doubts were connected with my growing awareness of the existence of people called the Poor, who did not share the pleasant sheltered life that I enjoyed at Heathcroft [the Pinto house in Hampstead]. In the reign of Edward VII, as in the time of Disraeli, there were two nations in England. One was the nation which was waited on by servants, possessed banking accounts and cheque-books and paid for the education of its children at private and "public" schools—the nation of "ladies" and "gentlemen." The other was the much larger nation consisting of people who worked for weekly wages, did their own domestic chores or had them done for them by their wives and daughters, sent their children to get a free primary education at "board schools" and lived under the menace of incarceration in the workhouse if they failed to get employment. . . .

Now the sincerity of Pinto's humanitarian instincts is not in question here. Obviously, the passage of more than a half century has led him, in retrospect, to see things from a different (educated) social and cultural angle. Still, the pages relating to Pinto's Edwardian world that are the most luminous are not those which bemoan "the condition of England," but rather those which call back the quality of one's emotional and intellectual life—a life that, in this case, was fortunate enough to gain from and absorb all those advantages that an affluent England bestowed on its middle class. It is this England that, in *The City That Shone*, really comes through with an almost iridescent quality and that discloses the ethos and the history of an age.

The inescapable fact is that Pinto's recollections ring more persuasively when he talks about his early childhood; his generous and kindly father, who prospered in his West End tobacco business (the royal family as well as Oscar Wilde traded there); his beautiful mother, who was poetic and musical (an "advanced woman" who "smoked cigarettes and played billiards"); his love for his vivacious Scottish nursery governess, Agnes Peffers, who helped manage the family after his mother's sudden death in 1900; his fascination with Punch and Judy shows, with a hurdy-gurdy operated by clockwork, or with "bathing machines," those "vehicles like small Noah's arks" drawn by horses into the water; his evocation of death, which "was still a solemn ritual in those days when hearses were drawn by black-plumed horses and attended by mutes wearing top hats draped with crepe"; his fondness for the country on the side directly opposite his house, where

> there were, in those days, open fields where cattle grazed. They were separated from the road only by a wooden fence over which a very small boy could easily climb. Beautiful undulating meadows, they were full of deep grass with plenty of buttercups, dandelions and daisies in the summer and shaded by hawthorn bushes, great oaks and elms. In my early boyhood "the other side of the road" was an enchanted country for me, where I could wander through acres of unspoilt meadow land and enjoy the thrill of squeezing through gaps in hedges and climbing over stiles to find myself in new and exciting surroundings. I can still shut my eyes and dream that I am lying in the deep grass of those meadows on a summer day and listening to the hum of insects, the crowing of distant cocks and other pleasant country noises.

Pastoral passages on English landscapes like this underscore, almost unconsciously, the germane quality of Pinto's loyalty to an England that elsewhere he claims made him feel guilty and uncomfortable. Indeed, Pinto's later circle of friends and the center of his activity were precisely those which were identified with and stamped by that England in which the "civilization of the mind" and a higher aesthetic taste and ethic prevailed. And it is to this England that Pinto belongs and that ultimately makes his aesthetics superior to his dialectics. In the long run, *The City That Shone* epitomizes in tone and in temper that profession of a gentle faith that Clive Bell once equated with

> a taste for truth and beauty, tolerance, intellectual honesty, fastidiousness, a sense of humour, good manners, curiosity, a dislike of vulgarity, brutality, and over-emphasis, freedom from superstition and prudery, a fearless acceptance of the good things of life, a desire for complete self-expression and for a liberal education, a contempt for utilitarianism and philistinism, in two words—sweetness and light.[11]

Pinto's intellectual awakenings, with the Edwardian world serving as the immediate background, can be seen occurring from the time that he got into the habit of reading in his book-filled Hampstead house, Heathcroft. His father's library was very Victorian in taste, with "finely bound sets of the works of Carlyle and Macaulay, the histories of Hallam, Lecky and Stubbs, Prescott's *Conquest of Mexico,* Motley's *Rise of the Dutch Republic* and such solid Victorian classics as Mill on *Liberty,* Darwin on *The Origin of Species* and Buckle's *History of Civilisation.* The eighteenth century was represented by noble sets of Johnson with Boswell's *Life,* Gibbon, Goldsmith and Burke." That Pinto was able to pursue his two loves of reading and solitude—no line of English poetry, he confesses, appeals to him more than Sidney's "O sweet woods, the delight of solitariness"—was largely owed to his father's favorable economic position, with all its consequent emoluments, and also to some of the prevailing Edwardian literary and intellectual fashions. His father's library contributed more to his education than any formal schooling, he feels.

In 1900 this house "was still a symbol of liberation from the stuffiness of stucco and the dinginess of the dark or yellowish brick of the older London residential areas." In every way this late Victorian, almost early Edwardian red-brick house bore the impress of William Morris' influential ideas. A big rectangular building with three floors, with a large basement and a loft under a high-pitched roof, it stood in a garden of about a quarter of an acre. Pinto's picture of the interior of the house is at its best and most illuminating when he describes his father's library: "a sort of refuge and haven of peace . . . [where] some of my happiest hours were spent . . . lying on the ottoman with a book, or stretched out full length on the thickly carpeted floor, or exploring the endless delights of the bookcases."

Similar to other English autobiographers who recall their school experiences with special and intense feeling, bitter as well as affectionate—e.g., Basil Willey's picture in *Spots of Time* of his attendance at University College School, a day school in London; Cyril Connolly's spirited account in *Enemies of Promise* of his years at Eton College; or the reminiscences about their private and public school experiences by men like William Plomer (Rugby) and Sir Harold Nicolson (Wellington), included in Graham Greene's enchanting symposium *The Old School*—Pinto devotes a long section in his memoir to his Edwardian school days which, like Willey, he spent at University College School. (His father, not untypical of other fathers in the middle and upper classes, planned for his son to go later to an ancient university and, after taking a degree, to try for a place in the Higher Division of the Civil Service either at home or in India.) It should also be pointed out that Pinto was fortunate in his private preparatory school training at Wykeham House in West Hampstead where he luxuriated in "an atmosphere of calmness, humanity and civilisation." His private school contrasts sharply with that of George

Orwell, for instance, whose experiences at Saint Cyprian's, in East-bourne, on the Sussex coast, left him, as he later reflected, with "memories of disgust" and remained "like an awful nightmare." "I've always held that the public schools aren't so bad," Orwell wrote to Cyril Connolly, a contemporary both at Saint Cyprian's and at Eton, "but people are wrecked by those filthy private schools long before they get to public school age."[12]

In writing about his years spent at University College School, Pinto is not as enthusiastic as another distinguished "old boy," Stephen Spender. ("This gentlest of schools," Spender has written, made him feel "freer . . . than I ever did in the snobbish environment of Oxford."[13]) Pinto began his studies at University College School in September 1906. The boys here were bigger and rougher, "and a good deal of mild bullying of the smaller ones took place in the grimy, gravelled playground," then located on the school grounds on Gower Street. At first he found the masters rather unkind and frightening, and the homework set in the lower forms was excessively heavy. The teaching at the school during this time, Pinto observes, was uneven and in a state of transition. One group of masters consisted of "old stagers," elderly, gray, bearded, or bewhiskered. "They were obviously tired and cynical and held for the most part what I would describe as the penal view of education." The other group of masters consisted of younger men, recent university graduates, enthusiastic and committed in their teaching. These younger and better qualified teachers taught in the higher forms. Pinto's appreciative portrait of his drawing master, F. J. Kell, suggests the reasons for teaching success and, at the same time, gives us insight into the relations between teacher and pupil. To Pinto, Kell "radiated vitality" and "communicated" with and "stimulated" his students. An accomplished painter and a vigorous, unassuming teacher,

> he [Pinto states] taught me to draw and to paint after a fashion in water and oil colours. But even more valuable than any executive skill which I acquired from him was a new kind of vision. This is a gift for which I shall always be grateful. It has enabled me, ever since those distant Edwardian days, to get endless pleasure from the contemplation of the most ordinary sights: a mass of trees, a patch of sky, a brick wall or a perfectly commonplace building transfigured by the magic of light and shade. It was an emancipation of the sense of vision from the bondage of the dusty abstractions of everyday life.

The years extending from the death of Edward VII in 1910 until "the fateful August of 1914" marked for Pinto the period of intellectual discovery. More and more he turned to the world of poetry, books, painting, and "quiet communion with nature." Though he chose to study classical languages and literatures, he did not neglect to broaden his interest in English poets. The Pre-Raphaelite poets and painters he found especially fascinating. His discovery of and passion for Swinburne is charmingly rendered, and his description of finding in a bookshop Swinburne's play *Atalanta in Calydon,* the opening lines of which—

> Maiden and mistress of the months and stars
> Now folded in the flowerless fields of heaven . . .

—"went to my head like a draft of champagne," clearly underlined Pinto's own poetic temperament and literary directions. In the pages that tell of his intellectual discoveries, there is an exalted sense of adventure experienced in a world that, in itself, was essentially poetic. Particularly delightful is Pinto's recollection of his buying inexpensive editions "including most of Stevenson's works in leatherette bindings, the Oxford poets and many other tempting baits for the young bibliophile." His account of his picking up and reading books containing poems by Robert Bridges, W. B. Yeats, and Ezra Pound (a poet whose slim volume of verse called *Personae* "struck me as being a rather attractive if eccentric follower of Browning") is equally refreshing in its intensity of recall. And, too, one will feel Pinto's sense of excitement in his account of how he now began to buy *The Athenaeum,* "a stimulating weekly called *The New Age,* edited by A. R. Orage," and "a monthly with a blue cover called *The English Review* in which I read Masefield's early narrative poems and D. H. Lawrence's early poems and stories." Here, indeed, we are reminded of great days in English literary and cultural history, full of expectancy, when experiment and innovation were in the upswing.

In October 1914, Pinto, "sick of school and of the London suburbs," enrolled as a student at Christ Church, Oxford. He found his new environment exhilarating. "Here, at last, it was no longer necessary for me to wear any kind of mask. At home I had to be a schoolboy, a son and a brother. At Oxford I only had to be a student and I was naturally a student." His newly acquired independence gave him greater opportunity to pursue his bent for solitude, meditation, and reading. The buildings of Oxford and the beauty of the place made a deep impression on him, and his

> imagination could feed upon such splendours as Tom Quad, black and silver by moonlight, Magdalen tower rising like a great lily against a

sun-drenched sky and those two contrasting and equally splendid giants, so nobly juxtaposed, St. Mary's spire and the Radcliffe dome. I loved the gloom and peace of the great grey buildings, the shaded walks by the Cherwell, the majestic flow of the Isis and the equally glorious "streamlike wanderings" of the High, at that time not yet fouled by endless processions of motor traffic.

Oxford in the autumn of 1914, as Pinto shows, still retained in all essentials its prewar quality. The undergraduate population was not yet depleted because of the coming of the Great War in August. But, increasingly, most of the young men who remained in Oxford had been rejected as unfit for military service. Pinto tried repeatedly to volunteer, but was turned down because of a myopic impairment. "The British Army had no use for spectacled soldiers in August, 1914," he states.

Not having been awarded a scholarship "to read for Honour Moderations," Pinto accepted a place as a "commoner" at Christ Church. His educational background in the ancient classics and in English literature gave him sound preparation for his new studies. In particular he notes his debt to his tutor at Christ Church, John Davidson Beazley, afterwards Sir John Beazley, the distinguished professor of archaeology. For Beazley, Pinto wrote weekly papers on classical themes and English literature. Their common enthusiasm for poetry eventually led to their becoming friends. It was Beazley who introduced Pinto to some of the modern French poets, especially the Parnassians and the Symbolists. None of the other dons interested him as much as Beazley did, though Pinto singles out Gilbert Murray, whose course on the Greek epic was "an unforgettable intellectual experience." Though life at Oxford during this period was still pleasant, intellectually and socially, it was an "unreal" life. "The only reality was the war." Pinto, like so many of his contemporaries, longed to leave Oxford and take his place along the side of the men fighting and dying in France. The old world of the Pax Britannica belonged to the past and had lost its relevance. Its unreality now steadily gave way to "a sense of release from an intolerable tension, of liberation from the deadly stuffiness of commercialised 'civilisation' and of participation in a great heroic adventure. Here, it seemed, was a chance for a wonderful renovation of human life, almost an apocalypse."

In this initial response to the war Pinto underlines the idealism which stamped his generation. Only as the war went on and as the slaughter on the Western Front increased did "young enthusiasts" come, too late, to realize that the war was useless and wrong; that it was a war advantageous to "the 'hard-faced' men in key positions";

that, in the end, the war was a "betrayal"—"one of the great disasters of history . . . [that] was to lead ultimately to the miserable reversion to the older game of power politics in the post-war period with all the terrible results that followed." But in 1914 and in 1915 "young enthusiasts" like Pinto could not possibly foresee the deeper consequences of the war. Their idealism was as youthful as it was naïve.

> Life is no life to him that dares not die,
> And death no death to him that dares not live.

Sir Henry Newbolt's words capture the spirit of those early heroic responses to the Great War that Pinto expressed. Not all Englishmen were as heroic or enthusiastic, however. E. M. Forster, refusing to be intimidated by "braying patriots of the moment," saw the war for all it was: "that terrible thing Armadillo-Armageddon."[14] And Forster's good friend G. Lowes Dickinson's feelings, when the war broke out, "resembled the feelings which arise when a promise has been broken by a person whom one loves."[15] But Pinto—*expectans, expectavi*— was nineteen in 1914; Forster was thirty-five and Dickinson was fifty-two. If age is to have its wisdom, youth must first have its high hour.

Pinto finally succeeded in volunteering for military service in the spring of 1915. During his medical examination the doctor left him alone for a few minutes with the eyesight testing card before asking the young recruit to remove his glasses. "In those few minutes I memorised the first four lines of letters on the card and was able to recite them glibly when the doctor returned and my glasses were removed." For several weeks Pinto served as a "rifleman" in the Inns of Court battalion. Then he was invited to accept a commission as an infantry officer in the Royal Welch Fusiliers, in which "ancient and famous regiment" he served until 1919. Now his family and life in suburban London, as well as "that pleasant Oxford dream-world," had been left behind. "Nevertheless," Pinto reflects, "I was glad that I had been able to spend two terms there before going into the Army. It gave me a glimpse of the old leisurely 'pre-war' Oxford, it provided me with the 'civvy' status of a university student when I was in the Army, and, most valuable of all, it gave me images of beauty and happiness to refresh my mind during the endless drab tedium and mechanised misery of army life."

Pinto's recollection of his war service takes up one-third of the length of his autobiography. Throughout this account he writes with a controlled vigor, avoiding overstatement and gratuitous drama, as if, to quote one reviewer, "Pinto's business is with life, not death, with everything that supports and dignifies the human spirit, not destroys it."[16] In the words of Siegfried Sassoon, he gives "that insane old war the damnation it deserves, while recollecting its redeeming humanities."[17] His experience in the Gallipoli campaign during "those dreary autumn days of 1915" is particularly memorable, as Pinto recounts some of the horrors and the blunders of that ill-fated operation. It was during this campaign that Pinto, with a working party, came on a number of decomposed corpses of English soldiers, lying unburied since the first landings in August. "These corpses," he writes, "haunted my memory; henceforward I was proof against the clichés about sacrifice, glory, victory and 'never sheathing the sword.' All such expressions were for me now permanently tainted by the thought of those vigorous young human beings transformed into objects of horror." In this campaign Pinto suffered frostbite and dysentery. In January and February of 1916 he convalesced in Alexandria and then in Luxor. Soon after this he also took part "in that curious little 'side-show,' the war against the Senussi," a tribe of Libyan Arabs incited by German and Turkish agents to declare a Holy War against the Allies. At the end of May this conflict in the Western desert ceased, after the leader of the Senussi realized he had been fighting on the wrong side. Pinto's division returned to Cairo in June and in the following month took part in the Sinai campaign, during which he suffered sunstroke and, once more, acute dysentery. In October he returned to England for three months' sick leave.

This "Eastern Adventure" was followed by a long period of active service on the Western Front, where Pinto eventually suffered from shrapnel wounds and gas poisoning. During one convalescent leave, spent in Dieppe, he relates how one day in the summer of 1917 he picked up a magazine in a hotel, now transformed into a hospital. In the pages of the magazine he came across "a poem by a writer with the resonant name of Siegfried Sassoon, of whom I had never heard before." Pinto liked the verse:

> Return to greet me, colours that were my joy,
> Not in the woeful crimson of men slain,
> But shining as a garden; come with streaming
> Banners of dawn, and sundown after rain.
>
> I want to fill my gaze with blue and silver,
> Radiance through living roses, spires of green
> Rising in young-limbed copse and lovely wood
> Where the hueless wind pauses and cries unseen.

Sassoon's poem expressed "the longing for beautiful things that many sensitive spirits felt amid the drabness of trench warfare." Here "was a poet to be watched." Not long after his return to the base at Rouen,

Pinto happened to read a review of a recently published volume by Sassoon, *The Old Huntsman* (1917). The reviewer quoted in full a war poem, "Blighters," not only quite unlike Sassoon's earlier poem which Pinto admired but also unlike any other war poem which he had read:

> The House is crammed: tier beyond tier they grin
> And cackle at the Show, while prancing ranks
> Of harlots shrill the chorus, drunk with din;
> "We're sure the Kaiser loves our dear old Tanks!"
>
> I'd like to see a Tank come down the stalls,
> Lurching to rag-time tunes, or "Home, sweet Home,"
> And there'd be no more jokes in Music-halls
> To mock the riddled corpses round Bapaume.

Sassoon's poem made a profound impression on Pinto. In it he intuited a poetic genius who "found the supremely right words for the growing indignation of the men of the front line at the heartless vulgarity of the people at home who were enjoying 'a lovely war.'" Literary history was to confirm Pinto's initial estimate of Sassoon's uniqueness as a war poet. *The Old Huntsman* achieved immediate success and Sassoon became a leading poet. Though this volume contained poems that were idyllic, it also contained the first poems, like "Blighters," in Sassoon's final war style, noted for the satiric and bitter qualities consummated in his most famous and influential volume of antiwar poems, *Counter-Attack* (1918), the title poem of which was to exemplify the full power and intensity of a new poetic idiom, rejecting the Georgian lyrical introversion and emphasizing, to quote Sassoon's own words of advice to another major war poet, Wilfred Owen, a "compassionate and challenging realism":

> The place was rotten with dead; green clumsy legs
> High-booted, sprawled and grovelled along the saps;
> And trunks, face downward, in the sucking mud,
> Wallowed like trodden sand-bags loosely filled;
> And naked sodden buttocks, mats of hair,
> Bulged, clotted heads slept in the plastering slime.
> And then the rain began,—the jolly old rain!

Pinto's knowledge of Sassoon was not to be limited to a knowledge of and sympathy with the latter's poetic vision. As one of those incredible ironies of fate would have it, he was assigned as second-in-command to Captain Siegfried Sassoon's unit, "A" Company of the Royal 25th Welch Fusiliers, on the Western Front in the summer of 1918. Pinto's response to Sassoon, whose reckless courage earned him the sobriquet "Mad Jack," as well as the Military Cross for rescuing wounded men while under fire, captures all the drama of one's first encounter with a great soldier-poet: "That splendid, erect figure, that noble head with the mane of dark hair, piercing black eyes and finely sculptured features could only belong to a poet." Pinto's account of his relation to Sassoon is characteristically modest, even reticent. It is in Sassoon's own autobiographical book, *Sherston's Progress*, that we find a more detailed portrait of his second-in-command, called Velmore in the book, and that, at the same time, gives us an appreciation of a subaltern who proved to be "never anything else but a consolation to me." But it was not merely Pinto's competence which Sassoon valued; he also appreciated his second-in-command's love of poetry. "To hear poetry talked about in our Company Mess was indeed a new experience for me." To gauge the extent of Sassoon's affection for Pinto, whose "beneficent presence" undoubtedly helped to mitigate "this human tragedy which sprawled across France," one need only consider these words of tribute:

> ... I very soon began to say to myself that I really didn't know what I'd have done without him. It was like having an extra head and a duplicate pair of eyes. Velmore was a tall, dark, young man who had been up at Oxford for an academic year when the outbreak of war interrupted his studies. More scholastic than soldierlike in appearance (mainly because he wore spectacles), he had the look of one who might someday occupy a professorial chair. His previous experience at the Front gave him a solid basis of usefulness, and to this was added a temperament in which kindliness, humour, and intelligence divided the honours equally, with gentleness and modesty in readiness to assert themselves by the power of nonassertion.[18]

With the end of the war Pinto returned to England to begin anew his civilian life. His re-creation of his life in those postwar years is in no way colored by inordinate self-pity or despair. To be sure, the memory of the war could not easily or ever be forgotten, such was the nightmare that that cataclysm provoked. Robert Graves recalls that after his return to civilian life, "I was still mentally and nervously organized for war. Shells used to come bursting on my bed at midnight ... strangers in daytime would assume the faces of friends who had been killed."[19] These lines from Siegfried Sassoon's poem "Aftermath," dated March 1919, must have captured the feelings of many of the returning veterans:

> *But the past is just the same—and War's a bloody game ...*
> *Have you forgotten yet? ...*
> *Look down, and swear by the slain of the War that you'll never forget.*[20]

But, as Pinto shows in *The City That Shone*, though the memory of the war could never be erased, life itself had to go on and men had to rebuild shattered beliefs and visions. "One must speak for life and growth, amid all this mass of destruction and disintegration," wrote D. H. Lawrence.[21] Pinto's own life in the postwar years testifies to the positive spirit embodied in Lawrence's words. Thus, "on a cold, grey morning in January 1919," Pinto was in "Oxford again." After having discussed his future with Siegfried Sassoon, he had been persuaded to return to Christ Church and to give up "some vague notions of trying to become a painter or a doctor." So now he formally enrolled to read for the Honour School of English Language and Literature. Beazley would continue to be his "moral tutor"; Percy Simpson, the great Elizabethan scholar, would be his "English tutor."

Pinto's picture of Oxford in the early 1920's is done with a charm and an authenticity that bring to mind those superb pages on Oxford undergraduate society found in L. P. Hartley's novel, *The Sixth Heaven*. Life at Oxford was much more austere than it had been in 1914. "Gone were the lavish breakfast parties and breakfast was now a communal meal eaten in Hall. The winter of 1918–1919 was cold and wet; coal was rationed and we often had to sit in our old army overcoats in unheated rooms." Pinto's love of literature and his facility for making friends with some of the more scholarly and gifted Oxford undergraduates (for instance, Owen Barfield) helped to diminish these material discomforts. While living in rooms at Christ Church, Pinto had as a neighbor "a very young, silent, pale undergraduate called William Walton . . . who was known to be a musical genius. Sometimes he would take Cecil Harwood and Toronto [F. J. Prewett] and me to the organ loft in the cathedral and ravish us with heavenly strains of Bach, Handel or his own compositions."

Through Sasson he was introduced to some of the most interesting people in Oxford at that time, particularly the Sitwells. "The great meeting place of the Sitwells at Oxford," Pinto recalls, "was that delightful old inn the Golden Cross near Carfax where the Marian martyrs are supposed to have slept on the night before their execution." It was at one of these parties in February 1919 that Pinto met Ronald Firbank, a *fin de siècle* writer who, according to Arthur Waley, "hover[ed] . . . an inch or two above the surface of things." (His writing, Forster has said, "is frivolous stuff, and how rare, how precious is frivolity!"[22]) This sketch of Firbank by Pinto is fascinating, especially to those aware of Firbank's personality and work:

> He refused to eat anything but consented to drink a glass of port. Sitting sideways on a chair and clutching sometimes nervously at his tie with

his beautiful white hands, he began to read to us an extract from a work which he afterwards published under the title of *Valmouth*. He did not read well but there was, nevertheless, a peculiar charm in his hesitant manner and low voice, and we were entranced by the quality of his writing. For nearly an hour we were living in a strange, fantastic world inhabited by the Negress Mrs. Yajnavalkya and her centenarian patients, Lady Parvula de Panzoust and Mrs. Hurstpierpont. It was a creation as original and moving as a fantasy of Watteau or Goya.

Through Sassoon, too, Pinto was introduced "into the world of Garsington Manor, the home of the famous Lady Ottoline Morrell, near Sutton Courtenay, about twelve miles from Oxford." His visits to Garsington Manor comprised only brief interludes in his quiet, studious life in postwar Oxford. But if they were brief, they were also extraordinary interludes. For here Pinto became acquainted with figures—"Bertrand Russell with his prominent Adam's apple and the lanky, stooping figure of Lytton Strachey with his red beard"—whose accomplishments are celebrated. Here, too, Pinto had the first occasion to meet and talk with pacifists and conscientious objectors, including no doubt those (at times ungrateful) Bloomsburies who, L. P. Hartley claims, "discharged their 'social duty' in the comfortable, beautiful and ducal surroundings of Garsington Manor, where Lady Ottoline Morrell gave them shelter, on her farm or on her husband's farm . . . from the inconveniences and dangers of war."[23] In any case, Pinto could hardly accept some of the nonsense that these people mouthed: "To hear them talk one would think that a poor defenceless Germany had been wantonly attacked by the wicked capitalists of the Entente!" Those who have read D. H. Lawrence's description of Garsington Manor and of the circle that gathered there around Lady Ottoline in his *Women in Love* (1920), in the chapter entitled "Breadalby"—Bertrand Russell, to his enduring distress, appears here as Sir Joshua, "a learned, dry Baronet of fifty, who was always making witticisms and laughing at them in a harsh, horse-laugh . . . talking . . . endlessly, endlessly, always with a strong mentality working, always interesting, and yet always known"—will recognize Pinto's picture:

> It was one fine afternoon in the early summer of 1919 when Siegfried [Sassoon], Osbert [Sitwell] . . . and I drove in an Oxford taxi through the lovely Oxfordshire country, still at that time untainted by industrialism, to one of Lady Ottoline's Thursday afternoon parties. I called Garsington a magic world and magical indeed was my first impression on that sunny May afternoon of this perfectly proportioned Tudor manor house built of silver-grey stone with its three gables and mullioned windows. The celebrated red-panelled room was crowded with people who

overflowed on to the terrace and into the gardens. Hanging on the walls were pictures of Augustus John, Richard Sickert and other modern English masters. When Siegfried presented me to my hostess I was confronted by an astonishing figure, very tall, with a long, rather heavily painted face, large ear-rings and dyed auburn hair hanging in short locks on either side of her temples. She was dressed in a bright scarlet frock in a style suggestive of the Elizabethan period and a sort of hoop or small crinoline. Her voice was as remarkable as her appearance. I can only describe it as a richly musical drawl. All this may seem to add up to a kind of grotesque but the impression made on me by Lady Ottoline was far from grotesque. She had an aura of radiant charm, vitality and intellectual power, and I felt I was in the presence of the modern equivalent of Fox's Duchess of Devonshire or Byron's Lady Oxford.

Since Pinto had an open invitation to visit Garsington Manor on any Sunday afternoon, he was able to meet other famous figures in Lady Ottoline's circle. H. H. Asquith, the former Liberal prime minister; Mark Gertler and Dorothy Brett, two young painters and friends of D. H. Lawrence; J. B. S. Haldane, Edward Sackville-West, Princess Bibesco—these were some of the persons whom he recalls in his memoir. Pinto's picture of one of Yeats's periodic visits to Garsington Manor is particularly interesting. "I was a little surprised to find that he was quite unlike the willowy dreamer of the Celtic Twilight as I had pictured him in my boyhood. Instead, I was confronted by a burly, genial, humorous Irishman. One day he arrived rather late for tea at Garsington, and when Ottoline asked him why he looked so depressed he said, 'I have just been listening to four hundred Boy Scouts singing "Innisfree." ' " And who will not recognize the great poet, in the course of a discussion on the *Odyssey*, insisting that "Homer was not 'primitive' but represented the culmination of a civilisation which worked towards unity in all things while ours works towards disunity and variety"?

The reminiscences about intellectual life in Oxford are also enthralling. Quite rightly Pinto observes that in the whole of the long history of Oxford, "rarely [had there] been such a concentration of poetic talent as there was in the city and the surrounding country in 1919–21." He mentions in this connection leading poets like Yeats, Robert Bridges, John Masefield, and Robert Graves, as well as promising poets like Wilfred Childe, Edgell Rickword, Alan Porter, Edmund Blunden, and Roy Campbell. In the 1930's, Pinto asserts, most Oxford undergraduates were politically minded, and in the 1940's they were nearly all religious. But after 1918 "it seemed that salvation could only come from the arts." Students in the 1960's, he agrees, can be described as being "apolitical, areligious and contemptuous of all

systems." This was also a prevailing attitude among Oxford undergraduates in the post-1918 years; but, as Pinto adds, "we did believe
passionately in the Arts, especially in poetry as well as in the critical
spirit, Arnold's 'disinterested endeavour to learn and propagate the
best that is known . . . and thus establish a current of fresh and true
ideas.' " What these pages of *The City That Shone* emphasize is that
in the years after 1918 Pinto and his generation attempted through
their studies and literary pursuits to formulate an ethos of life and
work that would strengthen them not only in overcoming all the anguish that the war had brought, but also in their attempt to find new
life-values to replace those wrecked by the war.

A number of other distinguished Oxford dons, besides those already
mentioned, appear in Pinto's memoir. David Nichol Smith, a chief
lecturer in the English school, is depicted as a "dry and formal" lecturer, as well as a "masterful, ambitious Scot." C. T. Onions, lecturer
in Middle English, gave helpful, learned, but unexciting lectures,
"seasoned by a pleasant dry humour." By far the most interesting of
Pinto's recollections is that of Walter Raleigh, the chief lecturer in
and head of the English School. "In 1919 he was one of the great
sights of Oxford, comparable with Magdalen Tower or St. Mary's
spire, a giant of humane learning." Pinto speaks of his name as one
that "was full of romance and the man seemed almost as legendary
and poetic as his Elizabethan namesake." Raleigh, "a huge, towering
figure, nearly seven feet tall, with a remarkably long head, short grey
hair and a small grey moustache," lectured twice a week "in the great
hall of the Examination Schools which was always crowded." As Pinto
vividly shows, Raleigh was admired immensely by students who were
stirred by his generous and undonnish manner, as well as by his enthusiasm for literature. ("Literature," he said, "is the record of man's adventures on the edge of things."[24]) His lectures were invariably stimulating. "He was not an instructor preparing us for examinations,"
Pinto declares, "but a princely host making us share with him his delight in a feast of the power and the glory of the masterpieces of English verse and prose. He read superbly and his comments on what he
read were not 'evaluations' but rich emanations of his generous personality, his immense learning and his knowledge of life."

For some academics and critics, Raleigh, like some of his close and
influential friends who belonged to the Cambridge-Bloomsbury circle,
was (and is) considered too much of an epicure in his literary taste and
criticism. But to many of the ex-servicemen studying at Oxford after
the war he was something of a hero, because, as Pinto contends, even if

he displayed a "rather old-fashioned insular patriotism" and "never passed beyond the attitudes of 1914" (Raleigh rejected the poetry of Sassoon and Owen, for instance, since like Yeats he did not believe that the suffering of war was a fit subject for poetry), "he was so obviously on our side in the war against pedantry, pettiness, philistinism and prudery." Raleigh's concept of what education in the university should be—"To escape from the eternal personal judgements which make a school a place of torment is to walk upon air. The schoolmaster looks at you; the college professor looks the way you are looking,"[25] —inspired his students. The sincerity and honesty of his approach to *paideia* undoubtedly influenced the men who fought in the war and who had now returned to complete their education and, if possible, salvage humane civilization. He thus acquired the respect of those men who, like Pinto, believed that Raleigh "provided an unforgettable image of the true university, a place of intellectual freshness, freedom and the disinterested pursuit of learning."

In June 1921, Pinto took the final examination for Honours in English. The week in which this written examination, "embodied in about fourteen papers," was administered also saw some very sultry and sweltering weather. For Pinto and the other examinees, "wearing the regulation gowns, 'subflux' suits and white bow ties," the examination was physically trying. Then, following a few weeks of rest, Pinto appeared at the beginning of July for his *viva voce* examination. The External examiners were Sir Arthur Quiller-Couch (or Q., as he was known) and Professor R. W. Chambers; the Internal examiners were Professor H. C. Wyld and Raleigh. "I approached these deities," Pinto writes, "in a somewhat dazed condition but my ordeal was brief." The examiners themselves, it appears, must have forgotten Pinto in the course of expressing their own strong feelings about Lord Byron, whose name had come up: "Raleigh, addressing himself to Q., said he didn't care much for Byron himself and Q. launched out into an impassioned defence of Byron's poetry while I listened humbly to this dispute between the Olympians till I was dismissed." If the examiners disagreed over Byron, they had no doubt at all as to Pinto's own achievement. He was awarded a first class Honours degree. He recalls that later when he presented himself at the commencement ceremonies, he found himself "with a batch of Christ Church graduands. . . . 1921 was the year when the first women received official degrees at Oxford." The novelty of this departure from tradition during the degree ceremony was undoubtedly too much for the Vice-Chancellor, Dr. Farnell, a distinguished classical scholar.

"He kept referring to blushing undergraduates as *'hunc dominum'* and being corrected by a prompting official who whispered audibly *'hanc dominam.'*"

Pinto arranged to remain at Oxford to read for a Higher Degree. Raleigh agreed to his choice of the Restoration poet Sir Charles Sedley as the subject of his thesis, under the supervision of Sir Charles Firth, the great authority on seventeenth-century history. In the meantime, during the summer of 1921, he decided to spend a holiday in Switzerland. His old family physician advised him to go to Les Avants, a charming village in the heights above Montreux, where the air would be beneficial to his health, especially as Pinto had suffered from bronchial attacks ever since he was gassed in 1918. During this idyllic holiday he met his future wife, a Swiss peasant girl, Irène Adeline Pittet. The romance led quickly to an agreement to regard themselves as engaged. They would marry only after Pinto had secured a regular salaried post. "In those days we still had what many people would regard as the Victorian notion that a man should not marry till he was capable of earning a livelihood." Pinto accepted a position as *lecteur d'anglais* at the Sorbonne in 1922–23. On August 26, 1922, he and Irène were married at Montreux in the Église Libre, the branch of Swiss Calvinism to which the Pittet family belonged. The marriage caused several complications. It alienated Pinto to some extent from his father and sister, who objected on the grounds that the marriage was "outside the sacred bounds of English middle-class suburbia" and that Irène's "working-class" background was "beyond the pale of civilisation." In addition, Pinto was denied either a tutorship at Christ Church or a Research Fellowship because he refused to delay his marriage for several years. Raleigh's sudden death in the summer of 1922 also robbed Pinto of necessary support. (Because of his association with Sassoon, the Sitwells, and the Garsington set, Pinto believes that his appointment to the English Faculty was opposed by David Nichol Smith.) With these events *The City That Shone* comes to an end. "The book started in the garden of childhood," Pinto reflects; "it ends in the holy garden of marriage."

Pinto notes that shortly before his marriage he had a dream in which he saw for a moment the Shining City that Bunyan describes in *The Pilgrim's Progress*. On two earlier occasions, when he was eight or nine years old and when he was an undergraduate at Oxford, soon after the Great War, Pinto had had "a vision enclosed in a kind of circular frame. I described it to myself as a shining city full of people moving about among wonderful coloured flames. . . . I did not merely see this place but I seemed to be in it and to be actually close to the 'shining people' and one of them." This vision, as Pinto points out, "had a considerable effect on my character and mentality. Far more than any religious creed or philosophic argument it has given me the assurance that, whatever appearances may be to the contrary, there is some sort of divine reality and that I am in touch with it and, indeed, in some sense, a part of it." Pinto's experience can be seen as being essentially religious both in its meaning and its consciousness of what is wholly other—an experience that, William James says, man has in solitude, insofar as he apprehends himself to stand in relation to whatever he may consider the divine.[26]

Pinto suggests that he was to undergo through his own visionary experience an awareness that "the eternal beatitude is the state where seeing and eating are the same thing." If vision touches and transforms life, it also delivers life. Vivian de Sola Pinto belonged to that small remnant of seekers whose vision of humane civilization's "bright day" is inspired by

> . . . hope that can never die,
> Effort, and expectation, and desire,
> And something evermore about to be.[27]

With Bunyan, he could also sing: "I told him that I was a Pilgrim, going to the Celestial City."

LEONARD WOOLF

I went to Rodmell [Leonard and Virginia Woolf's house near Lewes, Sussex] for last night, and very nice it was too. We sat out in the garden watching the late sunlight making the corn all golden over the Downs. . . . Oh my dear, what an enchanting person Virginia is! How she weaves magic into life! Whenever I see her, she raises life to a higher level. . . . And Leonard too: with his schoolboyish love for pets and toys (gadgets), he is irresistibly young and attractive. How wrong people are about Bloomsbury, saying that it is devitalised or devitalising. You couldn't find two people less devitalised or devitalising than the Wolves. . . .

The force of the truth of these words, from a letter of August 3, 1938, by Vita Sackville-West to her husband, Harold Nicholson,[28] comes to mind as one reads *Downhill All the Way*, the fourth volume of Leonard Woolf's autobiography.*

*Downhill All the Way. An Autobiography of the Years 1919–1939 (New York, 1967). For a fine critical discussion of the five volumes that comprise Woolf's auto-

Her words underline not only the vitality but also the dignity that his autobiography communicates.

Downhill All the Way covers twenty years of an energetic involvement in the intellectual life of England. It is an autobiography which brings us into contact with a man who speaks for the "civilization of mind" and for the things that matter, that really matter, as E. M. Forster, a good friend of Woolf, has insisted: tolerance, good temper, and sympathy. Woolf's reactions to life are always reactions to the different states of human consciousness and to a concern with human values. Invariably his writing reflects the thought and actions of a man dedicated to the continuity of civilization, which he sees ravaged by war, technology, vulgarization, and mediocrity. His world was not the modern world in which, as Henry James complained, life has become "an awful game of grab," with its "greedy wants, timid ideas and fishy passions." At once much higher and better, Woolf's world was characterized by a search for excellence, to be found in a free mind, in good taste, faith in the human race, a passion for honesty, a sense of humor, and in political and artistic accomplishment. His was "the world of Bloomsbury," which, according to J. K. Johnstone, "was 'arty' in that its members believed art to be the most important thing in the world, the highest expression to which man has attained. What is more, they practised this belief. But they were not exclusively 'arty.' They have made contributions at least equally important to economics and to international affairs."[29] In turn Bloomsbury was associated with Cambridge University and an ethos of which it was essentially an extension. Thus, the writings of two famous Cambridge dons, G. Lowes Dickinson and G. E. Moore—particularly the latter's *Principia Ethica*—occupied a central place in Bloomsbury thinking.

That Woolf belonged to Bloomsbury—*belonged*, for it has vanished from the English scene—is evident. From 1919 to 1939 his friends were writers and intellectuals, usually products of the public schools and the ancient universities. His social life was spent in high society, with its elegant parties, given by Lady Ottoline Morrell or Lady Sibyl Colefax, where one enjoyed "intimate, intense, and rather intensive talk about books and writers and the arts generally," and met "the Prime Minister and half the cabinet, Mary Pritchard, Margot Asquith, the editor of *The Times*, Max Beerbohm, and Augustus John." Mrs. Woolf thoroughly enjoyed these occasions, and her husband

---

biography, *Sowing* (1961), *Growing* (1964), *Beginning Again* (1965), *Downhill All the Way* (1967), *The Journey Not the Arrival Matters* (1969), see David Gervais' "Leonard Woolf's Autobiography," *The Cambridge Quarterly* (Spring/Summer 1970), pp. 82–98.

quotes her description of a fancy-dress party to which they went in Gordon Square in January 1923:

> We collided, when we met; we went pop, used Christian names, flattered, praised, and thought (or I did) of Shakespeare. At any rate I thought of him when the singing was going. Shakespeare I thought would have liked us all tonight. . . . My luck was in though and I found good quarters with Frankie [Francis Birrell] and Sheppard and Bunny [David Garnett] and Lydia [Lopokova]—all my friends in short. But what we talked about I hardly know. Bunny asked me to be his child's godmother. And a Belgian wants to translate me. . . . Jumbo [Marjorie Strachey] distorted nursery rhymes: Lydia danced: there were charades: Sickert acted Hamlet. We were all easy and gifted and like good children rewarded by having the capacity for enjoying ourselves thus.

With its love of intellect, discussion, books, and paintings; with its financial stability, its leisure, comfort, and travel; with its country and London houses and its love of the countryside; with its traditions and its quiet unorthodoxies—Woolf's world was undoubtedly aristocratic. But its aristocracy was that of culture and the inner life. In it the life of the mind and the estate of poetry were primary objects of attention, and personal relationships were revered as effective answers to violence and chaos. "To someone like myself born in the comparative civilization of the nineteenth century," he observes, "one of the horrors of life since 1920 is its senseless savagery." That we see dignity in life; that we love one another; that we protect our gentle imaginings in a crowded, jostling world—these are the ways in which we strengthen life as much as we give value to it, Woolf iterates.

Of course there are those who will always detest what Bloomsbury represented and refuse to accept John Maynard Keynes's belief that the members of Bloomsbury were "the forerunners of a new dispensation." Anthony Burgess, in an interview appearing in *Book World* (March 21, 1971), underlines the continuing hostility to Bloomsbury when he says: "I know that people like Virginia Woolf and E. M. Forster belong to a kind of society which I can't understand, I can't possibly touch, and fundamentally loathe. I find it makes my skin creep to even consider touching any member of that class. It's as physical as that. I can't help it, I just can't justify it, but there it is; it's just another world." This hostility is not entirely unwarranted. Snobbism flourished in the Bloomsbury milieu. Virginia Woolf was undeniably guilty of it—"a colossal snob," L. P. Hartley has charged.[30] English fiction, she said, would be an arid waste "without the nieces of Earls and the cousins of generals." She dismissed some of Lawrence's poems as "the sayings that small boys scribble upon stiles to make housemaids jump and titter." In a shriller tone she castigated Arnold

Bennett's "shopkeeper's view of literature." "I like the old creature," she wrote. "I do my best, as a writer, to detect signs of genius in his smoky brown eye...." She preferred "those trusty Cambridge fellows." (The same "Frankie" and "Bunny" whom Mrs. Woolf admired, Lawrence found exasperating. "Their attitude is so irreverent and blatant," he grumbled. "They made me dream in the night of a beetle that bites like a scorpion. But I killed it—a very large beetle. I scotched it and it ran off—but I came upon it again and killed it."[31])

Undoubtedly, too, the Cambridge-Bloomsbury world was guilty of tittle-tattle and of the more insidious element of self-congratulation that caused it to make so much fuss over the writings of Lytton Strachey, and even of Virginia Woolf herself. ("*The Voyage Out*," Lord Oxford said, "is a second-rate novel about second-rate people."[32]) Woolf speaks of David Garnett "at the beginning of a distinguished career." But "distinguished"? Surely the judgment is honorific, a testament of friendship and not a discriminating literary judgment. Still, we must realize that Woolf's world, even if it failed to compel a transcendent, impersonalizing scrutiny of its members' literary achievements, was a world in which friendship was a paramount goal. "We must not approve either those who are always for friendship," Epicurus tells us, "or those who hang back, but for friendship's sake we must even run risks." His words capture the place of personal relationships in Bloomsbury. In his autobiography Woolf shows his capacity for friendship and loyalty, even if wrongly placed. Always and first of all he is a gentleman, and his example reminds us how far modern man has strayed from good manners—simultaneously "destroying our ancient edifices," as Eliot notes, "to make ready the ground upon which the barbarian nomads of the future will encamp in their mechanised caravans."

What Woolf makes us further aware of is that an advanced culture can be identified with a certain stability of life. Culture and stability are interpenetrating and interdependent; one gives impetus to the other. Together they check the violence that, like goblin footfalls, always threatens. Hence Woolf observes that a house, in which he includes its material and spiritual environment, can mold the lives of its inhabitants. He identifies periods of his life by the houses he has lived in. Particularly arresting is his account of how while living in London he feuded with the management of a nearby hotel from which every evening, from eight to twelve, when a jazz band was playing full blast, "the Bedlam of noise, funnelled into our room even with the double windows closed." Woolf took his case to court—and won. "But," he says with a sigh, "the proceedings made me realize, as I had not before, the precariousness and helplessness of the individual in modern life."

As Woolf affirms the dignity of life, he affirms the dignity of work. Whether he is engaged in politics, preaching the need for social reform and for the abolition of fanaticism and of war; whether he is commenting on his work as an editor or on the progress of his own writings (the failure of which he views with good-humored disappointment); or whether he is talking about how in 1917 he and his wife established the Hogarth Press, he conveys happy absorption. (Edmund Blunden recalls "those old days, with the new Press . . . [when] the romance of life seemed to be a certainty.") Indifference and boredom, those blights on so much of modern life, were never his. The following account of how Leonard and Virginia Woolf carried out their printing chores pinpoints a charismatic intelligence that was as competent as it was clever, and as imaginative as it was practical:

> We ran it in our spare time on lines invented by myself without staff and without premises; we printed in the larder, bound books in the dining-room, interviewed printers, binders, and authors in a sitting-room. I kept the accounts, records of sales, etc., myself in my own way, which was from the chartered accountant's view unorthodox, but when it was challenged by the Inland Revenue and I took my books to the Inspector of Taxes, he agreed that they showed accurately the profit or loss on each book published, the revenue and expenditure of the business, and the annual profit or loss. . . .

On the basis of long experience as a writer, an editor, and a publisher, Woolf had deep interest in the psychology of authorship. Hence the pages describing his wife's working habits are engrossing, from the moment when the creative impulse occurred till the moment when the piece of writing had assumed shape and form, and from there going on to the agony of "cold proof," followed by the reviews and her reactions to these. Her first draft of a novel was written in a notebook with pen and ink in the mornings. Later each day she typed out what she had written, revising as she typed. At this stage she ignored her surroundings; her attitude toward her writing was controlled and dispassionate. "In the process of her writings—of her artistic creation—there were long periods of, first, quiet and intense dreamlike rumination when she drifted through London streets or walked across the Sussex water-meadows or merely sat silent by the fire, and secondly of intense, analytical, critical revision of what she had written."

Writing, for Virginia Woolf, was torture. She wrote with such intensity that, as she noted, "I seemed to stumble after my own voice, or almost after some sort of speaker (as when I was mad). I was almost afraid, remembering the voices that fly ahead." This tension produced mental exhaustion and made her writing a constant menace to her mental stability. Despite precautions, and despite Woolf's devoted care, she was often ill. In this entry in her diary for August 8, 1921, we can gauge her suffering:

> These, this morning, the first words I have written—to call writing—for 60 days; and those days spent in wearisome headache, jumping pulse, aching back, frets, fidgets, lying awake, sleeping draughts, sedatives, digitalis, going for a little walk, and plunging back into bed again—all the horrors of the dark cupboard of illness once more displayed for my diversion.

Woolf's account of his wife's illnesses is done with dignified compassion. Nowhere is this quality more evident than in the words recording her death: "On February 26, 1941, she finished *Between the Acts* and, as had happened four years before, she fell into the depths of despair. On March 28 she drowned herself in the Ouse." (In the first chapter of the final volume of his autobiography covering the years 1939–69, *The Journey Not the Arrival Matters*, Woolf gives the grim details surrounding his wife's last illness and suicide. Here he also talks about World War II, a period of history that he connects with a "feeling of hopelessness and helplessness" and with unparalleled cruelty and barbarism. Virginia Woolf no doubt had all these facts in mind when in her last novel she observed: "*Look at ourselves, Ladies and gentlemen! Then at the wall; and ask how's this wall, the great wall, which we call, miscall, civilization to be built by . . . orts, scraps and fragments like ourselves?*")

Downhill All the Way has as its epigraph these words from St. Luke, Chapter 8:33: "The herd ran violently down a steep place into the lake, and were choked." Here the words refer to the aftermath of the Great War, which Woolf thinks destroyed the foundations of European civilization: "When the maroons boomed on November 11, 1918, we were no longer the same people who, on August 4, 1914, heard with amazed despair that the guns had begun to boom." The years between 1919 and 1939 registered the disintegration of the moderate optimism he had felt before 1914; worst of all, they signalized the admission "into the privacy of one's mind or soul an iron fatalistic acquiescence and barbarism." Because of the anguish of these years, Woolf teaches us that we must accede to a certain "despair in virile acceptance," to use Albert Camus' terminology, but that we can accede with that faith in human dignity that gives meaning and power to man even in his darkest hours.

6

Notes on Eliot and Lawrence 1915–1924

ᔕ

The Hogarth Press published the first English edition of T. S. Eliot's *The Waste Land* on September 12, 1923. The book was hand-printed by Leonard and Virginia Woolf, who had founded this famous publishing house in 1917 as a diversionary activity. In 1919 they had hand-printed and hand-bound Eliot's *Poems*, containing, among others, "Sweeney Among the Nightingales," of which Leonard Woolf many years later wrote: "But I never tired and still do not tire of those lines which were a new note in poetry and came from the heart of the Eliot of those days (and sounded with even greater depth and volume in . . . the poem which had greater influence upon English poetry, indeed upon English literature, than any other in the 20th century, *The Waste Land*):

> The host with someone indistinct
> Converses at the door apart,
> The nightingales are singing near
> The Convent of the Sacred Heart,
>
> And sang within the bloody wood
> When Agamemnon cried aloud,
> And let their liquid siftings fall
> To stain the stiff dishonoured shroud."[1]

Woolf goes on to tell how he and his wife first got to know Eliot, liked him, but were "a little afraid of him." Their relations with him slowly changed from "extreme formality" to "real intimacy." Eliot, it is made clear, at first baffled everyone who got to know him. "The odd thing about Eliot," wrote Virginia Woolf, "is that his eyes are lively and youthful when the cast of his face and the shape of his sentences are formal and even heavy. Rather like a sculpted face—no upper lip; formidable, powerful; pale. Then those hazel eyes, seeming to escape from the rest of him."[2] And Lytton Strachey wrote of one of their early meetings in London: "Poet Eliot had dinner with me on Monday—rather ill and rather American: altogether not quite gay enough for my taste. But by no means to be sniffed at."[3]

"The more we know of Eliot, the better." So reads the first sentence of Ezra Pound's Preface to *The Waste Land. A Facsimile and Transcript of the Original Drafts Including the Annotations of Ezra Pound*.[4] With the appearance of this volume, edited by Valerie Eliot with a scholarly tact and an excellence that "would have delighted her husband," again to quote Pound, we are just beginning to "know" Eliot. Especially within the epochal years between 1915 and 1924, this book does a great deal in clarifying his life. Like his famous contemporary, D. H. Lawrence (though for different reasons), Eliot has been misunderstood and misrepresented. Thus, even in as respectable a journal as the *Times Literary Supplement*, the anonymous reviewer of the facsimile edition, injecting into his review irresponsible insinuations, imperiously concludes with a question that he chooses to follow with an almost shameless comment: "What is there to hide? Whatever it is, it cannot be worse than what is commonly alleged in whispers."[5] The reviewer insists that the time has come for Eliot's widow to reveal the secrets of his private life.

Many and by now well-known are the epithets applied to Eliot by critics and academics. Besides, he has been singled out for "special" treatment by the liberal ideologues of contemporary culture. In a political sense he is no less suspect of totalitarianism than, say, Baron Ernest Seillière, T. E. Hulme, Julien Benda, Irving Babbitt, and Charles Maurras and *L'Action française*. At the root of this reaction is the hostility that Eliot's cultural politics generates. Eliot will never be forgiven by the liberal ideologues for the "orthodoxy" of *The Idea of a Christian Society* and of *Notes Towards the Definition of Culture*, which they equate with political reaction. Nor will he ever be forgiven for his defense of the "moral imagination," as Russell Kirk has said, with its roots in religious insights and in the continuity of civilization.[6] Making "the last twist of the knife," therefore, has become a favorite pastime of those who see in Eliot an enemy of the "democratic ideology" and of the radical direction that Western society has been taking in the twentieth century. Eliot has become, in a word, a marked man because of pronouncements like the following:

> In a society like ours, wormeaten with Liberalism, the only thing possible for a person with strong convictions, is to state a point of view and leave it like that.

> Thought, study, mortification, sacrifice: it is such notions as these that should be impressed upon the young—who differ from the young of other times merely in having a different middle-aged generation behind

them. You will never attract the young by making Christianity easy; but a good many can be attracted by finding it difficult: difficult both to the disorderly mind and to the unruly.

... so long as we consider "education" as good in itself ..., without any ideal of the good life for society or for the individual, we shall move from one uneasy compromise to another. To the quick and simple organization of society for ends which, being only material and worldly, must be as ephemeral as worldly success, there is only one alternative. As political philosophy derives its sanctions from ethics, and ethics from the truth of religion, it is only by returning to the eternal source of truth that we can hope for any social organization which will not, to its ultimate destruction, ignore some essential aspect of reality.

But the difficult discipline is the discipline and training of emotion; this the modern world has great need of; so great need that it hardly understands what the word means; and this I have found is only attainable through dogmatic religion.

... what gives me concern, in the modern world, is not so much the growth of sexual laxity, or even of financial corruption, as the disappearance of the *sense* of sin.... I am not so much alarmed today at there being so many sinners as I am by there being so many people who feel virtuous. I can hardly think that there was ever a time before when so many people felt virtuous. And when people feel virtuous, civilization totters.[7]

Essentially, the opposition to Eliot, or rather the antithesis to his thought, temperament, and cultural "points of view," is posited by the life and work of D. H. Lawrence. "Lawrence and Eliot," John Middleton Murry writes, "are indeed antithetical: they repudiate one another, I would almost say they annihilate one another."[8] Indeed, it can even be said that the twentieth century, as an age of conflicting ideas and ways of living and behaving, comprises what can be called the Age of Lawrence and the Age of Eliot. What Lawrence represents, in stark contrast to Eliot, is a rebellious defiance of whatever is accepted and time-honored. Lawrence's charge that Eliot's "classiosity is bunkum, but still more cowardice" underlines what sets apart these two literary representatives of the modern age.

Lawrence, Eliot charges in *After Strange Gods*, which contains the core of his harshest pronouncements against Lawrence, is guilty of "heresy," which is "apt to have a seductive simplicity, to make a direct and persuasive appeal to intellect and emotions, and to be altogether more plausible than truth."[9] Eliot thought that Lawrence had a "sense of the moment" but lacked a "sense of history," which Joyce, in contrast, had. He always insisted that the continuity of culture was tied to the responsible person rooted in the full European tradition, which Lawrence said was "dull, old, dead." As Murry contended, both

Lawrence and Eliot, in their reactions to the broken world that came out of the war of 1914–18, were rooted in despair; but Lawrence's was "a romanticism of despair," Eliot's, "a classicism of despair." For Lawrence, however, the answer to the problems of human existence was to be found in a frantic search, on new levels of emotional and intellectual consciousness, an "adventure in consciousness" as he phrased it, which meant finally that men, as "life-adventurers," would be able to achieve "communion together . . . [in] something holy."

Eliot recognized the validity of and learned, referentially and procedurally, from Lawrence's poetic vision. (Scholars have shown how Eliot turned to Lawrence when he wanted to express his spiritual experience in sensual terms or in image-structures of the "moment." Like Lawrence, too, Eliot absorbed Heracleitean formulas, but, unlike Lawrence, he infused them with Christian meaning, as seen in *Four Quartets*.) Nevertheless, he refused to accept the constituents of Lawrence's message. And even if he could find a place for the world of Lawrence, it has been remarked, he could not bring it to life. "M. Lawrence est un démoniaque," Eliot wrote in *La Nouvelle Revue Française*, "un démoniaque simple et naturel muni d'un évangile. Quand ses personnages font l'amour—ou du moins accomplissent ce qui chez M. Lawrence est l'équivalent de l'amour (et ils ne font pas autre chose)—non seulement ils perdent toutes les aménités, raffinements et grâces que plusieurs siècles ont élaborés afin de rendre l'amour supportable, mais ils semblent remonter le cours de l'évolution et de ses métamorphoses, rétrogradant audelà du singe et du poisson jusqu'à quelque hideux accouplement de protoplasme."[10]

Lawrence's answer, he saw, was culturally rootless, ignorant above all of a full European tradition. It went the same way as Romanticism, the Romanticism that, as Eliot had learned from Hulme, was "spilt religion." Such an answer, Eliot believed, contained risks and dangers that man, by his very nature, his "indiscipline," would never be able to overcome. Not to go unnoticed in this respect is Eliot's implicit approval of this passage from Hulme, which he quotes in his essay "Baudelaire" and which stands in stark opposition to Lawrence's fundamental concept of "the pristine incomparable nature of every individual soul":

> "In the light of these absolute values, man himself is judged to be essentially limited and imperfect. He is endowed with Original Sin. While he can occasionally accomplish acts which partake of perfection, he can never himself *be* perfect. Certain secondary results in regard to ordinary human action in society follow from this. A man is essentially bad, he can only accomplish anything of value by discipline—ethical and politi-

cal. Order is thus not merely negative, but creative and liberating. Institutions are necessary."[11]

The Romantic, Eliot said in his review of George Wyndham's *Essays in Romantic Literature*, could no doubt "ride to hounds across his prose, looking with wonder upon the world as upon a fairyland."[12] The element of curiosity is a positive quality of Romanticism: "a curiosity which recognizes that any life, if accurately and profoundly penetrated, is interesting and always strange." Yet, as Eliot maintained, Romanticism ends in a perverse incompleteness. It travels in circles and has (in existentialist terminology, existentialism being a distended form of Romanticism) "no exit." "Romanticism is a short cut to the strangeness without the reality," Eliot concludes, "and it leads its disciples only back upon themselves." Perhaps no other words better sum up Eliot's indictment of the Lawrentian position. Although Eliot accepted Lawrence's diagnosis of the modern world, especially as found in a book like *Fantasia of the Unconscious* ("a book to keep at hand and re-read," Eliot said), he rejected as "untrustworthy" and "deceitful" the answers of Lawrence the "medicine man." He confessed in a later essay that Lawrence was an indefatigable "investigator of the religious life," "a kind of *contemplative* rather than a theologian," who wanted a "world in which religion would be something deeper than belief, in which life would be a kind of religious behaviourism." But, in profound disagreement, Eliot also felt that the religion which Lawrence sought to achieve "is a religion of power and magic, of control rather than propitiation." Lawrence, then, attained "only a religion of autotherapy" and his religious quest was in the end an "individualistic misdirection of will."[13]

Lawrence's message, Eliot insisted, was that of a heretic, a "person who seizes upon a truth and pushes it to the point at which it becomes a falsehood," and whose work is "the denial or neglect of tradition," the denial or neglect giving rein to a "disastrous" individuality. "With these two odd handicaps—the will against Christianity that was a residue of childhood and adolescence, and the temperament of *un*education—Lawrence started out life on a lifelong search for a religion."[14] Lawrence's vision had "a fluctuating ability of diagnosis, without the further and total ability of prescription and régime"; it lacked what Eliot believed to be the mainstay of the "classical ideal," that of "maturity"—"Maturity of mind: this needs history and the consciousness of history."[15] Eliot did concede that Lawrence wanted "something deeper than belief," but to Lawrence it was "more important really to feel terror than sing comminatory psalms." To Lawrence it was the progress of the emotional soul that mattered, or, as he himself expresses it in his essay "On Human Destiny":

> We have to struggle down to the heart of things, where the everlasting flame is, and kindle ourselves another beam of light. In short, we have to make another better adventure in pulsating thought, far, far to the one central pole of energy. We have to germinate inside us, between our undaunted mind and our reckless, genuine passions, a new germ. The germ of a new idea.[16]

Eliot's deepest beliefs stand in threatened opposition to Lawrence's "manifesto" here. Eliot thought that Lawrence's emphasis on "the dark consciousness" and on "the resurrection of the flesh," constituting "progress," stopped short of being fulfilled in "*other*-worldly wisdom." Such progress of the emotional soul lacked, in the end, "amplitude," "catholicity." Lawrence's "new unknown," he concluded, was incompatible with the "supervision of the tradition by orthodoxy." It rejected the final spiritual consummation of history, for the individual, for the race, and for the material universe. As Eliot writes in *Little Gidding*,

> ... all shall be well and
> All manner of thing shall be well
> When the tongues of flame are in-folded
> Into the crowned knot of fire
> And the fire and the rose are one.

Lawrence, above all, lacked the discipline of orthodoxy and hence reacted against "the process of the mind" in the diligent acquisition of faith described by Eliot in one of his most biographically revealing essays, "The *Pensées* of Pascal":

> The Christian thinker—and I mean the man who is trying consciously and conscientiously to explain to himself the sequence which culminates in faith, rather than the public apologist—proceeds by rejection and elimination. He finds the world to be so and so; he finds its character inexplicable by any non-religious theory: among religions he finds Christianity, and Catholic Christianity, to account most satisfactorily for the world and especially for the moral world within; and thus, by what Newman calls "powerful and concurrent" reasons, he finds himself inexorably committed to the dogma of the Incarnation.[17]

The cultural and intellectual debate between the two men has been carried on by contemporary critics. At a most responsible level, F. R. Leavis ("I am not an uncritical admirer of T. S. Eliot; I hope that is well understood") has accused Eliot of "pusillanimity" and of "inner dividedness," especially through his support of "the boys (and the Dame E. Sitwell) of the contemptible London literary world." In

Eliot, Leavis believes, "an essential part of the drive behind his poetry was self-contempt." Stoutly defending Lawrence against Eliot's charge of displaying in his life and work "the crippling effect . . . of not having been born and brought up in the environment of a living and central tradition," Leavis insists that

> To turn, as Lawrence did, the earnestness and moral seriousness of that tradition to the powering of a strenuous intellectual inquiringness was all in the tradition. That the Lawrences were Congregationalists is a relevant point—their Nonconformity was very far from being the debased tin-chapel salvationism that Mr. Eliot appears to think it. . . . And for those young people in the eighteen-nineties their intellectual education was intimately bound up with a social training which, even if it didn't give them Wykehamist or Etonian or even Harvard manners, I see no reason for supposing inferior to that enjoyed by Mr. Eliot. Moreover, they met and talked and read in a setting of family life such as, to judge from *The Cocktail Party*, Mr. Eliot cannot imagine to have existed—a family life beset by poverty and the day-to-day exigencies of breadwinning, yet quite finely civilized. . . . Lawrence knew every day of his life in intimate experience the confrontation, the interpenetration, of the old agricultural England with the industrial; the contrast of the organic forms and rhythms and the old beauty of human adaptation with what had supervened.[18]

The Lawrentian, and the Leavisite, disagreements with Eliot have not always been sustained either by the genius of the novelist or by the intransigent judgments of a great moral critic. What is sad is that, as in the case of the reviewer in the *Times Literary Supplement*, small minds are always busily at work chipping away at Eliot's literary reputation, as well as at his personal life. This infection spreads among the academics who condemn Eliot's views as being "irrelevant" and "reactionary." What is equally sad is that some academics unknowingly abet the "party line" regarding Eliot. Even distinguished American scholar-critics will single out Stanley Edgar Hyman's *The Armed Vision* as an authoritative history of criticism. When one turns to this book, the force that for so long has been seeking to dislodge Eliot is there, setting the tone, perpetuating the misconceptions. "The personality [of Eliot] that emerges finally is not," Hyman contends, "as we should expect, that of the triumphant great artist who has achieved, in the *Quartets*, one of the authentic masterpieces of our time, but that of a sick, defeated, and suffering man; the discipline and impersonality of the poetry, the 'tradition' of the criticism, chiefly props to sustain him."[19]

"A sick, defeated, and suffering man": the words bear repeating, for they express the informing and the perpetuating misconception which one comes across repeatedly in estimates of Eliot's achievement.

Eliot's attitude to life, to the life of the senses in particular, we are reminded *ad nauseam,* is one of "distaste" and "disgust." We must choose the other way, the "dark night," and

> Descend lower, descend only
> Into the world of perpetual solitude,
> . . . .
> Internal darkness, deprivation
> And destitution of all property,
> Dessication of the world of sense.

This attitude, in effect, assumes too often a narrow biographical application, so that the "revulsion" and the "distaste" and the "disgust" poetically communicated are turned back to Eliot's private emotions. "T. S. Eliot to me," wrote Lawrence's widow in 1951, "is like a beautifully carved skeleton—no blood, no guts, no marrow, no flesh."[20] The echoes of her statement reverberate when Eliot's work is being appraised. Precisely the Romanticism that Eliot distrusted becomes a part of his art being critically gauged. "There may be a good deal to be said for Romanticism in life," to recall Eliot's words; "there is no place for it in letters." But, like Lawrence, Eliot is unable to escape personally, biographically, from his work.

That there are paradoxes in Eliot's work, as in the work of any literary genius, goes without saying. Eliot's friend Paul Elmer More was bothered by the "cleft Eliot," that is, the "lyric poet of chaos" as opposed to the critic who judged the world as a classicist, a royalist, and an Anglo-Catholic. The legitimacy of such a view—or of Leavis' "distinction between the creative genius and the Eliot who can't escape from his consciousness of the social world"—cannot be challenged. Eliot himself affirmed the need for "internal *cultural* bickering if it is to achieve anything in the way of art, thought and spiritual activity." But in these matters what Eliot has called "the responsibility of the man of letters at the present time" has been steadily disappearing. The cultural disagreement between Lawrence and Eliot, or Eliot's critical inconsistencies posited by More and Leavis, must be seen in terms of problematic issues, indicative of what, critically and culturally, requires from the man of letters the "exercise [of] constant surveillance," to borrow Eliot's own words.[21]

But the spirit of the present is Romantic. It follows, therefore, that in artistic aspects Lawrence is as misapplied as the critical qualms of More and Leavis, apropos of Eliot, are misapplied. This contemporary Romanticism is, in other and ominous ways, anthropological, precisely in the dangerous ways that Eliot foresaw. Such a climate is not conducive to an understanding of "the achievement of T. S. Eliot." Because of this climate of hostility and of ignorance, because of the fallacy of a prevailing anthropological relativism, "the more we know of Eliot, the better." For the more we know about Eliot the more we come to know about the immense cultural and spiritual problems (and quarrels) that beset contemporary civilization, with its emptiness of meaning, perhaps nowhere better posed than in the opening stanza of the third section of *East Coker*:

> O dark, dark, dark. They all go into the dark
> The vacant interstellar spaces, the vacant into the vacant,
> The captains, merchant bankers, eminent men of letters,
> The generous patrons of art, the statesmen and the rulers,
> Distinguished civil servants, chairmen of many committees,
> Industrial lords and petty contractors, all go into the dark,
> And dark the Sun and Moon, and the Almanach de Gotha
> And the Stock Exchange Gazette, the Directory of Directors,
> And cold the sense and lost the motive of action.

The published version of *The Waste Land*, in the light of what Pound calls "the occultation" of the original drafts, will receive in time the diligent appraisal of scholarly minds commanding the history of its bibliographical sources and details. How the text was shortened and edited; what roles Pound and Eliot's first wife played in this process; what the events were that surrounded the suspenseful fate of the "lost" original typescript; what new and valuable clues can now be garnered in tracing the development of Eliot's creative process and the divagations of his thought—these are matters that critics will be increasingly reconsidering. Thus, the history of *The Waste Land* is just beginning to be written.

Once again we are reminded that the years between 1915 and 1924 encompassed a period of history leaving a permanent mark on English civilization. No understanding of *The Waste Land* can be complete without due recognition of the historical forces crashing then with each other. One's personal life, particularly an artist's, could hardly escape being caught up in the events of the age and all their consequences, direct or indirect, small or large. How to live one's own life and yet give transcendent form to one's creativeness was a major problem. For if, as it is said, crisis impels the artistic consciousness, it also stamps the personal consciousness with suffering. Poets may leap over death, but not over suffering. Lawrence's suffering during the years 1915–24, particularly during the war years—as seen notably in his relations with Lady Cynthia Asquith and with others like Bertrand

Russell, John Middleton Murry, and Lady Ottoline Morrell—was so deep that he labored under the burden of this suffering till the very end. Eliot likewise reflects the overwhelming urgencies and changes of these years. His life and his art, like Lawrence's, can in fact be fully comprehended not only in direct relation to his disillusionments, as occasioned by the events of this period, but also, and more importantly, in terms of the creative process, in direct relation to his shedding of illusions. Each of them characterizes, in its origins, the operative consciousness of the idol of illusion and the pain of disillusion.

Mrs. Eliot's Introduction, in the form of "life and letters," tells us as many things about Eliot himself as about his writing of the poem. It tells us, simply yet intensely, about devotion, strength, and suffering; about the history of an epoch and of a poet bearing the marks of this epoch. Quiet truths, not impressions, are the basis of Mrs. Eliot's Introduction. And the man and the mind that shine through this Introduction, deftly achieved through Mrs. Eliot's careful sifting of and quoting from Eliot's letters, written during the years 1915–24, will be seen to be far different from the man and the mind we have been led to expect. The man seen here holds resolutely to the letter and spirit of the motto of the Eliot family, *Tace et fac.* And the mind at work is dedicated to the attainment of the style that Alfred North Whitehead defines as "the ultimate morality of mind."

Hagiography is far from intended here. The quiet resolve that inspirits this Introduction reinforces the power of the personality with the same kind of extraordinary toughness and resilience that, according to D. W. Harding, underlie *The Waste Land.* Poverty, bad health, war, performing onerous jobs, often concurrently (schoolmastering, lecturing, banking), the perils of publication and the wiles of publishers, physical exhaustion, emotional collapse—"I am satisfied, since being here," Eliot wrote in 1921 to Richard Aldington from Margate, where he was taking a rest cure, "that my 'nerves' are a very mild affair, due not to over-work but to an aboulie and emotional derangement which has been a lifelong affliction. Nothing wrong with my mind"—are duly recorded in these pages to chronicle the various facets of Eliot's life during these years, emotionally, socially, and intellectually. Some details regarding his first marriage, in 1915, to Vivien Haigh-Wood, are also provided. A constitutional instability in her made for problems. As Pound once wrote: "His wife hasn't a cent and is an invalid always cracking up, & needing doctors, & incapable of earning anything—though she has tried." Bertrand Russell recalls the peculiar nature of Eliot's first marriage in ways underscoring its difficulties:

> He [Eliot] has a profound and quite unselfish devotion to his wife, and she is really very fond of him, but has impulses of cruelty to him from time to time. It is a Dostojevsky type of cruelty, not a straightforward everyday kind.... She is a person who lives on a knife-edge, and will end as a criminal or a saint—I don't know which yet. She has a perfect capacity for both.[22]

Yet, given all these problems, Eliot carried on with his work as a poet and critic, and in 1921 he even undertook "a new literary venture," the founding of *The Criterion*. The picture of Eliot that comes through is of a man of considerable resourcefulness and endurance, in spite of a certain physical frailty. "I am worn out. I cannot go on," we hear him crying out in 1923. Still, he did press on with his work—

> Since our concern was speech, and speech impelled us
> To purify the dialect of the tribe
> And urge the mind to aftersight and foresight

—with the same undeviating devotion that one finds in great poets. "He has more entrails than might appear from his quiet exterior," we hear Pound remarking of Eliot's inner strength.

That this strength was able to sustain him was due in large part to two of Eliot's supporters, Ezra Pound and John Quinn. Pound's help during these years was inestimable, for he extended to Eliot personal and material support, without which Eliot would have been lost, and also vital creative support, without which *The Waste Land* would not be what it is. Pound was as diligent as he was adroit in pressing and pressing the poem's essences, to employ here Eliot's own phrase. (And yet, as one commentator stresses, "Eliot was not Pound's puppet. He used, he exploited, the miraculously tuned literary sensibility that Pound then was. He used it; he was not used, nor manipulated, by it."[23])

Eliot never failed to affirm his debt to Pound, even as his dedication of *The Waste Land* to him indicates. Consistently clear and recurrent evidence of this recognition is also found in Eliot's little-known lecture "Leadership and Letters," the War Memorial Address that he delivered at Milton Academy, his old preparatory school in Massachusetts, on November 3, 1948. Among the various forms of leadership in the arts, particularly the art of literature, Eliot begins by singling out the contribution of Pound (without actually naming him, though the reference is indisputable):

There is a place for a kind of deliberate leadership in the advancement of literature. I think of a friend who, in the early days, was as much concerned with the encouragement and improvement of the work of unknown writers in whom he discerned talent, as with his own creative work; who formulated for a generation of poets, the principles of good writing most needful for their time; who tried to bring these writers together for their reciprocal benefit; who, in the face of many obstacles, saw that their writings were published; saw that they were reviewed somewhere by critics who could appreciate them; organized or supported little magazines in which their work could appear—and incidentally, liked to give a good dinner to those who he thought could not afford it, and sometimes even supplied the more needy with articles of clothing out of his own meagre store. To him, several other authors, since famous, have owed a very great deal. I am sure that he enjoyed his activity in these kinds; he very likely enjoyed a sense of power in their exercise; but if he had been motivated by the love of power, he would have been of no use to anybody, for kind actions which are performed *in order that* the benefactor may enjoy a sense of power are oppressive and humiliating to the recipient, resented even when accepted and futile or harmful in the end.[24]

In 1922, upon being given the annual *Dial* award of two thousand dollars for *The Waste Land*, Eliot wrote to his patron, the New York lawyer and collector John Quinn, of his regret that Pound was not the recipient: "I feel that he deserves the recognition much more than I do, certainly 'for his services to Letters,' and I feel that I ought to have been made to wait until after he had received this public testimony." Aware of the crucial differences Pound's criticism had made in forming the final version of *The Waste Land*, Eliot stressed his reasons for preserving the original drafts of the poem. "In the manuscript of *The Waste Land* which I am sending you, you will see the evidences of his work, and I think that this manuscript is worth preserving in its present form solely for the reason that it is the only evidence of the difference which his criticism has made to this poem. . . ."

It was through Pound, "my dear and brotherly friend," that Eliot came to know, though not personally, "the man from New York," whose help to Eliot was second only to Pound's. Like Pound, Quinn was another selfless "angel." He both appreciated Eliot's poetry and persuaded American publishers to accept the work of a relatively unknown poet. In terms both of money and other practical matters, Quinn underwrote Eliot's early career. Eliot acknowledged his great debt to Quinn by giving to him the original drafts of *The Waste Land*. Contrary to the charge that Eliot never fully affirmed his debts to Quinn, that he "shamelessly sponged" on him (and on Pound), the existing evidence, as found in the letters quoted, corroborates Eliot's gratitude. "I am quite overwhelmed by your letter, by all that you have done for me, by the results you have effected, and by your endless kindness," Eliot wrote to Quinn on September 21, 1922. "In fact, the greatest pleasure of all that it has given me is the thought that there should be anybody in the world who would take such an immense amount of pains on my behalf. The thought of this will be a permanent satisfaction to me."

These facts regarding Eliot's life between 1915 and 1924 are stated here to show the complexity of the suffering that *The Waste Land* communicates. E. M. Forster concludes that *The Waste Land* "is a poem of horror . . . a personal comment on the universe, as individual and as isolated as Shelley's *Prometheus*." Forster goes on to make these careful distinctions concerning a visionary's experience:

> In respect to the horror that they find in life, men can be divided into three classes. In the first class are those who have not suffered often or acutely; in the second, those who have escaped through horror into a further vision; in the third, those who continue to suffer. Most of us belong to the first class. . . . The mystics, such as Dostoevsky and Blake, belong to the second class. Mr. Eliot, their equal in sensitiveness, distinct from them in fate, belongs to the third.

Eliot, according to Forster, had "seen something terrible." Thus, to know about Eliot's life in the period 1915–24 is to perceive the dimension of that "something terrible" which he could never forget and which is organic to what he renders in *The Waste Land*. This rendering is a complete poetic statement that comes out of the deepest personal and visionary suffering, which Forster explains in this remarkable way:

> I have called that terrible thing Armadillo-Armageddon, and perhaps another personal reminiscence may conclude this very personal approach. It is of a very bright August morning in 1914. I am lying in bed. The milkman below calls as usual with the milk, and through the clink of the handle I hear him say: "We've gone in." This, in its small way, is the kind of experience that must have beset Mr. Eliot, and rooted itself in the soil of his mind.[25]

For Eliot the years between 1915 and 1924 crystallized precisely the distressing incoherence dominant in one's inner life and in the world around one. There was no escape from this disorder in the soul and in the commonwealth, as *The Waste Land* dramatizes with such terror of truth:

> What are the roots that clutch, what branches grow
> Out of this stony rubbish? Son of man,
> You cannot say, or guess, for you know only
> A heap of broken images, where the sun beats,
> And the dead tree gives no shelter, the cricket no relief,
> And the dry stone no sound of water.

The original manuscript of the poem contained an epigraph from Joseph Conrad's *The Heart of Darkness*:

> Did he live his life again in every detail of desire, temptation, and surrender during that supreme moment of complete knowledge? He cried in a whisper at some image, at some vision,—he cried out twice, a cry that was no more than a breath—
> "The horror! the horror!"

Eliot wrote to Pound that the epigraph from Conrad was "the most appropriate" he could find, "and somewhat elucidative." Pound disagreed. He felt that Conrad was not "weighty enough to stand the citation," though he stated, "Do as you like about the Conrad; who am I to grudge him his Laurel crown?" In the final version of *The Waste Land* the quotation was replaced by one from the *Satyricon*.

But the passage from Conrad must not be lost sight of. It has historical significance both in Eliot's poetic vision and in that of the artist who, according to Eliot, "never succeeded in making a work of art"—D. H. Lawrence. (*Sons and Lovers* is dismissed as "that sickly and morally unintelligible book"; and Lawrence's poetry, though "very interesting amateur work, is only notes for poems.") For when one thinks of the years 1915–24, and of the anguish, the futility, the uprootedness, the breakdown, the nihilism that prevailed, there is that other work which, like *The Waste Land*, recaptures the horror of that period. That work is Lawrence's novel *Women in Love* (1920), of which it can also be said, to apply here Leavis' view of *The Waste Land*, that "it would be difficult to imagine a completer transcendence of the individual self, a completer projection of awareness." One can say straight out that these two works, as "dramatic poems," contain a presentation of twentieth-century European civilization. For Eliot these were years of isolation, when

> I sat upon the shore
> Fishing, with the arid plain behind me
> Shall I at least set my lands in order?
> . . . .
> These fragments I have shored against my ruins
> Why then Ile fit you. Hieronymo's mad againe.

For Lawrence, as seen in *Women in Love*, these were years that also embodied the "horror of the completely negative," to apply words which Leavis uses to describe *The Waste Land*. Or as Lawrence himself writes, his words capturing a total view of the horror and the death that these years brought: "The 'world' has no life to offer."

Lawrence no less than Eliot felt the terror described by Forster. No less than Eliot, he too had "seen something terrible." *Women in Love*, which had as one of its early titles *Dies Irae*, was Lawrence's *The Waste Land*. "The book frightens me: it is so end-of-the-world," Lawrence wrote of his novel. His comment is especially relevant, for this novel projects his vision of a period that for him signified that now "We have no history." Horror followed horror for Lawrence during these years. No sooner had he come out of the experiences he relates in *Sons and Lovers*, than the outer world around him started to collapse with the coming of World War I. "The War came like an avalanche," Lady Ottoline Morrell states, "overturning all his hopes, and gradually more and more bewildered him and horrified him to the extreme limit of his ultra-sensitive being."[26]

Unquestionably *The Waste Land* is not the creative equivalent of *Women in Love*. The greatness of this prose creation in all its breadth in exploring human sensibility has the kind of sustained artistic wholeness that, by way of comparison, shows *The Waste Land* to be the fragment that it is. Lawrence, of course, rejected the fixing of "any definite line," and this rejection informs the creative power, the immense range of artistic and human possibilities, of *Women in Love*. Neither in his poetry nor in his verse plays was Eliot as capable of rendering the completeness of human experience as was Lawrence. His was, as *The Waste Land* proves, a fragmented vision, lacking the creative magnitude of *Women in Love*. As such his exploration of human sensibility was limited (or contained), limited like Dante's in comparison with Shakespeare's. (Eliot's championing of Joyce, at Lawrence's expense, is symptomatic of this fragmented view in its disquieting critical context.)

If these qualifying contrasts are further explored, the personal reactions, the attitudes of Lawrence and Eliot to these two works are further revealing, in catching a sense of the seriousness of total commitment on Lawrence's part and the limiting sense of commitment Eliot felt with respect to *The Waste Land*. "I know it is true, the book," Lawrence wrote. "And it is another world, in which I can live apart from this foul world which I will not accept or acknowledge or even enter. The world of my novel is big and fearless—yes, I love it, and love it passionately."[27] How pale are Eliot's afterthoughts regarding *The Waste Land*: "Various critics have done me the honour to interpret the poem in terms of criticism of the world, have considered it, indeed, as an important bit of social criticism. To me it was only the relief of a personal and wholly insignificant grouse against life; it is just a piece of rhythmical grumbling."[28] (A statement like this makes understandable the insipidity of Eliot's essay "Tradition and the Individual Talent," especially his belief that "the more perfect the artist, the more completely separate in him will be the man who suffers and the mind which creates.")

In Lawrence's vision of horror, as in Eliot's, it is death that remains the inescapable condition. "The touch of death is very cold and horrible on us all," Lawrence wrote early in 1915. He saw and felt death everywhere: "The passionate dead act within and with us. . . . Of the dead who really live, whose presence we know, we can hardly speak—we know their hush." Writing to John Middleton Murry in February 1923, upon learning of the death of Murry's wife, Katherine Mansfield, Lawrence discloses exactly how intense and yet inspiring his vision, indeed his experience, has been. "It has been a savage enough pilgrimage these last four years. Perhaps K. has taken the only way for her. We keep faith—I always feel death only strengthens that, the faith between those who have it. . . . I feel like the Sicilians. They always cry for help from their dead. We shall have to cry to ours: we do cry. . . . The dead don't die. They look on and help."[29]

Toward the end of his life Eliot was reappraising his earlier, peculiarly Bloomsbury, views of Lawrence, e.g., that he was "an incompetent writer" who seems "often to write very badly," "the most erratic and uneven . . . writer of our generation"; that the "false prophet" in him destroyed the "true artist"; that Lawrence was, in short, "an impatient and impulsive man . . . a man of fitful and profound insights rather than ratiocinative powers . . . an ignorant man in the sense that he was unaware of how much he did not know." As late as July 1961, in the sixth Convocation Lecture delivered at the University of Leeds, Eliot affirmed the ambivalence of his attitude toward Lawrence. "There is however one contemporary writer," he told his audience, "about whom my mind will, I fear, always waver between dislike, exasperation, boredom, and admiration. That is D. H. Lawrence."[30] And yet Eliot admitted that there were, in his literary criticism through the years, "errors of judgment, and, what I regret more, errors of tone." In light of these later feelings, it should not be hard to understand Eliot's willingness to testify as a witness for the defense during the trial of *Lady Chatterley's Lover* at the Old Bailey in late October and early November 1960.

In organizing the Defence, Michael Rubinstein recollects that he called on Eliot at the offices of Faber and Faber at 3:00 P.M. on September 14, 1960. "I talked to him," he writes, "in his rather cramped office and made notes from our conversation from which his proof of evidence was later prepared by me and submitted to him in draft for amplification or correction." When Counsel was able to decide that Eliot might be called to testify, according to the prearranged order of witnesses and their availability, Rubinstein further explains, "Mr. Eliot came to the Old Bailey and remained for some while (I have no idea how long) on one of the uncomfortable benches outside the Courtroom itself."[31] Eliot was not called. As for the reasons for such a decision by the Defence, it is Eliot himself who gives the best explanation:

> Perhaps the counsel for the defence were well advised not to put me into the witness box, as it might have been rather difficult to make my views clear to a jury by this form of inquisition, and a really wily prosecutor might have tied me up in knots. I felt then, as I feel now, that the prosecution of such a book—a book of most serious and highly moral *intention*—was a deplorable blunder, the consequences of which would be most unfortunate whatever the verdict, and give the book a kind of vogue which would have been abhorrent to the author. But my antipathy to the author remains, on the ground of what seems to me egotism, a strain of cruelty, and a failing in common with Thomas Hardy—the lack of a sense of humour.[32]

Leavis contends that Lawrence is our "last great writer," Eliot our "last great poet." In terms of English language and literature in the twentieth century, this contention has a validity few persons could reject. In a larger sense, Lawrence and Eliot are also our last great religious visionaries and seekers, if not the two most important men of religion of the modern age. Their very meaning must in the end be judged in terms of their work as sacred personal testaments defying a secular world. As a religious seeker, as well as a believer in an elect, each went his own way. Lawrence's way led him back to the "dark gods," to the Etruscan tombs in "the dead city of Cerveteri," when "Everything was in terms of life, of living." Lawrence believed that he had found the true religious quality in the Etruscan time: "ease, naturalness, and an abundance of life, no need to force the mind or the soul in any direction." Eliot's way led him to the Christian Fathers and martyrs, to the belief that "the modern dilemma" could be resolved only through the reemergence of a "Christian Society," for "the Community of Christians," wherein supernatural religion "must aim to lead its followers to something above the human." "We need to know how to see the world as the Christian Fathers saw it," Eliot insists; "and the purpose of reascending to origins is that we should be able to return, with greater spiritual knowledge, to our own situation. We need to recover the sense of religious fear, so that it may be overcome by religious hope."[33]

Their doctrinal attitudes notwithstanding—Lawrence's prehistoric, even nonhuman, spirituality as opposed to Eliot's Christian spirituality—an underlying sympathy of religious vision ultimately unites the two. Like "lilacs out of the dead land," their insights grew out of a common ground of isolation and pain. Eliot's awareness that he "was never anything anywhere" and Lawrence's that he was "torn off from the body of mankind" are central to each writer's comprehension of the age's spiritual homelessness and dispossession, epitomized by Eliot's "broken bundle of mirrors" and by Lawrence's "dance of living death." And yet both had to experience this suffering in order to attain the religious understanding that, as Eliot remarked in his essay "Francis Herbert Bradley," consists of "scepticism and uncynical disillusion."

The formative experience of horror was for Eliot and Lawrence an inclusive one to be suffered continuously, to the end. But, as religious seekers, they were able to resist surrendering to the horror, even as their vision absorbed and reintegrated the horror, so that they could see beyond it. Eliot reintegrated it eschatologically, absolutely, through his "sense of an ending," since, as he wrote in praise of Dante, one had to learn "not to expect from *life* more than it can give or more from *human* beings than they can give; to look to *death* for what life cannot give."[34] (The classicist, Eliot said, lives "without illusions, without day-dreams, without hope, without bitterness, and with an abundant resignation.") Thus, for Eliot the horror was another of the "historical moments of intemporal significance" in the expectation that time and change are redeemed and fulfilled in God. "The end is where we start from," he writes in the last stanza of *Little Gidding*:

> We die with the dying:
> See, they depart, and we go with them.
> We are born with the dead:
> See, they return, and bring us with them.
> The moment of the rose and the moment of the yew-tree
> Are of equal duration. A people without history
> Is not redeemed from time, for history is a pattern
> Of timeless moments.

Lawrence, on the other hand, reintegrated the horror cyclically, affirming the never-ending spatial movement of life in terms of creation and destruction, and of destruction and creation. He steadfastly rejected any theory of "the end of the world" associated with "thought-forms" and with "the dark side of Christianity." He sought for "a new knowledge of Eternity in the flux of time," for that "great imaginative world where we feel free and delighted," where God is neither fate nor redemption, neither "weal" nor "woe," but "only a great imaginative experience."

The final clue to their religious visions must be looked for not in their formative experiences of suffering, but rather in their ability to see through it in the years after 1924. Eliot's religious consciousness culminated in what has been called an attempt "to comprehend devotion rather than clutch religion." It culminated in the meditativeness of *Ash Wednesday*:

> Teach us to care and not to care
> Teach us to sit still

and finally in the "sudden illumination" of *Four Quartets*:

> I said to my soul, be still, and wait without hope
> For hope would be hope for the wrong thing; wait without love
> For love would be love of the wrong thing; there is yet faith
> But the faith and the love and the hope are all in the waiting.
> Wait without thought, for you are not ready for thought:
> So the darkness shall be the light, and the stillness the dancing.

Lawrence's religious consciousness culminated in the spiritual contemplations, the "absolute reverence," of his *Last Poems*, and in his no less prayerful "waiting" for the "stillness":

> Come, holy Silence! reach, reach
> From the presence of God, and envelop us.
> . . . .
> Ah! the holy silence—it is meet!
> It is very fitting! there is nought beside!
> For now we are passing through the gate, stilly,
> in the sacred silence of gates
> in the silence of passing through doors,
> in the great hush of going from this into that,
> in the suspension of wholeness, in the moment of division within the
>   whole!

Nowhere in his writings does Eliot mention Lawrence's *Women in Love*. He saves his "blesses" for James Joyce's *Ulysses*, which, for Eliot, was "the most important expression which the present age has found; it is a book to which we are all indebted and from which none of us can escape . . . it has given me all the surprise, delight, and terror that I can require."[35] (Joyce himself called *The Waste Land* "an unacknowledged parody of *Ulysses*.") Why, one must ask, did the apocalyptic poet of *The Waste Land* ignore the apocalyptic novel *Women in Love*? Whatever the reasons, or rather in spite of them, whether these be dereliction of critical judgment or antipathy against a writer whose "personality" Eliot found demonic and threatening—indeed, overpowering—the fact remains that he was never to "escape" from Lawrence. A second question is perhaps also in order here: Was Eliot, toward the end of his life, preparing to recognize, preparing at long last to admit, a debt to the novelist from whom he had surely gained as much as from Dante, Jules Laforgue, Baudelaire, and Pound, but to whom he had grudgingly refused to pay tribute for reasons that must constitute a future chapter in English literary history—and recantation for

> . . . all that you have done, and been; the shame
> Of motives late revealed, and the awareness
> Of things ill done and done to others' harm.

Answers to these questions belong to the realm of biographical speculation.

It is to each man's art, to his texts, that one must return for the "impersonal" truth. When, therefore, the concluding paragraphs from the chapter "Snowed Up" in *Women in Love* and several stanzas from "What the Thunder Said" in *The Waste Land*, quoted below, are placed side by side, it is possible to see two great masters of the English language at work. And it is possible, too, to extricate from the texts answers to questions of affinities and of debts, precisely those questions that Eliot must have been asking himself, especially after 1934, when his destructive indictment of Lawrence appeared in *After Strange Gods*. (There was no second printing of this book; it went out of print on August 3, 1944, expressly by Eliot's own wish: "I regarded the tone of much of its contents as much too violent and sweeping: some of my assertions I should qualify and some I should withdraw."[36])

What Lawrence's *Women in Love* and Eliot's *The Waste Land* reveal more than anything else is an apocalyptic moment in each writer's vision, at its source, in its beginnings, so to speak. It is as modern apocalyptists that Lawrence and Eliot respond to and render here a civilization in crisis. Each must, to repeat, absorb the moment of apocalypse before he can proceed. It is all a part of a soul's supreme struggle, as well as recovery, in the "divine darkness." At this point of his religious vision each writer experiences historical crisis, experiences the historical negation. As evidenced in the passages that follow, *Women in Love* and *The Waste Land* are experiences of and in negation, when the historical consciousness and the personal consciousness converge toward *blick ins chaos*.

WOMEN IN LOVE

He [Gerald Crich] slithered down a sheer snowslope. That frightened him. He had no Alpenstock, nothing. But having come safely to rest, he began to walk on, in the illuminated darkness. It was as cold as sleep. He was between two ridges, in a hollow. So he swerved. Should he climb the other ridge, or wander along the hollow? How frail the thread of his being was stretched! He would perhaps climb the ridge. The snow was firm and simple. He went along. There was something standing out of the snow. He approached, with dimmest curiosity.

It was a half-buried Crucifix, a little Christ under a little sloping hood, at the top of a pole. He sheered away. Somebody was going to murder him. He had a great dread of being murdered. But it was a dread which stood outside him, like his own ghost. Yet why be afraid? It was bound to happen. To be murdered! He looked round in terror at the snow, the rocking, pale, shadowy slopes of the upper world. This was the moment when the death was uplifted, and there was no escape.

Lord Jesus, was it then bound to be—Lord Jesus! He could feel the blow descending, he knew he was murdered. Vaguely wandering forward, his hands lifted as if to feel what would happen, he was waiting for the moment when he would stop, when it would cease. It was not over yet.

He had come to the hollow basing of snow, surrounded by sheer slopes and precipices, out of which rose a track that brought one to the top of the mountain. But he wandered unconsciously, till he slipped and fell down, and as soon as he fell something broke in his soul, and immediately he went to sleep.

THE WASTE LAND

Who is the third who walks always beside you?
When I count, there are only you and I together
But when I look ahead up the white road
There is always another one walking beside you
Gliding wrapt in a brown mantle, hooded
I do not know whether a man or a woman
—But who is that on the other side of you?

The Reverent Discipline

What is that sound high in the air
Murmur of maternal lamentation
Who are those hooded hordes swarming
Over endless plains, stumbling in cracked earth
Ringed by the flat horizon only

What is the city over the mountains
Cracks and reforms and bursts in the violent area
Falling towers
Jerusalem   Athens   Alexandria
Vienna   London
Unreal.
. . . .

In this decayed hole among the mountains
In the faint moonlight, the grass is singing
Over the tumbled graves, about the chapel
There is the empty chapel, only the wind's home.

7

E. M. Forster and D. H. Lawrence: Their Views on Education

There is a teacher for boys at school, but we, the poets, are teachers of men.
—ARISTOPHANES

ᔐ

In his admirable study, *Freedom and Authority in Education*, G. H. Bantock reminds us that "artists are so much better guides than the professional educators."[1] Two artists who testify eloquently to the truth of this observation are E. M. Forster and D. H. Lawrence. Although no high-sounding treatises on educational topics appear among the works of either writer, both disclose an intense and steadfast concern with the meaning, the needs, and the trends of education in the twentieth century. Poetic insights, not scientific statements, give expression to their attitudes. If Forster and Lawrence do not diagnose educational issues in strictly academic or scientific terms, they nevertheless dramatize in their writings the tensions emanating from an educational technocracy that inevitably emerges in a universe that Lawrence describes as:

> The world of reason and science, the moon, a dead lump of earth, the sun, so much gas with spots: this is the dry and sterile little world the abstracted mind inhabits.[2]

Forster's educational aims might best be termed corrective; that is, his main aspiration is to correct a bad condition, a "muddle," and to emphasize "the belief that man is, or rather can be, rational, and that the mind can and should guide the passions towards civilization." Accordingly, Forster feels, education should serve as a kind of antidote against the realization that "all life is perhaps a knot, a tangle, a blemish in the eternal smoothness." At the same time it should assist human beings, who are "fighting to reach one another," to ameliorate the human condition by cultivating the "generous impulses" —"tolerance, good temper and sympathy." In this respect, Forster's educational thinking, echoing Cardinal Newman's concept of a humane and liberal education enhanced by "freedom, equitableness, moderation and wisdom," focuses on the idea of enlightening a world grown "uncomfortable," "miserable and indignant," "disordered"— a world in which violence "is, alas! the ultimate reality on this earth, but it does not always get to the front." His total vision is rooted in his recognition of the periods in life when a goblin walks "quietly over the universe from end to end" and the intervals when force and violence are absent. It is these intervals which produce "civilization." In the effort to preserve this civilization and to resist and to contain "the armies of darkness," Forster sees in education perhaps his most effective instrument.

When we turn to Lawrence's educational preoccupations, on the other hand, we shift from a lyrical orientation to a prophetic awareness. Not only is there a difference of vision, but also a difference of energy in Lawrence's response: the reticent strain is replaced by the passional; the controlled tone gives way to prophetic song, which, as Forster tells us in *Aspects of the Novel*, "is bound to give us a shock." This shock is endemic to the sense of mission in the prophet's desire "to root out, and to pull down, and to destroy, and to throw down, to build, and to plant."[3] The fact is that Lawrence seeks not to change a particular condition but to cure it. *"Cure the pain, don't give the poetry."*[4] This is Lawrence's advice to Forster, and no words better indicate his variance from Forster in their approaches to education. To the question "What has gone wrong?" Lawrence replies:

> Our education from the start has *taught* us a certain range of emotions, what to feel and what not to feel, and how to feel the feelings we allow ourselves to feel.[5]

Hence to solve the problems of education, of civilization, it is first necessary, he insists, to redefine concepts, to achieve new meaning:

> Education means leading out the individual nature in each man and woman to its true fullness. You can't do that by stimulating the mind. To pump education into the mind is fatal. That which sublimates from the dynamic consciousness into the mental consciousness has alone any value.[6]

Strongly autobiographical factors pervading and influencing Forster's and Lawrence's treatment of education cannot go unnoticed. Forster's dislike of the public school system, for instance, goes back to his own years as a day boy at Tonbridge School (1893–97). The unhappiness that he associates with public school life is reflected in *The Longest Journey*, mainly in the character of Rickie Elliott, who "crept cold and friendless and ignorant out of a great school, and praying as a highest favour that he might be left alone." Sawston School, as depicted in this novel, epitomizes Forster's explicit criticisms of a "beneficent machine" which inflicts physical pain ("We can just bear it when it comes by accident or for our good . . . except at school"[7]) and which shouts, "Organize," "Systematize," "Fill up every minute," "Induce *esprit de corps*." Its loneliness and its bullying are especially intolerable:

> An apple-pie bed is nothing; pinches, kicks, boxed ears, twisted arms, pulled hair, ghosts at night, inky books, befouled photographs, amount to very little by themselves. But let them be united and continuous, and you have a hell that no grown-up devil can devise.[8]

In particular the unkind treatment of day boys is poignantly rendered in an episode in which Mr. Pembroke ends an assembly of students with the singing of the recently composed school anthem (the words of which Forster appropriated from his own school song, *Carmen Tonbridgiense*). Having given the "right intonation" to the lines "Perish each sluggard! Let it not be said / That Sawston such within her halls hath bred," he notes sarcastically to his young audience: "You're as tuneful as—as day boys!"

Upon the death in 1887 of his great-aunt, Marianne Thornton, Forster received a legacy of eight thousand pounds, which later enabled him to study at Cambridge and thereafter to travel for a few years. In 1897 he entered King's College, where he took Second Class Honours in the Classical Tripos in 1900, Second Class Honours in the History Tripos in 1901, and an M.A. in 1910. He was elected a Fellow in 1927, during which year he was Clark Lecturer at Trinity College. Cambridge, Frank Swinnerton has remarked, was "the most wonderful thing that ever happened to him."[9] Forster leaves no doubt concerning the veracity of this statement. Somehow his vision of education always reverts to the "magic years" re-created in the first part of *The Longest Journey*—to the Cambridge which "had taken and soothed him, warmed him, had laughed at him a little, saying that he must not be so tragic yet awhile, for his boyhood had been but a dusty corridor that led to the spacious halls of youth"; which had taught him "that the public school is not infinite and eternal." Above all, it brought him into contact with tutors and resident fellows "who treated with rare dexterity the products that came up from the public schools," teaching them to respect a man's efforts "not so much to acquire knowledge as to dispel a little of the darkness by which we and all our acquisitions are surrounded."

Studying classics under the tutelage of Nathaniel Wedd, Forster, like Mr. Lucas in his short story "The Road from Colonus," "caught the fever of Hellenism." In its beginnings his Hellenism must likewise be linked with that of his close friend, the don G. Lowes Dickinson. To understand the following passage from Dickinson's *The Greek View of Life* (first published in 1896) is to become aware of the impact that the ideas of this book had on Forster and that helped eventually to shape a generous part of his educational outlook as well as the idiom of his art:

> Harmony, in a word, was the end they [the Greeks] pursued, harmony of the soul with the body and of the body with its environment; and it is this that distinguishes their ethical ideal from that which in later times has insisted on the fundamental antagonism of the inner to the outer life, and made the perfection of the spirit depend on the mortification of the flesh.[10]

Doubtless, Hellenism of this kind inheres in Forster's belief that we must sustain at all costs those values in education which he objectifies in generosity and kindness; in warmth, "without which all education is senseless"; in respect for the "delicate imaginings" and the "relaxed will."

However, it must be emphasized that Forster's early Hellenism—the simple and idealizing sort as embodied in the Panlike figure of a Stephen Wonham—changed through the years, so that when we move from *Howards End* (1910) to *Pharos and Pharillon* (1923), we become increasingly aware of a Hellenism that "implies a recognition and acceptance of complexity," as one critic puts it.[11] In some ways Forster's Introduction to William Golding's *Lord of the Flies* underscores the evolvement of this less romantic and less idealized Hellenism as it reacts against the Hellenism "so drubbed into us at school" and "against the tyranny of Classicism—Pericles and Aspasia and Themistocles and all those bores," to quote from his essay on C. P. Cavafy.[12] Forster's admiration of Piggy, though it evokes the Hellenism preached by Dickinson, cannot fail to show a demanding sense of historical reality:

> He knows that nothing is safe, nothing is neatly ticketed. He is the human spirit, aware that the universe has not been created for his convenience, and doing the best he can. And as long as he survives there is some semblance of intelligence.[13]

As is well known, Lawrence did not attend a famous public school. A "scholarship boy" with a County Council stipend of fifteen pounds a year, he studied at Nottingham High School (1898–1901), a "purely bourgeois school," he later observed. In his early work he does not say very much about the school, and unlike Forster, he re-creates no memorable schoolboy experiences.

It is evident that although Lawrence received excellent instruction at the High School, he was unhappy there. With the exception of George H. Neville, a close friend during the Eastwood and the Croydon years, he was not intimate with the other boys. Besides, the daily trips from Eastwood to Nottingham must have proved exhausting for a frail youth. Neville recalls this period in these words:

> Then followed our High School days together, starting from home shortly after seven o'clock in the morning and returning just before seven at night with always a pile of lessons to do later. . . . Even in those days, Lawrence had that little, troublesome, hacking cough that used to bring his left hand so sharply to his mouth—a cough and an action that he never lost.[14]

Lawrence was not destined to attend Cambridge and "to see up there," in Forster's phraseology, "what you couldn't see before and mayn't ever see again." After leaving Nottingham High School, he served for a few years as a pupil-teacher and as an uncertified teacher in Ilkeston and in Eastwood. In 1906 he enrolled in the "normal course" at Nottingham University College, obtaining a "teacher's certificate" in 1908. For Lawrence these were not "magic years": "College gave me nothing, even nothing to do—I had a damnable time there, bitter so deep with disappointment that I have lost forever my sincere boyish reverence for men in position."[15] If Cambridge constituted for Forster a recovery of values, Nottingham University College led to Lawrence's loss of reverence. Chapter XV in *The Rainbow*, "The Bitterness of Ecstasy," crystallizes this bleak fact. Yet his disillusionment must not be construed as a criticism of the standard of instruction he received. We need only read Jessie Chambers' memoir to appreciate both the intellectual depth and the cultural vitality of Lawrence's educational background.

At first Lawrence was enthusiastic about his studies. In *The Rainbow* the early response of Ursula Brangwen to Nottingham University College (a re-creation of Lawrence's own) is of the same quality as Forster's response to Cambridge: "She scribbled her notes with joy, almost with ecstasy"; the black-gowned lecturer was a "priest"; the college was "holy ground":

> Her soul flew straight back to the medieval times, when the monks of God held the learning of men and imparted it within the shadow of religion. In this spirit she entered college. . . . Here, within the great, whispering sea-shell, that whispered all the while with reminiscence of

all the centuries, time faded away, and the echo of knowledge filled the timeless silence.[16]

But perhaps because Ursula had too much reverence did "a harsh and ugly disillusion" overcome her as she gradually became aware that college was

> a second-hand dealer's shop, and one bought an equipment for an examination. This was only a little side-show to the factories of the town.... This was no religious retreat, no perception of pure learning ... it was a sham store, a sham warehouse, with a single motive of material gain, and no productivity.... And barrenly, the professors in their gowns offered commercial commodity that could be turned to good account in the examination room; ready-made stuff too, and not really worth the money it was intended to fetch; which they all knew.[17]

Lawrence's words in "Education of the People (1918) that "The choice is between system and system, mechanical or organic,"[18] return us to their dramatic context in *The Rainbow,* to the laboratory scene that finds the physics instructor, Dr. Frankstone, talking to Ursula. That we should not find a special mystery in life, that life should consist in merely a complexity of physical and chemical activities already known to science—these are the bare facts of existence which the good instructor imparts to a dismayed Ursula. Is it any wonder, then, that Lawrence condemns an educational system for surrendering to a "process of derangement" and "sheer mechanical materialism" which force "all human energy into a competition of mere acquisition"?

Whereas Lawrence's reactions to education developed in the midst of working-class life in the English Midlands, with its great nonconformist tradition, Forster's reactions were shaped by the gentlemanly middle class, with its public schools and its ancient universities:

> I belong to the fag-end of Victorian liberalism [Forster writes], and can look back to an age whose challenges were moderate in their tone, and the cloud on whose horizon was no bigger than a man's hand. In many ways it was an admirable age. It practised benevolence and philanthropy, was humane and intellectually curious, upheld free speech, had little colour-prejudice, believed that individuals are and should be different, and entertained a sincere faith in the progress of society.[19]

Forster's bent, furthermore, belongs to the Cambridge-Bloomsbury ethos: the Cambridge which produced Rupert Brooke, a King's man and "a young Apollo, golden-haired," pitiably unready for the crisis of 1914, and as Lawrence wrote, "a Greek god under a Japanese sunshade, reading poetry in his pyjamas, at Grantchester—at Grantchester upon the lawn where the river goes";[20] the Bloomsbury which in time of crisis, as Professor Johnstone has commented, "remembered boating parties and summer days when all the good things of life seemed to have coalesced."[21] Forster's attitude was shaped by a "civilization" typified by intelligence and by humane liberalism, but also by a softness that, to be properly understood, is best defined by Lionel Trilling's statement that Forster "is content with the human possibility and content with its limitations."[22] Forster says of himself:

> The education I received in those far-off and fantastic days made me soft and I am very glad it did, for I have seen plenty of hardness since, and I know it does not even pay.[23]

Again and again he returns to these Cambridge years to reexperience that exhilaration which in *Howards End* touches even the harried and squalid life of Leonard Bast:

> Perhaps the keenest happiness he had ever known was during a railway-journey to Cambridge, where a decent-mannered undergraduate had spoken to him.[24]

It is this Cambridge which Forster wants to be preserved:

> Cambridge still keeps her antique shape. No idealistic millionaire has yet raped her.... O leave her where she is and as she is, leave her to her peculiar destiny.[25]

In all likelihood Lawrence's criticisms of Forster, who spent a few days with the Lawrences in Greatham, Sussex, in February 1915, could be interpreted as an arraignment of the Cambridge ethos, of Cambridge education, of the Cambridge "type" ("Through good report and ill such men work on, following the light of truth as they see it; able to be sceptical without being paralysed,"[26] etc., if one wants to persevere with Dickinson's sonorous description). "There is something real in him," Lawrence wrote of Forster, but "the grip has gone out of him," "the man is dying of inanition"; "he tries to dodge himself—the sight is pitiful":

> Foster is not poor, but he is bound hand and foot bodily. Why? *Because he does not believe that any beauty or any divine utterance is any good any more.* Why? Because the world is suffering from bonds, and birds of foul desire which gnaw its liver. Forster knows, as every thinking man now knows, that all his thinking and his passion for humanity amounts to no more than trying to soothe with poetry a man raging with pain which can be cured.... Will all the poetry in the world satisfy the manhood of Forster, when Forster knows that his implicit manhood is to be satisfied by nothing but immediate physical action.[27]

("Perhaps my character did not pass the test of the Sussex Downs ...," Forster ruefully observed fifteen years later.[28])

What must remain obvious is that Forster's views of education are anchored in the pre-1914 Cambridge, when, to quote John Maynard Keynes, "We were living in the specious present, nor had begun to play the game of consequences."[29] Indeed, Forster's peculiar shying away from "the game of consequences," so clearly detected by Lawrence, is visible in his fictional characters like Philip Herriton and Rickie Elliot. Always, Forster speaks for the survival of institutions, for a leisurely process of education, for a Cambridge that molded his humanity and his fairmindedness (he was one of the very few in 1930 to defend Lawrence's artistic genius against the "obituary-mongers," as H. J. Massingham aptly termed them[30]), but that in other ways contributed to his "general lack of vitality."

Still, the frequently cited "perils" to and "limitations" of Forster's liberalism and humanism cannot enfeeble either the integrity or the maturity of his vision.[31] The so-called softness of his attitude, furthermore, should not be confused with the decomposition portrayed in the character of Sir Michael in the story "The Point of It," who, having "mistaken self-criticism for self-discipline . . . had muffled in himself and others the keen, heroic edge." Education can produce persons like Mr. Pembroke, the organizer whose "plump finger was in every pie"; Cecil Vyse, who plays "tricks on people, on the most sacred form of life that he can find"; and even Tibby Schlegel, who though "he had lost his peevishness [and] . . . hid his indifference to people . . . had not grown more human." These characters stand for the shabbiest aspects of education, in which a public school accent remains constant, and remind us of what can go wrong. These, Forster is saying, represent tendencies and dangers which to ignore is to surrender to a debility synonymous with irresponsibility, a "sign of decay," so to speak. But that a choice is possible; that there are positive values of education which can sustain life against the Pembrokes and the Vyses; that there exist persons like Stewart Ansell, who has a "glimpse of comradeship," and a humane schoolmaster like Mr. Jackson, with whom students "remained friends . . . throughout their lives"—these are redeeming alternatives which need to be affirmed.

Cantabrigian society was revealed to Lawrence during a visit arranged by Bertrand Russell in March 1915. But Lawrence's reaction, particularly to the Cambridge "type," was far from agreeable. He felt that "Fabianism, Socialism, Cambridgism and advancedism of all sorts" were "like poison," "a nasty form of dry rot on the human species."[32] When we remember the Cambridge of this period—and the constellation formed by Russell, Keynes, Lytton Strachey, Leonard Woolf, G. E. Moore, J. M. E. McTaggart and Dickinson—when, as

Keynes declares, "Cambridge rationalism and cynicism [were] . . . at their height," with victory resting exclusively "with those who could speak with the greatest appearance of clear, undoubting conviction and could best use the accents of infallibility,"[33] it is not in the least difficult to understand why Lawrence could not approve of Cambridge "civilization." To Lawrence, Cambridge constituted "one of the crises of my life": "It . . . made me very black and down. I cannot bear its smell of rottenness, marsh-stagnancy. I get a melancholic malaria. How can so sick people rise up? They must die first."[34] His words underscore an intuitive response to and rejection of a "civilization," of an education (with its "accents of infallibility"), which Lawrence equated with a temper devoid of reverence and with a cast of mind that Keynes himself, on later reflection, censured for its thinness and superficiality: "I can see us as water-spiders, gracefully skimming, as light and reasonable as air, the surface of the stream without any contact at all with the eddies and currents underneath."[35]

Lawrence's reactions to the social order of his time resulted from intense personal involvement. "For him . . . the *whole* process had been lived," Raymond Williams rightly insists, "and he was the more conscious of the general failure, and thus of the general character of the system."[36] Indeed the Lawrence of 1915 had already served as a schoolmaster at the Davidson Road School at Croydon (1908–11); had, as is re-created in Ursula Brangwen's teaching experiences, come face to face with "the man's world"; had suffered the weariness, the grim realities of a "hard, malevolent system"—the days of "battle and hate and violence," "the sums, the grammar, the quarterly examinations, the registers." That he had been a teacher who had also experienced "the passion of instruction" is apparent to anyone who reads the school chapters in *The Rainbow* and in *Women in Love* or ponders lines like the following from one of Lawrence's school poems, "The Best of School":

> This morning, sweet it is
> To feel the lads' looks light on me,
> Then back in a swift, bright flutter to work:
> Each one darting away with his
> Discovery, like birds that steal and flee.
> Touch after touch I feel on me
> As their eyes glance at me for the grain
> Of rigours they taste delightedly.
>
> . . . .
>
> I feel them cling and cleave to me
> As vines going eagerly up; they twine

> My life with other leaves, my time
> Is hidden in theirs, their thrills are mine.[37]

To repeat: "The *whole* process had been lived." Surely it is in the pain and the truth of these words that we find Lawrence's remarkable grasp of the innermost issues of education, of a system in which

> The first great task was to reduce sixty children to one state of mind, or being. This state must be produced automatically, through the will of the teacher, and the will of the whole school authority, imposed upon the will of the children—

as well as a system in which the teacher was often

> liable to attack from either side at any minute, or from both at once, for the authorities would listen to the complaints of parents, and both would turn round on the mongrel authority, the teacher.[38]

It was precisely with such intelligence and such experience that Lawrence, in March 1915, confronted Cambridge "civilization." Yet Russell and Keynes deliberately aimed their conversation *"at Lawrence,"* and Professor G. E. Moore, who sat next to Lawrence in Hall, "found nothing to say to him!"[39]

Unfortunately, the lie that Lawrence was "an ignorant man in the sense that he was unaware of how much he did not know," as T. S. Eliot believed,[40] and as the literary establishment has maintained for years and years, still gains in circulation. J. I. M. Stewart in his *Eight Modern Writers* perpetuates the same dreary old lie, the same misrepresentation concerning Lawrence's working-class background, with this assertion: "But humble birth, plebian manners, and irregular education can never be other than disadvantageous circumstances, and Lawrence seldom forgot they had been his."[41] (Stewart, no doubt, feels it his task here to remind his readers that Lawrence had not seen "the light of Cambridge"—or, worse, had never been in attendance at Christ Church, Oxford!)

Any comparison of the educational views of these two writers cannot avoid the fact that in Forster the vision is mediate, which is to say, the result of delicate interweavings of and tensions between "actions and meditations." In shunning the extremes of "contending assertions," Forster allows a necessary place for the mind. Indeed, the habit of intellect and a predisposition toward introspection are basic elements of his art. He could not repudiate them without seriously menacing his regard for the continuity of life. "I am speaking like an intellectual, but the intellectual . . . is more in touch with humanity than is the cultural scientist. . . ."[42] He considers the intellect useful, for it can become a light penetrating the emotions. Ultimately, therefore, Forster salutes the intellect because of its potentialities in the scheme of things. It is with especial approbation that he quotes from his Cambridge teacher Oscar Browning, whose words at the same time define an important aspect of Forster's own attitude:

> "I have been drawn to think rather of the tens who have failed than of the units who have succeeded, and of the ore that lies buried in our social strata rather than of the bright coins that circulate from hand to hand. If a field of coal or of some other material lies unworked and unused, yet it is always there. It may be kept for some future age when its wealth will be more needed, and posterity will bless the prescience and parsimony of their ancestors who refrained from using it. But the human mind is born and lives and perishes. If it is unenlightened, it passes away into its native darkness."[43]

Indeed, the endurance of "belief in the human race," Forster says, is directly related to the need for exploring and cultivating available human resources before they pass into extinction.

In contrast, Lawrence's vision is immediate. There can be neither respect for nor compromise with a way of life in a "state of funk": "For all strife between things old is pure death."[44] Tensions in Lawrence are not relieved in a perilous balance between action and meditation, between the passion and the prose. "The last three thousand years of mankind," he declares, "have been an excursion into ideals, bodilessness, and tragedy, and now the excursion is over."[45] To Lawrence the problems of education require instant, total action, inasmuch as man has fallen "from spontaneous reality into dead or material reality." "All our education should be a guarding against this fall."[46] The reorientation of education, he says, must begin with the premise that "mental consciousness" is not a goal but a cul-de-sac. By no means, however, does Lawrence discredit the use of the mind, for it can be "a great indicator and instrument"; but "the mind as author and director of life is anathema." Conventional learning for Lawrence becomes "intellectual understanding" rather than "living understanding," and it is too often attached to some imposed *"standard* of instruction," to "regulation patterns," to "moral bullying":

> There should be no effort made to teach children to think, to have ideas. Only to lift them and urge them into dynamic activity. The voice of dynamic sound, not the words of understanding. Damn understanding. Gestures, and touch, and expression of the face, not theory. Never have ideas about children—and never have ideas *for* them.[47]

Again and again he exposes the inconsistencies of educators who "talk of free-expression, and . . . proceed to force all natures into ideal and aesthetic expression." Hence, he feels that a disbalance has led to children's degenerating "into physical cloddishness or mechanical affectation or fluttered nervousness," into "the nervous, twisting, wistful, pathetic, centreless children we are cursed with." The cure, as Lawrence envisions it, must entail a severe deintellectualization, the restoration of a "non-ideal, passional" element to human relations, and the sparking of an "emotional *rapport*," a certain fearlessness and openness in dealing with the young: a display of "clean, fierce rage" coexistent with "all love and tenderness"; a willingness, as well, to *"leave the child alone*, in his own soul." Were one to choose an epigraph for Lawrence's educational views, these words from William Blake's "The Proverbs of Hell" would be appropriate: "The tigers of wrath are wiser than the horses of instruction"—a sentiment which finds its parallel in Lawrence's declaration in *Etruscan Places* that "what one wants is the actual vital touch. I don't want to be 'instructed'; nor do many other people."[48]

As critics of education, Forster and Lawrence together yield a completeness and a sympathy of vision arising from a direct concern with the tasks and the responsibilities of the system. A primary impulse behind their reactions is a distress with increasing mechanization in the educational process, epitomized by a belief that "school is [or should be] the world in miniature." But that education can be something more than the external world, that it is "a sacred business"—these, Forster and Lawrence agree, are irrevocable truths. It is their belief that education has a greater destiny than is generally allowed it which unites them. "Educators . . . will be the priests of life," writes Lawrence, "deep in the wisdom of life. They will be the life-priests of the new era."[49] For Forster education means "the help of good will plus culture and intelligence" and "the good sense that persists in the human organism even when it is heated by passion." For Lawrence education means the attainment of "a perfect correspondence between the spontaneous, yearning, impulsive-desirous soul and the automatic *mind* which runs on little wheels of ideas." Forster protests against a system leading to "the tragedy of ugliness." Forster speaks to the heart; Lawrence speaks to the "man alive." Both voice warnings that cannot be ignored, except at our peril.

Although they approach educational problems from often opposing positions, they stand together in their reverence for an underlying mystery in human life that defies what Forster speaks of as the "implacable offensive of Science" and what Lawrence terms "an outward system of nullity," when, "Living as we do entirely in the light of the mental consciousness, we think everything is as we see it and as we think it."[50] It is awareness of the need to renew contact with the values beneath standardized instruction that is an impelling force in the educational attitudes of these two writers. In order to renew this contact Forster and Lawrence do not flinch from asking basic questions of our civilization: "What is education all about? What is it doing? Does anybody know?"[51] If not always or not fully satisfactory, their answers are indispensable to the debate that continues, and must continue, if modern education is to mean more than just enabling us to get jam today and—more jam tomorrow.

8

Ideologues of Mediocrity

And no observation of the decline in academic confidence can leave out of account the effect of a tendency which of recent years has established itself within the academic community, among teachers as well as students, the ideological trend which rejects and seeks to discredit the very concept of mind.

—LIONEL TRILLING, *Mind in the Modern World*

∽

"Standards" and "discipline" are not popular words nowadays. To judge by the present cultural climate, they are very much in neglect, as much absent as chaos and barbarism are present. Even sadder than that they are absent is that among intellectuals themselves, and in institutions traditionally the upholders of culture, "standards" and "discipline" are often treated as "irrelevant" words as useless and dead as, say, "metaphysics." When, therefore, one thinks of these two words, one must immediately think of the intellectuals' betrayal of them; one must think, that is, of all the grim connotations of Julien Benda's phrase, *la trahison des clercs*. Hence, more than ever one needs to recall the special meanings of these words in their cultural contexts. They require the courage of our attention now, even at this midnight hour of a "dissolving society," the dissolution being made evident in everything around us: in tastelessness, in insensibility, in ugliness, in what the British poet Roy Fuller has (too politely) called the "new nihilism."

There are those, we know only too well, who would dismiss the validity of this indictment of the cultural state. Any glance at the (monolithic) liberal press should be telling enough. Such a glance returns us to the need for definitions of the words "standards" and "discipline," our liberal spokesmen being their most flagrant violators. And it is perhaps best to start with standards, always the arch-enemy of the meretricious. Standards are what are resistant to the transient and the merely experimental. They *stand* for what is immutable, the proved and the transcendent; for what is of ultimate and permanent worth; for what gives form and order to value and vision, to judgment and principle, faithful in promise yet cognizant of limits. Standards are the discriminating formulation of truths that measure man against the greater truths of eternity. They are a bulwark against formlessness and falseness; inevitably they are rooted in hierarchy—a hierarchy of merit. Discipline, on the other hand, embodies the informing presence and application of standards. It is their next of kin, so to speak, the active transmitter of achieved forms, the supreme refiner and refinement of the order of life and thought, of the conditions of man and his civilization. It is a consubstantiating rigor operating between the defined and the undefined. Thus it is the power of exertion that refines what it defines. Discipline in its best and absolute sense is an antidote against extremes, for it must work in terms of limits.

These definitions are called for here not because there is need for some exercise in words, but rather because a small but important spirit of protest needs to be heard. Not all intellectuals, after all, are dupes of the liberal line. Not all intellectuals have betrayed either their cultural charge or their understanding of what values make for organic cultural continuity. There is yet a remnant that survives and warns of dire cultural consequences emerging from the erosion of standards and of discipline. The situation, as they try to make us aware, is rotting. Their warnings, like the two words they revere, are equally unpopular. But they are both diagnostic and necessary, and it is one of the infrequent good fortunes of this bleak phase of culture, and specifically American culture (though the whole of Western culture fits the diagnosis), that voices of a remnant can still be heard, in spite of the oracles of the liberal press and in spite of the liberal coterie-world dictating American taste and style (a bizarre style to boot).

John W. Aldridge in his *In the Country of the Young** and Robert Brustein in his *Revolution As Theatre: Notes on the New Radical Style*† are representative of those few intellectuals (others are Jacques Barzun, Daniel Boorstin, Oscar Handlin, and Sidney Hook) willing to question the way things have been going in the United States, especially during the 1960's. Aldridge and Brustein are distinguished educators and writers, the former a professor of English at the University of Michigan, the latter Dean of the Yale Drama School. Both are in touch with the young and are eminently aware of what is happening in higher education—and both are profoundly disturbed by what is happening. In advancing what Aldridge calls

---

* New York, 1970.
† New York, 1971.

"the case of critical skepticism" and in speaking up for standards and for discipline, they are certainly not going to receive accolades from "the current armies of self-righteous puberty and dissident studentism," to quote Aldridge's description. Likewise, the response of intellectuals themselves to those who, in Brustein's words, believe that "it is not just the cult of amateurism that is beginning to breach the walls of professionalism, but that the professionals are throwing over ladders and helping their assailants over the top," will not be enthusiastic, to say the least. For the concept of professionalism, as Brustein iterates, is under assault today not only by the young, but also by professionals who have succumbed to the "radical style." This bastard alliance of the clenched fist and the clenched mind can lead but to disintegration in the cultural sense that Aldridge discloses in the first quotation below as well as in the attendant educational problems that Brustein points to in the second quotation:

> ... their [youth's] actions derive not from a coherent ideology or even a coherent emotional attitude but more nearly resemble a series of random gestures enacted in a climate of metaphysical confusion. One notices, for example, that although they are passionate about causes and issues—especially as these relate to the quantitative, material problems of society—they are strangely indifferent to questions of quality, as well as to the process of intellectual discrimination and analysis by which qualitative judgments are made. (10–11)

> Education is used not for the acquisition of knowledge or for the development of the critical temperament, but rather for experiments in life styles, political manipulation and social engineering, while men of reason founder in a miasma of doubts, uncertainties, and petty surrenders. (6)

To some readers these observations will sound strange, even heretical, accustomed as they are to equate the "thoughts" of a Jerry Rubin and a Herbert Marcuse (or any other "infantile leftist"* who may come along) with wisdom. And we are reminded once more that demands for standards and discipline can hardly have the priority of "revolution for the hell of it" or the excitement of the "guerrilla theatre" in Chicago and elsewhere. But, then, exponents of standards and discipline in a century that has increasingly enshrined

---

*I owe this phrase to Oscar Handlin's "The Vulnerability of the American University," *Encounter* (July 1970), 22–30. His description of the "turtle-necked worshippers" of the young must be quoted, such is its insight into the American professoriate of the recent decade: "They see love in the eyes of the Visigoths who storm through their offices. To act otherwise would jeopardize the gains so recently made, the pleasures so little enjoyed. Accommodate! Better to yield a little here, give away a little there. It can't be called rape so long as the victim yells loudly enough that he likes it."

mediocrity have not fared well. One thinks of the derisive smiles on the faces of some professionals (and of the young, when and if they can recognize the names) when, for example, T. E. Hulme, Irving Babbitt, and T. S. Eliot are mentioned. (Interestingly, students are initially responsive to Eliot until their professors "tell it like it is" regarding Eliot's élitist "sociological" views!) For the professionals it would be particularly worthwhile to be persuaded to read these books by Aldridge and Brustein. Odd that they should need any persuasion at all, but dispassionate habits of scholarship do not seem to go with "the new radical style" (not even at Harvard), and ours is a time when intellectual work in higher education is surrendering to what Brustein calls a "monochromatic amateurism in which everybody has opinions, few have facts, nobody has an idea."

Brustein's book, since it centers on particular conditions in contemporary education, must be read in the light of Aldridge's, which examines some of the cultural conditions that give rise to cultural and intellectual breakdown. Aldridge's book has the added benefit of going to the roots of our cultural malaise, insofar as it is concerned with the ultimate question of values, cultural and personal. His preoccupation is with standards of culture and with their problematic role in contemporary American culture and, consequently, with their impingement on the manners, morals, and social concerns of the young. The essentially metaphysical artifacts of contemporary American culture are the object of his attention. Undoubtedly this is an old-fashioned approach, yet it is one that takes courage these days. With an honesty and a courage that few professionals dare assert and fewer dare practice, Aldridge expresses a minority view of culture; but it is the view of the minority that alone speaks for and transmits the cultural values that a collectivized society abhors and invariably submits to the reductionist processes of democratization and standardization. Although he is primarily concerned with today's "country of the young," he treats the whole American cultural scene since World War II. The power that the young wield today, Aldridge believes, is pervasive—"programming our minds to work within alternatives which *they* have invented, and forcing us to conform to *their* authoritarianism and bureaucratic plans for the renovation of the modern world." Throughout his book Aldridge is hardhitting, and his tone is uncompromising but refreshing at a time when the "radical style" remains largely unchallenged.

For some of the major causes of the sad condition of American culture today Aldridge fixes his attention on the war and postwar years: "We had brought no resources with us out of the past, no norms or precedents of conduct, no tradition of amenities or graces, luxuries or even comforts." As a result, what has prevailed is a lack of qualitative attitudes; "life in America became frozen—apparently for good—at the level of utilitarian existence." This reliance on the utilitarian, on "social engineering," he stresses, has led to a life style antagonistic to aesthetic and civilizing standards. Growing affluence and permissiveness, moreover, have overwhelmed any sense of standards or discipline, without which American society, in both its inner and outer semblances, has steadily given way to the ugly, the amorphous, the expedient. The emerging American cultural ethos in the years after 1945 was based essentially on a materialistic dream world. Such an ethos could hardly be anything less than specious, as parents and children saw their problems in terms of mechanical and technical solutions, "through legislative and programmatic action and the acquisition of higher incomes, bigger houses, better cars, and more goods and services."

The speciousness of such an ethos is characterized by a romanticism and a naturalism that lead to loss of control and that Babbitt equates with "a merely temperamental insurrection against convention." This is another way of saying that the tragic vision was gradually replaced by the absurd on the one hand and the progressivist on the other. (The disappearance of the religious element in life has its relevance here. "We introduce into human things," T. E. Hulme observed, "the *Perfection* that properly belongs only to the divine, and thus confuse both human and divine things by not clearly separating them.") It is precisely the speciousness of the contemporary American cultural ethos that Aldridge focuses on in this observation:

> They [parents] would scarcely be in a position to instruct their children in the unpopular but necessary wisdom that man is innately weak and imperfect, that human progress is slow and may even be illusory, that political systems cannot always be depended upon to cure the world's ills, that measures cannot always be taken, and that sometimes the most serious problems a man may face are those that exist between himself and his courage or conscience. . . . And because they did not, their children have grown up with apparently no awareness of, or tolerance for, human limitation, and no understanding of the obstacles that may stand in the way of the changes they are so anxious to bring about in our society. They think today in morally purist and naive terms perhaps because they have never experienced the impurities of the human condition, as those impurities might have been represented to them by their parents. (56–57)

Aldridge's small book could have been subtitled "Notes on the Shaping of the American Character." His conclusions are nothing less than sobering in conveying what is currently very much a malaise in the country, particularly among young people. Since the end of World War II it has been downhill all the way, it would appear, as far as "the humane life . . . the life of feeling and the life of thought" are concerned. Not only a debased aesthetic sensibility, but also a corrosive anti-intellectualism—a detestation of cultural standards and discipline—have characterized American attitudes, formed as they have been by quantitative concerns. Young people today, Aldridge shows, as the inheritors of such an ethos, may be "passionate about causes and issues—especially as these relate to the quantitative, material problems of society—[but] they are strangely indifferent to questions of quality, as well as to the processes of intellectual discrimination and analysis by which qualitative judgments are made." Hence, too, one can understand the reasons for all the fuss over legislative and administrative actions, cultural surrogates that do not require a discriminating, critical faculty, and the reasons for the absence of the standards and the discipline that give any permanence of cultural value to existence beyond animality. D. H. Lawrence summarized this problem nearly a half-century ago: "The tortures of psychic starvation which civilized people proceed to suffer, once they have solved the bread-and-butter problem of alimentation, will not bear thought."

That Aldridge is right to observe that the young, lacking the discriminating quality, "have very little sense of personal life and an overwhelming sense of collective life" is not to be denied when one thinks of their public actions in the last few years. A boring sameness of looks, dress, speech, movement, and taste is pervasive, defying, with sanctimonious arrogance (and a delusive piety, which the young seem to have assumed as their special moral province), finely civilized conduct and, even more, all sense of *pudeur*. Indeed, what Aldridge makes us see is that the young often lack a sense of moderation, that it is extremism that dictates their attitudes and gestures. If not ignorance, then it is surely irreverence that, as Aldridge suggests, dominates them. At the root of this irreverence, he points out, is the long-recognized fact (hardly ever admitted by parents, teachers, or leaders, except in *sotto voce*) that the "children of affluence and permissiveness" have never had to contend at any point of their lives with "the irritant of necessity" in their physical environment or with "the irritant of guilt" in their emotional environment.

And we are reminded once again of the absence of the tragic sense of life and why simplistic formulas for changing the world are so abundant; why the body and not the soul is the sole standard of measure today (even, alas, in the great conservatrix of tradition, the Roman Catholic Church, to judge by some of the demands and the actions of some of the clergy). Relativism, subjectivism, inordinate self-righteousness, naïve idealism, pragmatism, and perhaps worst of all sentimentalism have been steadily removing the tragic principle to the extreme that, as Aldridge reminds us, the modern inheritors of such an ethos illustrate in their lives and actions. Dostoevsky's prophetic passage in his Epilogue to *Crime and Punishment* has much truth for our time, such are the frightening parallels of Raskolnikov's vision of evil in this novel of 1866 and the enactment of that vision in its peculiarly American contexts as seen by Aldridge in *In the Country of the Young*:

> But never [Dostoevsky writes] had people considered themselves as wise and as strong in their pursuit of truth as these plague-ridden people. Never had they thought their decisions, their scientific conclusions, and their moral convictions so unshakeable or so incontestably right. Whole villages, whole towns and peoples became infected and went mad. They were in a state of constant alarm. They did not understand each other. Each of them believed that the truth only resided in him, and was miserable looking at the others, and smote his breast, wept, and wrung his hands. . . . In the cities the tocsin was sounded all day long: they called everyone together, but no one knew who had summoned them or why they had been summoned, and all were in a state of great alarm.

What, in the present cultural drift and portent, becomes especially distressing to consider is the future of humanity. Where are we going? This is a question that Aldridge asks. And the question becomes desperate when one finds that the traditional upholders of cultural standards and discipline—e.g., the Church and our educational institutions—are no longer either respected or respectable, the latter trait being of their own making, as these institutions have consistently surrendered to and placated the young in the guise of an "orthodoxy of enlightenment" (to apply here a phrase of the British critic F. R. Leavis). Professionals by training, experience, skill, and achievement, who should know the values of standards and of discipline, have willingly allowed these values to crumble. This is the major point made by Brustein, and in it he validates the warnings voiced by Aldridge. By abrogating their responsibilities, professionals capitulate to amateurs and to "the cult of amateurism" that prevails in the educational field: ". . . the system of hierarchy—so infuriating to a democratic society, yet so essential to its survival—begins to break down, and men cannot hold firmly to their judgments, values, and standards."

A society succumbing to the attitudes—the malaise—that Aldridge analyzes must inevitably come to the precarious conditions that Brustein describes as an educational crisis. Educators themselves must share the shame (along, to be sure, with parents and administrators— the deans and their deaneries that constitute such a top-heavy and expensive segment of education); they must share the blame for this crisis by continually sacrificing standards and discipline, which comprise the foundation of any culture and which Irving Babbitt, writing on "President Eliot and American Education" in *Forum* (January 1929), scrutinized in the way that brought him so much animosity, particularly from his teaching colleagues:

> At the bottom of the whole educational debate, as I have been trying to show, is the debate between a religious-humanistic and a utilitarian-sentimental philosophy. This opposition, involving as it does first principles, is not subject to compromise or mediation. Those who attempt such mediation are not humanists but Laodiceans. Many persons who deem themselves moderate are in fact only muddled.

(Since the time of President Eliot educators have become even more muddled, more vacillating, more timid, flabby, cowardly, and deserving of the fate of trimmers: *Sed quia tepidus es, et nec frigidus, nec calidus, incipiam te evomere ex ore meo* [Rev. 3:16].)

The problems besetting American education today are neither new nor immediate; they have been developing in scope and gravity during the last fifty years. Of course, the main problem on the American cultural scene has always been that of mediocrity, and it is an enforced, one could say regulated *and* plotted, mediocrity that has been gradually allowed to strangle American education in its qualitative sense. How to protect educational quality has been a battle of standards and discipline fought by the remnant during this long period. But the battle has been a losing one. Mediocrities in the profession have made for more mediocrity—a compulsive mediocrity. For a long time public school education was the battleground of the quantitative versus the qualitative. In the late 1940's and early 1950's, when the problem of education—what kind of education—had reached its climactic point, a few brave minds managed to focus on the problems and in some ways to encourage debate. Mortimer Smith's *And Madly Teach* (1949), Bernard Iddings Bell's *Crisis in Education* (1949), Gordon Keith Chalmers' *The Republic and the Person* (1952), Albert Lynd's *Quackery in the Public Schools* (1953), Arthur E. Bestor's *Educational Wastelands* (1953), and Russell Kirk's *Academic Freedom* (1955) did much to underline a minority view. The results of their efforts were another matter. For, to judge by today's young people, who are the products of the subsequent educational process in the public schools, something went wrong. Educational standards and discipline have steadily given way to nominalism and "progressivism." Indeed, what is happening at the present time in the American university is the culmination of a destructive process that, initially occurring in public school education, weakens the entire educational process until it may become inoperative.

The "pernicious utilitarianism," the egalitarian ethos (it is, in essence, a malaise) that Brustein sees destroying the very concept of university education—

> The idea [he writes]—so central to scholarship—that there is an inherited body of knowledge to be transmitted from one generation to another—loses favor because it puts the student in an unacceptably subordinate position, with the result that the learning process gives way to a general free-for-all in which one man's opinion is as good as another's. (91)

—is the legacy from the past, the epitomizing adulterative philosophy of a theoretical and applied mediocrity. The Hellenic concept of excellence, always central to the humanities, has been replaced by the specious programmatic measurement of the social sciences, an ultimate result of what in earlier years was termed the "democracy of the subjects." It is precisely this inherited "democracy" that is now being felt in the breaking down, or the proletarianization, of a hierarchy of merit and a hierarchy of values. Neither standards nor discipline, as the foundation of any hierarchy in its richest cultural sense (spiritual, intellectual, humane), can be tolerated by the proletarian attitude.

To capture and devastate American university education is the final stage of the attack on American cultural life itself. (Indeed, the bureaucratization of the university structure, in terms of an endless creation of student-faculty committees, as Aldridge and Brustein indicate, is symptomatic of what the educational ideologues have been conspiring to do all along, with the schools of education being perhaps the most notorious breeding ground for the disdainers of standards and discipline and for the canon of collectivized attitude.) In this respect it is not hard to trace the collectivist (mob!) tendencies of the young and their failure "to develop the perspective of otherness," in Aldridge's phrase. How, surely, can the young be otherwise than what they are, as Aldridge shows in the following passage, when their formative setting has all along been a dehumanized group consciousness:

> In fact, they must be the first generation in history to see itself from the outset as a herd rather than as an aggregate of private persons who happen to be the same age. Consequently instead of feeling separate and aloof from the masses and contemptuous of the concerns of the masses,

they identify psychologically with the masses, and so quite naturally conceive of the world's salvation in collective terms. (48–49)

And how, it will be asked, has all this been allowed to happen? A utilitarian-sentimental society no doubt hates to admit to failure and thus makes for the "irresponsibles." Indeed, modern American society, far from being a "great society," is thoroughly irresponsible. It is a society that, as both Aldridge and Brustein depict, has consistently allowed the ideologues of mediocrity to shake foundations and to destroy "ancient edifices." In the end the origin of this cultural destructiveness remains as it was thirty years ago, when Lewis Mumford exposed it in *The New Republic* (April 29, 1940): "the corruption of liberalism." The ideologues, then and today, are precisely those "pragmatic liberals" whose doctrines, rooted in Voltaire and Rousseau, "grew up in the eighteenth century out of a rather adolescent pride in the scientific conquest of nature and the invention of power machinery." Unlike "ideal liberalism," the principles of which belong to Western and Christian humanist tradition and have as their strength universality and historical continuity, "pragmatic Liberalism," Mumford maintains, is preoccupied with the machinery of life. And he continues in terms that help crystallize the kind of unstable thinking that has led to the cultural collapse that, in its most immediate offshoots, *In the Country of the Young* and *Revolution As Theatre* dramatically render:

> It was characteristic of this creed to overemphasize the part played by political and mechanical invention, by abstract thought and political contrivance. And accordingly it minimized the role of instinct, tradition, history; it was unaware of the dark forces of the unconscious, it was suspicious of either the capricious or the incalculable, for the only universe it could rule was a measured one, and the only type of human character it could understand was the utilitarian one. That there are modes of insight into man and into the cosmos which science does not possess, the liberal did not suspect; he took for granted that the emotional and spiritual life of man needs no other foundation than the rational, utilitarian activities associated with the getting of a living. Hence, finally, liberalism's progressive neglect of the fields of esthetics, ethics and religion.

The disintegration of standards and discipline in contemporary American culture reflects the irrevocable influences of the ideology of a disintegrated liberalism. It remains that cultural disintegration and educational mediocrity go hand-in-hand, that they are the result of the pragmatic liberal's unclear and often confused, as well as sentimental, awareness of ethical ideas, borrowing, as Mumford notes, "here a scrap of Kant or Bentham or again a dash of Machiavelli, pacifist Quakers one moment and quaking Nietzscheans the next." The worst characteristic of pragmatic liberalism is its lack of firm ethical judgments, hence its sentimentality and its immaturity of vision. Hence, too, esthetic concerns, moral discipline, the habit of contemplation and of diligent evaluation are to the pragmatic liberal "mere spiritual gymnastics." Their panaceas are based on simplistic external solutions: the machine, measurement, legislative actions, "methods of production"—"the mere surface of living." Pragmatic liberals have failed "to deal with the first and last things," as Mumford asserts: to deal with internal human experience in its corruption, its evil, its irrationalism, or even its fact of death. Yet the ideology of this pragmatic liberalism has been able, year by year and decade by decade, to displace cultural standards and discipline to the point of chaos and anarchy that Aldridge and Brustein bemoan. Its Marxist illusions, its dialectic, are precisely what have led to the failure found everywhere in American cultural life, particularly in its most vulnerable area—education. Mumford thus notes the central weakness of pragmatic liberalism: "Its color-blindness to moral values is its most serious weakness today; hence it cannot distinguish between barbarism and civilization."

Now the extent and the gravity of this barbarism are what the books by Aldridge and Brustein are all about. In a deep sense the ascendant barbarism is tantamount to the subordination of humane culture in a proletarian victory. Undoubtedly Aldridge and Brustein will be dubbed Luddites by pragmatic liberals. Nevertheless the need for resisting barbarism, technological, sexual, or institutional, for resisting a leveling process, is an acute one. "A general impoverishment of life —that is the threat," observes Leavis, "that, ironically, accompanies the technological advance and the rising standard of living; and we are all involved." This same impoverishment today poses for American—for Western—civilization, and for education, the university especially, the great dilemma. Can the university, to paraphrase Brustein's words, continue to rest on the rock on which it is founded—the search for truth—and not the implementation of ideology? Is it possible to preserve the private side of university professionalism that, like the private side of man, is not so easily adapted to social and political purposes? Are the universities, to cite here Aldridge's words, to be "primarily rebel encampments, forums of political debate, or media for the distribution of pamphlets ... [or] institutions whose first function is to train intelligence and preserve cultural standards"?

These are paramount questions in an age of the diminution of cultural standards and of a hostility to discipline. And the responses to

these questions so far are not encouraging. The ideologues of pragmatic liberalism, for all their naïveté and delusion, have been doing
their job with a vengeance. In marshaling support for their so-called
reforms these ideologues have even insisted that the young today, reflecting the "positive" cultural transformations evolving during the
last fifty years, are more sensitive, more committed, more aware, more
involved, and more intelligent than preceding generations. Aldridge's
and Brustein's books puncture this myth. They also call to mind the
need for what Mumford speaks of as "a recrystallization of the positive values of life, and an understanding of the basic issues of good
and evil, of power and form, of force and grace, in the actual world."
They remind one of the need for the reaffirmation of standards and
the reassertion of discipline, without which American culture will
continue to drift from barbarism to nightmare.

It may well be that the present battle in and for the university is
one that will decide whether what might be called the *meta*-barbaric
world to which the liberal ideologues are leading us will be the final
reality or not. Will America's educators have the guts to fight off the
drift into this *meta*-barbaric world? This is the overarching question
that Aldridge and Brustein are asking, "in fear and trembling" so to
speak. Developments in the 1960's, unfortunately, have hastened the
drift, even as the pusillanimity of the American professoriate has led
to a surrender of responsibility. Indeed, this pusillanimity is one of
the great scandals of the age. It would be as foolhardy as it is unreal
to paint an optimistic picture of American education today. The situation is as dismal as it was back in the early 1930's, when T. S. Eliot
wrote in *The Criterion*:

> We seem nowadays to be committed to the task of giving some sort of
> education to everybody. Education is a training of the mind and of the
> sensibility, an intellectual and an emotional discipline. In a society in
> which this discipline is neglected, a society which uses words instead
> of thoughts and feelings, one may expect any sort of religious, moral,
> social and political aberration, and eventual decomposition or petrifi-
> cation. And we seem to have little to hope from the official representa-
> tives of education.

The modern situation, in confirming Eliot's note of hopelessness, remains generally unchanged; it has even worsened. *Meta*-barbaric man
now dances and fornicates in the streets, and the remnant, protesting
but "very small and feeble," waits to be called.

PART TWO

Art and Morality

Writers do not have to be professors of morals, but they do have to express the human condition. And nothing concerns human life so essentially, for every man at every moment, as good and evil. When literature becomes deliberately indifferent to the opposition of good and evil it betrays its function and forfeits all claim to excellence.

—SIMONE WEIL

9

Toward a Metaphysics of Art

In vain do our modern positivists go about slashing the flowers of immortality and metaphysics; the selfsame flowers spring up under their passing feet.

—M. C. D'ARCY

ॐ

I

The Roman Catholic philosopher Étienne Gilson defines metaphysics as "the science of existence beyond the sciences of the ways of existing." He goes on to say that metaphysics requires its own principle of explanation; that it is "distinct from the other sciences"; that, in fact, it "dominates them because its object is the problem without which there would be no other problems."[1] This definition is not unusual, or revolutionary. But it is eminently concise, almost a miracle of brevity in a domain of philosophy that for the past twenty-five hundred years has variously preoccupied such luminaries as Parmenides, Plato, and Aristotle in the classical period; Saint Thomas Aquinas and William of Ockham in the Middle Ages; Descartes, Locke, Hume, and Kant in the Age of Enlightenment; and Josiah Royce, F. H. Bradley, and Henri Bergson in the modern period.

Gilson's words are especially relevant to the condition of "man in the modern age," for one of the central problems of modern man has been the "conceptual conflicts" emanating from his attempts to find "a way of speaking which will enable us to express the true nature of the universe."[2] Modern literature, more than theology or philosophy, has dramatized the intensity of these conflicts, whether they relate to general problems of "the true nature of the world," or to particular "problems of the human conscience in our time." Gilson's words help to define metaphysics and to characterize the tenor and the aspirations of some of the major works of literature since 1859, the year in which Charles Darwin's *The Origin of Species* marked a turning-point in Western civilization, as the voices of a new world began to be heard.

Modern literature has consistently demonstrated astonishingly imaginative genius in responding to metaphysical problems—to a view of the universe and of man's place in it, his relationship to what lies beyond it, to the transcending and transcendent. In short, modern literature has reflected a view "concerned ... with the *ultimate* nature of the *whole* of Reality, with the *first* cause, the *final* explanation, the *complete* account."[3] When art ignores or rejects a concern with "final things" and an awareness of the "accursed questions," to use a favorite nineteenth-century Russian phrase, it diminishes itself and its communicated value. Literature is but life in imagination and life in dialogue; and life as a total human experience comprises the seen and the unseen.

Boris Pasternak declares that art "always meditates on death and thus always creates life. All great, genuine art resembles and continues the Revelation of St. John."[4] But he is not necessarily Christianizing the creative conception. Rather, he is seeking to establish the highest function of the creative act by focusing on literature as revelation, the apocalyptic portrayal of existential and experiential truths, even as he points to the artist's burden of vision, which is seminally metaphysical in inspiration.

Pasternak believes that "great, genuine art" is "revelation." This is true of the works of some of the greatest artists through the centuries—Aeschylus, Sophocles, Virgil, Dante, Milton, Goethe, Dostoevsky, Tolstoy, D. H. Lawrence, T. S. Eliot. Great artists are rarely metaphysically neutral. Nor can they be neutral if their revelation is to be an authentic "gift to the future," as Albert Camus would have it. This does not mean that a great artist dramatizes a particular doctrine, that he gives us "philosophy in action," as it has been phrased. A great artist does not "state." He enables us to see and to understand by giving us a presentation of human reality in a dramatically organized manner. His presentation, ordered aesthetically, is what constitutes the criterion of true art as opposed to false art. Nevertheless, his presentation, to be fully effective, to achieve a shared vision and a sympathy of response, must give creative expression to the problematic aspects of "the true nature of the world." It is in a conjoined seeing and articulating that the meaning of metaphysics in art assumes inestimable value—and principle. "Your form is your meaning," to recall Joyce Cary, "and your meaning dictates the form."[5]

In his essay on William Faulkner's *The Sound and the Fury*, Jean-Paul Sartre declares that "the technique of the novel always refers us back to the metaphysics of the artist." He suggests also that before evaluating his technique, the critic must define the artist's metaphysics.[6] This statement may sound paradoxical, coming from one who asserts unreservedly that the God who once "spoke to us . . . now is silent, [and] all that we touch now is his corpse." Still, his statement is not surprising or incongruous, for it brings out one aspect of the struggle of modern man to comprehend "the universe of human subjectivity" in the face of the "silence of the transcendent."

If Sartre replaces "religious need" with "creative freedom" and "the sincerity which aims at itself in present immanence," he accentuates at the same time the abiding place of metaphysics in human experience. He accepts the need for a metaphysics of values, or as Sartre says: "Life has no meaning *a priori* . . . it is up to you to give it a meaning, and value is nothing else than this meaning which you choose."[7] Sartre's words here help to explain his demand that one should be "faithful to the earth" and show a defiant integrity in the face of human tragedy and absurdity. His words also help to explain much of modern literature, for if there is one constant among great modern artists, it is the place of values in direct relation to human experience.

Daily life, observes E. M. Forster, is "composed of two lives—the life in time and the life by values. . . . And what the story does is to narrate the life in time. And what the entire novel does—if it is a good novel—is to include the life by values as well."[8] By values we mean man's quest for a way of life, for an ethic that, though aware of and grounded in the everyday world, must also transcend it. Value is what embodies the full range of man's attempt to weigh the worth of himself and of others and to judge the importance of those qualities affecting the purpose and the direction of life. Value gives significance to life; it is what saves life from nothingness. It is the means for perception and for discrimination which must clarify and assess meaning.

Literature is the re-creation of the life of man and the life of values in a ceaseless struggle for synthesis. For some persons, as for Sartre, this struggle is one in which "man exists, encounters himself, surges up in the world—and defines himself afterwards." For others this struggle is the struggle for grace, for salvation when "old things are passed away; behold, all things are becom[ing] new."[9] The first is a metaphysics of self-value, often occurring, as Martin Buber notes, during "the historic hour through which the world is passing"—the "eclipse of the light of heaven, [the] eclipse of God." The second is a metaphysics of faith, when "something is taking place between heaven and earth" and when one "submit[s] himself to the effective reality of the transcendence."[10] Literature can render for us the experience of these two metaphysics, within and beyond the world, in a finite act of courage and in the infinite mystery of faith. When Sartre speaks of the need to define the artist's metaphysics before evaluating his technique, he is pointing to the artist's inner experience of the metaphysics of his encounter with values and his reaction to the encounter. The artist's technique is the aesthetic, sensitizing expression of the encounter and the epiphanizing of the metaphysics.

Sartre's statement concerning the relationship between technique and metaphysics brings to mind Jacques Maritain's emphasis on the relationship between art and poetry: Art as "the creative or producing, work-making activity of the human mind," Poetry as "the intercommunication between the inner beings of things and the inner being of the human Self which is a kind of divination."[11] In this "age of criticism" Sartre has pointed out the essential task of a critic. No matter how hard he tries to assess literature objectively, scientifically, no matter how diligently he wants to be concerned with "the black marks on the page," the art, a critic can hardly deny, though he may ignore, a novelist's metaphysics, the poetry. Clearly he cannot deny the indwelling essences either in the artist's creative process or in the subject matter of his art which relate to metaphysics. An artist cannot write in a void, and a work of art, to have any human pertinence, to be more than an autonomous and autotelic object, can escape neither the pain and the wonder of existence nor the problematic nature of existence. Indeed, the beginning and the end of life are the major preoccupations rendered in art. They constitute the passions and the visions which give birth to the creative art and which ultimately inhere in literary achievement.

II

Undoubtedly it is dangerous, as Eliseo Vivas warns, for a critic to look on literature as social, political, historical, moralistic, or theological documents. Art, he maintains, "reveals"; "it tears the veil" and discloses meanings and values. "But at the moment of revelation if the transaction is successful, we make no comment. We behold. The comment, the digestion of the meanings and values, their critical, which is to say, their transitive appreciation or assessment, comes later." The product of the creative imagination is not a patchwork of bare facts or a recitation of causal relationships within a suprahistorical or supraobjective framework. Creative art transcends, must transcend, the particularities, the esotericisms, the specialisms of social prognosis or diagnosis. Obviously, Vivas' belief that "poetry uniquely reveals a world which is self-sufficient" can help a critic avoid equating literature with epistemological and nonimaginative writings.[12]

It should be said that Vivas, carefully avoiding the dead-ends of formalism, allows for critical "comment" when one is evaluating a work of art. Without this comment, this "disciplined speculation," as G. Wilson Knight calls it, the full understanding and meaning of art remain incomplete. If, with Vivas, we recognize the power of art at the "moment of [our] rapt and intransitive grasp of it," we must also recognize the long-range need to contemplate and to comment on its meaning in sequence. In this connection, we must be brave enough to return to "the old criticism," recalling us, as George Steiner has shown, "to the remembrance of our great lineage," to "the old definitions, the long-founded categories of meaning," to a sense of love and admiration, to something philosophic in range and temper— above all, to the belief that the great writers "have been men impelled either to acquiescence or rebellion by the mystery of God" and that "there is at the heart of the creative process a religious paradox."[13]

A great work of art has more than one life and, to be great and universally sensitive, must continue its "grasp" in the unconscious and conscious, in the realm of aesthetic wonder and in that of thought, which ensues. Whether a work of art consists in a structure of meanings, forms, sounds, or ideas, it has, as Denis de Rougemont declares, the transcending function of "the bribing of the attention, the magnetizing of the sensibility, the fascinating of the meditation." A work of art, he concludes, is *"a calculated trap for meditation"* which "must orient existence toward something which transcends sounds and forms, or the words so assembled." What de Rougemont is getting at here is that the experience of and the reaction to the aesthetic act require an extension in time, a spatial enlargement, if the artist's work is to be more than a tour de force. In fact, de Rougemont insists that "criticism ought to be at one and the same time *technical*, on the one hand, and on the other metaphysical or ethical— which is to say, in the end, *theological*."[14]

His statement takes us directly back to Sartre. It stresses the ever-emerging fact that an artist's metaphysics, in its relation to technique, requires a special critical approach, a meditation. Meditative criticism seeks to achieve a breakthrough to the life beneath and beyond the artist's craft and to reach into the recesses of his cosmos which are not immediately definable "at the moment of the presentation," when a work holds us, to employ Vivas' image, "as a snake is said to hold the bird, quiveringly alive and so intent on the fascinating eyes that it does not know it is in rigid panic." The aesthetic experience in form exerts spontaneous power, at the instant moment. The technical expertise of the artist aids in securing this power and in tightening this grasp.

But this power must wane and the grasp must weaken as the forces of cognition begin their work. Precisely at this point, however, meditative criticism can penetrate the ironies, the tensions, the paradoxes, the controlling metaphor, the thematic structure, and the symbolic action with which technique is identified. In his breakthrough to the ground of the artist's metaphysics, the meditative critic helps to release a part of the artist's energy of vision, to approach closer to the center of the creative impulse, that part of his vision which attains organic artistic wholeness through a "rage for order."

Criticism that is at once technical and metaphysical and that is willing to define an artist's metaphysics before evaluating his technique is not solely meditative. It is "sapiential," as Thomas Merton would have it, approaching what can be said to be the first estate of criticism: *sapientia*, or wisdom. To quote Merton's observation:

> It [*sapientia*] goes beyond *scientia*, which is systematic knowledge, beyond *intellectus*, which is intuitive understanding. It has deeper penetration and wider range than either of these. It embraces the entire scope of man's life and all its meaning. It grasps the ultimate truths to which science and intuition only point. In ancient terms, it seeks the "ultimate causes," not simply efficient causes which make things happen, but the ultimate reasons why they happen and the ultimate values which their happening reveals to us.[15]

Both imaginative writing and criticism, Merton adds, "provide a privileged area for wisdom in the modern world." His words heighten the importance, if not the challenge, of Sartre's observation. A critic who sees through technique to metaphysics, through form to insight, thus seeks the "ultimate causes." He helps capture that "wisdom" in the writer which has meaning beyond aesthetic fact. Such a critic is not merely meditative or sapiential; he is a critic who encourages great art.[16]

We must ask ourselves, too, what constitutes art and what makes an artist great. Greatness implies a certain excellence and an ultimate. This ultimate coexists with intense and piercing vision, a peculiar seeing that includes not only the here but the beyond. The totality and the steadfastness of an artist's vision, if we read Sartre correctly, cannot be limited to the immediate, but must be followed to the hidden sources of his experience, which in time becomes converted, hypostatized, into expression, when, to use Erich Auerbach's phrase, "style is vision." The metaphysics embodies the rage and produces in the artist a fermentation, which, if the creative imagination's experience is as genuine as it is intense, spills over the frontier of the unconscious into the conscious. "The experience itself," I. A. Richards tells us, "the tide of impulses sweeping through the mind, is the source and the sanction of the words."[17]

The creative act is a direct response to "ultimate concerns" which vibrate in the metaphysics. These words give a picture of the artist as a seer, one who may see more than he should see: who sees startlingly, sees ultimately. A large part of this seeing is closely tied to the artist's metaphysics. His metaphysics epitomizes a crisis, that is, a decisive stage in the artist's confrontation of universal questions, as well as a peril, when the larger dangers and tensions, subsequent to the confrontation, crystallize the power of the metaphysics in the communication of creative insight.

An artist lives and creates in a state of crisis and in a condition of peril. He sees and expresses the semblances of the outer life, and he suffers the desperate secrets and questionings of the inner life. As a result of his metaphysical journeys and discoveries, his responsiveness and sensitivity to metaphysic-crisis and metaphysic-peril, his vision has explosive clarity and miraculous power—power that is even theurgic in its reaches. An artist is both a creator, *homo faber*, and a traveler, *homo viator*. His art, his craft, arises out of his vision: a vision which travels back to the metaphysics, to its crisis and peril, in time and outside time, in history and outside history.

For a critic to appraise the technique (the style) and not the metaphysics (the vision) is to miss completely the ceaseless rhythm of life in the flesh and in the spirit, to miss, in a word, the totality of being and becoming—*physis* and *meta-physis*; beginning and end, *archē* and *telos*. A great artist, in short, experiences a total existence, which, with all its known and unknown potencies, surges in his inspiration. To maintain the need of defining the artist's metaphysics before evaluating his technique is to guard the creative act against the reductive process. It is to maintain, provided we are willing to take the necessary "leap" with Gabriel Marcel, and provided we are to gauge the immeasurable significance of metaphysics,

> that in so far as we are not things, in so far as we refuse to allow ourselves to be reduced to the condition of things, we belong to an entirely different world-dimension, and it is this dimension which can and must be called supratemporal.[18]

To relate the artist to metaphysics is to see his form in an integral relationship to the "search for identity," the "search for meaning," the "search for transcendence," the "search for values." Metaphysics, as such, presupposes the principle of reality and the ultimate constituents of the universe. It also points out an inevitable interpenetration of the human and the divine. The key word here is search, for metaphysics entails the quintessential need to find the supratemporal values of existence. A metaphysical writer renders these values in his art. He dramatizes the generic interworkings of search and values, moving from existential and experimental modes of being, from a secular dynamics, to the conceptual effort to think about and to express what transcends him.

Here I use the word *effort* in the context of William Blake's supposition that "if the doors of perception were cleansed everything would appear to man as it is, infinite."[19] It is this infinite that tantalizes artists who are at the same time religious seekers—religious in the metaphysical sense I have been noting, in the sense of perceiving a "religious need" and a search. Many modern writers disclose in their art exactly this process. Their technique is the measure and the medium of the desideratum to comprehend and approach the transcendent. The technique is the artist creating in the finite world, whereas the metaphysics is the transcendent and infinite world in which the artist contemplates. The creative imagination achieves discipline in the finite but is nourished and inspired by the infinite. This metaphysical world defies circumspection, computerization, to use a popular word these days, and in this defiance we view a metaphysics of art, in short, the miracle of artistic imagination.

More than anything else, a metaphysics of art (in a synthesis of form and insight), hinting at a sacred view of man, helps to save man from his thingness, from his meaningless existence in a mechanical universe, identifiable on the basis of its technic authenticity or, as Alain Robbe-Grillet believes, its "contamination," its reduction to a " 'black box' of cybernetics, where only the relations of input and output matter."[20] A metaphysics of art leads to some experience of the transcendent, whereas its technique instances the evaluative dimensions and nuances of the experience. In the end, the experience of the transcendent embodies for the artist the burden of vision; the technique of his art embodies the proof of the vision, "the instrument of a recognition." The first is tantamount to a more or less mystic revelation; the second is a mode of apprehension and external evidence, the visibilizing determinants of the process of creation and the discovery "of ourselves and of our origins."[21]

"Of ourselves and of our origins": these words crystallize what for the metaphysical artist must be a longing for universals and what, in the function of criticism, purveys the need to define a writer's metaphysics. Art which gets away from ourselves and from origins gets away from metaphysics—what in a theological context Paul Tillich speaks of as man's ultimate concern for the ground and abyss of all finite being and the receptory of meaning, or what in an artistic context D. H. Lawrence speaks of as the necessity for men "to know how to go out and meet one another upon the third ground, the holy ground." It gets away from language that is memory and metaphor, from "the experience of the race." A demanding truth of transcendence, once separated from self and origin, must disintegrate into antivision and antilife.

By a metaphysics of art we also mean a metaphysics that is an implicit part of the creative vision and, hence, a natural and animistic facet of an artist's "seeing" which occupies its ordered place in "a presentation of human reality in a dramatically organized manner," to use Vivas' words. A metaphysics of art must not be confused with the superimposition of "concept" or "doctrine" or "idea." The metaphysics is to be seen as working within the artist's creative imagination, the point at which the artist is immersed in a refining activity, during which he achieves a discipline of aesthetic direction in his view of and dramatization of human experience in relation to a metaphysics of values.

A metaphysics of art is a metaphysics belonging to the internal world of the creative imagination, and not to the outer world of a philosophy or an ideology, in which, to quote Martin Heidegger, "metaphysics thinks about beings as beings."[22] These words summarize a ratiocinative process antithetical to a metaphysics of art, which does not "think" its way but, altering Heidegger's words, renders beings as beings and values as values. "Never trust the artist," D. H. Lawrence emphasizes. "Trust the tale. The proper function of a critic is to save the tale from the artist who created it."[23] A metaphysics of art does not begin with some metaphysical proposition, for this would distort "the meaning of the creative act" and transform a work of art into a prosaic document or an abstract treatise.

III

In a metaphysics of art we discern the artist's insights into the life of man, into the human condition. Even as it portrays life, art also functions as a dramatic medium for attaining and then transmitting understanding. An artist fuses in his imaginative achievement the

193

creative and the metaphysical, that is, a rendering of the human scene which complements the eternal. What an artist sees constitutes a response to the metaphysics of the human situation. How he expresses what he sees constitutes his technique. His function, Theodore M. Greene observes, is "not only to delight his fellows with new decorative patterns but to revitalize them, resensitize them, rehumanize them, respiritualize them, within the limits of possibility of his times and culture."[24]

A metaphysics of art is closely tied to the multidimensional patterns of life that the artist first re-creates. The greatness of his art is in the end judged by the integrity and the purity of his transcendent vision. For it is in the power of his creativeness that an artist's success must be measured and that tells us to what extent the act of his art has won over "the heaviness of the 'world' " and achieved "the liberation" that Nicolas Berdyaev speaks about.[25] The failure of art results from an artist's "adaptation" to the "world," specifically to some peculiar part of a metaphysics. The triumph of art comes from the artist's "fulness of imaginative responsibility" (the phrase is Leavis') which permits him, aesthetically, to possess a metaphysics without being possessed by it.

The metaphysics of the artist, as opposed to that of the philosopher, contains modalities of and insights into human experience, disclosed, presented, in dramatic contexts, furiously and intensely (like the creative and destructive rhythms of life) rather than systematically, in the form of premise and documentation, of what Wordsworth calls "the spiritless shape of fact." "In the novel," Sartre declares, "the dice are not loaded, for fictional man is free. He develops before our eyes; our impatience, our ignorance, our expectancy are the same as the hero's. . . . The fictional event is a nameless presence; there is nothing one can say about it, for it develops."[26] In this observation by Sartre, and in that by Berdyaev, the stress falls on freedom. Art is the supreme imaginative activity and, consubstantially, the act of freedom itself.

Indeed, it is initially a metaphysics of freedom that inheres in the creative process. This freedom is of vast importance in the artist's craft, in the way he expresses poetic intuitions, to his imaginative vision. It is a freedom no less intense and no less liberating than the creative process, which can be imaged as "a little like looking into a microscope and attempting to bring an unknown object into focus."[27] In art the act of freedom is gradually transposed into an act of order, that is, the craft. Yet a work of art, to achieve authentic communication with the reader, functions as a "trans-action": "Our relationship or 'inter-course' with art is a 'trans-action,' in which each term affects the other."[28] The act and the communication of art demand freedom and in the end synthesize into a condition of freedom—a metaphysics of freedom.

This metaphysics of freedom plays a role both in the creative process and in the creative substance, specifically in the words which reveal a vision of experience. Any discussion of the use and the function of words can hardly ignore the relevancy of one writer's contention that "words themselves do not convey meaning . . . they are but a gesture we make, a dumb show like any other."[29] Nevertheless, with all their limitations, words must give tangible, structural form to the artist's imagination. They are used to "create beauty" and to "tell the truth," and they become a "trans-acting" medium for relationship and communication between a work of art and the reader. Words are the vehicle for revelation, when, as it were, *logos* becomes *apocalypsis*. In a word we can "behold" a whole world. It signifies value. It catches expression. It discourses. It sings. It reveals, as it makes mystery "intelligible." A word is at once a weighted measure of something it discloses and a wonder. Although it contains a world in itself, it also belongs to different worlds and becomes, as in the famous case of James Joyce, a "wonderful vocable." Words are to the artist the tools for rendering "life in time" and "life by values." They enable the artist to "withdraw" into himself and "look," as Plotinus puts it, and then give concretization to his special vision. They render a creative process that is a testament of the endurance of faith, a concentrated visionary experience born in *ecstasis* and consummated in *askesis*.

Virginia Woolf, in an exquisite essay, "Craftsmanship," discusses the power of words and shows that they have a metaphysics of their own: transcendent powers soaring beyond boundaries of absolute meaning and coinage.[30] Words, she says, "live in the mind," and we can merely "peer at them over the edge of that deep, dark and only fitfully illuminated cavern in which they live." To the creative artist words are never a prison, or confined to a prison; they are a means of revelation, "many-sided, flashing this way, then that." What Mrs. Woolf is emphasizing is the metaphysics of freedom which is vital to the creative imagination—a reverence for the tradition of craft achieved through the power and the freedom of the words used by an artist who attempts to capture reality's "luminous halo."

Words can convey meaning and help us achieve a dialogue; but it is, it must be, a dialogue in freedom. As such, according to Mrs. Woolf, we should be wary about pinning a word down to one mean-

ing, for "when words are pinned down they fold their wings and die."
It is for this reason, too, that meditative criticism (almost a religious
act in itself, a literary appreciation that intuits the mystery of creative art at the same time that it conveys its meaning) is necessary.
Nowhere else in the consideration of art is there more need for this
meditativeness than in an awareness of the combined freedom and
mystery that actualize the experience of the artist's words and that
relate to the metaphysics of the artist's *logos*. "Finally and most emphatically," concludes Mrs. Woolf, "words like ourselves, in order to
live at their ease, need privacy. Undoubtedly they like us to think,
and they like us to feel, before we use them; but they also like us to
pause; to become unconscious. Our unconsciousness is their privacy;
our darkness is their light. . . ."

These remarks are helpful here as we turn to two modern novelists: James Joyce and D. H. Lawrence. The uses to which they put
language illustrate some of the metaphysical elements which inform
their art. Joyce's accomplishment becomes clear only by our realizing that his metaphysics is primarily a metaphysics of nihilism, of
negation, but one that, according to Carl Gustav Jung, becomes "a
creative destruction." When Jung further observes that in *Ulysses*—
a work, he adds, that "has the character of a worm cut in half, that
can grow a new head or a new tail as required"—Joyce seeks "an almost universal 'restratification' of modern man, who is in the process
of shaking off a world that has become absolute"; or when he writes
that Joyce seeks a "detachment of consciousness" as the "goal that
shimmers through the fog of this book," his comments help us to
comprehend the metaphysics that inspirits Joyce's technique.[31] His
technique, it is clear from *A Portrait of the Artist as a Young Man*
and from *Ulysses*, inevitably relates back to his metaphysics, to his
view of the world in which the "dominant note is the melancholy of
abstract objectivity" (Jung).

E. M. Forster goes so far as to declare that in *Ulysses* the aim "is
to degrade all things and more particularly civilization and art, by
turning them inside out and upside down."[32] And Lawrence calls
Joyce "a clumsy *olla putrida* . . . Nothing but old fags and cabbage-
stumps . . . stewed in the juice of deliberate, journalistic dirty-mind-
edness. . . ."[33] Such conclusions are harsh and angry and not entirely
fair. They come from writers whose metaphysics is antithetical to
Joyce's: Forster with his emphasis on wisdom, eclectic and distilled,
Lawrence with his emphasis on the blood and on life as an unending
"adventure in consciousness." It is evident that Joyce is seeking for
something entirely different. He is not interested in being merely

"wise" or "alive." The word "restratification" captures what he demands and what inheres in his metaphysics and in his language. Joyce's metaphysics of "creative destruction," his attempt to overcome "the tyranny of tradition," his "restratification" above all—these are ever present in his "way of controlling, of ordering, of giving shape and a significance to the immense panorama of futility and anarchy which is contemporary history," to quote Eliot.[34] Hence, when Joyce remarks, "I'd like a language which is above all language, a language to which all will do service,"[35] he indicates the far limits of what he desires to "restratify" in art and life. Throughout the process of his "restratifying," he is fervently seeking for an "epiphany," a sudden, even divine revelation about the nature of the universe.

Joyce's metaphysics ends in a call to the mystery of the priesthood—the priesthood of the artist. "He [Stephen Daedalus] would never swing the thurible before the tabernacle as priest," Joyce writes in *Portrait*. "The wisdom of the priest's appeal did not touch him to the quick. He was destined to learn his own wisdom apart from others or to learn the wisdom of others himself wandering among the snares of the world." Joyce is the priest-as-artist, who vows, "I shall express myself as I am." And it is, Joyce contends, "in the virgin womb of the imagination [that] the word was made flesh." His technique, an uncompromising vindication of this belief, is achieved by "a priest of eternal imagination" transmuting "the daily bread of experience into the radiant body of everliving life." His technique is continually colored on the one hand by an elemental religionism, a pious Catholicism, to be exact, and on the other by a ferocious independence of creative effort, which Joyce sums up in the words, ". . . I will try to express myself in some mode of life or art as freely and as wholly as I can, using for my defense the only arms I allow myself to use—silence, exile, and cunning."[36]

Joyce's art reveals a double process in an artistic imagination that is mythically and symbolically churched, or, as Joyce himself says, "supersatuated with the religion in which you say you disbelieve," and of an ideational dissent proceeding from an epiphanous view of the life of man as "a Vast Human Tragedy . . . in which a profound anthropological sense of the mystery and power of death takes the place of the Christian's traditional faith in union with God and the life everlasting."[37] This process evidences the objective substances and the measure of an artist's technique, in Joyce's case the levels of language and structure through which he finds the means of exploring his vision, of conveying its meaning, and of appraising it. For Joyce it is the self-centered word that achieves precisely the transcendence which he denies in the universe. For him, the word assumes hierophantic powers and signifies the metaphysical quest for the final restoration.

Like Joyce, Lawrence searches for new life-values, and for him the novel is a means of achieving them in a world which has gone "dead." "The novel," he writes, "is a perfect medium for revealing to us the changing rainbow of our living relationships. The novel can help us to live, as nothing else can. . . ."[38] In contrast to that of Joyce, Lawrence's metaphysical quest is nonintellectual. He is not interested in stratifying or restratifying, in dividing, in forming, in ordering the universe. His vision of the universe is characterized by a belief that "culture and civilisation are tested by vital consciousness," and his concern is with "revitalization." How can we overcome the "old, dead things" of the cosmos? How can we fathom "the unknown modes of being" by traveling beyond "the long mean marginal stretches of our existence"? How can we achieve, in a final, transcendent sense, "the new unknown," "the sensuous flame of life"? These are questions which pervade Lawrence's art and thought.

Blake's words, "Awake! awake O Sleeper of the land of shadows, wake! expand!"[39] capture Lawrence's view of the role of his art in relation to his vision of the universe and of man's possibilities in life. What Lawrence is doing in his art is reminding man of his need to "awake" and to "expand," to seek for the kind of revitalization, of "resurrection," which the Christ figure experiences in *The Man Who Died*. That man is capable of "moving back to consciousness" and of experiencing "the everlasting wonder in things" is what Lawrence insists upon and what conveys the nonintrospective metaphysical orientation of his art and message.

In his Foreword to *Women in Love* he views man "in a period of crisis." This crisis is enacted between people who struggle or must struggle to "speak out to one another." There are those who "fix themselves in the old idea" and who will consequently "perish with the new life strangled unborn within them." But there are also those who "can bring forth the new passion, the new idea." For Lawrence there is always an enduring "remnant" in the world that has "the courage of ultimate truth." His art at its best renders the metaphysics of a "life-courage" as opposed to a "death-courage." The following passage from his Foreword contains in essence Lawrence's view of the world as it informs the whole of his art:

Man struggles with unborn needs and fulfilment. New unfoldings struggle up in torment in him, as buds struggle forth from the midst of a plant. Any man of real individuality tries to know and to understand what is happening, even in himself as he goes along. This struggle for verbal consciousness should not be left out in art. It is a very great part of life. It is not superimposition of a theory. It is the passionate struggle into conscious being.

Lawrence discloses a profound awareness of the mystery of life. No examination of his cosmos, in which, as Elizabeth Bowen has observed, "every bush burns," can escape the "numinous awe" which Lawrence communicates. No aspect of life fails to excite his wonder; "awe," "awefulness," "overpoweringness," to use Rudolf Otto's touchstones,[40] inhere in Lawrence's re-creation of life, in his striving to touch the "emotional soul" and to come closer to the primordial truths which he associates with the "intuitional consciousness." If Joyce can be likened to the priest of the word, Lawrence can be likened to the priest of the passions. His novels become fervent sermons exhorting man to move closer to the numinous essences of life, there to "touch and wonder and ponder" the very meaning of existence. "What ails us," Lawrence complains, "is that our sense of beauty is so bruised and blunted, we miss all the best."[41]

With its spontaneous, rhythmic flow of words and emotions, "its pulsing, frictional to-and-fro which works up to culmination," his sermonic art feverishly strives to save the numen from the forces of antilife, from technology, industrialism, intellectualism, and scientism. The numen, as Lawrence sees and reveals it, is found ultimately not in the *logos* (as in Joyce's work), but in the flesh. Or as Lawrence writes in his unpublished Foreword to *Sons and Lovers*: "... not the Word made Flesh, but the Flesh made Word. Out of the Flesh cometh the Word, and the Word is finite, as a piece of carpentry, and hath an end. But the Flesh is infinite and has no end."[42]

In his view of the universe Lawrence attempts to help man understand that "the vast marvel is to be alive."[43] The metaphysics of this Lawrentian world-view is constantly expressed in his language and technique. His claim that "work is produced by passion with me" is not difficult to comprehend when we consider that Lawrence, from first to last, employed a technique of art that had as its source of inspiration the need of teaching man that "the magnificent here and now of life in the flesh is ours, and ours alone, and ours only for a time." Lawrence preaches the sermon of the flesh in a language and a form which continually echo his nonconformist Protestant upbringing and which at the same time achieve freedom from the limitations of doctrine.[44] His final position, as effected in his art and his message, is a metamorphosed religion of the instant, the living moment when man is "alive and in the flesh, and part of the living, incarnate cosmos."

Contrary to Joyce's concept of man's isolation—of his being, as Joyce asserts at the end of *Portrait*, "Alone, quite alone. You have no fear of that. And you know what the word means? Not only to be separate from all others but to have not even one friend"—Lawrence's concept of man emphasizes a communal and dialogic relationship. Man, he says repeatedly, fails himself and the world around him by asserting his separateness, physically or spiritually. Only when man accepts the fact of his relationship to the world about him will he understand his meaning and his destiny.

> My soul [we read in Lawrence's last prose work, *Apocalypse*] knows that I am part of the human race, my soul is an organic part of the great human soul, as my spirit is part of my nation. In my own very self, I am part of my family. There is nothing of me that is alone and absolute except my mind, and we shall find that the mind has no existence by itself, it is only the glitter of the sun on the surface of the waters.

No words better show the differences between the metaphysics of Lawrence and that of Joyce. (One recalls here Leavis' contention that "if you took Joyce for a major creative writer, then . . . you had no use for Lawrence, and if you judged Lawrence a great writer, then you could hardly take a sustained interest in Joyce."[45] When we compare the metaphysics and the techniques of the two, we can appreciate J. I. M. Stewart's observation that Joyce's achievement "is the work of a man who has lived too much alone with his own daemon."[46] In Lawrence's art, on the other hand, we are always in the presence of a creative genius whose daemon exists only as it participates in "the great relationship," in "the true relatedness to the other," "the relation itself," which comprises "the quick and the central clue to life" and which reveals the "Courage to accept the life-thrust from within oneself, and from the other person."[47]

IV

Modern literature shows that metaphysical issues cannot be easily dismissed, that all too often "the physical opens on the metaphysical." One of the ironies of the modern age is that imaginative artists have nourished and sustained the relevance of metaphysics, in the face of, even in defiance of, the style of the times. Of course, as Frederick J. Hoffman has shown in *The Mortal No*, the intruding presence of the secular in the midst of the religious—e.g., the paradoxes of "secular grace," the merging of "assailant" and "victim," the spatialization of time, the transposition of "the metaphysical properties of the Trinity into areas of secular improvisation"—discloses that traditional concepts of man and his universe are radically changing in the modern novel. "Man looks at the world," Robbe-Grillet wryly observes, "and the world does not return his glance."[48] Yet, when we read Hoffman's study, we can hardly miss the implicit conclusion that modern writers are obsessed with their views of the world; that whether their conceptions of the world are metaphysically organic or inorganic, man has once again been

> forced to speculate upon the possibility of a means of transcendence, since he [cannot] long suffer the thought of mortality in and of itself; he [is] forced back upon the initial experiencing of the self in time, and [is] impelled to work in terms of a sensed immediacy of his participation in tempered flow; he [becomes] more and more interested in himself *as process*, and he [attempts] to rescue a value from the fact that he [exists] in the apparently endlessly repetitive process of becoming something else. . . .[49]

Whatever the differences in their artistic visions, novelists as different as Tolstoy, Dostoevsky, Thomas Mann, Franz Kafka, Hermann Hesse, Nikos Kazantzakis, Ignazio Silone, and William Faulkner (to mention some representative figures) have powerful things to say about such questions as: What kind of universe do we inhabit? What constitutes the relationship of the immediate to the eternal? These novelists are concerned with "the situation of our time" and with "the terrible things of life": boredom, incommunicability, loneliness, anxiety, alienation, despair. Consciously or unconsciously, they express in their art the metaphysical tensions that arise on the one hand from a view of the universe which concludes that "there's no way out," and on the other hand from a view which, like that of Charles Williams, François Mauriac, Graham Greene, J. F. Powers, and Flannery O'Connor, affirms "salvation with diligence." ("The poet is traditionally a blind man," Miss O'Connor remarks, "but the Christian poet is like the blind man cured in the Gospels, who looked then and saw men as if they were trees, but walking. This is the beginning of vision."[50])

Through a continuing preoccupation with metaphysical problems, modern literature attests to what Pascal speaks of as *l'esprit de finesse* (the acute, or subtle spirit) as opposed to *l'esprit géométrique* (the geometric spirit). One of the ironies of this century is that creative writers have seen fit to express metaphysical concerns at a time when strident forces both in theological and philosophical circles have increasingly rejected metaphysics. We need look only at "new radical theologians" like Thomas J. J. Altizer, William Hamilton, and Paul M. van Buren, who advocate a "secularized Christianity" and a theology in which God "is not simply hidden from view ... [but] is truly dead," to comprehend a style which seeks for a reconstruction of metaphysics. Specifically, we are told that theology can be an empirical science; that our "image" of God must go; that speculative and abstract language must be cleansed, with words like "God," "transcendence," "redemption," "creation" seen in a new light and terms like "up there" and "out there" repudiated; that we now live in a "secular city" and must give stress to "the secular meaning of the Gospel." This is a "time for Christian candor," Bishop James A. Pike informs us.[51]

Among modern philosophers *l'esprit géométrique* has been particularly strong in the movement known as logical positivism (e.g., in the works of Ludwig Wittgenstein, Rudolf Carnap, and A. J. Ayer). For the logical positivists, concerned as they are with verbal analysis, grammatical schemata, logical rules, the nature of mathematics, the meanings of "meaning," the exactitudes of $2 + 2 = 4$, metaphysics lies outside the range of quantitative measurement and is consequently meaningless, inconsistent, and incommensurate with what G. E. Moore once spoke of as "the Common Sense view of the world." Metaphysics as a term has, at the hands of the positivists, taken on pejorative connotations. It contains, to recall Hume's famous attack, "nothing but sophistry and illusion." "The acme of *abstract* speculation," it signifies what is "neither true nor false but 'literally senseless,' " a "senseless obscurantism," the result of "mental cramp." Such have been the charges brought against metaphysics in the modern period; they embody what has been called the style of the times: a style which has been in evidence since the breakdown of the traditional structure of values and the "single standard of faith," and which emerged with the Renaissance and triumphed in the post-Enlightenment world, when metaphysical meaning was negated through the substitution of the "dynamics of *becoming*" for "static being."[52]

That one should remain aloof from metaphysics, inasmuch as it is untenable and intangible, is an attitude that many modern theologians and philosophers have emphasized. "Trust the world;" say "yes to the world"—this is the counsel of the radical theologians as well as of the logical positivists. (We are reminded here of Maritain's criticism of Teilhard de Chardin's "chronolatry," which he sees as part of the new trend in theology and ecclesiastic thinking, "a genuflection before the world."[53]) It is counsel that underlines an outlook, a style, that yearns for safeness and accuracy and comfort, secular qualities which preclude a quest for what lies beyond the sensible. "Matter," as Simone Weil astutely observes, "is [now] a machine for manufacturing good."

Imaginative art, however, is doomed to failure, to sterility, once it surrenders to such a style. "To create today," Camus insists, "is to create dangerously." His words bear heed. They focus on the mission of artists who are intensely preoccupied with the meaning of the world: "the world is everything—this is the contradictory and tireless cry of every true artist—the cry that keeps him on his feet with eyes ever open." A metaphysics of art demands that a writer speak up— that he speak up, or speak forth in a prophetic sense. "One may long, as I do," Camus reflects, "for a gentler flame, a respite, a pause for musing. But perhaps there is no other peace for the artist than what he finds in the heat of combat."[54]

If modern theologians and philosophers have surrendered to the style of the times, to "literal-minded analysis" and "cautious 'empiricism' "—to the dictates of the geometric spirit—there are creative writers who have chosen to express their views of the universe in dangerous terms. By "dangerous" one means yielding to the creative urge to respond to the world without limiting vision to the secular dynamics of life. A modern *alittérateur* like Samuel Beckett illustrates in his drama and fiction just how dangerous the metaphysical quest for human meaning and truth can be. He is concerned with conveying a "sense of mystery, bewilderment, and anxiety when confronted with the human condition, and . . . despair at being unable to find a meaning in existence." Thus, in metaphysical terms, Beckett sees "man as [a] lost soul," haunted by "an intolerable deprivation" and "an irreparable absence." His is a desacralized world when, as Nietzsche would have it, the shadow of God, lurking in caves, has been "conquered" at last.[55] Helplessness, worthlessness, meaninglessness, Beckett tells us, epitomize the condition of man. "But what matter," we read in *Malone Dies*, "whether I was born or not, have lived or not, am dead or merely dying, I shall go on doing as I have always done, not knowing what it is I do, nor who I am nor where I come from, nor if I am."[56]

But even "at his zero-point [when] there *is* no grace," Beckett is not unlike "a 'shepherd of being' unto our time . . . enhanced by the very resoluteness with which he plunges us into the Dark."[57] More than anything else, Beckett is a writer whose metaphysical search leads to the lowermost depths in his hope of somehow finding "the fundamental reality which would remain, once what is accessory in man has been destroyed." "By dropping down into the elementary void of existence, perhaps it is the soul that he hopes to find in the end," Claude Mauriac says of Beckett.[58]

What we experience in Beckett's work is indeed the danger, the heightened and terrifying metaphysical danger, which Camus emphasizes. The quest for metaphysical truth, we must realize, refuses to bow to "aggressive reason" or be satisfied with "straight answers." This refusal constitutes the strength and the glory of the artist, and it is what compels us to "face the full force of our existence." Surely, Beckett "has materialized the impalpable . . . has almost enabled us to touch the walls of our prisons."[59] Such is the power of an artist whose metaphysics must thrust him into "the heat of combat," into a world which is so close to us, yet so distant, so elusive—a world in which "the blind man's stick" is perhaps the only hope that one has, or needs, as he taps his way slowly and falteringly toward the real truth beckoning from behind boundaries of darkness. "For where I found truth," says Saint Augustine, "there I found my God, Who is Truth itself."

A metaphysics of art implies an artist's willingness to travel beyond the known world into the unknown, the unexpected, and to explore both worlds with an aim of realizing ultimate reality; to embark on that "expedition of truth" which Kafka envisioned; to combine the highest functions of poetry and prophecy; and to perceive the other world which some modern theologians and philosophers have been evading for fear of learning the real truth of the self and of the world. "To-day, as always," Karl Jaspers declares, "art must . . . make Transcendence perceptible, doing so at all times in the form which arouses contemporary faith. It may well be that the moment draws near when art will again tell man what his God is and what himself is."[60] Modern creative literature helps to bring us nearer to the moment of which Jaspers speaks and simultaneously reminds us of the timeless verity that "art is the grandchild of God."[61]

10

F. M. Dostoevsky and D. H. Lawrence: Their Visions of Evil

For of the last stage of this cultural development, it might well be truly said: "Specialists without spirit, sensualists without heart; this nullity imagines that it has attained a level of civilization never before achieved."

—Max Weber, *The Protestant Ethic and the Spirit of Capitalism*

∽

"Art itself doesn't interest me," D. H. Lawrence asserts, "only the spiritual content."[1] His words testify to a lifelong preoccupation with a metaphysics of art. Not surprisingly, Fyodor Mikhailovich Dostoevsky, perhaps the most metaphysical of nineteenth-century Russian novelists, always disturbed and fascinated Lawrence. Rejecting as "foul" Dostoevsky's "moral scheme," Lawrence satirized the Russian's view of "Christian ecstasy" and dismissed Dostoevsky's novels as "great parables" but "false art": "I don't like Dostoevsky. He is again like the rat, slithering along in hate, in the shadows, and, in order to belong to the light, professing love, all love. But his nose is sharp with hate, his running is shadowy, and rat-like, he is a will fixed and gripped like a trap. He is not nice."[2] Dostoevsky was, in short, an artist in whom "amazing perspicacity is mixed with ugly perversity," and yet an artist, Lawrence admitted, whose "diagnosis of human nature is simple and unanswerable."[3] Clearly, though Lawrence detested the Russian novelist, he could not get away from him, and no other novelist ever got as much attention from Lawrence as did Dostoevsky.*

E. T. (Jessie Chambers) notes in her Memoir that Lawrence, while

---

*Reflecting on the origins and the composition of this essay, I want to record that the writing—in the winter and spring of 1961, in Nottingham, England, on those "strange marvellous black nights of the north Midlands," to use Lawrence's description—occurred simultaneously with my careful study of G. Wilson Knight's *The Wheel of Fire*, particularly of his essays on *Hamlet*, *Macbeth*, and *King Lear*. The observant reader should be able to detect the influence of that great book in my essay.

still a young schoolmaster in Croydon, read the English translation of Dostoevsky's *Crime and Punishment*. She also recalls that the novel puzzled him, that he frowned and said: "It's very great, but I don't like it. I don't quite understand it. I must read it again."[4] It is difficult to say if Lawrence did reread this great Russian novel, as he did *The Brothers Karamazov*. Yet there is a very strong probability that one character from this book exerted—even within the process that Lawrence once referred to as his remembering "hints" from others' works and then proceeding by "intuition"[5]—a profound and extraordinary influence on at least one of Lawrence's subordinate characters, who appears at the end of *Women in Love*. Indeed, when one thinks of this character, Herr Loerke, a German sculptor, it is difficult to deny that his affinities with the notorious voluptuary Svidrigaylov in *Crime and Punishment* are remarkable. Both characters, though subsidiary figures in the novels, are denizens of the underworld, with an almost sinister importance, and the superb characterization of each carries with it an implicit message and warning of major proportions. They are evil beings with menacing, immoral, demonic powers, and they inevitably remain in the reader's memory like some nightmarish phenomenon. In Svidrigaylov, Dostoevsky sought to depict the most lamentable excessiveness and innate moral depravity and evil. In his notes to this novel, he writes of this character: "Svidrigaylov is conscious of mysterious horrors within himself which he will tell no one but lets slip out as facts. He has convulsive, animal-like urges to rend and to kill; coldly passionate. A wild beast. A tiger."[6] Lawrence's Loerke, likewise, shares the immorality of Svidrigaylov, and in a sense embodies and carries forward that particular pattern of moral bankruptcy that appears in Svidrigaylov.

As prophetic novelists and seers, Dostoevsky and Lawrence often portrayed the disintegration of the human condition in its most naked and horrifying forms. And their visions of evil reached terrifying effectiveness in their depictions of Svidrigaylov and Loerke, who, as the embodiments of unbridled depravity and immorality, indicate that ultimate point of no return in the breakdown of human life and the triumph of the forces of antilife. Dostoevsky was preoccupied with this great problem in the nineteenth century, and his portrayal of Svidrigaylov underscores his concern. Lawrence was also fiercely concerned with the same problem; his portrayal of Loerke served, in some ways, to update Svidrigaylov by focusing a clearer light on the same Dostoevskian evil and putting it in a more modern setting. Thus, although Lawrence did not like what he had read in *Crime and Punishment* (in a letter to Blanche Jennings he refers to it as a "tract, a treatise, a pamphlet compared to Tolstoy's *Anna Karenina* or *War and Peace*"[7]), he nonetheless was to be tormented and haunted by the same vision of evil, the same nightmare, the same excessiveness. In this respect, of course, Lawrence, being the rebellious nonconformist that he was, refused to acknowledge the truths of his teacher. The fact remains that he was unable to deny their validity. To some extent his portrayal of Loerke can be interpreted both as an admission of his debt to Dostoevsky and as an acknowledgment and vindication of the Russian novelist's visionary powers.

Philip Rahv has correctly pointed out that Svidrigaylov should not be treated merely as the alter ego of Raskolnikov, that, as a character who is admittedly subordinate, he is "invested with originality and expressive form" and exercises an appeal that nearly matches that of the hero.[8] The same could be said of Loerke, who becomes the center of interest in the last three chapters of *Women in Love*. In fact, when he does appear, he not only stirs the interest of Rupert Birkin, Gerald Crich, and Ursula and Gudrun Brangwen, but also at times overshadows them. As a subordinate character, he is as brilliantly and uniquely drawn (disproving the familiar but indefensible charge that Lawrence failed to create memorable and distinguishable minor characters) as other unforgettable and great Lawrentian figures, such as Mrs. Witt in *St. Mawr* and Mrs. Bolton in *Lady Chatterley's Lover*. Whereas these two women induce much sympathy and tenderness, Loerke arouses the deepest fear and dismay, and this is no doubt precisely what Lawrence aimed at. The circumstances and milieux in which Svidrigaylov and Loerke appear also tend to emphasize the evils that they embody and the threats they present to the life and well-being of society. Svidrigaylov is seen in the blighted slum areas of St. Petersburg, where he lives and moves about in the cellars and filth of that city. The blackness of night seems always to hover about him. Flies and mice seem to be his companions.[9] The beauty and iridescence of the natural world seem to sigh and shrivel in his presence. It is as if this creature, as George Gibian has aptly observed,[10] violates and defiles by his very presence God's world itself, not only the human beings who live in it. Svidrigaylov hates all of God's creation, the light of the sun, and the beauty of the earth and the sea. "I've been abroad before," he says, "and I always got sick of it. Not that I didn't like it there; but the sunrise, the bay of Naples, the sea—all that makes you feel so damnably depressed" (IV, 1).[11] A former nobleman who served two years in the cavalry, a cardsharper, and now a widower, he has gone to Petersburg "for the sake of women." He cares about nothing except the satisfaction of his lust and physical urges ("I put all my hopes on anatomy now"). From the moment that he reaches Petersburg he shows a devouring passion for carnal pleasure and seeks for "a whiff of the familiar smells" in the familiar dens of vice. "I like my dens to be dirty," he admits. Understandably Raskolnikov speaks of Svidrigaylov as "that dirty villain and voluptuous *roué* and scoundrel." His outward appearance, however, tends to be delusive; it is as if he is wearing a mask, the inevitable mask worn by villains and evil-doers from time immemorial. In appearance he is a handsome, dandified man of about fifty years of age, over medium height, and he looks much younger than his years. This is what Raskolnikov sees when he scrutinizes Svidrigaylov:

> It was a peculiar kind of a face, which looked like a mask: white, with red cheeks, with bright-red lips, a light, flaxen beard, and still very thick, fair hair. His eyes were, somehow, a little too blue, and their expression was, somehow, too heavy and motionless. There was something repulsive in this handsome and, to judge by his age, extremely young face. Svidrigaylov's clothes were very smart, of light summer material, and he seemed to be particularly proud of his fine linen. One of his fingers was adorned by a huge ring with a valuable stone (VI, 3).

Lawrence's Loerke arouses much the same kind of terror and despair, although his excessiveness is far more cerebral than carnal. He first appears in the hostel in the Tyrolese Alps, where he is one of ten guests, all Germans, who are eventually joined by Gerald, Birkin, Gudrun, and Ursula. Unlike Svidrigaylov, who inhabits the dens of vices in Petersburg, Loerke is to be seen in the cold, silent world of snow and ice "in the heart of the mountains." Just as the slums of Petersburg become the evil workshop for Svidrigaylov, so does the "deep and silent snow" of the Alps accentuate the barrenness and living death that Loerke represents. For Loerke nothing really matters any longer; his own emotional world is as desolate as that which is actually covered over by snow and ice, producing "a silence and sheer whiteness exhilarating to madness." It is the kind of "silence," or inertia, that comes when human life has disintegrated and human contact and connection are nonexistent, when the excesses of sensuality and intellect leave very little room for the healthy relationships of creative and intuitive being. It is this sense of isolation and alienation that the dehumanized Loerke represents. The snow, ice, and frigid winds of the Alps merely underscore the brutal truth of his death-in-life. The typically Dostoevskian practice of blending human degradation with the depiction of various insects and lower animals is adopted with notable success by Lawrence in his portrayal of Loerke. When any allusion is made to him, there is often, and at the same time, a reference to some sort of insect or lower animal. Loerke looks like "a lop-eared rabbit," "a troll," "a bat," "a little obscene monster of the darkness," a "wizard rat that swims ahead," a "noxious insect," "a gnawing little negation, gnawing at the roots of life," a "little vermin," a "little dry snake," "a hopping flea with a proboscis." Even "his thin, brown, nervous hands were prehensile, and somehow like talons, like griffes, inhuman." Lawrence takes endless pains to portray Loerke as "the rock-bottom of all life." Like Svidrigaylov he is a cynic and a denier of the values and beauty of life. In appearance Loerke is deceptive; he, too, is a skillful wearer of the mask to cover inner ugliness and irreverence, evil and depravity. And like Svidrigaylov he is middle-aged; yet, with his boyish figure and slight, unformed body, he, too, exhibits a peculiar, if repelling, kind of youthfulness. For Gudrun, especially, though he has "the look of a little wastrel about him" and an "uncanny ugliness," he nevertheless has a curious and mysterious attraction that becomes even more pronounced as she begins to realize and repudiate the kind of deadness inherent in Gerald Crich's world. Certainly Lawrence's physical depiction of Herr Loerke is no less effective in its observations of the life-denier than that of Dostoevsky in the case of Svidrigaylov. This is how Loerke appears on the afternoon when he and Gudrun are going on a toboggan ride (this day is also fatal for Gerald):

> In his brown velvet cap, that made his head as round as a chestnut, with the brown velvet flaps loose and wild over his ears, and a wisp of elf-like, thin hair blowing above his full, elf-like eyes, the shiny, transparent brown skin crinkling up into odd grimaces on his small-featured face, he looked an odd little boy-man, a bat. But in his figure, in the greeny loden suit, he looked *chétif* and puny, still strangely different from the rest (XXX).[12]

Both Svidrigaylov and Loerke stand for the forces of negation and deterioration. The way of life that they represent, Dostoevsky and Lawrence are warning, leads to the complete breakdown of human fellowship and organic harmony. This is made quite clear in their everyday actions, their general outlook on life, and their relations to other human beings. Svidrigaylov, who sets the pattern of such a subterranean type, has surrendered himself to Satanism. Utterly unscrupulous and self-willed, he sees no distinction between good and evil. Human dignity and reverence for life have no meaning for him whatsoever. He places his faith in the forces of evil and vice. He confesses in the course of one of his conversations with Raskolnikov: "There is something permanent in this vice; something that is founded on nature and not subject to the whims of fancy: something that is always there in your blood, like a piece of red-hot coal; something that sets it on fire and that you won't perhaps be able to put out for a long time, even with years" (VI, 3). By his actions he shows the extent to which he is captivated by his belief in the absoluteness of permanent evil. In the course of his life, he has seduced young girls, maids, and married women; he has caused the death of his own wife, whom he married only because she promised to pay his gambling debts and whom he continually and flagrantly dishonored by his behavior. It is implied, too, that the death of Philip, his servant, had been the result of Svidrigaylov's abusive meanness. Perhaps even worse is the fate of a deaf-and-dumb girl of fourteen or fifteen who committed suicide after Svidrigaylov had violated her. Indeed, his appetite for young girls is as unquenchable as it is outrageous; he finds their innocence and beauty "tempting." "I don't know what you think of female faces," he says to Raskolnikov, "but to me a girl of sixteen—those still childish eyes, shyness, and tears of bashfulness—to me this is much better than beauty..." (VI, 4). This particular craving and uncontrolled self-indulgence lead him to become engaged to a sixteen-year-old girl. It is with unashamed carnal delight that Svidrigaylov describes this poor creature: "I put her on my knees yesterday, but I suppose a little too unceremoniously—she flushed all over, and tears started to her eyes, but she did not want to show it, she was on fire herself" (VI, 4). But it is not enough that he actively seeks in every way to satisfy his voluptuousness. Even his nightmares relate to his molesting of girls, one fourteen years of age and the other five. One can well understand why Sonia, whose neighbor Svidrigaylov happens to be during his stay in Petersburg, is disturbed by his presence: "She felt ashamed for some reason, and also somehow frightened."

Here, once more, Svidrigaylov's similarities with Loerke are unmistakably close. Loerke "seems to be the very stuff of the underworld of life. There was no going beyond him." He embodies the forces of negation and evil, and in him Lawrence seeks to show the ultimate point of human degradation and nothingness. "In the last issue he cared about nothing, he was troubled about nothing, he made not the slightest attempt to be at one with anything. He existed a pure, unconnected will, stoical and momentaneous. There was only his work" (XXIX). When we first meet Loerke, we find that he is accompanied by "a very fair young man," "his penniless dependent," Leitner. Although Lawrence does not go into detail, the implications of the homosexual relationship between Loerke and Leitner are sufficiently clear and devastating: "It was evident that the two men who had travelled and lived together in the last degree of intimacy, had now reached the stage of loathing" (XXIX). It is evident, furthermore, that Loerke's homosexuality is as purely mechanical and functional as that of André Gide's Corydon, for example, is passionate and intense. What is even more remarkable in the affinity between Svidrigaylov and Loerke is the comparable delight that the latter finds in the beauty of girls "at sixteen, seventeen, eighteen—after that they are no use to me." The central difference, however, is that whereas Dostoevsky is showing the carnal purposes of Svidrigaylov in his physical passion for young girls, Lawrence seeks to show Loerke's adulteration of physical beauty in the "aesthetic" pursuit of his goals as a master-sculptor. This can be seen when Loerke shows to Gudrun a photogravure reproduction of a statuette that he has done:

> The statuette was of a naked girl, small, finely made, sitting on a great naked horse. The girl was young and tender, a mere bud. She was sitting sideways on the horse, her face in her hands, as if in shame and grief, in a little abandon. Her hair, which was short and must be flaxen, fell forward, divided, half covering her head.
>
> Her limbs were young and tender. Her legs scarcely formed yet, the legs of a maiden just passing towards cruel womanhood, dangled childishly over the side of the powerful horse, pathetically, the small feet folded one over the other, as if to hide. But there was no hiding. There she was exposed naked on the naked flank of the horse (XXIX).

Svidrigaylov embodies the excesses of physical corruption at its worst; Loerke embodies the corruption and deterioration that come as a result of the excesses of intellect. For the purposes of art he will utilize anything. Things that are beautiful are beautiful to him only insofar as they can be used to form his art. Beauty thus becomes mere mechanism and pure embellishment to him. Like his counterpart, Svidrigaylov, he sees nothing sacred and reverent in the mystery and wonder of living beauty, human or otherwise. Beauty for him, therefore, is not at all creative, but rather utilitarian and instrumental in his attaining purely mechanical, inorganic ends. Svidrigaylov finds that beauty is "tempting," and he strives to violate it purely for pleasure. Loerke seeks to employ beauty in the depiction and satisfaction of exoteric form, not organic life. Even the horse, he says, *"is part of a work of art, it has no relation to anything outside that work of art."* Loerke is one of those dehumanized artists who see no connection between art and the organic expression of life. His concept of art indicates an arrogant hostility to life, from which it is totally separated. (It is a characteristic violation, as well, of Lawrence's own concept of art, the task of which, he says in his essay "Morality and the Novel," "is to reveal the relation between man and his circumambient universe, at the living moment."[13]) In his portrayal of Loerke, Lawrence is trying to show that final point of human decadence and sterility when life becomes a mere instrument of mental goals and concepts. To Ursula, Loerke's picture of the naked girl is especially depressing; she sees in it a picture of Loerke himself. To this reaction the enraged sculptor replies in words that actually serve to justify her fears and suspicions:

> "A picture of myself!" he repeated, in derision. "Wissen sie, gnädige Frau, that is a Kunstwerk, a work of art. It is a work of art, it is a picture of nothing, of absolutely nothing. It has nothing to do with anything but itself, it has no relation with the everyday world of this and other, there is no connection between them, absolutely none, they are two different and distinct planes of existence, and to translate one into the other is worse than foolish, it is a darkening of all counsel, a making confusion everywhere. Do you see, you *must not* confuse the relative world of action, with the absolute world of art. That you *must not do*" (XXIX).

Svidrigaylov and Loerke are cynical and indifferent men who have chosen to cut themselves from the body of humanity. Each is dedicated to his own functional ends and to these alone: Loerke to his sculpture ("the absolute world of art") and Svidrigaylov to his physical appetites ("all my hopes on anatomy"). For them life can have no living values whatsoever. Svidrigaylov lives for only the immediate experience and experiment of his debaucheries; beyond these there is nothing at all that has merit. His is a self-willed, ruthless arrogance that results in utter denial and negation. He is, inevitably, bored by life. "I feel rather," he says, "like joining an expedition to the North Pole; for drink makes me miserable, and I hate drinking and there's nothing left for me to do except get drunk" (IV, 1). He is an unrelenting cynic who has come to distrust everything and everyone outside the immediate reach of his own sensual demoralization. "But you can never be sure of anything," he cries, "that may take place between a husband and wife or a lover and his lass. There's always a little corner which remains hidden from the rest of the world and which is only known to the two of them" (VI, 4).[14] He is a life-denier for whom any nobility of thought and deed is sheer fantasy. "We're always thinking of eternity as an idea that cannot be understood, something immense. But why must it be? What if, instead of all this, you suddenly find just a little room there, something like a village bathhouse, grimy, and spiders in every corner, and that's all eternity is. Sometimes, you know, I can't help feeling that that's probably what it is" (IV, 1).

Similarly, Loerke has chosen to isolate himself from the stream of life, for outside of his work there is nothing that really matters. The natural world around him is dead. His capacity for love and human contact and fellowship, his recognition and appreciation of natural and creative beauty, his sense of any joy and wonder through participation in the flow of life, are all those great manifestations of the human spirit and purpose that he will never attain, for he has chosen to go beyond the creative springs of life. Even his attraction to Gudrun is one that is based on "a little companionship in intelligence." Gudrun herself "knew that Loerke, in his innermost soul, was detached from everything, for him there was neither heaven nor earth nor hell. He admitted no allegiance, he gave no adherence anywhere. He was single and, by abstraction from the rest, absolute in himself" (XXX). Loerke, too, depicts an excessiveness of selfishness, of will and intellect. The necessary and vital give-and-take of human life must be avoided: he is incapable of giving himself to others. He lacks the kind of spontaneous, innate generosity and magnanimity that is needed to make any experience of life rich and meaningful. He is not only that isolated human being but also that alienated artist in life who lives to serve ascendant mechanical powers. Eternity to him, as to Svidrigaylov, is a "dream of fear" when "the world went cold, and snow fell everywhere, and only white creatures, polar-bears, white foxes, and men like awful white snow-birds, persisted in ice cruelty" (XXX). In effect, he is that growing phenomenon of the modern age, the man who acknowledges no master except the mechanics and science of his art and the dialectics of the intellect. Utterly barren of human warmth and large-heartedness, he is a central figure in Lawrence's vision of evil and the embodiment of that final human catastrophe. "He lives like a rat," Birkin says to Gerald, "in the river of corruption, just where it falls over into the bottomless pit. He's further on than we are. He hates the ideal more acutely. He *hates* the ideal utterly, yet it still dominates him" (XXIX).

The meaning of Birkin's words can be more fully understood when one considers Loerke's whole outlook toward and his philosophy of work and art. As a master-sculptor, Loerke, who had risen in the social world from very humble circumstances, has now surrendered himself entirely to the machine. Vivid human relationships have been completely *displaced* by the mechanics of work, and to this, and this alone, he has given selflessly. "No," Loerke cries out, "it is noth-

ing but this, serving a machine, or enjoying the motion of a machine—
motion, that is all." And just as Svidrigaylov finds reality and eternity
only in impermanent sensual pleasure, so does Loerke find the same
in his mechanical work. What, then, is Loerke's basic principle of art?
His answer to this question is that art in the modern industrial age
should interpret industry, as art once did religion. "Sculpture and
architecture," he believes, "must go together. . . . And since churches
are all museum stuff, since industry is our business, now, then let us
make our places of industry our art—our factory-area our Parthenon,
ecco!" (XXIX). As a sculptor he applies this principle to his own
work with zealous faith. We can see this from the following description of his sculpturing on a great granite frieze that he has done for
a factory in Cologne: "It was a representation of a fair, with peasants
and artisans in an orgy of enjoyment, drunk and absurd in their modern dress, whirling ridiculously in roundabouts, gaping at shows, kissing and staggering and rolling in knots, swinging in swing-boats, and
firing down shooting galleries, a frenzy of chaotic motion" (XXIX).
Here, indeed, Lawrence again shows the prophetic power and vision
of his art, for is this not that modern nightmare in which the Loerkes
(and Svidrigaylovs) destroy all semblance of the creative mystery of
and reverence for life? Is this not the mechanical prostitution of life
that follows the excessiveness and deification of the will and ego, be
it Svidrigaylov's self-willed debauchery or Loerke's monomania for
"beautiful machine-houses"? Loerke's frieze, depicting the "frenzy of
chaotic motion," is essentially the embodiment of the doom of modern industrial society in which there is little choice left for anything
else. What, Loerke asks, is man doing at a "fair" like this? His reply,
with its almost agonizing and indelicate frankness, is certainly a prophetic one: "He is fulfilling the counterpart of labor—the machine
works him instead of he the machine. He enjoys the mechanical motion, in his own body" (XXIX).

Loerke denies life by placing his faith in automatism. Svidrigaylov
denies life by seeking to demoralize every vestige of goodness that is
inherent in man. Loerke has no God, except the machine. Svidrigaylov is his own god, the Dostoevskian Man-God. Both embody that
"evil world-soul," as Lawrence calls it, that annihilates all capacity
for redemptive action in life. In the case of Svidrigaylov, however,
one cannot escape the fact that he has a certain "atrophied grandeur"
about him, as Richard Curle has remarked.[15] This is to be seen, for
example, in his financial help to the poverty-stricken Marmeladovs,
his willingness to bear the funeral expenses after Mrs. Marmeladov's
death, his efforts to place the three children in good orphanages, even

his plans to help Sonia. But Svidrigaylov's acts of kindness, if the word itself can be used, do not indicate a repentant or heroic nature, nor are they the elements of redemption. They are simply acts that are closely related to Svidrigaylov's devouring passion for Dunya, Raskolnikov's sister. They are an integral part of the deceptiveness of his own evil personality, in all likelihood the last attempt of such men, to quote Shakespeare's words, "to mask their brows and hide their infamy."[16] Svidrigaylov, in short, is a totally ruined and damned human being whose abuse of human relationships has been so absolute and so devastating that, even when he is willing to help others, he is acting not out of an instinctive and inherent sense of deep-seated altruism and generosity, as is the case with Raskolnikov, but rather out of the urge to do something to lessen his own boredom. His are acts that too often stem from the task at hand, characteristic of the whole nature of his transient reactions to life. In reality, they are kind deeds with a price; they are not spontaneous and humane outbursts of the magnanimity of the human spirit, but rather the cynical reactions of an egotist who unequivocally knows that he is *playing* with human life and experience. "The man," Raskolnikov thought, "was always full of all sorts of plans and projects." (In this respect, Svidrigaylov's acts anticipate Stavrogin's marriage to the feebleminded Marya Timofyevna in *The Devils*, "a new experiment of a blasé man, with the object of finding out what you can bring a crazy cripple to," as Pyotr Verhovensky puts it.) However, when Svidrigaylov's monstrous egotism suffers a setback after Dunya has unhesitatingly denied his advances and has even fired a revolver at him, there is nothing left for him, for all along he has calculated his every gesture and action on the premise of his egocentrism and its necessary satisfaction. At this crucial point, Svidrigaylov is a defeated fiend whose mask has been stripped away and whose ego has been subjected to defeat. His failure to force Dunya to submit to him is too great a blow to his evil being. It is for him a humiliation that burdens him now with his own sense of egoistic failure and nothingness. It is his cynicism, *not* his conscience, that is dealt a fatal blow at this point. He is the kind of strong man who is essentially weak, too weak to cope with life that will not always cringe and bow before brute will or fall into the pattern of his own cynical nature and expectations. His sole recourse, then, is suicide, for only this remains as the last bastion of a perverse form of courage necessary to the superhuman Man-God. It is a self-inflicted death, as Mochulsky has noted, that comes from a feeling that is "mean-spirited" (*malodushie*) and not from one of "remorse" (*raskayanie*).[17] Thus, with the coming of dawn, in the cold dampness of a Petersburg street, when a "thick, milky mist hung over the city," Svidrigaylov put the revolver to his right temple and pulled the trigger. To the poor, bewildered sentry, who happened to be standing by, Svidrigaylov had said, "When they ask you about it, tell them he's gone to America." With these parting words Svidrigaylov conveys the moral bankruptcy of the perennial life-denier.

In their portrayals of Svidrigaylov and Loerke, Dostoevsky and Lawrence sought to depict the despair and doom that *can* paralyze man. With these figures, one well understands the kind of impasse that can be reached in modern civilization, for both personify the dangers that are inherent in the world, as well as the dangers that must be transcended if life is to remain meaningful. Svidrigaylov and Loerke are religionless men in that for them belief in life and in man is synonymous with negation, cynicism, and violation. Dostoevsky's stress on the mystery of life and Lawrence's on "vivid life" are far beyond their comprehension. And it is their special brand of diabolical cleverness that makes it impossible for either of these two monomaniacs to maintain and sustain the sanctity of human contact. Svidrigaylov is that chaotic force in life which, prompted by an insatiable urge to satisfy its own selfish ends, destroys the harmony and balance of creation. He is an evil which stalks and violates life, ever ready to subvert and vitiate what is clean, healthy, and innocent in human relationships. When Raskolnikov admits to Svidrigaylov that "I can't help feeling that in some way you are very like me," or that the latter seemed to have some power over him, the implication is incontestably clear that heroic effort is vitally needed to overcome what is debased and evil. For Raskolnikov, therefore, there is the choice between Svidrigaylov and all that he stands for, and Sonia, who almost miraculously communicates to him the beauty and order that are immanent in life. Her message is one of affirmation, of rebirth and rediscovery, of life that has "taken the place of dialectics." Svidrigaylov epitomizes the defilement of universal harmony, and his very presence perverts and distorts the "good life." Sonia, however, counsels Raskolnikov to make his peace with life, with all of creation and all of its creatures. "Go at once," she says to him with the genuine conviction that Svidrigaylov lacks in his acts of charity, "this very minute, and stand at the cross-roads, bow down, first kiss the earth which you have defiled, and then bow down to all the four corners of the world—and say to all men aloud, I am a murderer! Then God will send you life again" (V, 4).[18]

In the same manner, Loerke also symbolizes the perversity of boundless freedom and power. His superficial charm (the special *charme* that is the particular hallmark of the successful modern artistic "personality"—successful, that is, only if it is sufficiently "counterfeit" and disengaged from real positive life-action) is as fascinating as Svidrigaylov's sinister benevolence, but it is merely part of his mask and certainly just as sinister. He makes people rock with laughter. He is always amusing and clever in his use of words: "a chatterer, a magpie, a maker of mischievous word-jokes." He and Gudrun enjoy escaping into the pure mental delights of conversation about literature, sculpture, and painting. "They played with the past, and with the great figures of the past, a sort of little game of chess, or marionettes, all to please themselves. They had all the great men for their marionettes, and they two were the God of the show, working it all" (XXX). He himself realizes that he is not strong and attractive, but his mental vanity, he implies, is different from the ordinary, and it is this talent in him that must be satisfied—"my *me* is watching for the thee of the mistress, for the match to my particular intelligence." Svidrigaylov suffers from an excess of sensual appetite, Loerke from an excess of mentality. The latter has transcended the bloodstream of humanity and the "creative wonder" of the universe. He has dedicated himself to the machine and to his work, which in turn have led to the dehumanized values that are now triumphant in his nature and in his separation from life—"the machine works him, instead of he the machine." Life, excluding his "work," has neither meaning nor joy nor wonder for him because nothing matters outside the "reality" of his art. "What one does in one's art," he says, "that is the breath of one's being. What one does in one's life, that is bagatelle for the outsiders to fuss about" (XXX). To Ursula, it is important to note, Loerke stands for a dehumanized world of "eternal snow," of "machinery and the acts of labour." When she becomes terrified by Loerke's discourse on his statuette of the naked girl on the green bronze horse, she reaches out rather desperately for the *restorative* experience of a living relationship. She seeks to free herself from Loerke's world and all that it represents. "She wanted to see the dark earth, to smell its earthy fecundity, to see the patient wintry vegetation, to feel the sunshine touch a response in the buds" (XXIX).

The fact cannot be escaped that Loerke, like Svidrigaylov, serves to depict the completely unregenerative side of man who has surrendered to the powers of automatism. Gerald Crich, the modern industrial magnate, especially detests Loerke, as can readily be seen in their encounters, but the detestation is in reality his bitter and highly disturbing recognition of an evil and life-negation that he himself has made possible through his own apotheosis of the industrial machine. Both are willing victims of excessive will and ego. Both serve the same master, the machine. Both treat life with the same irreverence and disdain. In one respect, however, Loerke has gone far beyond Gerald Crich, and that is in the absolute degree of his separation from the life-stream. Loerke has jumped beyond all human frontiers and fellowship; he has surmounted *"the deadly space between,"* as it were. His dehumanization is so absolute and so irrevocable that he has no need whatsoever of anything except "for a little companionship in intelligence." It is this that Gerald Crich ultimately sees, and it is this that frightens him to the point of death. For Loerke is that part of Gerald's human consciousness and being that can no longer defy or escape self-recognition and self-examination. In Loerke, "that little insect," "that little scum of a sculptor," Gerald at last grasps the utter magnitude and the supreme and now uncontrollable evil of his own crime against all life. Loerke is the evil that men like Gerald Crich bring to pass. It is this disastrous distortion, this mutation of human kind, that Gerald Crich, the would-be superman, sees and despairs of, his despair leading finally to his own self-inflicted death in "the great shallow among the precipices and slopes near the summit of the pass."

Gerald Crich, like Rodion Raskolnikov, must be viewed as the superman who has failed. The parallel here between the two tragic figures is a decisive one, especially because both men do believe in the cult of the strong-man. Raskolnikov bludgeons to death the moneylender, Alyona Ivanova, and her simple and devout sister, Lisaveta, in order to prove his theory that to chosen and extraordinary natures it is permissible to commit any crime, to transgress any law, "to eliminate all obstacles." "But," he says, "if for the sake of his idea such a man has to step over a corpse or wade through blood, he is, in my opinion, absolutely entitled, in accordance with the dictates of his conscience, to permit himself to wade through blood, all depending of course on the nature and scale of his idea . . ." (III, 5). Raskolnikov looked on his crimes as the inevitable test of a great and strong man who, in order to be a Napoleon and not some "aesthetic louse," does not kill an insignificant human being but a principle. The attainment of such a goal, he feels, releases the strong-man from any inhibitive moral and human responsibility, and it secures for him what is ultimate in "Freedom and power—power above all. Power over all the tumbling vermin and over all the ant-hill." In murdering the two women, Raskolnikov protests against the principle of human equality and moral conscience, and he strives at the same time to proclaim his independence in isolation from all things. Raskolnikov is the superman who kills human beings in order to gain moral independence; Gerald Crich is the superman, the man who "would be a Napoleon of peace, or a Bismarck," who appoints himself to be god of the machine and seeks to organize and manipulate life as mere function through the struggle with and subjugation of nature and man. As the owner of mines at Beldover, Selby, Whatmore, and Lethley Bank, this "promoter of industry" sets out to enact his "vision of power." "He discovered at last a real adventure in the coalmines." Raskolnikov sees himself as a superman in the realm of ethics and morality, which he believes must no longer hinder his theories and action. Gerald Crich sees himself as a superman in the realm of industry and the machine, and he devotes himself to the "eternal mills of God" and to the "pure instrumentality" of life. "The unifying principle," this modern captain of industry announces, "was the work in hand. Only work, the business of production, held men together. It was mechanical, but their society *was* a mechanism" (VIII). Although Raskolnikov and Gerald Crich are supermen who do battle in different fields of action, they both seek to assert their power and will over the whole of life itself. Raskolnikov seeks to become a master of Theory; Gerald Crich seeks to become a master of a System. In the end the Theory not only shatters the one, but brings about his exile and imprisonment, whereas the System destroys the other.

Raskolnikov's fate in comparison with that of Crich is less disastrous, for he is never fully certain whether his acts of murder were instances of altruistic yearnings or of outright revolt. There is in him an innate humanity and a conscience that cling to and refuse to disown him. Raskolnikov does remain divided in this respect to the very end, and the conflict between his renunciation of all human values and his need to repent for misdeeds against one's fellowmen tortures him even after his confession and imprisonment. The fact that this conflict *is* going on in Raskolnikov serves to show that he is not completely damned. Moreover, for him the matter of choice is still a potent one, for the paradigmatic presence of Sonia serves all the time to lighten his burden and shed a ray of light in an otherwise bleak future in Siberia. Marmeladov's words in the early part of the novel, "For every man must have at least somewhere to go," have a relevant place here. Sonia, by remaining loyal to Raskolnikov and following him to Siberia, where he is to remain eight years, personifies this "somewhere to go." Otherwise, the result for Raskolnikov might be the utter isolation and lack of conscience that prevail in Svidrigaylov. Sonia, then, remains close by Raskolnikov's side in the time of his crises; she nurses him in his illness, she aids him to battle with his doubts, she labors to awaken his sense of goodness. All along, in fact, Sonia has been with Raskolnikov, fighting for his soul against the demonic forces that have besieged and battered his intellect. For Raskolnikov there was the path of Svidrigaylov, leading to moral chaos, but this he unhesitatingly recognized and rejected. There was also the path of Sonia. That he realized at least some measure of its greater meaning and merit can be seen in his decision to ask forgiveness of Man and "the great Mother Earth," when "He knelt down in the middle of the square, bowed down to the earth, and kissed the filthy earth with joy and rapture. Then he got up, and bowed down once more." Raskolnikov is the potential superman who remains within the human pale, if somewhat precariously. When, at last, Sonia's love and devotion for Raskolnikov begin to turn the tide, "now their hands did not part." And this in itself is symbolic of the affirmation of life through the tie of love and "all-togetherness." "It was love that brought them back to life: the heart of one held inexhaustible sources of life for the heart of the other." Now, too, "Life had taken the place of dialectics, and something quite different had to work itself out in his mind." Most significant is the vision of the new life that Raskolnikov, while a prisoner in Siberia, has early one morning when sitting down at the bank of a river. (The vision of felicity found in Dostoevsky's Epilogue is, like the endings of Lawrence's *The Rainbow*, of E. M. Forster's *Howards End*, and of Hardy's *The Dynasts*, not at all incongruous in the light of the strife and tension that have preceded, but is a great and ringing note of hope that is an indispensable part of the prophetic art of the writer whose work is founded on life and not despair.) Hitherto, Raskolnikov has been in a state of agony and has had frightening dreams of killings and human horror. The terror of doubt and disbelief is now replaced by a growing serenity and hope, by the acceptance of man, and by the affirmation of life. The nightmare of the past slowly gives way to the affirmation of the present and the vision of the future:

> From the steep bank a wide stretch of the countryside opened up before him. Snatches of a song floated faintly across from the distant bank of the river. There in the vast steppe, flooded with sunlight, he could see the black tents of the nomads which appeared like dots in the distance. There there was freedom, there other people were living, people who were not a bit like the people he knew; there time itself seemed to stand still as though the age of Abraham and his flocks had not passed (Epilogue, 2).

Unlike Raskolnikov, who still has a choice in life, as embodied in the person of Sonia, Gerald Crich has none, for it is now too late. He failed earlier to respond to the bond of fellowship offered him by Birkin, and on the basis of which his life could have, if only partially, achieved some meaning through the joy and harmony that are given only in genuine human friendship. This is the kind of friendship that Lawrence describes as "the real implicit reliance of one man on another: as sacred a unison as marriage: only it must be deeper, more ultimate than emotion and personality, cool separateness and yet the ultimate reliance."[19] He has lost Gudrun, who cannot love him precisely because he cannot really love her as a person. "There was a league between them, abhorrent to them both. They were implicated with each other in abhorrent mysteries" (XVIII). To her he can offer nothing, as she claims, but "a very madness of dead mechanical monotony and meaninglessness." Herein, too, can be seen the real tragedy of Gerald Crich, for in his attempt to be a master-builder of industry and a *princeps* of the System, he has submitted to an immoderateness of will and ego from which there can be no turning back. Undoubtedly, he does attain the supreme goal of translating "the mystic word harmony into the practical word organization"— which is now otherwise known as "progress." With the help of experts and the latest scientific discoveries, Gerald has at last

> found his eternal and his infinite in the pure machine-principle of perfect co-ordination into one pure, complex infinitely repeated motion, like the spinning of a wheel; but a productive spinning, as the revolving of the universe may be called a productive spinning, a productive repetition through eternity, to infinity. And this is the God-motion, this productive repetition ad infinitum. And Gerald was the God of the machine, Deus ex Machina. And the whole productive will of man was the Godhead (XVII).

Mechanical perfection, the Godhead in process, "the pure working out of the problem," are to him the only goals and values in life. He becomes the "high priest" of a new social and economic order who translates everything into sheer mechanization. "Terrible and inhuman were his examinations into every detail; there was no privacy he would spare, no old sentiment but he would turn it over. The old grey managers, the old grey clerks, the doddering old pensioners, he looked at them and removed them as so much lumber. The whole concern seemed like a hospital of invalid employees. He had no emotional qualms" (XVII). His approach to the entire problem is the reverse of his father's: Thomas Crich wanted the mining industry to be run on love and "wanted to be a father of loving kindness and sacrificial benevolence." Mr. Crich's *raison d'être* was one of helping out the miserable, whereas that of his son was of arrogant mastery. Yet, the father's world was crushed when he found that the gap between religious creed (which in his case was pervaded by an excessive, life-sapping sentimentalism) and the grim reality of material necessity was unbridgeable. His son, on the other hand, who "vibrated with zest before the challenge" and who looked on the problems of life as being no different from those in geometry, was able to create his own world of pure instrumentality. It was a new and inhuman world, mechanically perfect but devoid of human warmth and feeling, one in which human fellowship was no longer even a memory. It

> was the first step in undoing, the first great phase of chaos, the substitution of the mechanical principle for the organic, the destruction of the organic purpose, the organic unity, and the subordination of every organic unit to the great mechanical purpose. It was pure organic disintegration and pure mechanical organisation. This is the first and finest state of chaos (XVII).

However, with the attainment of "the subordination of every organic unit to the great mechanical purpose," Gerald Crich was to experience the disillusionment that is inevitable when the creative and spontaneous fullness of being has been sacrificed to a theory and a formula. It is the case of the superman who overestimates and overreaches himself. Here we are reminded of Birkin's prophetic words to Gerald at the beginning of the novel: "And what's your work? Getting so many more thousands of tons of coal out of the earth every day. And when we've got all the coal we want, and all the plush furniture, and pianofortes, and the rabbits are all stewed and eaten, and we're all warm and our bellies are filled and we're listening to the young lady performing on the pianoforte—what then? What then, when you've made a real fair start with your material things?" (V). Gerald Crich ultimately becomes the victim of his own creation and isolation, and it is the evil presence of Loerke that dogs his path as a reminder of this. Unlike Raskolnikov, who has "somewhere to go," Gerald Crich has nothing left and no one to turn to ("What then, when you've made a real fair start with your material things?"). His great schemes of reform have sullied the world, and he, the "supreme instrument of control," and the people around him who are now beyond feeling or reason, "something really godlike," can no longer meet on a common ground. It is this ironical fate of the master and the mastered, the victim and the victimizer, that Gudrun realizes when she repudiates Gerald Crich and seeks the underground world of Loerke:

He was to her the most crucial instance of the existing world, the *ne plus ultra* of the world of man as it existed for her. In him she knew the world, and had done with it. Knowing him finally she was the Alexander seeking new worlds. But there *were* no new worlds, there were no more *men*, there were only creatures, little, ultimate *creatures* like Loerke. The world was finished now, for her. There was only the inner, individual darkness, sensation within the ego, the obscene religious mystery of ultimate reduction, the mystic frictional activities of diabolic reducing down, disintegrating the vital organic body of life (XXX).

Yet, of all of Lawrence's characters, Gerald Crich is the only one who approaches any great stature as a tragic hero. And, like the tragic heroes of old, he is not beyond the pangs of conscience and moral struggle nor the realization of what his hubris has brought forth. The moral struggle must be insisted upon on the basis of the unerring evidence of this novel, even in spite of T. S. Eliot, who declared in *After Strange Gods* (1934)—with the dogmatism that characterizes that little "primer of modern heresy"—that Lawrence's work was devoid of moral struggle. Indeed, even at the time he was destroying "true spontaneous life," and deifying the power of the machine, Gerald Crich was not without the vague and mysterious, but nonetheless present, feeling that he was overstepping certain human limits and moral boundaries. *"In a strangely indifferent, sterile way, he was frightened."* And in these few words of the "still small voice" of conscience, he was to reveal a humanity containing the sparks of heroism itself, the heroism that is implicit even in the grudging comprehension of the inexorable powers of *nomos* and *physis*. Gerald Crich's "power-intoxication" is ultimately limited by a humanity immanent in him, by his inability to repudiate, fully and finally, the organic unity of life and fellowship which he is unable to attain but which he can never deny in an absolute sense. He suffers from an egoism or conceit that is one of function but not one of substance. What he says and what he does belie what is innate in his mind and heart, and this is what made him "frightened." For this very reason, Gerald is not the superman triumphant at all, but the suffering witness to his own human limitation. Indeed, it is this limitation that Gudrun sees in him:

Whereas in Gerald's soul there still lingered some attachment to the rest, to the whole. And this was his limitation. He was limited, borné, subject to his necessity, in the last issue, for goodness, for righteousness, for oneness with the ultimate purpose. That the ultimate purpose might be the perfect and subtle experience of the process of death, the will being kept unimpaired, that was not allowed in him. And this was his limitation (XXX).

It is this limitation, likewise, that allies Gerald Crich with Raskolnikov, for both cannot ascend beyond the boundaries of human life. In them, in one degree or another, the conflict between supreme intellect and a moral sense of belonging to human kind is not a decisively concluded one, as it is in Loerke and Svidrigaylov; nor is the evil that enthralls them as unmitigating or irredeemable as, for instance, the malignity of Shakespeare's Iago in *Othello* or the malevolent envy of Melville's Claggart in *Billy Budd*. Gerald Crich, like Raskolnikov, *suffers* the tortures of his human limitation and succumbs to them.

As a would-be superman and tragic hero, Gerald Crich produces a feeling of pity that is as gripping as that evoked by Raskolnikov, and even more terrifying because of the singular circumstances of his fate in those great and incomparable last chapters of *Women in Love*. Raskolnikov, it is seen, is not alone and unfriended, for he has Sonia. Gerald's fate, however, is one of total isolation, and it is he, ironically, who becomes an outsider in the very world he has sought to master. In the end, Gerald can turn to no one because the world that he has defied through his cruel reforms has been robbed of its human feelings and fellowship which Gerald learns, *too late*, that he cannot do without. In such a world of terror, there is only Loerke to turn to, and it is he who symbolizes the impasse that comes with the extinction of all that is creative and alive. There is no going beyond Loerke, for he is that "beyond," that "finest state of chaos," of mechanized petrification, that Gerald has begotten through his sacrifices to the will and the intellect. To view Loerke is for Gerald to view the final result of "working out the problem." All along, Gerald has been a sort of productive agent, the great modern "Specialist," who in service to the System has bestowed upon himself and others the fruits of his labor. The System, the machine, has made Gerald too weak; conversely, it has produced in Loerke a "man" who has no responsibility whatsoever to human life. Loerke is the "free individual," amoral and absolute in himself. His is a "machine consciousness," but Gerald's ties, despite the onslaught of his theories and the working out of problems, are still those of a struggling humanity. Gerald is the begetter of the Loerkes as a result of an excess of will and idea. Loerke is born out of wedlock: he is the dissonant future, the man of tomorrow. Gerald Crich is a vainglorious rebel who meets challenge after challenge, and Loerke is the dangerous by-product of this lust for power. The former relies on masterful will and material strength to arm him in his daring feats. But the latter, who neither commands nor feels, who neither loves nor is loved, knows greater and deeper secrets. "Loerke knew a secret beyond these things. The greatest power is the one that is subtle and adjusts itself, not one which blindly attacks" (XXX).

When, at the end, Gerald Crich views his own product, the picture is so horrifying and the agony of the crime that he has committed is so painful and distressing, that death, which he brings on himself, is inevitable. It is at this point, more than at any other, that Gerald Crich is a tragic figure who realizes that in killing life, he has killed the thing he has loved most. "The man had killed the thing he loved, / And so he had to die," writes Oscar Wilde in "The Ballad of Reading Gaol." But in condemning himself to die, Gerald Crich indicates the heroic capacity to recognize the vanity of his hubris and the enormity of his *hamartia* against life. In some ways Gerald is like the tragic Byronic figure Manfred, that "Magian of great power, and fearful skill," heaping "knowledge from forbidden mines of lore" and passing "the nights of years in sciences untaught." Like him who had but "slight communion with other men" and no sympathy "with breathing life" and who placed all his faith in "the power and joy of this most bright intelligence," Gerald Crich must make amends for his crime against life, in the tragic destiny of the realization that

> . . . his knowledge, and his power, and will
> As far as is compatible with clay,
> Which clogs the ethereal essence, have been such
> As clay hath seldom borne; his aspirations
> Have been beyond the dwellers of the earth,
> And they have only taught him what we know—
> That knowledge is not happiness, and science
> But an exchange of ignorance for that
> Which is another kind of ignorance.[20]

Thus, when Gerald Crich chooses a "death by perfect cold," it is a choice that becomes as much a moral relenting as a departure from the life he has molded. His choice is not only "an omen of the universal dissolution into whiteness and snow," but, even more, a sign of the highest suffering that follows the realization that intellect "*avails him not.*" Gerald Crich is no longer "the gleaming" but the penitent sufferer whose memory of what he has done serves as his condemnation and his mind as his hell. ("There are shades," Lord Byron writes, "which will not vanish / there are thoughts thou canst not banish.") "I've had enough," Gerald cries, "I want to go to sleep. I've had enough." It is the "sleep of death" that he seeks at last. This in itself is Gerald's admission and confession, as he has now realized his own limitations before the "creative mystery" of life and the cosmos. He commits himself to a higher judgment and answers to a higher summons.

In the final analysis, Gerald Crich is, as Mark Schorer has noted, a sinner.[21] Yet, in choosing to die, he at the same time indicates a rejection of the inhuman world that he has fostered, the world of the Loerkes. In this, too, Gerald acknowledges his responsibility to man and the universe. Like Rodion Raskolnikov, he remains by his action a dweller in the realm of redemption, for he is a sinner who has ultimately recognized his crime against life. But unlike Raskolnikov, who is being redeemed through the saving grace of Sonia, Gerald waits to be redeemed. The question asked of Cain, "What hast thou done?" remains, then, to be answered.[22] Gerald Crich, it should be remembered, had as a child accidentally shot and killed his brother, and like Cain he was in the end to be "a fugitive and a vagabond in the earth." But as a sinner and sufferer, he was to choose death, in a scene that is perhaps one of the greatest in the twentieth-century novel. Like Cain, who had cried out, "My punishment is greater than I can bear," Gerald was to recognize in the last and perhaps most redeeming moments of his earthly life that the punishment he was bearing all along was the agonizing burden of his crime against himself and against man and the universe. In death he was to be "surrounded by sheer slopes and precipices." As "he fell something broke in his soul, and immediately he went to sleep." And indeed, it is sleep, *not* annihilation, that begins a new experience for Gerald Crich; it is the sojourn of the penitent superman who *is to be* cleansed and then reborn "in touch" with other men.

In his excellent study of Dostoevsky, the Russian poet and critic Vyacheslav Ivanov, discussing the meaning and degree of evil, makes the important point of distinguishing between the evil in Raskolnikov and that in Svidrigaylov. He believes that in Raskolnikov it is the dynamic evil of Lucifer, the archetype of isolation, that is lurking, whereas in Svidrigaylov it is the stagnant evil of Ahriman, the archetype of destruction, that is supreme. Luciferian evil, he says, is the tempter and seducer, a force that impels man and denotes defection but not ruination, sharp conflict but not complete victory. "The influence of Lucifer can therefore be described as inversionary, and that of Ahriman as perversionary." (It is exactly this "inversionary" evil that is found in Raskolnikov and Gerald Crich.) Again, later on, he writes: "Lucifer is 'the Prince of this World,' Ahriman is his executioner, his Satrap, and—so he hopes—his royal successor."[23] Svidrigaylov and Loerke embody that vision of evil when the creative meaning of beauty and love has been defiled beyond recognition. In them the

utter reduction to stagnation is complete and final: Arkady Ivanovitch Svidrigaylov embodies limitless evil in which animality becomes
bestiality, and in Herr Loerke there is a progressive decomposition of
a mentality that becomes inhuman. Their condition of evil is unmit-
igable; it is that which comes *meta*, the *meta*-evil, as it were, when
overwhelming evil slips "over the ocean and round the world," as
E. M. Forster appropriately describes it.[24] Indeed, the beauty of this
world, which Lawrence associates with an immanent "tenderness"
and Dostoevsky with "gladness," has now been transposed into the
"insect-lust" that Svidrigaylov stands for and the "insect-like comprehension" that Loerke deifies. Contrary to Raskolnikov and Gerald
Crich, in whom the rage of Luciferian evil has now come to a halt
with the realization that superhuman Theory and System are not the
highest absolutes and values of life, the evil of Ahriman in Svidrigaylov and Loerke is that "royal successor," that "finest state of chaos,"
when there can be no turning back or seeing ahead, when hell itself
is that new realm of life.

Lawrence time and again criticized Fyodor Dostoevsky. His comment in his Preface to *The Grand Inquisitor*, which was one of the
last things he wrote, is quite characteristic: "Dostoevsky is always perverse, always impure, always an evil thinker and marvellous seer."[25]
In those last two significant words, "marvellous seer," Lawrence admits, despite everything else, his real debt to the Russian novelist, as
well as his kinship to his great precursor and teacher. Both writers
were concerned with the breakdown of life; both revered the creative
mysteries of man and the universe; both refused to bow to the greater
forces of science and the intellect; both were religious seekers who
sought to revive the real, living meaning of religion as the bond of
human fellowship and connection. They were prophets and seers who
utilized their art as both a contemplation of life and an exploration of
the depths of human existence and experience. Dostoevsky was a great
seer who was to define the predicament of modern society; Lawrence,
in grasping the great creative accomplishment and message of his
precursor, was in his own unique way to apply the definition to the
ever-increasing, ever-baffling problems of contemporary civilization.
Their visions of evil united them in the search for a solution to the
lacerations and violations of what is good and true in life. In a large
sense, Dostoevsky was a witness to the gathering storm of the breakdown of modern life, and Lawrence was to become its unwilling victim. Still, in the face of all that was happening, Dostoevsky and
Lawrence refused to submit to the relentless reality of their visions
of evil. This brave refusal to surrender to those forces that would de-

stroy creative life is a source of the greatness of their art, and it lends to their prophetic visions a quality of heroism that carries with it the seeds of hope and redemption.

11

Dostoevsky and Satanism

ἀλλὰ ῥῦσαι ἡμᾶς ἀπὸ τοῦ πονηροῦ·
—MATTHEW 6:13

∾

I

In Dostoevsky's vision of evil the figure of the devil assumes a powerful role and brings to mind the contention that a writer's obsessive
concern with the devil can result in "indelible burns" and "incur-
able wounds." In a trenchant essay, "The Devil in Contemporary
Literature," Claude-Edmonde Magny declares that an artist who has
too strong a desire to look the devil in the face may even seek "to vie
in cunning with him." "Once the mere thought of evil is present in
the mind," she goes on to observe, "it loses no time in invading the
imagination; then the soul, which has taken delight in the thought,
makes a movement towards it, and ends by consenting to it."[1] In a
more realistic and conciliatory vein Friedrich Schleiermacher has
remarked that the poetic use of the devil is to be accounted the least
harmful, and "no disadvantage is to be feared from an emphatic use
of this idea in pious moods."[2] André Gide, in his *Journal des Faux-
Monnayeurs*, has also expressed a keen interest in this subject (though
from another angle of aesthetic vision), pointing out that the devil is
best served when he is unperceived. The devil's securest hiding place,
Gide stresses, is behind any approach that dismisses him as *une
puérile simplification*, that argues his non-being according to *expli-
cations rationnelles*, and that relegates him to *l'hypothèse gratuite*.[3]
Indeed, no less an authority than Saint Ignatius Loyola, in his *Spiritual Exercises* ("Discernment of Spirits," R. 13), has vigorously asserted, "Unmask Satan and you vanquish him."

Perhaps in no other novelist has the figure of Satan been as conspicuous or inexorable as in Dostoevsky. Indeed, the whole range of life
depicted in his novel *The Devils* (1873) must be regarded as fundamentally a product of satanic activity when, as Dostoevsky quotes
from Pushkin in one of the two epigraphs to the novel,

We've lost the way,
Demons have bewitched our horses,
Led us in the wilds astray.[4]

In this work Satan is supremely active in human experience. "Like a roaring lion, seeking whom he may devour" (Eph. 6:11–12), Dostoevsky's devil has in a very large and true sense "gone round about the earth and walked through it" (Job 1:7). The meaning of human existence seems irremediably violated to the point that "the very laws of the planet are a lie and the vaudeville of devils" (*samye zakony planety lozh i diavolov vodevil'*), as the God-tormented Alexey Nilitch Kirillov has direly concluded. In *The Devils* in general and in the person of Nikolay Vsyevolodovitch Stavrogin in particular, Dostoevsky tremblingly but relentlessly confronts Satan as the Evil One, the Adversary, the Accuser, the Tempter, the Liar, the Murderer, the Tormentor, the Prince of this World, the Prince of Darkness. This confrontation is achieved with extraordinary artistic success, and for Dostoevsky the medium of art thus becomes the frightening reality of struggling with that infinitely diabolical phenomenon whose *raison d'être* is best expressed by the Greek word ὁ Πονηρός. Surely, it was not accidental that Dostoevsky entitled his novel *Besy—The Devils*.

Dostoevsky's use of Satan must be seen in a decidedly different light from that of artists like Milton, Goethe, Shelley, Byron, Hugo, Carducci, and Baudelaire. It must be seen as transcending the applicability of H. G. Wells's statement in *The Undying Fire*: "Satan is a celestial *raconteur*. He alone makes stories." For Dostoevsky, Satan was not a literary device or problem. Nor, in his portrait of Satan in the figure of Stavrogin, was he striving for aesthetic effects per se, such as the invocation of a Radcliffian terror or the evocation of the weird, the macabre, the startling, the grotesque, the gloomy, or the terrifying. What he was attempting was chiefly motivated by Christian values and a Christian consciousness; his response and vision were preponderantly religious and moral. Stavrogin must not be approached in the Miltonic framework of a creature "majestic though in ruin," endowed with and admired for his "heroic energy." Neither is he to be coupled with Lord Byron's "fatal" man, that mighty outlaw lingering on the misty borders of vice and virtue. Stavrogin, it will be seen, is in severe contrast to any romantic archetype of Satan as a fiery rebel or a composite of a Typhon and a Prometheus, defying divinity for the sake of an oppressed humanity. He is Dostoevsky's vision of evil and of the innermost reality of sin. The Russian writer does not try to show the origin of this evil, but rather its alluring and hideous aspects, above all its *present* existence as an actual fact, as a "falling away." The total scheme of *The Devils*, Dostoevsky seems to bring out, was justified theologically and poetically because it not only gave the truth about evil, but also induced an examination of conscience, a profound spiritual experience, and a thirsting and hungering for God.

Appraisals of Stavrogin are consistently and overwhelmingly timid and irresolute. Conclusions to the effect that to "settle on any prototype would be hazardous" and that Stavrogin is "a complex amalgam of many literary characters" summarize precisely the approaches of most critics.[5] To them Stavrogin is a kind of disenchanted character— he is full of mystery; he is not only below but also beyond good and evil; he is beset by boredom; he is a tragic figure; he is a man with a curse on him, his "greatness nullified by his split personality"; he is a divided, Russian Luciferian type, perhaps an offshoot of a Speshnev or a Bakunin; he is "a typically modern personality haunted by the 'demon of irony' "; he is a "victim of romantic *ennui*"; he is the "most complete development of the romantic, 'Byronic,' egoist"; he is the victim of a "hopeless solitude."[6] "Wrapped in indifference, lost in an egotism he does not value, he passes by, simply but deadly, as if he were the inhabitant of another planet, spreading around him, impassively, a miasma as he goes."[7] There seems to be almost common rhetorical agreement that Stavrogin cannot be categorized either as a man or as a *homo fictus*. He has become an enigma fascinating to behold and explore, a wonderful opportunity for clever critical exercises and semantics—clever, that is, as long as critics disregard moral value judgments, religious awareness, and definite ethical and theological elements, without which, as T. S. Eliot has well noted, literary criticism remains incomplete. The proper, more adaptable critical approach to Dostoevsky, as one eminent comparatist has phrased it in a collection of essays, is "to avoid fierce commitments of the Russians [e.g., Merejkowski, Ivanov, Berdyaev, and Zander[8]], to make compromises, to combine approaches, to suggest shadings of meaning."[9] But the results of such an attitude are, to say the least, all too apparent in the excessively secularized critical pronouncements of the skeptic, the aesthete, the formalist, the rationalist, the positivist—for such comprise the gang that has continually made of Stavrogin everything and nothing.[10]

It would, of course, be a presumption to deny Dostoevsky's debts to the Western literary tradition and the profound influences made on him by such writers as Balzac, Dickens, George Sand, Hugo, Sue, E. T. A. Hoffmann, Byron, Schiller, Racine, and Corneille. That Dostoevsky borrowed and adapted freely from other writers is quite obvious; yet, as Charles E. Passage has noted in his interesting study, Dostoevsky was a creator, not an imitator. Hoffmann's *Die Elixiere des Teufels*, for instance, persisted as an inspiring influence in much of the Russian's work, but as Passage also brings out, "It is of silver; Dostoevski turns it into gold."[11] The claim, furthermore, that Dostoevsky is, as artist and thinker, in the stream of Western thought and literature, though not essentially inaccurate, fails far too often to take an informed or sympathetic view of Dostoevsky's obligations to "Orthodox culture" (*Pravoslavnaia kul'tura*), to the philosophical and spiritual realities of which Dostoevsky had been exposed since his early youth and from which he was unable and unwilling to separate himself throughout his life and work. What needs to be insisted upon, in the face of the increasing attempts to make Dostoevsky into just another commodity for the consumption of Western readers and more grist for Western critics, is that Dostoevsky's greatest and primary debts were to "Orthodox culture" and that before his art and the people of his cosmos are understood, readers will have to have some idea of what constitutes an Eastern Orthodox milieu and metaphysic. "In Dostoyevsky," as Professor Zenkovsky has very aptly declared, ". . . we see philosophic creativity *growing out* of the womb of the religious consciousness."[12]

In the Eastern Orthodox tradition the devil is the personification of a fierce evil that besieges human life. Every measure must be taken to keep him away. When we consider "The Office of Holy Baptism" and "The Prayers at the Reception of Catechumens," as found in Eastern Orthodox rites, we can ascertain how formidable and threatening the figure of the devil is. For example, in the First Exorcism there appears this typical passage, as the devil is adjured: "Fear, begone and depart from this creature, and return not again, neither hide thyself in him, neither seek though to meet him, nor to influence him, either by night or by day; either in the morning, or at noonday: but depart hence to thine own Tartarus, until the great Day of Judgment which is ordained."[13]

Satan is able to assume human attributes that enable him to descend upon man "in a mighty rage" (Rev. 12:12). He is not only a κοσμοκράτωρ but also a δύναμις that must be constantly reckoned with and fought: a disturbing force that ceaselessly harasses man by day and by night. He is an "unclean spirit" (Rev. 16:13) with a "deceitful tongue" (Isa. 14:13, 14), seducing, subverting, frustrating, destroying life at every opportunity—"a murderer from the beginning." Often he "disguises himself as an angel of light" (II Cor. 11:14) who, in the words of Saint Tychon of Zadonsk, "offers evil under the semblance of good, like poison steeped in honey."[14] "The angel of the bottom-less pit," he afflicts, infects, and maims life. He incessantly emerges from the abyss to become a prowler in life. Even when he takes human shape, Satan represents a completely unregenerate humanity, a humanity that has "known the 'deep things' of Satan" and has died, never to wear the "crown of eternal life." Ultimately, too, Satan must transhumanize himself and return to his domain of darkness, despair, and impiety. He stands outside of time and is exempt from responsi-bility: he is that "lawless one" and everlasting κατήγορος.

If some of his critics have been deluded by the person of Stavrogin, Dostoevsky at any rate was not. In his portrayal of Stavrogin, the Russian novelist was actually participating in the unending conflict with evil and concurrently resisting it and acquiring "patient endur-ance" (Rev. 2:1, 2). For Dostoevsky a profound lesson was to be learned in this confrontation, a lesson which is nowhere more simply and poignantly phrased than in the words of James (4:7), "Resist the devil and he will flee you." Stavrogin illuminates perfectly the im-mense difficulties of viewing satanism in its various enigmatic guises. In this respect, Dostoevsky indicates that the powers of Satan are not mere theories or explorations, not mere questions and answers, but rather manifestations that must be directly encountered, seen for what they are, judged, and resisted. In *The Devils*, then, Dostoevsky is firmly committed to waging a battle with the devil and with the evil that the devil perpetrates. In it he also discerns the epiphenomena of the warfare that one must enter into with πειρασμός, not merely with the devil as a personality but with the devil as the embodiment of those terrifying energies, "principalities and powers" which assail and brutalize life. "For we wrestle not against flesh and blood," Saint Paul reminds us, "but against principalities, against powers, against the rulers of the darkness of this world ... against the prince and power of the air" (Eph. 6:12). Dostoevsky fiercely probes these pow-ers and energies, neither sentimentalizing nor romanticizing them. And the implicit, unwavering moral judgments of his novel indicate the deepest religious convictions of the artist, in spite of the nagging doubts, insecurities, and tensions of faith that periodically burst into the whole of his art and message.

The stress on the irreducible in Stavrogin and the persistent at-tempts to enigmatize and humanize him have failed to perceive the dimensions of the evil he represents. All too often Stavrogin's activity is not seen in the light of the impelling value that he has made of evil; rather it is subordinated to what must presumably remain as an ab-surdity or a riddle. Both the dimensions and the intensity of Stavrogin's crimes remain unexplained, and serious omissions relating to Dostoevsky's own intentions as a religious artist result. Yet, to explain evil merely as what is inexplicable in life abrogates religious faith itself and moral responsibility. One of the most constant demands exacted by Dostoevsky's novels is that evil should be apprehended in its exterior and interior forms. Dostoevsky's approach to evil was a profoundly vital one, resting firmly on the belief that, in contrast to the good-natured Tolstoian attitude of nonresistance, evil must be confronted and challenged. It should be stipulated that in his depiction of evil Dostoevsky did not preach an eschatology of vengeance and torment, did not fail to bring out the mysterious, unending interpenetration of the clean and the unclean. His recognition of human error and frailty and the acuteness of his vision itself are far from being narrowly moralistic, and his art affirms that man, through penitence and purification, can recover the image of God.

Just as Dostoevsky disclosed a strong optimism in his belief in "the perfection of the human soul" and in the redemption of humanity through Christ, he also recognized the existence of limitations in the doctrine of divine economy. His portrayal of Stavrogin reveals the limitations of compassion and charity in this doctrine. In a sense, it can be asserted that Dostoevsky is at times groping in his delineation of Stavrogin's character. His steadfast belief that under rough exteriors there is to be found some gold comes to the surface time and again, perhaps even to salvage Stavrogin, perhaps to diminish the implacability of his sins, perhaps to find some niche for him in God's infinite mercy. However, when we consider the Eastern Orthodox concept of evil, we can comprehend not only just how steeped Dostoevsky was in its doctrine, but also how it enabled him to see through and unmask "the spirit of error, the spirit of guile, the spirit of idolatry and of every concupiscence." The figure of Stavrogin accentuates the whole truth of this, for he is precisely the unmitigating evil that is synonymous with satanism. Above all he illustrates the absence of goodness and the consequent darkness and disintegration that fill the realm of hell and Satan. John of Damascus in his *Exposition of the Orthodox Faith* (II, iv) makes note of this absence in words that could easily serve as an epigraph to the whole of Dostoevsky's art and message: "For evil is nothing else than absence of goodness, just as darkness also is absence of light. For goodness is the light of the mind, and similarly, evil is the darkness of the mind." Stavrogin's diabolism is attested to by his inability to appreciate what Kirillov speaks of as "moments of eternal harmony" (*minuty vechnoĭ garmonii*) and by his own admission that "from me nothing has come but negation, with no magnanimity and no force. . . . Everything has always been petty and lifeless" (III, viii).[15]

II

The biblical statement "My name is Legion: for we are many" (Mark 5:9) is especially applicable to Dostoevsky's "sons of disobedience" in *The Devils*. Stavrogin serves as an archetype of the various satanic disguises, shapes, and images. Indeed, so incredibly sly and clever is he that there is even the tendency on the part of readers to sympathize with him, to forgive his well-nigh unmentionable sins and crimes, and to ignore his moral depravity, his "brutal conduct," his outrages against society, his disdain for all spiritual values. Stavrogin, in the light of such a response, should be neither judged nor condemned. He merely personifies the paradoxes of the burden of mortality; he is man cruelly trapped by his doubts, conflicting loyalties, questionings, anxieties, ambivalences; he is a mirror of poor mankind's frailty and plight and fatefulness. He is that pitiably and helplessly *human* element. Such an approach to Stavrogin not only deemphasizes moral and spiritual responsibilities, but also encourages an indifference and a rationalizing that lead to an escapism of the most serious consequences. This not uncommon response to Stavrogin renders one defenseless to the many "wiles" and "snares" and "devices" employed by the devil, whose central aim is to debase all human significance and to bring death to the soul. "For he is insatiable," Saint Gregory Nazianzen observes; "he grasps at every thing. He fawns upon you with fair pretences, but he ends in evil; this is the manner of his fighting" (*The Oration on Holy Baptism*, X).

To Dostoevsky satanism is not only the absence of goodness and of magnanimity, but also of impelling, active love, which recalls Father Zossima's words in *The Brothers Karamazov*: "What is hell? I maintain that it is the suffering of being unable to love."[16] It is in such a "hell" that Stavrogin finds himself, for if there is one quality he lacks throughout, it is love. Unlike a Svidrigaylov, who seems to be furiously groping in his depravity so that he may satisfy his "insect-lust," Stavrogin is (in Stefan Zweig's memorable phrase) "the calculating tactician of debauchery."[17] Stavrogin has come to a full stop: he neither questions nor answers what is evil; he *knows* that he lives and is evil: "Indignation and shame I can never feel, therefore not despair, either" (III, 8). He is the evil that ultimately has transcended all distinctions and has passed beyond the morality and immorality of this universe into the amorality and conscienceless being of a satanic

235

realm. Stavrogin has "decayed and corrupted children," has made "no distinction in beauty between some voluptuous and brutish act and any heroic exploit, even the sacrifice of life for the good of humanity" (II, 1, 7). He has leaped beyond all boundaries of compassion and the charity of divine largesse. His calm, his indifference, his composure, his pride, even his boredom are the consequences of a satanism that wallows in the abyss. "Oh, you never walk at the edge of the abyss, but precipitate yourself over it boldly, head downwards," Shatov says to Stavrogin (II, 1, 7), and his words underline the true condition of the satanic. Dostoevsky, in his delineation of Stavrogin, ventures into the abyss, but his purpose is not of alliance with its infernal creature but of spiritual warfare, which St. Macarius the Great describes as follows: "The most important work in spiritual struggle is to enter the heart and there to wage war with Satan; to hate Satan, and to fight him by opposing his thoughts."[18]

On numerous occasions Stavrogin is called "Prince," but the title, like the name Stavrogin, which comes from the Greek word for cross (σταυρός), is grimly ironical. Dostoevsky's peculiar use of the word "Prince" (ἄρχων) compares with the traditional Christian treatment of Satan as the prince of demons, as the ruler of this world, as the prince of the power of the air. Stavrogin is the artistic counterpart of the "fallen Lucifer," the "awful Aristocrat," the creature who as lightning fell from Heaven (Luke 10:18). He, too, contains a certain element of charm and of grandeur, an aristocratic appearance, a handsome and glittering exterior that have traditionally been associated with Satan and that led Dante to the depiction of Satan as the "paragon of all creation." On one occasion Stavrogin is imaged as "a diamond on the filthy background of . . . life" (I, 5, 6). Even Shatov once admired him: "You, you alone could have raised the banner!" (II, 1, 7). And like the biblical Satan, Stavrogin is very much the aristocrat surrounded by mystery and spoken of in fear and awe. Dostoevsky's description of Stavrogin in the following passage is certainly in line with that of the "fallen Lucifer":

> . . . his hair was just a little too black, his light-coloured eyes a little too calm and clear, his complexion a little too tender and white, his colour a little too dazzling and pure, his teeth like pearls, his lips like coral— he would seem to be a paragon of beauty, yet at the same time there was something hideous about him. People said his face reminded them of a mask; there was, by the way, a great deal of talk about his amazing physical strength (I, 2, 1).

The atmosphere generated by the presence or actions of Stavrogin is unmistakably one of murkiness and putrefaction, heightening and deepening the titanic evil which he contains and which blasphemes majesty (Jude 8). When Stavrogin appears, when he encounters other figures, when he is related to episodes of the past and present, when he conjures up the future, it is hideousness and fear that permeate the scene. Ugliness and decay become, in association with him, recurrent images. Often, too, references to him have the effect of linking him with the lowest animal life: he is imaged as a wild beast showing its claws, a monster, a serpent, a spider, a vampire. His presence incites the consciousness of evil, of instinctive fear of contact with the demonic. This consciousness becomes evident when Marya Timofyevna Lebyadkin says to Stavrogin: "As soon as I saw your mean face when I fell and you picked me up—it was as if a worm had crawled into my heart" (II, 2, 4). On one occasion, when Captain Lebyadkin leaves a gathering, he accidentally collides with Stavrogin in the doorway: "The Captain somehow suddenly cowered before him and stopped dead in his tracks without taking his eyes off him, like a rabbit in front of a boa-constrictor" (I, 5, 6). One night, when Stavrogin goes out, Dostoevsky describes the scene in these words: "The wind howled and tossed the almost denuded tops of the trees, and the little, sand-covered paths were soggy and slippery" (II, 1, 4). And when Stavrogin arrives to talk with Kirillov he is "covered with mud." Entering the room, he sees Kirillov playing with an eighteen-month-old baby held by a woman. "The child, catching sight of him, clung to the old woman and went off into a prolonged childish cry; the woman at once carried it out of the room" (II, 1, 4). Toward the end of the novel, in a letter to Dasha, Stavrogin expresses a desire to leave Russia and to live in the canton of Uri in Switzerland: "The place is very dull, a narrow valley, the mountains constrict both vision and thought. It is very gloomy" (III, 8). Stavrogin is inevitably identified with darkness, and with him we make the descent into the abyss.

Stavrogin communicates the experience of hell itself; his presence, directly or indirectly, engenders a relentless spirit of destructiveness, of terror and hideousness. Often he is not even on the scene, but his dark shadow seems to fall on all the other characters and on all the episodes of the novel. He seems to stand fixed in the center of a universe, and yet he also seems to propel the fate of those whom he addresses, touches, or looks at. The mystery and fear that immediately emerge in relation to him are no doubt the projection of what is sinister and woeful. It is obvious that his stagnancy is of the most perverse form and cannot hide the realization that the evil in him is supreme and powerful to the degree that it automatically overflows into all avenues of human activity. Stavrogin is thus the chief source of the poison that brings contamination and death. His very nature stands in direct opposition to the creative and the beautiful. Stavroginism, then, signifies the inability to suffer or love or feel. Consistently he refuses to make any positive struggle or decision for the good. His woeful effortlessness, consequently, is conducive to a state of soul in which, to use Martin Buber's sage words, "Intensification and confirmation of indecision is decision to evil."[19] Stavrogin embodies the brutal entity of whatever is malevolent and beyond hope, and this accounts for the fact that he is receptive to no expression or action kindled with human passion. "His malice was cold, calm, and, if one may put it that way, *rational*, which means that it was the most abominable and most terrible kind of malice" (II, 5, 8). His whole existence revolves around this malice—it is his only world, his only nourishment. We recall Byron's Lucifer crying to Cain: "Mortal! My brotherhood's with those who have no children."[20] Everything must pale and recoil before this infernal spirit, which remains ageless and unmoved in its evil. Even as we happen to cross his path, arouse "his faint smile," or hear his "gentle, melodious voice," we can discern "strange screams of death" and "the smoke of a great furnace" as it blackens the sun and air. To know Stavrogin is to know "the torment of a scorpion." Very likely it is the terrifying knowledge of this truth that grips Varvara Petrovna Stavrogin when she chances to see her son as he sleeps:

> His face was pale and stern, but it looked completely frozen and immobile; his brows were slightly drawn together and frowning; he certainly looked like a lifeless wax figure. She stood over him for about three minutes, hardly daring to breathe, and suddenly she was seized with panic; she tiptoed out of the room, stopped for a moment at the doorway, hurriedly made the sign of the cross over him, and went away unobserved, with a new heavy feeling and with a new anguish (II, 1, 4).

When Dmitri Karamazov cries out to his brother Alyosha, "The awful thing is that beauty is mysterious as well as terrible. God and the devil are fighting there and the battlefield is the heart of man,"[21] he expresses a belief that pervades the totality of Dostoevsky's thinking. The devil is integral to Dostoevsky's artistic and moral vision, and the Russian novelist continuously converses and clashes with him. When the devil appears, he can do so *in persona*, mysteriously but distinctly visible to a particular figure, as in the case of Ivan Karamazov, or within another character, as in the case of Stavrogin in *The Devils*. In the first, Satan takes the form of a nightmare; in the second, he is an ontological reality. Combined, these two manifestations embody a complete picture of satanism. Whereas the devil is *with* Ivan, pulling him, tugging at him, lacerating him, he is *in* Stavrogin, commanding him, regulating him, impelling him.

Ivan epitomizes the satanic element which leads to the ultimate self-betrayal of the soul. Ivan's devil coexists with a rending inner yearning for deliverance in a man who embodies an agonizing "riddle." Dostoevsky's Christian view of sin is also brought out in his characterization of Ivan, for evil is not inherent in this man but is the result of a corruptive, pervasive process of wrong-doing and the tyranny of a "Euclidean earthly mind." The devil encountered in Ivan's nightmare is eloquent, witty, affable, clever; both in speech and form he contains the most sophisticated elements which Dostoevsky equated with "rational egoism." Certainly, the description of the devil sitting on Ivan's sofa "against the opposite wall" reinforces the "idea" of a Satan endowed with gentility and sophistication:

> This was a person or, more accurately speaking, a Russian gentleman of a particular kind, no longer young, *qui faisait la cinquantaine,* as the French say, with rather long, still thick, dark hair, slightly streaked with grey and a small pointed beard. He was wearing a brownish reefer jacket, rather shabby, evidently made by a good tailor though, and of a fashion at least three years old, that had been discarded by smart and well-to-do people for the last two years. His linen and his long scarf-like neck-tie were all such as are worn by people who aim at being stylish, but on closer inspection his linen was not over clean and his wide scarf was very threadbare. The visitor's check trousers were of excellent cut, but were too light in colour and too tight for the present fashion. His soft fluffy white hat was out of keeping with the season.[22]

Ivan's devil wanders in the secret recesses of the mind and heart in search of a refuge, a victim. "I suffer," he tells the distraught Ivan, "but still, I don't live. I am x in an indeterminate equation. I am a sort of phantom in life who has lost all beginning and end, and who has even forgotten his own name." Of course, Ivan wants the devil to be a "dream, not a living creature," and he thus hopes to equate him with *l'hypothèse gratuite,* to recall Gide's words. The devil, however, stubbornly clings to Ivan exactly because the latter has all along been advancing the theory that "all things are lawful." Ivan's assumption, then, embodies an inviting shelter to the satanic, extends a welcome to a "visitor" who is always willing to "enter into the world" and to take a seat on a sofa, "to keep his host company at tea," "ready for any affable conversation as soon as his host should begin it." Satan's central aim is to give living reality to this theory from the very moment it is entertained. To promulgate such a theory, the devil will adopt diverse guises, indulge in all sorts of charming postures and gestures ("I lead you to belief and disbelief by turns, and I have my motive in it. It's the new method"). Nevertheless, his final aim is unmistakable and his unflagging cynicism overshadows all outward amicability. Even a deracinated Ivan cannot help perceiving the devil's real goal. He suddenly snatches a glass from the table and flings it at the devil, who, quoting Ivan's own past utterances, ends with these words:

> There is no law for God. Where God stands, the place is holy. Where I stand will be at once the foremost place . . . "all things are lawful" and that's the end of it! That's all very charming; but if you want to swindle why do you want a moral sanction for doing it? But that's our modern Russian all over. He can't bring himself to swindle without a moral sanction. He is so in love with truth.

This quotation is particularly important, for it not only adumbrates a conspiracy of feelings in Ivan, but also, by way of contrast, indicates how in Stavrogin evil is *the* condition of existence, "without a moral sanction." Contrary to Ivan Karamazov, Stavrogin is not plagued by an "earnest conscience" or torn by a division of soul. In him there is absent "the anguish of proud determination" which we find in Ivan. The satanic is an inextricable condition of Stavrogin's existence, and its power over and in him is as unquestioned as it is unyielding. Stavrogin has totally resigned himself to his lostness, his cynicism, his denial of God. He is a creature who no longer resists Satan but has abjectly surrendered himself to him. He represents a defeat concurrent with the triumph of deception and denial. "To cook a hare—you must catch it, to believe in God—you must have God" (II, 1, 7). This, we are told, is one of his favorite sayings. Stavrogin's condition, furthermore, has passed beyond the ramifications of struggle between a Champion and an Oppressor. The aridity of disbelief is his "infinity of endless ages": " 'If Stavrogin believes in God, then he doesn't believe that he believes. And if he doesn't believe, then he doesn't believe' " (III, 6, 2). No wonder he is an alien in the human realm: "I have nothing to keep me in Russia—everything is as foreign to me there as anywhere else" (III, 8). No wonder that Lisa Tushin, after spending a night with him, senses how barren he is of human feeling, of love: "I always imagined that you would take me to some place where there was a huge, wicked spider, as big as a man, and we should spend the rest of our lives looking at it and being afraid of it. That's what our love would be wasted on" (III, 3, 1). No wonder, finally, that Varvara Stavrogin must wail, "I have no son!" (III, 7, 3). Companion of Satan and denizen of hell, Stavrogin is the epitome of dismemberment from God and from life, and he must suffer the fate of those whom Father Zossima has so well described in one of his "exhortations":

> Oh, . . . there are some fearful ones who have given themselves over to Satan and his proud spirit entirely. For such, hell is voluntary and ever consuming; they are tortured by their own choice. For they have cursed themselves, cursing God and life. They live upon their vindictive pride like a starving man in the desert sucking blood out of his own body. But they are never satisfied, and they refuse forgiveness, they curse God Who calls them. They cannot behold the living God without hatred, and they cry out that the God of life should be annihilated, that God should destroy Himself and His Own creation. And they will burn in the fire of their own wrath for ever and yearn for death and annihilation.[23]

The last two chapters of the third and final part of *The Devils* show the depth of the horrifying void in Stavrogin. It is especially seen when we compare Stepan Trofimovitch Verhovensky's last days of life with Stavrogin's. In the death of Stepan, Dostoevsky evinces a deep note of compassion for human loss, and an implicit sense of forgiveness resounds in the course of Stepan's sickness and death. What starts off with his almost comical decision to reject Varvara Petrovna's charity and "luxurious provision," and to hold aloft "the standard of a great idea and . . . to die for it on the open road" ends up as an inherently spiritual pilgrimage, achieving a sense of redemption and even nobility. Stepan, in the course of his "last wandering," is imaged as a sick man freed from the devils and now come to sit "at the feet of Jesus." As he approaches his end, he is more and more the picture of a pilgrim who has suddenly felt bright rays of light shining warmly on him. Stepan has at last confronted decision and has, as a result, gained insight into his heart and mind. "The hardest thing in life," he says to the gospel woman, Sofya Matveyevna, who cares for him during these last days, "is to live without telling lies . . . and without believing in one's lies" (III, 7, 2). At this point, above all, Stepan is juxtaposed to Stavrogin. He now radiates the innate humanity and warmth and magnanimity which are totally absent in Stavrogin. There is a positive note in Stepan's utterances, especially in his affirmation of life, and he dies blessing life and the mystery of existence: "Every minute, every instant of life ought to be a blessing to man . . . they ought to be, they certainly ought to be! It's the duty of man to make it so; that's the law of his nature which always exists even if hidden" (III, 7, 3). Stepan indicates the power of renewal and belief that girds him in the presence of much pain. And this paradigmatic power stems from a realization of human limitations:

The one essential condition of human existence is that man should always be able to bow down before something infinitely great. If men are deprived of the infinitely great they will not go on living and will die of despair. The Infinite and the Eternal are as essential for man as the little planet on which he dwells. My friends, all, all: hail to the Great Idea! The Eternal, Infinite Idea! It is essential to every man, whoever he may be, to bow down before what is the Great Idea (III, 7, 3).

In contrast, Stavrogin, as the end approaches, reveals his desperate aloneness and lostness, his betrayal of life. "One may argue about everything endlessly," he confides to Darya Pavlovna in a letter, "but from me nothing has come but negation, with no greatness of soul, no force. Even negation has not come from me. Everything has always been petty and spiritless" (III, 8). At the core of Stepan there is an indwelling power that allows him to rediscover the kinship with and the necessity of "the Eternal, Infinite Idea" (*Vechnaia, bessmertnaia Mysl'*) that lies in all persons. In short, he acknowledges in the most reverent terms a community of feelings that all men must share in the end, in spite of the obstacles and misfortunes of "cruel history." Whereas Stepan speaks from the depths of his heart and from an overpowering love and a religious need, necessarily and finally surmounting all hatred and despair, Stavrogin, through his suicide, reveals the inner desolation of his heart and the false pronouncements of his soul.[24] Stepan dies in reverent affirmation of life; Stavrogin hangs himself, the only witness to his own isolation in the loft: "The citizen of the canton of Uri was hanging there behind the door. On the table lay a piece of paper with the words in pencil: 'No one is to blame, I did it myself.' Beside it on the table lay a hammer, a piece of soap, and a large nail" (III, 8). Self-murder is for him the final act and the final death, the quintessence of his satanism, his Hell—that Hell which, as Nicolas Berdyaev writes, "is continuous dying, the last agony which never ends."[25] In destroying himself, Stavrogin simply discloses his separation from life and his denial of what Dostoevsky often spoke of as its "gladness."

III

Stavrogin's decision to go to Bishop Tihon and to confess his sins brings into focus Dostoevsky's severest testing of the doctrine of divine economy. A mere surface view of the meeting of sinner and holy man will perhaps tend to induce compassion for Stavrogin as he utters some "wild and incoherent" disclosures "with unaccustomed frankness." His inner sufferings, his terrifying hallucinations, his expression of love for the monk, his sense of transgression, even his recognition of God—all of these would tend ostensibly to suggest a repentant, guilt-stricken nature in Stavrogin, as well as a feeling that he bears within him seeds of redemption. It is the picture of the persecuted, not the persecutor, that we supposedly have. With that remarkable aesthetic distance and objective vision which pervade his art, Dostoevsky strives to give a dispassionate depiction of a man in the agonizing act of confession. But the revelations and dialogue, especially as they evolve from Stavrogin himself, ultimately speak for themselves, and the feeling that we are in the presence of a "liar," a "misanthropic demon" (in the words of Justin Martyr) becomes indisputable. Slowly we grasp just how complete Stavrogin's separation from and renunciation of God and life are, how much he is frozen in his abyss. "I don't invite anybody into my soul," he snarls at one point; "I do not need anybody, I can shift for myself."[26] His meeting with Tihon confirms the magnitude of his violations of life and of his mania to pervert truth. The informing response to this entire scene and to Stavrogin himself is crystallized in a little-noticed incident occurring in the course of Tihon's reading of the pamphlet documenting the confession: "Meanwhile, Stavrogin stopped at the writing-table, and taking up a small ivory crucifix, began to turn it about in his fingers, and suddenly broke it in half." This is a profoundly meaningful happening, which accents the discrepancy between Stavrogin's words and actions and further shatters any image of him as an erring human being. The incident also illustrates both a conscious and an unconscious condition of a creature of evil that ruins everything with which it comes into contact, and we are duly reminded of Denis de Rougemont's comment in his work concerning Satan: "Everything he annexes to himself he destroys."[27]

What we especially find in Stavrogin during his visit to Tihon is the fully developed evil that "shows different faces and assumes different characters, and yet is always the same." His decision to go to the monastery is a facet of this definition, another instance of the role and power of Satan as the Tempter and Tormentor. Stavrogin is not at all sincere, repentant, or humble, but wholly blasphemous and cynical throughout his talk with Tihon. It is significant that Dostoevsky's narrator interprets Stavrogin's purpose in having Tihon read the document relating his crimes as one that seeks "to exchange one kind of suffering for another. . . . Indeed, in the very existence of such a document one senses a new, unexpected and irreverent challenge to society." The document, "vile, crawling and abominable," forcefully underlines the irreversibility of Stavrogin's crimes, the self-centeredness and self-absorption of all his actions and dissimulations. The picture of Stavrogin on these pages is confirmation of evil; from it we are able to grasp how restless and unsatisfied is his yearning to subvert and harm life. It is the "criminal energy" of Stavroginism that we see here, and its scourge is both inversionary and perversionary. Stavrogin's violation of the twelve-year-old Matryosha validates this "criminal energy" and discloses a diabolic scorn of all human decency. His actions, too, are always the product of his free will, of his choice of and responsibility for evil: "I was in full possession of my faculties, and that consequently I was not a madman, and that I am responsible for everything."

When Stavrogin admits, even after Matryosha has hanged herself, that "I was able to master my memories and ... became callous to them," the satanic element in him becomes absolutely clear. Later on, while traveling in Germany, he dreams of the "Golden Age," but the vision is the fleeting and inconsequential one of a man who has already suffered the "death of the soul" and who has abandoned all hope and given up the struggle. Such a dream cannot really comfort or renew a man who has moved beyond the frontier of religious vision and affirmation. The truth of this conclusion is measured by Stavrogin's own cynical, despairing response to the dream as a "lofty illusion," as "the most improbable of all visions, to which mankind throughout its existence has given its best energies, for which it has sacrificed everything, for which it has pined and been tormented, for which its prophets were crucified and killed, without which nations will not desire to live, and without which they cannot even die!" Ironically, this dream is immediately followed by an apparition of "Matryosha, grown haggard and with feverish eyes, precisely as she had looked at the moment when she stood on the threshold of my room, and shaking her head, had lifted her tiny fist against me." He admits that this image of Matryosha, especially with her "threatening gesture," stabbed him with "a maddening pity." But he also admits—and the significance of this admission can hardly be overstressed—that the fundamental reason for his pity and remorse is not a humane one at all, but one that is interlinked with his overweening pride ("the beginning of all sin"). It is Stavrogin's sadism and shamelessness that are predominant here; and to Tihon, at one point, the confession smacks of arrogance and insincerity:

> Even in the very intention of this great penitence there is something ridiculous, something false, as it were ... not to speak of the form, which is loose, vague, unsustained because it is weakened by fear, as it were.

Oh, don't doubt but that "you'll conquer." ... Even this form ... will avail, if only you will sincerely accept the blows and the spittle, if you will endure it! It was always thus, that the most degrading cross became a great glory and a great power, if only the humility of the act was sincere. But is it? Is it? Will it be sincere? Oh, what you should have is not a challenging attitude, but measureless humility and self-abasement! What you should do is not despise your judges, but sincerely believe in them, as in a great Church, then you would conquer them and draw them to you and unite them in love. ... Oh, if only you could endure it.

Stavrogin's central aim in his confession is not to evoke forgiveness. His aim stems from his boundless egoism, his titanic pride, his obsession with self-glorification and self-blessing: "Listen to me, Father Tihon: I want to forgive myself. That's my chief object, that's my whole aim!" He categorically refuses to "wash" his heart (Jer. 4:14) and he makes a mockery of "confession" itself. The entire incident should be imaged as a flagrant desecration of the sanctity that Tihon represents. What Saint Athanasius writes of the devil in his *Life of Antony* is appurtenant to Stavrogin's encounter with Tihon: "Let us then heed not his words, for he is a liar: and let us not fear his visions, seeing that they themselves are deceptive." The meeting of Tihon and Stavrogin is, as Mochulsky has noted, an intense struggle between disbelief and belief, the collision of two ideas embodied in two personalities: the atheist Stavrogin and the mystic Tihon.[28] Throughout the meeting, Stavrogin's behavior accords with the mold of his character and attitude, into which the poor cripple, Marya Timofyevna, has amazing prophetic insight. He is, in her words, "an owl and a shop-keeper," a "mask," an "imposter," a "pretender," a "Grishka Otrep-yev," anathematized in seven cathedrals. No, Stavrogin's confession must not be misconstrued as an act heroic in scope and noble in gesture. For he is mocking and profaning the Λόγος of God (to the point, in fact, that even the kindly and naïve Tihon is fooled or outwitted). Like Satan he refuses to "hate the evil" (Amos 5:15) in his heart and to embrace the meaning of the Psalmist's injunction, "Stand in awe, and sin not" (Ps. 4:4). His confession embodies the uttermost limits of impiety (ἀσέβεια) and moral deception, and like Satan he ultimately deceives himself. In the brilliantly perceptive words of Romano Guardini,

> He is the poorest of all men. One feels great compassion for him, yet Satan truly has no majesty! What modern apologists for satanism and for moral transvaluations say about the greatness of evil is simply not true. For Satan is the one who is being cheated, cheated by himself. He is absolutely empty. He is not great in anything. He is the wretched "simius Dei."[29]

It needs to be reemphasized that Stavrogin is always composed, unenthusiastic, cold. Above all else, he lacks tenderness and reverence, those particular graces of kenotic religion that are embodied in the Russian word *umilenie*. He can hardly share Kirillov's love of children and nature, or Shatov's faith in the "God-bearing" people of Russia. His marriage to a poor cripple, "after a drunken dinner, for a bet, for a bottle of wine," and his silence in permitting a little girl to be punished after being wrongly accused of stealing his knife, which he knew he had misplaced, also clearly bring out his sadistic impulses. The inexhaustible presence of Satan in Stavrogin is especially to be seen in the latter's lack of compassion. The puny extent of his concern for other human beings is captured in the course of his meeting with Captain Lebyadkin. Having come to the Lebyadkin lodgings to talk with Marya Timofyevna and having conversed with the Captain (her brother) for a time, Stavrogin tells him to go out while he speaks in private with Marya Timofyevna. Because it is raining, he tells the Captain to take his (Stavrogin's) umbrella:

> "Your umbrella? But, sir, am I worth it?" the Captain said ingratiatingly.
> "Every man has a right to an umbrella."
> "You've defined the minimum of human rights in one short sentence, sir" (II, 2, 2).

There is no doubt that Stavrogin shows "unnatural strength," both in his physical prowess and in his social relations with other figures. In this respect, he embodies the strength and cunning inevitably associated with the "evil spirit" and its cosmic power. Though he is often "quiet, listless, and rather morose," looking even "abstracted," he is constantly "watching and listening." In him we are made aware of the coalescent principle and obtrusiveness of evil. To generate itself in God's creation, the "evil spirit" must fulfill itself in an outer substance, achieve a peculiar fullness of being in an external body. Stavrogin's relation to Pyotr Stepanovitch Verhovensky illustrates such an hypostatization. Pyotr is the exteriorized evil that Stavroginism inspires and breeds: an actual, identifiable force and entity in life. "You're my leader," he cries out to Stavrogin; "you're my sun, and I am your worm" (II, 8). He is the fleshly, substantive body of evil ("a scoundrel and a sophist," "a filthy human louse," "a rogue," "a political seducer") as it appears in a particular time and place. There is nothing abstract about Pyotr, and his goals are tangible ones. He plots to cripple the physical body of life—"to level mountains," to create "political disturbances," to cause such "an upheaval that the foundations of the State will be cracked wide open," to inaugurate a new system of "monstrous, disgusting vice which turns man into an abject, cowardly, cruel, and selfish wretch":

> The thing we want is obedience. The only thing that's wanting in the world is obedience. The desire for education is an aristocratic desire. The moment a man falls in love or has a family, he gets a desire for private property. We will destroy that desire; we'll resort to drunkenness, slander, denunciations; we'll resort to unheard-of depravity; we shall smother every genius in infancy. We shall reduce everything to one common denominator (II, 8).

Stavrogin stands for the death of life. Pyotr, whom Stavroginism torments and actuates, is the murderer of life. Totally "absorbed in his sensations," Pyotr personifies the cruelest bestiality of evil. Even in the midst of treachery and killing, this executioner must satisfy his appetite with a beefsteak. Who can ever forget the picture of Pyotr, accompanied by another conspirator, Liputin, eating heartily in a restaurant:

> Pyotr Stepanovitch did not hurry himself; he ate with relish, rang the bell, asked for a different kind of mustard, then for beer, without saying a word to Liputin. He was pondering deeply. He was capable of doing two things at once—eating with relish and pondering deeply. Liputin loathed him so intensely at last that he could not tear himself away. It was like a nervous obsession. He counted every morsel of beefsteak that Pyotr Stepanovitch put into his mouth; he loathed him for the way he opened it, for the way he chewed, for the way he smacked his lips over the fat morsels, he loathed the steak itself (III, 4, 2).

From the beginning to the end of the novel, Stavrogin's actions and thoughts lead in the direction of utter breakdown, chaos, and death. In him there is no sense of aspiration at all, no ascent of the "living soul" (Gen. 2:7). He fears nothing, he doubts everything. Ἀγάπη, πνεῦμα, πίστις—those eternal verities that provide a sense of direction and that stand for the victory of belief over disbelief—are to him senseless and unattainable. His character shows a complete lack of positive development, not because of any structural deficiencies or artistic failures on Dostoevsky's part, but because of the kind of creatureliness and evil that Stavrogin must represent and re-create. Stavrogin can travel in only one direction, out of a primordial past into a primordial chaos, evincing the total denial of the possibility of *new life*. It could be said that his very existence is a cyclical one, inasmuch as he refuses to appeal to transcendence, to reach out for or to desire what is above him. It is an existence that reacts only to what lies around it, to what can be manipulated and grasped from immediate levels. Stavrogin cannot *respond to* or *commune with* others; he can merely appear as an aspect of evil that is incarnated in a Pyotr Verhovensky or in a Kirillov.

Irremediably "dwelling in evil things," Stavrogin is unable to find a "place of rest." In his terrible restlessness and dissatisfaction, he seems to be a tormented wanderer, in constant flux and turmoil. For him there can be no inner peace or outer stability. Plagued by demonic impulses and hatred, he is in everlasting pursuit of hostage and victim. He travels in the Orient; he goes to Mount Athos and stands through interminable night services; he visits Egypt, moves on to Jerusalem, stays in Switzerland, journeys as far as Iceland, attends the University of Göttingen for an academic year. And yet for him there is no surcease, no content, no "gladness," no destination. Whether he is in Russia or abroad, he is unhappy, possessed, loveless. And whether he is a student, a soldier, a traveler, or a rebel, he must needs be the irreconcilable enemy of life and of man. His existence metamorphoses into a demonism that is destined to make him homeless and hopeless. Not all the power in the world can save him from his admission to Dasha that "Nothing comes to an end in this world" (II, 3, 4). But, then, the satanic as found in Stavroginism has bound itself to a wheel of sin which never stops turning. Evil feeds on life: its appetite is endless: its thirst quenchless. Stavrogin dramatizes, in effect, the burden of sin, of impenitence, of negation.

By no means must Stavroginism be assessed as a desperate "search for values."[30] To make such a claim, as unfortunately so many critics do, is to ignore the satanism of a figure who blandly realizes that he cannot even "play at magnanimity." "I know that it will be another delusion again," he confesses, "a delusion in an infinite sequence of delusions" (III, 8). The desire of some critics to excuse Stavrogin may very well be prompted by an optimism and a charity which, though commendable, are essentially misguided and illusionary. This desire may also arise from a preeminently relativistic appraisal of evil and from a belief that the satanic element in life is an insignificant element or an ancient superstition which can no longer harmonize with the modern scientific world.[31] The figure of Satan and the problem of evil remain real and adamant in life, as real and adamant as Dostoevsky's Stavrogin. Surely, it is grievous to believe that in Stavrogin lies the story of a "spiritual adventure."[32] It is grievous, too, that modern man refuses to acknowledge the real Satan till he must feel him at his own throat. "The fire is in the minds of men and not in the roofs of houses," Dostoevsky writes at one point in *The Devils* (III, 2, 4). The fact remains that for the great Russian novelist art was a theurgical function interdependent with the state of the soul. In this connection, his recognition of evil must at once be witnessed as a charismatic quality of a visionary artist who, with Saint Cyril of Jerusalem, clearly realized that God suffers the devil to wrestle with men that they who conquer him may be crowned (Lecture VIII, 4).[33]

12

Pater Seraphicus: Dostoevsky's Metaphysics of a "New Saintliness"

Then flew one of the seraphims unto me, having a live coal in his hand, which he had taken with the tongs from off the altar: And he laid it upon my mouth, and said, Lo, this hath touched thy lips; and thine iniquity is taken away, and thy sin purged.

—Isaiah 6:6–7

For not one sparrow can suffer & the whole Universe not suffer also In all its Regions, & its Father & Saviour not pity and weep.

—William Blake, *Jerusalem*

ॐ

The Brothers Karamazov (1879–80), Dostoevsky's last novel, shows how affirmation comes out of denial, and, above all, how saintliness overcomes satanism. Maxim Gorky goes so far as to call *The Brothers Karamazov* "a fifth Gospel" in which Dostoevsky's "preoccupation with supra-moral goodness, Christ-like-ness,"[1] attains its greatest intensity, its paradiso. In this novel he is doing some extraordinary things as a great visionary artist and prophetic novelist—as a "realist of distances" who sees "near things with their extensions of meaning and thus ... [sees] far things close up."[2] That is to say, Dostoevsky undertakes to defy categorically the threats and the arrogance of "rational assertions" in the course of his envisioning and then affirming the ultimate reality of the sacred, the spiritual, the numinous, the theonomous.

Essentially this affirmation is derived from a vision that "is genuinely and radically dialectical," or as one writer would have it: "... it is by means of the very power of the demonic—of the profane—that an epiphany of the sacred occurs."[3] The passage from an immersion in the profane, "the non-religious mood of everyday experience," to a yielding to and a reconciliation with the ultimate, "the depth of one's experience, the awareness of the holy," in Paul Tillich's phraseology, constitutes the evolving and the major pattern of experience in *The Brothers Karamazov*. For in this novel, which must signify for Dostoevsky as well as for his readers the highest state of spiritual progression, he comes as close as one can to touching the *mysterium tremendum*, and hence to intuiting what is hidden and esoteric, what is beyond conception or understanding, what is nonrational or suprarational—to a growing and profound "consciousness of a 'wholly other,' " or a divine otherness. This experience, "thrillingly vibrant and resonant"[4] while it lasts, must be seen as being a struggle to approach the holy and to glimpse the nature and modes of its manifestations, its numina. On the outcome of this encounter depends the ultimate, the eschatological, experience which Dostoevsky viewed as crystallizing in the miracle of redemption.

"Miracle is the dearest child of Faith," declares Schiller. In his notebooks relating to *The Brothers Karamazov* Dostoevsky writes that "much is inexplicable in this world without miracles."[5] (It was with good reason that Thomas Mann coupled Dostoevsky and Schiller as "children of spirit," as "saintlike.") He renders precisely the miraculous in the person of Father Zossima. And it is through the old monk that he strives to achieve a dual interacting process belonging to the highest function of a religious poetry that breaks for us the shackles of habit. Artistically, this breakthrough is communicated as an epiphany of the sacred. Religiously, or spiritually, it is transposed into the experience of the holy, which in the end, according to Rudolf Otto, must be "recognized as that which commands our respect, as that whose real value is to be acknowledged *inwardly*."[6] Father Zossima, embodying both the experiential and the epiphanous facets of an artistic process that the German poet Richard Dehmel identified with "embrac[ing] the world in love and lift[ing] it up to God," contains Dostoevsky's consummate view of the whole of "human existence as a tension between earthly suffering and a striving for a lofty ideal."[7]

Father Zossima dramatizes Dostoevsky's continual efforts to make the Word become flesh. In him we recognize the furthest advancement of Dostoevsky's concept of the sacred and the mysterious as everpresent numinal energies in the universe. "I am a frightful hunter after mysteries,"[8] Dostoevsky wrote of himself. Father Zossima is Dostoevsky's ecstatic conception of the world, is the image in which—and the point at which—mystery and miracle, holiness and redemption cohere in presaging the "subsurface unexpressed future Word." In him the aesthetic, or the secular, element is converted by the spiritual, or the religious element when, Dostoevsky states, "the Holy Spirit is the direct understanding of beauty, the prophetic cognition of harmony and, therefore, a constant striving for it."[9] Father Zossima epiphanizes the most mystical dimension of Dostoevsky's spiritual art. Aesthetically and ideologically he becomes the medium of and for the experience of the holy, when the artistic proximity to the divine wondrously approximates the religious experience of the divine. Once again Otto helps us to gauge the intensity and value of the experience, the transfiguration, when he writes:

> The point is that the "holy man" or the "prophet" is from the outset, as regards the experience of the circle of his devotees, something more than a "mere man." . . . He is the being of wonder and mystery, who somehow or other is felt to belong to the higher order of things, to the side of the numen itself. It is not that he himself teaches that he is such, but that he is experienced as such.[10]

"That he is experienced as such": these words indicate the very nature and significance of Father Zossima, a type "of the universally human," Stephen Zweig declares, "soaring upward towards God."[11] As a form of the beautiful containing measure and harmony, he represents an essential facet of Dostoevsky's belief (as well as of his aesthetics) that "the world will become the beauty of Christ."[12] Through Father Zossima, Dostoevsky reveals an intuitive, and symbolic, apprehension of paradisiacal heights, just as in the figure of Stavrogin in *The Devils* he reveals a knowledge of "satanic depths." The "religious" experience that Dostoevsky seeks to portray in Father Zossima instances at the same time a meditation on the "double eternity," Death and Resurrection. Father Zossima is a fictionalized meditation as well as a meditative *homo fictus* lifted up to a metaphysical plane. Both as an image of reconciliation and as an image of redemption he personifies the miracle of how "the eternal penetrates . . . life in time,"[13] to use Romano Guardini's words.

Undoubtedly Father Zossima constitutes an integral part of a novel in which the applied Christian content of Dostoevsky's aesthetic theory is readily observed. He stands for something real and yet ideal, transcendental and timeless. To Dostoevsky he exemplifies the Christian aesthetic which lies beyond the pale of Russian Orthodoxy per se. That is, Father Zossima is Dostoevsky's vision of a Christianity refined and purified to its highest point, a universalized vision, when Dostoevsky has overcome his own prejudices and limitations, his own religious idiosyncrasies necessarily occasioned by such excrescences as Slavophilism and some of the rigid traditions of the Eastern church. With Father Zossima, Dostoevsky soars, even if precariously, into a realm of pristine Christianity, but only after purging himself of religionist elements that are mere secularizations—personality, dogma, legalism, and ritual, for example, those inevitable entrapments of temporalized *ecclesia*, Eastern as well as Western. Father

Zossima, in short, is Dostoevsky's vision of prophetic Christianity, and of Christianity beyond historicism. Indeed, in Father Zossima he meditates on the whole religious process of this de-creation, on the promise of redemption, from a fallen and philistine Christianity. The purity of this vision, this pan-Christian vision, it needs constant stressing, is arrived at through the artistic process, and arrived at in a novel in which, as R. P. Blackmur remarks, "it is the novelistic force which gives poetic justice to the religious."[14]

With Bishop Tikhon in *The Devils* and with the old pilgrim Makar Ivanovitch Dolgoruky in *A Raw Youth*, Father Zossima comprises "the most wise teachers of life." Actually, the figure of Father Zossima enlarges upon the earlier figure of Makar, intensifying and heightening the kerygmatic qualities of the "beautiful serenity" and the "positively beautiful" which comprise that "old monk" ("a very grey-headed old man, with a big and very white beard") in his life and travels. That Makar is a precursor of Father Zossima is not difficult to see. Like Zossima he has a "benign serenity, an evenness of temper, and what was more surprising than anything, something almost like gaiety" (I, vii, 2).[15] And like Father Zossima, "he retains a pure position," "a sinless heart,"[16] in the face of inextinguishable pain and suffering in life. In his love of man and of the whole of nature, which he sees garbed in a boundless and radiant mystery—

> "What is the mystery? [Makar asks, and then goes on to reply:] Everything is mystery, dear; in all is God's mystery. In every tree, in every blade of grass that same mystery lies hid. Whether the tiny bird of the air is singing, or the stars in all their multitudes shine at night in heaven, the mystery is one, ever the same. And the greatest mystery of all is what awaiteth the soul of man in the world beyond" (III, i, 3)

—he anticipates both physically and pneumatically the holiness consummated in the figure of Father Zossima.

More, Makar anticipates a monastic ideal foreign to Byzantine Christian austerity and asceticism. His "gaiety of heart, and therefore 'seemliness,' " looks directly ahead to Father Zossima's sanctification of the "gladness" of life when, as the *staretz* affirms, "every day that is left me I feel how my earthly life is in touch with a new infinite, unknown, but approaching life" (VI, 1).[17] From Makar to Father Zossima we view an organic pattern of development, a steadily evolving spiritual vision and emerging Christian ethos, rooted in the sacred mystery of the created world. It is a vision and a world that are detheologized, freed from the restrictions of creed and the particularizations of dogma, and that embrace "living life" in communion with the Divine.

Makar and Father Zossima are images of a divine *sophia*, earthly and yet metaphysical. Dramatically they reflect Dostoevsky's own contemplation of the theme of mystical naturalism that is intrinsic in a spiritual vision which never loses sight of a supernal power, but that concurrently bathes in the majesty of the immediate physical world in which God's immanence remains as an irrevocable, interpenetrating hint of a higher dimension—and as gleams of an ultimate experience that must have their beginning in sensuous ways. The recognition of this fact is tantamount to an "experiential transformation," as Guardini expresses it. Similarly, Mochulsky conceives of it in these words: "To the pure heart paradise opens itself on that ground." Which is to say, "on that ground" of theophanic experience which Makar describes ecstatically with reference to his pilgrimage to the monastery of Our Lady for the holy festival:

> We spent the night, brother, in the open country, and I waked up early in the morning when all was still sleeping and the dear sun had not yet peeped out from behind the forest. I lifted up my head, dear, I gazed about me and sighed. Everywhere beauty passing all utterance! All was still, the air was light; the grass grows—Grow, grass of God, the bird sings—Sing, bird of God, the babe cries in the woman's arms—God be with you, little man; grow and be happy, little babe! (III, i, 3)

An "inspirer of Dostoevsky" was the great Russian Saint Tikhon Zadonsky (1724–83). The first drafts of both *The Life of a Great Sinner* and *The Brothers Karamazov* contain the name "Tikhon," which was subsequently changed to "the Hermit" and then to the "Elder Zossima." Dostoevsky was well acquainted with the life of Saint Tikhon and it is probable that during his years in Siberia he had heard of or read the saint's writings (e.g., *Of True Christianity, The Spiritual Treasury, Letters from a Cell*), the style of which definitely colored the writing of Book VI, "The Russian Monk," in *The Brothers Karamazov*. Dostoevsky "found in the simple Russian saint his initial idea of perfection"[18] and, as he noted in *The Diary of an Author*, a great "historical ideal" from which the Russian people "would be learning beautiful things."[19] In a letter to A. N. Maikov, dated March 25, 1870, he clearly shows just how much Saint Tikhon meant to him, to the extent that this saint had furnished him with a prototypal image and ideal aesthetically and spiritually realized in *The Brothers Karamazov*:

> The whole of the second story [in *The Life of a Great Sinner*] will take place in a monastery. I have fostered all my hopes upon this second story. . . . I wish, in this second story, to portray as its main figure Tikhon Zadonsky, naturally under a different name, but he will also be

a bishop and will live in retirement in a monastery. . . . I know the monastic world, I have known the Russian monastery since childhood. . . . If only I could depict a *positive* holy figure. . . . It is true that I am not going to create but only portray a real Tikhon whom, long ago, with deep delight, I received into my heart. If I succeed I shall account it a great achievement.[20]

Nor is it difficult to see the high qualities of Saint Tikhon's life and writings which Dostoevsky found attractive and which influenced the creation of the figure of Father Zossima. Professor G. P. Fedotov rightly speaks of this attraction in terms of Saint Tikhon's "charitable and kenotic personality." Saint Tikhon, it should be pointed out, lived during a time of spiritual and monastic revival in Russia, following a period of religious lassitude and doctrinaire religionism, all too often apparent only as external signs of piety and morality, which gripped Russian Orthodox society throughout the seventeenth century. In many ways his solitary life of prayer and his acts of charity to the poor, his guidance of and exhortations to the many visitors and pilgrims who came to see him at the monastery of the Blessed Virgin at Zadonsk, his preaching of and attempts to effect a national regeneration, epitomized the direction of this spiritual revival. Indeed, Saint Tikhon, stressing the radiance of Christlike life and divine love, was "a living reply"[21] to those who embraced atheism and antireligionism. As James H. Billington asserts, "at Zadonsk, Tikhon took the role of the spiritual elder out of the narrow confines of the monastery into the world of affairs, becoming the friend and counselor of lay people as well as monastic apprentices."[22]

Billington's words accentuate the broader basis of interrelationship between the historical role of Saint Tikhon ("a Westernizing kenotic") and the fictional image of Father Zossima. Of course, it cannot be denied that any comparison of these two figures shows, as has been remarked, "a disparity which is greater than the likeness": viz., Father Zossima contains "a Christian humanism, a serene freedom and cosmic mysticism of Mother Earth, which were entirely foreign to the melancholy recluse of Zadonsk."[23] But the point that needs to be understood is that Father Zossima served for Dostoevsky as an artistic transfiguration. Thus he went far beyond mere historical reality or fact, originally acting as a spermatic inspiration. "In the ecstatic Pater Seraphicus," Nadejda Gorodetzky reminds us, "the novelist revealed something at which St. Tikhon, out of the depths of his hidden spiritual life, only hinted."[24] Father Zossima, then, renders a metamorphosed Saint Tikhon without doctrinal curtailment or presuppositions. He is a "hint" of a new spiritual conscience, and he lives in the light of the coming resurrection.[25] He is a culminating, seraphic vision of peace and reconciliation, the point at which, it can be said with Saint Paul, "The night is far spent, the day is at hand."[26]

If it is Saint Tikhon who inspired some of the deeper religious ramifications of Father Zossima's significance, it is Father Ambrose (1812–92), elder of the famous monastery of Optina Pustyn ("the desert of Optina"), who actually provided some of Father Zossima's exterior qualities. Dostoevsky visited this monastery for a few days in June 1878, not long after his little son Alyosha had died and just as he had started writing *The Brothers Karamazov*. Accompanied by his young friend Vladimir Soloviev, at the time a promising philosopher, he went to the Optina for consolation. During his stay he was particularly impressed by the *staretz* Ambrose,[27] with whom he had three meetings. The visual and atmospheric aspects of the hermitage, located near the small town of Kozelsk, in the province of Kaluga, are amply reproduced in Dostoevsky's own description of the physical properties of the hermitage and of the particular cell in which Father Zossima lived.

Dostoevsky and Soloviev were not the only ones making a pilgrimage to the Optina. The Slavophile publicist Ivan Kireevsky, the novelist N. V. Gogol, the critic N. N. Strakhov, and the "aesthetic monoman" (as he called himself) Konstantin Leontiev had also, at one time or another, visited the hermitage in order to seek spiritual comfort. And during his lifetime Count Leo Tolstoy repeatedly visited the monastery, located some hundred miles from Yasnaya Polyana. His discussions with Father Ambrose prompted him on one occasion to praise the elder as a "holy man." "I talked with him and my soul felt light and joyous. When one speaks with such a man one really feels the nearness of God."[28] At the end of October in the fateful year 1910, when he left his family for good, Tolstoy again set out for the Optina. (His sister Marya was a nun at the convent of Sharmandino, approximately eight miles from the monastery.) "Apart from everything else," he now wrote to his wife, "I can no longer live in these conditions of luxury ... and I am doing what old men of my age commonly do: leaving the worldly life to spend the last days of my life in peace and solitude."[29] Tolstoy died on November 7, 1910, at the railroad station of Astapovo, still in the neighborhood of Optina Pustyn and still possessed by that inner turmoil, that "infinite, irresistible despair and loneliness," which tortured him to the very end.

Both the figure of Father Ambrose, bearded, tall, thin, and stooping, and the surroundings of Optina Pustyn, simple and poor, made a profound impression on Dostoevsky's religious consciousness and his aesthetic sensibility. Father Zossima bodies forth the strength of this impression. In his preachings and in his religious position, he is a composite of Saint Tikhon and Father Ambrose, who in turn belong to a special tradition of Russian Orthodox monasticism. This tradition goes back to Saint Nil Sorsky (1433–1508), who advocated a monastic life based on spiritual freedom, on tolerance of heretics, on compassionate love, and on moderation.[30] "There is a time for silence," Saint Nil taught his followers, whom he treated as friends, "and a time for quiet conversation, a time for prayer and a time for sincere obedience."[31] Some of his other teachings were these: "With regard to eating and drinking, let the practice of each monk be adjusted to his physical and spiritual capacity, avoiding satiety and greediness."[32] "It is a mistake to seek a more advanced state than our progress justifies; we should pursue the middle way and await the right moment."[33] "Therefore neither should we have gold and silver and other unnecessary ornaments in our possession, but only what is necessary to the church."[34] These teachings and the spiritual principles inherent in them are echoed by Father Zossima's "exhortations": "Equality is to be found only in the spiritual dignity of man, and that will only be understood among us" (VI, iii). "Remember particularly that you cannot be a judge of any one. For no one can judge a criminal, until he recognises that he is just such a criminal as the man standing before him, and that he perhaps is more than all men to blame for that crime" (VI, iii). "Seek no reward, for great is your reward on this earth: the spiritual joy which is only vouchsafed to the righteous man. Fear not the great nor the mighty, but be wise and ever serene" (VI, iii). "Always decide to use humble love. If you resolve on that once for all, you may subdue the whole world" (VI, iii).

By his opposition to ritualistic formalism and to monastic authoritarianism and discipline, as well as by his repudiation of living authorities (for he considered the "Holy Writings" as the only true authority), Saint Nil went counter to the Byzantine-Muscovite religious thinking which had prevailed in Russia for hundreds of years. (It is not difficult to see why the Russian liberal intelligentsia admired him.) In this connection he was vigorously opposed by Saint Joseph of Volokolamsk (1439–1515) and his followers, the so-called "Josephites," who stressed order, discipline, obedience, and autocracy. Saint Nil and his "friends," it should be noted, formed what is called a "skete" (or "skit"), a monastic way of life "neither eremitical nor cenobitical, but a middle way which avoided the disadvantages of both."[35] Their retreat was located in a wild and solitary spot in the forest bordering the Sora River, in northern Russia. Saint Nil remained here till the end of his life. In 1503 he attended an ecclesiastical council held in Moscow. Saint Joseph was also among those present. At this gathering Saint Nil advocated various controversial monastic reforms, including the dispossession of lands by the monasteries. His radical proposals were defeated by Saint Joseph and his administration-minded sympathizers, who were also responsible for the subsequent persecutions of Saint Nil and his followers.

The ideology of the Josephites remained firm until the eighteenth century, when the inherently liberal religious thinking of Saint Nil reappeared in the persons of Saint Tikhon and Father Païsius Velichkovsky (1722–94), the latter a great Optina elder whose Slavonic translation of a Greek ascetic-mystical anthology entitled the *Philokalia* played an important part in the Russian monastic revival at the end of the eighteenth and the beginning of the nineteenth centuries. The form of this contemplative monastic life and Orthodox culture flourished throughout this period in Optina Pustyn, which "held itself to be the heir and depository in a special sense of Païsius' tradition."[36] In the person of Father Zossima, Dostoevsky dramatized some aspects of this revived spiritual tradition, with its stress on prayer and love and on the interior life, which embraced not only Saint Nil, but also Isaac the Syrian, Saint Sergius of Radonezh, Saint Tikhon of Zadonsk, and Father Ambrose. "By the power of his artistic insight," Father Georges Florovsky writes in his *Puti russkogo bogoslovia*, "Dostoevsky discovered and understood this seraphic current in Russian piety and prophetically continued it."[37]

Dostoevsky himself considered Book V, "Pro and Contra," which contains the celebrated Legend of the Grand Inquisitor, and Book VI, "The Russian Monk," as the quintessential parts of *The Brothers Karamazov*. Both parts comprise antithetical energies, or rhythms: the first is one of negation and destruction, whereas the second is one of affirmation and creation—an "opposed heartbeat" to Ivan's prose poem. To his influential friend C. P. Pobedonostev, whom he called "a healing spirit" and who, it is sometimes claimed, though somewhat tenuously, not only influenced the composition of the novel but also "suggested" the creation of the figure of Father Zossima, Dostoevsky wrote concerning Book VI, "I have written this book for the few and consider it to be the culminating point of my work."[38] The fact remains that on "The Russian Monk" Dostoevsky "expended more effort" than on any other book in the novel. The reasons for his extra effort are not hard to understand. In a letter dated September 13, 1879, he comments on the extraordinary nature and aims in writing Book VI. "My main worry and care just now is with regard to the necessity of refuting the atheistic thesis. I intend to give the answer to the whole negative side in *The Russian Monk*. I tremble for it and wonder whether it will be a *sufficient* answer. . . ."[39] And in another letter he again wrote concerning the role of Father Zossima: "Pater Seraphicus. The death of the Elder. I consider this the climax of the novel."[40]

Dostoevsky fully knew, as only a prophet can, the irrevocable reality of the facts of the history of his time; he knew, that is, that what he was trying to do in "The Russian Monk" ran counter to the tendencies and actualities of an age seeking after new gods. That he had his doubts as to what he was doing in his presentation of Father Zossima is clearly indicated. "I think I have not sinned against reality," he wrote to Liubimov. "I only wonder if I have succeeded."[41] For Dostoevsky, Father Zossima was a figure who embodied something larger than life, who transcended everyday experience in communion with a greater power and a greater world. In Father Zossima he envisioned the organic metamorphosis of the human condition—a redeeming moment of encounter with the manifestly divine. No wonder that words failed to disclose the significance of his purpose. "I myself think that I have not expressed even a tenth part of what I wanted."

It would not be excessive to suggest that, in Father Zossima, Dostoevsky was searching for those converging aesthetic and religious levels of meaning that in visual art appear in the Pancreator of the Byzantine mosaic at Ravenna; or in El Greco's painting of Christ dead in the arms of the eternal Father; or in William Blake's "Promise of Redemption." A comparable stillness of contemplation seems to surround Dostoevsky's "Pater Seraphicus," who speaks to all time and all men. Hence, Father Zossima is not merely a dramatic figure, an artistic portrayal, but a visionary, universal power, both permanent and immanent, that speaks from "out of the whirlwind." Hence, also, he must be defiant of the transient demands of particular dramatic usage and idiom, because he says what he says from the center of a universal experience and a meaning for all time and all men. And for these reasons, too, Dostoevsky can hardly violate on aesthetic levels the supernatural experience of sanctity that Father Zossima captures, precisely because it is an experience of "the alpha and the omega" that in its depth arises from the beginning of time and will continue to the end of time. Such an experience cannot, must not, be personalized, subjected to a Heracleitian flux, for it challenges art. Rather, it must be rendered in its immemorial wisdom and purity, in its spiritual depth and permanence. Dostoevsky in his letter to Liubimov seems to be underlining precisely these elements when he writes: "Although I myself hold the same opinions which he [Father Zossima] expresses, yet if I expressed them personally *from* myself, I should express them in a different form and in a different style. But he could not speak in a different style, nor *express himself in a different spirit* than the one which I have given him."

Essentially, Father Zossima must be viewed as experience beyond art, vision beyond reality, spirit beyond flesh, life beyond death. Not only the skills of the craft of fiction but the eternals of spiritual art go into the portrayal of the old monk. If he signals for Dostoevsky the metamorphosis of the human condition, he also signals the metamorphosis of art—when art itself becomes a contemplation of the divine. As a prophetic figure Father Zossima contains those intuitive powers of discernment and truth that make him "the great healer," "the saint and custodian of God's truth," to quote Dostoevsky. André Gide has observed that there is not a single great man in all of Dostoevsky's novels, with the exception of Father Zossima, "the noblest figure the Russian novelist had drawn."[42] But his greatness, Gide insists, is not as the world generally reckons it. Rather, it is the greatness that we must associate with saintliness, with holiness. Father Zossima, in a word, represents spiritual greatness and is the product of spiritual art. In this respect he signifies for Dostoevsky a spiritual force, invisible and unregarded, that, as rendered in art, lives and breathes in the very destiny of man. As such the figure of Father Zossima is also the moment of confrontation, or as Dostoevsky wrote to Liubimov: "If I succeed, I shall achieve a good work: *I will compel people to admit* that a pure, ideal Christian is not an abstraction, but a vivid reality, possible, clearly near at hand. . . ."[43]

Understandably, Dostoevsky was concerned with the response that the figure of Father Zossima would generate. He was writing, after all, in an age in which moral crisis was in the air, and precisely that social, intellectual, and religious crisis in Western society that exploded with the Great War of 1914. How authentic, how effective, how convincing would Father Zossima be? Would he be able to withstand the kind of gospel that the archintellectual Ivan Karamazov espoused, or the brutally compromised religious philosophy that the Grand Inquisitor promulgated? Would his doctrine of love and compassion, of "lovingkindness," be able to militate against the increasing emphasis on the dynamics of power increasingly pervading European civilization? Father Zossima, Dostoevsky well realized, was an abstract image of a believing faith in an age on the threshold of the "crisis of faith," the age that Raskolnikov envisioned with prophetic terror in his dream, as found in the Epilogue to *Crime and Punishment*, and that Dostoevsky had first reflected on in his *Winter Notes on Summer Impressions*. Hard questions and hard facts seemed to constitute the real meaning of existence as the nineteenth century was coming to its ominous end. And Father Zossima, speaking for the joys of a life of faith and prayer, was ostensibly an anachronism with which a "modern age" would have little patience.

Since the publication of *The Brothers Karamazov*, Father Zossima has aroused precisely the impatience that modern man has continually disclosed in response to metaphysics as a whole and to figures like Father Zossima who are rooted in metaphysics. Thus he has gone the way of metaphysics in modern times, into the realm of the obscure, the unreal, the intangible, the senseless. Most modern critics have seen to it! Interestingly, his dismissal can be traced back as early as 1882, when Konstantin Leontiev's *Nashi Vovye Khristiane* appeared. Leontiev (1831–91), a Russian writer and thinker, a military surgeon in the Crimean War, a consular official in the Near East, underwent a spiritual crisis in 1871 and lived for a time at Mount Athos. Prior to his death he took monastic orders at the Optina Monastery. Espousing formal aesthetic criticism and admiring the pagan art of Hellas and Constantinople and the spirit of the Renaissance, Leontiev considered Tolstoy's *Anna Karenina* the most artistically perfect work of art; and for a model of aesthetic simplicity, he believed that one had to go to George Sand's *Lucrèce Floriana*.

In Leontiev, Nicolas Berdyaev concludes, we sense "a pointless aristocratic squeamishness and superficial aestheticism."[44] These elements are clearly communicated in Leontiev's judgment of Dostoevsky's "monstrous" novels, which can "only excite a few psychopaths, living in badly furnished rooms."[45] He claimed that they were "non-beautiful," inelegant, joyless, oppressive; that they re-created in tone, atmosphere, and characterization what was dissolute and debased; and that they continued some of the vulgar techniques and elements of the Gogolian school of writing. He felt that *The Brothers Karamazov* failed to pass the tests of "true Orthodoxy" or to perpetuate the Christianity of the Holy Fathers and of the Elders of Mount Athos and the Optina. (J. Middleton Murry, advancing a similar thesis, later suggested that Father Zossima—and Dostoevsky with him—was "a Christian after the order of Ernest Renan."[46]) Father Zossima, Leontiev charged, was neither Father Ambrose nor an authentic Orthodox "type," but an offshoot of the overall "superficial and sentimental make-believe" of the novel: an aspect, in a word, of Dosto-evsky's "rosy Christianity."

Most of the modern criticism of the figure of Father Zossima and of the artistry of Book VI in the novel stands in direct succession to Leontiev's. The most common criticism is that Father Zossima lacks convincing reality and offers unrealistic solutions to spiritual problems. The part of the novel in which he appears is said to be disordered, strange, prolix, digressive, "an endless dissertation, introduced apparently *à propos de bottes,* on the duties of a Russian monk."[47] Dostoevsky, it is charged, "is carried away by the moral-religious didactic element in Zosima."[48] Even a sympathetic and penetrating critic like Ernest J. Simmons describes Father Zossima's religious philosophy as stagnant and humiliating: "It is a negation of the whole ideal of progress."[49] Another critic calls the section on the Russian monk "unfortunate." The life and maxims of Father Zossima, he goes on to assert, are presented in "the naïve meandering style of a sermon," which lacks depth and focus and which runs toward "spiritual diffusion and boring prolixity." "The style excludes dimensions of personality, moreover, which are vital to substantive argument."[50] Still another critic, in a shriller vein, summarizing the typical, if arrogant, impatience of many modern critics and readers in the West, avers that "there are times when Father Zosima is dangerously near to becoming an intolerable old bore and his 'Conversations and Exhortations' are an inartistic excrescence"![51] In fact, the entire novel is, according to Joseph Conrad, "an impossible lump of valuable matter. It's terrifically bad and impressive and exasperating. . . . It sounds to me like some fierce mouthings from prehistoric ages."[52]

Such evaluations of Father Zossima inevitably disclose sharp misconceptions and misunderstandings and are a part of the debased values and loyalties in modern society. They are symptomatic of the crisis of faith that has gripped Western civilization since the middle of the nineteenth century. In this connection they are the distillation of a skeptical, often cynical, and prejudiced spirit as opposed to the prophetic spirit and that "new and dangerous faith" which, Hermann Hesse believed, Father Zossima announced. But the "modernism" of the assessments of Father Zossima is strangely paradoxical. Dismissing the old monk as an image that is dead and no longer relevant, this criticism fails to see that Father Zossima is indicative of Dostoevsky's struggle to abolish time itself and that he personifies "that inner man who has emerged from a rebirth."[53] (The significance of the biblical epigraph to the novel—"Verily, verily, I say unto you, except a corn of wheat fall into the ground and die, it abideth alone: but if it die,

it bringeth forth much fruit" [John 12:24]—assumes its proper relevance here.) Indeed, Father Zossima can be described in terms of a
"new revelation," a "new Christianity," as well as a reborn Orthodoxy, and a new freedom. In him Dostoevsky not only anticipated the
demands of the modern spirit for something that is religiously existential, as both the history and the ambitions of religious thought in the
twentieth century have revealed, but also went beyond modernism, to
defy, it can be said, a static modernism (and a static criticism as well).

Dostoevsky invests Father Zossima with the burden of vision. His
presence in the novel is prophetic. It must stir up something new and
reverberate against a spirit of religious decay and sterility; it must
energize, like some "Holy Event," a change in man; it must act like
a prophetic "announcement" and contain, concurrently, what is peculiar to prophecy—a mission and a function, a declaration and meditation. And we must bear in mind that as a prophetic figure Father
Zossima is also the bearer of the "charismatic" power, the power of
grace, the "splendor" of which is transmitted after his death to another man[54]—to Alyosha—"in whom there is spirit." To miss the
point of this prophetic power in Father Zossima, and in Alyosha, is
to miss the continuing dramatic movement of the novel itself, from
beginning to end, and which gives it its justification and meaning.

From a surface look Father Zossima appears to lack vitality and to
suffer from inanition. He is imaged as a "dying saint." Death hovers
in his presence, and he is pictured as "dying of weakness and disease."
Even his cell has "a faded look." Death and life, life and death—these
are the great tensions that he embodies. He is of this world, but at the
same time he belongs to the other, the next world. His knowledge of
life is temporal and supratemporal. Infinite understanding and compassion radiate from him; blessed tranquillity, profound patience,
abiding and pure love, and reverence are not only the qualities of his
being but also the conditions of the realm that he personifies and inspires. To the old Karamazov he is "the most honest monk among
them." To the youngest Karamazov, Alyosha, he is that "some one or
something holy to fall down before and worship." The immediate
physical projection of the elder, as rendered by Dostoevsky, consists
of traits that underline suffering, venerability, wisdom. The details
of his physical appearance inevitably bring to mind portraits of famous saints found in Byzantine iconography, with which Dostoevsky
was undoubtedly familiar:

He was a short, bent, little man, with very weak legs, and though he was only sixty-five, he looked at least ten years older. His face was very thin and covered with a network of fine wrinkles, particularly numerous about his eyes, which were small, light-coloured, quick, and shining like two bright points. He had a sprinkling of grey hair about his temples. His pointed beard was small and scanty, and his lips, which smiled frequently, were as thin as two threads. His nose was not long, but sharp, like a bird's beak (II, ii).

There is nothing, however, in Father Zossima that communicates sadness, pessimism, or ethereal detachment. A rigoristic Byzantine asceticism does not inform his life or message; he is "not at all stern" but "always gay," "joyful," "smiling." "His mind was quite clear; his face looked very tired, yet bright and almost joyful" (IV, 1). Though sick and weary, he remains active in his ministry, exhorting, imposing penance, absolving, reconciling, blessing. A divine *sophia* inheres in him as he teaches the importance of "infinite, universal, inexhaustible love." The tone of his teachings is distinctly human and humble, bringing to mind affinities with Saint Nil Sorsky. Indeed, Father Zossima is not averse to jesting as he talks with his fellow monks and with visitors. "I've been teaching you so many years," he says, "and therefore I've been talking aloud so many years, that I've got into the habit of talking, and so much so that it's almost more difficult for me to hold my tongue than to talk, even now, in spite of my weakness, dear fathers and brothers" (IV, 1).

Whatever he says is part of a constant attempt not so much to instruct others as "to share with all men and all creation his joy and ecstasy, and once more in his life to open his whole heart" (IV, 1). His view of those who follow the monastic life is balanced and existential: "For monks are not a special sort of men, but only what all men ought to be" (IV, 1). Both his person and his teachings are the antithesis of the religious extremism of Father Ferapont—"kneeling all day long at prayer without looking round," living on bread and water, and wearing irons weighing thirty pounds under his coat. It is not necessarily the life of devoutness or of fasting and observing silence, Father Zossima insists, in word and practice, which gives meaning to religion; for such a life can all too often ignore the most intrinsic relation, the finest harmony, that exists among all men. "For know, dear ones, that every one of us is undoubtedly responsible for all men and everything on earth, not merely through the general sinfulness of creation, but each one personally for all mankind and every individual man" (IV, 1). The knowledge of this responsibility, he stresses, "is the crown of life for the monk and for every man" (IV, 1).

When we consider the structure of *The Brothers Karamazov*, and chiefly the fact that "The Russian Monk" constitutes exactly the middle part of a novel containing twelve books and an epilogue, we must be impressed by the centralizing importance of Father Zossima's role. For he is, in essence, the one who seeks to reconcile the factious elements of a family that in itself dramatizes a schism of soul. He understands completely the nature of human suffering: "Alyosha noticed that many, almost all, went in to the elder for the first time with apprehension and uneasiness, but came out with bright and happy faces" (I, 5). Instinctively aware of the nature of sin, he "was more drawn to those who were more sinful, and the greater the sinner the more he loved him" (I, 5). His compassion, his patience, his understanding and wisdom are infinite, as well as steadfast in the face of the mockery, the cynicism, the boisterous indifference, and the sarcasm of some of those whom inevitably he meets. Yet "he blessed them all and bowed low to them" (II, 3). Significantly, he tells his young disciple Alyosha "to care for most people exactly as one would for children, and for some of them as one would for the sick in hospitals" (V, 1). (Indeed, are not the Karamazovs "children of darkness," childlike and sickly in their illusions, their rebellion, their urges? Do they not need to be cared for?)

If Father Zossima is a healing spirit, if he represents an enduring sacredness in the midst of the profane, he is also that marvelous sanctifying force in the novel that absorbs the recurring blows of life. Disbelief, disharmony, and cruelty rage all around him; he is at the very center of turmoil and hatred. Yet, he endures all and signifies hope and connection. Quietly but perseveringly, even heroically, he withstands the cynical and ruthless subversions of his meaning and message, the pitiless defiance of his gospel of love and belief and hope by the "Euclidean earthly mind," with its abrasive rational assertions, its terrifying end-of-the-world conceptualizings—the cold, cruel, grim, hopeless negativisms which Ivan Karamazov voices with an indignation and authority that seem to defy rebuttal, so forceful are his "conclusions" and his view of life and man. "To my thinking, Christ-like love for men is a miracle impossible on earth. He was God. But we are not gods" (V, 4). "It's not that I don't accept God . . . it's the world created by Him. I don't and cannot accept [it]" (V, 3). "If all must suffer to pay for the eternal harmony, what have children to do with it, tell me, please?"

Far from being a dull or pedestrian sermon, "The Russian Monk" constitutes the most visionary part of the novel. Its quietness, perhaps even its passivity, is the true source of its strength, for it reminds us of the need for meditation if life itself is to be saved from nothingness. Father Zossima serves as the antithesis to the obsession with flesh that we observe in the old Karamazov and to the riot of mind that possesses Ivan. In a way he stands at midpoint between the sensual and the rational, and he dramatizes what is immutable. He provides in his own life-experience and in his teachings the occasion to reflect on the meaning of existence. His presence in the novel is a sustaining counterpoint to shrill extremes. Father Zossima stands for contemplation, when man seeks to attain himself beyond flesh and beyond mind, as well as for conscience, when man must summon himself to himself. Too, he reminds us that the drama of life includes meaning that lies outside the domain of the purely functional demands of existence. Life is something more than flesh or mentality, something more than the excitation of sense. And he reminds us that contemplation of life verges on contemplation of the mystery of death. In short, Father Zossima reminds us that "Dostoevsky is the prophet of the *other life*."[55]

Dostoevsky, it has been remarked, "stands deep within the uncertainties of his work, not somewhere above them or beside them."[56] The Karamazovs depict the secular dimensions of uncertainties connected primarily with the problems of flesh and mind. They embody earthly entities and preoccupations which consume various stages of the seen life. It is their thingness that we feel throughout the novel. With them we experience the multifaceted, the relentless immediacies of life. They are our elemental, our urgent encounters with the elements—with the world, and in it. They are our longings and disappointments, our struggles, our sinnings, our hopes, our naked selves and requirements. With the world, and in it, the Karamazovs are this world, the world reacting to and against itself in the most elemental ways. As a family and as individuals, the Karamazovs are witnesses to and participants in the spectacle of life. In the depth and breadth of their experiences, small and great, they portray for us the human condition in all its fleeting variability—economic, social, emotional, religious. In the Karamazovs we know ourselves as we are and as we live, creatures of a day. Their passions are our passions; their joys are our joys; their nights are our nights. Unwavering necessities of existence, in the face of the uncertainties of existence, color and distort their responses to the world. The limits of time itself make them captives. The Karamazovs are prisoners of life in time.

Father Zossima is more than just an elder; he is also a great teacher.

His teachings are passed on and propagated by his followers, especially Alyosha. It is the life of the spirit that he teaches. So uplifting are his teachings that Alyosha and the other monks "had unquestioning faith in . . . [his] miraculous power." The story of Father Zossima's life, which Alyosha recorded on the basis of the old monk's last conversation with his friends and which appears under the heading "Biographical Notes," constitutes a kind of holy book on which one is asked to meditate. What is emphasized is the way in which Father Zossima, who came of a family of landowners, had been in the army in his youth, and served as an officer in the Caucasus, recalls some "precious memories" of his home and of his study of the Bible and of books of Scriptural history. Throughout the novel these memories achieve an epiphanous role and serve to underscore revelations that take on deeply spiritual connotations and lead to the affirmation of spiritual values. They record miraculous moments, prophetic encounters, sacred signs and numina, that crystallize spiritual change and conversion and lead to an awareness of the divine and to an experience of otherness. Awe, wonder, and gladness accompany these memories, which assume the form of a human link.

Martin Buber has remarked that the spark which leaps from him who teaches to him who listens and learns "rekindles a spark of that fire which lifted the mountain of revelation 'to the very heart of heaven.' "[57] Such a transmission evidences the relationship between Father Zossima and Alyosha (and later between Alyosha and the schoolboys). Together they represent the continuity of the values of spirit, as well as the encounter of generations. Time and again, to recall Buber, an older generation "comes to a younger with the desire to teach, waken, and shape it; then the holy spark leaps across the gap."[58] In this respect Father Zossima must be viewed as a *didaskalos* whose teachings, touched by eternity, return us to the *Logos*. In himself he is the great reminder, the great memory, the great teaching. In "The Russian Monk" Dostoevsky seeks to evoke precisely the wisdom and the strength of this teaching. But Alyosha is not the only pupil whom Father Zossima is "forming" and "making."[59] All men are the object of his concern; his world-view is both prophetic and universal. Indeed, Father Zossima's teaching has as its purpose that of affording one rebirth into a better life. "Spirit begets and gives birth; spirit is begotten and born; spirit becomes body."[60]

"The Russian Monk" follows Book V, "Pro and Contra." It follows, that is, the exposition of Ivan Karamazov's rebellion and his famous "poem in prose," "The Grand Inquisitor." In this light the meaning of rebirth is enhanced. Nor is it insignificant that at the end of Ivan's "poem" Jesus approached the Inquisitor "in silence and softly kissed him on his bloodless aged lips. That was all his answer." Father Zossima represents an added aspect of this "answer." He is the rendering of religious life, and religious "answer," the holding fast to the God that Ivan repudiates, the essence of the humility which refuses to exist outside God. He is faith emerging in the midst of unfaith, an answer to the possibility of nothingness. In his life and work Father Zossima shows the importance of making a choice in the world and of accepting the reality of the world, of living at harmony with the powers of the world but not of becoming absorbed by them as Ivan did. Alienation from the world leads to the rejection of the world. Thus, Father Zossima declares, Alyosha will go forth from the walls of the monastery and "live like a monk in the world." "You will have many enemies, but even your foes will love you," he tells his young disciple. "Life will bring you many misfortunes, but you will find your happiness in them, and will bless life and will make others bless it—which is what matters most" (VI, 1). And here we are reminded of Karl Jaspers' contention that remoteness from the world gives an inward distinction, whereas immersion in it awakens what is human in selfhood. "The former demands self-discipline; but the latter is love."[61]

For Father Zossima the word "love" connotes *kerygma* and *pistēs*: it is the only answer, the only struggle, the only mystery, the only redemption. "Brothers, love is a teacher; but one must know how to acquire it, for it is hard to acquire, it is dearly bought, it is won slowly by long labour. For we must love not only occasionally, for a moment, but for ever. Everyone can love occasionally, even the wicked can" (VI, 3). Love conquers pride (of the kind that we find in Father Ferapont, for instance) and overcomes despair. It serves as the beginning of life, in "kindness and mercy."[62] It reveals God to man; it relates man to God. It frees man and announces a new "way"—"the way of hallowing." "Love a man even in his sin," Father Zossima exhorts, "for that is the semblance of Divine Love and is the highest love on earth. Love all God's creation, the whole and every grain of sand in it. Love every leaf, every ray of God's light. Love the animals, love the plants, love everything. If you love everything, you will perceive the divine mystery in things" (VI, 3). For Father Zossima love assumes the highest spiritual value, and it arouses an experiential transformation, the "experience of paradise," of divine immanence. The failure of love is tantamount to damnation, to hell. "Fathers and teachers, I ponder 'What is hell?' I maintain that it is the suffering of being unable to love" (VI, 3). Father Zossima's words here crystallize the innermost conflict and crisis of the novel. They also give a clue to a knowledge that comes from a higher dimension and that is transposed into spiritual art.

And yet in *The Brothers Karamazov* love also presents the overwhelming paradox. The struggle for and the absence of love: these comprise the terrible conditions of life; these are the very problems of human nature that make of life the dichotomy that it is and that practically devour poor Ivan. Father Zossima affords the knowledge of this desperation. Through him we are able to share in a vision that in itself objectifies the burden of mortality. Father Zossima asks to help and to sustain us under the crushing weight of this burden. Pater Seraphicus! Truly, he is such, as Ivan claims, for Alyosha—and for us. Father Zossima's preoccupation with love adumbrates its difficulties, its elusiveness. Ivan's contention that "for any one to love a man, he must be hidden, for as soon as he shows his face, love is gone" (V, 4) is not without relevance here. Throughout the novel love is there and is not there, as Dmitri Karamazov discovers to his grief. Its presence is as painful as its absence. It requires so much of one, Father Zossima indicates, that it becomes a trial to which not only Dmitri but all men are summoned. (We can well recall Miguel De Unamuno's sage words: "Love is the child of illusion and the parent of disillusion; love is consolation in desolation; it is the sole medicine against death, for it is death's brother."[63]) When the prosecutor in the course of the trial speaks of "the broad Karamazov character" as "capable of combining the most incongruous contradictions, and capable of the greatest heights and of the greatest depths," he is at the same time describing the paradox of love. Of all the characters in the novel only Father Zossima is fully aware of this truth. Seeking to alleviate the human condition, he is also striving to renew it, to save it from itself.

The story of Father Zossima's life serves to emphasize the place of spiritual illumination as it alters one's vision of life. In particular, Father Zossima notes the great importance of certain "precious memories" in his life, such as his fond recollections of his study of the Bible (for instance, the parts relating to Abraham and Sarah, to Job, to the parables of Jesus Christ, and to the conversion of Saint Paul) and of his study of a book of Scriptural history, *A Hundred and Four Stories From the Old and New Testament*. Through these recollections he strives to show how his own life was transformed and saved. "Only a little tiny seed is needed," he says, and life can take a new direction. He recounts how as a youth he spent eight years in a military cadet school at St. Petersburg and how he later became an officer. "Drunkenness, debauchery and devilry were what we almost prided ourselves on," he confesses. He tells of falling in love with a girl who later marries another man, while Zossima is away on military duty. Eventually, he insults his rival, an action that brings on a duel. Just before the duel, in a bad temper, he cruelly beats Afanasy, his orderly. Guilt-stricken, he thinks: "This is what a man has been brought to, and that was a man beating a fellow creature! What a crime! It was as though a sharp dagger had pierced me right through" (VI, 2). And then he thinks, too, of his brother, seventeen-year-old Markel, who had died when Zossima was still a child. He remembers what Markel said on his deathbed to his servants: "My dear ones, why do you wait on me, why do you love me, am I worth your waiting on me?" (VI, 2)

From Afanasy, Zossima now begs forgiveness and drops at his servant's feet and bows his head to the ground. Other crucial words uttered by Markel have further impact on Zossima: ". . . in truth we are each responsible to all for all, it's only that men don't know this. If they knew it, the world would be a paradise at once" (VI, 2). When the duel takes place, his rival "had the first shot," which just grazes Zossima's cheek and ear. Zossima thereupon takes his own pistol and flings it far away into the woods. A new form of courage emanates from Zossima as a result of these experiences. For in making the decision to bow to his orderly and not to shoot at his rival, Zossima has overcome his own proud will. More importantly, he has come to grips with a difficult question, that of human dignity—the question that is so central to the novel. In the story of Father Zossima's early years, especially up to the age of twenty-five when he became a monk, human dignity is finally affirmed. This affirmation, Dostoevsky shows, can be the process of a good, precious memory, which in itself is touched by God.

At the end of the novel, during Ilusha's funeral, Alyosha similarly returns to the meaning of a good memory in life, especially a memory of childhood and of home. A sacred memory preserved from childhood, Alyosha says to the boys who gather around him at Ilusha's stone, can be the best education for one. "If a man carries many such memories with him into life," Alyosha declares, "he is safe to the end of his days, and if one has only one good memory left in one's heart, even that may sometime be the means of saving us" (Epilogue, 3). In *The Brothers Karamazov* memory is seen to assume mystical and spiritual significances. As a vehicle of grace in an Augustinian sense, it connects not only life and life but also life and eternity. It fuses the conscious and the unconscious. It exempts us from oblivion and reaffirms divine immanence. It generates hierophantic powers, when, as Mircea Eliade points out, *"something sacred shows itself to us,"*[64]

evoking and revealing the power of the *Logos* in life. The hierophantic, in this respect, is a major esoteric element of spiritual art. "Poets
are the hierophants of an unapprehended inspiration," Shelley declares. His words summarize a special function of Dostoevsky's work.

With the approach of Father Zossima's death, Alyosha and the
other monks "anticipated miracles and great glory to the monastery
in the immediate future from his relics" (I, 5). When he does die,
however, "a smell of decomposition began to come from the coffin."
This incident shatters the hopes of his followers. To Alyosha it is
"one of the bitterest and most fatal days of his life," for Father Zossima, he felt, "instead of receiving the glory that was his due, was
suddenly degraded and dishonoured." It was as if Providence had
suddenly hidden its face "at the most critical moment." If "the breath
of corruption" proves to be such a terribly disappointing episode for
Father Zossima's supporters, it serves to sharpen the "frantic outcries
of bigots" like Father Ferapont. "The unbelievers rejoiced, and as
for the believers some of them rejoiced even more than the unbelievers, for 'men love the downfall and disgrace of the righteous,' as
the deceased elder had said in one of his exhortations" (VII, 1). For
Alyosha the "unseemly" incident is "a crisis and turning-point in his
spiritual development." His immediate reaction is one of abject disillusionment, and at one point he even repeats Ivan's words to the
effect that he rebels not against God but simply against His world.
("He is rebelling against his God and ready to eat sausages," quips
the wily Rakitin.)

Returning again to the elder's cell where the coffin is standing,
Alyosha falls on his knees and prays. In the meantime Father Païssy
reads from the biblical story of the marriage at Cana in Galilee when
Jesus works "the first miracle" of turning water into wine. As Father
Païssy reads, Alyosha starts to listen, but, exhausted, he begins to
doze. The pages of this chapter recounting this episode exemplify
what has already been called the hierophantic power and function of
spiritual art. They also illustrate Dostoevsky's use of biblical language and meaning under the guise of fiction. The entire episode
synthesizes vision and miracle, life and eternity. At the same time the
role of Father Zossima in the novel and story is further heightened.
For Alyosha suddenly has a vision of "the little, thin old man, with
tiny wrinkles on his face" coming up to him. The elder appears joyful and laughs softly: ". . . he, too, had been called to the feast. He,
too, at the marriage of Cana in Galilee . . ." (VII, 4). He speaks to
Alyosha and raises him by the hand. From every aspect the incident
breathes mystical joy and ecstasy; there is a pervasive, even over-

powering, spiritual mood created in these pages. The emphasis is on rebirth, on a renewed faith, dramatically rendered in a thoroughly hierophantic scene.

Father Zossima, as he appears to Alyosha, personifies miracle. These moments, as they are described, are moments of holiness, of revelation, when art converts and is converted. ("Artistic and religious vision," R. L. Jackson tells us in his study *Dostoevsky's Quest for Form*, "are ultimately one vision, reveal the same absolute reality.") Father Zossima constitutes the miracle of vision at a point of infinite significance in Alyosha's life. "We are rejoicing," he tells Alyosha. "We are drinking the new wine, the wine of new, great gladness . . ." (VII, 4). The hierophantic power of Dostoevsky's art here is crystallized as divinity itself is glimpsed, as in a dream, or in a memory that flashes in the mind and communicates to us some meaningful experience. For in a very deep sense Father Zossima is now part of the Spirit when something happens to man—to Alyosha. He pleads with his young disciple to make the beginning, to see Him, to believe in Him, to be reborn in Him. "Do not fear Him," he counsels Alyosha. "He is terrible in His greatness, awful in His sublimity, but infinitely merciful. He has made Himself like unto us from love and rejoices with us. He is changing the water into wine that the gladness of the guests may not be cut short. He is expecting new guests, He is calling new ones unceasingly for ever and ever. . . . There they are bringing new wine" (VII, 4).

"Changing," "expecting," "calling," "bringing": these words are essentially hierophantic words which attempt to capture the charged significance of the entire episode that is Alyosha's vision. And likewise they inform the nature of his response. Something "glows" in his heart and "fills" it with rapture. "He stretched out his hands, uttered a cry and waked up" (VII, 4). Suddenly, "as though thrown forward," he goes right up to the coffin. "Something strange was happening to the boy." The momentousness of the happening, dramatized with artistic skill, is consummated in a majestic passage that directly follows Alyosha's gazing "for half a minute at the coffin, at the covered, motionless dead man that lay in the coffin, with the ikon on his breast and the peaked cap with the octangular cross on his head":

> He did not stop on the steps either, but went quickly down: his soul, overflowing with rapture, yearned for freedom, space, openness. The vault of heaven, full of soft, shining stars, stretched vast and fathomless above him. The Milky Way ran in two pale streams from the zenith to the horizon. The fresh, motionless, still night enfolded the earth. The

white towers and golden domes of the cathedral gleamed out against the sapphire sky. The gorgeous autumn flowers, in the beds round the house, were slumbering till morning. The silence of earth seemed to melt into the silence of the heavens. The mystery of earth was one with the mystery of the stars . . . (VII, 4).

As mystical as this part of *The Brothers Karamazov* is—possibly the most mystical of anything Dostoevsky wrote—it does not end on a passive note. We see Alyosha suddenly throwing himself down on the earth, embracing it, kissing it, "sobbing and watering it with his tears." Father Zossima's words, "Water the earth with the tears of your joy and love those tears," return to him and echo "in his soul."

For Alyosha this mystical experience has as its media vision and voice, supersensual auditory and visual intuitions which bring man's finite being, his "seeing self," into contact with the Infinite Being, the Absolute. What Dostoevsky seeks to dramatize here is what is paramount to such an experience in the mystic life; visionaries from Saint Teresa to Blake and down to John Masefield believed that the messengers of the invisible world knock persistently at the doors of the senses, with visions and voices, symptoms of transcendental activity.[65] Alyosha apprehends "that other world," "in a flash," as it were. "And never, never, all his life long," writes Dostoevsky, "could Alyosha forget that minute. 'Some one visited my soul in that hour,' he used to say afterwards, with implicit faith in his words" (VII, 4). That "some one," of course, is Father Zossima, who, as Mochulsky declares, "teaches about the soul's ascent to God."[66] For Alyosha this ascent is now marked by the discovery of a great new strength, all the more required to steel him against the subsequent happenings in the tragic history of the Karamazov family. His visionary experience is energizing in its ultimate contexts: ". . . something firm and unshakable as that vault of heaven had entered into his soul. It was as though some idea had seized the sovereignty of his mind—and it was for all his life and for ever and ever. He had fallen on the earth a weak boy, but he rose up a resolute champion, and he knew and felt it suddenly at the very moment of his ecstasy" (VII, 4).

As a result of what is termed "the organic growth of his transcendental consciousness,"[67] Alyosha now "longed to forgive every one and for everything, and to beg forgiveness. Oh, not for himself, but for all men, for all and for everything" (VII, 4). His vision cannot be viewed as exclusively God-conscious. It is that, and something more, in the sense that Alyosha's very purpose and task, from this point on in the story, will revolve around what Father Zossima had earlier told him: ". . . to care for most people exactly as one would for children, and for some of them as one would for the sick in hospitals" (V, 1). Alyosha's visionary experience has enabled him to make his ascent and to experience the mystic states of ecstasy ("a synonym for joyous exaltation, for the inebriation of the Infinite") and rapture ("a violent and uncontrollable expression of genius for the Absolute"; "the violent uprush of subliminal intuitions"). But the end of this vision for Alyosha is not the attainment per se of what mystics term the "Unitive Life," or that "final triumph of the spirit, the flower of mysticism, humanity's top note: the consummation towards which the contemplative life, with its long slow growth and costly training, has moved from the first."[68] The highest and most perfect in its forms, "standing at the highest point of the mystic ladder," the Unitive Life, "though so often lived in the world, is never of it. It belongs to another plane of being, moves securely upon levels unrelated to our speech; and hence eludes the measuring powers of humanity."

For if we are to judge by what befalls Alyosha after his mystic experience, not the contemplative (and ultimately the unitive) life but rather the familiar, concrete, everyday life is to be his fate. His *askesis*, the "dark night of the soul" when the "mysterious death of selfhood" occurs and the soul is "initiated into the atmosphere of Eternity, united with the Absolute," is merely antecedent to his own interior and exterior exposure, in the fullest sense, to "the primitive force of the Karamazovs," "a crude, unbridled, earthly force." For good reason does Dostoevsky stress in his Author's Note that Alyosha "carries within himself the very heart of the universal." His vision has enabled him to touch the divine and, in effect, to gain another "breath of life" by which he is renewed and strengthened to face, to withstand, the travails he is to undergo: the murder of his father, the prosecution of his brother Dmitri, the brain sickness of Ivan—in short, the whole gamut of affliction and catastrophe endemic to the human condition: doubt and death, hatred and cruelty, despair and destruction, temptation and sin. Alyosha's destiny, as Father Zossima prophesies in the early pages of the novel, will not be easy. "I bless you for great service in the world," the elder tells him. "Yours will be a long pilgrimage. And you will have to take a wife, too. You will have to bear *all* before you come back. There will be much to do. . . . You will see great sorrow, and in that sorrow you will be happy" (II, 7). And indeed, to contend with this sorrow, to care for man "as one would for the sick in hospitals," Alyosha's Divine Encounter serves quintessentially as a strengthening, as a preparation for his "sojourn in the world."

His mystic vision, thus, does not fall into quietism, so dynamic is it in its roots and its potentiality, so extraordinary is its meaning as seen in the light of the movement of the novel and Alyosha's role in it—a role so dynamic that one is surprised that it is little remarked on by critics who are satisfied merely to complain that Alyosha and Father Zossima do not provide a "clear moral guide."[69] Evelyn Underhill in her book *Mysticism* gives the best explanation of the kind of visionary experience that Alyosha had and, at the same time, clarifies the thrust of its direction and the nature of its meaning:

> Whereas vision of the passive kind is the expression of thought, perception, or desire on the part of the deeper self: active vision is the expression of a change in that self, and generally accompanies some psychological crisis. In this vision, which always has a dramatic character, the self seems to itself to act, not merely to look on.[70]

In the persons of Father Zossima and Alyosha we have a single positive spiritual-earthly force. Alyosha is an extension of Father Zossima in a secular way. To view and to estimate Alyosha's actions in the novel is really to comprehend a transfiguration of Father Zossima himself. That is, Alyosha continues his elder's work as "the great healer," continues it in another arena, one certainly more problematic and dangerous than that of the monastery. Whereas Father Zossima bows down at Dmitri's feet—a prophetic symbol of this unhappy man's future suffering—Alyosha is an active witness to his brother's search for salvation and actually helps to give him "new life," as seen in this dialogue:

> Once more they kissed hurriedly, and Alyosha was just going out, when Mitya suddenly called him back.
> "Stand facing me! That's right!" And again he seized Alyosha, putting both hands on his shoulders. His face became suddenly quite pale, so that it was dreadfully apparent, even through the gathering darkness. His lips twitched, his eyes fastened upon Alyosha.
> "Alyosha, tell me the whole truth, as you would before God. Do you believe I did it [the murder of the father]? Do you, do you in yourself, believe it? The whole truth, don't lie!" he cried desperately.
> Everything seemed heaving before Alyosha, and he felt something like a stab at his heart.
> "Hush! What do you mean?" he faltered helplessly.
> "The whole truth, the whole, don't lie!" repeated Mitya.
> "I've never for one instant believed that you were the murderer!" broke in a shaking voice from Alyosha's breast, and he raised his right hand in the air, as though calling God to witness his words.
> Mitya's whole face was lighted up with bliss.
> "Thank you!" he articulated slowly, as though letting a sigh escape him after fainting. "Now you have given me new life. Would you be-

lieve it, till this moment I've been afraid to ask you, you, even you. Well, go! You've given me strength for to-morrow. God bless you! Come, go along! Love Ivan!" was Mitya's last word (XI, 5).

The center of Father Zossima's *raison d'être,* giving him flesh and purpose, is his hope for "that grand and simple-hearted unity." His spiritual ideal, however, is all along rejected primarily by Ivan Karamazov's blasphemy in the denial of the meaning of God's creation. Ivan, to quote Camus, "incarnates the refusal of salvation."[71] Another critic goes so far as to say that though unable "to receive Alyosha," because of "Dostoevsky's unclarity or our blindness," modern man can receive Ivan with "a terrible kind of delight." For Ivan, he contends, "is a true gift to us all, perhaps Dostoevsky's supreme gift."[72] In him one finds his self-portrait, inasmuch as "the God that is dead for him is dead for us; and his Karamazov-God of tension and terror is often the only one we are able to find."[73] These arguments, which for Dostoevsky would have been symptomatic of the logic emerging from the Crystal Palace, his image of a debased materialistic culture, particularly as it is found in his *Winter Notes on Summer Impressions* instance the kind of reaction both Father Zossima and Alyosha draw forth. Too often there has been precisely this refusal to accept the role and significance of the elder, as well as that of his follower, within the economy of *The Brothers Karamazov.* Implicit in this refusal is an insistence on the abstract quality of the saintly figure.

Undoubtedly one reason for the denigration of Father Zossima is that his pastoral work, on which basis he can be judged, is not only inconclusive but even negative, insofar as it does not provide clearly defined and estimable advantages or remedies. The message of suffering, of love, humility, and patience hardly (ever) qualifies alone for actualized success. Even Father Zossima's own example of life, as well as his message, contributes to turmoil, as seen in the hostility of some other monks, like Father Ferapont, who felt that the elder failed in monastic asceticism characterized and ultimately judged by the presence or the absence of "invisible warfare." "He did not keep the fasts according to the rule . . . ," Father Ferapont screams. "He was seduced by sweetmeats ladies brought . . . to him in their pockets, he sipped tea, he worshipped his belly, filling it with sweet things and his mind with haughty thought . . ." (VII, 1).

If Father Zossima was too radical in his behavior, he was also too radical in his doctrines. In his notebooks Dostoevsky planned for Father Zossima to say: "Love men in their sin, love even their sins."[74] Although the second part of this injunction was later eliminated from the text, its appearance in the notebooks further predicates Dostoevsky's radical intention to give Father Zossima a revolutionary religious significance—that "new saintliness" the modern world has yet to comprehend. No words can better summarize the daring of what Dostoevsky had in mind, what he sought to personify in the figure and purposefulness of Father Zossima, than these of a later religious thinker and prophetic genius, Simone Weil (1909–43): "We live in an age which is quite without precedent: to-day there is nothing in being a saint. We need a saintliness proper to the present moment, a new saintliness, which is also without precedent."[75]

Obviously, this "new saintliness," of which Father Zossima is very much a prototype in modern literature, was alien to Father Ferapont, who represents a moribund ecclesiasticism. Dostoevsky dramatizes in Father Zossima the problematic aspects of faith even as he renders in the entire novel the crisis of faith. The old monk, Eduard Thurneysen notes, embodies "the eschatological tension that gives life its meaning"; indeed, this "eschatological tension develops into eschatology itself."[76] And for Dostoevsky the religious situation, with all its paradoxes and uncertainties, as rendered in Father Zossima and subsequently in Alyosha, comprised the focal point of this tension. To a great extent Father Zossima is Dostoevsky's answer to Ivan; he provides the occasion for reflection on the "eternal questions," particularly on the opposition of good and evil. Father Zossima embodies the metaphysical view of and concern with human life. He symbolizes proximity to God, just as Ivan symbolizes distance from God. In a deeply dramatic sense Dostoevsky uses Father Zossima, whether as an active presence or as a name on the lips of some other characters, as a means of keeping one's attention fixed upon divine truth. He constitutes for Dostoevsky, in the metaphysics of his art, a sacred force comprising love and attention in the midst of immense evil. As we come to see in the various confrontations in *The Brothers Karamazov*, Father Zossima is not only a sacred force but also a contact with purity, effecting a transformation in evil. "But if through attention and love," Simone Weil tells us, "we project a part of our evil upon something perfectly pure, it cannot be defiled by it; it remains pure and does not reflect the evil back on us; and so we are delivered from the evil."[77]

It is Simone Weil who helps us most to discover the various and subtle levels of meaning in Father Zossima. When Berdyaev divided people into two classes, the "dostoievskites" and the "non-dostoievskites," he pronounced a truth which the modern world has witnessed with ever-increasing urgency. In Simone Weil, whom Camus saluted as "the only great spirit of our time," we have a paragon "dostoievskite" whose own writings are in themselves astonishing commentaries on the Russian novelist's metaphysics. Perhaps it would be best to conclude this interpretation of Father Zossima, and of *The Brothers Karamazov*, in the light of some of her writings, particularly her essay "The Love of God and Affliction." Affliction (*malheur*), she says, though inseparable from physical suffering, "is something apart, specific and irreducible," an uprooting of life, a destroyer of personality. It takes possession of the soul, destroys it, and then marks it for slavery. "Affliction is above all anonymous; it deprives its victims of their personality and turns them into things. It is indifferent, and it is the chill of this indifference—a metallic chill—which freezes all those it touches, down to the depth of their soul."[78] Primarily, it contains the truth of the human condition; that is, it epitomizes man's infinite fragility and his constant exposure to "the mechanism of necessity." It is not a psychological state, but rather "a pulverization of the soul by the mechanical brutality of circumstances." The possibility of affliction, writes Simone Weil in words which deserve to be quoted, is always present:

> All the three sides of our being are always exposed to it. Our flesh is fragile; it can be pierced or torn or crushed, or one of its internal mechanisms can be permanently deranged, by any piece of matter in motion. Our soul is vulnerable, being subject to fits of depression without cause and pitifully dependent upon all sorts of objects, inanimate and animate, which are themselves fragile and capricious. Our social personality, upon which our sense of existence almost depends, is always and entirely exposed to every hazard. These three parts of us are linked with the very centre of our being in such a way that it bleeds for any wound of the slightest consequence which they suffer. Above all, anything which diminishes or destroys our social prestige, our right to consideration, seems to impair or abolish our very essence—so much is our whole substance an affair of illusion.[79]

It is true that the themes of purgation, resurrection, holiness, repentance, and theodicy run throughout and interpenetrate in *The Brothers Karamazov*. But these themes are mainly the manifestations and constituents of what must remain basic in the structure and in the intended purpose of the novel—to dramatize a condition of affliction in life. No character in this novel of affliction is spared affliction—physically, socially, or spiritually. Each endures in the most painful, unexpected, and inexplicable ways a sense of deracination, depersonalization, weakness, or disintegration. The fragility of each character, even of the saintly ones, appears in numerous and sometimes enigmatic ways. The supreme victimizer, as well as the ultimate human process, affliction has "the power to seize the very souls of the innocent and to possess them as sovereign master. At the very best, he who is branded by affliction will only keep half his soul." Father Zossima (and eventually Alyosha) is the only one of the major figures in the novel who comprehends this condition. The power of his vision, and hence of his prophetic faith, is rooted in his own experiences of suffering and joy and in his recognition of the fact, to quote Simone Weil, "that the substance of the universe is necessity and that the substance of necessity is obedience to a perfectly wise Love."[80]

The so-called passivity attributed to Father Zossima is not that at all. In contrast to the rebelliousness, even the madness, that grips the other characters in *The Brothers Karamazov*, it is his acceptance of the universe and his obedience to God that give Father Zossima quietude and confidence. He sees the universe as no other person sees it: he accepts the fact that man by himself has not created the world nor can he control it. Again, Simone Weil's remarks are invaluable here in illuminating Father Zossima's power—the mysterious, hierophantic power that Dostoevsky endows him with in the novel: "It is affliction that reveals, suddenly and to our very great surprise, that we are totally mistaken" ["that the world is created and controlled by ourselves"]. . . . "To be a created thing is not necessarily to be afflicted, but it is necessarily to be exposed to affliction. Only the uncreated is indestructible."[81] Man is vulnerable, and thus afflictive, Father Zossima teaches; hence, he must also accept this condition. "Affliction, when it is consented to and accepted and loved, is truly a baptism."[82] The two poles, the two essential truths of Christianity, are the Trinity ("perfect joy") and the Cross ("perfect affliction"), Simone Weil emphasizes. "It is necessary to know both the one and the other and their mysterious unity, but the human condition in this world places us infinitely far from the Trinity, at the very foot of the Cross. Our country is the Cross."[83]

She also notes that "affliction without the Cross is hell," that the one thing enabling man to accept affliction "is the contemplation of Christ's Cross."[84] Father Zossima's knowledge of this truth, it can be said, opens the door to the wholly "other reality," whereas Ivan's rejection of any "mysterious unity," or "higher harmony" as he puts it, ends in the cul-de-sac of rebellion. "What good can hell do," Ivan cries to Alyosha as he expounds his theory of the "unatoned" suffering of children, "since those children have already been tortured? And what becomes of harmony if there is hell? I want to forgive. I want to embrace. I don't want more suffering. And if the sufferings of children go to swell the sum of sufferings which was necessary to pay for truth, then I protest that the truth is not worth such a price" (V, 4). Ivan, surely the most afflicted of Dostoevsky's characters, here protests against the hell of affliction. For him there can be neither contemplation nor consolation, inasmuch as he believes that God is absent. Even if Ivan can agree with Father Zossima that man is the slave of necessity, he disagrees, violently, that man is also the son of her Master. Unlike Father Zossima, he cannot be obedient to God.

In *The Brothers Karamazov* Dostoevsky's vision of evil in the world, in the forms of affliction and crime, achieves its consummate prophetic validity. In the person of Father Zossima, in the essence of his utter goodness and compassion, Dostoevsky strives to show how immensely difficult and painful it is for us to accept his spiritual insights or sympathize with his spiritual values. Our distance from Father Zossima reflects the distance between us and God. This, in effect, is what accounts for Father Zossima's so-called "unreality," "unclarity," "immobility."[85] Father Zossima's constant awareness of the inseparability of, even the dialogue between, Creation and Passion is that which gives him meaning and prophecy in the novel. His message of love attests to the Creation; his own death attests to the Passion. "The tremendous greatness of Christianity comes from the fact that it does not seek a supernatural remedy against suffering, but a supernatural use of suffering."[86] Thus Simone Weil wrote in her notebooks. Her words underline Father Zossima's unique place in *The Brothers Karamazov* as well as Dostoevsky's own religious orientation, which, as it emerges in this novel, transcends any religious system.

Man must not, Father Zossima shows, struggle against the Absolute. Nor must afflicted man expect final answers to requite his fears and degradation. In a sense man must wait for God in silence. "He who is capable not only of listening," Simone Weil declares, "but also of loving hears this silence as the word of God. The speech of created beings is with sounds. The word of God is silence. God's secret word of love can be nothing else but silence. Christ is the silence of God."[87] Father Zossima personifies this silence in the midst of affliction: ". . . the Lord *is* in his holy temple: let all the earth keep silence before him,"[88] a Hebrew prophet admonishes. The numinous value of this silence is suggested by Father Zossima's attitude and by the manner in which he communicates with and counsels others.[89] His silence of waiting is what enables him to break through the horror and ugliness of the affliction around him. He sees and understands this affliction without ceasing to love. This is a secret of his power. This is why he remains in constant touch with God. This contact, in turn, gives him a profounder knowledge of man's suffering. Thus, Father Zossima also knows the last secret of this suffering. He knows, in Simone Weil's words, that if man, "remains constant, what he will discover buried deep under the sound of his own lamentations is the pearl of the silence of God."[90]

The pain of affliction and the cry of terror prevail in Dostoevsky's last novel. Again and again he seems to be saying that the possibility of escaping or defeating this human condition is remote, if at all existent. Even if man can follow after God, he cannot be God. For one seeking to defy such a truth will meet with Ivan's fate. This fate—the common fate of all men—is reflected in the crushed, twisted, terrified, broken world in view in *The Brothers Karamazov*. The frenzied movement, the lacerations, the grim dialogue, the questionings of Dostoevsky's people—young and old, sons and fathers, men and women—testify repeatedly to the extent of man's affliction and to the forms of his protest against it. But all human actions and reactions must ultimately be viewed in the framework of chronology. "Time's violence rends the soul: by the rent eternity enters," it is said. Father Zossima represents Eternity in so far as his teachings transcend *chronos*. We can understand, therefore, why he is always characterized by pure and absolute goodness, by quietness, by patience—virtues which he gladly shares with others even as he shares the burden of their sin and affliction. Father Zossima, writes Dostoevsky, "had acquired the keenest intuition and could tell from an unknown face what a new comer wanted, and what was the suffering on his conscience. He sometimes astounded and almost alarmed his visitors by his knowledge of their secrets before they had spoken a word" (I, 5).

Father Zossima embodies Dostoevsky's concept of a new kind of sanctity. He has emptied himself of any false divinity and social idolatry. For him there is no such thing as an easy or safe Christianity reached by institutionalized conventions or means. "It is necessary to uproot oneself. To cut down the tree and make of it a cross, and then to carry it every day."[91] It is this process of de-creation that Father Zossima undergoes and that gives him a clear understanding of human destiny and of the "greater reality." To be sure, Christianity is for him the changeless Word of peace, but it is first of all the Word of suffering, of affliction. He stands at the point where Christianity meets the world of the Karamazovs, the real world. And it is at this point of confrontation that divine truth and the absurdity of the human condition itself must reach each other across the abyss. Father Zossima is terribly aware of this chasm in time and space, just as he is aware of the supreme fact that, as Simone Weil phrases it, "Sin is nothing else but the failure to recognize human wretchedness."[92] (The whole of Dostoevsky's art and thought are, in fact, encompassed by these words.) Father Zossima is thus also aware of the impossibility and the contradiction made implicit in life by the mystery of suffering. His function is to connect the divine and the created worlds, to act as intermediary whose very essence and meaning must be experienced as a regeneration of religious consciousness. In him the sacred and the profane conjoin.

Far from being ineffectual, Father Zossima's Christianity is radical and existential. It could be said that his Christianity is Dostoevsky's answer to the inert Christianity that Ivan Karamazov castigates and refuses. That *this* Christianity can enter profane life and alter it: such is Father Zossima's message and at the same time the poetic, the creative, significance assigned to him in the novel. As a prophet Dostoevsky felt the poetic need, which he related to what is spiritual, to create in *The Brothers Karamazov* a religious figure pertinent to a world in which increasingly both philosopher and theologian were surrendering to the dialectics of a modern cosmology. "When the philosophers abandon the metaphysical threshold," St.-John Perse has said, "it falls to the poet to take upon himself the role of metaphysician: at such times it is poetry, not philosophy, that is revealed as the true 'Daughter of Wonder.' . . ."[93] This is the role which Dostoevsky assumes in this novel more than in any other in his pentalogy; and Father Zossima is, more than any other of his people, the poetic revelation of the novelist's metaphysics of a "new saintliness."

13

Boris Pasternak's Protest and Affirmation

We have all become people according to the measure in which we have loved people and have had occasion for loving.

—BORIS PASTERNAK, *Safe Conduct*

∽

"It is not the clash of generations or classes," the Russian poet and critic Vladimir Markov writes of Boris Pasternak's *Doctor Zhivago*, "but that of eternal truth vs. false ideals which forms the central interest of the novel."[1] Yet from the moment that the Swedish Royal Academy selected Boris Pasternak to receive the Nobel Prize for Literature in 1958, his name was utilized as a kind of battle slogan by literary warriors seeking to exploit art as a weapon in the ideological warfare between East and West. The consequence was a strong tendency in many circles to categorize Pasternak as a political novelist and his acclaimed work, *Doctor Zhivago*, as perhaps the most noteworthy political novel of the twentieth century. Critics and criticism of this sort can be pardoned for such thinking, in light of the extreme political consciousness that has characterized almost all facets of life and thought since the end of World War II. Yet it cannot be denied that it is one of the great misfortunes of modern times that ideological labels, classifications, and creeds—the dogmatics of politics—have been applied, indiscriminately at times, to artists and their works. It is especially unfortunate when works of art that are of philosophical significance and are stirring testaments of man's spiritual meaning and nobility become confused with the narrow and stringent partisanship of political power struggles and skirmishes.

In *Doctor Zhivago*, Pasternak's first novel, it is not unusual to see that the poet sometimes finds it difficult to be at home in prose. Through the years Pasternak built up an excellent reputation in Russia as a poet; he especially captured the imagination of Russian youth. It is said that even Stalin was a little in awe of him. In addition to being a poet, he was a translator of Verlaine, Goethe, Kleist,

Rilke, Shelley, and Shakespeare, and this work also made him a notable figure in the Russian literary world. In fact, a reading of *Doctor Zhivago* brings out in places a Shakespearean sense of tragedy. Zhivago is not only a modern Hamlet desperately caught up in a terrifying dilemma, but also a modern Lear who is a tragic witness to the conflict between the old and the new. In *Doctor Zhivago*, Pasternak writes not only of the politics of modern times, or even of Russia and the Russians in particular. In the great tradition of Turgeniev, Dostoevsky, Tolstoy, and Chekhov, Pasternak deals with the "accursed questions" of life and love, good and evil, freedom and slavery, belief and disbelief, spirit and matter.

Pasternak's message to modern man is without doubt the result of his own search for truth, his devotion to the freedom of the artist, his unwavering belief in the greatness of man. His message and meaning must be understood in the light of their Christian humility and simplicity. Unlike André Gide, Marcel Proust, or James Joyce, Pasternak developed a creed of art that found ultimate truth in Christ and in the Gospels. "The final point of Pasternak's vision," one critic declares, "is the message of Christ, and what Christ means to him is absolute faith in man's innerness and freedom."[2] Pasternak's concept of love is complete precisely because it must be seen in the unity that is found in Christ. Nikolai Nikolaievich, a former priest, unfrocked at his own request, underscores this theme early in the book when he says: "Gregariousness is always the refuge of mediocrities, whether they swear by Soloviev or Kant or Marx. Only individuals seek the truth, and they shun those whose sole concern is not the truth. How many things in the world deserve our loyalty? Very few indeed. I think one should be loyal to immortality, which is another word for life, a stronger word for it. One must be true to immortality—true to Christ!"[3]

That Pasternak managed to survive the terrors of the Soviet world since its inception was miraculous when one considers the inevitable fate of the creator-artist under the Stalinist system. Yet, during most of his life Pasternak lived and worked in his native Russia; he found strength in the Russian land and countryside, in the Russian people; and it was basically his vigorous devotion to the land and its people that prompted him to reject the Nobel Prize rather than to live in exile. Russia nurtured not only Pasternak, but his art as well. Born in Moscow in 1890, the eldest son of Leonid Pasternak (a celebrated painter of Rilke, Rachmaninoff, and Lenin) and of Rosa Kaufman-Pasternak, a concert pianist, young Pasternak was exposed to unique influences and figures that influenced him immeasurably.[4] Botany "appeared as his first passion." Later the great musician and family friend Scriabin, with his "incommunicable music," hauntingly inspired the young Pasternak, who would run "along the dark Myasnitzkaya to make him come back or see him just once more."[5]

Pasternak's love for music was great indeed, but since he did not possess "absolute pitch," he turned to the study of law at the University of Moscow. Law did not appeal to him, so he abandoned it and went to study philosophy in Germany at the University of Marburg under the neo-Kantian scholar Hermann Cohen, who strongly influenced Pasternak's idealism in the early stages. Later, when he traveled to Italy and became acquainted with Italian art, he gained "a sense of the tangible unity of our culture." "I came to understand," Pasternak wrote in his autobiographical sketch, "that the Bible is not so much a book with a hard and fast text, as the notebook of humanity, and also what is the nature of everything eternal."[6] In this connection, it is interesting to note that although Pasternak came from a Jewish family, he was unable to accept Cohen's loyalty to their common Judaic tradition. This point of view is clearly delineated by Pasternak in a significant passage in *Doctor Zhivago*:

> It's so strange that these people who once liberated mankind from the yoke of idolatry, and so many of whom now devote themselves to its liberation from injustice, should be incapable of liberating themselves from their loyalty to an obsolete, antediluvian identity that has lost all meaning, that they should not rise above themselves and dissolve among all the rest whose religion they have founded and who would be so close to them, if they knew them better.[7]

Early in his life Pasternak became involved with avant-garde literary groups and had a very brief encounter in 1912 with Futurism, a literary movement in Russia which called for a repudiation of the old culture, which experimented with language, rhyme, and metrics, and which took keen interest in the realities of modern life. Among the leaders of this movement were Velemir Khlebnikov, Alexey Kruchonykh, David Burlyuk, and Vladimir Mayakovski. A leading poet of the Russian Revolution and a passionate defender of the Bolshevist cause, Mayakovski as a man and an artist had a strange magnetism that was felt by Pasternak, who, though he was devoted to him as a friend, was quite removed from his politics. Pasternak's description of Mayakovski and his tragic suicide in April 1930 is beautifully recalled in words that place the writer and his life in the framework of the agony of thought and action then found in the Soviet system. Pasternak was to write, in prose that would repeat itself in *Doctor Zhivago*:

And it occurred to me then in the same irrelevant way that this man was perhaps this State's unique citizen. The novelty of the age flowed climatically through his blood. His strangeness was the strangeness of our times of which half is as yet to be fulfilled. I began to recall traits in his character, his independence, which in many ways, was completely original. All these were explained by his familiarity with states of mind which though inherent in our time, have not yet reached full maturity. He was spoilt from childhood by the future, which he mastered rather early and apparently without great difficulty.[8]

As a writer Pasternak was often censured by Soviet literary authorities for his "decadent formalism," his "rotten decadence," his "alienation from the masses." Such official criticism, as can be expected, forced him to center his literary efforts in translations, short stories, and poetry; and from 1933 until his death in 1960, he lived in retirement, detached as it were from the literary and cultural movements and experiments of contemporary times. Yet this retirement and detachment gave birth to *Doctor Zhivago*, which Victor S. Frank calls "a miracle of non-conformity and aloofness."[9] And as Stuart Hampshire so well observes, "Perhaps only a long isolation in a cultural desert could have produced this result, this slow maturing of a work that is independent of any distracting contemporary influences."[10] A reading of *Doctor Zhivago* is not only a "meditation on history," as Nichola Chiaromonte describes it, but also a very stirring spiritual experience, as the reader views the life of a self-sacrificing man which spans the history of Russia during the years 1903–43. Zhivago, the protagonist, is an indefatigable witness to the peaceful years before 1905, to the emergence of socialism and collectivism, to World War I, when, to quote Rilke, "the world . . . passed out of the hands of God into the hands of men," to the revolution of 1917, and to the Soviet systematization of life in Russia that has been going on since the fall of Tsarism.

Without doubt, there was a pronounced tendency, as has been mentioned, to appraise *Doctor Zhivago* as a political document that deals with the terrors of the Soviet police state. In addition to political critics, there were also those who attack the book's stylistic and artistic defects. Writing in *The Kenyon Review*, Richard G. Stern cited "narrative sins which succeed in blighting almost every breath of life which Pasternak's handsome imagination began to conjure."[11] He went on to specify such shortcomings as unwarranted and unsignaled transitions, unjustified coincidences, inability to relate an incident, lack of proper sequence, and "intolerable profusion of simile and metaphor." To limit oneself to the stylistic weaknesses of a work can create an impasse and can also restrict appreciation of the novel to

its technical characteristics and qualities, or lack of same. The meaning and the message of *Doctor Zhivago* are much deeper than the
immediate manifestations and connotations of words and stylistic
devices. To condemn a work on these principles alone leads to a sort
of oversimplified literary license, which, were it applied to other writers and their works, would lead to wholesale literary deprecation. No,
the difficulties and weaknesses of Pasternak's style are too insignificant to interfere with an appreciation of the great themes with which
his novel deals.

Pasternak's heroes and heroines are concerned with absolutes, with
the soul, with love and faith. *Doctor Zhivago*, like Dostoevsky's *The
Devils*, depicts not only a social epidemic, in which man becomes the
victim of historical changes and of the external accidents of time,
place, and fashion, but also, and above all, a moral affirmation of the
spiritual verities of love, honor, pity, compassion, and sacrifice that
since 1914 have come under increasing attack. When Pasternak pictures the Russian Revolution as subjugating the human will, inevitably suppressing nonconformity by force, he shows, as Dostoevsky
prophesied, that this subjugation is a declaration of war on the moral
and spiritual aspects of man. But this war on man, this negation of
man, is not a Russian phenomenon alone—it is a universal fact; it is
mankind in its sin and weakness.

In rejecting the "heroic" epic of the Russian Revolution, Pasternak
shows how war is an endless, frustrating, meaningless affair which denies man's humanity and divinity. In particular, he shows in *Doctor
Zhivago* how life is killed as a result of a revolution that begins with
a vision of future amelioration, which Zhivago himself shares, and
that ends in the cannibalism that Dostoevsky foresaw. The characters
in this novel bear the inevitable scars of all the slaughter. Human
dignity and the innate goodness of man give way to the law of the
jungle, and a satanic way of life distorts men as they struggle to survive in a society torn asunder by viciousness and ideological amorality and barbarism. "That period confirmed the ancient proverb,"
writes Pasternak, " 'Man is a wolf to man.' Traveller turned off the
road at the sight of traveller, stranger meeting stranger killed for fear
of being killed. There were isolated cases of cannibalism. The laws
of human civilization were suspended. The jungle law was in force.
Man dreamed the prehistoric dreams of the cave dweller."[12]

In the midst of this killing and dying, those that remain behind
gradually lose their human identity and become orphans of life, cut
off from family and friends, from love, from God. This motif of loss
runs throughout the novel.[13] From the very beginning of the work,

when young Yurii Andreievich Zhivago's mother is buried (his dissolute father commits suicide), we find that his relatively short lifetime, 1891–1929, is a series of cruel dispossessions. To see Zhivago
is, in the words of Tiutchev's poem "The Abyss," to

> Behold man, without home,
> orphaned, alone, impotent,
> facing the dark abyss; . . .
> And in this strange mysterious night
> he sees and knows a fatal heritage.[14]

In the course of the story we find that Zhivago's marriage to Tonia
Gromeko is interrupted by World War I, during which, while serving
as a medical officer in Galicia, he is wounded and cared for by Larisa
(Lara). Later, when the revolution breaks out in 1917, and Zhivago
returns to a desolate Moscow, he and his family make a desperate,
even epic, attempt to survive the carnage and bestiality of the revolution by traveling across Russia, in a nightmarish train ride that
takes weeks, to the industrial town of Yuratin in the Urals. But in
the spring of 1919, after being forcibly kidnapped by Red forces and
conscripted as a medical officer, Zhivago loses all contact with his
wife and infant son, who eventually emigrate to France. "I can't go
on. I can't stop crying. Well, goodbye. Let me make the sign of the
cross over you," Tonia writes to her lost husband, "and bless you for
all the years ahead, for the endless parting, the trials, the uncertainties, for all your long, long, dark way."[15]

Other characters in this work also depict the effects of loss and
isolation. Parallel to Zhivago's own turmoil is the tragic, unhappy
marriage of Lara and Antipov, a schoolteacher. Lara loses all sight
of her husband after he enlists for front-line duty in 1914 and then
is reported missing and presumably dead. However, Antipov, who
escapes his captors in 1917, is to become known as Strelnikov ("The
Shooter"), a notorious Bolshevist leader whose task it is to suppress
rebellious peasants and White resistance forces. Never to return to
his wife, Lara, this ambitious and confused figure—an enigma and
a victim of the revolutionary period—who had been "filled with
the loftiest aspirations from his childhood" and who "had looked
upon the world as a vast arena where everyone competed for perfection, keeping scrupulously to the rules," finds that it is not so.
"He nursed the grievance and with it the ambition to judge between
life and the dark forces that distorted it, and to be life's champion
and avenger. Embittered by his disappointment, he was armed by the
revolution."[16]

Throughout Zhivago is portrayed as a man who makes one sacrifice after another, yet one who, despite all the upheaval and disaster in a confused world, does not lose faith in the principle that "unshared happiness is not happiness." The sacrifices of Zhivago are portrayed in the background of furious, blinding snow storms, which bring to mind Alexander Blok's descriptive passage in his famous poem "The Twelve":

> Mischief lashed into a fury,
> Drives the snow, storms the snow!
> Folk move hidden, groping slow,
> Blind in gusty veils of snow.[17]

When Zhivago condemns the Russian Revolution, he condemns its travesties of justice, its deceptions, its "madness," its "loyalty to forms." In an eloquent and significant conversation between Zhivago and Lara, whose unusual love affair occupies a large portion of the book, an affair which ends in dispossession when Lara is brought to temporary safety (in the end she disappears and dies in a northern concentration camp) by her old seducer, Victor Ippolitovitch Komarovsky, Lara Antipova's words epitomize the breakdown of human life and human values in modern times:

> But it's strange that I, an ordinary woman, should explain to you, who are so wise, what is happening to human life in general and to life in Russia and why families get broken up, including yours and mine. Ah, it isn't a matter of individuals, of being alike or different in temperament, of loving or not loving! All customs and traditions, all our way of life, everything to do with home and order, has crumbled into dust in the general upheaval and reorganization of society. The whole human way of life has been destroyed and ruined. All that's left is the naked soul stripped to the last shred, for which nothing has changed because it was always cold and shivering and reaching out to its nearest neighbor, as cold and lonely as itself. You and I are like Adam and Eve, the first two people on earth who at the beginning of the world had nothing to cover themselves with—and now at the end of it we are just as naked and homeless. And you and I are the last remembrance of all that immeasurable greatness which has been created in the world in all the thousands of years between them and us, and it is in memory of all those vanished marvels that we live and love and weep and cling to one another.[18]

Other writers, such as E. I. Zamyatin, Arthur Koestler, George Orwell, and Aldous Huxley, have attacked and laid bare the horror of the mass-man. As a religiously oriented writer, however, Pasternak viewed this same horror but went beyond the nightmare visions of these other writers. He is a poet of belief, and his art, like his conception of man, is Christian and humane, not dogmatically but ethically and morally. Dmitri Merejkowski's depiction of Dostoevsky as a "seer of the spirit" might well apply to Pasternak.[19] To him, as to Dostoevsky, man's divinity cannot be trammeled and transmuted by brute force or permanently molded by great social schemes and systems. As Zhivago says to his Red captor, Liberius Mikulitsyn: "Reshaping life! People who can say that have never understood a thing about life—they have never felt its breath, its heartbeat—however much they have seen or done. They look on it as a lump of raw material that needs to be processed by them, to be ennobled by their touch. But life is never a material, a substance to be molded. If you want to know, life is the principle of self-renewal, it is constantly renewing and remaking and changing itself, it is infinitely beyond your or my obtuse theories about it."[20]

Pasternak's message to the modern world, in which life, art, and faith have frequently been uprooted by the forces of evil, is one of moral and spiritual affirmation. What strengthens Pasternak, and Pasternak's Zhivago, is a belief in immortality, in the final victory of life over evil. Indeed, Zhivago, the doctor and poet, the humanist and creator, is the embodiment of the perennial struggle between freedom and despotism, between belief in man and belief in dehumanizing force. As Professor Loose states, "Zhivago thus embodies that grave spiritual dilemma of our age: the deep concern with essence and quintessence, with ultimate meaning and transcending purpose."[21] He refuses to betray his humanity and his soul. He bravely and heroically labors and sacrifices to the very end, when he is felled by a heart attack; he realizes the need to live and commune with man, for all men live together and are responsible to each other. Zhivago sacrifices all and gives up all advantage for the higher aims of life, for a life in which faith has value and purpose, in which men respect and love and forgive one another. When Pasternak writes in his *Notes on Translations of Shakespeare's Tragedies* that "*Hamlet* is not a drama of a lack of will, but a drama of duty and self-abnegation . . . of a lofty destiny, of an assigned duty, of an entrusted appointment,"[22] he is surely speaking of his own hero, Zhivago. And in a poem entitled "Hamlet"—one of the twenty-four poems written by Zhivago and included at the end of the novel—Pasternak portrays himself as well as his hero:

> I stand alone. All else is swamped by Pharisaism.
> To live life to the end is not a childish task.[23]

Zhivago's struggles and sacrifices are never in vain. When some five or ten years after the end of World War II, two of Zhivago's old friends, Dudorov and Gordon, are rereading a book of Yurii's writings, collected and published by Evgraf, Zhivago's half-brother, now an important Soviet official, these writings are living and positive proof of the endurability of Zhivago's struggle and affirmation. As these men sit at an open window above Moscow one quiet summer evening, they realize the historical significance of the postwar period, when "portents of freedom filled the air." Pasternak's epilogue ends with words that echo their optimism:

> To the two old friends, as they sat by the window, it seemed that this freedom of the soul was already there, as if that very evening the future had tangibly moved into the streets below them, that they themselves had entered it and were now part of it. Thinking of this holy city and of the entire earth, of the still-living protagonists of this story, and their children, they were filled with tenderness and peace, and they were enveloped by the unheard music of happiness that flowed all about them and into the distance. And the book they held seemed to confirm and encourage their feeling.[24]

Doctor Zhivago contains within it ideological, historical, political, and cultural problems. But these are secondary to the main theme— love and faith, truth and immortality, things of the spirit that remain eternal. "It has always been assumed," Uncle Kolia observes, "that the most important things in the Gospels are the ethical maxims and commandments. But for me the most important thing is that Christ speaks in parables taken from life, that He explains the truth in terms of everyday reality. The idea that underlies this is that communion between mortals is immortal, and the whole of life is symbolic because it is meaningful."[25] Zhivago's protest is an affirmation of the higher life. His life symbolizes the immemorial protest against the dehumanization of man; his death immortalizes the struggle of man to free himself from those things and systems that would destroy the human soul. In this protest and in this affirmation Boris Pasternak built a monument to the divinity of all men. Quite appropriately the last poem in *Doctor Zhivago* is entitled "Garden of Gethsemane" and ends with these words:

> Seest thou, the passing of the ages is like a parable
> And in its passing it may burst to flame.
> In the name, then, of its awesome majesty
> I shall, in voluntary torments, descend into my grave.
>
> I shall descend into my grave. And on the third day rise again.
> And, even as rafts float down a river,
> So shall the centuries drift, trailing like a caravan,
> Coming for judgment, out of the dark, to me.[26]

14

J. D. Salinger and the Russian Pilgrim

࿐

Critical estimates of J. D. Salinger's *Franny and Zooey* invariably contain references to the profound influence made on Franny Glass by a little book of Russian Orthodox spirituality, *The Way of a Pilgrim*.[1] It is obvious that Salinger attaches much significance to this work of Russian piety, as is clearly registered in his depiction of Franny's response to the book. This influence, however, does not necessarily prove distinct structural affinities or parallels, but rather reveals a sensitive recognition on Salinger's part of the moving spirit and message of *The Way of a Pilgrim*. That is to say, Salinger, in showing the influence of this book on Franny, confesses at the same time a decidedly sympathetic and intuitive understanding of the Russian work. He seems to have found in it what might be called a transcending religious meaning and experience; and in his characterization of Franny he re-creates the form, direction, and power of such an experience. *Franny and Zooey* is, then, another example of how modern fiction can affirm the divinity of all men.

The difficulties and the doubts that Salinger must have experienced in order to achieve a positive realization of *The Way of a Pilgrim* are readily seen at the beginning of *Franny and Zooey*, where allusions to the Russian book are couched in obscure, even suspicious terms. Like Franny, Salinger seems at first somewhat ashamed of the "small pea-green clothbound book," which Lane Coutell notices Franny carrying in her left hand when he meets her on the station platform. She has come to join him for "the weekend of the Yale game." He questions her about the book, but she avoids discussing it and quickly stuffs it into her handbag. Yet, by the end of Salinger's book, *The Way of a Pilgrim* is freed from this preliminary obscurity and suspicion. Gradually, its title and content are referred to freely and fearlessly, and its growing significance becomes incontestable. Indeed, at the conclusion of *Franny and Zooey* the spirit and inspiration of *The Way of a Pilgrim* have become convincing and impelling, and the earlier process of grudging discovery is transformed into an undoubting triumph of affirmation. *The Way of a Pilgrim* is no longer "just something," but the way to redemption and the very beauty and wisdom that Franny desperately and painfully longed for.

It would be best at this point to say a few things about *The Way of a Pilgrim* before going on to appraise its significance in Salinger's work. The complete title of the book is *The Way of a Pilgrim and The Pilgrim Continues His Way*, translated from the Russian by R. M. French. The first translation of *The Way of a Pilgrim* was published in 1930, and its sequel, *The Pilgrim Continues His Way*, was published separately at a later date; in 1941 both were published for the first time as a continuous narrative in one volume. The Pilgrim's story was first discovered in manuscript form at a Greek Orthodox monastery on Mount Athos by a Russian abbot, who copied the manuscript, on the basis of which a book was published in Kazan in 1884. This volume narrates the experiences of a Russian wanderer over the steppes and fields of Russia at some time prior to the liberation of the serfs in 1861. In particular it is the story of the Pilgrim's practicing a way of prayer which arises out of his desire to understand the words "Pray without ceasing," from the first Epistle of Saint Paul to the Thessalonians. In the process of learning the meaning of "unceasing interior prayer," the Pilgrim seeks the advice of a monk (*staretz*) known for his wisdom and spiritual counsel. "Learn first to acquire the power of prayer," he is advised, "and you will easily practise all the other virtues" (8). The monk also tells him that the essence of the prayer is found in the words "Lord Jesus Christ, have mercy on me." Soon the Pilgrim obtains a copy of the *Philokalia*, or *The Love of Spiritual Beauty*, a collection of mystical and ascetic writings by the Fathers of the Eastern Orthodox Church. Compiled in the eighteenth century, the Greek *Philokalia* was first published in Venice in 1782; in the nineteenth century it was translated into Russian (*Dobrotolubiye*), and this translation was to play an important role in Russian religious life and thought.

Often described as "the foremost and best manual of the contemplative spiritual life," the *Philokalia* was to be for the Pilgrim a major guide in his attaining purification and in his comprehending more fully the Jesus Prayer. This achievement was no easy matter, for the Pilgrim was to experience the inevitable assaults of laziness, boredom, and distraction. It was not merely a matter of learning and repeating the Jesus Prayer, but of making it become a "self-acting spiritual prayer." Constant effort and stern self-discipline are necessary for the Pilgrim to purge his soul. In the end, with the understanding and assistance of his *staretz*, the Pilgrim discovers the mystery of prayer.

He gradually reaches a state of happiness and innocence, free from evil-thinking and an ego-tainted consciousness. Although he is only thirty-three years of age, the Pilgrim is a widower. He has a withered left arm. His sole worldly possessions are a knapsack containing some dried bread, a Bible, and the *Philokalia*. Nevertheless, in his arduous travels and in his encounters with all kinds of persons, he meets with success; for the Jesus Prayer has become an organic part of his life and purpose, enabling him to see and feel God everywhere.

From all this it should not be inferred that Salinger has adopted Russian mysticism as a kind of religious prop or that he has been experimenting with Eastern Orthodoxy as a means of religious conversion. On the contrary, his approach is entirely nonsectarian: it is mainly a search for religious meaning and for spiritual vision on higher levels of experience. It is expressed in a preeminently modern idiom and context. The fact remains that *Franny and Zooey* is not a "devotional manual," but rather a creative work of art that transcends religious doctrine, creed, and so-called theological dimensions. Its preoccupation is with religious sensibility, with vital emotions, responses, and instincts outside the pale of the rational and the empirical. Any attempt to treat Salinger's work on a religious plane should be detached from the strictly theological and homiletic. Religion, *not* religiosity, is what distinguishes *Franny and Zooey*; and it is religion in the spirit of Alfred North Whitehead's admirable definition, which sees it as

> the vision of something which stands beyond, behind, and within the passing flux of immediate things; something which is real, and yet waiting to be realised; something which is a remote possibility, and yet the greatest of present facts; something that gives meaning to all that passes, and yet eludes apprehension; something whose possession is the final good, and yet is beyond all reach; something which is the ultimate ideal, and the hopeless quest.[2]

Let us turn again to *Franny and Zooey*, particularly to the first scene. In it we find Franny and her boy friend, Lane Coutell, sitting at a table in a downtown restaurant called Sickler's, an eating place specializing in snails—"a highly favored place among, chiefly, the intellectual fringe of students at the college." This setting is identified by what Salinger describes as college students "talking in voices that, almost without exception, sounded collegiately dogmatic." Lane Coutell personifies this haughty dogmatism and pseudosophistication; he is very much a product of an educational system that, Salinger charges, is "all the most incredible farce." In the words of Franny's brother Zooey, Lane is "a charm boy and a fake," and "it's paid off!"

He even reminds Franny of "pedants and conceited little tearer-downers," a potential "section man," with "his little button-down-collar shirt and striped tie." Franny becomes ill in the course of their conversation—a conversation that inevitably reveals to her the crassness and impoverishment of Lane's state. Upon finishing with the words "I'm sick of just liking people. I wish to God I could meet somebody I could respect...," she excuses herself and goes to the ladies' room. Here *The Way of a Pilgrim* comes into view a second time, directly after Franny has gone into "the farthest and most anonymous-looking" enclosure: "She cried without trying to suppress any of the noisier manifestations of grief and confusion, with all the convulsive throat sounds that a hysterical child makes when the breath is trying to get up through a partly closed epiglottis" (22). Then she "picked up her handbag from the floor, opened it, and took out the small peagreen clothbound book," *The Way of a Pilgrim.* "She picked up the book, raised it chest-high, and pressed it to her—firmly, and quite briefly" (22). Then she returned the book to her handbag, stood up and came out of the enclosure. After washing her face, applying fresh lipstick, and combing her hair, she left the room. "She looked quite stunning as she walked across the dining room to the table, not at all unlike a girl on the *qui vive* appropriate to a big college weekend" (23).

As if strengthened by the "small pea-green clothbound book," Franny returns to the table. From the menu she selects a chicken sandwich and a glass of milk, much to the surprise of Lane. "This is going to be a real little doll of a weekend," he exclaims ominously. A moment later he orders frogs' legs, snails, and a salad for himself. Their conversation continues as Lane confidently outlines plans that include meeting his college friend Wally Campbell for a drink and then going to the stadium for the football game. Franny's immediate response is none too favorable; she begins to condemn a society flooded with Wally Campbells:

> "I don't mean there's anything horrible about him or anything like that. It's just that for four solid years I've kept seeing Wally Campbells wherever I go. I know when they're going to be *charming*, I know when they're going to start telling you some really nasty gossip about some girl that lives in your dorm, I know when they're going to ask me what I did over the summer, I know when they're going to pull up a chair and straddle it backward and start bragging in a terribly terribly quiet voice—or *name*-dropping in a terribly quiet, *casual* voice" (25).

To Lane this outcry sounds incredible—although it makes little appreciable difference in his enjoyment of the snails he is relishing while listening to an increasingly pale and haggard Franny. When he learns, however, that she has abandoned all her interests in drama and the theater, he is perturbed. The reason for Franny's decision, in spite of the fact that she has had notable acting success, especially in summer stock, is made explicit in her remark that she is "just sick of ego, ego, ego. My own and everybody else's. I'm sick of everybody that wants to *get* somewhere, do something distinguished and all, be somebody interesting" (29). To this assertion Lane reacts with a typical smugness and he glibly implies that Franny is afraid of competing. He proclaims that her statements would reveal something very serious to a psychoanalyst! Franny's rejoinder rings with honesty. "That's why I quit the Theatre Department," she declares with feeling and resolution. "Just because I'm so horribly conditioned to accept everybody else's values, and just because I like applause and people to rave about me, doesn't make it right. I'm ashamed of it. I'm sick of it. I'm sick of not having the courage to be an absolute nobody. I'm sick of myself and everybody else that wants to make some kind of a splash" (30). As she utters these words, her forehead is perspiring conspicuously, and she unloads a few things from her handbag in order to find some Kleenex. In "the disorderly little pile of handbag freight on the tablecloth," there comes into view again "the little clothbound book."

The third appearance of the book is in every way revealing. No longer is *The Way of a Pilgrim* a shadowy form hovering sadly in the background, but it is an immanent, living force. Indeed, all that has been said up to this point has had as a silent but compassionate witness the Russian Pilgrim. Doubtless he has been kept undercover, hidden from actual sight, and Franny's handbag has been like a gray, oppressive shroud imprisoning a spirit of enlightenment and joy. Bowing at last to Lane's demands, Franny begins to explain the history and meaning of *The Way of a Pilgrim*. Her summary of it becomes increasingly enthusiastic, in spite of occasional interruptions by Lane as he eats his frogs' legs, which he even admonishes at one time to hold still. "I hate to mention it," he breaks in to say, "but I'm going to reek of garlic." Bravely Franny continues with her exposition of *The Way of a Pilgrim*, even when Lane blatantly interferes again to ask Franny whether she will read in the near future a psychoanalytic paper of his on Flaubert, which his instructor had suggested was publishable. Franny, very tolerant and patient, agrees to do so as she watches him butter another piece of bread. "You might like this book," she suddenly says. "It's so simple, I mean" (35). Nonchalantly, he opines that it "sounds interesting," at the same time asking, "You don't want your butter, do you?" But despite the gross indifference that captivates a self-centered Lane, who is now smoking as he sits rather slouched in his chair, Franny goes on to give special emphasis to the Jesus Prayer. She notes that the power of this prayer is no less effective than the words, "Namu Amida Butsu," in praise of Buddha. The same thing happens, she says, in "The Cloud of Unknowing" with the word "God."

Lane's reaction is in keeping with the character and malady of a negator. "You actually believe that stuff, or what?" he inquires. What, he demands to know, are the concrete results of "All this synchronization business and mumbo-jumbo." Accustomed as he is to suprarational formulas, to inviolable answers and systems of thought, he discloses a condition of mind that automatically suspects experiences and responses of a visionary and intuitive nature. Nevertheless, Franny is in no way wholly discouraged or frightened by Lane's cold and calculating doubts and questions. Her reply to him has an enhancing grace and simplicity; in its innocence it is both lovely and touching: "You get to see God. Something happens in some absolutely nonphysical part of the heart—where the Hindus say that Atman resides . . . and you see God, that's all" (39). Lane responds with the question, "You want some dessert, or coffee?" noticing, too, that Franny has not touched her chicken sandwich. He also looks at his watch and states that there isn't much time left to get to the game. And only then does he in any way attempt to refer to Franny's impassioned remarks on "seeing God." He notes condescendingly, and with the kind of toleration which masks a sinister sneering and a heartrending insolence, that what Franny has been saying is perhaps "interesting" but doesn't "leave any margin for the most elementary psychology."

It is evident that Franny has been unsuccessful in communicating with Lane, and it is the brutal realization of an unshared sensibility that drives her once again from the table. She walks briskly through the dining room and stops short at the small bar at the far end of the room. Here she faints and collapses to the floor. Five minutes later she finds herself on a couch in the manager's office, with Lane sitting beside her. Now when she realizes that they have missed the cocktail party and the football game, she apologizes. Lane shrugs it off with the advice that she should return to her lodgings and get some rest— after all, "that's the important thing." Likewise, he tells her that once she has rested and regained her strength, she will be in good condition to meet him that night. Getting to her will be no problem: a man of wide experience and accomplishment, he can easily find out about some back staircase. "His hot little ivy league intellect," after all, should be able to come up with something! (Remember, too, he handles martinis as easily as he does Flaubert!) His real purpose, finally, becomes crystal clear in the remark that follows, and reveals, concurrently, a creatureliness with only one thing in mind: "You know how long it's been?" he asks. "When was that Friday night? Way the hell early last month, wasn't it? . . . That's no good. Too goddam long between drinks. To put it crassly" (42). Soon he leaves the room, and an agonized Franny lies very still, looking at the ceiling. And when the first part of the book concludes, we have a vivid picture of Franny, her lips tremblingly "forming soundless words"—the words of the Jesus Prayer: "Lord Jesus Christ, have mercy on me."

The first part of *Franny and Zooey* may be likened to an encounter between the profane and the sacred. On the one hand, Lane Coutell represents a degenerated consciousness that is irrevocably insensitive and contaminated. On the other hand, Franny represents a consciousness that, even when faltering and fearful, seeks for purposive meanings in human relationships. In her encounter with Lane, therefore, Salinger is attempting to show the difference between what is debased and what is potentially good. Franny embodies the potentiality for good, and Lane personifies the spirit of ruin. He will utilize every devious device and means at his command to achieve his aims. He can be considerate and charming, but his manner hides an ulterior purpose. He has many other weapons at his disposal: derision, cajolery, innuendo, deception, slander. Before such awesome power, Franny appears somewhat limp and overmatched. And yet, we can say that at the end of the first stage of her pilgrimage, Franny has managed to survive the attacks brought to bear on her. This is not to claim that she is triumphant, but rather that she has succeeded in confronting the real nature of debasement. Concerning Franny's triumph we must look to the second, longer part of Salinger's work.

This second part, "Zooey," serves as a kind of sequel to the first story. The time is a November morning in 1955, and the setting is an old but not unfashionable apartment house in the East Seventies of Manhattan. Here we come face to face with Franny's brother Zooey and her mother, Bessie. We also derive information about the other members of the Glass family: Seymour, the eldest and most brilliant brother who had committed suicide; Buddy, a writer-in-residence in a girls' junior college in upstate New York; Boo-Boo, the mother of three children; and the twins, Walt and Waker, the former of whom had been accidentally killed in Japan while serving with the army of occupation. Concerning Mr. Glass, we learn that

"He thinks anything pe*cul*iar or un*pleas*ant will just go away if he turns on the radio and some little schnook starts *sing*ing" (82). We learn, too, that all the Glass children, during the period 1927–43, participated on a popular radio quiz program, "It's a Wise Child." For the most part, however, it is Zooey, a handsome twenty-five-year-old television actor and leading man, who occupies the central place in this story. His role, however, is closely interlinked with Franny's, for they both respond to the problems of life with an intensity, even a desperation, that makes them allies and fellow-sufferers. When Franny at one point tells him that "we're not bothered by exactly the same things, but by the same kind of things . . . and for the same reasons" (143), she is emphasizing a truth that becomes increasingly clear by the end of the book.

Now, the most painful and serious problem confronting Zooey is that of ego. Zooey is without doubt an egoistic young man with strong and violent prejudices and dislikes. Extremely intelligent, he holds an M.A. in mathematics and could easily go on to obtain a Ph.D. in Greek that would permit him to become a member of what Salinger speaks of as "a brass-hat, brass-mortarboard world." He is a quick thinker and a ruthless conversationalist. But, as he himself admits, "We don't talk, we hold forth. We don't converse, we expound" (139). He lacks an active and energizing humanity, not because he is innately bad but because he is too arrogantly intellectualized to allow his instinctive goodness to blossom forth naturally. "If you don't like somebody in two minutes, you're done with them forever," Mrs. Glass declares to him on one occasion (99). Defiant and impatient in his approach to human relationships, Zooey needs to be schooled in lessons of humility. He has lost a sense of wonder that would help him overcome his deep-seated bitterness and cynicism. And yet these are negative traits that he has adopted through the years as a defensive mechanism. His deficiency is understandable when we recall that the Glass children were always in the public eye, were always looked on as young geniuses, and as such were expected to provide answers and solutions to "alternately deadly-bookish and deadly-cute questions" sent in by listeners. Moreover, all seven of the children "had been fair game for the kind of child psychologist or professional educator who takes a special interest in extra-precocious children" (54). Zooey, who had the "most precocious wit and fancy," had especially been the victim of examinations and research, one diagnosis concluding that at the age of twelve he "had an English vocabulary on an exact par with Mary Baker Eddy's, if he could be urged to use it" (55). No wonder that he describes both Franny and himself as "freaks."

Nevertheless, Zooey's ego is essentially a disguise; like Franny, he would like to renounce this disguise and rediscover that inmost part of his being which still retains its humanity, its naturalness. Zooey's awareness of his own condition becomes clear in proportion to his recognition of the spiritual metamorphosis in Franny, who has now left college and returned home. According to her mother, she is continually "crying" and "mumbling" and has become a "run-down, overwrought little college girl that's been reading too many religious books." Zooey's mounting concern for Franny is self-concern as well: he senses that her agony mirrors the same kind of deep inner turmoil that he is suffering. Not without reason, therefore, he comes to Franny's defense when Mrs. Glass is critical of her daughter's behavior and implies that her present state is unnatural and abnormal. She suggests that it would be helpful to consult "a *very* devout *Cat*holic psychoanalyst" who might "save" Franny. To this suggestion Zooey replies in words that not only throb with imprecation but also indict a conditioned response to an age that is characterized by an imperious psychology with its manufactured panaceas and bedside beneficence:

> "You just do that [Zooey cries to his mother]. You just call in some analyst who's experienced in adjusting people to the joys of television, and *Life* magazine every Wednesday, and European travel, and the H-bomb, and Presidential elections, and the front page of the *Times*, and the responsibilities of the Westport and Oyster Bay Parent-Teacher Association, and God knows what else that's gloriously normal—you just do that, and I swear to you, in not more than a year Franny'll either be in a *nut* ward or she'll be wandering off into some goddam desert with a burning cross in her hands" (107–8).

It is characteristic of Zooey that his vocabulary drips with spleen not only when he is speaking to his mother but also when he is counseling Franny. "You're beginning to give off a little stink of piousness"; "all this hysteria business is unattractive as hell"; "this [is a] little snotty crusade you think you're leading against everybody" (160)—these are statements which comprise Zooey's criticism of Franny's religious crisis. Strongly critical of Franny's use of the Jesus Prayer, he questions her motives. He accuses her of using the prayer as a means of laying up "some kind of treasure" and even making it "as negotiable as all those other, more material things." "As a matter of simple logic," he says to Franny, "there's no difference at all, that *I* can see, between the man who's greedy for material treasure—or even intellectual treasure—and the man who's greedy for spiritual treasure" (147).

But Franny's honesty and integrity are her greatest strengths in her pilgrimage. She makes no attempt to find all the answers to the great problems and enigmas of life. Nor does she try to be presumptuous or cute in her discussions with her brother. She has, as she confesses, definite human weaknesses. For example, she admits to her brother that she abhors the man who has been teaching her in a religion seminar, a Professor Tupper. She sarcastically describes him as being "charming and Oxfordish," "on lend-lease or something from Oxford." What she mainly dislikes about him is that "He has no enthusiasm whatever for his subject. Ego, yes. Enthusiasm, no" (127). To her he represents a false teacher who is comparable to a false poet—one of those poets who, she asserts, "get published and anthologized all over the place," but who fail "to do something beautiful," "to *leave* something beautiful after you get off the page and everything." The whole problem of education is for Franny a crucial one. The pursuit of knowledge for the sake of knowledge, she charges, is one of the worst faults of the modern educational system. "I don't think it would have all got me quite so down," she cries, "if just *once* in a while—just *once* in a while—there was at least some polite little per*func*tory implication that knowledge *should* lead to *wisdom*, and that if it *doesn't*, it's just a disgusting waste of time" (145–46).

Consequently, Franny's chief problem is that of reconciling her ostensible lack of charity for people with her earnest efforts to purify her outlook on life. Zooey recognizes her dilemma and summarizes his case against Franny when he criticizes the way she talks about others. "I mean," he says to her, "you don't just despise what they represent—you despise *them*" (161). What Zooey fails to perceive at first is that Franny has an intrinsic awareness of her dilemma. She does see that somehow she must overcome the personal limitations of her response to people. She does see that if the Jesus Prayer is to be really effective and redeeming, she must struggle to overcome these shortcomings. After all, she cries out to Zooey, one of the reasons for her agony is that she has been worrying all along "about my motives for saying the prayer." "That's exactly what's *both*ering me so," she remarks. "Just because I'm choosy about what I want—in this case, en*light*enment, or *peace*, instead of money or pres*tige* or *fame* or any of those things—doesn't mean I'm not as egotistical and self-seeking as everybody else. If anything, I'm more so" (148). When she realizes, finally, that Zooey is not able to help her, she balefully asks to talk to her brother Seymour, who has been dead for seven years. And indeed, we have at this point a concomitant feeling of gloom and despair. Both Franny and Zooey are precariously groping for a restorative religious meaning and experience.

In spite of all the gloom, there occurs in the course of their conversation an episode that contains a saving grace and foreshadows an ultimate note of affirmation. This episode reveals that Zooey is not beyond the reach of those glad moments in life that suddenly burst forth to sustain faith in humanity. It takes place after Franny's frantic request to talk to Seymour. Dazed and puzzled by what has preceded, Zooey lets his attention be drawn "to a little scene that was being acted out sublimely, unhampered by writers and directors and producers, five stories below the window and across the street" (150). There he notices a girl of seven or eight hiding behind a maple tree in front of a girls' private school. Some fifteen feet away her dog is scurrying and sniffing to find her. The anguish of separation is scarcely bearable for him. When he finds the little girl, he gives a little yelp, then cringes, "shimmying with ecstasy, till his mistress ... stepped hurriedly over the wire guard surrounding the tree and picked him up" (151). Zooey is profoundly stirred by the charm and beauty of this scene; in a very deep sense it conveys to him a message of hope—of hope reborn. It also demonstrates that he has an essential sensibility that is not doomed or dead but is capable of being aroused and energized. "God damn it," he says, "there are *nice* things in the world—and I mean nice things. We're all such morons to get so sidetracked. Always, always, always referring every goddam thing that has happened right back to our lousy little egos" (151).

Zooey's experience, in this respect, is comparable to Franny's reactions to a family that the Russian Pilgrim meets in *The Way of a Pilgrim*. It is a family, as Franny said to Lane Coutell at the beginning of the book, that she loved more than anybody she had ever read about. As an "instructive experience" in the wanderings of the Russian Pilgrim, this scene takes place one day as he is seen passing through a poor village, where he stops to pray at a small wooden church. At the side of the church, he sees two little children who cry out to him, "Dear little beggar! Dear little beggar! Stop!" The two youngsters then run after him and take him by the hand to their house, where their mother greets him warmly and with her own hands takes off his knapsack and offers him the hospitality of her home and family. She then asks him to join her family in attending church on the following day, Sunday, and to share their meal after the services. What impresses the Pilgrim most during this scene is the meal that he shares at the dining table not only with the family but also with four other women guests who are present. He learns that the four, who are treated as sisters by the mistress of the house, are respectively the cook, the coachman's wife, the woman who has charge of the keys, and the maid. To Franny this meal in *The Way of a Pilgrim* serves as a memorable picture of simplicity and harmony. It is truly a "feast of love," undefiled by any artificiality. Taken together, then, both episodes comprise for Franny and Zooey what can be termed as brilliant gleams of illumination, those "graces of light," as François Mauriac has called them, that are given to man "at moments of tribulations and uncertainty—at the hour, as it were, of darkness."[3]

Doubtless, it is not easy for Zooey to realize the profundity of Franny's religious sensibility, or to fathom the influence on her by *The Way of a Pilgrim*. Often and too quickly, he tends to ignore and dismiss the manifestations of these influences and to subject them to cruel rational dialectic. Zooey's reactions are, as a result, a reflection of the atrophy of his own sensibility. He has for too long subjected the meaning of *all* religious experiences to an intellectualized, forensic process and has subordinated it to the irritability and pettiness that often condition and inform his response. The result is that he is really unprepared and unable to appreciate Franny's efforts to respond to the voices of "the emotional soul," "the spontaneous, living, individual soul," and to embrace a "gentle faith in life," to quote D. H. Lawrence's terminology. This is especially noticeable in his reactions to the Jesus Prayer. He does *know*, to be sure, what the Prayer is, but he does not comprehend the delicacy and sensitivity of the feelings behind it. Thus he reflects the acquired hardness and harshness all too common in modern technological civilization.

In the main Franny's conduct is at all times an offshoot of what she has read and reverenced in *The Way of a Pilgrim*, just as the Russian Pilgrim himself had been immensely influenced by his study and absorption of the *Philokalia*. When, therefore, Franny refuses to eat very much, she is merely doing something that the Russian Pilgrim does as a result of the instruction of St. Gregory of Sinai that "the practiser of silence should always be starved, never allowing himself to eat his fill" (*Philokalia*, 78).[4] When Franny is seen weeping, she, like the Russian Pilgrim, is adhering to the instruction that "a man striving to attain pure prayer in silence must proceed towards it with great trepidation . . . constantly shedding tears for his sins, in sorrowful contrition" (*Philokalia*, 82). Franny's self-imposed silence and solitude parallel the Russian Pilgrim's response to the injunction "sit silently in your cell and it will teach you everything" (224). Beyond this, Franny's silence is completely in line with the spirit of *The Way of a Pilgrim* which stresses that "the silent recluse teaches by his very silence, and by his very life he benefits, edifies and persuades to the search of God" (226). Even Franny's relationship to Zooey, for that matter, is at all times epitomized by an unerring faith in the saying that *"spirit can give to spirit"* (230), a saying that is the very essence of the Russian Pilgrim's travels and that becomes the supreme inspiration of one's attempt "to reach the harbor of the good father" (*Philokalia*, 98).

Although Zooey is not in complete rapport with these phases of Franny's religious sensibility, he is not able to repudiate their sincerity. Ultimately, this sincerity is communicated to him. In sharp contrast to a Lane Coutell, he is not an uncompromising negator of the marvels and mysteries that distinguish the development of "self and soul." Inevitably, the form and substance of this communication progress into a greater vision of life. It remains for the ending of Salinger's book to depict the process and achievement of this vision, as well as to underline the concept that "spirit can give to spirit."

We should stop to recall here that in the final phase of his conversation with Franny, Zooey had accused her of misapplying the Jesus Prayer by "using it to ask for a world full of dolls and saints and no Professor Tuppers." Surely, there was much truth in Zooey's diagnosis—and Franny knew it was true. She knew, furthermore, that spiritual egotism is as onerous a condition as evil itself. But Zooey's diagnosis was rooted in disheartenment and led, in turn, to abstraction from life. It was this disheartenment that Franny sensed in her brother's attempt to counsel her, and it was *this* disheartenment, and not her brother, that she rejected. Of necessity, then, Zooey leaves Franny on a note of failure—a failure that "had suddenly filled the room with its invariably sickening smell."

Not long after this conversation takes place, Zooey goes into his brothers' old room. It is obvious that he is now deeply disturbed by his inability to help Franny in her problems. He is undergoing much self-questioning, and he realizes that if he is able to help Franny, he will also be helping himself. Soon we find him taking up the telephone on Buddy's old desk to call Franny, who answers on the telephone in her parents' bedroom. Zooey begins by saying that it is Buddy who is speaking, and Franny seems unaware of the impersonation. It does not take long for her to realize that it is Zooey who is speaking: his celebrated verbal stunts finally give him away. But she also realizes that Zooey's usual bravado is missing, that even reconciliation and atoning echo in his words. By the conclusion of his telephone call, Zooey is able to describe to his sister an incident which informs the conversation with a redeeming magnanimity. He relates that as a youngster appearing on "It's a Wise Child," he had on one occasion acted very hostile after being told by his eldest brother,

Seymour, to shine his shoes before the program was to begin. His immediate reaction to this request was furious, and he recalled: "The studio audience were all morons and I just damn well wasn't going to shine my shoes for them . . ." (198–99). Seymour told him to shine them anyway—to shine them for the Fat Lady. Although Seymour didn't tell him who the Fat Lady was, Zooey did shine his shoes finally and continued to do so on later programs. He envisaged the Fat Lady as a person suffering from cancer, sitting on her porch all day, swatting flies, and listening to her radio playing full blast from morning to night. Zooey then goes on to tell Franny "a terrible secret," namely, "*There isn't anyone out there who isn't Seymour's Fat Lady*" (200)—including even Professor Tupper. Indeed, he asserts, the Fat Lady is Christ Himself!

To Zooey's final comment, Franny reacts with instantaneous and ecstatic gladness. She is "filled with joy" at "the good news," for Zooey's remark is in every possible way a victory over his disheartenment, a vindication of the Jesus Prayer itself. Franny has been waiting and praying for this all along, and now she "rises upward," as it were, purged of the engulfing spirit of negation and cynicism. This is the moment of victory in the lives of two young people when both are released from "the abyss of hell even before death" (*Philokalia*, 63). It is a moment that testifies to the message and inspiration which Franny received through her study of and meditation on the life of the Russian Pilgrim. Like the Russian Pilgrim she has been on a pilgrimage that has taken her from death into life. Like him she has grasped the tremendous implications of the Jesus Prayer. At the end of the book we are able to feel the serenity and beauty that accompany this affirmation. We also discover the joy and wonder of having reached at last "the royal road." When Salinger's book concludes with Franny's falling "into a deep, dreamless sleep," we too are blessed with the sweet slumber that comes at the end of a long journey into the very heart of human existence. And, in effect, we become Pilgrims in Eternity.

PART THREE

Ancients and Moderns

Everywhere we see the beginnings of confusion, and we want a clue to some sound order and authority. This we can only get by going back upon the actual instincts and forces which rule our life, seeing them as they really are, connecting them with other instincts and forces, and enlarging our whole view and rule of life.

—MATTHEW ARNOLD

15

Henry More:
Cambridge Platonist

ᔭ

The seventeenth century was a period of change; it saw the impact of modernism upon medievalism; it embodied strong and insistent demands for scientific explanation; it was an age in which divine mystery was questioned by those seeking "release from traditional hauntings"; in short, there was taking place "a general transference of interest from metaphysics to physics, from the contemplation of Being to the observation of Becoming."[1] Yet, in the face of these new yearnings and demands, there was in England a significant school of thought—the Cambridge Platonists—that was striving to formulate a philosophy of religion and to stress the divine inspiration of human reason. Though neglected and ignored by critics and scholars, the Cambridge School, including Benjamin Whichcote (1609–83), Henry More (1614–87), John Smith (1616?–52), Ralph Cudworth (1617–88), Nathaniel Culverwel (1618/19–51?), John Worthington (1618–71), and George Rust (1626?–70), sought to show the existence of order in the individual soul, in society, in the cosmos; to prove the existence of spiritual being; and to strengthen the belief that there is an incorporeal world and that incorporeal substances transcend and embrace earthly phenomena. In the process of accomplishing such a goal, "it was the peculiar service of the Cambridge Platonists to ignore the Roman theology, which through Augustine and Calvin dominated in the western church, and to revive the spirit of Greek interpretation."[2] In the revival of the Greek spirit, especially as found in the thought of Plato and in the neoplatonic thought of Plotinus, the Cambridge Platonists did not explain mysteries in the mechanico-materialistic sense, but rather sought a mystical communion with the Mind of God. Plato's words "Wherefore, also, we ought to fly away thither, and to fly thither is to become like God, as far as this is possible; and to become like him, is to become holy and wise"[3] definitively characterize the spiritual and intellectual aspirations of the English Platonists. They were concerned mainly with attaining a holy life, with being dead to the flesh and the vanities of living; above all, they desired a religious experience that had as its aim divine ecstasy made possible through a separation of the soul from the body.

In addition to the revival of the Greek spirit of interpretation, Cambridge Platonism represents the quintessence of religious mysticism in the seventeenth century. Despite the fact that the Cambridge Platonists lived in a period of narrowness and bigotry, a period characterized by the conflict of religious ceremonialism and dogmatism, extreme and militant Anglicanism contending with extreme and rampant Puritanism, they sought to climb the spiritual ladder from earth to heaven, seeking the purgative, illuminative, and unitive states of divine being, rather than worldly possession, power, and prestige. It may well be said that the conversation of the Cambridge Platonists was of a divine quality; like sages of old they gave themselves up to sublime speculations and gracious affections. Through prayer and meditation they sought to transform themselves into the likeness of Him in whose image they were created. Theirs was a true mysticism, which can be defined as "a temper rather than a doctrine, an atmosphere rather than a system of philosophy";[4] as "the attempt to realise the presence of the living God in the soul and in nature, or, more generally, as *the attempt to realise, in thought and feeling, the immanence of the temporal in the eternal, and of the eternal in the temporal.*"[5]

In his essay on "Anglicanism in the Seventeenth Century," Felix R. Arnott concludes: "It was the religious aspirations of the Seventeenth-Century divines which made the *Via Media* become a glorious reality instead of a barren philosophical theory. They desired to gather up all that was best in the Church's past, and to adapt it for English use. . . ."[6] Without doubt, the task of the Cambridge mystics was a difficult one since they found themselves in the midst of strife of two sorts. First, there was the growing attachment to the scientific and mechanistic interpretation of phenomena, giving rise to materialism and atheism; and second, there was the bitter struggle going on between the Anglicans and the Puritans. The Anglicans sought to gather churchmen together on the basis of ritual, ceremonial observances, and Episcopal church government. The Puritans maintained that the essentials of Christianity were to be found in the Scriptures and in the Presbyterian form of church government. The Church thus lacked decisiveness and became involved in theological battles relating to dogma and church administration. Angry voices often became shrill and defiant, and wordy debates turned into riotous action, as Puritans, who certainly made no boast of passiveness, refused to kneel at communion, challenged the interpretation of the Lord's Supper, openly opposed theological decrees, and tore down painted windows in churches and college chapels. The Cambridge Platonists, however, realized the theological paradox of the Anglican insistence upon liberty of belief, without liberty of worship, and the Puritan insistence upon liberty of worship, without liberty of belief.

This was a period when the flood of "enthusiasm" swept England and parts of the continent, as if in reaction against the strict theological structure of creeds and dogmas. The consequent rise of Familists, Anti-Scripturists, Antinomians, Anti-Trinitarians, Arians, Anabaptists, and Quakers caused dismay, and the new religious groups were looked upon as propagators of "abominable errors, damnable heresies, and horrid blasphemies, to be lamented if it were possible with tears of blood."[7] Both the social-political and religious situations were not helped at all by the eruption of other difficulties, such as the Petition of Right in 1628, the infamous Star Chamber sentences, the Civil War of 1642, the execution of Archbishop Laud in 1645, the rule of Cromwell, 1653–58, and the growing rivalry between England, France, and Spain, nations continually seeking empire and colonization. The Cambridge Platonists sought, in the face of these increasing controversies and dangers, to remove religion from the external world and to make it an internal working force. From the contemplative peace of their study at Cambridge University, the Latitudemen, or Latitudinarians, so called because of their emphasis on theological tolerance and broad-mindedness, labored to reconcile opposing schools of religious thought. Theirs was a message of spiritual peace and joy at a time when man's religious attitudes were in need of reappraisal.

The Cambridge Platonists, motivated by Ralph Cudworth's famous sermon in which he stated that "The spirit of man is the candle of the Lord, lighted by God, and lighting man to God,"[8] preached that God was to be sought and found through the faculties that man possessed rather than through a simple acceptance of external religious ceremony. For the Cambridge Platonists, so strongly influenced by the Greek spirit, religion was a living force in the human soul, an inward peace and an outward expression of love, an emotional experience based upon a vision of the eternal and immutable. They believed that human ideas were copies of divine ideas and that human knowledge was produced by an active exertion of the human mind and not through the passive reception of sense data. The intellectual love of God, the *amor dei intellectualis*, was an important part of their theosophy and mysticism; yet they stressed that religious knowledge could not be derived from the power of thinking alone, without the fundamental disposition of the will. Without doubt they would have assented to Pascal's famous definition of faith, *voilà ce que c'est que la foi: Dieu sensible au coeur non à la raison*, for faith to them was felt in the heart ("order of the heart"), not in the head ("order of understanding"). The Cambridge Platonists opposed logical as well as theological dogmatics; they did not see any difference between natural and intelligible being, that is, between the rational and the spiritual, since for them the spiritual was the highest form of the rational.

Rejoicing in the thought and experience of divine immanence, which brought the transcendent God of Augustinianism near as Immanuel, or God with us, the Cambridge Platonists as religious moralists recognized no separation between God and Man and helped to rescue from oblivion the ethical mysticism of Saint Paul and his blessed experience of vital union with Christ. The Platonists thus form "a sort of connecting link between minds and epochs," since "they preserved a nucleus of genuine ancient philosophical tradition and passed it on uncontaminated to the centuries to come."[9] In their emphasis on the metaphysics of Plato, the English Platonists found an ally to oppose Hobbesian materialism and empiricism, but as moralists they found in him authority for their thesis that conduct mattered more than creed. Stressing values, the Platonists proved the existence of God through ontological and cosmological arguments, especially brought out in the poetry of Henry More:

> But true Religion sprong from God above
> Is like her fountain full of charity,
> Embracing all things with a tender love,
> Full of good will and meek expectancy,
> Full of true justice and sure verity,
> In heart and voice; free, large, even infinite,
> Not wedg'd in strait particularity,
> But grasping all in her vast active spright,
> Bright lamp of God! that men would joy in thy pure light![10]

In many respects the Cambridge Platonists were transitional in their philosophical and religious thought, since they stood at a point marking the end of the domination of the scholastic system of learning and the beginning of modern thought. During this period the English Platonists opposed the sophistic system of learning, the overemphasis of logic, the seeking after knowledge for the sake of power and excitement—the Hobbesian *scientia propter potentiam*. More, who in many ways embodied the culmination of the thought of the English Platonists, spoke of "the ridiculous folly of this present Sophism." Other voices too joined the chorus decrying the dangers and menace of sophism. Francis Bacon attacked this as "contentious learning," and John Milton spoke of it as "an asinine feast of sow-thistles and brambles." To the English Platonists knowledge of things was not the supreme felicity of man, a fact which was especially underscored in the life of More. To these men, these mystics and divines, the highest knowledge was won not merely, or mainly, by the study of things, but by the purgation of the mind from all sorts of vices and evil. Piety, reverence for the mysterious, and sincere modesty were first necessary before the illumination of the truth. More expresses this in his poem "Charity and Humility," where he concludes:

> Lord, thrust me deeper into dust,
> That thou maist raise me with the just.[11]

John Tulloch speaks of Henry More not only as the most vital and interesting of all the Cambridge School, but also as "the most Platonical of the Platonic sect, and at the same time the most genial, natural, and perfect man of them all."[12] The protégé and biographer of More, Richard Ward, refers to him as a "shining light," a "Celestial Herald," a sort of Christian Elias, sent into the world to promote truths, whether in philosophy or theology.[13] Although Ward is somewhat euphoric in his admiration of More, there is no doubt that the latter's rapturous mysticism and profound piety distinguish him from the other English Platonists. Born at Grantham, Lincolnshire, on October 12, 1614, he came of a good Calvinist family. From childhood he was a thoughtful and remarkably proficient student at both Eton and Cambridge, from which he graduated M.A. in 1639. While a student at Eton, he boldly disputed the concept of fate and Calvinistic predestination: "But neither there, nor yet any where else, could I ever swallow down that hard doctrine concerning Fate."[14] In his thirst after knowledge, More immersed himself in philosophy, studying especially the works of Aristotle, Cardan, and Julius Scaliger. It is interesting to note that while at Cambridge, More was somewhat of a skeptic regarding the origin and end of life, although he never doubted the existence of God. More read a great deal of philosophy; yet he remained unsatisfied and uncertain, and he recorded his thoughts in poetic form under the title 'Απορία, the Greek signifying "Perplexity":

Οὐκ ἔγνων πόθεν εἰμὶ ὁ δύσμορος, οὐδὲ τίς εἰμί,
῍Ω τῆς ἀφροσύνης, οὐδὲ τῇ ἐρχόμενος.
'Αλλ' ὀδύνης τε γόου τε πολυγνάμπτοις ὀνύχεσσι,
Ζώω, ἔμοιγε δοκεῖ πανταχοῖ ἑλκόμενος·
῍Ισα ἐγρηγόρσεις καὶ ὀνείρατα, ὦ πάτερ, ὦ Ζεῦ,
'Ως σεμνὸν· χ' ἡμεῖς ζώομεν ἐν νεφέλαις.
Ψεύδεα, φαντασίη, κενότης, τερετίσματ', ἀνάγκη,
Τἄλλα μὲν ἀγνώσας τὸν βίον οἶδα μόνον.[15]

Eventually More began to suspect that knowledge of things was not the supreme happiness of man. He concluded, after a painstaking study of the writings of the Platonists, especially Marsilius Ficinus and Plotinus, that it was best to purge the mind of all vices so as to achieve the mystical illumination of full union with the eternity of Divine and celestial Being. More's early skepticism concerning the origin and the end of the world ceased, and he realized that true holiness was the only safe entrance into divine knowledge. This more optimistic mood was expressed by his poem Εὐπορία, "Facility":

Οὐρανόθεν γέγονα προθορὼν, θεοῦ ἄμβροτος ἀκτὶς,
Κ', ὦ τῆς εὐφροσύνης, πρὸς θεὸν εἶμι πάλιν.
Νῦν δε τ' ἔρως με πτεροισι θεόσυτος ἐξυπερείδει,
Ζῶ δ' ἐπ' ἀληθείᾳ, παντοτε τερπόμενος.
Νὺξ ἀπέβη μὲν ὄναρ τε. Πάτερ θεοδερκέος αὐγῆς,
'Αΐδιον χ' ἡμᾶς ἀμφικάλυψε φάος.
Πίστις ναὶ σοφίη, θεότης, χαρὰ, εὔπτερος ἀλκὴ,
Ταῦτα ζωή, ἅδης τἄλλα καὶ οὐδενία.[16]

The importance of the "Divine Presence" in More's thought, as well as his abandonment of skepticism, was strongly established by his reading of the well-known mystical work *Theologia Germanica*, "that Golden little Book," which had also moved Luther.[17] It was this work, along with the works of Plotinus, that further convinced More of the necessity of extinguishing the will of the ordinary self, this being dead to one's self, so that union with the Divine Being might be gained. More was never to forget the inherent meaning of the *Theologia Germanica* and its insistence that "blessedness lieth not in much and many, but in One and oneness. . . . Therefore I must wait only on God and His work, and leave on one side all creatures with their works, and first of all myself."[18]

More agreed in theory and practice with the *Theologia Germanica* and with Plotinus that man should die unto himself and detach himself, by prayer and meditation, from elements and fragments of worldly life, pleasure, and profit. He himself lived and died a private Fellow of Christ's College, Cambridge, where "he spent his time in an

Angelical way." More's religious mysticism was characterized by a "mystical aloneness," a religion of personal piety and intense contemplation, whereby a union with the Divine Being could come about. The designs of ambition and the entanglements of the body did not affect More in the least. His life was a long contemplation, a life of unbroken prayer that sought the spiritual joys that emanate from divine reason and holiness. More refused to accept numerous titles and honors; he turned down the Deanery of Christ Church, the Provostship of Dublin College, and the Deanery of St. Patrick's in Ireland. Although he was ascetic by temperament and habits, he did not indulge in the extreme self-denial practiced by other mystics. More had a healthy constitution and his mysticism did not become at all pathological; rather, he always indicated to those who came into contact with him a certain wholesomeness and tranquillity. Ward reports that when More died on September 1, 1687, at the age of seventy-three, following a lingering illness, it was with the deepest feeling of spiritual fulfillment.

According to Dean Inge, More belongs to that kind of mystic, akin to Plato,[19] who tries to rise through the visible to the invisible, through Nature to God, who finds "in earthly beauty the truest symbol of the heavenly. . . ." In his readings of mystical literature, More realized that to annihilate the human will it was necessary to go through the three stages of purification, enlightenment, and union, especially as expressed in the *Theologia Germanica*:

> The purification concerneth those who are beginning or repenting, and is brought to pass in a threefold wise; by contrition and sorrow for sin, by full confession, by hearty amendment. The enlightenment belongeth to such as are growing, and also taketh place in three ways: to wit, by the eschewal of sin, by the practice of virtue and good works, and by the willing endurance of all manner of temptation and trials. The union belongeth to such as are perfect, and also is brought to pass in three ways: to wit, by pureness and singleness of heart, by love, and by the contemplation of God, the Creator of all things.[20]

However, it must be said that More's mysticism was of a sound proportion; he did not permit his heart to "run away with his head, or for that matter with his body either."[21] In his *Enchiridion Ethicum*, More advised man "to have wherewithal to live well and happily."[22] In his concept of the three stages, this *scala perfectionis*, More thought of humility in the sense of the mystics, that is, an acknowledgment of the utter inability of man and of the complete submission of man's self to God. In respect to purity, More stressed the moderation of all appetites (of "animal life") and the steadfast affection for the perfect ideal of celestial beauty set up by God in our hearts. This is an ideal born in man: we do not create it; we can only find it.

More felt that a mystical oneness with God, following the stages leading to such a union, was the highest step in the process of divine enlightenment. Be this divine ecstasy or the Plotinian beatific vision, More believed absolutely in the union with the goodness of God. In his poem "Philosopher's Devotion" he wrote:

> God is good, is wise, is strong,
> Witnesse all the creature-throng,
> Is confess'd by every Tongue.
> All things back from whence they sprong,
> As the thankfull rivers pay
> What they borrowed of the Sea,
>   Now myself I do resigne,
> Take me whole, I am thine.
> Save me, God! from Self-desire,
> Death's pit, dark Hells raging fire,
> Envy, Hatred, Vengeance, Ire.
> Let not Lust my soul bemire.[23]

More's "Now myself I do resigne / Take me whole, I am thine," clearly points out that vision, or ecstasy, "begins when thought ceases, *to our consciousness*, to proceed from ourselves."[24] Though close to Plato's philosophy, More's mysticism is not to be separated from Saint Paul's mysticism, although the former's is not Christocentric in essence. More's mysticism does not depart from the Pauline view that man is "the image and glory of God" (I Cor. 11:7).

Platonic philosophy has often been identified as the "old loving nurse" of the Church. The Cambridge Platonists appealed to Plato, condemned by some in the course of the centuries as the "mad theologian" and "bombastic poet," as a confederate against the empiricism, sensualism, and materialism which negated access to religious experience. More and the other Cambridge men, embodying the Greek spirit, venerated both Plato and Plotinus, in contradistinction to the Calvinists and Puritans who took careful precautions to give Christianity unquestioned precedence over antiquity. The goal of More and the other English Platonists was the discovery of being. In order to achieve this discovery, as Cassirer points out, they did not hesitate "to say that the good will of a heathen is godlier than the angry zeal of a Christian."[25] The fact is that More and the others did not openly distinguish between Plato and Plotinus, Platonism and Plotinianism. But both of these, especially to More, were philosophies of values, not form; and both supplemented Christianity in relation to certain eternal values and a common indifference to worldly preoccupations. More and his colleagues at Cambridge did not seek to superimpose Platonism upon Christianity. They simply wished to find philosophical support in a system which was essentially religious, which taught the sole reality of the spiritual world, and which proclaimed the immortality of the soul and the upward ascent of the soul in the quest for divine union.

Religious mysticism owes a great deal to Plotinus, to whom the phenomenal world was not evil nor burdened with the defilement of original sin, but was simply the "image" or reflection of the highest perfection of the world above, a realm sought beyond all images, from the image to the prototype. Henry More was strongly influenced by Plotinus, and his poems of 1642 and 1647 show this throughout. More's conception of the Trinity was comparable to Plotinus' trinity of the One or the Good, above existence, or God as the Absolute; the Intelligence, the sphere of real existence, or the organic unity; and the Soul, the sphere of appearance, of imperfect reality, or God as action. More's Plotinianism is clearly brought out in a stanza from his poem *Psychathanasia* showing the flowing, emanating, goodness of God:

> When nothing can to Gods own self accrew,
> Who's infinitely happy; sure the end
> Of this creation simply was to shew
> His flowing goodness, which he doth out-send
> Not for himself; for naught can him amend;
> But to his creature doth his good impart,
> This infinite Good through all the world doth wend
> To fill with heavenly blisse each willing heart:
> So the free Sunne doth 'light and 'liven every part.[26]

In the thinking of More and the other Platonists the soul was looked upon as the Plotinian principle of motion, the vital ἀρχὴ τῆς κικήσεως. More further argued, always drawing on Plotinus, that the soul was immaterial and immortal because it was independent of the body. First of all, More believed that the body, which was dependent on the soul, was in the soul; second, that the soul could be occupied with its own thoughts without affecting the body, thus centering its attention upon the contemplative quest of its own well-being; third, that since the soul does not emanate from sensual things, it could resist the desires of the body, sublimating material lusts and devoting itself to the intellectual love of divine qualities; and fourth, that the soul was a continuum of existence, growing in force and strength, whereas sense, fancy, and memory faded away with the gradual disintegration of the body. More refers to the soul's independence of the body in the following:

> What disadvantage then can the decay
> Of this poore carcase do, when it doth fade?
> The soul no more depends on this frail clay
> Then on our eye depends bright Phoebus glist'ring ray.[27]

More also believed in the preexistence of the soul. He contended that God was good; and if the soul was also good, as he believed, God would naturally have created the soul early in the divine scheme. For More the pilgrimage of the soul through earthly life was primarily a "return to the source from which all being emerged and . . . [a] unification with the realm of divine entities above the world of material things."[28] The end of this pilgrimage was marked by spiritual catharsis and mystical union with God. More realized that this ecstatic vision would not be granted without one's fulfilling certain conditions which Plotinus best describes: "The very soul, once it has conceived the straining love towards this, lays aside all shape it has taken, even to the intellectual shape that has informed it. There is no vision, no union, for those handling or acting by any thing other; the soul must see before it neither evil nor any thing else, that alone it may receive the Alone."[29] Also, in true Plotinian fashion, More argued in favor of three realms of the soul: the *terrestrial*, the combination of soul and body; the *aereal*, the separation of the soul and body and the former's attachment to the particles in the air; and the *ethereal*, the union with the highest category of Being, above reason and intelligence.

In further trying to substantiate the Plotinian concept that the "footprints" of the universal soul could be found everywhere, More in his later years began to give credence to the "proofs" of apparitions and witches, that is, proofs of the existence of spirit as a substance distinct from matter. Willey in his analysis of this writes: "The fact is that in appealing to demonology More, like Browne and Glanville, was tapping a reservoir of traditional supernatural belief which lay deeper in the national consciousness than Christianity itself, and deeper, certainly, than the new ice-crust of rationalism which now covered it."[30] More not only reported but accepted such "proofs" as bricks flying in a room; stones being hurled by unseen hands from a roof; pots traveling to and from the fire; violent flappings of a chest cover; tablecloths and sheets blowing in the air on a calm day; boxes locking, then unlocking themselves; and a vomiting of cloth stuck with pins, nails, needles, glass, iron, and hair. One cannot fail to mention that More was not alone in these beliefs. Bacon trusted in charms and amulets. Dr. Johnson believed in ghosts, witches, and second sight. Boyle recommended the thighbone of a hanged man as a cure for a violent disease. Berkeley had an honest faith in tar water. And Dr. Rush prescribed cloves and mace to strengthen the memory.

Essentially More's concept of God was Plotinian: God was the force producing all things but produced by none, the source of all beauty, the end of all things, the highest good and wisdom, the transcendence of all existence itself, the highest abstraction, superior even to the Platonic Idea. To More, as to Plotinus, the human mind would return to and unite with the absolute only after passage between vulgar opinion and philosophical knowledge. More believed that the innate idea of God existed in man. "It remains therefore undeniable," he wrote, "that there is an inseparable Idea of a Being absolutely Perfect ever residing, though not always acting, in the Soul of Man."[31] More, closely adhering to Plotinian emanatistic theory, looked upon the world as an *overflow* of the divine life, and believed in the return of the being to its divine source, made possible through contemplation. He believed that the mind of man is as the image of God, drawn and descending from Him. More's faith in the Holiness and greatness of God is seen in his lines:

> From thy Works my Joy proceeds:
> How I triumphed in thy Deeds!
> Who thy Wonders can express?
> All thy Thoughts are fathomless,
> Hid from Men in Knowledge blind,
> Hid from Fools to Vice inclin'd.[32]

With Philo, More agreed that man's rational faculty was a temple of God, and with Plotinus that the human intellect was an image of the divine rationality which was the emanation of God. Indeed, More believed in the excellence and necessity of reason for the maintaining of the truth of Christian religion. He enthusiastically quoted Cicero's saying *"Rationem, quo ea me cunque ducet, sequar"* in his attempts to bolster the "two grand pillars"[33] of religion, the existence of God and the immortality of the soul. But he was convinced that piety was the key to knowledge, that keenness of insight proceeded from purity of life, that the life of contemplation was superior to that of pleasure and statesmanship. Being religious was to More of supreme importance in a life that was really a struggle between the lofty and the low, between the sacred and the profane. More's emphasis on reason, however, did not become an arrogant and impossible demand for a foolproof system of theology free from mystery. More felt that reason should "construct a philosophy round these two pivots, God and

Man."[34] And even when More sought to establish a free intercourse between religion and the natural sciences and philosophies, he kept uppermost in his mind that scientific discoveries were nothing more than the revelations of the immanence, beneficence, and wisdom of God.

The Greek concept of man's life as a continual effort to achieve the beautiful and good was central to More's ethical point of view. Ethical living was part of divine living, and the harmonious unity of both brought man to a point of perfection. Goodness and happiness were identical to More. Along with Cudworth he felt that human nature was inherently divine: "I come from Heaven; am an immortal Ray / of God; O Joy! and back to God shall goe."[35] Both stressed that all appetites and passions "yet fall into proper subordination to the higher divine faculty or reason, which distinguishes man, and stamps him a moral being. More observed in his *Enchiridion Ethicum* ("a middle ground of ethical doctrine"[36]), which was really an answer to Hobbesianism, that "Passions therefore are not only good, but singularly needful to the perfecting of human life."[37] He emphasized that proper guidance and regulation were necessary at all times, in order to avoid sensualism of an extreme sort. He did not fail to introduce an element of mysticism and religious faith into his ethics, pointing out that the end of human life was purification and assimilation with divinity. The existence of a divine moral faculty in man was always a primary belief in More's thinking. He called this the "Boniform Faculty of the Soul," which represented the moral sense of the soul, and which was the image of God in man's soul, containing right reason.

Henry More steadfastly believed in absolutes: absolute good, absolute evil, absolute values, absolute justice. The publication of Thomas Hobbes's *Leviathan* in 1651 contributed a great deal to the maturity of More and the Cambridge Platonists, since they had not only to answer Hobbes's materialism, which denied the existence of the soul and the freedom of the will, but also to combat his belief that the source of all moral obligation lay in power and civil authority. Hobbes's materialistic theory of perception affirmed the reality of the "body," but More affirmed the reality of the spirit. The ideological struggle, therefore, between Cambridge Platonism and Hobbesianism resulted in bitter feelings during the seventeenth century. Hobbes believed that thinking was in reality feeling; that an incorporeal spirit does not exist; that there can be no "image made of a thing invisible"; that the natural state helps to keep order amid instinctive struggle, *bellum omnium contra omnes*; that the death of the body is the death of the soul. "For him the word of God is really little but a symbol of the philosopher's fatigue."[38] Hobbes' philosophy is one of negation, whereas that expressed by More is an affirmation of absolutes. Tulloch reports, strangely enough, that Hobbes "was in the habit of saying that if ever he found his own opinions untenable, he would embrace the philosophy of Dr. More."[39]

The Cambridge Platonists wished to look on nature as plastic, not mechanical; More, wishing to reunite matter and spirit, looked on spirit as an active force, penetrating and moving matter. In the work of his contemporary René Descartes, More sought an ally, one whose science might augment the metaphysical beliefs of the English Platonists. At first More admired the rational clearness of the Cartesian speculations which had departed from the scholastic tradition and which unified and reconciled philosophical truths through reason. Descartes' ideas especially fascinated More because they affirmed the existence of the soul and of God as fundamental certainties. "By the name God," said Descartes, "I understand a substance infinite [eternal, immutable], independent, all-knowing, all-powerful, and by which I myself, and every other thing exists, if any such there be, were created. . . . And thus . . . God exists: for though the idea of substance be in my mind owing to this, that I myself am a substance, I should not, however, have the idea of an infinite substance, seeing I am a finite being, unless it were given me by some substance in reality infinite."[40]

However, when More began to reflect upon Descartes' findings, it became clear that the work of the latter was rooted in logic and epistemology, not in metaphysics and theology. More strongly believed that all existence, spiritual or material substance, was extended, *res extensa*; for if God were unextended, He was necessarily nowhere. More's early admiration of Cartesianism was dampened when Descartes' dualistic system was understood; for how could More ever separate, as did Descartes, *res cognitans*, the realm of thought and knowledge of God and soul, from *res extensa*, the realm of physical phenomena? More and the other English Platonists felt that Cartesianism condemned nature to a standstill, since in Descartes' mechanistic system spiritual substance was put in a realm of its own with no unifying and spiritual bond with the phenomenal world. "There would be no purposive deity. There would be no causative spiritual power. There would be no organizing force."[41] More felt that Descartes was guilty of the unpardonable sin of denuding the spirit of all attributes, and placing God in a spiritual realm that was not attached to the natural world of phenomena. Thus Descartes was affirming God as a mere abstraction. The Cartesians, to More, were "Nullubists" who affirmed that a spirit is "nullubi," *nowhere.* He had no choice but to oppose Cartesianism because it excluded the influence of every nonmaterial cause of natural phenomena.

Henry More was throughout his life a contemplative mystic, a "divinely intoxicated genius." His love of God was made fuller and truer by his reverence for the Greek spirit of interpretation and for the ancient and divinely inspired philosophers. He fought atheism, skepticism, and materialism in every possible way, and he upheld absolutes without fear or hesitation. Culture of itself was not enough for More, since his was the life of theological mysticism. In true Platonic fashion, he cried out:

> O thou eternall Spright, cleave ope the skie,
> And take thy flight into my feeble breast,
> Enlarge my thoughts, enlight my dimmer eye,
> That wisely of that burthen closely prest
> In my straight mind, I may be dispossest:
> My Muse must sing of things of mickle weight;
> The souls eternity is my quest:
> Do thou me guide, that art the souls sure light,
> Grant that I never erre, but ever wend aright![42]

Henry More was the embodiment of the Christian spirit in his sincerity and devotion, and his life exemplified and realized the excellence of Christian virtue in its pristine beauty. His life was of "an inwardness too deep for words."[43]

16

Simone Weil: A Passionate Platonist

〜

I

Simone Weil, according to André Gide, was "the most spiritual writer of this century." She was, Albert Camus asserted, "the only great spirit of our time." T. S. Eliot went so far as to sanctify her life and thought by stating, "We must simply expose ourselves to the personality of a woman of genius, of a kind of genius akin to that of a saint." And Leslie Fiedler, emphasizing Simone Weil's peculiar relevance to the present, has concluded, "Simone Weil has come to seem more and more a special exemplar of sanctity for our time—the Outsider as Saint in an age of alienation, our kind of saint." Simone Weil herself was perhaps most aware of her own place and purpose in life, and in history, when she wrote, "Today it is not nearly enough to be a saint, but we must have the saintliness demanded by the present moment, a new saintliness, itself also without precedent." Teacher, classical scholar, intellectual *par excellence*, and French-Jewish genius; political and religious nonconformist, Spanish Civil War participant, Free French Movement worker; factory and farm laborer; poet, visionary, mystic, suffering "friend of God," religious thinker and philosopher precariously situated at "the intersection of Christianity and everything that is not Christianity" (to quote her own words): Simone Weil in her short span of life, 1909–43, combined brilliantly, enigmatically, all of these roles as no other religious thinker has quite combined them in the twentieth century.

Simone Weil has been increasingly appreciated, if we are to judge by the continuing, posthumous publication of her writings covering an astonishingly wide area of knowledge and cultural thought: philosophy, literature, history, art, classics, psychology, politics, mathematics, economics, education. Most of her writings have now been made available in English; and her life and thought have been sensitively evaluated by a sympathetic intermediary, Sir Richard Rees, who has translated and edited *Selected Essays 1934–1943* (1962), *Simone Weil: Seventy Letters* (1965), and *First and Last Notebooks* (1970). He is also author of *Simone Weil: A Sketch for a Portrait* (1965), the most lucid introduction to her life and thought yet to appear in English.

For Simone Weil the ultimate questions relating to the human condition were existential spiritual questions. She had little faith, and rightly so, in the philosophy of those who believed that, as she well expressed it, "matter is a machine for manufacturing good." In her frantic quest for answers, for wisdom, she returned to ancient sources and tradition, particularly to Hellenism and Christianity. Indeed, it can be said that Simone Weil is the great Christian Hellenist of modern times, occupying a place commensurate with that of Christian Hellenists like Justin Martyr, Athenagoras, Clement of Alexandria, and Origen (*ille vir tantus*, as St. Augustine described him) in the early centuries of the Christian era. It is in the line of this great Christian tradition that Simone Weil should be placed. Not unlike her illustrious predecessors she too maintained that Christian theology itself was the fruit of Greek genius, that Greek philosophy contained a direct divine revelation, the *logos spermatikos*, that Christianity is the fulfillment of philosophy, divine wisdom being the first of the *charismata* of God. "From the flash of genius of Thales until the time when they were crushed by the armed force of Rome," Simone Weil writes, the Greeks "searched everywhere—in the regular recurrence of the stars, in sound, in equilibrium, in floating bodies—for proportions in order to love God." "The whole of Greek civilization," she further states, "is a search for bridges to relate human misery with divine perfection." It is in Plato, in particular, that Simone Weil sees the crux of "Greek spirituality." His philosophy "is nothing else but an act of love towards God." "Plato's wisdom," she thus stipulates, "is not a philosophy, a research for God by means of human reason. That research was carried out as well as it can be done by Aristotle. But the wisdom of Plato is nothing other than orientation of the soul towards grace." "This is the discovery that intoxicated the Greeks," she concludes: "that the reality of the sensible universe is constituted by a necessity whose laws are the symbolic expression of the mysteries of faith." Observations like these typify Simone Weil's view of life and Greek philosophy and return us to their earliest prototypes in the writings, say, of Clement of Alexandria, who wrote: "And by reflection and direct vision, those among the Greeks who have philosophized accurately, see God." "Now the Greek philosophy, as it were, purges the soul, and prepares it beforehand for the reception of faith, on which the Truth builds up the edifice of knowledge." The high place that Simone Weil gives to Plato, "an authentic mystic . . . the father of Western mysticism," accords with that of the Fathers of the Eastern Church who not only admitted to being disciples of Plato but also saw him as a precursor of Christ—a philosopher who, Clement claimed, was truly noble and divinely inspired.

On Science, Necessity, and the Love of God is divided into two parts, the first containing Simone Weil's essays on science, the second containing her essays on ancient Greek culture.* Yet, as Rees correctly emphasizes, "the subject of the two parts of this book is really the same. It is a conception of human destiny—which is approached in the first part mainly from a scientific point of view and in the second mainly from a religious and philosophical point of view." Her conception is precisely that which emerges from coalescent Christian and Hellenic elements. She notes that whereas for the Greeks, science, art, and the search for God were united, they are separate for us. Hence the fragmentation of our modern culture. The development of technology, she goes on to claim in her difficult but illuminating essay "Reflections on Quantum Theory," can offer no hope of happiness "until we have learnt how to prevent men from using technology to dominate their fellows instead of nature." Her relevant modernism, as Fiedler would have it, is one that undoubtedly makes her fully aware of the world in which she lived, one in which "moral crisis and a subservience to purely political values" was (is?) the predominant condition. Values, she claims, are uprooted or allowed to decay, their hierarchy disrupted:

> Everything is oriented towards utility, which nobody thinks of defining; public opinion reigns supreme, in the village of scientists as in the great nations. It is as though we had returned to the age of Protagoras and the Sophists, the age when the art of persuasion—whose modern equivalent is advertising slogans, publicity, propaganda meetings, the press, the cinema, and radio—took the place of thought and controlled the fate of cities and accomplished coups d'etat.

Invariably, Simone Weil's criticisms expose those intellectual and scientific aspects of modern culture which betray a moral sense, a

*Ed. and trans. Richard Rees (London, 1968). Rees traces the profound impact of Simone Weil's writings on his own life and thought in *A Theory of My Time. An Essay in Didactic Reminiscence* (London, 1963). His first book was *Brave Men. A Study of D. H. Lawrence and Simone Weil* (Carbondale, Ill., 1959), "a comparative study of two minds which appear to me to be almost completely disintoxicated from decadent progressivism, though retaining most of what is valuable in progressivism and conservatism."

"sense of values." The fashion today, she points out, is to progress, to evolve, technically and socially. Metaphysics must consequently surrender to techniques and schemata conducive to progress. "To find a place in the budget for the eternal," she laments, "is not in the spirit of our age." Her strongest criticisms, however, she aims at science, and these breathe the essentially Greek spirit of *sophrosyne*. She begins her premise with an uncompromising statement: "Limitation is the law of the manifested world. Only God . . . is without limits." Deliverance, she goes on to say, "consists in reading limit in all sensible phenomena without exception with the same clarity and immediacy as a meaning in a printed text." A true science, which must have as its essential idea that of equilibrium, which defines limits, should serve as "a preparation for deliverance." Science itself will always depend upon man's intelligence and physique, which are themselves permanently limited. Hence,

> it is absurd to believe that science is capable of unlimited progress. It is limited, like all human things, except that point in man which is assimilated to God; and it is well that it should be limited because it is not an end to which many men ought to devote themselves; it is a means, for every man. What is needed now is not to try to extend it further, but to bring thought to bear upon it.

The limitations which Simone Weil believes should circumscribe science, though scientists themselves may refuse to acknowledge them, are implicit in the essays comprising the second part of *On Science, Necessity, and the Love of God*. For here, whether she is writing about Greek philosophy, art, morality, or the "love of God," her purpose is to show the ultimate truth of the transcendent, the supernatural. Thus, "Greek spirituality" as found in Plato accentuates man's limitations, that is, man's subordination to God. Again and again Simone Weil attempts to differentiate between "social morality" and "supernatural morality." (In this connection she makes use of Plato's simile of the "Great Beast," which she identifies with the collective "social morality," as instanced by ancient Rome's atheistic materialist culture, and by Israel's deified national state in religious disguise.) The true religious consciousness, she maintains, must be characterized by the need to achieve "supernatural love," insofar as "The Love of God is the unique source of all certainties." And with Plato as her mainstay, Simone Weil discloses an unmistakable Christian Hellenist orientation when she states: ". . . it is total detachment that is the condition for the love of God, and when once the soul has performed the motion of totally detaching itself from the world so as to turn entirely towards God, it is illumined by the truth which comes down to it from God."

The creative imagination and art itself, she also believes, reflect the profound difference between adherence to "social morality" and to "supernatural morality": instance, that is to say, the need for limits. Her conclusions with respect to morality and literature will no doubt strike many readers as being inordinately purist, although this should not be surprising in one who admired Cathar civilization in the twelfth century. Writers of genius can produce works in which "the force of gravity" governs our souls. One discovers this "sense of gravity," as well as genius oriented toward the good, in Aeschylus, Sophocles, Racine, Villon, in some of whose works "good and evil appear in their truth." Above all she notes her belief "in the responsibility of the writers of recent years for the disaster of our time." She contends that the amorality of modern literature, with its dadaism and its surrealism—"such easy morals in literature, such tolerance of baseness"—has contributed to "the disappearance of the idea of value." Thinking no doubt of writers like D. H. Lawrence, James Joyce, Marcel Proust, and André Gide, she goes on to observe: "Such words as spontaneity, sincerity, gratuitousness, richness, enrichment—words which imply an almost total indifference to contrasts of value—have come more often from their pens than words which . . . contain a reference to good and evil." Conversely, words which refer to the good (e.g., virtue, nobility, honor, honesty, generosity) have become almost impossible to use or else "have acquired bastard meanings." "Language," she indignantly but wisely observes, "is no longer equipped for legitimately praising a man's character. . . . The fate of words is a touchstone of the progressive weakening of the idea of value, and although the fate of words does not depend upon writers one cannot help attributing a special responsibility to them, since words are their business." Modern literature, she concludes, has been essentially psychological, "and psychology consists in describing states of soul by displaying them all on the same plane without any discrimination of value."

Simone Weil's life and work was contemporary with that of Jean-Paul Sartre's (b. 1905) and of Albert Camus' (1913–60). It is hardly necessary to note that though her writings have been steadily published and acclaimed—acclaimed more than they are read, it would seem—Simone Weil does not command the sympathy of popular response accorded her two contemporaries. The reasons for this neglect should be clear. She is not, of course, a creative artist, and her writing style is marred by a certain philosophical abstruseness. More importantly, unlike Sartre, who affirms man's integrity and commitment in *this* world, despite the absurdity of the human situation, and Camus, who affirms the dignity and the (absurd) heroism of man in the face of all his despair and futility, Simone Weil does not find her solutions in an existential Now. Her final recourse is not to the brutal truth of experience in a world in which Sartre and Camus, who like Simone Weil also addressed themselves to the crises of "corrupt history" in the "terrible twentieth century," found the possibility of "no exit." In this respect Simone Weil's view of life is metaphysical, or better eschatological, rather than immediate, or what might be termed (without seeking to oversimplify) the natural and political view of life when we view life purely in time and hence in its incompleteness. For Sartre and Camus life was to constitute a final form of adventure in the guise of "metaphysical revolt" when, as Camus writes in *The Rebel*, one "refuses divinity in order to participate in the common struggles and common destiny," that consummate adventure in progress and evolution that grips the imagination and makes of man, even as he has the worm in his heart, a "saint without God."

For Simone Weil, as the final and perhaps the most important essay, certainly the most provocative, in *On Science, Necessity, and the Love of God*, "The Love of God and Affliction," makes clear, human life is characterized by its affliction (*malheur*), in short, the absence of God and the condition of anonymity which "deprives its victims of their personality and turns them into things" and places them "at the foot of the Cross, almost at the greatest possible distance from God." Man, according to Simone Weil, can overcome this affliction, but not in ways prescribed by a Sartre or a Camus. And how this is done sums up her metaphysics, her spiritual quest and meaning, which must be seen against a permanent pattern—"the feeling for a permanence above the permanence of one human existence," to borrow Edwin Muir's words. In other words, Simone Weil, as even Martin Buber bitterly complained, sought in the end flight from nature as well as from society. "Reality," writes Buber, "had become intolerable to her, and for her, God was the power which led her away from it." Simone Weil in fact asserted: "We possess nothing in this world other than the power to say I. This is what we should yield up to God, and that is what we should destroy." For her, then, it is the destruction, the repudiation, the "decreation" of the I that must be attained. This de-creation enjoins upon one an uprooting: "It is necessary to uproot oneself. To cut down the tree and make a cross, and then to carry it every day.... To exile oneself from every earthly country . . . [for] by uprooting oneself one seeks greater reality."

Buber's complaints against Simone Weil crystallize some of the reasons why her writings have not always aroused sympathy. Man, after all, seems to prefer being an adventurer in this rather than in some other world. In a sense, Simone Weil's answers to the paradox of existence entail a repudiation of that very existence. "All that man vainly desires here below is perfectly realized in God," she declares. "We have all those impossible desires within us as a mark of our destination, and they are good for us provided we no longer hope to fulfill them." Only when man recognizes the state of his affliction, containing "the truth about our condition," "only by looking upon the Cross" for "our country is the cross," will he be propelled toward the ultimate reality. "They alone will see God who prefer to recognize the truth and die, instead of living a long and happy existence in a state of illusion." Simone Weil sought to find her answers to the meaning of life in her acceptance of "the infinite sweetness of obedience": "For us, this obedience of things in relation to God is what the transparency of a window pane is in relation to light. As soon as we feel this obedience with our whole being, we see God." Her words are finally addressed to those who would be greater than heroes, who would, in a word, accept their affliction, their limit-situation: "Our existence is made up only of his [God's] waiting for our acceptance not to exist. He is perpetually begging from us that existence which he gives. He gives it to us in order to beg it from us."

T. S. Eliot has written in his essay "Second Thoughts About Humanism": "Man is man because he can recognise supernatural realities, not because he can invent them. Either everything in man can be traced as a development from below, or something must come from above. There is no avoiding that dilemma: you must either be a naturalist or a supernaturalist." Simone Weil chose to be a supernaturalist. This choice enabled her to see life as being much more than, as one modern novelist has described it, "a strip of pavement over an abyss." Surely, Simone Weil has been one of the few to assert the greater courage, beyond mere tenacity and endurance, by leaping across the abyss from out of "the hands of men" into "the hands of God."

II

Simone Weil did not express her religious philosophy in essays alone. She was always writing down her thoughts—her meditations—in single words, in phrases, sentences, extended paragraphs. One can find these fragments in her *Notebooks* (*Cahiers*), containing the notes she made in France in 1940–42, translated by Arthur Wills and published in two volumes in 1954, and in her *First and Last Notebooks* (*La Connaissance surnaturelle*).* The latter volume consists of notes for the years 1933–39 and for 1942–43, when she was in the United States and in England. As one would expect, these notes are unsystematic, often repetitious, at times obscure, and at other times imprecise. They are fragments that should be considered as a whole, however, if their full import is to be assessed. "Taken all together," Rees writes in his Introduction, "the notebooks provide an unselfconscious and unintentional self-portrait of one of the most remarkable minds and characters of this century." One should add that, as fragments, the notes are as noble as they are pious. They show a religious mind reflecting, struggling with words to crystallize thought and then, more importantly, to render the meaning and the variety of unified religious experience.

First and Last Notebooks points not only to Simone Weil's remarkable mind and thought, but also to her sustained concern with human problems approached in the light of ultimate religious perception. For her the "earthly life" is ever in "great need of the supersubstantial bread." "Through our fleshly veils," she writes in one of her letters, found in her book *Waiting for God*, "we receive from above presages of eternity which are enough to efface all doubts on the subject." There is always present an interaction between secular and eschatological tensions: between an awareness of matter as "our infallible judge" and the final certitude that "Waiting patiently in expectation is the foundation of the spiritual life." And here, as in all her writings, there are certain "tracks" that cross in and out of her work and thought. The one that is the most manifest is her preoccupation with "waiting" (as opposed, it might be pointed out, to Samuel Beckett's "languishing"). For Simone Weil waiting implies an intense spiritual condition, indeed a final religious state on the edge of redemption.

As such, the experience of waiting—"waiting humbly"—is one by which man is made similar to God. For Simone Weil, waiting is "the Mystical Way." It marks the ultimate perception, the transcendental consciousness, or "the movement of consciousness from lower to higher levels of reality," the awakening of the Self to the consciousness of Divine Reality, of the "deified life," as Evelyn Underhill observes in her great book *Mysticism*. Thus, waiting is identified with humility and expresses in action a certain passivity of thought.

*Trans. Richard Rees (London, 1970).

"There is no attitude of greater humility than to wait in silence and patience. . . . It is the patience which transmutes time into eternity." Beyond humility, and beyond "the tension accepted in perpetuity," waiting also signifies obedience to time. "Total obedience to time obliges God to bestow eternity." All men, according to Simone Weil's concept, are abandoned in time, which epitomizes the act of abdication by God, who "emptied himself of his divinity and filled us with a false divinity." By his creative will God maintains man in existence that he may renounce it. "God waits like a beggar who stands motionless and silent before someone who will perhaps give him a piece of bread. Time is that waiting. Time is God's waiting as a beggar for our love." The contemplation of time is the key to human life, "the irreducible mystery, upon which no science can get a hold. Humility is inevitable when one knows that one is not sure of oneself for the future. There is no stability unless one abandons the 'I' which is subject to time and modifiable."

It is always as a religious philosopher, not as a theologian, that Simone Weil thinks and writes. That is to say, her "vision philosophy," as it can be called, must be appreciated in terms of personal intuition and meditation, rather than in terms of dogma. (In the earlier published *Notebooks* she quotes with approval the remark that " 'the science of religions has not yet begun,' " and she insists that "To be able to study the supernatural, one must first be capable of discerning it.") As a philosopher who is at once concerned with the problems of history and the religious meaning of life, and who refuses to separate religion from history or history from religion, Simone Weil adheres to a spiritual criterion. Her adherence to this criterion is uncompromising and nonliberal. "The Gospel," she asserts, "contains a conception of human life, not a theology." Earthly things are the criterion of spiritual things. "The value of a religious or, more generally, a spiritual way of life is appreciated by the amount of illumination thrown upon the things of this world." Yet she is never unaware of the inherent resistance of the secular attitude to such a truth: "This is what we generally don't want to recognize, because we are frightened of a criterion." Iris Murdoch perceives an essential quality in the whole of Simone Weil's thought when she writes: "To read her is to be reminded of a standard."

When she applies her criterion to history, to the world, Simone Weil finds that spiritual poverty is the pervading condition of life. As she puts it succinctly, "We no longer know how to receive grace." Hence her conclusions regarding both human history and historic reality are profoundly pessimistic. Sadness, a rending spiritual sadness, inevitably describes Simone Weil's own condition as she looks at the world. In *Waiting for God* she explains the threefold nature of this sadness when she admits that fate has permanently stamped it upon her nature; that her own "miserable and conscious sins" are inescapable; that "the miseries of this epoch and all those of all past epochs" make this sadness terrifying. At the same time it is precisely this sadness that makes her social-cultural observations acute and prophetic. Indeed, Simone Weil has a kind of bifurcated vision that in a historical sense is deeply prophetic, particularly as found in works like *The Need for Roots, Oppression and Liberty*, and *Selected Essays, 1934–1943*, and that in a religious sense is mystical, as found in works like *Gravity and Grace, Waiting for God*, and in her letters and notebooks. In the end her mystic vision is triumphant and leads to her stern rejection of the temporal world and an escape from what Plato, her favorite philosopher, calls the "Cave of Illusion." This bifurcated vision, in all its tensions, helps to explain the violent and aggressive aspect of her prophetic utterances and the pure and saintly aspect of her synthesizing religious search—her final grasp of a transcendent religious faith, which is Christian in the inspirational sense and which she superbly defines as "the submission of those parts which have had no contact with God to the one which has."

In her *First and Last Notebooks* Simone Weil's views of the historical situation recur as they are found in her essays relating to cultural and social questions. These views are largely negative, and the note of hopelessness is never far away. What she particularly focuses on, in ways that bring Dostoevsky to mind, is man's arrogance and his self-corruption through the manipulation of power, which contains "the unlimited" and turns man into a thing. Man's love of power distorts his sense of proportion and accounts for what is a base phenomenon, of which physical "gravity" is symbolic. "Humanism," she asserts, "was not wrong in thinking that truth, beauty, equality are of infinite worth, but in thinking that man can obtain them for himself without grace." Such an attitude (in Dostoevsky's novels the "Titans," with Ivan Karamazov as the best example, illustrate this process) leads to human breakdown in various forms. It leads to the most dangerous consequence of all: the plight when collectivity dispossesses man and, in effect, corrupts everything. "Outside the sphere of external observances (bourgeois formality) the whole moral trend of the post-war years (and even before) has been an *apology* for *intemperance* (surrealism) and therefore, ultimately, for madness." Any critical survey of our civilization will "bring to light exactly how it is that man has become the slave of his own creations." Methodical thought and action have surrendered to the quantitative, with man losing control of science and technique and thus building (to borrow Dostoevsky's images) his "Crystal Palace" and becoming part of the "ant-hill." "When humanity fell away from a civilization illumined by faith, probably the first thing it lost was the spirituality of labour." Disequilibrium and alienation are, therefore, in ascendancy, because

> The conditions of modern life destroy the mind-body equilibrium in everything, in thought and in action—in all actions: in work, in fighting . . . and in love, which is now a luxurious sensation and a game. . . . In its every aspect, the civilization we live in overwhelms the human *body*. Mind and body have become strangers to one another. Contact has been lost.

Gustave Thibon, the religious thinker who befriended Simone Weil and, along with the Reverend Father J. M. Perrin, acted as her spiritual legatee, observes that "Simone Weil oscillates between a pessimism which reduces man to nothingness and an optimism which raises him prematurely to divinity." If, then, she sees the social order as essentially evil, she emphasizes that "The world must be regarded as containing something of a void in order that it may have need of God." Her thoughts are always God-oriented, and she insists that "only the unconditioned leads to God," since no resolution can transport one to eternity. The "unconditioned" is contact with God, is the absolute. All sins, Simone Weil affirms, are attempts to escape from time and to fill the void; at the bottom of each sin there is anger against God. "If we forgive God for his crime against us, which is to have made us finite creatures, He will forgive our crime against him, which is that we are finite creatures." God and humanity she images as "two lovers who have missed their rendezvous. Each is there before the time, but each at a different place, and they wait and wait and wait." Indeed, she concludes, the crucifixion of Christ "is the image of this fixity of God." The distance that separates God from the created, she adds, is spanned by compassion, which "should have the same dimension as the act of creation. It cannot exclude a single creature."

No reader will fail to appreciate the aphorisms interspersed throughout Simone Weil's *Notebooks*. Interest in her philosophic thought should not blind one to the stylistic excellence of her writing, particularly its simplicity and lucidity. Examples of her aphorisms and the language in which her thinking is expressed are in constant evidence: "Without humility, all the virtues are finite. Only humility makes them infinite." "In another use of the word, justice is the exercise of supernatural love." "Impossibility is what limits possibles; limit is necessity abstracted from time." "Nothing is more difficult than prayer. In all other tasks of the religious life, however exacting, one can sometimes rest; but there is no rest in prayer, up to the end of one's life." "To give a piece of bread is more than preaching a sermon, as Christ's Cross is more than his parables." "Beauty is a providential dispensation by which truth and justice, while still unrecognized, call silently for our attention." "Once we have understood how it develops minute personal failings into public crimes, then nothing is a minute personal failing. One's little faults can only be crimes."

Invariably, as one follows the various tracks leading through Simone Weil's *Notebooks*, one is aware of being, as T. S. Eliot said, in "contact with a great soul." But, beyond this, she is the kind of mystic and saint ("the saint of the churchless," as she has been called) who serves as a guide leading the soul toward God. Admittedly, hers are concerns so unyielding and relentless in their spiritual essences—she has been described as suffering from "vertigo of the absolute"—that her conception of what is human is distorted by an excess of love for the superhuman. To insist on such a view, however, is to ignore the peculiar quality of her thought and of her mysticism which Rees speaks of as "an uncommonly refined common sense." One need only think of Simone Weil's belief in the need "To love men in the same way as the sun would love us if it saw us"; or her insistence, in the last sentence of the *Notebooks*, that "The most important part of teaching = to teach what it is to *know* (in the scientific sense)"—to know, that is, "with one's whole soul"—to understand why, in spite of her "immoderate affirmations" (to quote Eliot again), she is always looking behind her, beckoning men tormented by the demon of doubt to follow her in the last and greatest quest.

Simone Weil's *Notebooks*, though they contain fragments, the rough drafts of her thought, are nonetheless paradigms of spiritual progress won through meditation. As stark and severe as her meditations are, they have much to say about the glory of the inner life; and to meditate on her meditations is to participate in an experience of the inner life that modern man has ignored to his impoverishment. If Simone Weil's works remind us of a standard, they also remind us of an inner, reverent discipline without which life is incomplete. "Depths of silence," writes Thibon, "have to be traversed in order to grasp the authentic meaning of her words." But when we have grasped it, we are able to communicate with one whose meditations on the life of man and "the needs of the soul" place her among the first philosophers of our civilization.

17

D. H. Lawrence and the Ancient Greeks

*We always return to Greece because it fulfils some need of our own
life, although that need may be very different at different epochs.*

—WERNER JAEGER, *Paideia*

∽

To think of D. H. Lawrence in connection with the ancient Greeks
would for some compound already existing "unclassical incongru-
ities." For others Lawrence's creative art, with its almost frenzied prophetic appeals and its addiction to the call and answer of "pure and
passionate experience," could hardly be viewed in the same framework as Hellenism, with its pervasive sense of *sophrosyne* and *sophia*,
and with what Matthew Arnold, in his famous phrase, spoke of as its
"aerial ease, clearness, and radiancy ... full of ... sweetness and
light."[1] And for still others, who continue to look on Lawrence as an
"untutored phoenix" and an "inspired provincial genius," lacking
grace and culture, it would be wise to look at Lawrence only among
those writers whose specialties are illicit love and four-letter words.
Surely, it can even be claimed that to link Lawrence and classical
Greek accomplishment would be a travesty of literary propriety, as undignified and indefensible as having had Lawrence become a don at
Cambridge, where, according to the fearful T. S. Eliot, "his ignorance
might have had frightful consequences for himself and for the world,
'rotten and rotting others.' "[2]

Lawrence's education, though a good, solid one, did not include
Greek, to be mastered in that "grand, old, fortifying classical curriculum," as seen in the lives of Milton, Shelley, and Swinburne. Lawrence, like Keats, knew no Greek and had to rely on translations for
his understanding of Greek literature. Nevertheless, the fact is that he
read widely and deeply among Greek writers. Some of his earliest letters reveal a response to Greek literature which was remarkable for its
intensity and its spontaneity of thought and expression. *Trojan Wom-
en*, he writes, is "the finest study of women from ancient times"; *Oedi-
pus* is "the finest drama of *all* times ... terrible in its accumulation—

like a great big wave coming up—and then crash!"; the *Bacchae* is remembered best "for its flashing poetry."[3] To the end, Lawrence's reaction to the Greeks was motivated by passion, by an intuitive sense of wonder, and by an enthusiasm surpassing the conventional and academic. In this respect, Lawrence's attitudes toward Hellenism can be related to those of another fiery, rebellious artist, Lord Byron. For, like Byron, Lawrence appreciated Greek culture in its living aspects.

Non-intellectual rather than *anti*-intellectual would best characterize Lawrence's feelings toward the Greeks. That is to say, Lawrence insisted that one should respond to literature with "emotion, not reason," for literature affects "sincere and vital emotion and nothing else." In the Greeks, then, Lawrence sought for emotional rapport, for sensuous sympathy of experience, for "actual vital touch." What Lawrence writes of the Etruscans—"They are not a theory or a thesis. If they are anything, they are an experience"—comes especially to mind at this point.[4] Lawrence associated cerebral aesthetic appreciation with a debasing systematization of experience and the attempt "to force the mind or the soul in any direction." Unlike Keats, whose eyes had feasted on the Elgin Marbles and whose rapturous aesthetic imagination had equated Greek art and myth with physical and spiritual beauty, Lawrence gained "more real" pleasure from an Etruscan ash chest than from the Parthenon frieze, because it brought him into contact with "the old physical world," with "the whole Etruscan pulse and rhythm." In short, Lawrence did not seek either in ancient literature or in ancient Greek life for an aesthetic or intellectual experience. The test of any true impact on experience, he maintained, was not the carry-over of an "ecstatic proportion of the mental and spiritual consciousness," but rather the emotional depth of "the natural beauty of proportion of the phallic consciousness." He even criticized Greek accomplishment because he felt that at times a great deal of pure Greek beauty was "too much cooked in the artistic consciousness": "One wearies of the aesthetic quality—a quality which takes the edge off everything and makes it seem 'boiled down.' A great deal of pure Greek beauty has this boiled down effect."[5]

Lawrence did not seek in Greek literature and life for the metaphysical values of freedom, as did Shelley; or of spiritual nobility, as did Wordsworth; or of harmony, as did Matthew Arnold. The fact is that Lawrence disliked Shelley. We can understand this dislike when we consider Shelley's Platonism and the inspiration that touched and then tremulously overcame him as he stood amid ancient ruins. This inspiration led to his unmatched esteem for things Greek, which he expressed in these words: "The human form and the human mind attained to a perfection in Greece which has impressed its image on those faultless productions, whose very fragments are the despair of modern art, and has propagated impulses which cannot cease, through a thousand channels of manifest or imperceptible operation, to ennoble and delight mankind until the extinction of the race."[6] Lawrence's concern with the "pure present" forbade the approximation of such sentiments. Precisely because Lawrence wrote in the framework of the nonintellectual, he was never able to write prose like Shelley's, or to write an ode in the manner of Wordsworth, whose Greek influence certainly resounds in his "emotion recollected *in tranquillity.*" Poetry, Lawrence claimed, was not the result of control and discipline but of an *"emotional pattern,"* depending not on the ear "but on the sensitive soul," on "the finest instinct imaginable, much finer than the skill of the craftsmen." In this light, we can understand and regret why Lawrence was incapable of composing the kind of poetry that we find in the last, mighty lines of Shelley's *Hellas*:

> Oh, cease! must hate and death return?
> Cease! must men kill and die?
> Cease! drain not to its dregs the urn
> Of bitter prophecy.
> The world is weary of the past,
> Oh, might it die or rest at last![7]

Lawrence's responses to the ancient Greeks were inevitably pregnant with an immediacy of feeling and with an intuitiveness that were not in the least concerned with reconciling the Apollonian and the Dionysian. In language recalling Tolstoy's, he admired Homer simply because his epic poems are "the supreme old novels." "These are," he continues, "all things to all men. Which means that in their wholeness they affect the whole man alive, which is the man himself, beyond any part of him."[8] In Hector and Menelaus he applauded the "emotional reaction"; in Achilles he saw a hero "of passionate and beautiful death," one of the "royal lions and tigers of our life." How refreshing is Lawrence's reaction to Achilles, in contrast with that kind of paltry, impudent judgment of, say, Lord Chesterfield, who held that Achilles

was both a brute and a scoundrel, and consequently, an improper character for the hero of an epic poem; for he had so little regard for his country, that he would not act in defence of it because he had quarrelled with Agamemnon about a whore.[9]

In his reaction to Cassandra, Lawrence likewise revealed equally refreshing and stimulating insights. To him she was a "great woman saint," "one of the world's great figures," a medium "of the deepest truth": "Through Cassandra," he says, "the truth came as through a fissure from the depths and the burning darkness that lies out of the depth of time." He continues:

> It is necessary for this great type to re-assert itself on the face of the earth. It is not the salon lady and the blue stocking—it is not the critic and judge, but the priestess, the medium, the prophetess. . . . She is one of the world's great figures, and what the Greeks and Agamemnon did to her is symbolic of what mankind has done to her since—raped and despoiled and mocked her, to their own ruin.[10]

The critic A. Alvarez has noted the "complete truth to feeling" in Lawrence's art and thought. This truth permits no intellectualization of response, no puttering in the ruins of antiquity, no futile debate between "two voices." For Lawrence, the ancient Greeks were not the depository of those verities providing partial relief for the moral and religious uncertainties of an Arnold, as Douglas Bush has observed.[11] Instead, they were living experience, a "book of life," so to speak, which "can make the whole man alive tremble." In his response to the Greeks, Lawrence, unlike many Englishmen in the centuries before him, was not concerned with formulating "observations," "contemplations," "accounts," "hymns," "meditations," "estimates," "elegies," "odes," "inquiries," "memoirs," but rather with experiencing direct contact with what he termed "the everlasting *wonder* in things."

Lawrence's reactions to the Greeks disclose the perceptiveness of true genius, of an integrity and an intensity of feeling permeating each word, each revelation. In his reading of and response to Thucydides, for example, we are able to see that marvelous quickness of insight, that acute ability to go straight to the heart of things, that sureness of touch and economy of language that must place Lawrence in the first order of critics. Thucydides "is a very splendid and noble writer," Lawrence writes, "with simplicity and the directness of the most complete culture and the widest consciousness. I salute him. More and more I admire the true classic dignity and self-responsibility."[12] Surely, this is a response without equivocation; it is intelligent, honest, sound, as is this statement also: "I read Thucydides . . . when I have courage to face the fact of these wars of a collapsing era, of a dying idea. He is very good, and very present to one's soul."[13]

Lawrence's reaction to Plato was altogether different. Time and again he expressed a strong dislike of Plato. Lawrence saw in the philosophy of Plato an escapism that ended in the annihilation of all vital human experience through an ecstatic flight to some celestial region.

Lawrence strove always to transcend the classic ideal of human balance that figures so strongly in Plato and to try to achieve a different kind of balance, one consistent with human imperfections. He believed that the lion was indispensable to the unicorn, that each quality was kept in equilibrium by its opposite. "And there is no rest, no cessation from the conflict," he declares. "For we are two opposites which exist by virtue of our inter-opposition. Remove the opposition and there is collapse, a sudden crumbling into universal nothingness."[14] For many Plato has been and continues to be an "old, loving nurse," to be honored and esteemed to the end of all time and the judgment of all nations. Clement of Alexandria spoke of him as ὁ πάντα ἄριστος Πλάτων; and Saint Augustine was able to discover in the *libri Platonici* not only a refuge but also a liberation from error. However, Lawrence's "mystical materialism," as Aldous Huxley labeled it, could not possibly permit him to appreciate or to understand fully the essence of Platonism. Lawrence believed that "Life, the ever-present, knows no finality, no finished crystallization." "Tell me of the mystery of the inexhaustible, forever unfolding creative spark . . . of the incarnate disclosure of the flux, mutation in blossom, laughter and decay perfectly open in their transit, nude in their movement before us."[15] In a sense, such utterances indicate what for Lawrence constituted the "highest good," in contradistinction to Plato's belief that the highest good is the progressive "assimilation to God." Certainly, in the following comment we can understand the honesty of Lawrence's feelings about Plato, though we can hardly excuse his harsh tone:

> If in Plato's *Dialogues*, somebody had suddenly stood on his head and given Plato a kick in the wind, and set the whole school in an uproar, then Plato would have been put into a much truer relation to the universe.[16]

Lawrence bitterly attacked Platonism as a "religion of renunciation," with its stress on the need to quell what the ancient philosopher spoke of as "the savage, many-headed monster" residing in all human beings. Lawrence's constant reminders that "The promised land, if it be anywhere, lies away beneath. No more prancing upwards," and that "By willing and intellectualizing . . . we only exhaust ourselves and lose our lives . . ." crystallized his inability to be a "devoted disciple" of Plato. Instinctively his "animistic vision" finds Platonism utterly alien. "Mentality and ideas are death," he insists. No amount of study would have drawn Lawrence to Plato, and he could never have shared Emerson's belief that Plato's "merits multiply with study.

When we say, here is a fine collection of fables; or, when we praise the style; or the common sense . . . we speak as boys. . . ."[17]

Lawrence's attitude toward Plato must not be thought unusual. His distrust of the Hellenism of Plato or Aristotle had long before been voiced by other figures in Western thought. Indeed, in his denigration of Plato, Lawrence underscores his Protestant nonconformist heritage, from which he never freed himself completely, and in which concerted attempts to deintellectualize religious life and to purify theology have long occupied an important role. Some early Protestant reformers, we should remember, were strongly critical of "Hellenic accumulations," and Aristotle, in fact, was regarded as a "godless bulwark of the Papists." Luther went so far as to declare that "if Aristotle had not been of flesh, I should not hesitate to affirm him to have been truly a devil." A later Protestant theologian, Edwin Hatch, even charged that Christianity's "darkest pages are those which record the story of its endeavoring to force its transformed Greek metaphysics upon men or upon races to whom they were alien."[18]

Still, it is not without a measure of truth that Shelley once noted that "We are all Greeks." This statement holds true for Lawrence in spite of his belief that everything of importance lies *"in ourselves, or nowhere."* For sustenance and inspiration, Lawrence, unable to tolerate the Platonic "excursion into ideals, bodilessness, and tragedy," turned to the pre-Socratic Greeks, who personified the "tremendous days of Greece." Contending that "With the coming of Socrates and 'the spirit,' the cosmos died," Lawrence felt that among the pre-Socratic Greeks there was the kind of "living understanding" that harmonized with his own vision of a vital existence. In these early Greeks, as in the Etruscans, the Aztecs, and the American Indians, Lawrence found an inviting atmosphere, a vehemence and an abundance of life untainted by any doctrinal "thought-forms."

Lawrence's introduction to the pre-Socratic philosophers came in 1915, when Bertrand Russell gave him a copy of John Burnet's *Early Greek Philosophy.* As can be gathered from the numerous references to it in his correspondence and the quotations from it in his works, this volume both delighted and influenced him. Of course, it should be noted that the direction of Lawrence's thought and art was already established by 1915, as evidenced in his early poems, stories, and essays, in *Sons and Lovers,* and in the early version of *The Rainbow,* and *Women in Love.* To pinpoint absolute influences or borrowings from literary sources would be difficult in the work of an artist who admitted that "I only remember hints [from other writers] and I proceed by intuition."[19] Nevertheless, it is quite obvious that reading Burnet's volume, with its inclusion of the fragments and its appraisal of pre-Socratic philosophers like Heracleitus and Empedocles, gave Lawrence an intense satisfaction, like that with which André Gide first read William Blake, finding in him, as he tells us in the *Journals*, "a revelation and a confirmation of certain thoughts that have long been stirring within me."[20] To Lawrence the pre-Socratic philosophers were not a text, so to speak, but as he says, "a step onwards in untravelled space"; through them he achieved a proximity to "the old cosmic and elemental world" and rediscovered "the great and intricately developed sensual awareness, or sense-awareness, and sense-knowledge of the ancients."

Of the pre-Socratic philosophers, Heracleitus is closest in spirit to Lawrence. Heracleitus was called in Greek ὁ σκοτεινός, "the obscure." The element of obscurity would seem to ally the ancient Greek with the modern Lawrence, whose work so appalled T. S. Eliot that he said, "The man's vision is spiritual, but spiritually sick," and caused I. A. Richards to attribute to him "the mentality of a bushman."[21] If Heracleitus confused the ancients by asserting that the living and the dead are always changing places and by saying that real rest is change, Lawrence in such books as *Psychoanalysis and the Unconscious* and *Fantasia of the Unconscious* was equally obscure in his obsession with what he termed "solar plexus," "lumbar ganglion," "terrestrial volution," and "upper sympathetic centre." We can be sure that the gamekeeper Oliver Mellors in *Lady Chatterley's Lover* would have heartily endorsed Heracleitus' precept "I have sought for myself."[22]

Lawrence was a modern Heracleitus, except that he had the dialect of the English Midlands. To understand the truth of such an observation, we need only examine those existing fragments of Heracleitus which Lawrence, consciously or unconsciously, incorporated in much of his work. Heracleitus' disdain for "polymathy," that is, his belief that the learning of many things does not teach understanding, found in Lawrence an enthusiastic adherent. For in the whole of his work Lawrence continually decries "mental activity," maintaining that "The mind as author and director of life is anathema," and going so far, at one point, as to demand that "all schools be closed at once." Another concept of Heracleitus, that strife is the father of all things, reverberates in Lawrence's work. It is recognized in his pronouncements that man is "a creature of conflict, like a cataract," and that

while we live
the kissing and communing cannot cease
nor yet the striving and the horrid strife.[23]

Lawrence's reiteration of man's need for a "gentle soul" and for "delicate sensitiveness" is not without parallel in Heracleitus' observation that "Eyes and ears are bad witnesses to men if they have souls that understand not their language." Heracleitus' deemphasis of the Delphic precept "Know thyself" finds an echo in Lawrence's counsel to modern man: "The goal is *not* ideal. . . . The final aim is not *to know*, but *to be*. There never was a more risky motto than that: Know thyself. . . . 'BE yourself' is the last motto."[24] Not one content with the mere exposition of such a philosophy, Lawrence tried to convert his friend Bertrand Russell to it. "For heaven's sake," he wrote to Russell, "don't think . . . be a baby, and not a savant any more. Don't *do* anything any more—but for heaven's sake begin to *be*—start at the very beginning and be a perfect baby: in the name of courage."[25]

In Lawrence's work the references to Greek life and myths are abundant, especially in his poems. He did not use myths, however, for ornamentation or allegory; nor did he turn to them for rhetorical and dramatic patterns, as the Renaissance writers did. By no means did he hark back to the ancient Greeks for style, in the sense of imitating a specific form or technique. To do so would have been for Lawrence totally inconceivable, even immoral, a defilement of the artist's integrity and artistic vision. "They want me to have form," he wrote while still a struggling writer; "that means, they want me to have *their* pernicious ossiferous skin-and-grief form, and I won't."[26] Lawrence's purpose was not to find a style or to evoke some spiritual malady or attitude or to teach political or moral lessons. He reacted to myths on the basis of their cult-lore, and simply because, as he says, "it was all part of the active, actual, everyday, normal life—not something apart." He embraced the ancient idea not only that love and existence were rooted in the same ground, but also that the divine was not to be superimposed on natural events but was revealed in the essence of life. In Lawrence's claim that "The old Greeks were very fine image-thinkers, as the myths prove. Their images were wonderfully natural and harmonious,"[27] we can see the real nature of his admiration and can gain a strong hint of what the Greek poets really meant to him. The problem, as Lawrence saw it, was how "to get back the grand orbs of the soul's heavens": "How are we to get back Apollo, and Attis, Demeter, Persephone, and the halls of Dis?"[28]

Hence Lawrence made no attempt to move back into the ancient Greek past, as did the nineteenth-century French Parnassians, but rather tried to evoke its elemental wonder in order to corroborate his belief that "For man, the vast marvel is to be alive. . . . The dead may look after the afterwards. But the magnificent here and now of life in the flesh is ours, and ours alone, and ours only for a time."[29]

Throughout his poems Lawrence makes it clear that he was unable to forget the Greek gods and heroes. When he glorifies the "delicious rottenness" of medlars and sorb-apples, he thinks of Orpheus and Dionysus, gods whom he sees as "drenched with mystery." When he pictures bare fig trees, "nude with the dim light of full healthy life," he thinks of "the snakes on Medusa's head." When he describes himself returning home as the house sleeps in darkness, he suddenly sees "Tall black Bacchae of midnight" rushing at him.[30] The Greek gods are to Lawrence symbolic of the bloom of youth, of the instinctive life of the senses, of fertility, of the "eternal return" of the seasons. It is the god Pan who especially appeals to his imagination, as Pan once appealed to Lord Byron, who lamented:

> The gods of old are silent on their shore,
> Since the great Pan expired, and through the roar
> Of the Ionian waters broke a dread
> Voice which proclaim'd 'the mighty Pan is dead.'[31]

To Lawrence "Rustic Pan," the god of flocks, pastures, wild life, shepherds, and the countryside, personifies the "power" and "mystery" of physical being, the "vivid relatedness between man and the living universe." The death of Pan connotes for Lawrence the ascendancy of "idea," "engine," "abstraction," "the triumph of the machine" and "the dark, satanic mills" when "the iron has entered the soul of man."[32]

Above all, it is in Lawrence's *Last Poems* that the ancient Greeks figure prominently. These poems, written in southern France in the last years of his life, when Lawrence was reading the Bible in James Moffatt's translation, Dean Inge's *The Philosophy of Plotinus*, and Gilbert Murray's *Five Stages of Greek Religion*, comprise the final chapter of an artist's spiritual autobiography.[33] Even in the presence of death, Lawrence thought of the Greeks and longed for the physical immediacy of their way of life. He envisioned the ancients as men of action, as Aegean mariners "with archaic pointed beards." He recalled "the Argonauts' sea" at dawn when "Odysseus calls the commands, as he steers past those foamy islands." He thought of the Mediterranean Sea, which

will never die, neither will it ever grow old
nor cease to be blue, nor in the dawn
cease to lift up its hills
and let the slim black ships of Dionysos come sailing in
with grape-vines up the mast, the dolphins leaping.[34]

"The Greeks are coming," he cries, and, "Hark!" he hears

the low and shattering laughter of bearded men
with slim waists of warriors and the long feet
of moon-lit dancers.[35]

Close by him

the Minoan gods and the gods of Tiryns
are heard softly laughing and chatting.[36]

The god Hermes, "with his cloak over his arm," comes to visit him, filling him with "such loveliness." With words that recall Heracleitus, as well as the ancient Greek concept of θεοί—of the gods to be found in all facets of life—Lawrence cries that

God is the great urge that has not yet found a body
but urges towards incarnation with the great creative urge

And becomes at last a clove carnation: lo! that is god!
and becomes at last Helen, or Ninon: any lovely and generous woman
at her best and her most beautiful, being god, made manifest,
any clear and fearless man being god, very god.

There is no god
apart from poppies and flying fish,
men singing songs, and women brushing their hair in the sun.
The lovely things are god that has come to pass, like Jesus came.
The rest, the undiscoverable, is the demi-urge.[37]

In his poem "Bavarian Gentians," it is Pluto, Demeter, and Persephone who appear as the poet pleads, "lead me then, lead me the way." The concluding lines of this poem are memorable not only for their beauty and tenderness but also for their inherent Hellenism, the Hellenism which, as Gilbert Murray has said, imbues all "regions of imagination and aspiration":

Reach me a gentian, give me a torch!
let me guide myself with the blue-forked torch of this flower
down the darker and darker stairs, where blue is darkened on blueness
even where Persephone goes, just now, from the frosted September
to the sightless realm where darkness is awake upon the dark
and Persephone herself is but a voice
or a darkness invisible enfolded in the deeper dark
of the arms Plutonic, and pierced with the passion of dense gloom,
among the splendour of torches of darkness, shedding darkness on
the lost bride and her groom.[38]

In his *Last Poems,* Lawrence's concern with death is predominant. Death is for him the "utter and absolute dark," a "silence," a "sheer oblivion," a "silent sheer cessation of all awareness," a sleep in which there is "a hint of lovely oblivion," the "sleep of God!" when "the world is created afresh":

> And if tonight my soul may find her peace
> in sleep, and sink in good oblivion,
> and in the morning wake like a new-opened flower
> then I have been dipped again in God, and new-created.
>
> And if, as weeks go round, in the dark of the moon
> my spirit darkens and goes out, and soft strange gloom
> pervades my movements and my thoughts and words
> then I shall know that I am walking still
> with God, we are close together now the moon's in shadow.[39]

When we come to his celebrated death-poem, "The Ship of Death," we can certainly appreciate his invocation of the Greek gods and his reading of Greek philosophy. The tone of this poem is not one of despair or cynicism, but of wonder as "the sojourn in the after-life" is about to begin. We can understand, too, Lawrence's interest in Plotinus, who was preoccupied with the soul's departure from life, the soul that the neo-Platonist imaged as a traveler from the realm of sensual beauty to the supersensual. "The soul," Plotinus declares, "must see before it neither evil nor anything else, that alone it may receive the alone."[40] Nor should it be forgotten that the "journey of the soul" which Lawrence depicts in this poem is indeed that mysterious "adventure of death" that took the Homeric heroes to the "islands of the blest," where, as the epic poet says, "life is easiest for men: no snow is there, nor yet any great storm, nor any rain; but always ocean sendeth forth the breeze of the shrill West to blow cool on men."[41] There is no doubt that in their spirit and movement, and with their sense of reverence, wonder, mystery, and endurance, Lawrence's concluding lines in "The Ship of Death" suggest a Hellenism that remains ageless and undying:

> The flood subsides, and the body, like a worn sea-shell
> emerges strange and lovely.
> And the little ship wings home, faltering and lapsing
> on the pink flood,
> and the frail soul steps out, into the house again
> filling the heart with peace.
>
> Swings the heart renewed with peace
> even of oblivion.

Oh build your ship of death. Oh build it!
for you will need it.
For the voyage of oblivion awaits you.[42]

When we come to the final phase of Lawrence's creative art, we cannot fail to recognize that a contemplative mood prevails. Lawrence is no longer only a poet of emotion, of the creative urge, of that poetry arising in all its splendor and all its pain from the dictates of the flesh, from, as Robert Graves expresses it,

> . . . lust frightful, past belief,
> Lurking unforgotten,
> Unrestrainable endless grief.[43]

Lawrence is here an apocalyptic poet transcending empirical realities, and in the words of his poem "Loneliness,"

> . . . seeing the world beyond
> and feeling oneself uninterrupted in the rooted connection
> with the centre of all things.[44]

The Preacher's words that there is "a time to embrace, and a time to refrain from embracing," capture Lawrence's feeling of serenity. There comes to mind Lawrence's observation that "There is something in the Greek sculpture that any soul is hungry for—something of the eternal stillness that lies under all movement, under all life, like a source, uncorruptible and inexhaustible."[45] In the end, Lawrence's "screams of the soul" are under control, and it is "stillness" and yearning for the "uncorruptible" that grip the poet. And, ironically, Lawrence shows at the same time that he cannot avoid coming back to Plato. For what Plato speaks of as the "rehearsal for death" is very much in evidence in Lawrence's final work. And just as Plato longed for the Word, just as he traveled from the seen to the unseen, so too does Lawrence now ponder "the voyage of discovery towards the real and eternal and unknown land." His work, his thought, his mood now radiate with those Platonic virtues of wisdom, courage, and moderation. At the end Lawrence shows a sage, mature, calm, in short, Hellenic understanding of "the rhythm of life," of "the long neuter spell of Lent, when the blood," as he writes, "is low, and the delight of the Easter kiss, the sexual revel of spring, the passion of mid-summer, the slow recoil, revolt, and grief of autumn, greyness again, then the sharp stimulus of winter of the long nights."[46]

To Lawrence the ancient Greeks epitomized virile, vital experience. He returned to them again and again in order to possess even a moment of life at the full, to catch a glimpse of a way of life that had not been condemned to what he felt was the ugliness of the modern industrial world. The ancient Greeks and the south of Europe, Lawrence felt, embodied beauty and music and warmth and sun. The Mediterranean world enchanted Lawrence in much the same way it enchanted Keats, Byron, Shelley, the Brownings, Landor, Norman Douglas, and E. M. Forster. It provided release from the somber, dark, damp North, from "the great black pine forests" of Germany, from London and Paris, "the bursten cities" where

> the dead tread heavily through the muddy air
> through the mire of fumes
> heavily, stepping weary on our hearts.[47]

It was a world "eternally young, the very symbol of youth." Lawrence's memorable image of England as "a grey, dreary-grey coffin sinking in the sea behind, with her dead grey cliffs and the white worn-out cloth of snow above,"[48] encompasses his rejection of the North and explains in some ways the reasons for his "savage pilgrimage." When in the North he yearned "to be back in the South . . . beyond the Straits of Messina, in the shadow of Etna, and with the Ionian Sea in front: the lovely, lovely dawn-sea where the sun does nothing but rise towards Greece, in the morning-past, and towards the east."[49]

Lawrence's debt to the ancient Greeks must be seen in the framework of special qualifications. Lawrence was, of course, always sensitive to great cultural influences. But he metamorphosed influences, which he designated as "hints" and "suggestions," according to his belief that "the spark is from dead wisdom, but the fire is life." His view of tragedy especially underlines one way in which he sought to transform "old vision" into "new living utterance." Lawrence was intensely concerned with tragedy, and *Women in Love* exemplifies his tragic vision at its height of artistic execution. He defines his view of tragedy in the Preface to his play *Touch and Go* (1920): Tragedy is a "profound struggle"; it embodies dignity, beauty, satisfaction; it is a "creative crisis," a form of "creative activity in which death is a climax in the progression towards new being." Lawrence felt that tragedy is noble only if man endures, "comes through," is "reborn." Essentially, then, he sought to de-eschatologize tragedy, to cleanse it of any taint of sin or of guilt. He wanted tragedy purged of the metaphysics of fatalism. "The man [Lawrence asserts] is caught in the wheels of his part, his fate, he may be torn asunder. He may be killed, but the resistant, integral soul in him is not destroyed. He comes through, though he dies. He goes through with his fate, though death swallows him. And it is in this facing of fate, this going through with it, that tragedy lies. Tragedy is not disaster.... Tragedy is the working out of some immediate passional problem within the soul of man.... There must be a supreme *struggle*."

Like any tragedian, Lawrence was filled with moral purpose, but one that was secular, without *telos*. His religious nonconformity overcame his sacramental longings, which he transmuted into his "dark gods" and his myths rooted in *physis* and *eros*. Hence, it is understandable why tragedy for Lawrence signified the liberating discovery of one's deeper self; why, too, it is in its last offshoot passional in its revelation of "forgotten wisdom." Hence, too, for Lawrence the need for struggle into consciousness is tied to an active awareness. Insisting on writing his own "apocalypse," he conduces meditation, even as his "doctrine" repudiates its essences. Accepting mystery, he refuses to accept a "theology of mysteries."

Lawrence as tragic poet can be seen in *The Rainbow* and, above all, in *Women in Love*; indeed, even in *Sons and Lovers* he shows capacity for the presentation of tragic emotion. What this statement means is that Lawrence accepted tragedy in its traditional form roughly through 1920, i.e., through the period immediately following World War I. *Women in Love* belongs to this period, as seen in its rendering of suffering, its view of modern man's collective hubris, its concept of demonic power, of human destiny, and, above all, of the fact of death. Adhering to the ancient metaphysic, no other modern novel better portrays what happens when human limits are scorned, individually and collectively. *Women in Love* is the story not only of the fall of men but also of the fall of civilization. One of its great lessons is that knowledge is acquired through suffering and through death.

It was particularly fitting that during the war years Lawrence turned to ancient Greek literature, philosophy, and history. Where else could he have better grasped the tragic element? What other writers could have better satisfied him during "the first civil war of the West," as it has been described? If the Hebrew prophets schooled Lawrence in his mastery of their idiom, the Greek poets enlarged and intensified his tragic vision of man in history. Under the circumstances Lawrence's sympathetic reading of Thucydides during these years is particularly revealing. In writing about the Peloponnesian Wars, Thucydides disclosed the universal meaning of historical crisis, especially in his description of the pathology of war and of its demoralization. Lawrence read Thucydides as a tragic poet (not as a political philosopher) who possessed "true classic dignity and self-responsibility" in describing "the death-agony of Greece ... [and] not her life struggle." For Lawrence, Thucydides had the value of confirming the tragic drama of twentieth-century Europe. He was an important aspect of Lawrence's "Greek experience," from which his concept of the tragic principle of life largely derived.

Lawrence chose to reject Hellenism. Hellenism, with its message of moderation, did not satisfy him in a world he believed had gone dead. "We must have the courage," he pleaded, "to cast off the old symbols, the old traditions. . . . There is something beyond the past. The past is no justification. Unless from us the future takes place, we are death only." For Lawrence the Great War marked the death of the past as well as of tragedy. The war signified the complete irrelevance of everything that European civilization included. To cling to old forms meant to cling to dead ideals, and this meant the death of all adventure. The 1920's, then, dramatize Lawrence's "savage pilgrimage," his ceaseless adventure into consciousness, untouched (he hoped) by the past and by all it had meant.

In abandoning the Hellenic concept of tragedy, Lawrence in effect abandoned a sustaining life- and art-force that would have made his writing in 1920–30 far different from what it was. To be sure, he always retained the power to render tragic emotion (as in "The Nightmare" chapter of *Kangaroo*), but he could not accept the tragic human condition. His "screams of soul" and "deaths in belief," during and after World War I, were so acute that the staying power of "the Greek view of life" was inadequate. Thus, he chose to count *phallus* superior to *sophia*, as his fiction, especially *The Plumed Serpent* (1926), *Lady Chatterley's Lover* (1928), and *The Man Who Died* (1929), illustrates. In these works the flow of Lawrence's vision reaches flood proportions. "We have to go back, a long way," he cries in *A Propos of Lady Chatterley's Lover* (1930), "before the idealist conceptions begin, before Plato, before the tragic idea of life arose, to get on to our feet again. For the gospel of salvation through the Ideals and escape from the body coincided with the tragic conception of human life. Salvation and tragedy are the same thing, and they are now both beside the point."

But Lawrence, to repeat, failed as an artist during this period. He chose to trivialize his art by negating the tragic view of life. *The Plumed Serpent* consists of phallic confusion; *Lady Chatterley's Lover* teaches a perverse phallicism; *The Man Who Died* posits a simplistic myth of phallic optimism. Although Lawrence retained to the end his tragic vision, it was molded and crabbed by its modernism, so that it became, in Murray Krieger's words, both a "protestant vision" and a "romantic vision." In other words, Lawrence grasped fully the essences of tragedy: evil, suffering, treachery, death. Yet his art never came to terms with the tragic: the artist remained so bitterly dissatisfied with his vision of tragedy that he became too intimately concerned about "the tormented ecstasy of seeking." Lawrence could not accept the tragic destiny of man, which Sophocles equated with "phantoms" and "mere fleeting shadows," with the fate that warns one "to call no earthly creature blest." For Lawrence this tragic apprehension was equivalent to a *stasis* he disdained no less than the classical idea, which he dismissed as cowardly.

Lawrence tried to transcend "the tragic sense of life" by resurrecting "the man who died." Though never completely escaping from the Christianity of his youth, he chose in his last years a non-Christian form of transcendence to overcome the death-cry *Consummatum est!* To the vision of tragedy he gave his own answer: "Look! We have come through!" And he rooted this answer in the phallic—in that experience which contains no real or lasting accommodation between experience and conscience. In this tendency Lawrence reflected the "modern temper" as opposed to the "Greek temper," the tragic element in the former characterized by the conviction of innocence and in the latter by the conviction of guilt. Lawrence's characters, after *Women in Love*, are involved in "passional" struggles but not in moral struggles, even as his novels depict passional but not moral problems. By attempting to separate the passional from the moral, Lawrence attempted to evade tragic destiny. He was not altogether successful in his effort.

Some essences of the tragic spirit, nevertheless, reappear in his *Last Poems*. In these poems we find Lawrence's release from the waste land, as he slowly reasserts the religious faith that gives rise to the tragic faith. Tragic dilemmas no longer rend the artist's consciousness; his view of man is softened by a tragic contemplativeness as he hears "the music of lost languages." He now affirms the greatness of the human soul, the possibilities of harmony, the omnipresence of God as the natural and the supernatural worlds coalesce—"and the silent soul / may sink into god at last, having passed the veils." Here Lawrence again discloses a tragic faith of serenity, "after the bitter passage of oblivion," and reincorporates its constituents in his poetic vision. Appropriately enough the protagonist of these poems is a spiritual hero.

18

A Tribute to Gilbert Murray

∽

The death of Sir Gilbert Murray at the age of ninety-one on May 20, 1957, marked the passing of a scholar who, from the time he learned the *Agamemnon* by heart as a schoolboy,[1] spent a lifetime studying and embracing Hellenism as a way of life. To Murray, Hellenism was, in the words of Matthew Arnold, the renowned Hellenist of the nineteenth century, that "spontaneity of consciousness," that "sweetness and light," and "the best that is known and taught in the world";[2] yet Murray's own life of scholarship and teaching and, above all, his adherence to Hellenism as the highest mode of living, were not in the least a flight into quietude and did not negate an active role in politics[3] and the promotion of world peace. This foremost classicist of modern times was a rare kind of scholar. His was that rarity associated with the writer and teacher who unhesitatingly moves out of his intellectual niche in order to crusade openly and bravely for the ideals and values he espouses, but that are all too often relegated to the quiet confines of a lecture hall or the pages of a book.

In every respect Gilbert Murray was a Hellenist, and his loyalty to the spirit of Hellenism, which he said was the "real moving power" of the Western world, remained steadfast to the end. During a radio broadcast on his ninetieth birthday, he stated: "There has never been a day, I suppose, when I have failed to give thought to the work both for peace and for Hellenism. The one is a matter of life and death for all of us, the other of maintaining amid all the dust of modern industrial life our love and appreciation of eternal values."[4] As Professor of Greek at Glasgow University during the years 1889–99, as Regius Professor of Greek at Oxford University from 1908 until his retirement in 1936, and as Charles Eliot Norton Professor of Poetry at Harvard in 1926, he resolutely stressed that the three major goals of Hellenism—humanizing the brutal masses, effecting universal concord, and proclaiming a unified world—were the very same aspirations of the modern world.[5]

To Murray the past was a rich source of "high thoughts" and "great emotions," and even the elements of the past that had become, with the passage of time, obsolete and worthless, still retained the qualities of beauty and truth which remain eternal. It cannot be said that Murray adopted Hellenism as a refuge from the modern world, a world that was "stamped by the institution of war, by the degradation of the poor, by drink, gambling, vice: above all, ever since the industrial revolution, by a strange lack of beauty, a lack of self-respect and human dignity."[6] Neither can it be said that he ignored the present, for he clearly realized that man can easily become, in essence, a witless captive of the "material present," that "great Jailer and Imprisoner of man's mind." Murray was only too much aware of the vulgarity of a "dull and sad" modern world, and he felt that it was the scholar's great task to find direction and meaning.

The scholar, Murray asserted, did not lose either his freedom or his effectiveness by reverting to the past. This he made very clear in his eloquent presidential address to the Classical Association on January 8, 1918. He insisted that it was the scholar's duty to keep hold of the past and to treasure the best of the past, for only in this way would the "man of letters" secure his freedom. The cacophony and the violence of an angry and sordid present, he pointed out, would be less frightening when the scholar called back memories of the spirit with which brave men long ago faced the same evils.[7] Murray, as George Sarton pointed out, sought to interpret Greek wisdom, not only as a teacher and a poet, but as a friend, as one who did not take flight from the present, but rather emerged "from the beloved past to mingle with the living men of today and share their burdens."[8] To the charge that his life was one of intellectual retreat, Murray answered emphatically: "No: to search the past is not to go into prison. It is to escape out of prison, because it compels us to compare the ways of our own age with other ways."[9]

Spiritual rebirth, lasting values, intellectual inspiration, and laboring for the sake of the beautiful were integral facets of the Hellenic spirit which, Murray realized, insisted that the world was something more than a mere planet. In choosing Hellenism as the basis of world order and peace, as the prime example of free speech, liberty, and equality before the law, he acted as a bridgespan "from the ancient world . . . over into our distracted epoch."[10] In Hellenism, Murray saw the qualitative brilliance of an ancient way of life as opposed and superior to the quantitative mediocrity of the modern world. The megalomania of the modern day was happily lacking in Hellenism, a "humane civilization" that was not sullied by dogmatism and fanaticism. Free of extremism, Hellenism was a way of life in which there was genuine freedom of thought and speech and in which there was always a spirit of understanding and tolerance. One of the finest qualities in the Greek written record was its *intimacy*, for, as he points out, "You can only speak freely and intimately when you are not afraid, afraid of spies, of enemies, of friends who may turn and betray you."[11]

It has been well said that Murray, through his translations of the great Greek dramas, "brought Greek drama back to the modern stage."[12] Of course, critical opinions concerning the merits and defects of Murray's translations have ranged from the tribute by George Bernard Shaw[13] to the condemnation by T. S. Eliot. Shaw regarded Murray's translations, especially of Aeschylus and Euripides, as masterpieces; Hesketh Pearson in his biography writes that "Shaw ranked these translations as being in a class by themselves, and that the highest, in twentieth-century drama."[14] On the other hand, Eliot strongly criticized Murray's translations; he said that if the classics are to survive in literature and as a part of the European mind, they need persons "capable of expounding them," and that "Professor Gilbert Murray is not the man for this." Eliot criticized Murray on the score that "the Greek actor spoke in his own language, and our actors were forced to speak in the language of Professor Gilbert Murray."[15]

It is not the purpose here to analyze Murray's abilities as a translator. The fact remains that the continuity of Greek thought has been made possible by the contributions of men like Gilbert Murray, who, in the words of Christopher Dawson, recognized that "apart from Hellenism, the European idea of man would be inconceivable."[16] To Murray, Hellenism and Progress were synonymous; time and again he pointed out that by reading the works of such ancient writers as Thucydides, Herodotus, Aeschylus, and Euripides, modern man might be able to find some of the answers that would help to solve current problems. In Hellenism he saw spiritual values and efforts transcending the babble of the marketplace, and he concisely expressed this view when he wrote:

> This is the true message of our Hellenic and European tradition. Serve humanity: glorify God; go forth, not so much to convert, but to contribute. Live in the service of something higher and more enduring, so that when the tragic transcience of life at last breaks in upon you, you can feel that the thing for which you have lived does not die.[17]

Murray strongly felt that modern society was addicted to material power and possession, to selfishness and rapacity. He felt that in the twentieth century, much that was good—standards, values, absolutes—was dissolving.[18] Concerned with the higher side of human life, he said that the daily business of the student and the teacher was "to read, study, think, enjoy—not to fight or to bargain."[19] His preoccupation with Hellenism as a way of life led him to the conclusion that "the classical view is that there is such a thing as quality, that the highest quality is a thing of almost priceless value and worth taking trouble about."[20] It is pertinent to note here that while lecturing at Harvard in 1926, Murray was critical of the American educational system, first because the president of Harvard, Charles W. Eliot, had discontinued Greek as a required subject at the university and second because the American educational scene noticeably lacked a clear-cut affirmation of Hellenic principles—the result being a basic ignorance on the part of Americans of the art of living. Yet he underscored the fact that Hellenism, though neglected, was a necessity in the modern world and a cultural force of eternal value. In a lecture given to the Royal Academy of Arts in 1941, he voiced this feeling when he said: "And surely, we may without self-flattery claim that in the high civilization which Europe has inherited and passed on to her kindred across the ocean is a Hellenism which the barbarian rejects but still longs to understand and assimilate."[21]

In the thought and achievement of ancient Greece, Murray found that the artist had secured that measure of freedom and respect denied elsewhere, both in ancient and modern societies. Thus, Hellenism was characterized by one of its finest and noblest qualities, for whereas modern society treats the artist as a "distinguished alien," the artist in Greece was looked on as a "friend and fellow worker." Murray found this all the more remarkable in view of the fact that Greece was surrounded by savagery and backwardness and the "swampy level of the neighbouring peoples." That the artist was able to survive in Greece, amid the "remnants of the primaeval slime from which Hellenism was trying to make mankind clean," was to him an achievement of unequaled and inestimable importance. The Greek artist was able to secure his freedom in a small white-hot center of spiritual life, a way of life that was still beset by primitive institutions: by slavery, which was criticized in Greece some two thousand years before it was abolished in Europe (in "Greece alone men's consciences were troubled by slavery"); by the subjugation of women, who in Greece found a certain degree of freedom and were treated with respect and sympathy and even as heroines in Greek tragedy (e.g., Clytemnestra, Antigone, Alcestis, Polyxena, Jocasta, Phaedra, Medea); by sexual license, which the Greeks strived to diminish, so as to end the barbarities and human sacrifices connected with this perverted kind of life.[22]

Murray had special admiration for the Greek artist because he personified *sophrosyne* and his intellectual inquiry was always restrained by the combination of "a spirit of intense enjoyment with a tempering wisdom." In combining the appreciation of good things and the power to refuse them—characteristic of the spirit of progress and of Greek civilization—Murray viewed Greek art as embodying the antithesis of puritanism. Nevertheless, in Hellenism and in puritanism he also saw two spirits that fight with one another, but "are parts of one truth." The Hellenic love of moderation, sobriety, temperance, and self-discipline symbolized to Murray the greatest accomplishment a civilization is capable of, for

> There is a way of thinking which destroys and a way which saves. The man or woman who is sóphrōn walks among the beauties and perils of the world, feeling the love, joy, anger, and the rest; and through all he has that in his mind which saves. —Whom does it save? Not him only, but, as we should say, the whole situation. It saves the imminent evil from coming to be.[23]

In speaking of the beauty, freedom, and flexibility of the Greek language, he aptly observed: "It would be almost impossible to discuss a modern political or philosophical problem in classical Hebrew, difficult even in Latin. But in Greek it can always be done...."[24] Murray believed Greek a finer language because it expresses the minds of finer and nobler men,[25] and he thought Greek poetry, like Greek art, distinguished for its beauty of structure, its rightness and simplicity, free from lavish ornamentation and exaggeration. Masterpieces of Western literature, including *Paradise Lost* (the language of which Murray found "elaborately twisted and embellished into loftiness and rarity," lacking the simplicity and straightforward direction of a Greek poem[26]), *Prometheus Unbound,* and even *Hamlet* and *A Midsummer Night's Dream,* "are the children of Vergil and Homer, of Aeschylus and Plato."[27] He could not compromise, furthermore, in respect to being content with a knowledge of Latin and not Greek, since "the *exemplaria Graeca* are so extraordinarily good. They are our best pearls." In Greek literature Murray found that quality of inspiration and beauty, where "the soul of man stands at the door and knocks; it is for each one of us to open or not to open, and if we do not open, the message that should have been immortal dies."[28]

Murray went so far as to assert that many problems of the modern world remain unsolved because twentieth-century man is ignorant of the classics and because some statesmen have not "drunk at the eternal springs" of classical knowledge and inspiration.[29] There is no doubt, of course, as Horace M. Kallen points out, that ancient peoples outside of Greece could never become Greeks and that to them Hellas would be only an ambition and an accomplishment, a discipline and a doctrine of their schools, a cherished source of imitation and adoption.[30] This holds true also today. Yet, one of the great disasters of modern times, Murray claimed, has been the failure of the Western world to adopt qualities of Hellenism. The avoidance of World War III, the famous classicist said, is the supreme responsibility of a generation that "must use all its strengths, all its wisdom, to see that the main drift of the world is Hellenic and not barbarous."[31]

To Murray, ethics, morality, and good will—the essential attributes of Hellenism—embodied the inner meaning of Western civilization, and his university lectures, as a result, took the form of international pronouncements when Murray, who was president of the League of Nations Union from 1923 to 1938 and the first president of the United Nations Association General Council, sought with intense devotion to promote global peace.[32] His Hellenism was too much a part of him to accept the inevitability of war. He saw that in the world there is something of higher value than our own lives; he emphasized the futility of war, for "the weakest, if they care to use it, have the power to destroy." Indeed, even the scholar, who not only spends himself upon the advances and understanding of the things of the spirit, but also seeks a solution to social problems, finds that all his activities and aspirations are utterly annihilated by war. Murray's words "Civilization created war, and has now reached a point where it must discard war" become all the more important today, although they were written in the twenties, after the First World War and before the Second.

In Greek culture, even as in the Greek landscape, Murray found the quality of eternity. Striving to show the importance of high values in everyday living, he said, "If Shakespeare, Plato and Homer, if St. Paul and the New Testament, are not of value, then nothing is."[33] Murray's lifetime of devotion to Greek ideals was a noble example of dedication to *humanitas*. A man like him lives on after death, and his monument is not in marble or triple bronze, but in the texture of thought which he has woven into the very stuff of other men's lives. In his tribute to Gilbert Murray, John Masefield echoed the sentiment of many when he wrote:

> Surely, in some great quietude afar,
> Above Man's madness and the creed of night,
> Wisdom will crown this spirit with her star
> In conqueror's peace, in her undying light.[34]

19

Graven Images

༄

When Mario Praz's *The Romantic Agony* appeared (1933), some critics felt that it was ingenuity rather than excellence which distinguished this work. Other critics believed that the book was an extreme oddity in literary criticism. Wyndham Lewis described it as a "gigantic pile of satanic bric-à-brac," and Montague Summers dismissed it as "disjointed gimcrack." Works of excellence, however, have a fortunate habit of refusing to perish, and today the author of *The Romantic Agony* has been vindicated. The book remains as an accomplishment of the first order and as a testimony of rare ability.

In *The Romantic Agony* Praz sought to provide "a study of certain states of mind and peculiarities of behaviour" based on observations gathered from three literatures: French, English, and Italian. His intimate examinations of "particular tendencies of sensibility" underlined the charisma of a comparatist seldom found in literary studies. In *The House of Life,** when Praz focuses attention on his own life, the faculties and percipience that he demonstrated in *The Romantic Agony* are again in evidence.

The House of Life is an unusual autobiography. Actually it is an elaborate description of Praz's flat in Via Giulia in Rome, where he has lived for more than thirty years.[1] "This journey round my home," he writes, "is to me like a Via Crucis; each Station has its own special prayer." Each room, with its furnishings, its art objects, its historical relics, is examined with an affection and a tenderness that characterize the life of a connoisseur. In particular, it is the items in the Empire and the Regency styles that he seeks to describe. Often an item recalls an event in Praz's life. His recollections are rendered with disarming candor and with radiant charm.

Born in Rome in 1896, Praz belongs to a generation that has witnessed tremendous technological upheavals. "When I think now of those first wavering, short-winded flutterings by the new successors

---

*Trans. Angus Davidson (New York, 1964).

of Icarus," he declares, "when I reflect upon what man can accomplish in the sky today, aspiring already to the conquest of other planets, I feel I have lived for centuries: what other generation has seen, as mine has seen, so great a change in the face of the world?" In many ways Praz's life reflects the scourges of change and the impact of contemporary technocracy. Essentially scholarly and aesthetic, his responses disclose time and again an occasional touch of regret, of sadness and disenchantment. They disclose a mood that commences on the first page with Praz's recalling the years when he was studying law in Rome and living in dreary lodgings: "...my memory of them is anyhow dim, but there remains the vague, numb feeling of squalor."

Although the squalor disappeared from Praz's own life, it did not disappear from the life around him; today he sees it subsisting in technology and modernism. Praz indicates an acute, fearful awareness of this squalor, which fills him with exasperation and dismay. But his protests against modern civilization are generally passive, and he accentuates them by evoking "the serene silence of Via Giulia which had lingered in my mind ever since that distant day in 1917 when I visited it for the first time, that silence which had a physiognomy of its own, a rhythm like that of a tune once heard which one has always longed to hear again."

Nevertheless, for Praz the recovery of the past can be desperately tenuous. Old memories grudgingly surrender; nostalgia must ever give way to realities. Although "the atmosphere of Via Giulia ... has remained that of bygone days," and although "it might be said that, in this crevice of a street like a deep trench, the mist of the past has lingered and stagnated," there remain those bitter and ugly reminders that this is an amorphous world in which man lives in the twentieth century. Modern cities have changed; now they offer unending "perils and disasters": Florence is nauseating, "with its din of motorcars and its modern, vulgar shops in streets where once quiet and dignity and good taste ... held sway." Modern houses have changed and have lost all effect of "sumptuousness": "A house today is 'a machine for living in,' a beehive of neat, rather clinical-looking cells which, to anyone who is used to the ample breathing-space of an old palace, can indeed give a feeling of claustrophobic constriction." Modern taste, too, has changed, and a positive sense of values has surrendered to "sham perspectives":

> ... today everything is sham, everything is a substitute; the fur that you think is mink or beaver is nylon, the dress that you think is made of silk is made of metal, the eyes that you think are sparkling are made so

by invisible lenses which are slipped out in the evening before the wearer goes to sleep, the word "democratic" is used equally for totalitarian as for constitutional regimes, painters show a board riddled with holes or a piece of raw canvas with a few clots of colour on it and call them pictures, and a sculptor takes a lavatory seat, combines it with a stovepipe and calls it a statue.

Some of the most vivid pages of the book recount Praz's experiences in Rome during World War II. As for those during World War I, it is interesting to note that Praz's reactions bordered on the indifferent, for "that war, apart from the disaster of Caporetto, did not make itself truly felt as did the second." During the years 1914–18, when Western civilization was in a state of collapse, Praz's "great adventures" were the walks which enabled him to discover Rome and especially Via Giulia, a street that deeply impressed him and that someday would share in his destiny: "it was quiet like some noble street in a provincial town; quiet like a corridor between rooms which were the courtyards of palaces, or like the nave of a church with chapels on either hand." (His attitude toward World War I was in sharp contrast to that of many of his European contemporaries, especially those young Englishmen to whom the declaration of war seemed at the time to signal a deliverance from the shabbiness of "civilization.") For Praz, World War II was also the time of "new discoveries," for war again brought him into contact with "the wonder of Rome," the Rome as found one night in 1940:

> Everything was now secret and adventurous. Portions of the great palaces, caught in the moonlight, looked like spectres from a world of giants. Everything became enormous: walls like indestructible cliffs, magic canals cut in the rock. . . Such a sight revealed the true face of the city: without artificial light, without the light of day and its seductive veil of colour, Rome appeared as she was, an ancient and somewhat sinister tomb, a city which, in spite of everything, still belonged to the past.

For Praz the war constituted more an aesthetic than a human tragedy. His concern was not so much with what happened to the human victims of air raids, but with the damage, for example, done to the Basilica of San Lorenzo: "that destroyed façade, that work of art, now vanished, which had endured for so many centuries that for me it was identified almost with eternity, moved me more than the deaths of human beings."

These reactions to war are quintessential, for they both reveal and typify many of Praz's attitudes and particularly what some might term a displaced passion. It is quite clear that Praz has chosen, as he himself admits, to "put so much of my mind into the cult of things which to most people seem devoid of life, such as furniture, why I have sinned by 'bowing down to graven images.'" He derives his greatest satisfaction in obtaining a "beautiful thing": "I cannot resist it, I must have it." With mirrors, furniture, and books it is a matter of being able to afford them; "with human beings, unfortunately, things do not go so smoothly."

Praz's passion for things is evidenced continually in the book. In a very large sense, he infuses things with a separate, soulful existence that can even arouse his compassion. When he speaks of a little dressing table that he has to part with, he hopes that it has not been punished by cruel contacts with human beings. At the same time, he laments that its looking glass cannot be saved "from the punishment of reflecting human faces that are unattractive or wicked." With almost agonizing honesty he distinguishes (*and* chooses) between the inanimate and the animate, between things and people. Recognizing a person or remembering a name, he confesses, is a talent he lacks,

> ... whereas I am capable of remembering, with great precision, the appearance and whereabouts of objects of art, pictures, furniture and things of even less importance. Things remain impressed in my memory more than people. Things which have no soul, or rather, which have the soul with which we endow them, and which can also disappoint us when one day the scales fall from our eyes; but people disappoint us too often, for it is only very rarely that we come to know them, and when we think we know them and feel ourselves in unison with them, it is because it is the thickest scales of all which then cover our eyes—the scales of love.

In general, Praz subordinates human beings to things; yet his awareness of other persons lacks neither richness nor vitality of response. If he seems to avoid human involvement, by no means does he ignore the human scene. His recollections of his encounters with other writers, for instance, are eminently perceptive. He remembers a conversation with Charles Du Bos, "who conferred an appearance of profundity even on the simplest things and who, indeed, talked like a printed book." He describes an episode with Benedetto Croce: "Once in Florence he came himself to look for me at my home; he did not find me, for I had already gone away again; but he left a note which filled me with pride. He knew very well how to fish for proselytes, that St. Peter of philosophy!" He pictures Edmund Gosse as one who has grown "very old, and his whole life has become concentrated in a kind of refined mockery that shows itself, when he speaks of other men of letters, in the play of his eyelids and in the cut of his lip, which is shadowed by the meagre wisps of his flowing moustache." He recalls a meeting with Robert Bridges, "and what with his untidy hair, his woolly beard, his flashing eye and his warlike frown, I imagined myself in the presence of a holy anchorite or an old buccaneer, or a sort of Count of Monte Cristo such as you see in popular illustrations to that novel." He finds John Masefield "not so interesting," "a rather wooden-looking little man, dressed a little like a porter on a Sunday, with short nut-brown trousers above his ankles and an impossible collar, who stuck his head forward like someone about to take a dive—and with a lock of hair falling down his forehead as if he had just come out of the water." He depicts Vernon Lee in her old age, "no longer a person but the diffused degeneration of an organ. A grotesque figure, if her cantankerous expression had not given her a certain tragic intensity." He senses in F. O. Matthiessen "a restless, ardent soul, unable to find peace and devoid of self-assurance, strangely different . . . from the gentle, smiling mask that he showed in public."

In line with the temper of Praz's life and his reactions to other people, his recollections are not the result of an "adventure in consciousness," but rather of the casting of a cold eye on life. Always, then, his response to the human scene is the outgrowth of sensitive but detached intelligence, the result not of an active commitment to or a passionate realization of human life, but of a cautious recognition of it. "Mine, alas, is one of these temperaments that are lazy in human relationships," he admits, "too content to take things for granted, to consider as fixed, once and for all, the thing which for others has to be a fresh conquest each day, the delicate balance of living forces in continual motion." It will be unmistakably apparent that Praz is wary of personal relationships, of the complications of intimacy, of the acceptance of the fact that all human lives flow into each other. He is decidedly unlike, say, D. H. Lawrence, who could write: "I get mixed up in people's lives so—it's very interesting, sometimes a bit painful, often jolly. But I run to such close intimacy with folk, it is complicating. But I love to have myself in a bit of a tangle."[2] In sharp contrast, Praz discloses a desire to escape the harassments of human relations. *"O miseras hominum mentes, O pectora caeca!"* undoubtedly expresses a sentiment which threads its way through this book.

To some readers Praz will bring to mind a Forster-like figure who remains content merely to view the spectacle of life. "Some souls," he writes, "are like tenacious plants that can split stones; others are like flowers, which droop if they lack air and light. I am not ashamed to say that my soul is not among the first." Still, if Praz seems to lack a certain robustness and grittiness, if he seems to slink "out of the race where that immortal garland is to be run for," it cannot be assumed that in any way he is a victim of ennui or a detachment which precludes concern. His great contributions to literary criticism would refute any charge of inanition.[3] There are present in his life redeeming virtues and energies that in their own way equip him with a refined vitality and a gentle sensitiveness which transcend the dust and the heat of the workaday world. Praz belongs to an aesthetic aristocracy and to that realm of splendor and perfect form that Plotinus envisioned as "the stainless shrine."

His search for order, for inner freedom and enrichment, for the preservation of the hidden life is characterized by infinite delicateness, by good taste, and by courage of humility and self-recognition:

> This person who looks into the mirror is myself [his concluding paragraph reads], and this book that I have written is like a conspectus, in a convex mirror, of a life and a house. . . . I see myself as having myself become an object and an image, a museum piece among museum pieces, already detached and remote, and . . . like Adam in the graffito on the marble floor of the church of San Domenico at Sienna, I have looked at myself in a convex mirror, and have seen myself as no bigger than a handful of dust.

Praz's world represents not only a leisurely, contemplative way of experiencing life but also a condemnation of the vulgarity, the insensitiveness, the rubbish that cumber so much of modern living. His reverence for things is an integral part of a quest for that *ataraxia* which ancient philosophers equated with "the tranquil face and the placid breath." But it is primarily his reverence for beauty that lends *The House of Life* its dignity and strength. In seeking to endue life with beauty, Praz speaks earnestly but gently, with the rapture of the poet and not with the frenzy of the prophet. He reminds us that it is not too late for beauty to save the world.

20

Interpreter of Genius

It is, it is, some angel. Vanished again!
Oh, come back, ravishing boy! bright messenger!
Thou hast, by these mine eyes fix'd on thy beauty,
Illumined all my soul.

—Philip Massinger and Thomas Dekker,
The Virgin Martyr

〜

"Of what use, or uses, is literary criticism, is a question worth asking again and again, even if we find no answer satisfactory," writes T. S. Eliot.[1] For many today there is no answer satisfactory, especially concerning the criticism of our own century. The relevance of the New Critics is doubted, and the New Humanists are hardly mentioned. This depreciation is part of a prevalent distaste for moral criteria, felt most vehemently by those who find their high priestess in Susan Sontag, who, as Martin Green remarks, "rejoices . . . in the extinction of the Matthew Arnold idea of culture, in which literature was so central; she rejoices in the decline of conscience and the rise of aesthetic autonomy in the arts."[2] Critics like J. Middleton Murry, T. S. Eliot, I. A. Richards, and even F. R. Leavis, William Empson, Cleanth Brooks, Kenneth Burke, and R. P. Blackmur are now of interest only in the history of literary criticism. They have had their say; they have exerted their influence; but today they no longer count.

It is not the purpose here to provide a reconciliation of different schools of criticism. Those seeking a "synoptic view" can refer to Northrop Frye's *Anatomy of Criticism* (1957). Nor is it the purpose here to recite a history of twentieth-century criticism. Such information can be found in the appropriate sections in, say, George Watson's *The Literary Critics*; in René Wellek's monumental *A History of Modern Criticism*, as well as in his *Concepts of Criticism*; and in Stanley Edgar Hyman's *The Armed Vision*. If some facts are given, it is for the purpose of approaching the contributions of G. Wilson Knight (b. 1897). Somehow, Knight, though a major critical force—especially in Shakespeare studies—since the publication of *The Wheel of Fire* (1930), does not quite fit in among the various other critics and their schools. There is something unorthodox in his work. He is not "academic," to start with, and this, we know, always causes problems! Indeed, for forty years he has been registering his dissatisfaction with "literary criticism," which, he says, "has always been my peculiar bête noire." In its place he has been offering something else; the results of his efforts have both dazzled and infuriated other critics. By and large they have been fascinated by his findings, but at the same time they have not always gauged their worth.

Watson, with hasty oversimplification, concludes that "the vast school of Shakespearean criticism inspired since 1930 by G. Wilson Knight has ambitiously interpreted dramatic characters as if they are philosophical ideas."[3] Wellek, with more ambitious, and narrow, critical strictures, declares that Knight transposes criticism into "something like a total world view or even a system of philosophy." "We have learned from Wilson Knight," Wellek states, ". . . But most of us have become increasingly dissatisfied with the arbitrariness of his associations, the intrusion of a crude psychoanalysis and of a strangely misused Nietzsche."[4] Hyman, with an arrogance that actually compromises his reliability, goes so far as to say, "The most extreme and instructive case of a critic ridden by his crotchet, and a particularly odd one, is G. Wilson Knight."[5]

Not only has Knight been disparaged; he has also been neglected in critical anthologies—omitted, for instance, from *Modern Criticism: Theory and Practice* (1963), edited by Walter Sutton and Richard Foster, and slighted in *The Modern Age*, edited by Boris Ford, specifically in John Holloway's essay "The Literary Scene," in which he is fleetingly recognized for "his detailed if often erratic analyses of poetry and symbolism in Shakespeare."[6] It is encouraging, nevertheless, that in more recent collections of critical essays such as *Shakespeare: The Tragedies* (1965), edited and with an Introduction by Clifford Leech, and *His Infinite Variety: Major Shakespearean Criticism Since Johnson* (1964), edited by Paul N. Siegel, Knight's work is being duly included—and appreciated.

But despite the neglect of Knight, it is sure that countless students and scholars have been greatly helped in their understanding of Shakespeare by their study of Knight's seven magisterial volumes: *The Wheel of Fire*, a continuation of his monograph *Myth and Miracle* (1929), which "interprets" Shakespeare's major tragedies; *The Imperial Theme* (1931), which centers on the tragedies and Roman plays and in which the "life theme" prevails; *The Shakespearian Tempest* (1932), which attempts to show a unity in the ever-recurring symbolism of the "tempest-music opposition"; *Principles of Shake-spearian Production* (1936), which discusses theories of and gives outlines for the production of particular works, especially the tragedies; *The Crown of Life* (1947), which examines Shakespeare's final plays (*Pericles, The Winter's Tale, The Tempest, Cymbeline,* and *Henry VIII*); *The Mutual Flame* (1955), which discusses the sonnets, along with *The Phoenix and the Turtle,* in relation to the dramas and Shakespeare's personality; and *The Sovereign Flower* (1958), which deals with Shakespeare as a poet of royalism.

If Knight has been criticized for being too enthusiastic, if he has been rebuked for not being "interested in sources" (as Mario Praz has complained), if his style has been called "at once fervid and overcharged with detail" (according to the late H. I'A. Fausset), if he is seen on occasion as just an updated J. Middleton Murry, he has nevertheless become one of the most imaginative and provocative Shakespearean commentators, without whose contributions Shakespeare studies today would be impoverished. Mark Van Doren, in recognizing these contributions, has declared that Knight's works "contain some of the most brilliant and illuminating remarks ever made about the poetry of the plays."[7] F. R. Leavis, that "severe magistrate of literature," has on several occasions, both in the pages of *Scrutiny* and in *The Common Pursuit* (1952), singled out Knight's achievement. Bonamy Dobrée, writing in *Criterion,* has observed that even "Coleridge ... would no longer have found *Measure for Measure* 'painful' had he read Mr. Knight's surprisingly convincing chapter '*Measure for Measure* and the Gospels' " (in *The Wheel of Fire*).[8]

"One may say that his interpretations are always likely to be right," states Edmund Blunden, "for he reveals an intense patience in choosing and linking his evidence; and where there is doubt, the doubt itself probably does him honour."[9] Obviously, not all readers will accept Knight's "interpretive criticisms." But, in the phraseology of the *Times Literary Supplement,* "there is more illumination to be derived from disagreement with Mr. Knight than from agreement with a host of 'safer' critics." These words crystallize the achievement of G. Wilson Knight; they are corroborated by another eminent Shakespearean critic, L. C. Knights:

> Perhaps more than any other writer Mr. Wilson Knight has shaped the contemporary approach to Shakespeare, not only by prompting new insights into individual plays but by widening and deepening our conception of the kind of experience that the plays offer; so that many of us who find ourselves in disagreement with him on important matters retain a sense of gratitude and indebtedness.[10]

Nor should it be overlooked that T. S. Eliot played a role in the publication of *The Wheel of Fire*. In a fascinating essay, "T. S. Eliot: Some Literary Impressions," appearing in a commemorative issue of *The Sewanee Review*, Knight relates some of his early connections with Eliot, who was editing *Criterion*.[11] In the main he viewed Eliot as a "critic," in contrast to Murry, then editing the *Adelphi*, whom he viewed as an "interpreter." Eliot's approach was "more objective and intellectual," Murry's "personal and emotional." And the essays in *The Sacred Wood* (1920) and *For Lancelot Andrewes* (1928) were "cool and urbane in manner ... objectifying, even distancing, the literatures discussed." "The prophetic element in literature," Knight adds, "all important to Murry, seemed to be scanted by Eliot. This was my impression, and there was little doubt in my mind to which camp I belonged." There was little doubt, that is, that Knight favored the position of Murry, "the apostle of a new age."

Yet it was Eliot who made possible the publication of *The Wheel of Fire*, even though his own empirical approach was not naturally attuned to Knight's "mystical interpretations." (Eliot proposed, as he wrote at the end of his "Tradition and the Individual Talent" [1919], "to halt at the frontier of metaphysics or mysticism.") Nevertheless, having received with a "degree of approval" Knight's brochure *Myth and Miracle: On the Mystic Symbolism of Shakespeare* (actually a shortened version of an earlier, unpublished, book-length manuscript, "Thaisa," "which found no support"), Eliot offered to recommend and to take Knight's other Shakespearean essays to Oxford University Press, where they were published as *The Wheel of Fire*. Knight notes how impressed he was by "the extraordinary power Eliot had even then, for though I had earlier received a dubious reply from the Press regarding the prospect of their doing such a book, a word from Eliot and all went smoothly." He was also impressed by Eliot's "generosity in so putting himself out to forward a line of research diverging from his own critical tenets."

As Knight points out, Eliot agreed that "a necessary distinction" needed to be drawn between "criticism and interpretation." When the publisher suggested that he write an introduction to *The Wheel of Fire*, he complied. This introduction "was not written from the standpoint of the essays themselves; it engaged in complications which I, rightly or wrongly, do not feel to be necessary; but the status which it gave, and still gives, my life's work has been invaluable."[12] In the Introduction, Eliot frankly admits, "It has taken me a long time to recognize the justification of what Mr. Wilson Knight calls 'interpretation.' " Not uncharacteristically he stresses, "It is also the prejudice or preference of anyone who practises, though humbly, the art of verse, to be sceptical of all 'interpretations' of poetry, even his own interpretations; and to rely upon his sense of power and accomplishment in language to guide him." He adds, "So, finally, the sceptical practitioner of verse tends to limit his criticism of poetry to the appreciation of vocabulary and syntax, the analysis of line, metric and cadence; to stick as closely to the more trustworthy senses as possible."

At the same time Eliot does not insist "that *nothing* solid and enduring can be arrived at in interpretation," though he avers "that there must be in every effort of interpretation, some part which can be accepted and necessarily some part which other readers can reject." Eliot also declares that Knight's work is of value in insisting "upon the right way to interpret poetic drama"; in pursuing "the right line for his own plane of investigation, not hypostasizing 'character' and 'plot' "; in disclosing "the results of the passive, and more critical, poetic understanding"; in not falling "into the error of presenting the work of Shakespeare as a series of mystical treatises in cryptogram, to be filed away once the cipher is read." The following words accentuate Eliot's estimation of Knight's work and suggest the reasons why he was so forceful in helping to introduce Knight to the reading public. "But I confess that reading his essays seems to me to have enlarged my understanding of the Shakespeare pattern; which, after all, is quite the main thing."

Indeed, one of the most impressive results of Knight's discovery of new depths of spiritual meaning in Shakespeare's late plays, particularly as myths of immortality, was evidenced by Eliot's poem "Marina" (1930), an inscribed copy of which he sent to Knight. Not only did Eliot, as Knight believes, compose in this poem "a perfect poetical commentary on those Shakespearian meanings which I had unveiled," but he also underlined his critical acceptance of those meanings in his essay "John Ford" (1932) and in a later essay, "To Criticize the Critic" (1961). After the publication of "Marina," furthermore, Eliot asked to see Knight's commentary on *Coriolanus*, then in preparation, for at the time he was working on a poem inspired by Beethoven's *Coriolan*. After Knight had sent him some notes, and soon afterward the entire essay, he received a reply (dated December 30, 1930) in which Eliot wrote that "what the complete essay adds for me is chiefly the detailed and convincing analysis of the type of imagery. That does increase my understanding and appreciation."

Undoubtedly he was referring to Knight's treatment of stone, metal, and city imagery in *Coriolanus*, imagery which also occurs in Eliot's "Triumphal March":

> Stone, bronze, stone, steel, stone, oakleaves, horses' heels
> Over the paving.
> And the flags. And the trumpets. And so many eagles.
> How many? Count them. And such a press of people.

Eliot was pleased, too, when in an appendix to *The Christian Renaissance* (1933) Knight wrote that Eliot's was "a small, but intense, poetic world of the same quality as Shakespeare's and Dante's." "I was honoured," Knight recalls, "when I next saw him by his evident pleasure at this brief essay by so unrenowned an expositor."

As indicated above, it was probably J. Middleton Murry who provided Knight with the greatest stimulus, who was in any case a seminal influence, in the years 1923–28 when Knight was "searching for a new direction in Shakespearian commentary." This influence appeared in various forms, viz., in Murry's articles in the *Adelphi*, which he edited, and in volumes like *Discoveries: Essays in Literary Criticism* (1924), *To the Unknown God* (1924), and *Things to Come* (1928). In an appreciative essay, Knight expresses his debt to Murry's writings of this period—writings, he emphasizes, that "acted on me like an avatar." "Here was someone who without reservations was proclaiming the religious importance of literature in a voice of authority."[13] In 1926 Murry published in the *Adelphi* two pieces by Knight, one on Wordsworth's "Immortality Ode" and another on *Julius Caesar*, "which won a competition on a point of interpretation." Additional pieces on Shakespeare were also printed in its quarterly successor, *The New Adelphi*.

That Knight should have responded so sympathetically to Murry is not difficult to comprehend when, for instance, one reads the first essay in *Discoveries*, "The Nature of Poetry," in which Murry communicates something of the enthusiasm, the mysticism, the critical genius that touch and reecho with such spark and revelation in Knight's subsequent works. In Murry, Knight sensed qualities of critical vision and energy, an attempt by a critic, to quote Murry himself, to experience the "excitement of losing oneself in exploration, the elation of being possessed by the very process of discovery ... the most precious thing ... found in criticism."

For aspiring young critics in the England of this era, there was not only the *via rata* of Eliot, but also the *via mystica* of Murry. To read Murry's contention that "the more we understand him [Shakespeare], the more we can understand the essential laws of poetic genius, and the nature of poetry itself," is to anticipate the direction of Knight's own work. To ponder the following statement—or, better, credo, for that is precisely what Murry is formulating in it—is to comprehend the nature, impact, and excitement of Murry's "discoveries" and their influence on a young critic seeking to travel a different road from that of Eliot:

> ...the fact is that there are moments when criticism of a particular kind, the only kind I care for, utterly absorbs me. I feel that I am touching a mystery. There is a wall, as it were, of dense, warm darkness before me—a darkness which is secretly alive and thrilling to the sense. This, I believe, is the reflection in myself of the darkness which broods over the poet's creative mind. It forms slowly and gradually gathers while I read his work. The sense of mystery deepens and deepens; but the quality of the mystery becomes more plain. There is a moment when, as though unconsciously and out of my control, the deeper rhythm of a poet's work, the rise and fall of the great moods which determined what he was and what he wrote, enter into me also. I feel his presence; I am obedient to it, and it seems to me as though the breathing of my spirit is at one with his.[14]

Again and again Knight expresses his debt to Murry as he describes his own emerging approach to Shakespeare. His terminology, his feeling of exhilaration, his sense of "touching a mystery" communicate the measure of his response. To achieve his own "discoveries," to which he gave the name "interpretation," Knight surmounted "the critical faculties" and accepted "what was there, in detail and major outline alike." Indeed, no words better crystallize Murry's own critical orientation. New significances and insights "were seen unrolling in the tragedies and plays of Shakespeare's final period." "I looked at images and symbols," Knight recalls, "as entities speaking in their own right, almost, one might say, out of context; and thrilled to the coming-alive of Hermione's statue as keenly as I responded to the death of Lear. My results countered what was generally supposed; but, in tune with Murry's own gospel, I refused to let the intellect interfere."

Interestingly, and paradoxically, though there was this intuitive, magnetic attraction to Murry's work, Knight found Murry's reactions becoming "less favourable." Specifically, Knight's piece on Wordsworth "contained the germ of a divergence, for in it I referred to spiritualism." Thus, when Knight's *Myth and Miracle* appeared, Murry reviewed it adversely in *The Times Literary Supplement*, as he reviewed *The Wheel of Fire* in the *Adelphi*. The latter volume, he felt, "wants to prove too much, to delve too deep. He [Knight] forgets the great maxim of Goethe: *Am farbigen Abglanz haben wir das Leben.* It is the first and last commandment in Shakespeare criticism. Delve as deep as we will, we must come back to the surface, to be sure of our own discoveries: for the surface is clean."[15]

Murry regarded Knight as too "intellectual." In turn, Knight claimed that Murry's own system lacked "the picture-language of imagination and the mystery of symbol." Knight "preferred the multi-coloured qualities of literature to the one soul-centre on which Murry concentrated." And he contended, in reply to Murry's fears of intellect, that it nevertheless could be "a glass through which we may focus reality; or as a prism to split the unsearchable golden fire into blending tints." In summarizing his essential disagreement with Murry, Knight writes:

> My divergence from Murry, as a writer, was this: he wrote from his own spiritual experience, I from the imagination. My reading of Shakespeare's last plays originated from an acceptance of what others, and sometimes my own instinct, regarded as impossible. Imagination is precisely the faculty for apprehending and accepting what is *not* covered by one's own experience. It might be said to offer substitutes for the mystical experience, and such substitutes Murry would not accept.

John Masefield's Romanes Lecture *Shakespeare and Spiritual Life* (1924) was another decisive influence on Knight, who is unfailing in citing his debt to this memorable piece of only thirty-two pages. A reading of it readily discloses why he refers to it with loyalty and respect. On its own Masefield's *Shakespeare and Spiritual Life* has lasting value; the prose has a faultless clarity and cogency that show how debilitated, how insensitive and uninspiring criticism has since become. What Leavis has said of Pound's *Cantos* (that they are "little more than a game—a game serious with the seriousness of pedantry" [16]) could just as easily describe the writing of much literary criticism today. (One is aptly reminded here also of Allen Tate's decrying "the reduction of the republic [of letters] to a raw democracy of competition and aggression . . . of 'vanity and impudence.' "[17])

Certainly, Masefield's definition of "spiritual life," that is to say "all imagined or apprehended Life which, without known, sensible, physical character, affects, or is imagined to affect, the lives of men and women in this world," has been undiminishingly sustained by Knight's own interpretation of Shakespeare's spiritual development and the spiritual truth that can be found in his work. When Masefield, speaking of *Julius Caesar* as a "visionary play," notes that "Shakespeare in all this was following his fable closely, but seeing it [life] startlingly, so that to us, as to him, the storm is the very thunder of the power of life, more than any truth, more real than any reality known to us," his words become almost prophetic glimpses of what Knight does in his interpretation of Shakespeare's tragic symbolism. When Masefield comments that Shakespeare "had . . . intense zest for the beauty and the rush of life. On the top of these two zests, sex ran in him like a sea," he seems to be looking ahead to some of Knight's most impelling and revealing "poetic interpretations."[18]

An article entitled "The Principles of Shakespeare Interpretation," appearing in the September 1928 issue of *The Shakespeare Review*, was Knight's "first published manifesto." (It is now included as Appendix E in *The Sovereign Flower*.) In a footnote acknowledgment he expresses his indebtedness to the work of A. C. Bradley, of Masefield, and of Murry, to whom, he stresses, his criticisms do not apply. In this article, Knight clearly, if not definitively, announces the "principles" of his approach to Shakespeare, as sustained in his later volumes. Emphasizing the neglect of "the imaginative quality" and "the poetic meaning" of Shakespeare's plays, he goes on to outline five main principles that he believes would enable one to appreciate Shakespeare's "poetic and irrational meaning."

First: "We should observe absolute loyalty to our aesthetic reaction to the poetry." Second: "We must start our interpretation from the thing to be interpreted . . . and beware of losing ourselves in a morass of hypotheses and abstractions." Third: "We should give more detailed attention to the individual peculiarities of each play." Fourth: "The plays from 1599 (*Julius Caesar*) to 1611 (*The Tempest*) must be regarded not only individually, but also as a succession forming a closely consecutive relationship in which groups of plays and single plays shed mutual light on each other." And fifth: "An examination and correlation of Shakespeare's poetic imagery throughout his work" should be insisted on. The essay concludes significantly: "Especially do the plays demand and provide the new necessary synthesis of religious and aesthetic experience."[19]

From the time of the publication of this essay and of his first published book, *Myth and Miracle*, Knight has been consistently occupied with the analysis and interpretation of genius. The key word that resounds in his oeuvre is "interpretation"; and for the distinctions and clarifications that he patiently and diligently draws between "interpretations" and "criticism" readers and scholars must always be grateful. The distinction must be understood if the direction of his efforts is to be grasped. These two terms are defined on the first page of Chapter I in *The Wheel of Fire*: "On the Principles of Shakespeare Interpretation."[20]

With that "unusual sincerity" (the phrase is Hardin Craig's) which inevitably stamps his work, Knight begins by noting that "criticism" to him suggests a process of objectifying a work under consideration; this process invariably includes comparisons with other and similar works, its strengths and weaknesses, its "good" as opposed to its "bad" points, its validity. Criticism is active, it looks ahead, it treats past work "as material on which to base future standards and canons of art"; or, as he states in a later piece, "Literary criticism applies *ideas* to literature from outside." Hence, in a definition that has become as memorable as it is apposite (characteristic, too, of the care and depth with which Knight writes), "Criticism is a judgment of vision."

On the other hand, "interpretation" merges in the work it analyzes, attempts to "understand its subject in the light of its own nature," avoids a discussion of a work's merits, and "makes sense of our established acceptance of them *as* works of genius." As a result "interpretation is passive, and looks back, regarding only the imperative challenge of a poetic vision." Interpretation is "a quite definite act of mind." "I would even assert that all art of highest quality *demands* interpretation." Further, he counsels that we should not strive to see "faults" in works of genius, but instead "we should interpret our original imaginative experience into the slower consciousness of logic and intellect, preserving something of that child-like faith which we possess, or should possess, in the theatre." Interpretation performs exactly "this translation from one order of consciousness to another," and in the end assists "us to live intellectually what has already been experienced and ratified spiritually, or imaginatively." As such, interpretation, uncritical and passive, metaphysical rather than ethical, "receives" the whole of a poet's vision and then "re-expresses" this experience "in its own terms." "Interpretation," Knight insists, "reveals *substances*, hitherto unsuspected, within literature." In contrast to criticism—and his statement here completes the definition quoted above—"interpretation [is] a reconstruction of vision."

Another word that Knight uses frequently is "spatial."[21] To receive the whole poetic "vision into the intellectual consciousness" and to remember the "quality of the original poetic experience," we "must be prepared to see the whole play in space as well as in time." By just devoting attention to the temporal nature of drama or by just pursuing "the steps of the tale in sequence," we tend to ignore qualities that can be of great importance; for there are throughout a play "a set of correspondences which relate to each other independently of the time-sequence which is the story" and are that which Knight sometimes calls the play's "atmosphere."

Spatial analysis in poetic drama views and elucidates atmosphere;

its first concern is with the structure, the pattern, images, symbols, and the body of a work being considered, irrespective of the exact language used. Likewise, Knight sees it as a counterbalance to the increasingly obtrusive "critical mind-structure of our time [which] has little feeling for what might be called 'other dimensions' of being." "My use of the word 'spatial,' " he asserts, "really means just this: we must not let ourselves be *limited* by the temporal approach." The "spatial" approach, which, incidentally, Milton employed in his treatment of the New Testament in *De Doctrina Christiana*,

> performs a necessary function *beyond* what has already been accomplished by the poet. It is not content with what the poetry *says*; it attempts to reveal the meaning of what it *is*. It tends to see effects in depth, as significant in their own right, and not merely as logical or narrative links, though once attained, the new insight reacts sharply on logic and narrative.[22]

Striving to elucidate " 'other dimensions' of being" and to disclose "harmonies" and "substances," which criticism per se overlooks, Knight has not restricted his studies to Shakespeare. He has made analyses of Milton, Swift, and Byron in *The Burning Oracle* (1939); of Wordsworth, Coleridge, Shelley, and Keats in *The Starlit Dome* (1941); of Pope in *Laureate of Peace* (1954); and of John Cowper Powys in *The Saturnian Quest* (1964). His work, moreover, has depended on seeing and taking seriously supernatural and spiritual elements (e.g., in *Cymbeline* or in John Masefield's *King Cole* and *Melloney Holtspur*) which are generally dismissed. No literary student, he believes, can ignore "the more occult significances in which our dramatic and poetic traditions are saturated." And as he has established in *The Golden Labyrinth* (1962), Greek and Renaissance drama and the plays of Byron, Beddoes, Ibsen, and Masefield have found the occult "a natural language." Knight's most comprehensive statement regarding the relation of spiritualism to both Christianity and Renaissance literature occurs in the Epilogue to the 1962 reissue of *The Christian Renaissance*.

Knight's strong interest in Byron—"our greatest poet in the widest sense of the term since Shakespeare"—is attested to by three books: *Lord Byron: Christian Virtues* (1952), *Lord Byron's Marriage: The Evidence of Asterisks* (1957), and *Byron and Shakespeare* (1966). In the first he is concerned with Byron's personality and with the "dominant themes" and "dominant images" in the plays or poems. A corrective to existing biographies, this study captures Byron's greatness and seeks to put an end to some of the "misunderstandings" connected with his life and thought. "In his comprehensive personality," Knight observes, "nothing is omitted. . . . At any instant of his life all ages, and both sexes, all human compulsions, good and evil are co-present. In this sense he is the eternal, the universal man."[23]

In the second book, essentially a sequel to *Lord Byron: Christian Virtues*, Knight examines Byron's "vices," though by no means does he condemn the man. Rather, he questions some of the assumptions surrounding Byron's marriage and subsequent separation from his wife, primarily the assumption that the terrible secret of Byron's life was his incestuous relationship with his half-sister, Augusta Leigh. The secret, according to Knight, must be seen as lying "somewhere within the area of homosexuality," and he documents his findings eloquently and honestly, without in any way broaching the sensational as he brings out the "bisexual temperament" not only of Byron but of Lady Byron as well. (Elsewhere, with special reference to Powys, Oscar Wilde, Rupert Brooke, T. E. Lawrence, and T. S. Eliot, Knight has also written in detail of "the compulsion on man of the bisexual, or seraphic, vision which, though transmitted through human figures, speaks from a dimension beyond the biological."[24])

In *Byron and Shakespeare*, Knight continues with the task of displaying the truth that "Byron was the nearest personality we know of to what Nietzsche envisioned in his 'over-man.' " In the main he shows how Byron's life, thought, and "protagonist consciousness"—far from being either "disorderly" or "uninteresting," as T. S. Eliot believed—"expands Shakespeare." "We begin to understand what Shakespeare, what all great drama, is *for*: it exists for a human, and more than human, purpose, of which Byron is the exemplar." Above all, Knight feels, Byron's "universe, the world of his contemplation, was superficially at least far larger and more confusing than Shakespeare's; but what he did about it was, in both sweep and detail, Shakespearian." Knight is as much concerned with Byron the man as with Byron the poet, though, he admits, that with most poets it is dangerous to mix up biographical details with the fruits of their genius. With Byron the problem is profoundly different, for

> Any one of his greater poems can, like all poetry, be read in and as itself alone; but if we choose to relate it to his life there is no danger whatsoever of reducing it to a lower order since *his life exists in the poetic dimension*, and is itself potentially authoritative. That is the great, yet simple, difference. As a result the poetry, already great, becomes yet greater when related to his life; and his life and poetry together make something for which we have no name of staggering importance.[25]

What must be understood, Knight emphasizes in concentrating on Byron's "Shakespearian qualities," is that he was "kaleidoscopic," with good, evil, violence, innocence, worldliness, and asceticism mingling in his being. By turns or simultaneously he was Hamlet, Puck, Macbeth, Falstaff, Antony, Timon, Prospero—"an amazing comprehensiveness in strict correspondence to the main themes and persons of Shakespearian drama." And yet he was "a single, recognizable man," a literary genius tending naturally toward variety—a supremely synthesizing variety of the kind Keats well described: "Men of genius are great as certain ethical chemicals operating on the Mass of neutral intellect—but they have not any individuality, any determined Character—I would call the top and head of those who have a proper self Men of Power."[26]

Knight sees Byron as "a man of some new order, as yet unrecognized," whose ancestry can be traced to Greek tragedy, to Shakespeare's "dramatic supermen," to Dante, Milton, and Swift, men who tried "to inject literary genius into the world of politics and action." Surpassing the great figures of the past, Byron "is a hinge towards the future, pointing on to Ibsen and Nietzsche, both of whom had sense of a new kind of man in process of creation; and both were influenced by Byron." He points to what Ibsen in 1887 spoke of as "The Third Empire":

> I believe that poetry, philosophy and religion will be fused into a new
> category and a new vital force. . . . Particularly and especially do I be
> lieve that the ideals of our age, in passing away, are tending toward that
> which in my drama *Emperor and Galilean* I have tentatively called
> "The Third Empire."[27]

The difficulties of summing up, let alone appraising, the achievement of a scholar who has combined teaching with continuing and original work in criticism are many and complicated. But what is certain is that our debts to Knight are numerous; that even when these debts are ignored—for though his findings are echoed and borrowed by other critics, he is not always acknowledged—it is probably because we have, consciously and unconsciously, assimilated the wisdom and the illumination of his interpretations. It is the case, really, of a great master, to whom we gradually grow up.

During the past forty years, as his writings have appeared and as the variety of his responses to literature has richly expanded—and this in spite of the modern curse of "specialization" among men of letters—Knight's two greatest qualities of openness and inspiration have remained constant. In this respect he is a teacher of positive critical lessons, of the kind that literary scholarship sorely needs if it is to survive in an increasingly mechanical and de-creative age. Roy Walker's remark in *The Time Is Free. A Study of Macbeth*, that "The warmth of imagination that startled the literary world . . . when *The Wheel of Fire* first appeared is characteristic of the man as of his works,"[28] is made more meaningful when we consider Knight's view of his own efforts:

> *I have instinctively kept clear of the religious and mystical poets; also Blake, Yeats. . . .* WHY?? I have instead run after Shakespeare, Milton, Pope, Byron, Masefield. I like best those who are warm with human instincts and involvements, including *sex* and *politics*, or *adventure*. The point is, there must be *interpenetration*. . . . Also I like things simple, and prefer Powys to Joyce. . . . Powys of course is difficult in one way, but his language is *simple*—I don't like to be bothered in matters of communication and the unravellings of modern language complexities. I like what is *simple, sensuous*, and *spiritual*; colour, the elements, etc. I do not like *intellectual* conundrums—my mind is childish in a way.[29]

"Loyalty to the imagination"; the necessity of seeing "symbolic literature" with an "imaginative apprehension"; "our need of imaginative understanding: first of the prophets and poets, and next of life itself"; acceptance of the fact that all great literature is prophetic since it points to and creates the future—these are what Knight emphasizes in interpretations that ultimately constitute "a severely disciplined speculation." Hence, his pervasive concern is with ways of bringing out, of epiphanizing, as it were, the full, resplendent powers of the imagination, of the visionary process that becomes a work of art. Criticism, he shows, can violate and distort this vision by becoming a terminal, objectifying "ratiocinative process," and thus in its own peculiar manner becomes part of the destructive element. Interpretation, in transcending this element, harmonizes with the creative spirit of great writers. Even more, it encourages great art in the wonderful ways that Masefield envisioned when he wrote:

> Great art does not proceed from a great criticism, but from great encouragement. The great mind being given his opportunity, does great things, and it is from these that criticism derives such principles as it has. The great times of art are those when power has the intelligence to encourage it.[30]

Masefield's words epitomize the purpose and significance of Knight's work and should answer the critics who deprecate the goals of such interpretation. The mystery of literature cannot be fathomed by rationalist methodologies, for unquestionably it contains numinous qualities (and experiences) which defy circumscription. Critical "balance" and "judgment," as such, are not legitimate properties of interpretation, inasmuch as the interpreter is neither "discriminating" nor "evaluating" works of art. The encouragement, the reconstruction, the intensification of imaginative vision, after all, require the kind of energy and sensibility which only a gifted interpreter possesses. The process of interpretation is close to the creative process, which it does not judge but encourages and with which it merges. "It behoves everybody," again to quote Masefield, "to strive with the imagination, because only so do the Helpers come down to this earth; where many are striving, many help."[31] This "striving with the imagination" becomes the overwhelming task of interpretation, as Knight has consistently demonstrated, and transforms the relationship between a great artist and his interpreter into an adamantine *philia*.

The principles of interpretation return us ultimately to the attitudes of Longinus, particularly to the attitude that great writing "affects the reader not to persuade but to entrance," and when "fitly expressed, pierce[s] everything like a flash of lightning."[32] As an interpreter Knight is concerned with bringing to consciousness the experience of literature. "This is what good literature is for; not to serve the cause, or meet the demands of literary criticism," he maintains, "nor to provide the scholar with a living, but to distend and enlarge our minds, or souls."[33] No statement could better serve as an epigraph to the whole of his work or better testify to the dignity of literature, which Knight affirms with steadfastness and genuine passion.

21

The Leavisite Rubrics

*What governed our thinking and engaged our sense of urgency was
the inclusive, the underlying and overriding, preoccupation: the preoccupation with the critical function as it was performed, or not performed, for our civilization, our time, and us.*

—F. R. LEAVIS

Between 1932 and 1953 there appeared an English critical quarterly
called *Scrutiny*. Its founder was Dr. Frank Raymond Leavis (b. 1895),
and its editorial center, and indeed its center of being, was Cambridge
University. Its principal subject was the whole range of English literature. Its impelling concern was with "the business of criticism" and
the need for promulgating "standards," "discipline," "discrimination," "intelligence," "values"—words characterizing the significance
of two decades of literary (re)valuations by the "Scrutineers" (Dr.
Leavis, Q. D. Leavis [his wife], L. C. Knights, D. W. Harding, John
Peter, H. A. Mason, W. H. Mellers, R. G. Cox, James Smith, Denys
Thompson, D. A. Traversi, et al.). Its assessments were invariably
brilliant, invariably controversial, and to some, e.g., the Philistines,
distasteful. Its honesty, severity, polemicism, its refusal to compromise, its rejection of established literary reputations (and conventions), its fierce moral tone—such made *Scrutiny* something of an
"outlaws' enterprise," to use Leavis' own words. Its disdain for "theoretical criticism" and literary history, for belletristic, aesthetic, impressionistic, theological, and formalistic critical approaches, for the
dilettante literary attitudes of the Bloomsbury group, and for "the
major *trahison des clercs* of the *Criterion*," a quarterly edited by T. S.
Eliot from 1922 to 1939, was rooted in what has been termed "the
realist-empiricist tradition." Its inspiration came, of course, from "a
social critic of the radical missionary tradition"[1]—from a Cambridge
teacher and critic, a genius himself, Dr. Leavis.

In its lifetime *Scrutiny* enjoyed much fame and sympathy, as would
be expected of a journal defying the literary and academic establish-

ments. Against strong opposition, with paltry material resources, and in a situation that contained the conditions of a war (the Scrutineers on one side struggling against an entrenched coterie on the other side, the latter composed of the "Bloomsburies," the dry-as-dust academics, the London journalists, the Sunday reviewers, etc.—a militant republican spirit versus a decaying patrician spirit), *Scrutiny* battled for survival. What *Scrutiny* was attempting was not unprecedented: to give a sustaining moral direction to the study of literature and thus to the basic cultural artifacts of English life which had the Great War and the disillusionments of the 1920's in the immediate background; to give, that is, a moral consciousness and revitalization to society in a period demanding a value system resistant to failure of nerve, or heart, to deterioration and life-emptiness (precisely the breakdown re-created in D. H. Lawrence's *Women in Love*, in T. S. Eliot's *The Waste Land*, in Ezra Pound's *Hugh Selwyn Mauberley*— works that Leavis and his followers admired for their diagnoses of Western civilization). Earlier, in 1925-27, there was the *Calendar of Modern Letters*, which sought for "standards of criticism" to overcome growing social and cultural disintegration. And, too, there were the efforts of John Middleton Murry, who in his monthly *Adelphi* and in his book *Aspects of Literature* (1922) perceived "a sense of the needed [literary] direction." "But some lack of mental toughness," G. Wilson Knight has observed, "some failure in self-trust, prevented his developing it in terms that would smash the opacities of the contemporary intellect."[2]

Scrutiny succeeded where the *Calendar of Modern Letters* had failed; and Leavis exemplified that "mental toughness" and "self-trust" which failed Murry and which were indispensable to a journal that—according to the *Times Literary Supplement*, itself an object of derision in *Scrutiny* through the years—"in effect presented an entirely fresh approach to the history of English literature."[3] When *Scrutiny* ceased publication in 1953, it had succeeded in "placing" the works of creative artists; in holding the interest of teachers and scholars alike; in influencing critical studies; in making its energizing authority felt in education and in the practice of criticism both in England and abroad. World War II, obviously, heightened the quarterly's problems, and the consequences of the war were telling in dispersing "the connection of collaborators and contributors." "The post-war world was," Leavis wrote in his "Valedictory" editorial, "a preoccupying and distracting one for those who came back to civilian life." (Nevertheless, it is the experience of the Great War which figures more largely in the background of *Scrutiny* and of Leavis than that of World War II.)

In 1963 *Scrutiny* was reissued by the Cambridge University Press in twenty volumes, with an index and a retrospect. This reprinting was prompted not only by a demand for copies of the journal but also by a recognition of its permanent value. What had started out as a revolutionary movement in criticism had thus ended in acceptance; it was a vindication of what *Scrutiny* had stood for and struggled for, and a personal victory for its founder, Leavis, as a "reformer of English sensibility," as Frank Kermode has expressed it.[4] ". . . I've lived a life of battle—battle for what I stand for and battle for a living," Leavis wrote to this writer, in a letter dated September 21, 1970. "It has been *distrait* and often desperate: it's only these half-dozen yeas that I have been admitted to respectability (for which I didn't ask)." By and large the response to the reprinting was enthusiastic, though dissent was heard. Writing in the *New Yorker*, in a long review under the title "Insurrection," Harold Rosenberg asserted: "It was plain from the start that *Scrutiny* had set itself against Progress, democracy, and political liberalism, and that it occupied a sector in the battle line of anti-modernism established by *L'Action Française*, the New Humanism, the classicism-royalism-Catholicism formula of T. S. Eliot, the literary agrarianism of the Old South, and the cultural Fascism." Leavis' own rancor, he also suggested with befuddled naïveté, "made him a moral ancestor of Britain's angry young men."[5]

I quote Rosenberg in order to underline the strong feelings ignited by *Scrutiny* and to instance the kind of rantings that all along have led to a misunderstanding of Leavis and of his quarterly. (Here, Leavis' statement that "Where serious standards have lapsed, the insignificant [in criticism as well as elsewhere] can enjoy an importance to which otherwise they would aspire in vain" is a rejoinder that comes to mind with respect to Rosenberg.) Still, the general response to Leavis and to *Scrutiny*, before and after its republication, has been consistently serious and intelligent, complementing the seriousness and intelligence which Leavis' oeuvre and *Scrutiny* have instilled in the study and criticism of literature. Two well-argued chapters, "F. R. Leavis: Reality and Sincerity" and "F. R. Leavis: Impersonality and Values," in Vincent Buckley's book *Poetry and Morality* (London, 1959); a long, thoroughly researched essay, "Better History and Better Criticism: The Significance of F. R. Leavis," by G. S. Singh, in Volume 16 of Mario Praz's *English Miscellany: A Symposium of History, Literature, and the Arts* (Rome, 1965); and a valuable and objective study, "The Literary Criticism of Frank Raymond Leavis," by René Wellek, in *Literary Views*, edited by Carroll Camden (Chicago, 1964), are sound appraisals of Leavis' achievement. Also, *F. R. Leavis: Some Aspects of His Work*, edited by C. D. Narasimhaiah (Mysore, India, 1963), and devoted entirely to Leavis, contains helpful articles by Seymour Betsky, William Walsh, J. C. F. Littlewood, as well as by the editor. This book concludes with an essay by Leavis himself, "A Note on the Critical Function."

Earlier I spoke of the misunderstanding that sometimes surrounds Leavis and his Scrutineers. This misunderstanding arises from Leavis' overall style and tone as seen in his critical methodology or approach. At the center of his criticism, what lends to it both its stimulants and its constituents—its response and its idiom, its disquisition, its prose, its style, in a word—is Leavis' belief that in the criticism of literature "a judgment is personal or it is nothing; you cannot take over someone else's. The implicit form of a judgment is: This is so, isn't it? The question is an appeal for confirmation that the thing is *so*; implicitly that, though expecting, characteristically, an answer in the form, 'yes, but—,' the 'but' standing for qualifications, reserves, corrections." Such a concept dictates a style that seeks to persuade in rational, disinterested terms of composition—in terms focused on and excited by a passion for honesty (with D. H. Lawrence as the exemplar) and impersonality (with T. S. Eliot as the commanding voice)—for what Leavis terms a "transcendent impersonalizing intelligence," to which both writer and critic must submit imaginatively and critically. Displays of emotion, or what Leavis calls the "sentimental debauch"; hankerings for cute, memorable phrases, for light touches and humor; surrenders to rhetoric and impressionistic fancies, the "declamatory generality"; appeals to sophistication and smart poses of one sort or another—these are antipathetic to Leavis as discordant elements which produce the sham and the shallowness that he detects in a Rupert Brooke and a Lytton Strachey. His is a style, then, that becomes a metamorphosing process of intelligence and that in many ways characterizes the tutorial approach of a didactic.

Responses to such a style, to both its prose and content, have not always been favorable. Philip Rahv believes that Leavis "is plagued by all the defects of his virtues. What I have in mind is not his plain speaking, of course, but rather the *esprit de sérieux* animating many of his critical pronouncements. It expresses itself in a kind of provincial moralism (by no means to be equated with the 'marked moral intensity' he so esteems in his literary preferences), a protestant narrowness of sensibility."[6] Frank Swinnerton complains of Leavis' style as one "in which sentences, already involved, are swelled and made uncouth by parenthesis and divagation."[7] Father Martin Jarrett-Kerr, complaining on this same score, suggests that it is a style that takes it cue, and thus its faults, from Henry James, a Leavis favorite.[8] George Steiner observes that Leavis' writing has "a kind of noble ugliness and points a finger of Puritan scorn at the false glitter of Pater." "His refusal of elegance is the expression of a deep, underlying Puritanism."[9]

Perhaps the best illustration of Leavis at his fiercest is his Richmond Lecture, delivered at Downing College, Cambridge, on February 28, 1962, and later published in the *Spectator* under the title "The Significance of C. P. Snow." The content and the repercussions of this lecture are by now familiar; we need only recall a few of its statements which have a bearing on the matter of Leavis' style, which for some readers returns to a polemical pamphleteering tradition. Taking issue with Snow's 1959 Rede Lecture, *The Two Cultures and the Scientific Revolution*, also given at Cambridge University, Leavis cites Snow as a portent of our time (an "intellectual nullity"), characterized "not by insight and spiritual energy but by blindness and automatism. He doesn't know what he means, and doesn't know he doesn't know. This is what his intoxicating sense of a message and a public function, his inspiration, amounts to." Above all, "he doesn't know what literature is"; even "as a novelist he doesn't exist; he doesn't begin to exist."[10] For many, the attack on Snow further illustrated what *Scrutiny* had all along illustrated: a style, a tone, that was "severe," "angry," "scornful," "harsh," "quarrelsome" (in some respects echoing the strident note in D. H. Lawrence, whose novels Leavis ranks in "the great tradition" along with those of Jane Austen, Joseph Conrad, George Eliot, and Henry James). Aldous Huxley, opposing Leavis' views on Snow, resented the "violent and ill-mannered, the one-track, moralistic literarism of the Richmond Lecture."[11]

T. S. Eliot called Leavis "the Critic as Moralist."[12] Most literary scholars agree that Leavis is concerned essentially with the "moral imagination" and the "moral consciousness." (J. B. Priestley, whose writings Leavis had declared not worth reading, life being too short, terms Leavis "a sort of Calvinist theologian of contemporary culture."[13]) The critical act, Leavis believes, predicates "moral discrimination, and judgment of relative human value." In time the critic will be forced to become "explicitly a moralist" concerned with the "possibilities of life" ("life" being a term that according to both

Wellek and Eliseo Vivas lacks clear-cut definition as employed by Leavis); and "criticism, when it performs its function, not merely expresses and defines the contemporary sensibility, it helps to form it." Leavis' preoccupation with this moral sense of life can be discerned in *New Bearings in English Poetry*, in *The Great Tradition*, in *The Common Pursuit*, and in *D. H. Lawrence: Novelist*—studies in which he delivers moral judgments with such astringency, it is claimed, that his criticism takes on the character of a sermon. In this connection Leavis' moral criticism must be seen as a reaction to the Bloomsbury ethos emerging from the war of 1914–18, and it is for this reason that his work must also be read in the light of that war and its aftermath—the cultural malaise which, Leavis charges, Bloomsbury, as "the hardly questioned centre of the literary world— the conscious controlling centre of taste, enlightenment, and higher fashioned," purveyed in a world that lay morally disoriented and broken. Nor would it miss the mark to underline the so-called republican source of strength in Leavis' own temper, as it infoms his sensibility and cultural point of view, his own "Englishness," innately nonconformist and puritan, in opposition to the Bloomsbury "gang" and to the gentlemanly spirit of, say, a Sir Harold Nicolson or a Lord David Cecil. "Anglo-Saxon moralist" or "Anglo-Saxon rebel," Leavis evinces in his writings, to quote Martin Green's *A Mirror for Anglo-Saxons* (London, 1961), a puritanism (which makes more meaningful Leavis' admiration of Lawrence), "taking that to mean a concern with right and wrong so keen as to set the tone of the whole personality, an eagerness to draw sharp, exclusive lines, mapping out as much as possible of the world, a distrust of all connoisseurship in experience, all aestheticism."

If I have dwelled at such length on matters relating to Leavis and to the form and method of his criticism, I have done so to facilitate the discussion of the two books at hand. For what I have said up to this point achieves its necessary crystallization, its confirmation, in an examination of *A Selection from Scrutiny*.* For those who cannot afford the entire set, this *Selection* can serve the purpose, although Leavis says "it is not offered as a representative anthology." (A glance at the section headings tells us otherwise.) In fact, these two volumes reflect the primary critical positions of *Scrutiny* and of Leavis himself, as found consubstantially in his various books since 1930, from the appearance of *Mass Civilization and Minority Culture* through

*Comp. F. R. Leavis. 2 vols. (Cambridge, Eng., 1968).

the more recently published *Nor Shall My Sword*. These volumes contain not only the style and tone but, more importantly, the critical pattern and doctrines. As such, these volumes contain paradigmatic principles of criticism—the Leavisite Rubrics, so to speak. Needless to say, it is helpful to add these volumes to the canon.

The essays and reviews included delineate the critical directions taken by *Scrutiny* over the years, though no chronological pattern of selection is attempted. Rather, the value of this *Selection* lies in its thematic makeup and temper. Volume I begins with an examination of "The Cambridge Tradition," with all the essays written by Mrs. Leavis, whose combination of a brilliant mind and an acid pen makes for lively reading at the expense of a debilitating academicism in dons like George Gordon, "a green bay-tree specimen," and Walter Raleigh, "the most dangerous kind of academic." In contrast to the "academic politicians," Mrs. Leavis gives an admiring picture of Sir Leslie Stephen as a positive aspect of "Cambridge Criticism." "We believe with Stephen," she writes, "that literary criticism is not a mystic rapture but a process of the intelligence." This section of the book reminds us of Leavis' battles at Cambridge over English studies, their philosophy and teaching, and of the completely understandable anger and anguish that infuse statements like these: "But it is the academic with no vocation for teaching—with nothing to teach—who enjoys the power that can be exercised in committee rooms" and "The answer does seem to be that the academic world, like other worlds, is run by the politicians, and sensitively scrupulous people tend to leave politics to other people, while people with genuine work to do certainly have no time as well as no taste for committee-rigging and the associated techniques." (A detailed treatment of the subject is found in Leavis' highly influential book *Education and the University*.)

Other parts deal with T. S. Eliot, whose earlier criticism (*The Sacred Wood* and *Homage to John Dryden*, for example) is judged more penetrating and valuable than his later work (in essays such as "Thoughts After Lambeth," "Religion and Literature," "Modern Education and the Classics," as well as in his book *Notes Towards the Definition of Culture*), when Eliot, "de-routed," had "gone outside literature"; with William Butler Yeats, in whom there is, after 1930, a "slackening of tension" and a growing inability to sustain "the taut, delicate and difficult complexity" of "Sailing to Byzantium"; with Ezra Pound, who, in spite of his past services to literature, has increasingly exhibited in his writings (*How To Read, Active Anthology*) an absence of critical intelligence and "has become as incapable of disinterested re-orientation as the 'bureaucrats' whom he scorns"; with post-Eliot poets who are judged to have failed to develop, e.g., William Empson ("the exhibition of a fine intelligence applied and misapplied"), W. H. Auden ("immature," "adolescent"; "such a spectacle of dissolution must be profoundly depressing, even tragic"), and Dylan Thomas ("his progress has been swift, confident, and disastrous"). Still other sections set out to debunk T. E. Hulme ("as a thinker he was essentially an amateur"), Wyndham Lewis (he is called "a symptom, not a leader, of the age"), Lytton Strachey ("incapable of creation in life or literature, his writings were his substitute for both"), John Maynard Keynes ("he promoted in enormously influential ways the habit of substituting the social-personal values for the relevant ones"), Dorothy Sayers (her fiction "isn't mere detective story of an unimpressive kind, it is exactly that: stale, second-hand, hollow"), Stephen Spender (he has "an essential lack of literary gift, and a bent for cliché and ineptitude"). And throughout are attacks on persons and institutions comprising "the literary racket": Alan Pryce-Jones and the *Times Literary Supplement*, the British Council and the BBC, Bloomsbury and the Sunday papers. Mrs. Leavis, commenting on Edward Marsh, exemplifies the acrimonious tone of *Scrutiny*'s indictment of "the literary racket": "He is a beautiful specimen, a perfect litmus-paper without, as a literary critic, any individuality, personal taste or character."

Underlining all these attacks is Leavis' belief that there has been a steady breakdown of "serious standards in literary criticism." What these standards should be, in poetry for example, Leavis provides in three essays, "Thought and Emotional Quality," "Imagery and Movement," and "Reality and Sincerity." The great poet, he stresses, must refuse "the ready-made, the illusory and the spectral in the way of conceptual apparatus," and "keep his abstractions so fully charged with the concrete of experience and his thinking so unquestionably faithful to it." What criticism, on the other hand, should strive to emulate is to be found in the example set by Matthew Arnold, whose "critical intelligence" and "critical standards," in consonance with his idea of "centrality," provide the guidelines for a genuine critical spirit.

Volume II displays less virulent attitudes than Volume I does, perhaps because the latter can be seen as sounding the clarion call and, from an emotive angle, as proclaiming the conditions of the war with literary racketeers. Volume I traces the battle lines, reconnoiters the terrain, identifies the enemies, indicates the goals, shouts the commands—in short, declares war and begins action. Volume II contains the campaigns. In this volume are found some of *Scrutiny's* "revaluations," including Mrs. Leavis' remarkable essays on the writings of Jane Austen, essays that exemplify at their objective best the critical desiderata insisted upon by *Scrutiny*. Here, too, novelists are "placed": Richard Jefferies "goes further than any Victorian novelist towards the modern novel . . . the novel that seems to have significance for us other than as a mirror of manners and morals." Henry James and Edith Wharton are singled out for literary excellences: "The American novel grew up with Henry James and achieved a tradition with Mrs. Wharton." In contrast, Ernest Hemingway is judged as having the "values of a disintegrating society . . . a means of avoiding the complexity of human relations, of avoiding the necessity of living." Dorothy Richardson is seen as overpraised. George Gissing "is an example of how disastrous it may be for a writer whose talent is not of the first order to be born into a bad tradition." Virginia Woolf, after *To the Lighthouse*, shows "how little of human experience—how little of life—comes within . . . [her] scope."

In Volume II there is also a section, "The History of Critical Journalism," containing two essays by R. G. Cox on the "Great Reviews" and one essay by Denys Thompson on "A Hundred Years of Higher Journalism." Cox's contributions are particularly good. With reference to the nineteenth-century journals *Edinburgh Review, Quarterly Review,* and *Blackwood's Magazine,* Cox shows how "a serious, intelligent and responsible journalism" existed that helped to provide (1) a focus for current movements of thought and opinion, (2) "a means of livelihood and a field of action for the middleman," and (3) "an authoritative expression of critical standards." The great reviews, he feels, made it "still possible to write for the reading public as a whole" and to formulate at the same time critical judgments that disclose "a concern for the maintenance of the highest standards of thought and feeling" and "critical vigilance" and "standards of taste" "when faced with the unequal, the mediocre, or the utterly worthless." Cox's appraisal of the values of these famous reviews summarizes the values of *Scrutiny,* the inheritor and enhancer of the legacy.

Undoubtedly Leavis personifies hard critical positions constituting, in one critic's word, an "absolutism."[14] Steiner observes that "criticism must be, by Leavis' own definition, both central and humane. In his achievement the centrality is manifest; the humanity has often been tragically absent."[15] Leonard Woolf claims that "poor Dr. Leavis, who seems never able to keep going at all without someone to hate, has always happily found a willing Aunt Sally in Bloomsbury."[16] Certainly these protestations are not without their informing reasons. But Leavis' style and tone are grounded on a "critical consciousness" that eschews any moral hedgings. There is, Leavis insists in his *Mass Civilization and Minority Culture*, a small literary minority that, *pace* Snow's cultural thesis, is always capable of expressing, and must express, "unprompted, first-hand judgments." Upon this minority, which found a voice in *Scrutiny*, depends the power of profiting by the great experience of the past, as well as the continuity of "the implicit standards that order the finer living of an age, the sense that this is worth more than that, this rather than that is the direction in which to go, that the centre is here rather than there."

Such standards necessarily exempt no one from censure, and they point to the truth of Buckley's contention that in Leavis there appears "a trend which leads to a position of an almost religious kind."[17] Organic in this "religious" element is the moral strength, if not the moral ferocity, of Leavis' judgments. Thus F. W. Bateson is criticized for recommending Wellek and Warren's *Theory of Literature*: "And why does Mr. Bateson speaks of the 'thoroughness, the usefulness' and the 'general good sense' of Wellek and Warren's *Theory of Literature*? To have suggested that the student may go hopefully to it for help or enlightenment is an irresponsibility that ought to trouble Mr. Bateson's conscience. There are too many of these conventional values which, once established, are perpetuated by inertia, and it is *not* the function of criticism to countenance them." Harry T. Moore is reprimanded for presuming to dedicate *The Collected Letters of D. H. Lawrence* (1962) to Richard Aldrington, David Garnett, and Lawrence Pollinger: "Who is Professor Harry T. Moore, one asks, and what standing does he suppose he has in relation to the genius of whom he has taken academic possession, that he should dedicate a collection of Lawrence's letters? ... But Professor Moore takes over Lawrence as an established classic on whom he has been able to consolidate his own position as an 'authority' with immediate academic credit and munificent institutional support."[18] In statements like these we recognize the hard moral core of Leavis' criticism. Indeed, it is doubtful that he could ever relent from his critical positions to reveal the mellow and ingratiating qualities that inhere in, say, T. S. Eliot's essay "To Criticize the Critic."[19] Human warmth and grace per se are alien to Leavis and his followers insofar as these qualities do not lend themselves to a moral criticism of literature that, self-limited and -limiting, ignores metaphysical elements and, as Lionel Trilling points out, "those aspects of art which are gratuitous, which arise from high spirits and the impulse to play."[20]

For the shortcomings in Leavis' criticism we have cause for regret. Magnanimity, after all, is not without its place in the humane tradition of learning.[21] But genius, *mutatis mutandis*, has its failings. In the end, I think, we shall remember Leavis (and *Scrutiny*) not for his hardness, or his harassments, but for disciplining us in how to read; for trying to save us from that "spiritual Philistinism" with its "implicit belief that the only reality we need take account of in ordering human affairs is what can be measured, aggregated and averaged";[22] for helping us to travel beyond the shadow line separating what is dull and dead from what is compellingly alive in our responses to literature as it has its significances and values in our lives and ultimately in the continuity of our culture. No student of English literature, and surely of *any* literature, can ignore the nature of this achievement in all its greatness of strength and integrity.

It is within the province, indeed it is within the nature of prompting critical responsibility itself, for literary critics, as Leavis often points out, to respond to the great cultural problems of the world— of civilization at large. Matthew Arnold exemplified this critical dimension in the nineteenth century. In this century T. S. Eliot is cited as the exemplar, for his critical writings are both literary and "sociological." The latter adjective is perhaps not the best to use, but it is the one most likely to evoke a writer's extra-literary—or is it interdisciplinary?—concern with cultural problems as a whole, with what is and what makes for civilization, its orientation, its directions, its values and essences. Eliot, in any event, spoke out concerning political, economic, religious, educational, and social issues. His views are generally labeled as "conservative." He has even been attacked as a fascist by "enlightened" liberals, that is, by the liberal ideologues who object to any standards that may apply to themselves. But Eliot is now dead, and his fate at the hands of these spokesmen speaks for itself. (Yet in some ways this fate has been paradoxical, even as Eliot created the paradox, for as editor of *The Criterion* he made it possible for a curiously Marxizing position to be stated in the review section of his journal because of the writers to whom books were assigned— and positions thus postulated.)

Leavis is the only other modern critic who shares with Eliot the honor of representing the critical discipline at its influential best. Together these two men provide a picture of great practicing critics writing in the English language, concerned with the formulation and the maintenance of "standards of discrimination," with specifying principles, and with a discipline to adhere to in terms of constantly coalescing literary and cultural positions. Ultimately, it should be said, Eliot's profoundest strength appeared in his creative work, in his poems from *The Waste Land* to his greatest triumph, the *Four Quartets.* As a critic he was often divided and unsure of himself (with exceptions, no doubt, as his essays on the "Metaphysical Poets" and on the Elizabethan dramatists show)—the "cleft" Eliot, in other words, who irritated his friend Paul Elmer More. Eliot's essential heroism was not, in the end, critical but creative. As a critic he had his special loyalties and weaknesses (of inconstancy and of inconsistency), refined and purified only when the creative impulse took over as a total impersonalizing process of critical intelligence. The point is that Eliot lacked the vital inner strength able to guard him against the compromises in essays like that on a parlor-figure like Charles Whibley, or even in plays like *The Cocktail Party*—and that made him, to the acquiescing social (and coterie) world of his time the "Great Tom."

Eliot's greatness is not being questioned here. Rather, these necessarily qualifying references have their comparative force in establishing the critical place and worth of Leavis. For what Eliot lacked was a vigor, a critical heroism enabling him to overcome the Bloomsbury ethos:[23] e.g., to see Virginia Woolf's limitations as an artist, or to measure the mediocrity of David Garnett's novels, or, above all, to count D. H. Lawrence among the really great novelists of the age. It is precisely that power of conviction, of integrity, that Leavis has disclosed during the last forty years. Critically, socially (for the two go together), Eliot refused, or was emotionally unable, to pay the price that Leavis has been willing to pay in order to uphold his critical function with the honest severity that empowers it. Leavis' criticism has that kind of completeness that Eliot's has only erratically displayed. One need only study Leavis's *oeuvre* from, say, *New Bearings in English Poetry* to *English Literature in our Time and the University* to *Nor Shall My Sword* to understand the critical strengths that are not consistently there in, say, Eliot's *The Use of Poetry and the Use of Criticism, After Strange Gods, On Poetry and Poets.* There is in Leavis' work a constant refusal to compromise, to be a party to the *trahison des clercs,* in which single phrase, incidentally, is summed up some of the most glaring and even perverse manifestations of the critical stance that George Orwell possibly had in mind (after his early failures to find a publisher for his *Animal Farm,* which even Eliot's Faber and Faber rejected) when he complained that the liberal fears liberty and the intellectual strives to do dirt on the intellect.

There is, it will be seen, a correlation between Orwell's complaint and Leavis' continuing complaints in *Nor Shall My Sword*, in that they both have a common enemy in the heralds of modern progressivist enlightenment who reduce life to sheer material measurement, whether as a "New Deal" or as a "Great Society." Ideologues of enlightenment, wielding mighty political power (and found, ironically enough, in *all* political camps), often formulate their schemes for human progress without concern for any cultural and moral consequences. They fail, as Leavis insists, to engage in the "creative questioning"—"What for—what ultimately for? What, ultimately, do men live by?"—that must define the limits of mere "social hope" and that should, in the end, inform its deepest values. "But life in the civilization of an age for which such creative questioning is not done and is not influential on general sensibility," writes Leavis, "tends characteristically to lack dimension: it tends to have no depth—no depth against which it doesn't tacitly protect itself by the habit of unawareness. . . ." It is not material civilization in all its humane achievement that Leavis questions here. Rather, it is "the energy, the triumphant technology, the productivity, the high standard of living and the life-impoverishment—the human emptiness" that he seeks to focus on. He is questioning, then, the absence in modern life of the moral centrality that provides a perspective, indeed a "religious depth of thought and feeling," which civilization must have if life is not to be enjoyed "in a vacuum of disinheritance."

The world of enlightenment is, for Leavis, a world in which standards and discipline are sacrificed to the technological spirit, to the spirit of permissiveness, to an attitude "that can see nothing to be quarrelled with in believing, or wanting to believe, that [for example] a computer can write a poem." It is a complacent and self-indulgent attitude that is dialectically negative—that must negate the critical spirit and "the creativeness that is responsibility." In his criticisms Leavis, of course, focuses on the permissive and the sloppy attitudes that get attention as distinguished critical and creative attitudes and on the kind of values that are accepted and even required in the whole of culture. These are the attitudes and the values that play a crucial role in the making of civilization, the civilization that in its totality is identified by an ethos, a way of thought, of intelligence, of discrimination—the ways that say and tell (or do *not* say and tell, as the case may be) about man's view of himself and of the life around him, about those matters that must count and that inform the higher values of cultural continuity, which, in Leavis' words, "has its life in time, and transcending 'present' and 'past,' gives time its meaning and humanity its grasp of a real."

For some—the enemies and the destroyers—Leavis' assertions are greeted with derision. One academic thus dismisses *Nor Shall My Sword* for containing "a conspiratorial rhetoric for which no sufficient evidence has been produced." After all, few people, especially academics, want to be reminded of conditions they have made possible through their betrayal of moral, spiritual, educational values. There is nothing that touches enlightened ideologues to the quick more than the charge (or reminder) that they have encouraged the disorder and the indiscipline that shake the foundations of civilization. Yet an enlightened orthodoxy that insidiously creates a permissive spirit and that sanctifies, for the wrong reasons, a *Lady Chatterley's Lover* poses the danger that Leavis seeks to overcome. The danger is one of *uncritical* thought. Not Dickens but C. P. Snow is the model for emulation, the comprehender of what the modern world is, where it is going, how it can be saved. Surely Leavis emphasizes a timely truth in seeing Snow as a portent.

Leavis' critical concern is not with "literary values" but rather with "judgments about life." "What the critical discipline is concerned with," he insists, "is relevance and precision in making and developing them." The discipline of literary studies, then, is as genuine and as important as that of any of the sciences; without it "there can be no adequate attention paid to the problems of our civilization." In the study and the evaluation of the literature in one's own language (in the first place), one comes to recognize the nature and the priority of what Leavis calls "the third realm," a realm "which is neither merely private and personal nor public in the sense that it can be brought into the laboratory or pointed to." It is English literature, he maintains, that, in its diversity and range, fully registers changing life and shows the continuity of mind, spirit, and sensibility. Indeed, it is only in "the third realm" that a "cultural community of consciousness" can be attained, or as Leavis writes in *English Literature in our Time and the University*: ". . . unless society . . . develops by dint of sustained intelligent purpose the habit and the means of fostering in itself this collaborative and creative renewal, the cultural consciousness and the power of response will fade into nullity, and technological development, together with administrative convenience, will *impose* the effective ends and values of life. . . ."[24]

Leavis' lifetime work can be viewed as a reasoned and connected protest against those forces that would repress "the essential creativeness of life." In *Nor Shall My Sword* he again and again points to William Blake as an inspiration for contemporary society. Blake serves as the antithesis to Locke and Newton, and he points forward to, even as he is corroborated and reinforced by, the Dickens of *Hard Times* and the Lawrence of *Women in Love*. "To emphasize creativity as Blake did," Leavis states, "is to be committed to bringing home to the world, if in a world of Lockean or technologico-Benthamite blankness that can be done, that you can't generalize life, that individual lives can't be aggregated or averaged, and that only in individual lives is life 'there.' "[25] Human creativity and human responsibility: these are the recurring, the affirming preoccupations of Leavis' work and thought. Unlike Snow, he refuses to accept the existence of "two cultures," the humanist and the scientific. There is only "one culture," Leavis asserts: "The world we live in is not the world that forms a tiny part of the distinguished chemist's—the scientific—universe. It is a world, a reality, of human values and significances which is created and maintained by continuous collaborative human creativity. Without it there would have been no science."[26]

Like Arnold's, Leavis' best work is that of a literary critic, even when it is not literary criticism. This is so because it comes from an independent and disciplined intelligence, profoundly aware of humane values. How are humane values to be defended and to be passed on in our time? How are these values to be saved from the process of dehumanization that, in the technologico-Benthamite world, alters everything it comes into contact with? Leavis responds positively to these questions. If his view of contemporary developments is negative, his significance is not, for Leavis rises above negations. His work as a teacher-critic is a great plea for the affirmation of humane values and of humanistic culture. This plea has in it both latitude and depth, has centrality of unifying purpose and of relevance. Certainly it easily refutes the charge of provincialism that one hears used against him. But whenever it is a matter of maintaining standards and exercising discipline, an advocate of such a view is very apt to be charged with being "provincial" and "narrow." ("Puritano frenetico," for instance, is a description that has been applied to Leavis. The heralds of enlightenment have seen to that, the smear tactic being one of their major weapons.) What is now happening in the universities—and one thinks here of the portent of the "free university," or of the "open university," or of the "university without walls"—discloses precisely the representative consequences of the power of "enlightened" (mis) direction.

It should be noted that Leavis addresses himself mainly to an English audience and to "the condition of England." His diagnostic insights, however, have a much wider and, above all, a prophetic value, for they ultimately relate to the condition of both European and American civilizations, to the human condition itself. In this respect the prophetic spirit is shown not limited to visionaries like Blake and Lawrence. It has (and should have) an equally appropriate and endemic place in the critical spirit that Leavis exemplifies. The prophetic spirit that a great man possesses, Paul Tillich remarks, "exposes him to a terrible anxiety within himself, to severe and often deadly attacks from others, and to the charge of pessimism and defeatism on the part of the majority of the people. Men desire to hear good tidings; and the masses listen to those who bring them."[27] No words could better capture the difficulty of Leavis' labors nor better underline the burden of the instructive responsibility he bears, as well as the heroic mission he refuses to surrender.

22

Austin Warren: Man of Letters

∽

"To criticize is to appreciate, to appropriate, to take intellectual possession, to establish in fine a relation with the criticized thing and make it one's own." So writes Henry James concerning the critical function, and his statement typifies the wisdom, as well as the civilization, that inheres in his writings. Obversely, this statement calls attention to the all too frequent absence of the intensity, the sense of responsibility, and the sympathy of vision that James associates with the pursuit and values of criticism. Hence, we have always with us "imperfect critics," as T. S. Eliot would have it—"the propagandists for criticism," "the popularizers." Hence, too, it is always bracing to see a real critic when he is on the scene and to know that his work has worth and relevance in that sense James distinguishes as a mark of good criticism.

In his most recent work, *Connections** (a title that James would have appreciated), Austin Warren (b. 1899), one of the most respected of American critics, confirms the truth, the centrality, of James's "plea for Criticism, for Discrimination, for Appreciation." Warren reconfirms this truth, since for more than forty years now he has been a practicing scholar-critic whose work abounds with critical thought and insight—creative thought and creative insight. Any reading of his earlier volumes, such as *Alexander Pope As Critic and Humanist* (1929), *The Elder Henry James* (1934), *Richard Crashaw: A Study in Baroque Sensibility* (1939), *Rage for Order* (1948), as well as his two studies in "culture-history" that do not purport to be literary criticism, *New England Saints* (1956) and *The New England Conscience* (1966), will show the continuity of excellence and the coherence in Warren's critical achievement. With René Wellek, the well-known historian of criticism, Warren collaborated in writing the influential *Theory of Literature* (1942). This book, however, does not constitute the practice of criticism but is essentially a treatment of literary theory and methodology.

*Ann Arbor, Mich., 1970.

Connections contains critical essays written since 1948 and now largely and meticulously rewritten. Warren has intended it to be a sequel to *Rage for Order,* in which he writes on a number of poets (Edward Taylor, George Herbert, Gerard Manley Hopkins, William Butler Yeats) and novelists (Nathaniel Hawthorne, Franz Kafka, E. M. Forster, Henry James). In the earlier book Warren shows how great creative artists must reconcile "two contraries necessary to poetry or literature—intensity or calm, initial violence, sought and achieved discipline, which is not suppression but controlled and formal speech." Not incidentally Warren shows in this work that the critic must have "his own rage for order, a passionate desire to discover, by analysis and comparison, the systematic vision of the world which is the poet's construction, his equivalent of a philosophical or other conceptual system." What, in other words, Warren emphasizes here is the need for the critic himself to search for "a general principle of order," since the critic, like the poet, cannot write "without the search for an adequate poetics" that leads to the ordering of the literary heritage.

Warren sees E. M. Forster as a writer who "endeavoured to attain wholeness and steadiness of vision; his passion is for dispassionate comprehension." This view has its significance here. For it is precisely this view and this comprehension of the poet's world—"a concretely languaged, synoptically felt world; an ikon or image of the 'real world,' " as Warren describes it—that the critic must seek to "appropriate" in the way Henry James said it should be done. In this respect the critical process, as Warren succeeds in it, can be likened to the creative process that he describes in his essay "Henry James: Symbolic Imagery in the Later Novels" in *Rage for Order*:

> The tension in James between the dialectic and the mythic is an epistemological way of naming that rich interplay and reconciliation of impulses which constitutes his great achievement. As a person and as a writer, he matured slowly; he had to confront the long, slow business of synthesizing his impulse to merge and his impulse to withdraw, his shyness and his sociability, his romanticism (his first literary mode) and his realism, his humanism and his mysticism.

The critical process, as it is sustained in Warren's work, asserts an equivalent synthesis and integrity. And this is what makes for a "perfect critic." This is what is at work in Warren's literary criticism, as it evolves from scholarly to theoretical to literary and finally to religious exploration and discovery. The critical process here inevitably becomes the humanizing process that makes a literary scholar a critic and an educator as well. Criticism in itself must be a part of the edu-

cative process. It must help to order the mind and to lead others out
of darkness. It must civilize; it must humanize. If it cannot do so, it
can do little else.

> The practical conclusion [Warren concludes in his essay "The
> Teacher As a Critic"] isn't that we, as critics, should refrain from cur-
> rent polemics or expression of present conviction, prompted by present
> need, and, instead, utter generalities which, in a general kind of way,
> are always true—if one knows what they mean. It is rather that, with
> whatever sense of the past we really, and not merely "notionally," have,
> we should participate as teachers and critics in that archetypal balance
> which is tension, not compromise.

That Warren considers *Connections* a sequel to *Rage for Order*
should recall his view of the critic's need to construct, essay by essay
and book by book, a theory of criticism. *Connections* and its prede-
cessor indicate this construction. But more importantly these two
books show that such a construction need not end with aesthetic
formulas, that beyond principles and practice, beyond a discipline
that is at once technical and spiritual and unitive, there is a final
stage. In perhaps the highest and best sense, this is the stage a critic
should reach, when criticism becomes a humane discipline and when,
as with Warren, the critic addresses himself precisely to those coalescing ("interdisciplinary" is another way of putting it) literary connections that give to art and to criticism an informing humanity. Again
it is Henry James who gives the critical *donnée*. In the final sentence
of the passage that Warren uses as an epigraph James says, "Really,
universally, relations stop nowhere. . . ."

In his sequel to *Rage for Order*, Warren's concept of criticism is
enlarged and refined. If in *Rage for Order* he is preoccupied with
revealing an essential and an informing discipline that makes for
an ordering of the creative imagination—the discipline that unifies
sensibility and ultimately rarefies the "equilibrium which is also a
tension"—in *Connections* he shows the "relations," or "interness," between writers (this time critics as well as poets and novelists) and their
works. These "connections" he depicts particularly in the light of
literature as it is related to religion and to learning, either coinci-
dentally or coinherently. But the pattern of these "connections" is
not, he points out in his Preface, one of "sources and influences" nor
of "the shock of recognition." Rather, it is more nearly the desire "to
exhibit 'Literature as an Institution.' " Literary "connections," as a
result, are viewed by Warren in the light of "talent" and "tradition,"
as well as of "tradition" and "culture." John Donne, Sir Thomas
Browne, Cotton Mather, Nathaniel Hawthorne, Emily Dickinson,

M. R. James, A. C. Benson, Paul Elmer More, and T. S. Eliot—these are the subjects of Warren's essays. These writers reveal, even dramatize, the elements that relate them, sometimes directly, sometimes tangentially, sometimes peripherally—relations in terms of friendship, of style, and, paramountly, of spiritual and intellectual kinship.

Warren insists that as a literary critic he has neither "method" nor "specialty" but that he is a "generalist," a "general practitioner." (His assertion is undoubtedly true, as it is also undoubtedly modest—modesty being a normative quality of the whole of Warren's writing.) For what he abundantly shows in *Connections* is that he is finally, preeminently, a humanist, a "humanist" in its correlative religious sense inasmuch as he is acutely sensitive to the literary imagination and to the critical function in their broadly religious implications and in their specifically Christian or near-Christian determinants. Warren's criticism is heightened by his awareness of religious values in himself and in the authors whom he writes about. But what is of greater importance, from the standpoint of literary criticism's being disinterested and discriminating, is that Warren does not impose religious values on the writers whom he discusses. His religious humanism is implicit in his critical bearings without its being either repressive or oppressive. In a word, he judges by perception rather than by principles. "He is a good man to listen to," writes Lewis Leary, "persuasive even to those of us who cannot utterly submit to what seem limiting expectations in creed or for literature."

This humanism, to clarify a term that can be ambiguous and easily becomes claptrap, is very much in line with Eliot's contention that "Humanism makes for breadth, tolerance, equilibrium, and sanity. It operates against fanaticism." Warren's humanism is never uncritical in the way in which relativistic humanism can be. Indeed, his humanism helps to modify sensibility, simultaneously conserves values, and in effect transposes into a finer humanism. It is close in spirit to that of the Cambridge Platonists Henry More, John Smith, and Ralph Cudworth, who sought for a reconciliation of reason and imagination, as opposed to what, among the Puritans, was narrow and fanatical. Yet, if Warren's humanism is latitudinarian, if it is filled with respect and hope for human nature, it is also aware of human limits, and precisely those problematic limits that Warren himself underlines when he writes: ". . . it must be understood that I understand Humanism and Religion as at least as likely to be rivals or enemies as friends: their alliance, which I desire, I realize ever to be

unstable,—as precarious as—I think, along with Abbé Bremond—
desirable."

A book like *New England Saints* is not merely a scholarly work,
but also a work designed, as Warren notes, "primarily for edification."
Bronson Alcott, Ralph Waldo Emerson, Irving Babbitt, and John
Brooks Wheelwright, whom, among others, Warren treats in this
volume, are not "canonized," "but they are, whether priests, and of
whatever 'communion,' men I recognize, and celebrate, as those to
whom reality was the spiritual life, whose spiritual integrity was their
calling and vocation." A critical and a religious humanism is organic
in Warren's achievement, organic in the light of Eliot's further belief
that ". . . the humanistic point of view is auxiliary to and dependent
upon the religious point of view." Such a humanism is not only finer,
but also purer and older. It belongs to a tradition of critical and religious synthesis going back to the fusion of ancient Greek thought
(as humanism) and the religious view (as revelation) of Christian
Platonists like Clement of Alexandria and Origen.

It is this humanism that, in Warren's criticism, achieves in *Connections* a transcending direction and pattern. "There is no practice
without an implied theory, a theory under construction," he writes in
Rage for Order. His critical achievement discloses cumulatively the
evolving "construction" of this theory, as opposed to the more restricted critical "method" or "specialty." There is, then, in Warren's
criticism a definite theoretical ordering rooted not only in scholarship
but also in a moral perception of critical tasks and values. Clarity of
purpose is one way of summarizing Warren's objective in his work
as a critic. He is a humanist critic who, to judge by the writers he
examines, their particular works and themes and age, constantly discerns the inseparable relations of life and art. In his first book, *Alexander Pope As Critic and Humanist,* Warren was to anticipate, if not
to define, his attitude toward criticism when he writes:

> Being a humanist involves keeping one's balance between pedantry and
> dilettantism, confessedly a difficult and precarious position. I have not
> dared claim for Pope that he maintained this perfect balance. But I
> may claim for him that he comprehended the attitude, an attitude which
> is, in my opinion, inferior in dignity and value to few if any of the other
> possible attitudes toward life and art.

Warren is not a specialist critic, and his criticism is wary of specialisms. "Mind knows no ultimate distinctions into 'departments' of
knowledge; and what God hath joined together let no specialist pre-
sume to put asunder," he warns. To be sure, he is ever concerned with
the "intention of the text"; and, indeed, Warren has long been identi-

fied with the movement called the New Criticism. But, unlike the New Critics who have persisted in their anticognitive efforts and emphases, Warren has been less one-sided, less dogmatic. ("I often wish I could be a critic pure and simple," he reflects, "with all the advantage to boldness and ground-covering and personal dogmatism that would have afforded.") He has continually and vigorously responded to and assessed literature not only according to aesthetic, as well as ethical and philosophical criteria, but also according to humane and, in Warren's own words, "celebrational" and "edifying" values. These humane values of literature and, necessarily, of criticism have been his guiding lights. (This explains why Warren rejects any pretension to having a literary method or specialty. For once such a method or specialty is established, the critic—e.g., formalist or Marxist—limits the free play of his intelligence and his literary exploration. He sacrifices his freedom and circumscribes the humanizing goals of his work.)

In *The World's Body*, it might be noted here, John Crowe Ransom cites his admiration for Warren's writings, but at the same time he sees in them "diversionist" tendencies, particularly in Warren's attempt to synthesize the scholarly and the critical, or what Ransom calls "the academic development of the critical project." What Ransom admires is Warren's ability to remain close to the texts, to talk with the text before him in precisely those ways, Ransom insists, that enable criticism to "receive its own charter of rights and function independently." Yet, *pace* Ransom and the other New Critics, "the critical act" for Warren signifies a respect as well as a need for fathoming a poet's "meaning" by exploring all available resources, "the extra-poetic information." The "critical act" proper, therefore, has to operate on materials collected by scholarship and research, the scholarly work necessarily preceding the critical process of evaluation. "Erudition must affix glossaries," Warren writes in his Preface to *Richard Crashaw*, "explain allusions, supply the stylistic and ideological environment before the aesthetic experience or the critical judgment can, with surety, operate." Certainly, this study is a masterly example of Warren's critical approach to Crashaw the man and the poet. Though never losing sight of the text, Warren has always recognized that a critic must make connections that give to *Richard Crashaw* the strengths that, in Douglas Bush's opinion, make this book "the standard critical treatment."

Throughout his work Warren has stressed, interrelatedly, historical, moral, and religious backgrounds. In effect, and as one would expect of the work of a critic as humanist, Warren's criticism has attained a marvelously integrated form in the clarity of its purpose and of its vision. He has endowed his criticism, through careful inquiry over the years, with the intellectual order of discipline that must first be found and assimilated in one's work before it can become a humanizing process. This is, it would appear, what Warren denotes by a "theory under construction" in its aesthetic and intellectual aspects. Here it can be simply observed that a critic's final achievement and impact are to be judged by the way in which his work reaches a civilizing intellectual transport. If the critic's work sharpens the intelligence, it should also humanize it, as is often forgotten by literary scholars. In Warren's criticism we observe a harmony, in theory and in practice, that strikes its quintessence in the admirable ways in which Warren synthesizes literary history, literary theory, and literary criticism. Such a synthesis, a "theoretical eclecticism" as Emerson R. Marks terms it, once a critic formulates it, is more favorable to what is humane rather than to what is technical and specialistic. "There is a judgment of sensibility," Warren says in his chapter on "Evaluation" in *Theory of Literature*, "and there is a reasoned, a ratiocinative, judgement. They exist in no necessary contradiction: a sensibility can scarcely attain much critical force without being susceptible of considerable generalized statement; and a reasoned judgement, in matters of literature, cannot be formulated save on the basis of some sensibility, immediate or derivative."

Understandably Warren's work has been preoccupied with spiritual and moral entities in the literary imagination. (D. H. Lawrence no doubt best characterizes the forms of this vision when he writes, "But primarily I am a passionately religious man, and my novels must be written from the depth of my religious experience.") Understandably, too, this preoccupation has led to and centered in the metaphysics of art, those deep and impelling issues that imaginative vision revolves around. When Warren writes about "New England Saints" or the "New England Conscience," he is pursuing not only a motif or an "idea" in a "sociological" framework, but beyond it the indwelling moral energies that inspire and mold creative imagination. As a critic who has managed to create a synthesis, Warren is successful in weighing the moral import of art without at the same time becoming a moralist and thereby limiting himself. He is able to follow and augment the critical process in its moral, or its metaphysical, or its religious dimensions without destroying the process, in the way in which, as T. S. Eliot wrote in his Preface to *The Sacred Wood*, Arnold did "destructive work" by becoming a "critic tempted outside of criticism" and by seeing "the masters ... as canonical literature, rather than as masters."

As a critic who is preoccupied with literary connections, Warren's religious humanism has increasingly asserted itself in a concern with literary culture, in its American, British, and European edifices. His view of literary and of Christian culture is unitive as is Christopher Dawson's view of history and Christianity. ("If a true world-civilisation is ever to be created," Dawson insists in *The Making of Europe*, "it will not be by ignoring the existence of the great historic traditions of culture, but rather by an increase of mutual comprehension.") A unitive grasp of tradition particularly equips Warren to understand the thought and influence of Paul Elmer More, for example, and to see clearly the developing paths of More's critical and philosophical efforts. "In contrast to thinkers who start with designs for, and upon, society, More was in search of wisdom and—to use a word of yet higher intensity—'salvation.'" Likewise, in a long and brilliant essay on Eliot's criticism, Warren insists on a unifying and connecting pattern of development embracing Eliot's aesthetic theory, as a practicing poet and critic, and his conversion to Christianity in 1927, the latter decision having caused "surprise" and even "scandal" to many of his contemporaries.

The impelling religious essence, the spiritual capacity, of Eliot's thinking, if it is to be seen and judged for what it is, according to Warren, must not be seen as causing a disjunction in his critical position, or, as Eliot himself demurred, an arresting of his progress and an "unmistakably making off in the wrong direction." Nor must it be judged as Eliot's attempt to build a "schematic" system, or general theory. Rather, it is a qualitative and continuous development of "a first-rate mind intent upon the process of thinking." For those who have scoffed at Eliot's religious position as marking an "inexplicable" break in his critical astringency and have persistently opposed an early and revered Eliot (of *The Sacred Wood*) to a later and "unacceptable" Eliot (of *Notes Towards the Definition of Culture*), when Eliot progressively showed an "unhealthy detachment from facts," what Warren has to say about the evolving shape of Eliot's vision and experience— "his own literary experience, including (for he is no solipsist) his experience of the experience of others"—helps bring corrective insight into a question often complicated by muddled assessments:

> . . . [Eliot] sought for no merely verbal or even overtly logical consistency but one which should depend on the constant maintenance of spiritual integrity. And so, though he treats each of his prose pieces as "occasional," his mind is possessed by the occupation with a steady series of central topics. And each time he takes one of these up, he starts afresh to think it out, hoping to advance his development of thought

on this topic, and trusting that his mind has such a reasonable degree of continuity and coherence that there will be no really shocking break but some advance, at least some new distinctions and refinements.

Great American critics of the twentieth century are characterized by special qualities in their theory and practice. R. P. Blackmur has shown the interrelations of "language as gesture." Kenneth Burke has attempted to expand criticism into a total world-view and a philosophy of culture. Vernon Louis Parrington has examined literature along sociological lines with heavy emphasis on social history and the history of political ideas. Edmund Wilson and Lionel Trilling have disclosed a deep concern with social, political, and psychological problems. Irving Babbitt in stern, irrevocable ways (as his disciples attest to: "Having myself begun as a disciple of Mr. Babbitt, I feel that I have rejected nothing that seems to me positive in his teaching," T. S. Eliot declares) raked over those types of romanticism that he saw as threatening civilization, and he pleaded for the assertion of "discipline against the various forms of naturalistic excess." Yvor Winters, an "absolutist" decrying relativist literary and critical positions, has stressed rational elements and moral discipline as opposed to didactic, hedonistic, and romantic literary theories surrounding the nature of literature and the function of criticism. John Crowe Ransom, criticizing abstraction and distinguishing between structure and the "irrelevant" texture of a work of art, has, in Wellek's phrase, rejected "organistic aesthetics" and made a "rational defense of the concrete, of texture, of things and nature."

How does Warren fit into this constellation of major modern American critics? What is the special distinction of his body of work? Happily, he has avoided overexposure, the overwriting of David Daiches, for example. Consistently, his has been a careful critical inquiry and contemplation and an equally careful form of composition, sustainedly lucid (using "The common word exact without vulgarity, / The formal word precise but not pedantic," to recall Eliot) in contrast with R. P. Blackmur's, for example, which became turgid and confusing. Warren's comment on Cotton Mather is to the point here: "Yet what a pity that our Mather, copious and thrifty, could not have carved and cut and thrown away and disposed to form and order and proportion his memorable stones of remembrance. Even more than when he lovingly accumulates, the Lord is with the artist when, painfully, he discards."

As a literary stylist, as a craftsman, as a man of letters for whom writing, in T. S. Eliot's words, "is primarily an *art* . . . as much concerned with style as with content," Warren is almost without peer among American critics. He is always graceful in expression and economical of words, as instanced by his description of Saint Francis Xavier, who,

> winning repute for himself as a professor of philosophy at Paris, became, at the call of St. Ignatius, a Jesuit, labored for twelve years in India and Japan, embraced all Asia in his imagination and love, and died as he was about to enter upon the conquest of China;

or by this remark on Ralph Waldo Emerson:

> Though always, to himself, John the Baptist, ever in search of the Messiah to come, Emerson was no fool in his judgement of men, even when they were "idealists";

or, finally, but not least, by this statement in a review in 1935, in *The American Review*, of Nicolas Berdyaev's famous book *Dostoievski: An Interpretation*:

> Dostoievski's thought, and Berdyaev's book, are, therefore, not for the catechumens, and offer little of what the old Calvinistic sermons included under the head of Applications. They are concerned with first principles and Last Things.

Warren's is a meditative style that achieves an optimal excellence, persuasive in its eloquence, an eloquence of wisdom, so to speak. Never doctrinaire, ambivalent, circuitous, dishonest, or ranting, his style blends perfectly with the temper of a harmonizing critical approach—his humanism.

But, in a larger and impressive way Warren's importance as a critic has other (one could say *supra*-comparative) values. They lie in the unsecular tone and pattern of his criticism. American criticism has often been narrowly and (at its worst) reductively secular in its form and direction, inordinately preoccupied with judging literature in its naturalist and empirical contexts. Babbitt, Warren's old teacher at Harvard, decried this naturalist tendency, but his rigidities of thought precluded a total view of the literary process as instanced by his crippled poetic sensitivity. (It was ethical but defective.) Paul Elmer More, too, was aware of the secular tendency, as an examination of his *Shelburne Essays* shows; but his efforts adverted into the history of Greek philosophy—More's critics charged that he converted Aristotle into a Presbyterian elder—and Christian theology, areas that finally became tendentious and, indeed, escapist.

In contrast Warren has been able to balance an active, steady concern with cultural matters with a discriminating critical appreciation of literary imagination. His work has moved from his appraisal of the philosophical ideas of the elder Henry James to his appreciation of the poetry of Richard Crashaw, and later to the critical estimates of his subjects of the essays in *Rage for Order* and *Connections*. This has been, on the whole, the way in which Warren's dialectical process has moved: "Like theology and philosophy," he says, "criticism has to proceed dialectically, not pursue with steady zeal a single line." It has not veered into the cul-de-sacs of the New Humanists or of the New Critics. It has not, that is, bogged down in ideological or aesthetic positions and presuppositions. "... I think of myself in my latest period," Warren writes, "as *attempting to reconcile* ... the New Humanism (as revised by T. S. Eliot) with the New Criticism (as practiced by Eliot)."

Clearly, Warren's interests center on English and American literature, specifically on the English poets of the seventeenth century and on the New England divines and writers of the last three hundred years. His latter interest displays a definite cultural regionalism, and it could be said that for Warren, who is himself a native New Englander, there is a New England ethos that is permeated by a sense of community and meaning and that continues a rich cultural tradition in terms of values, standards, and, above all, moral discipline. Warren is a critic whose Americanness, in the light of the writers and the ethos that he obviously admires, has a classical bent, responsive, that is to say, to the classical qualities in literature that Eliot lists as "maturity of mind, maturity of manners, maturity of language and perfection of the common style." Warren's intellectual sympathies lie with what Philip Rahv has described as a "paleface" literature and a "solemn, semiclerical culture of Boston and Concord," hankering after "religious norms," with Henry James and Walt Whitman forming "a kind of fatal antipodes." As Warren's volumes on New England show, he is sympathetic to a literary culture that has roots and identity. No doubt it is this New England ethos that Eliot, whom Warren calls "my chief inspiration," favored and the diminution of which he bemoaned, in 1923, in

> ... the passing of the exclusive control of American letters out of the hands of a group of gentlemen in Boston closely associated with Harvard University, the decline of prestige of university professors, the increase of non-Anglo-Saxon elements in the population: various causes combined to give rise to styles of writing which are based on anything but contemporary English models.

Warren is an American critic; his New England, the home of "my spiritual ancestors and kinsmen," is his Americanness. His concern with the literary culture of a particular region, however, is not programmatic in the manner, say, of the Southern Agrarians, for whom Warren has always had warm feelings. For him New England is not a temple, but rather a humane temper illuminating and guiding the moral life. He has a reverence for the past and a recognition of its disciplines. "Life is not given to us for amusement," he says in his essay on Charles Eliot Norton, "but for responsibility; advantages confer obligations." Along with Perry Miller and F. O. Matthiessen, Warren belongs to a generation of scholars who rediscovered in the New England past not only abiding cultural values but also the referents of their own identities. "The spirit with which these men embarked upon their voyage of rediscovery," as David D. Hall has pointed out, "was not a parochial fixation with the immediate scene, but a cosmopolitan awareness of other possibilities." The point made here is important, for Warren's conception of New England is tied to a great living tradition, both as literary and general culture.

By no means is Warren sentimental or nostalgic in his view of this past; he does not remain inert in what is called a "parochialism in time." That is to say, Warren in his rediscovery of the New England past displays feelings and judgments culturally robust. Nowhere does he make his view more evident than in the careful distinctions he draws between the "sick" and the "healthy" sides of the New England conscience—the pathological, "neuralgic" conscience, "partly disease, partly sin," of a Michael Wigglesworth and the "healthy," "honest," and the "resilient" conscience, "that kind of conscience which the Puritans before their exodus and the early Quakers had," of a William Lloyd Garrison. Warren does not fall, and he does not allow himself to fall, into the illusory indulgences of a Van Wyck Brooks, who, as Alfred Kazin has observed in *On Native Grounds*, made of the nineteenth-century New England mind and past "a sweet and shining epic of a lost heroic tradition, a kind of American Nibelungenlied in which all the gods were literary men and women and all their passions revolved around a distinctive moral idealism." Warren is a conservator, not a lyricist. Not atmosphere and scene, but vital cultural thought and informed judgment are what count. For him New England is not "Country Pictures" but the reverent discipline that the past can exemplify and that can help in the continuity of a culture and in the health of a society.

Like Eliot's, Warren's tastes are classical and conservative, and his writings are similarly concerned with tradition and discipline in the controlling and the ordering of civilization (those elements that Henry James, whose work earns a high valuation in Warren's writings, found wanting in American life). But to say that Warren is classical and conservative is to say that he is aware of deep cultural lapses in American life; that he seeks for a form of civilization that is religious, respectful of tradition, and resistant to mass-mindedness, to the "redskin" aspects of American culture and literature that Rahv connects with "reactions [that] are primarily emotional, spontaneous, and lacking in personal culture." His critical conservatism is thus to be viewed in a temper and a line of thought that, religiously and intellectually, stresses, in Simone Weil's phrase, "the need for roots," as well as the "sanity, moderation, continuity, gradual change" that Warren praises in the social criticism of Norton. Its critical tools are those of clarity, ordonnance, precision, definition. Its standards of value are restraint, limitation, contemplation, order, commitment, orthodoxy, and civilization ("uncontaminated by the deluge of barbarism outside," to quote Eliot). Its enemies are sloppiness in all guises, romanticism, "dispersive" liberalism, anarchy, vulgarity, populism as well as popularity and mediocrity (in those special forms that modern American educators seem to take pride in fostering).

The critic as humanist communicates special insights, which are what really matter in the end. He is able to see things in imaginative art that other critics may fail to see, precisely because he has a vision that other critics do not understand. This vision is often religious not only in its creative nuances, as D. H. Lawrence insisted, but also in its critical offshoots. "Religion is the most important element in life," Eliot told an interviewer, "and it is in the light of religion that one understands anything." Warren's awareness of this truth is what equips him to appraise the underlying significance of Donne's sermonic art. "Donne was not an original or a systematic theologian; but he was a great preacher: I venture to think a greater preacher than poet—able to express in that medium, and in that middle period of life, a range and a depth to which the poems rarely reach." And there is, too, Warren's equally perceptive and "religious" insight into Emily Dickinson's poetry. "Her deepest poems are metaphysical or tragic; her mode of vision symbolist; her thinking, analogical. Emerson (whose *Essays* an early 'tutor' gave her) probably flexed her mind, encouraged her speculations and her questionings of orthodoxy; but her mythology remains—what Hawthorne's was, and Emerson's never— Biblical and Trinitarian. Though a rebel, she is not, like Emerson, a schismatic."

Critical comments, insights, like these are representative of Warren's work. It is often a religious dimension of art that he helps others to understand, and to understand in responsible critical ways—discriminatingly, judgmentally, morally. Warren's religious sensibility is, to be sure, there in his critical function. And as a critic concerned as he should be with discerning and conserving humane values, he uses this sensibility to lead to understanding in disciplined ways. His eye is always on the critical discipline that is itself rooted in his religious humanism in those rarefying ways that F. R. Leavis pinpoints in this observation: "If Christian belief and Christian attitudes have really affected the critic's sensibility, then they will play their due part in his perceptions and judgments, without his summoning his creeds and doctrines to the job of discriminating and pronouncing." No words could better define the significance, as well as the value, of Warren's achievement. What gives Warren's criticism relevance, reveals the merit of his critical pronouncements, and both strengthens and objectifies his positive critical process is the presence of a sensibility humanized by religious "belief" and "attitude," but also disciplined and refined by a critical intelligence faithful, immediately and finally, to what Eliot speaks of as the main business of the critic: "The critic, one would suppose, if he is to justify his existence, should endeavour to discipline his personal prejudices and cranks—tares to which we are all subject—and compose his differences with as many of his fellows as possible, in the common pursuit of true judgment."

A critic, if he is to be great, must assert the judgmental power that stamps the truth of his judgments and that sets him off from the ordinary, the dilettante, the specialist, or the academic critic. The greatness of Eliot's criticism lies in the power of the intellect to "urge the mind to aftersight and foresight." The greatness of Leavis' lies in the power of an "unafraid intelligence and vitality" of a "judging mind," to use his own words. The greatness of George Orwell's lies in the compelling power of an honesty that pushes to the side all pose and pedantry. "A critic must be able to *feel* the impact of a work of art in all its complexity and its force," Lawrence writes regarding some of the personal strengths contributing to a critic's integrity. "To do so, he must be a man of force and complexity himself . . . , a man of good faith. He must have the courage to admit what he feels, as well as the flexibility to *know* what he feels." Austin Warren's achievement reminds us that, beyond judgmental powers and personal qualities, or rather along with them, great criticism demands a great humanity: a great critic must also be a great humanist.*

---

*In a beautifully written memoir, "In Search of a Vocation" (published in the *Michigan Quarterly Review* [Fall 1972], 237–47), Warren traces his career as a teacher and a scholar-critic during the 1930's. He shows how in striving to define his "vocation" in terms of his critical writings, he had gradually to "renounce," that is, to subordinate and to reconcile, his interests in church music, in " 'philosophy,' abstract thought," and in speculative theology.

Acknowledgments

◡

"The Writer and Society: Some Reflections" was written as the Introduction to the volume of essays I edited under the title *The Politics of Twentieth-Century Novelists* (New York: Hawthorn Books, 1971).

"Promise of Greatness: The War of 1914–1918" was written as the Introduction to the volume of essays I edited under the same title (New York: The John Day Company, Inc., 1968).

"King of Bloomsbury" was first published in *Modern Age. A Quarterly Review*, Volume 13, Number 1, under the title "Epicurus' Owne Sone."

"Leonard Woolf" was first published in *Modern Age. A Quarterly Review*, Volume 12, Number 2, under the title "The Bloomsbury Cult."

"E. M. Forster and D. H. Lawrence: Their Views on Education" was written for *Renaissance and Modern Essays*, edited by G. R. Hibbard (London: Routledge and Kegan Paul, 1966).

"Ideologues of Mediocrity" was first published in *Modern Age. A Quarterly Review*, Volume 15, Numbers 3–4, under the title "The Cult of Mediocrity."

"Toward a Metaphysics of Art" was written for *The Vision Obscured: Perceptions of Some Twentieth-Century Catholic Novelists*, edited by Melvin J. Friedman (New York: Fordham University Press, 1970), under the title "A Metaphysics of Art."

"F. M. Dostoevsky and D. H. Lawrence: Their Visions of Evil" was first published in *Renaissance and Modern Studies* (Nottingham, England), Volume 5.

"Dostoevsky and Satanism" was first printed in *The Journal of Religion*, Volume 45, Number 1.

"Boris Pasternak's Protest and Affirmation" was first published in *The Greek Orthodox Theological Review*, Winter Issue, 1959.

"J. D. Salinger and the Russian Pilgrim" was first published in *The Greek Orthodox Theological Review*, Summer 1962–Winter 1963 Issue.

"Henry More: Cambridge Platonist" was first published in *The Greek Orthodox Theological Review*, Christmas Issue, 1956, under the title "The Greek Spirit and the Mysticism of Henry More."

"Simone Weil: A Passionate Platonist" was first published, in two parts, in *Modern Age. A Quarterly Review*, Volume 14, Numbers 3–4 and Volume 15, Number 2, under the titles "A Passionate Platonist" and "Saint of the Churchless," respectively.

"D. H. Lawrence and the Ancient Greeks" was first published in *English Miscellany. A Symposium of History, Literature, and the Arts* (Rome, Italy), Volume 16.

"A Tribute to Gilbert Murray" was first published in *The Classical Journal*, Volume 53, Number 2.

"Graven Images" was first published in *Comparative Literature Studies*, Volume 2, Number 2.

"Interpreter of Genius" was first published in *English Miscellany. A Symposium of History, Literature, and the Arts* (Rome, Italy), Volume 20, under the title "G. Wilson Knight: Interpreter of Genius."

"The Leavisite Rubrics" was first published in *Comparative Literature Studies*, Volume 6, Number 4.

The essays reprinted here appear essentially in their original forms. But all of them have been revised, chiefly through excision. Wherever possible and relevant, I have also tried to interconnect essays by the addition of transitional material. I have tried to make changes without altering value judgments or forcing an artificial unity, since these essays have, I believe, a coherent critical concern and direction.

The following essays were written specially for this volume and have not appeared elsewhere, with the date of composition given in parenthesis after each essay:

"The End of the Lamplight," with the exception of the last section, which was first published in *Modern Age. A Quarterly Review*, Volume 14, Number 1 (1969); "Arnold Toynbee" (1969); "Vivian de Sola Pinto" (1970); "Pater Seraphicus: Dostoevsky's Metaphysics of a 'New Saintliness'" (1968–70); "Austin Warren: Man of Letters" (1970); the introductory section of "Three English Lives," with the exception of some material first published in *Modern Age. A Quarterly Review*, Volume 13, Number 3, under the title "Approach to Avernus" (1972); and "Notes on Eliot and Lawrence, 1915–1924" (1970–72).

The concluding sections of "D. H. Lawrence and the Ancient Greeks" and "The Leavisite Rubrics" were written in 1972.

Acknowledgments

My association with *Modern Age* since 1965 has been for me a fortuitous one, insofar as this quarterly review has welcomed my writings and has provided an outlet for the expression of my literary and cultural ideas. Without *Modern Age* some of the central directions of my work would never have developed and portions of this book would never have been written. To be able to write for a journal that maintains critical and cultural standards with which one is also in accord is always a happy blessing. My debt to Dr. David S. Collier, editor and publisher of *Modern Age*, and to Joseph M. Lalley, literary editor, is such that even to state my gratitude is to state what is in the end illimitable.

For friendship, encouragement, suggestions, support, and, in a good number of instances, for the inspiration of some of the essays I have written, I owe a great deal to Professor A. Owen Aldridge, Professor John W. Aldridge, Archbishop Athenagoras, Seymour Barofsky, Michael S. Baron, Miss Hedy Bergida, Professor and Mrs. Milton Birnbaum, Mrs. H. D. Brewster, Stephen F. Cox, Eugene A. Davidson, Harold Flavin, Professor Morris Freedman, Professor Melvin J. Friedman, Professor G. R. Hibbard, Professor Richard B. Hovey, Professor G. Wilson Knight, Dr. F. R. Leavis, Professor Leonard Lutwack, Professor Charles D. Murphy, N. Frederick Nash, Mr. and Mrs. Andrew Panichas, Professor Mario Praz, Professor Norman T. Pratt, Professor Costas M. Proussis, Professor Nathan A. Scott, Jr., Professor Raymond Thorberg, Dr. Arnold Toynbee, Alan Tucker, Professor Eliseo Vivas, Professor Austin Warren, Professor Kurt G. Weber, and David D. Wicks.

To Mrs. Irene Cronin, Supervisor, Reference Department, and to the members of her Staff, City Library, Springfield, Massachusetts, I am grateful for the many kindnesses and the assistance so graciously extended to me during the past sixteen years.

Once more I am pleased to record my debt to Miss Martha Seabrook for giving so much of her time in editing my work. I count it a great fortune to have as an editor a friend whose own literary taste and sensibility, in addition to her editorial skill, have been such a rich and constant source of illumination for me through the years.

And once more, too, I wish to thank Miss Mary E. Slayton for her readiness to assist me in any way necessary to the demands of my work, particularly in all the various stages of the research for and the preparation and the completion of my writings, and for giving of herself in ways too numerous even to begin to list or to assess. I want this book to pay special tribute to her efforts.

Notes

∽

NOTES TO CHAPTER 1

1. New York (1942), 106.
2. *Selected Essays* (New York, 1950), 117.
3. *What Is Art?*, trans. Aylmer Maude (New York, 1960), 142.
4. See Dedication, *Axel's Castle: A Study of the Imaginative Literature of 1870–1930* (New York, 1931).
5. "Ivan Turgeniew," *The North American Review* (April 1874), 350.
6. *Beyond Culture: Essays on Literature and Learning* (New York, 1968), 13.
7. Trans. Eden and Cedar Paul (Garden City, N. Y., 1957), 1–2.
8. *Essays on Literature and Society* (Cambridge, Mass., 1965), 143–44.
9. *Ibid.*, 147.
10. *Ibid.*, 150.
11. Robert Alter in *The Politics of Twentieth-Century Novelists*, ed. George A. Panichas (New York, 1971), 334.
12. "The Idea of the Modern," *Literary Modernism*, ed. Irving Howe (New York, 1967), 18. *The Modern Tradition. Backgrounds of Modern Literature*, ed. Richard Ellmann and Charles Feidelson, Jr. (New York, 1965) is also indispensable to the discussion of what "modernism" means.
13. *What Is Literature?*, trans. Bernard Frechtman (New York, 1965), 61–62.
14. *The Betrayal of the Intellectuals*, trans. Richard Aldington (Boston, 1955, [1928]), 32.
15. *Selected Essays*, 13, 118.
16. G. Jean-Aubry, *Joseph Conrad: Life and Letters* (New York, 1927), 301–302.
17. Page 231.
18. Jeremiah 1:10.
19. *The Collected Essays, Journalism and Letters of George Orwell*, ed. Sonia Orwell and Ian Angus (New York, 1968), II, 41.
20. "What Happened in the 30's," *Commentary* (Sept. 1962), 204.
21. *Writers On the Left. Episodes in American Literary Communism* (New York, 1961), 4. See also Walter B. Rideout, *The Radical Novel in the United States, 1900–1954: Some Interrelations of Literature and Society* (Cambridge, Mass., 1956).
22. Oxford, Eng., 1968 [1938], 198, 200.
23. L. C. Knights, *Drama and Society in the Age of Johnson* (New York, 1968 [1937]), 177.

24. New York (1967), 33.

25. Sept. 9, 1966, p. 326.

26. June 1, 1967, p. 21. Rahv includes this essay under the title "An Open Secret" in his *Literature and the Sixth Sense* (Boston, 1969), 437–45.

27. *The Times Literary Supplement* (Sept. 15, 1966), 855.

28. *Partisan Review* (Summer 1967), 359–81.

29. Garden City, N.Y. (1953 [1944]), 212–13.

30. Garden City, N.Y. (1953 [1950]), 179.

31. New York (1947), 214.

32. *Ibid.*, 218.

33. *Ibid.*, 216–17.

34. *Language and Silence: Essays on Language, Literature, and the Inhuman* (New York, 1967), 322–23.

35. Albert Salomon, "Sociology and the Literary Artists," *Spiritual Problems in Contemporary Literature*, ed. Stanley Romaine Hopper (New York, 1952), 24.

36. *The Common Pursuit* (London, 1952), 194.

37. *The Collected Essays, Journalism and Letters of George Orwell*, II, 276.

38. *Ibid.*, II, 184–97.

39. *Ibid.*, II, 144–45.

40. "Rudyard Kipling," *On Poetry and Poets* (New York, 1961 [1957]), 284.

41. *Lectures in America* (New York, 1969), 7.

42. *Letters of James Joyce*, ed. Richard Ellmann (New York, 1966), II, 364.

43. *The God That Failed*, ed. Richard Crossman (New York, 1949), 81.

44. *The Necessity of Art: A Marxist Approach* (Baltimore, 1963), 214.

45. *Ezra Pound: Perspectives. Essays in Honor of His Eightieth Birthday*, ed. Noel Stock (Chicago, 1965), 87, 89.

46. *The Dissenting Academy*, ed. Theodore Roszak (New York, 1968), 36, 12, 13.

47. *Ibid.*, 59.

48. *Ibid.*, 58.

49. *One-Dimensional Man: Studies in the Ideology of Advanced Industrial Society* (Boston, 1966 [1964]).

50. "On the Steps of Low Library. Liberalism and the Revolution of the Young," *Commentary* (Nov. 1968), 36.

51. James F. Goldberg, " 'Culture' and 'Anarchy' and the Present Time," *The Kenyon Review*, 31 (1969), 607.

52. Bruce Franklin, "The Teaching of Literature in the Highest Academies of the Empire," *College English*, 32 (1970), 557. This essay is now included in *The Politics of Literature: Dissenting Essays in the Teaching of English*, ed. Louis Kampf and Paul Lauter (New York, 1972).

53. "The Failure of Left Criticism," *The New Republic* (Sept. 9, 1940), 346.

54. "The Critical Path: An Essay on the Social Context of Literary Criticism," *Daedalus* (Spring 1970), 342.

55. *Essays on Literature and Society*, 158.

56. Book V of *A Vision*, dated Feb. 1925.

57. "What Happened in the 30's," 212.
58. *Phoenix: The Posthumous Papers of D. H. Lawrence*, ed. Edward D. McDonald (London, 1936), 539.
59. "What Is English Studies, And If You Know What That Is, What Is English Literature," *Partisan Review*, 37 (1970), 58.
60. *Flannery O'Connor. Mystery and Manners*, ed. Sally and Robert Fitzgerald (New York, 1969), 131.
61. "The Central Problem in Literary Criticism," *College English*, 4 (1942), 163.
62. *Theodore Spencer: Selected Essays*, ed. Alan C. Purves (New Brunswick, N. J., 1966), 8–9.
63. *Speaking To Each Other* (New York, 1970), II, 259.

NOTES TO CHAPTER 2

1. New York (1922), 3.
2. Quoted in Virginia Woolf, "Walter Raleigh," *Collected Essays* (London, 1966), I, 318.
3. Ernest Jones, *The Life and Work of Sigmund Freud*, ed. and abr. Lionel Trilling and Steven Marcus (New York, 1963 [1961]), 336.
4. See Julien Benda, *The Betrayal of the Intellectuals*, trans. Richard Aldington (Boston, 1955 [1928]), 140.
5. Romain Rolland, *Above the Battle*, trans. C. K. Ogden (Chicago, 1916), 111 ff.
6. *Within the Rim* (London, 1918), 90.
7. *The Letters of Charles Sorley*, ed. W. R. Sorley (Cambridge, Eng., 1919), 232.
8. *Selected Letters of Robert Frost*, ed. Lawrance Thompson (New York, 1964), 134.
9. Guy Chapman, *A Passionate Prodigality* (London, 1965 [1933]), 226.
10. Pierre Teilhard de Chardin, *The Making of a Mind*, trans. René Hague (New York, 1961), 205, and *Hymn of the Universe*, trans. Simon Bartholomew (New York, 1961), 54.
11. *The Letters of Charles Sorley*, 220, 312.
12. Edward Marsh, *Rupert Brooke. A Memoir* (New York, 1926), 163.
13. *The War That Will End War* (New York, 1914), 14.
14. *Above the Battle*, 39.
15. Julian Symons, *Horatio Bottomley* (London, 1955), 174.
16. *Further Speculations*, ed. Sam Hynes (Lincoln, Neb., 1962), 184.
17. Preface to *Far From the Madding Crowd* (New York, 1960 [1874]), vii.
18. *The World of Yesterday. An Autobiography* (New York, 1943), 197.
19. New York, Modern Library Edition [1920], 254; Foreword, ix.
20. *The Memoirs of Raymond Poincaré*, trans. Sir George Arthur (London, 1929), III, 295.
21. *Siegfried's Journey, 1916–1920* (London, 1945), 69–70.
22. Dylan Thomas, "My World is Pyramid," *Collected Poems. 1934–1952* (London, 1966), 26.

23. *Seven Pillars of Wisdom* (New York, 1966 [1926]), 162–63.
24. Harmondsworth, Eng., 1960 [1924], 709.
25. London (1967), 9.
26. J. Middleton Murry, *Looking Before and After* (London, 1948), 155.
27. *The Soldier* (Norfolk, Conn., 1944), 16.
28. *A Passage to India* (London, 1953 [1924]), 156.
29. Trans. Fitzwater Wray (New York, 1917), 112.
30. Michael Holroyd, *Lytton Strachey. A Critical Biography* (New York, 1968), II, 148.
31. *The Collected Letters of D. H. Lawrence*, ed. Harry T. Moore (New York, 1962), I, 528.
32. Desmond MacCarthy, *Memories* (New York, 1953), 141.
33. *Kangaroo* (Harmondsworth, Eng., 1960 [1923]), 236.
34. See Ch. XXI in *A Study of History*, abr. D. C. Somervell (New York, **1946**).
35. Paul Valéry, *History and Politics*, trans. Denise Folliot and Jackson Mathews (New York, 1962), 115, 116.
36. *Ibid.*, 23.
37. *Ibid.*, 29.
38. Habakkuk 2:2.
39. *The Shaking of the Foundations* (New York, 1948), 7.
40. Jeremiah 8: 20.
41. *Pointing the Way: Collected Essays*, trans. Maurice S. Friedman (New York, 1956), 190.
42. *The Lie About the War*, Criterion Miscellany, no. 9 (London, 1930).
43. *Civilization* (Middlesex, Eng., 1947 [1928]), 137.
44. Quoted in Leonard Woolf, *The Journey Not the Arrival Matters. An Autobiography of the Years 1939–1969* (London, 1969), 93–94.
45. *Above the Battle*, 157.
46. *The Proud Tower* (New York, 1966), xiii.
47. *The Meaning of the War* (London, 1915), 47.
48. *Parade's End* (New York, 1961 [1925]), 307.
49. *History of Europe in the Nineteenth Century*, trans. Henry Furst (New York, 1933), 350.
50. *Max Ernst*, ed. William S. Lieberman (New York, 1961), 11.
51. *Antic Hay* (New York, 1965 [1923]), 283.
52. *Tragedy Is Not Enough*, trans. Harald A. T. Reiche, Harry T. Moore, and Karl W. Deutsch (Boston, 1952), 45.
53. "The Dead Heroes," *The Collected Poems of Isaac Rosenberg*, ed. Gordon Bottomley and Denys Harding (New York, 1949), 42.
54. *Tragedy Is Not Enough*, 104.
55. *Ibid.*, 105.

NOTES TO CHAPTER 3

1. *The Collected Essays, Journalism and Letters of George Orwell*, ed. Sonia Orwell and Ian Angus (New York, 1968), IV, 443.

2. Marghanita Laski, *Saturday Review* (July 6, 1968), 28.

3. Princeton, N. J. (1968), vii–viii.

4. Vera Brittain, "War Service in Perspective," *Promise of Greatness: The War of 1914–1918*, ed. George A. Panichas (New York, 1968), 369.

5. *The Collected Essays, Journalism and Letters of George Orwell*, IV, 446.

6. Edward Marsh, *A Number of People* (New York, 1939), 202.

7. *Soliloquies in England* (Ann Arbor, Mich., 1967 [1922]), 45.

8. *The Letters of Henry James*, ed. Percy Lubbock (New York, 1920), II, 379 ff.

9. *Downhill All the Way. An Autobiography of the Years 1919–1939* (New York, 1967), 14.

10. *Left Hand, Right Hand!* (Boston, 1944), 268–69.

11. *Up the Line to Death: The War Poets, 1914–1918*, ed. Brian Gardner (London, 1964), 7.

12. *Promise of Greatness*, 153, 154.

13. *Disenchantment* (New York, 1922), 15.

14. *Promise of Greatness*, vi.

15. New York (1938), 182.

16. *The Complete Poems of D. H. Lawrence*, ed. Vivian de Sola Pinto and Warren Roberts (New York, 1964), I, 554, 553.

17. *Women in Love* (1920), Ch. VIII.

18. *The Collected Letters of D. H. Lawrence*, ed. Harry T. Moore (New York, 1962), I, 215.

19. *Ibid.*, 309.

20. Harry T. Moore and Warren Roberts, *D. H. Lawrence and His World* (New York, 1966), 42.

21. *The Collected Letters of D. H. Lawrence*, I, 378.

22. *Ibid.*, 487.

23. *Phoenix: The Posthumous Papers of D. H. Lawrence*, ed. Edward D. McDonald (London, 1936), 703.

24. *D. H. Lawrence: A Composite Biography*, ed. Edward Nehls (Madison, Wis., 1957), I, 408, 409.

25. *The Collected Letters of D. H. Lawrence*, I, 490.

26. *A Mingled Chime* (New York, 1943), 161.

27. *Asquith. Portrait of a Man and An Era* (New York, 1964), 519.

28. G. Lowes Dickinson, *A Modern Symposium* (New York, 1967 [1905]), 24. Lord Cantilupe, the fictional speaker here, is based upon Lord Salisbury.

29. *Ibid.*, 25.

30. *Great Morning!* (Boston, 1947), 255.

31. *Heart of the Empire* (London, 1901), vii.

32. *The Collected Essays, Journalism and Letters of George Orwell*, II, 344.

33. *A Mirror for Anglo-Saxons* (New York, 1960), 99.

34. *Testament of Youth* (New York, 1937), 17.

35. Reproduced in H. W. Nevinson, *The Natives of England* (New York, 1931), opposite p. 20. The artist was the only son of H. W. Nevinson (1856–1941), essayist and journalist.

36. *Not I, but the Wind . . .* (New York, 1934), 68.

NOTES TO CHAPTER 4

1. Lady Cynthia Asquith, *Diaries 1915–1918*, ed. E. M. Horsley (New York, 1969), 459.

2. T. S. Eliot, *Selected Essays* (New York, 1950), 445.

3. *The Letters of Sir Walter Raleigh (1879–1922)*, ed. Lady Raleigh (London, 1926), II, 479, 481, 482, 489.

4. C. E. Baron, "Bloomsbury Revisited" (Winter 1967/68), 89.

5. *The Observer* (Oct. 1, 1967), 26.

6. *Scrutiny* (Cambridge, Eng., 1963), XVI, 243–44.

7. *A Selection from Scrutiny*, comp. F. R. Leavis (Cambridge, Eng., 1968), I, 138.

8. David Garnett, *The Flowers of the Forest* (London, 1955), 96.

9. *The Letters of D. H. Lawrence*, ed. Aldous Huxley (New York, 1932), 224, 241.

10. *A Selection from Scrutiny*, I, 140.

11. *Ibid.*, 25.

12. *Ibid.*, 185.

13. *Literary Views*, ed. Carroll Camden (Chicago, 1964), 175–93.

14. Michael Wilding, "The Literary Criticism of F. R. Leavis," *The Oxford Review*, No. 7 (1968), 78.

15. George A. Panichas, *Epicurus* (New York, 1967), 125.

16. *The Autobiography of Bertrand Russell. 1872–1914* (Boston, 1967), 94–95.

17. *Ibid.*, 129.

18. *The Letters of D. H. Lawrence*, 228.

19. *A Selection from Scrutiny*, I, 156, 160–62; II, 281.

20. "A Case for Treatment," *Encounter* (March 1968), 71–83.

21. David Williams, "Apostolic" (Oct. 25, 1967), 639.

22. *The New Statesman* (Oct. 6, 1967), 438.

23. *Vogue* (June 1968), 66.

24. *Carrington. Letters and Extracts from Her Diaries*, ed. David Garnett (New York, 1971), 183. See also pp. 11–12, 175–78.

NOTES TO CHAPTER 5

1. *Diaries and Letters*, ed. Nigel Nicolson (New York, 1968), III, 267.

2. London, 1967.

3. *The Moment and Other Essays* (New York, 1948), 136, 138.

4. *Two Cheers for Democracy* (New York, 1951), 228.

5. Arnold and Philip Toynbee, *Comparing Notes: A Dialogue Across a Generation* (London, 1963), 56.

6. *Ibid.*, 150.

7. New York and London, 1969.

8. George A. Panichas, *Epicurus* (New York, 1967), 75–76.

9. *Two Cheers for Democracy*, 56.

10. *Abinger Harvest* (New York, 1955 [1936]), 61.

11. *Civilization* (Middlesex, Eng., 1947 [1928]), 104.

12. *The Collected Essays, Journalism and Letters of George Orwell*, ed. Sonia Orwell and Ian Angus (New York, 1968), I, 363.

13. *The Old School*, ed. Graham Greene (London, 1934), 189, 193.

14. *Abinger Harvest*, 85.

15. E. M. Forster, *Goldsworthy Lowes Dickinson* (New York, 1934), 155.

16. Thomas Lask, *The New York Times* (Oct. 24, 1969), 45.

17. Letter to George A. Panichas, Jan. 31, 1967.

18. *Sherston's Progress* (New York, 1936), 200.

19. *Goodbye to All That* (London, 1960 [1929]), 235.

20. *Up the Line to Death. The War Poets: 1914–1918*, ed. Brian Gardner (London, 1964), 154.

21. *The Letters of D. H. Lawrence*, ed. Aldous Huxley (New York, 1932), 260.

22. *Abinger Harvest*, 111, 113.

23. "In Defence of Lady Cynthia," Letter to *The Listener* (May 30, 1968), 704.

24. Quoted in David Nichol Smith's Preface to *The Letters of Sir Walter Raleigh (1879–1922)*, ed. Lady Raleigh (London, 1926), I, xii.

25. *England and the War* (Oxford, 1918), 53.

26. *Varieties of Religious Experience* (New York, 1903), 31.

27. William Wordsworth, *The Prelude*, vi, 606–8.

28. Sir Harold Nicolson, *Diaries and Letters*, ed. Nigel Nicolson (London, 1966), I, 350–51.

29. Introduction, *The Bloomsbury Group* (New York, 1963).

30. *The Listener* (May 30, 1968), 703.

31. *The Letters of D. H. Lawrence*, 228.

32. Quoted in L. P. Hartley's letter to *The Listener*, 704.

NOTES TO CHAPTER 6

1. *Beginning Again. An Autobiography of the Years 1911–1918* (London, 1965), 243.

2. Leonard Woolf, *Downhill All the Way. An Autobiography of the Years 1919–1939* (London, 1967), 108.

3. Michael Holroyd, *Lytton Strachey. A Critical Biography* (New York, 1968), II, 364.

4. Ed. Valerie Eliot (New York, 1971), vii.

5. "T. S. Eliot and the 'Out There' " (Dec. 10, 1971), 1552.

6. *Eliot and His Age. T. S. Eliot's Moral Imagination in the Twentieth Century* (New York, 1971), 9. Following Kirk's line of thought, George Steiner declares that Picasso, Stravinsky, Pound, Eliot, and Joyce, as "the last classicists," were not destroyers but custodians of tradition. "What seems to us obvious in the genius of 'Personae' and the 'Cantos,' " Steiner writes, "in 'The Waste Land' and Eliot's essays, in 'Ulysses' is the overwhelming force of tradition, the explicit recourse to a body of epic and lyric poetry that goes back to Homer and Catullus." "The Cruellest Months," *The New Yorker* (April 22, 1972), 134.

7. *After Strange Gods. A Primer of Modern Heresy* (London, 1934), 13;

"Thoughts After Lambeth," *Selected Essays* (New York, 1950), 329; *The Idea of a Christian Society* (New York, 1940), 64; "Religion Without Humanism," *Humanism and America*, ed. Norman Foerster (New York, 1930), 110; "The Modern Dilemma," *The Christian Register*, Vol. 112, No. 41 (Boston, 1933), 676.

8. *Love, Freedom and Society* (London, 1957), 38.

9. *After Strange Gods*, 25.

10. "Le roman anglais contemporain," *XXVIII.* 164 (May 1, 1927), 671. "Mr. Lawrence is a demoniac, a natural and unsophisticated demoniac with a gospel. When his characters make love—or perform Mr. Lawrence's equivalent for love-making—and they do nothing else—they not only lose all the amenities, refinements and graces which many centuries have built up in order to make love-making tolerable; they seem to re-ascend the metamorphoses of evolution, passing backward beyond ape and fish to some hideous coition of protoplasm."

11. *Selected Essays*, 381.

12. *The Athenaeum* (May 2, 1919), 265–67.

13. *Revelation*, ed. John Baillie and Hugh Martin (London, 1937), 28 ff.

14. *Ibid.*, 29.

15. *On Poetry and Poets* (New York, 1961 [1957]), 62.

16. *Phoenix II. Uncollected, Unpublished, and Other Prose Works by D. H. Lawrence*, ed. Warren Roberts and Harry T. Moore (New York, 1970), 628–29.

17. *Selected Essays*, 360.

18. F. R. Leavis, *D. H. Lawrence: Novelist* (New York, 1956), 388–89.

19. New York (1948), 104–5.

20. *Frieda Lawrence. The Memoirs and Correspondence*, ed. E. W. Tedlock, Jr. (New York, 1964), 327.

21. "The Man of Letters and the Future of Europe," *Sewanee Review* (Summer 1945), 333–42.

22. *The Autobiography of Bertrand Russell. 1912–1944* (Boston, 1968), 64.

23. "T. S. Eliot and the 'Out There,' " 1552.

24. *The Milton Bulletin*, Vol. 12, No. 1 (Feb. 1949), 7.

25. *Abinger Harvest* (New York, 1955 [1936]), 84–91.

26. *D. H. Lawrence: A Composite Biography*, ed. Edward Nehls (Madison, Wis., 1957), I, 309.

27. *The Collected Letters of D. H. Lawrence*, ed. Harry T. Moore (New York, 1962), I, 477.

28. *The Waste Land. A Facsimile and Transcript of the Original Drafts Including the Annotations of Ezra Pound*, 1. Quoted by Theodore Spencer during a lecture at Harvard Univ., and recorded by the late Henry Ware Eliot, Jr., the poet's brother.

29. *The Letters of D. H. Lawrence*, ed. Aldous Huxley (New York, 1932), 568–69.

30. *To Criticize the Critic and Other Writings* (New York, 1965), 24.

31. Letter from Michael B. Rubinstein to George A. Panichas, Feb. 9, 1970.

32. *To Criticize the Critic and Other Writings*, 24–25.

33. *The Idea of a Christian Society*, 63. "Eliot's poetic life-work,"

G. Wilson Knight observes, "is an attempt to place the vision within the constrictions of contemporary man and his society; to assimilate the Christessence, Christ as tiger, to the Christian Church." "Thoughts on *The Waste Land*," *The Denver Quarterly* (Summer 1972), 13.

34. *Selected Essays*, 235.

35. "Ulysses, Order, and Myth," *Dial*, Vol. 75, No. 5 (Nov. 1923), 480.

36. This quotation comes from the statement of evidence by Eliot, prepared but not delivered on the occasion of the trial of Penguin Books Limited for the publication of the unexpurgated text of *Lady Chatterley's Lover* in Oct.-Nov. 1960. The quotation is from the copy corrected by Eliot in his autograph and deposited in the Univ. of Nottingham Library.

NOTES TO CHAPTER 7

1. London (1952), 162.

2. "A Propos of *Lady Chatterley's Lover*," *Sex, Literature, and Censorship*, ed. Harry T. Moore (New York, 1959), 107.

3. Jeremiah 1:10.

4. *The Collected Letters of D. H. Lawrence*, ed. Harry T. Moore (New York, 1962), I, 318. My italics.

5. *Sex, Literature, and Censorship*, 88.

6. *Fantasia of the Unconscious*, Introduction by Philip Rieff (New York, 1960), 112–13. This edition also contains *Psychoanalysis and the Unconscious*.

7. *Where Angels Fear to Tread* (1905), Ch. IX.

8. *The Longest Journey* (1907), Pt. I.

9. *The Georgian Scene* (New York, 1934), 391.

10. London (1957), 253–54.

11. G. D. Klingopulos, "E. M. Forster's Sense of History: and Cavafy," *Essays in Criticism*, VIII (April 1958), 156–65.

12. "The Poetry of C. P. Cavafy," *Pharos and Pharillon* (1923).

13. See Forster's Introduction to William Golding's *Lord of the Flies* (New York, 1962), x.

14. *D. H. Lawrence: A Composite Biography*, ed. Edward Nehls (Madison, Wis., 1957), I, 34.

15. *The Collected Letters of D. H. Lawrence*, I, 8–9.

16. *The Rainbow*, Ch. XV.

17. *Ibid.*

18. *Phoenix: The Posthumous Papers of D. H. Lawrence*, ed. Edward D. McDonald (London, 1936), 611.

19. *Two Cheers for Democracy* (New York, 1951), 56.

20. *The Collected Letters of D. H. Lawrence*, I, 337.

21. J. K. Johnstone, *The Bloomsbury Group* (New York, 1963), 18.

22. *E. M. Forster* (Norfolk, Conn., 1943), 22.

23. *Two Cheers for Democracy*, 56.

24. Ch. XIV.

25. *Two Cheers for Democracy*, 350. Cf. "A Letter [from] E. M. Forster," *The Twentieth Century*, CLVII (Feb. 1955), 99.

26. Quoted by Noel Gilroy Annan, *Leslie Stephen* (London, 1951), 286.

27. *The Collected Letters of D. H. Lawrence*, I, 317–18. Lawrence's italics. The posthumous publication of Forster's homosexual novel, *Maurice* (1971), begun in 1913 and finished in 1914 and "Dedicated to a Happier Year," sheds new light on the significance of Lawrence's observations, as expressed in his letter to Bertrand Russell, dated Feb. 12, 1915.

28. *The Nation and Athenaeum* (March 29, 1930), 888.

29. *Two Memoirs* (London, 1949), 95.

30. *The Nation and Athenaeum* (April 5, 1930), 12.

31. See Frederick C. Crews, *E. M. Forster: The Perils of Humanism* (Princeton, N. J., 1962); Donald Hannah, "The Limitations of Liberalism in E. M. Forster's Work," *English Miscellany*, XIII (Rome, 1962), 165–78; Alan Wilde, *Art and Order: A Study of E. M. Forster* (New York, 1964).

32. *D. H. Lawrence: A Composite Biography*, I, 407.

33. *Two Memoirs*, 85.

34. *The Collected Letters of D. H. Lawrence*, I, 330.

35. *Two Memoirs*, 103.

36. *Culture and Society 1780–1950* (Harmondsworth, Eng., 1961), 202.

37. *The Complete Poems of D. H. Lawrence*, ed. Vivian de Sola Pinto and F. Warren Roberts (New York, 1964), I, 51–52.

38. *The Rainbow*, Ch. XIII.

39. *D. H. Lawrence: A Composite Biography*, I, 286, 574 note 103.

40. See T. S. Eliot's Foreword to Father William Tiverton's [the Rev. Martin Jarrett-Kerr's] *D. H. Lawrence and Human Existence* (London, 1951).

41. New York (1963), 484.

42. *Two Cheers for Democracy*, 60.

43. *Ibid.*, 352.

44. *Phoenix*, 675.

45. *Sex, Literature, and Censorship*, 106.

46. *Phoenix*, 714.

47. *Fantasia of the Unconscious*, 114–15.

48. Ch. VI.

49. *Phoenix*, 606–7.

50. *Ibid.*, 634.

51. *Ibid.*, 587.

NOTES TO CHAPTER 9

1. *A Gilson Reader*, ed. Anton C. Pegis (Garden City, N. Y., 1957), 63.

2. *Encyclopedia of Philosophy*, ed. Paul Edwards (New York, 1967), V, 306.

3. *The Nature of Metaphysics*, ed. D. F. Pears (London, 1960), 131. José Ortega y Gasset's *Some Lessons in Metaphysics*, trans. Mildred Adams (New York, 1969), contains many valuable insights.

4. *Doctor Zhivago*, trans. Max Hayward and Manya Harari (New York, 1958), 90.

5. *Writers at Work. The Paris Review Interviews*, ed. Malcolm Cowley (New York, 1959), 55.

6. *Literary and Philosophical Essays*, trans. Annette Michelson (New York, 1962), 84–85.

D. H. Lawrence's concept of the relationship of art to metaphysics, as defined in his Foreword to *Fantasia of the Unconscious* (1922), is also pertinent here:

> And finally, it seems to me that even art is utterly dependent on philosophy: or if you prefer it, on a metaphysic. The metaphysic or philosophy may not be anywhere very accurately stated and may be quite unconscious, in the artist, yet it is a metaphysic that governs men at the time, and is by all men more or less comprehended, and lived. Men live and see according to some gradually developing and gradually withering vision. This vision exists also as a dynamic idea or metaphysic —exists first as such. Then it is unfolded into life and art.

Counted "among the handful of the best critics of this century," by Allen Tate, the late William Troy (1903–61) emphasized that to novelists like Lawrence, Gide, Proust, Mann, and Joyce "life still presented itself in terms of metaphysical problems. . . . No matter into what unpopularity metaphysics has fallen, it is the only relevant approach to these writers." He further claims: "Of the various approaches to literature—the technical or esthetic, the historical, the socio-economic—the metaphysical alone has the advantage of throwing light at one and the same time on both the form and the content of a work." *William Troy: Selected Essays*, ed. Stanley Edgar Hyman (New Brunswick, N. J., 1967), 123–24 and 19, in the order cited here.

7. See "Un nouveau mystique," *Situations I* (Paris, 1947); *Existentialism*, trans. Bernard Frechtman (New York, 1947), 58, 60. See also Martin Buber, *Eclipse of God*, trans. Maurice S. Friedman (New York, 1957), Ch. V, "Religion and Modern Thinking," 65–70.

8. *Aspects of the Novel* (New York, 1963 [1927]), 28–29.

9. II Corinthians 5:17.

10. *Eclipse of God*, 23, 24.

11. *Creative Intuition in Art and Poetry* (Cleveland, 1954), 3.

12. See Eliseo Vivas, "Philosophy of Culture, Aesthetics, and Criticism: Some Problems," *The Texas Quarterly* (Spring 1966), 231–41. See also his *D. H. Lawrence: The Failure and the Triumph of Art* (Evanston, Ill., 1960) and *Creation and Discovery* (Chicago, 1955).

13. *Tolstoy or Dostoevsky. An Essay in the Old Criticism* (New York, 1959), 4–7. See also Steiner's *Language and Silence. Essays on Language, Literature, and the Inhuman* (New York, 1967), particularly the first essay "Humane Literacy" delineating the functions of the critic: (1) "to show us what to reread, and how"; (2) to "act as an intermediary and custodian . . . [and] to establish the dialogue between past and present"; and (3) to make judgments on contemporary literature. Noting the existence of privation and uncertitude in the entire cultural situation, Steiner concludes: "Because the community of traditional values is splintered, because words themselves have been twisted and cheapened, because the classic forms of statement and metaphor are yielding to complex, transitional modes, the art of reading, of true literacy, must be reconstituted. It is the task of literary criticism to help us read as total human beings, by example of precision, fear, and delight.

Compared to the act of creation, that task is secondary. But it has never counted more. Without it, creation itself may fall upon silence" (7–11).

14. *The New Orpheus. Essays Toward a Christian Poetic*, ed. Nathan A. Scott, Jr. (New York, 1964), 59–73.

15. "Baptism in the Forest: Wisdom and Initiation in William Faulkner," *Mansions of the Spirit: Essays in Literature and Religion*, ed. George A. Panichas (New York, 1967), 25–26. Iris Murdoch's observation, in *The Sovereignty of Good Over Other Concepts* (Cambridge, Eng., 1967), is equally pertinent here: "A serious scholar has great merit. But a serious scholar who is also a good man knows not only his subject but the proper place of his subject in the whole of his life."

16. John Masefield, *Shakespeare and Spiritual Life* (Romanes Lecture; London, 1924), 24.

17. *Science and Poetry* (London, 1926), 31.

18. *The Mystery of Being*, trans. René Hague (Chicago, 1960), II, 208.

19. "A Memorable Fancy," *The Marriage of Heaven and Hell* (*ca.* 1793).

20. Ernst Fischer, *The Necessity of Art: A Marxist Approach* (Baltimore, 1963), 200. See also Martin Jarrett-Kerr, C. R., "The Conditions of Tragedy," *Comparative Literature Studies*, II, No. 4 (1965), 363–66; Claude Mauriac, "A. Robbe-Grillet," *The New Literature*, trans. Samuel I. Stone (New York, 1959), 225–34; Geoffrey Wagner, "Freedom to be a Thing: The 'New Novel' and Reality," and Thomas Molnar, "The 'New Novel' and the Future of Literature," in *The Intercollegiate Review*, III, No. 1 (1966), 23–29 and 30–34, respectively.

21. These words are from the concluding lines of Wallace Stevens' "The Idea of Order at Key West" (1935):

> Oh! Blessed rage for order, pale Ramon,
> The maker's rage to order words of the sea,
> Words of the fragrant portals, dimly-starred,
> And of ourselves and of our origins,
> In ghostlier demarcations, keener sounds.

22. "The Way Back into the Ground of Metaphysics," in Walter Kaufmann, *Existentialism from Dostoevsky to Sartre* (Cleveland, 1956), 207.

23. "The Spirit of Place," *Studies in Classic American Literature* (1923).

24. *Moral Principles of Action. Man's Ethical Imperative*, ed. Ruth Nanda Anshen (New York, 1952), 475.

25. *The Meaning of the Creative Act*, trans. Donald A. Lowrie (New York, 1962), especially Ch. X, "Creativity and Beauty: Art and Theurgy." See also Frank Kermode, *The Sense of An Ending. Studies in the Theory of Fiction* (New York, 1967). "*Il faudrait une renaissance dans les moeurs pour en avoir une dans les arts*," Eugène Delacroix writes in *Journal*, III (Paris, 1895), 215.

26. *Literary and Philosophical Essays*, 95–96.

27. Paul J. Marcotte, *The God Within. Essays in Speculative Literary Criticism* (Ottawa, 1964), 60–61.

28. Eliseo Vivas, *The Artistic Transaction and Essays on Theory of Literature* (Columbus, Ohio, 1963), vii.

29. D. H. Lawrence, *Women in Love* (1920), Ch. XIV.

30. *The Death of the Moth and Other Essays* (London, 1942), 126–32.

31. *The Spirit in Man, Art, and Literature,* trans. R. F. C. Hull (New York, 1966), 111, 112, 117, 119, 120, 124, 128.

32. *Aspects of the Novel,* 122.

33. *The Letters of D. H. Lawrence,* ed. Aldous Huxley (New York, 1932), 750.

34. *James Joyce: Two Decades of Criticism* (New York, 1948), 198–202.

35. Quoted in Richard Ellmann, *James Joyce* (New York, 1959), 410.

36. *A Portrait of the Artist as a Young Man* (1916), Ch. V.

37. Irene Hendry Chayes, in *Joyce's "Portrait." Criticisms and Critiques,* ed. Thomas E. Connolly (New York, 1962), 213.

38. *Phoenix: The Posthumous Papers of D. H. Lawrence,* ed. Edward D. McDonald (London, 1936), 532.

39. *Jerusalem* 4:6 (1804–20).

40. *The Idea of the Holy,* trans. John W. Harvey (New York, 1958).

41. *Assorted Articles* (London, 1930), 25.

42. *The Letters of D. H. Lawrence,* 97–98.

43. *Apocalypse* (Florence, 1931), Ch. 23.

44. George A. Panichas, *Adventure in Consciousness: The Meaning of D. H. Lawrence's Religious Quest* (The Hague, 1964), 31–61.

45. *D. H. Lawrence: Novelist* (New York, 1956), vii.

46. *Eight Modern Writers* (Oxford, Eng., 1963), 483.

47. *Phoenix,* 531.

48. Frederick J. Hoffman, *The Mortal No* (Princeton, N. J., 1964), 366.

49. *Ibid.,* 346–47. For an incisive appreciation of this book see Melvin J. Friedman, "The Achievement of Frederick Hoffman," *The Massachusetts Review,* VI, No. 4 (1965), 862–67.

50. "The Role of the Catholic Novelist," *Greyfriar* (Siena College, Loudonville, N. Y.), VII (1964), 12. See also "A Collection of Statements" in *The Added Dimension: The Art and Mind of Flannery O'Connor,* ed. Melvin J. Friedman and Lewis A. Lawson (New York, 1966), 226–37.

51. See Kenneth Hamilton's *Revolt Against Heaven* (Grand Rapids, Mich., 1965) and *God Is Dead: The Anatomy of a Slogan* (Grand Rapids, Mich., 1966) for a helpful discussion of the history of antisupernaturalism from pre-Reformation theology to neo-liberalism and for an analysis of the writings of the "Christian atheists."

52. W. H. Walsh, *Metaphysics* (London, 1963) and *The Nature of Metaphysics,* ed. D. F. Pears, contain excellent accounts of logical positivism in particular and of metaphysics in general.

53. Jacques Maritain, *The Peasant of the Garonne,* trans. Michael Cuddihy and Elizabeth Hughes (New York, 1968).

54. *Resistance, Rebellion, and Death,* trans. with an Introduction by Justin O'Brien (New York, 1961), 249–72.

55. *The Joyful Wisdom* (108):

New Struggles.—After Buddha was dead people showed his shadow for centuries afterwards in a cave,—an immense frightful shadow. God is dead: but as the human race is constituted, there will perhaps be caves for milleniums yet, in which people will show his shadow.—And we—we have still to overcome his shadow!

56. New York (1956), 52.

57. Nathan A. Scott, Jr., *Samuel Beckett* (London, 1965), 130. See also Josephine Jacobsen and William R. Mueller, *The Testament of Samuel Beckett* (London, 1966).

58. *The New Literature*, 85.

59. *Ibid.*, 89.

60. *Man in the Modern Age*, trans. Eden and Cedar Paul (New York, 1957), 141.

61. Dante, *The Divine Comedy. Inferno*, Canto XI, l. 105.

NOTES TO CHAPTER 10

1. Unpublished letter, July 27, 1917, from D. H. Lawrence to Eunice Tietjens. Tietjens Papers, Newberry Library, Chicago.

2. *The Letters of D. H. Lawrence*, ed. Aldous Huxley (New York, 1932), 242, 318, 331.

3. *Phoenix: The Posthumous Papers of D. H. Lawrence*, ed. Edward D. McDonald (London, 1936), 285.

4. E. T., *D. H. Lawrence: A Personal Record* (London, 1935), 123. For studies relating to Dostoevsky's role and influence in English literature, see Walter Neuschäffer, *Dostojewskijs Einfluss auf den englischen Roman* (Heidelberg, 1935); Helen Muchnic, *Dostoevsky's English Reputation (1881–1936)* (Northampton, Mass., 1939); Gilbert Phelps, *The Russian Novel in English Fiction* (London, 1956).

5. *Fantasia of the Unconscious*, 7–8.

6. Ernest J. Simmons, *Dostoevsky. The Making of a Novelist* (London, 1950), 141.

7. Kenneth and Miriam Allott, "D. H. Lawrence and Blanche Jennings," *A Review of English Literature* (July 1960), 75.

8. Philip Rahv, "Dostoevsky in *Crime and Punishment*," *Partisan Review* (Summer 1960), 407–9.

9. For an interesting study examining Dostoevsky's use of lower forms of insect and animal life (flies, beetles, cockroaches, spiders, snakes, tarantulas, scorpions, phalanges), so as to underscore a fundamental kinship to demonically dissolute characters, see Ralph E. Matlaw, "Recurrent Imagery in Dostoevskij," *Harvard Slavic Studies*, III (Cambridge, Mass., and The Hague, 1957), 201–25.

10. "Traditional Symbolism in *Crime and Punishment*," *PMLA* 70 (1955), 986.

11. All references to *Crime and Punishment* (1866) are included within the text, with Roman figures indicating the parts and Arabic figures the sections. Throughout David Magarshack's translation in Penguin Books (1960) is used.

12. All references to *Women in Love* (1920) are given in the text, with the chapter references indicated in Roman figures.

13. *Phoenix*, 527.

14. It is interesting to compare this with a remark in Dostoevsky's *Letters from the Underworld* (1864) : "Every man's reminiscences include things

which he reveals, not to all men and sundry, but to his friends alone. Again, every man's reminiscences include things which he does not reveal even to his friends, but to himself alone, and then under a close seal of secrecy. Lastly, every man's reminiscences include things which he hesitates to reveal even to himself." *Letters from the Underworld*, trans. C. J. Hogarth (London, 1913), Part I, xi.

15. Richard Curle, *Characters of Dostoevsky* (London, 1950), 40.

16. *The Rape of Lucrece*, I, 794.

17. K. Mochulsky, *Dostoevskii, Jizn' i Tvorchestvo* (Paris, 1947), 254.

18. For an excellent appraisal of Sofya (Sonia) Semyonovna Marmeladov's role in *Crime and Punishment*, see L. A. Zander, *Dostoevsky*, trans. Natalie Duddington (London, 1948), 66–98.

19. *D. H. Lawrence: A Composite Biography*, ed. Edward Nehls (Madison, Wis., 1957), I, 501.

20. *The Works of Lord Byron*, ed. Ernest Hartley Coleridge, IV (London, 1922), 114–15, Act II, Scene IV, ll. 55–63.

21. Mark Schorer, "*Women in Love*," *The Achievement of D. H. Lawrence*, ed. Frederick J. Hoffman and Harry T. Moore (Norman, Okla., 1953), 177.

22. Genesis 4:10, 13, 14.

23. Vyacheslav Ivanov, *Freedom and the Tragic Life: A Study in Dostoevsky*, trans. Norman Cameron with an Introduction by Sir Maurice Bowra (London, 1952), 125–31. See particularly Part III: "Theological Aspect," Ch. I: "Daemonology," 120–41.

24. E. M. Forster, *Aspects of the Novel* (London, 1949), 132.

25. *Phoenix*, 285. This should be compared with what Lawrence wrote of Dostoevsky in a letter to S. S. Koteliansky in the spring of 1915: "But he is a great man and I have the greatest admiration for him." "Letters to S. S. Koteliansky," *Encounter* (Dec. 1953), 29.

NOTES TO CHAPTER 11

1. *Satan*, ed. Père Bruno de Jesus-Marie, O.C.D. (New York, 1952), 455.

2. Friedrich Schleiermacher, *The Christian Faith*, ed. H. R. Mackintosh and J. S. Stewart (Edinburgh, 1928), 170.

3. André Gide, *Le Journal des Faux-Monnayeurs* (Paris, 1926), 141.

4. Khot' ubeĭ, sleda ne vidno,
   Sbilis' my, chto delat' nam?
   V pol'e bes nas vodit vidno
   Da kruzhit po storonam.

5. Ernest J. Simmons, *Dostoevsky. The Making of a Novelist* (New York, 1962), 247; Michael H. Futrell, "Dostoyevsky and Dickens," *English Miscellany*, VII (Rome, 1956), 78.

6. E. H. Carr, *Dostoevsky* (London, 1931), 227; Derek Traversi, "Dostoevsky," in *Dostoevsky: A Collection of Critical Essays*, ed. René Wellek (Englewood Cliffs, N.J., 1962), 168; Georg Lukács, *ibid.*, 155; Irving Howe, *Politics and the Novel* (New York, 1957), 63.

7. Richard Curle, *Characters of Dostoevsky* (London, 1950), 138.

8. Dmitri Merejkowski, *Tolstoi as Man and Artist: With an Essay on Dostoievski* (New York, 1902); Vyacheslav Ivanov, *Freedom and the Tragic Life: A Study in Dostoevsky*, trans. Norman Cameron (London, 1952); Nicolas Berdyaev, *Dostoevsky*, trans. Donald Attwater (New York, 1957); L. A. Zander, *Dostoevsky*, trans. Natalie Duddington (London, 1948).

9. René Wellek, *Dostoevsky: A Collection of Critical Essays*, 6.

10. We are reminded here of T. S. Eliot's comment: "The persons who enjoy these writings *solely* because of their literary merits are essentially parasites; and we know that parasites, when they become too numerous, are pests." *Selected Essays* (New York, 1950), 344.

11. Charles E. Passage, *Dostoevski the Adapter* (Chapel Hill, N.C., 1954), 175.

12. V. V. Zenkovsky, *A History of Russian Philosophy*, trans. George L. Kline (London, 1953), I, 415.

13. *Service Book of the Holy Orthodox-Catholic Apostolic Church*, comp., trans., and arranged from the Old Church-Slavonic Service Books of the Russian Church and collated with the Service Books of the Greek Church by Isabel Florence Hapgood (3d ed.; Syrian Antiochian Orthodox Archdiocese of New York and all North America, 1956), 272.

14. *A Treasury of Russian Spirituality*, comp. and ed. G. P. Fedotov (London, 1952), 227. The selections from St. Tychon were translated by Helen Iswolsky.

15. All quotations from Dostoevsky's novel are taken from Constance Garnett's translation of *The Possessed* (New York, 1936), containing a Foreword by Avrahm Yarmolinsky and his translation of the hitherto-suppressed chapter "At Tihon's"; and from David Magarshack's translation of *The Devils* (Baltimore, 1953). The references to *The Devils* are included in the text, with the Roman figures indicating the particular part and the Arabic figures the chapter and the section.

16. *The Brothers Karamazov*, trans. Constance Garnett (New York, 1950), VI, 3.

17. *Master Builders* (New York, 1939), 209–10.

18. *Writings from the Philokalia on Prayer of the Heart*, trans. E. Kadloubovsky and G. E. H. Palmer (London, 1951), 29.

19. Martin Buber, *Images of Good and Evil*, trans. Michael Bullock (London, 1952), 34.

20. *Cain: A Mystery* in *The Poetical Works of Lord Byron* (London, 1894), 459.

21. *The Brothers Karamazov*, III, 3.

22. All references relating to Ivan and the devil are from Book XI, ch. ix ("The Devil. Ivan's Nightmare"), pp. 771–91 in Mrs. Garnett's translation of *The Brothers Karamazov*.

23. *The Brothers Karamazov*, VI, iii. Cf. Rudolf Otto: "It might be said that Lucifer is 'fury,' the ὀργή, hypostatized, the *mysterium tremendum* cut loose from the other elements and intensified to *mysterium horrendum*." *The Idea of the Holy*, trans. John W. Harvey (New York, 1958 [1923]), n. 2, pp. 106–7.

24. "Immer stärker wird der Eindruck: Das Innere dieses Mannes ist

leer." (The impression becomes more and more strong: The man is empty inside.)

"Er besitzt einen scharfsehenden Verstand, eine mächtige Körperkraft, einen ungeheuren Willen aber sein Herz ist öde." (He possesses an acute intellect, powerful physical strength, a phenomenal will power, but his heart is desolate.) Romano Guardini, *Religiöse Gestalten in Dostojewskijs Werk* (Munich, 1951), 318.

25. Nicolas Berdyaev, *The Destiny of Man*, trans. Natalie Duddington (London, 1937), 280.

26. All references to Stavrogin's confession are from Avrahm Yarmolinsky's translation of "At Tihon's," found in Mrs. Garnett's translation of *The Possessed*, 689–736.

27. Denis de Rougemont, *The Devil's Share*, trans. Haakon Chevalier (Washington, D.C., 1944), 30.

28. "Vybroshennaia glava—kul'minatsiia v tragedii Stavrogina i vysochaĭshee khudozhestvennoe sozdanie Dostoevskogo. Bor'ba very s neveriem, narostavshaia na protiazhenii vsego romana, dostigaet zdes' svoego predel'nogo napriazheniia. Protivostavlenie dvukh ideĭ voploshchaetsia v stolknovenii dvukh lichnosteĭ—ateista Stavrogina i mistika Tikhona." K. Mochulsky, *Dostoevskii, Jizn' i Tvorchestvo* (Paris, 1947), 376. See also Paul Ramsey's illuminating study, "God's Grace and Man's Guilt," *The Journal of Religion* 31 (1951), 30–34.

29. "Er ist der ärmste aller Menschen. Ein grosses Mitleid kommt einem um ihn—aber der Satan ist ja auch wahrhastig keine Majestät! Was neuzeitliche Satanismen und Moralumwertungen von der 'Grösse des Bösen' sagen, ist nur Papier. Der Satan ist der Betrogene einfachhin; der von sich selbst Betrogene. Er ist ganz kahl. Er ist in gar nichts grossartig. Er ist der armselige 'simius Dei.' "

30. See Elizabeth Welt Trahan, "The Golden Age—Dream of a Ridiculous Man?" *Slavic and East European Journal* 18 (Winter 1959), 354.

31. "We are today lost in a pseudo-intellectualism which, by claiming a final authority and logical clarity that it in no sense possesses, has made chaos in the world of thought." G. Wilson Knight, *The Christian Renaissance* (New York, 1963), 4.

32. This phrase is from Albert Camus' Foreword to *The Possessed. A Play in Three Parts*, trans. Justin O'Brien (New York, 1960), vi. Thomas Merton, however, contends that Camus does not endorse Stavrogin's brand of evil: "It seems to me that in treating Stavrogin as 'the spiritual adventure and death of a modern hero' Camus is certainly speaking ironically. He certainly takes with the fullest seriousness the moral nihilism of Stavrogin, and even sees him as a prime example of the kind of evil forces in the world that you and I would characterize as satanic, and which Camus really condemns with all his force as disastrous nihilism. I do not by any means think that Camus considers Stavrogin a sort of sympathetic Promethean character or even a 'hero of the absurd' like his Sisyphus. Stavrogin represents the totalist revolutionary who uses violence to subject everything to pure will, the arbitrary application of the principle that 'if God is dead everything is permitted.' " Letter from Thomas Merton to George A. Panichas, April 3, 1967.

33. Cf. Josiah Royce: "It is not those innocent of evil who are fullest of the life of God, but those who in their own case have experienced the

triumph over evil. It is not those naturally ignorant of fear, or those who, like Siegfried, have never shivered, who possess the genuine experience of courage; but the brave are those who have fears, but control their fears. Such know the genuine virtues of the hero." *Studies of Good and Evil. A Series of Essays upon Problems of Philosophy and of Life* (New York, 1898), 1–28.

NOTES TO CHAPTER 12

1. *The Letters of T. E. Lawrence,* ed. David Garnett (New York, 1939), 492.

2. *The Added Dimension: The Art and Mind of Flannery O'Connor,* ed. Melvin J. Friedman and Lewis A. Lawson (New York, 1966), 237.

3. Thomas J. J. Altizer, *Mircea Eliade and the Dialectic of the Sacred* (Philadelphia, 1963), 114.

4. Rudolf Otto, *The Idea of the Holy* (New York, 1958 [1923]), 13 ff.

5. Robert L. Jackson, *Dostoevsky's Quest for Form* (New Haven, 1966), 90.

6. Otto, 51. (My italics.)

7. Jackson, 176.

8. *Ibid.,* 82.

9. *Ibid.,* 57.

10. Otto, 158.

11. *Three Masters,* trans. Eden and Cedar Paul (New York, 1930), 231.

12. Jackson, 56.

13. *Religiöse Gestalten in Dostojewskijs Werk* (Munich, 1951), 108. All references to this book were translated from the German by Herbert Schaumann.

14. *Eleven Essays in the European Novel* (New York, 1964), 217.

15. All references to *A Raw Youth* (1875) are included within the text, with uppercase Roman numerals indicating the part, lowercase Roman numerals the chapters, and Arabic numerals the sections. Throughout, the Modern Library Edition, trans. Constance Garnett (New York, 1956), is used.

16. Guardini, 95.

17. All references to *The Brothers Karamazov* (1880) are included within the text, with Roman numerals indicating the books and Arabic numerals the chapters. Throughout, the Modern Library Edition, trans. Constance Garnett (New York, 1950), is used.

18. Nadejda Gorodetzky, *Saint Tikhon Zadonsky* (London, 1951), 180.

19. Trans. and annotated Boris Brasol (New York, 1954), 203.

20. Gorodetzky, 183.

21. *Ibid.,* 193.

22. *The Icon and the Axe* (New York, 1966), 202.

23. *A Treasury of Russian Spirituality,* comp. and ed. G. P. Fedotov (London, 1952), 185.

24. Gorodetzky, 187.

25. K. Mochulsky, *Dostoevsky: His Life and Work,* trans. with an Introduction by Michael A. Minihan (Princeton, N.J., 1967), 636.

26. Romans 13:12.

27. Dmitry F. Grigorieff, "Dostoevsky's Elder Zosima and the Real Life Father Amvrosy," *St. Vladimir's Seminary Quarterly*, Vol. 11, No. 1 (1967), 22–24.

28. Aylmer Maude, *The Life of Tolstoy* (London, 1953), 75.

29. Countess Alexandra Tolstoy, *The Tragedy of Tolstoy*, trans. Elena Varneck (New Haven, 1933), 254.

30. Constantin de Grunwald, *Saints of Russia* (New York, 1960), 87–103.

31. *Ibid.*, 97.

32. Fedotov, 93.

33. Grunwald, 96.

34. Fedotov, 93.

35. *Ibid.*, 87.

36. *Ibid.*, 281.

37. Grigorieff, 32.

38. Gorodetzky, 185.

39. *Ibid.*, 185.

40. *Ibid.*, 186.

41. Ernest J. Simmons, *Dostoevsky. The Making of a Novelist* (New York, 1962), 358.

42. *Dostoevsky* (New York, 1961), 89.

43. Simmons, 357.

44. Nicolas Berdyaev, *Konstantin Leontiev* (London, 1940), 148.

45. *Ibid.*, 148.

46. *Fyodor Dostoevsky: A Critical Study* (London, 1916), 238.

47. Lytton Strachey, *Spectatorial Essays* (New York, 1964), 175.

48. Jackson, 121.

49. Simmons, 363.

50. Mark Spilka, "Human Worth in *The Brothers Karamazov*," *The Minnesota Review* (Jan.-April 1965), 42, 43.

51. Gerald Abraham, *Dostoevsky* (London, 1936), 132–33.

52. *Letters from Joseph Conrad, 1895–1924*, ed. Edward Garnett (Indianapolis, 1928), 240.

53. Guardini, 108.

54. *The Writings of Martin Buber*, ed. Will Herberg (New York, 1961), 170.

55. Henri de Lubac, *The Drama of Atheist Humanism* (New York, 1963), 245.

56. Eduard Thurneysen, *Dostoevsky* (Richmond, 1964), 83.

57. *The Writings of Martin Buber*, 324.

58. *Ibid.*, 319.

59. *Ibid.*, 318.

60. *Ibid.*, 318.

61. *Man in the Modern Age*, trans. Eden and Cedar Paul (London, 1951), 184.

62. Hosea 2:19.

63. *Tragic Sense of Life* (New York, 1954), 132.

64. Mircea Eliade, *The Sacred and the Profane* (New York, 1959), 11.

65. Evelyn Underhill, *Mysticism* (New York, 1955), 268, 270.

66. Mochulsky, 636.

67. Underhill, 380.

68. *Ibid.*, 413.

69. Thomas J. J. Altizer and William Hamilton, *Radical Theology and the Death of God* (Indianapolis, 1966), 81.

70. Underhill, 290.

71. *The Rebel*, trans. Anthony Bower (New York, 1954), 51.

72. Altizer and Hamilton, 84.

73. *Ibid.*, 84.

74. Mochulsky, 588–89.

75. *Waiting for God*, trans. Emma Craufurd (New York, 1951), 99.

76. Thurneysen, 44. For a detailed appraisal of some of the philosophical and existential problems found in *The Brothers Karamazov* see Ellis Sandoz, *Political Apocalypse: A Study of Dostoevsky's Grand Inquisitor* (Baton Rouge, La., 1971).

77. *On Science, Necessity, and the Love of God*, ed. and trans. Richard Rees (London, 1968), 149.

78. *Ibid.*, 170.

79. *Ibid.*, 184–85.

80. *Ibid.*, 187.

81. *Ibid.*, 193.

82. *Ibid.*, 191.

83. *Ibid.*, 187.

84. *Ibid.*, 194, 195.

85. *Ibid.*, 154.

86. *The Notebooks of Simone Weil*, trans. Arthur Wills (London, 1956), II, 386–87.

87. *Waiting for God*, 197.

88. Habakkuk ii.20.

89. Otto, 68 ff., 210 ff.

90. *On Science, Necessity, and the Love of God*, 198.

91. Simone Weil, *Gravity and Grace*, trans. Emma Craufurd (New York, 1952), 86.

92. *Ibid.*, 176.

93. St.-John Perse, *Two Addresses* (New York, 1966), 11.

NOTES TO CHAPTER 13

1. Vladimir Markov, "Notes on Pasternak's *Doctor Zhivago*," *The Russian Review* (Jan. 1959), 14.

2. Nichola Chiaromonte, "Pasternak's Message," *Partisan Review* (Winter 1958), 133. See also Chiaromonte's "Doctor Zhivago and Modern Sensibility," *Dissent* (Winter 1959), 35–44.

3. Boris Pasternak, *Doctor Zhivago*, trans. Max Hayward and Manya Harari; "The Poems of Yurii Zhivago," trans. Bernard Guilbert Guerney (New York, 1958), 9. The first edition of *Doctor Zhivago* appeared in Italy in 1957, and was published by Signor Gian Giacomo Feltrinelli, to whom Pasternak had sold the translation rights after Soviet authorities refused publication.

4. For an excellent biographical appreciation of Pasternak's life and his place in contemporary Russia, see Victor S. Frank, "The Meddlesome Poet: Boris Pasternak's Rise to Greatness," *The Dublin Review* (Spring 1958), 49–58.

5. Boris Pasternak, *Safe Conduct: An Autobiography and Other Writings*, trans. Beatrice Scott, Robert Payne, Babette Deutsch, and C. M. Bowra (New York, 1958), 18.

6. *Ibid.*, 101.

7. *Doctor Zhivago*, 300.

8. *Safe Conduct*, 146–47.

9. Victor S. Frank, "A Russian Hamlet," *The Dublin Review* (Autumn 1958), 212.

10. Stuart Hampshire, "*Doctor Zhivago* as From A Lost Culture," *Encounter* (Nov. 1958), 3. See also William Phillips, "Men and History," *Commentary* (Dec. 1958), 529–33.

11. Richard G. Stern, "*Doctor Zhivago* as a Novel," *The Kenyon Review* (Winter 1959), 157 ff.; cf. Lionel Abel, "On Doctor Zhivago," *Dissent* (Autumn 1958), 334–41. In this article, which is in the form of an open letter to Nichola Chiaromonte (see note 2), Abel stresses the reasons for his lack of admiration of *Doctor Zhivago*. He writes: "Certainly it is one of the most interesting novels that has appeared in many years. But it is as certainly not a great book; I do not find it great as a work of art or as a document. . . . My liking for this book is a personal fact without significance for literary judgment; it is an accident of my own intellectual history."

For the pro-Communist response to *Doctor Zhivago*, see Jack Lindsay, "Dr. Zhivago," *Anglo-Soviet Journal* (Winter 1958–59), 20–23; and Murray Young, "Dr. Zhivago," *New World Review* (Nov. 1958), 74–76. Both Lindsay and Young accuse Zhivago of egocentrism and middle-class selfishness. In general their comments follow the same Marxist pattern of literary valuation found in the statement of the Union of Soviet Writers explaining to Pasternak the reasons for not accepting his manuscript (*The Current Digest of the Soviet Press* [Dec. 3, 1958], 7–8, 11):

> It is our view that Doctor Zhivago is, in fact, the incarnation of a definite type of Russian intellectual of that day, a man fond of talking about the sufferings of the people and able to discuss them, but unable to cure those sufferings in either the literal or the figurative sense of the word. He is the type of man consumed with a sense of his own singularity, his intrinsic value, a man far removed from the people and ready to betray them in difficult times, to cut himself off from their sufferings and their cause. He is the type of the "highly intellectual" Philistine, tame when left alone but capable in thought as well as in deed of inflicting any wrong whatsoever on the people just as soon as he feels the slightest wrong—real or imagined—has been done to him.
>
> You are no stranger to symbolism, and the death, or rather the passing, of Doctor Zhivago in the late 1920's is for you, we feel, a symbol of the death of the Russian intelligentsia, destroyed by the revolution. Yes, it must be admitted that for the Doctor Zhivago you depicted in the novel the climate of the revolution is deadly. And our disagreement with you is not over this but, as we have already mentioned, over something quite different.

To you, Doctor Zhivago is the peak of the spirit of the Russian intelligentsia.

To us he is its swamp.

To you, the members of the Russian intelligentsia who took a different path from the one Doctor Zhivago took and who chose the course of serving the people, betrayed their true calling, committed spiritual suicide, and created nothing of value.

To us they found their true calling on precisely that path and continued to serve the people and to do for the people precisely the things that had been done for them—in laying the groundwork for the revolution—by the best segment of the Russian intelligentsia, which was then, and is today, infinitely remote from that conscious break with the people and ideological regnancy of which your Doctor Zhivago is the bearer.

12. *Doctor Zhivago*, 378.

13. "A Russian Hamlet," 215.

14. Nicolas Berdyaev, *The End of Our Time* (New York, 1933), 72.

15. *Doctor Zhivago*, 417.

16. *Ibid.*, 251.

17. Alexander Blok, *The Twelve*, trans. Babette Deutsch and Abraham Yarmolinsky (New York, 1920), 20.

18. *Doctor Zhivago*, 402–3.

19. Dmitri Merejkowski, *Tolstoi as a Man and Artist: With an Essay on Dostoievski* (New York, 1902).

20. *Doctor Zhivago*, 338.

21. Gerhard Loose, "Pasternak's *Doctor Zhivago*," *The Colorado Quarterly* (Winter 1959), 266.

22. "A Russian Hamlet," 218.

23. *Doctor Zhivago*, 523.

24. *Ibid.*, 519.

25. *Ibid.*, 42.

26. *Ibid.*, 558–59.

NOTES TO CHAPTER 14

1. J. D. Salinger, *Franny and Zooey* (Boston, 1961); *The Way of a Pilgrim and The Pilgrim Continues His Way*, trans. R. M. French (London, 1961). All page references are included in the text.

2. Alfred North Whitehead, *Science and the Modern World* (Cambridge, Eng., 1926), 267–68.

3. François Mauriac, *Cain, Where Is Your Brother?* (New York, 1962).

4. *Writings from the Philokalia on Prayer of the Heart*, trans. E. Kadloubovsky and G. E. H. Palmer (London, 1951).

NOTES TO CHAPTER 15

1. Douglas Bush, *English Literature in the Earlier Seventeenth Century*

(Oxford, Eng., 1945), 1; and Basil Willey, *The Seventeenth Century Background* (New York, 1955 [1934]), 15, 16.

2. Edward A. George, *Seventeenth Century Men of Latitude* (New York, 1908), 197.

3. *Theaetetus* 176 B.

4. The word "mysticism" was taken by the Neoplatonists from the ancient Greek mysteries. Μύστης was a name given to the initiate, since he was one who was securing a knowledge of divine phenomena about which he must keep his mouth shut—μύω, meaning to close the lips or eyes; thus can be seen the association of secrecy or mystery. See Caroline F. E. Spurgeon, *Mysticism in English Literature* (Cambridge, Eng., 1913), 2.

5. William R. Inge, *Christian Mysticism* (7th ed.; New York, 1956), 5. Italics are the author's.

6. *Anglicanism*, ed. Paul Elmer More and Frank Leslie Cross (Milwaukee, Wis., 1935), lxxii.

7. John Tulloch, *Rational Theology and Christian Philosophy in the Seventeenth Century* (London, 1874), II, 10.

8. Tulloch, II, 99. "The spirit in man is the candle of the Lord . . ." comes from Proverbs 20:27.

9. Ernst Cassirer, *The Platonic Renaissance in England*, trans. James P. Pettegrove (Austin, Tex., 1953), 8, 202.

10. *Psychathanasia*, Book II, Canto III, stanza. 6. The old spelling used by More will be followed throughout this essay.

11. Henry More, *Philosophical Poems* (Cambridge, Eng., 1647), 332.

12. Tulloch, II, 303.

13. Richard Ward, *The Life of the Learned and Pious Dr. Henry More* (London, 1710), 34–36.

14. Ward, 5–6.

15. "I, the wretched one, did not know from where I am, nor who am I, oh the folly! nor which way I am going. But I live in the much-twisting claws of grief and wailing, and it seems to me that I am dragged in every direction. Wakings and dreams are alike, father Zeus, how august it is! And we live in clouds. Falsehoods, apparition, emptiness, hummings of necessity—as for the other things unknown, I only know life" (*Philosophical Poems*, 334).

16. "I have sprung forward from heavens, an immortal ray of God, and, oh joy, back to God I shall go. And now love sent by God supports me with wings, and I live in truth, always enjoying myself. Night turned out and dream. Father of god-seeing dawn, eternal light enfolded us. Faith, wisdom, divinity, well-winged joy, strength—these are life; the others are Hades and nothingness" (*Philosophical Poems*, 334).

17. Trans. Susanna Winkworth (London, 1907), xi.

18. For years Luther was the sole authority for the text of this work, but about 1850 a manuscript of it was discovered at Wurtzburg by Professor Reuss, the librarian of the University there. This manuscript dates from 1497 and has been published verbatim by Professor Pfeiffer of Prague. The translator selected Dr. Pfeiffer's edition as the basis of this work. See *Theologia Germanica*, xxiv-xxv.

19. This type of mystic is one in whom there can be found "that the highest good is the greatest likeness to God—that the greatest happiness is

the vision of God—that we should seek holiness not for the sake of external reward, but because it is the health of the soul, while vice is its disease—that goodness is unity and harmony, while evil is discord and disintegration—that it is our duty and happiness to rise above the visible and transitory to the invisible and permanent." Inge, *Christian Mysticism*, 79.

20. *Theologia Germanica*, 47.

21. W. C. De Pauley, *The Candle of the Lord* (New York, 1937), 118.

22. Henry More, *Enchiridion Ethicum* (New York, 1930), 26. This book was first published in 1666.

23. *Philosophical Poems*, 330.

24. *Christian Mysticism*, 14.

25. Cassirer, 73.

26. *Psychathanasia*, Book III, Canto III, stanza 16.

27. *Ibid.*, Canto II, stanza 22.

28. Paul R. Anderson, *Science in Defense of Liberal Religion* (New York, 1933), 104.

29. *Enneads*, VI, 7, 34. The English translations are from *Plotinus. The Six Enneads*, trans. Stephen MacKenna and B. S. Page (Chicago, 1952), vol. 17 of *Great Books of the Western World*.

30. Willey, 170.

31. *Antidote Against Atheism*, 13.

32. *Divine Dialogues* (2nd ed.; London, 1668), 524.

33. *Collection of Several Philosophical Writings of Henry More* (4th ed.; London, 1712), v, iv.

34. De Pauley, 120–21.

35. Ward, 16.

36. Eugene M. Austin, *The Ethics of the Cambridge Platonists* (Philadelphia, 1935), 38.

37. *Enchiridion Ethicum*, 41.

38. Willey, 118.

39. Tulloch, II, 366. See also Ward, 80.

40. René Descartes, *A Discourse on Method and Selected Writings*, trans. John Veitch (New York, 1951), 115.

41. Anderson, 167.

42. *Psychathanasia*, Book I, Canto I, stanza 25.

43. George A. Craig, "Umbra Dei: Henry More and the Seventeenth-Century Struggle for Plainness," Diss. Harvard Univ., 1946, 425. For a sound assessment of More's place in the intellectual and religious history of his time, see Aharon Lichtenstein's *Henry More: The Rational Theology of a Cambridge Platonist* (Cambridge, Mass., 1962). This book, however, is badly marred by an appalling insensitiveness to the mystical aspects of More's religious thought and life. I discuss this weakness in a review of the book in *The Journal of Religion* (July 1963), 251–53.

NOTES TO CHAPTER 17

1. Matthew Arnold, *Culture and Anarchy* (New York, 1924 [1869]), 116.

2. T. S. Eliot, in his review of J. Middleton Murry's *Son of Woman* in *The Criterion* (July 1931).

3. *The Letters of D. H. Lawrence*, ed. Aldous Huxley (New York, 1932), 9.

4. D. H. Lawrence, *Etruscan Places* (New York, 1957), 185. "*Etruscan Places* is the record of a spiritual act of excavation. Among the treasures he exhumed there was something of his own essential being. The Etruscans provided him with a group of symbols," writes Christopher Hassall in his "D. H. Lawrence and the Etruscans," in *Essays by Divers Hands*, ed. Peter Green (Oxford, 1962), XXXI, 71.

5. *Ibid.*, 173–74.

6. *The Complete Poetical Works of Percy Bysshe Shelley*, ed. Thomas Hutchinson with Introduction and Notes by Benjamin P. Kurtz (New York, 1933), 447.

7. *Ibid.*, 478.

8. *Phoenix: The Posthumous Papers of D. H. Lawrence*, ed. Edward D. McDonald (London, 1936), 536.

9. *Letters*, no. 1621 (1749), IV, 1305–6.

10. *The Letters of D. H. Lawrence*, 236.

11. Douglas Bush, *Mythology and the Romantic Tradition in English Poetry* (Cambridge, Mass., 1937), 260.

12. *The Letters of D. H. Lawrence*, 347.

13. *The Collected Letters of D. H. Lawrence*, ed. Harry T. Moore (New York, 1962), I, 454.

14. D. H. Lawrence, *Reflections on the Death of a Porcupine and Other Essays* (Bloomington, Ind., 1963), 6.

15. *Phoenix*, 219.

16. *Reflections on the Death of a Porcupine*, 107.

17. Ralph Waldo Emerson, "Plato; or, the Philosopher," *Representative Men* (New York, n.d.), 71–72.

18. Edwin Hatch, *The Influence of Greek Ideas on Christianity* (New York, 1957[1890]), 349.

19. D. H. Lawrence, *Psychoanalysis and the Unconscious and Fantasia of the Unconscious* (New York, 1960), 54.

20. *The Journals of André Gide*, trans. and ed. Justin O'Brien (New York, 1956), I, 322.

21. T. S. Eliot, *After Strange Gods. A Primer of Modern Heresy* (London, 1934), 60; I. A. Richards, *Science and Society* (London, 1935), 79.

22. All quotations from Heracleitus in this essay are taken from John Burnet, *Early Greek Philosophy* (Cleveland, 1957), 130–68.

23. D. H. Lawrence, *Last Poems*, ed. Richard Aldington and Giusèppe Orioli (New York, 1933), 43.

24. *Fantasia of the Unconscious*, 105.

25. *The Collected Letters of D. H. Lawrence*, I, 433.

26. *The Letters of D. H. Lawrence*, 89.

27. D. H. Lawrence, *Apocalypse* (New York, 1932), 86.

28. D. H. Lawrence, *Sex, Literature, and Censorship*, ed. Harry T. Moore (New York, 1959), 107.

29. *Apocalypse*, 199–200.

30. D. H. Lawrence, *Collected Poems* (London, 1932), 354, 379, 177.

31. *The Complete Poetical Works of Byron* (Boston, 1933), 205.
32. *Phoenix*, 31.
33. See my article "Voyage of Oblivion: The Meaning of D. H. Lawrence's Death Poems," *English Miscellany*, ed. Mario Praz, XIII (Rome, 1962), 135–64; and my book *Adventure in Consciousness: The Meaning of D. H. Lawrence's Religious Quest* (The Hague, 1964).
34. *Last Poems*, 5.
35. *Ibid.*, 6.
36. *Ibid.*, 5.
37. *Ibid.*, 11.
38. *Ibid.*, 38.
39. *Ibid.*, 77–78.
40. *Enneads*, VI, 7, 34.
41. *The Odyssey*, Book IV.
42. *Last Poems*, 60–61.
43. Robert Graves, *Collected Poems* (New York, 1961), 24.
44. *Last Poems*, 106.
45. *The Collected Letters of D. H. Lawrence*, I, 241.
46. *Sex, Literature, and Censorship*, 99–100.
47. *Last Poems*, 32.
48. *Kangaroo* (1923), Ch. XII.
49. *The Letters of D. H. Lawrence*, 532.

NOTES TO CHAPTER 18

1. Murray was born on Jan. 2, 1866, in Sydney, Australia, and went to England when he was 11. He attended the Merchant Taylors' School, a London public school, where he read widely in the classics. Later he attended St. John's College, Oxford, attaining high honors in Latin and Greek.
2. Matthew Arnold, *Culture and Anarchy* (Cambridge, Eng., 1955 [1869]), 129–44.
3. He sought six times to be elected to the House of Commons from Oxford, but never succeeded.
4. *The New York Times* (May 21, 1957), 35.
5. *Hellenism and the Modern World* (Boston, 1954), 52 ff.
6. "The Next Set of Problems But One," *The Hibbert Journal* 25 (1927), 206.
7. *Tradition and Progress* (Boston, 1922), 13.
8. George Sarton, "Preface to Volume Thirty-Eight. A Tribute to Gilbert Murray and a Plea for Greek Studies," *Isis* 38 (1947), 5.
9. *Tradition and Progress*, 19.
10. Lucien Price, "Gilbert Murray at Ninety," *Atlantic Monthly* (Jan. 1956), 79.
11. *Greek Studies* (Oxford, 1946), 18.
12. *Encyclopaedia Britannica*, Vol. 15, pp. 978–79.
13. When Lucien Price compares Shaw and Murray, he observes that in spirit Shaw is Hebraist, Murray Hellenist. He writes: "Protagonist and deuteragonist in classic drama of our time, they exchange places. When

we are young and bellicose, Shaw is our man ... when we mature our man is Murray, urbane, patient, reasonable, and prepared in face of discouragement to keep at it for a life time" ("Gilbert Murray at Ninety," 77).

14. Hesketh Pearson, *G. B. S.: A Full-Length Portrait* (New York, 1942), 206. See also Stephen Spender's article, "The Riddle of Shaw" (1949), in *George Bernard Shaw: A Critical Survey*, ed. Louis Kronenberger (New York, 1953), 237.

15. T. S. Eliot, *Selected Essays* (New York, 1950), 47–48.

16. *The Making of Europe* (New York, 1932), 4.

17. "The Next Set of Problems But One," 206.

18. "The Classics," *The Fortnightly*, N.S. 152 (1942), 40.

19. "The Next Set of Problems But One," 193.

20. "The Classics," 37.

21. *Greek Studies*, 52–53.

22. The quotations and ideas in this paragraph are to be found in *The Rise of the Greek Epic* (3rd ed., Oxford, 1924), 3, 10, 15, 18, 19–21.

23. The quotations and ideas in this paragraph appear in *The Rise of the Greek Epic*, 24–26.

24. *Hellenism and the Modern World*, 34.

25. "The Value of Greece to the Future to the World," *The Art World* (Nov. 1916), 130.

26. *Ibid.*, 129.

27. *Tradition and Progress*, 27.

28. "Are Our Pearls Real?" *Atlantic Monthly* (June 1955), 46–47.

29. *Greek Studies*, 194.

30. Horace M. Kallen, *Art and Freedom* (New York, 1942), 47.

31. *Hellenism and the Modern World*, 58.

32. The following ideas and quotations appear in "The Next Set of Problems But One," 193, 195, 206–7.

33. *Ibid.*, 205.

34. *The New York Times* (May 21, 1957), 35.

NOTES TO CHAPTER 19

1. Praz no longer lives in Via Giulia. He has now moved to another flat located in Via Zanardelli. In a letter to me postmarked June 17, 1969, he writes: "I am much happier in this new flat, which is sunnier and affords the amenity of a (small) terrace."

2. *The Letters of D. H. Lawrence*, ed. Aldous Huxley (New York, 1932), 24.

3. Significantly, Edmund Wilson makes these qualifying remarks concerning Praz as a literary critic: "Yet to think of Mario Praz as primarily an English expert and a literary critic is largely to misconceive his role. He should be considered as primarily an artist—and I do not even say literary artist, for the results of his activities as a collector of furniture, pictures, and *objets d'art* are as much a part of his *oeuvre* as his books. He is an artist and a unique personality who expresses himself through his art in connection with any subject he is treating." "The Genie of the Via Giulia," *Friendship's*

Garland. Essays Presented to Mario Praz On His Seventieth Birthday, ed. Vittorio Gabrielli (Rome, 1966), I, 5–6.

NOTES TO CHAPTER 20

1. *To Criticize the Critic and Other Writings* (New York, 1965), 11.
2. "A New Sensibility," *Cambridge Quarterly* (Winter 1966/67), 56.
3. *The Literary Critics* (New York, 1964), 197.
4. *Concepts of Criticism* (New Haven, 1963), 34, 216.
5. *The Armed Vision* (New York, 1948), 236.
6. Harmondsworth, Middlesex, Eng., 1961, 90.
7. *The Private Reader* (New York, 1942), 183.
8. *The Criterion* 10 (1930–31), 345. Knight's *Shakespeare and Religion* (London, 1967) is dedicated to Bonamy Dobrée. This collection contains Knight's "occasional" writings and talks of the last forty years and centers on Shakespeare's spiritual meaning. An enhancing feature of this volume is the inclusion, under the title "Shakespeare and Religion," of "Six talks for the B.B.C. series *Lift Up Your Hearts* broadcast during the Quartercentenary Shakespeare birthday week, 20–25 April, 1964." No one who reads these talks will fail to appreciate Knight's belief that "They form the heart of the collection; that is, the heart of my life's work on Shakespeare."
9. "The World of Books," *The Nation and Athenaeum* (Aug. 9, 1930), 593.
10. *The Review of English Studies*, N. S. 8 (1957), 302. J. M. Newton, in "*Scrutiny*'s Failure With Shakespeare," *Cambridge Quarterly* (Spring 1966), 144–77, argues that "the exceptional value" of the Shakespeare studies of both A. C. Bradley and of Knight has yet to be fully recognized. He also tries to show that the "Shakespeare criticism" of Dr. Leavis, L. C. Knights, and D. A. Traversi is of inferior quality. *Scrutiny*'s Shakespeare criticism, Newton contends, recommended Knight, in spite of his "aberrations," but unjustly dismissed Bradley as "inadequate and wrong."
11. *The Sewanee Review* (Jan.-March 1966), A Special Issue ed. Allen Tate, 239–55.
12. *The Wheel of Fire* (London, 1949), xiii–xx.
13. *Of Books and Humankind*, ed. John Butt (London, 1964), 149–63.
14. *Discoveries. Essays in Literary Criticism* (London, 1924), 13–14.
15. *The Adelphi* (Jan. 1931), 347.
16. *New Bearings in English Poetry* (London, 1932), 155.
17. "Postscript by the Guest Editor," *The Sewanee Review*, 386.
18. *Shakespeare and Spiritual Life* (London, 1924), 3, 19, 10.
19. *The Sovereign Flower* (New York, 1958), 289, 290, 291, 292, 293.
20. See 1–16.
21. *The Wheel of Fire*, 3 ff.; *The Sovereign Flower*, 245–59; *Essays in Criticism*, III (1953), 382–95.
22. *The Sovereign Flower*, 256.
23. *Lord Byron: Christian Virtues* (New York, 1953), 48.
24. *The Christian Renaissance* (New York, 1963 [1933]), 284–300; *The*

Saturnian Quest (New York, 1964), 13; and *Promise of Greatness: The War of 1914–1918*, ed. George A. Panichas (New York, 1968).

25. *Byron and Shakespeare* (New York, 1966), 17–18.

26. *Ibid.*, 18.

27. Quoted by Knight, "Speech at the Dinner given for Retiring Members of Staff on 18th June, 1962," *University of Leeds Review* (Dec. 1962), no pagination.

28. London (1949), xiii.

29. Letter to George A. Panichas, Dec. 13, 1966. For Knight's own detailed statement on the significance of his literary viewpoint and labors, see his introductory chapter, "Poetry and Magic," in *Neglected Powers. Essays on Nineteenth and Twentieth Century Literature* (London, 1971), 17–109. Particularly apropos is this statement on page 25: "For myself, I am at least consistent. My own tendency has always been to honour lucidity; all my interpretations derive from *the will to clarify*; my own creative writing has always aimed, as my preface to my early poems in *Gold–Dust* [London, 1968] recently made clear, at simplicity. Meanwhile, I see our various cultural industries—I say 'cultural' because far more than literature is involved—lacking purpose and direction; and the more violently they assert themselves, the more deeply are they mazed and bogged." This remarkable collection of essays contains previously published essays on Tennyson, Brooke, Masefield, Eliot, and Francis Berry, as well as new essays on John Cowper Powys and T. E. Lawrence.

See "Criticism in the Cause of Conversion," *The Times Literary Supplement* (Oct. 10, 1971), 1171, for a discussion of *Neglected Powers*. This incisive review also assesses Knight's total literary contribution and his importance as an interpreter with a "genius for discovering new insights."

30. *Shakespeare and Spiritual Life*, 24.

31. *Ibid.*, 15.

32. *On the Sublime*, trans. Frank Granger (London, 1935), I, 4.

33. *Essays in Criticism*, 395.

NOTES TO CHAPTER 21

1. "Vindication: 'Yes, But—,'" *The Times Literary Supplement* (Nov. 1, 1963), 877.

2. G. Wilson Knight, "*Scrutiny* and Criticism," *Essays in Criticism*, XIV (1964), 32.

3. "Vindication: 'Yes, But—,'" 879.

4. Frank Kermode, "A Tradition of Scrutiny," *Commentary* (July 1968), 83.

5. Harold Rosenberg, "Insurrection," *The New Yorker* (March 14, 1964), 169, 187.

6. Philip Rahv, "On F. R. Leavis and D. H. Lawrence," *Literature and the Sixth Sense* (Boston, 1969), 290.

7. Frank Swinnerton, *Figures in the Foreground* (New York, 1964), 264.

8. Martin Jarrett-Kerr, "The Literary Criticism of F. R. Leavis," *Essays in Criticism*, II (1952), 360–61.

9. George Steiner, "F. R. Leavis," *Language and Silence* (New York, 1967), 224.

10. F. R. Leavis, in *Spectator* (March 9, 1962), 297, 302, 299.

11. Aldous Huxley, *Literature and Science* (New York, 1963), 1.

12. T. S. Eliot, *To Criticize the Critic* (New York, 1965), 13.

13. J. B. Priestley, *Thoughts in the Wilderness* (New York, 1957), 205.

14. Bernard C. Heyl, "The Absolutism of F. R. Leavis," *The Journal of Aesthetics and Art Criticism*, 13 (1954), 249–55. A vigorous defense of Dr. Leavis's "professional conduct," of his critical "tone" in terms of an inseparable "existential clarity," is included in John Fraser's "[F. R.] Leavis and [Yvor] Winters: Professional Manners," *The Cambridge Quarterly* (Spring/Summer 1970), 41–71.

15. Steiner, *Language and Silence*, 238.

16. Leonard Woolf, "Thugs and Beetles," *The New Statesman* (May 31, 1968), 729.

17. Vincent Buckley, *Poetry and Morality* (London, 1961), 196.

18. F. R. Leavis, " 'Lawrence Scholarship' and Lawrence," *Anna Karenina and Other Essays* (New York, 1968), 167.

19. The first essay in Eliot's *To Criticize the Critic*.

20. Lionel Trilling, "Science, Literature and Culture: A Comment on the Leavis-Snow Controversy," *Commentary* (June 1962), 464.

21. In implying here Leavis' lack of magnanimity, I think it only fair to remind readers of some of the personal problems that he had to contend with, and overcome, as a Cambridge teacher-critic. "I was, in my academic career (if that is the word), made to feel irretrievably an outlaw," he recalls, "and I remained to the end conscious of being looked on by those in power as a deplorable influence.... At my superannuation I was indeed a University Reader: I had been advanced to that status in my sixty-fifth year. As for my previous official standing, I was appointed an Assistant Lecturer in my early forties and full University Lecturer in my fifties. The financial consequences for my retired years, as well as for my previous life, of such an academic career constitute, in the nature of things, a fact that I and my wife ... can hardly regard as negligible." "The State of English," *The Times Literary Supplement* (March 3, 1972), 246.

22. F. R. Leavis, "T. S. Eliot and the Life of English Literature," *The Massachusetts Review*, X (1969), 26.

23. "What they [the Bloomsburies] were waiting for, quite crudely, was a victim and outsider," writes V. S. Pritchett in *The New Statesman* (July 16, 1972), 828. T. S. Eliot's view of the Bloomsbury Group is strikingly different: "Any group will appear more uniform, and probably more intolerant and exclusive from the outside than it really is; and here, certainly, no subscription of orthodoxy was imposed. Had it, indeed, been a matter of limited membership and exclusive doctrine, it would not have attracted the exasperated attention of those who objected to it on these supposed grounds." "Virginia Woolf," *Horizon* (May 1941), 315.

24. London (1969), 172.

25. *Nor Shall My Sword: Discourses on Pluralism, Compassion and Social Hope* (New York, 1972), 127–28.

26. *Ibid.*, 174.

27. *The Shaking of the Foundations* (New York, 1948), 8.

Index

〜

442